Understanding
Fiber Optics

Understanding Fiber Optics

Third Edition

Jeff Hecht

Prentice Hall
Upper Saddle River, New Jersey   *Columbus, Ohio*

Library of Congress Cataloging-in-Publication Data

Hecht, Jeff.
    Understanding fiber optics / Jeff Hecht.—3rd ed.
       p.   cm.
    Includes index.
    ISBN 0-13-956145-5
    1. Fiber optics.   I. Title.
TA1800.H43   1998
621.382'75—dc21
                                  98-39457
                                  CIP

Editor: Charles E. Stewart, Jr.
Production Editor: Alexandrina Benedicto Wolf
Cover photo: © H. Armstrong Roberts
Design Coordinator: Karrie M. Converse
Cover Designer: Jason Moore
Production Supervision: Lisa Garboski, Bookworks
Production Manager: Deidra M. Schwartz
Marketing Manager: Ben Leonard

This book was set in Garamond by The Clarinda Company and was printed and bound by
R. R. Donnelley & Sons Company. The cover was printed by Phoenix Color Corp.

Published by Prentice-Hall, Inc.
Upper Saddle River, New Jersey 07458

10 9 8 7 6

ISBN: 0-13-956145-5

Prentice-Hall International (UK) Limited, *London*
Prentice-Hall of Australia Pty. Limited, *Sydney*
Prentice-Hall of Canada, Inc., *Toronto*
Prentice-Hall Hispanoamericana, S. A., *Mexico*
Prentice-Hall of India Private Limited, *New Delhi*
Prentice-Hall of Japan, Inc., *Tokyo*
Pearson Education Asia Pte. Ltd., *Singapore*
Editora Prentice-Hall do Brasil, Ltda., *Rio de Janeiro*

This book is dedicated to the memory of Heather Williamson Messenger
gifted editor, friend, and victim of domestic violence.

Preface

Fiber optics has come a long way since I wrote the first edition of *Understanding Fiber Optics*. Optical-fiber communications was a radical new technology then, used mostly for high-capacity, long-distance transmission of telephone signals. As I finish the third edition, work crews have begun installing fiber cable down my street to distribute telephone, Internet, and cable-television signals for a new local communications carrier.

Over the years, I have been greatly impressed by the tremendous progress in developing practical fiber-optic equipment. The technology is interesting and elegant, as well as important. I find myself caught up in the advancing field, like a sports writer covering a team blazing its way to a championship. The thrill of technical achievement can be just as tangible to those of us involved with engineering or technology as the thrill of victory is to an athlete.

Although I wrote the first edition mainly for self-study, the book is now used in classrooms. My goal is to explain principles rather than to detail procedures. When you finish this book you should indeed *understand* fiber optics. You should be able to pick up a trade journal such as *Lightwave* or *Fiberoptic Product News* and understand what you read, just as you should be able to understand the duties of a fiber engineer, a network planner, or a cable installer. You will not be able to do their jobs, but you will be literate in the field. Think of this as Fiber Optics 101, a foundation for your understanding of a growing technology.

To explain the fundamentals of fiber optics, I start with some ideas that may seem basic to some readers. When introducing a relatively new field, it is better to explain too much than too little.

To make concepts accessible, I include drawings to show how things work, limit the mathematics to simple algebra, and step through some sample calculations so you can see how they work. I also compare fiber optics with other common technologies and highlight similarities and differences. I have also organized the book to facilitate cross referencing and review of concepts.

The book is structured to introduce you to basic concepts first, then covers fiber hardware and its applications. The chapters are organized as follows:

- The first three chapters present an overview, starting with a general introduction in Chapter 1, then the basics of light guiding and fiber applications in Chapters 2 and 3, respectively. These chapters assume you have little background in the field and are worth reading even if you think your background is adequate.

- Chapters 4 through 8 cover optical fibers, their properties, and how they are assembled into cables. The material is divided into five chapters to make it easier to digest. Chapters 4 through 6 are essential to understanding the fiber concepts found throughout the rest of the book. Chapter 7 covers fiber amplifiers, fiber lasers, and fiber gratings. Chapter 8 is an overview of cabling.

- Chapters 9 to 12 cover transmitters, receivers, light sources, optical amplifiers, and electro-optic regenerators. Chapter 12 compares and contrasts the operation of optical amplifiers and electro-optic regenerators.

- Chapters 13 to 16 cover other components that serve as the "nuts and bolts" of fiber-optic systems. They include connectors, splices, couplers, splitters, and an assortment of other passive and active components that you are likely to encounter.

- Chapter 17 covers fiber-optic measurements. It concentrates on the optical aspects of fiber measurements, and explains the general and background principles of optical measurements.

- Chapters 18 to 20 cover general principles of fiber-optic communications. Chapter 18 covers system principles, and Chapter 19 describes major communications standards. Chapter 20 outlines the principles of communication systems design with sample calculations, so you can understand how systems are assembled.

- Chapters 21 to 25 cover various aspects of telecommunications for telephone, cable-television, data, and Internet transmission. They are divided into different levels to keep the discussion manageable. Chapter 26 covers special systems that are not covered in other chapters.

- The last two chapters describe non-communication applications. Chapter 27 explains the principles and operation of fiber-optic sensors. Chapter 28 covers imaging and illumination applications of fiber optics.

The glossary at the back of the book provides a quick reference of specialized terms.

I have tried to keep everything current, but fiber optics is advancing so fast that some details are bound to become obsolete. When you finish *Understanding Fiber Optics,* you should be prepared to follow the new advances, and perhaps contribute to them as well.

Acknowledgments

Many people in the fiber-optics industry have given generously of their time to patiently answer my questions. I want especially to thank Jim Hayes, Marc Duchesne, John Schlager, and Mike Pepper for help with this edition and Robert Gallawa and David Charlton for help with earlier editions. I would also like to thank Eugene R. Bartlett of ITT Technical Institute for his invaluable feedback. I also owe thanks to the companies and consortia that post tutorials, application notes, standards, and other helpful information on World Wide Web sites where I could find them when questions arose outside normal working hours.

Jeff Hecht
Auburndale, MA

Contents

CHAPTER 3 APPLICATIONS OF FIBER OPTICS 39

CHAPTER 4 TYPES OF OPTICAL FIBERS 55

CHAPTER 5 PROPERTIES OF OPTICAL FIBERS 81

CHAPTER 6 FIBER MATERIALS AND MANUFACTURE 105

CHAPTER 7 SPECIAL-PURPOSE FIBERS 123

CHAPTER 8 CABLING 141

CHAPTER 9   LIGHT SOURCES   163

CHAPTER 10   TRANSMITTERS   187

CHAPTER 11   RECEIVERS   207

CHAPTER 12   REPEATERS, REGENERATORS, AND OPTICAL AMPLIFIERS   231

CHAPTER 13   CONNECTORS   251

CHAPTER 14   SPLICING   271

CHAPTER 18   INTRODUCTION TO SYSTEM CONCEPTS   367

CHAPTER 19   FIBER SYSTEM STANDARDS   389

CHAPTER 20   SYSTEM DESIGN   405

CHAPTER 24   LOCAL TELEPHONE NETWORKS 499

CHAPTER 25   COMPUTERS AND LOCAL-AREA NETWORKS 517

CHAPTER 26   VEHICLE AND MILITARY FIBER COMMUNICATIONS 539

CHAPTER 27   FIBER-OPTIC SENSORS   553

CHAPTER 28   IMAGING AND ILLUMINATING FIBER OPTICS   567

APPENDIX A: LASER SAFETY   583

GLOSSARY   585

INDEX   601

Understanding
Fiber Optics

Introduction to Fiber Optics

A Personal View

Light is an old friend. I've been fascinated with light and optics ever since I can remember. I started playing with lenses and prisms when I was about 12, and though my box of optical toys has spent some time in the closet over the years, I've added some new playthings, and many of them involve fiber-optic technology.

The first optical fibers I saw were in decorative lamps. A group of fibers was tied together at one end and splayed out in a fan at the other. A bulb at the tied end illuminated them, and the light emerging from the loose ends made them glitter. The effect was pretty enough that I bought one for my sister as a Christmas present but useless enough that I wandered away to explore other things.

When I next saw fiber optics, in the mid-1970s, the technology had come a long way. Fibers had been improved enough that telephone companies were looking at them for communications. Those were the days when phone companies were—with good reason—described as "traditionally conservative" in their use of technology. Cautiously, they probed and tested fiber optics, almost like a bomb squad examining a suspicious package. It was not until 1977 that, within a month, first GTE and then AT&T dared to venture down manholes and stick fiber-optic cables into telephone circuits carrying live traffic.

Looking back, the technology they used looks primitive. It was daring then, and it worked. Not only that, it worked flawlessly. The small armies of engineers monitoring those test beds came to countless technical meetings afterward repeating the same monotonous but thrilling conclusion: "It works. Nothing has gone wrong."

I was at the first fiber-optic trade show in the late 1970s and have watched the excitement spread since then. Each year the meetings have grown larger. For a few years, breakthroughs were almost routine. The first generation of systems was barely in the ground before a second generation was ready. A third generation followed and became standard by the mid-1980s. That technology remains in use, but a fourth generation has become common, and a fifth is now being installed, which sends many signals through one fiber at different wavelengths. The overall rate of change has varied over the years, but the accomplishments are incredible when measured on the scale of the first fiber-optic systems.

Looking back, it's been an incredible ride. I've watched a technology spring from the laboratory into the real world. Once I heard about fiber optics from research scientists; now I hear about fiber optics from telephone service people. But the fun isn't over yet. The fiber-optics revolution will continue until fiber comes all the way to homes. It won't come tomorrow, but when it does come, it will bring a wealth of new information services. Some fiber services already reach businesses; eventually they will go into homes. The visionaries who foresaw a wired city were wrong—we will have a fibered society instead. We can all watch it happen.

But that's enough of this visionary stuff. Let's get down to the nuts and bolts—and fiber.

About This Chapter

The idea of communication by light was around long before fiber optics, as were fibers of glass. It took many years for the ideas behind fiber optics to evolve from conventional optics. Even then, people were thinking more of making special optical devices than of optical communications. In this chapter you will see how fiber-optic technology evolved and how it can solve a wide variety of problems in communications.

How and Why Fiber Optics Evolved

Light normally travels in straight lines, but sometimes it is useful to make it go around corners.

Left alone, light will travel in straight lines. Even though lenses can bend light and mirrors can deflect it, light still travels in a straight line between optical devices. This is fine for most purposes. Cameras, binoculars, telescopes, and microscopes wouldn't form images properly if light didn't travel in straight lines.

However, there also are times when people want to look around corners or probe inside places that are not in a straight line from their eyes. Or they may just need to pipe light from place to place, for communicating, viewing, illuminating, or other purposes. That's when they need fiber optics.

Piping Light

The problem arose long before the solution was recognized. In 1880, a Concord, Massachusetts, engineer named William Wheeler patented a scheme for piping light through buildings. Evidently not believing that Thomas Edison's incandescent bulb would prove practical, Wheeler planned to use light from a bright electric arc to illuminate distant rooms. He devised a set of pipes with reflective linings and diffusing optics to carry light through a building, then diffuse it into other rooms, a concept shown in one of his patent drawings in Figure 1.1.

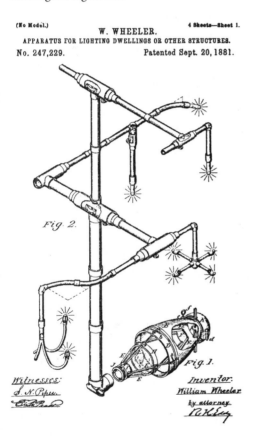

FIGURE 1.1

Wheeler's vision of piping light (U.S. Patent 247,229).

Although he was in his twenties when he received his patent, Wheeler had already helped found a Japanese engineering school. He founded a successful company that made street lamps, and went on to become a widely known hydraulic engineer. Nevertheless, light piping was not one of his successes. Incandescent bulbs proved so practical that they're still in use today. Even if they hadn't, Wheeler's light pipes probably wouldn't have reflected enough light to do the job. However, his idea of light piping reappeared again and again until it finally coalesced into the optical fiber.

Total Internal Reflection

Ironically, the fundamental concept underlying the optical fiber was known well before Wheeler's time. A phenomenon called total internal reflection, described in more detail in Chapter 2, can confine light inside glass or other transparent materials denser than air. If the light in the glass strikes the edge at a glancing angle, it cannot pass out of the material and is instead reflected back inside it. Glassblowers probably saw this effect long ago in bent glass rods, but it wasn't widely recognized until 1841, when Swiss physicist Daniel Colladon used it in his popular lectures on science.

Colladon's trick, shown in Figure 1.2, worked like this. He shone a bright light down a horizontal pipe leading out of a tank of water. When he turned the water on, the liquid flowed out, with the pull of gravity forming a parabolic arc. The light was trapped within the water by total internal reflection, first bouncing off the top surface of the jet, then off the lower surface, until the turbulence in the water broke up the beam.

FIGURE 1.2

Light guided down a water jet.

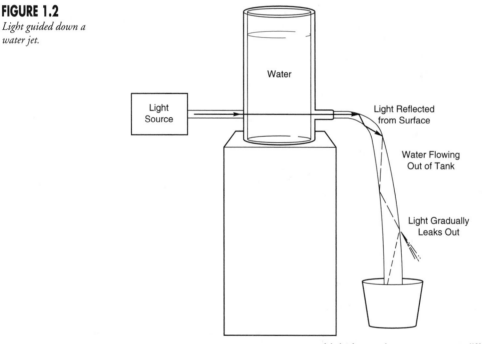

Light beam becomes more diffuse as it passes down the water jet, because turbulence breaks up surface.

Optical Communication

Meanwhile, in Washington, a young scientist who already had an international reputation was working on what he considered his greatest invention—the Photophone. Earlier, Alexander Graham Bell had used electricity to carry voices in the telephone. However, Bell was intrigued by the idea of sending signals without wires. He thought of optical communication, an idea that probably goes back to signal fires on prehistoric hilltops. The first "telegraph," devised by French engineer Claude Chappe in the 1790s, was an optical telegraph. Operators in towers relayed signals from one hilltop to the next by moving semaphore arms. Samuel Morse's electric telegraph put the optical telegraph out of business, but it left behind countless Telegraph Hills.

In 1880, Bell demonstrated that light could carry voices through the air without wires. Bell's Photophone reproduced voices by detecting variations in the amount of sunlight or artificial light reaching a receiver. It was the first "wireless" voice communication. However, it never proved practical because too many things could get in the way of the beam.

Later, others used light to carry voices through the open air, something that is now done with a few laser systems but it is not used widely. In the 1930s, another engineer, Norman R. French—ironically, an employee of the American Telephone & Telegraph Corp., the company built around Bell's telephone—patented the idea of communicating via light sent through pipes.

An optical telegraph was invented in France in the 1790s and made obsolete by the electric telegraph.

The Clad Fiber

Although Colladon could guide light in his stream of water, he couldn't do so very well. The rough boundary of the water broke up the light beam. Other effects also limited light guiding in bent glass rods. The problem is that light can leak out wherever the rod touches something other than air. Because the rod cannot hang unsupported in the air, it has to touch something.

Light leakage became a serious problem when engineers realized that a bundle of fibers could carry images from one end to the other as long as the fibers formed the same pattern on each end. Clarence W. Hansell, an American electrical engineer and prolific inventor, patented the concept in the late 1920s. Heinrich Lamm, a German medical student, made the first image-transmitting bundle in 1930. But the images were faint and hazy. When many bare fibers are bundled together, their surfaces touch, so light can leak from one into the other. The fibers also can scratch each other, and light leaks out at the scratches. Light even leaks out where fingerprint oils cling to the glass. The same problem plagued three men who independently reinvented imaging bundles in the early 1950s: a Danish engineer and inventor, Holger Møller Hansen, and two eminent professors of optics, Abraham van Heel in the Netherlands and Harold H. Hopkins in England.

The key development in making optical fibers usable was a cladding to keep the light from leaking out.

The solution to that problem seems painfully obvious with 20/20 hindsight. Everyone started by looking at total internal reflection at the boundary between glass and air. However, total internal reflection can occur at any surface where light tries to go from a material with a high refractive index to one with a lower refractive index. Air is convenient, and its refractive index of 1.00029 is much lower than 1.5, that of ordinary glass. But total internal reflection occurs as long as the material covering the glass has a refractive index smaller than the glass, as shown in Figure 1.3. Møller Hansen produced total internal reflection by coating glass fibers with margarine, but the results were impractically messy.

FIGURE 1.3

Light cannot leak out of clad fibers.

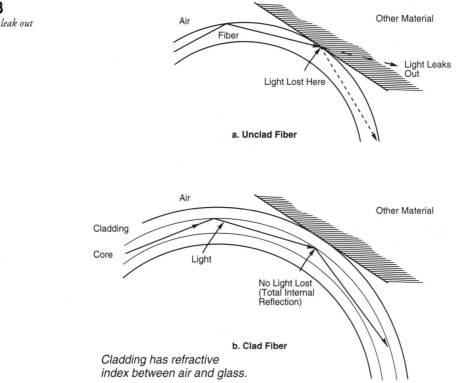

Brian O'Brien, a noted American optical physicist, separately suggested the cladding to van Heel in 1951. Van Heel used beeswax and plastic, which were more practical than margarine. In December 1956, Larry Curtiss, an undergraduate student at the University of Michigan, made the first good glass-clad fibers by melting a tube of low-index glass onto a rod of high-index glass. Glass cladding soon became standard, although a few fibers continue to be plastic-clad, and plastic is used to *coat* fibers to protect them mechanically.

Imaging Applications

Curtiss' fibers were used in fiber-optic endoscopes to look inside the human body, although many modern endoscopes use fibers only to carry light into the body, and return images using miniature electronic cameras. In an endoscope, the fibers are glued in place on each end but left loose in the middle, forming a thin, flexible bundle that can be inserted down the throat. The fiber-optic endoscope soon became an important medical tool.

Other applications soon emerged for bundles of optical fibers. Fibers could be drawn into rigid bundles, which are easier to make with thinner fibers, although they cannot be used where flexibility is vital. Bundles of fibers could "pipe" light for illumination into hard-to-reach spots. A whole industry grew around fiber-optic imaging and light piping in the 1960s. The technology, described in Chapter 28, remains in use, but it has largely been eclipsed by fiber-optic communications.

Many optical fibers can be bundled together to transmit images.

Reducing Fiber Loss

Recognizing Transmission Problems

One important fundamental limit remained: the glass-clad optical fibers used for medical imaging absorbed too much light for use in communications. That statement must be put into context. Today even comparatively high-loss fibers are much more transparent than ordinary window glass. (Ordinary windows are very thin, so they absorb little light; most light lost at windows is reflected from the glass.) Typically, half the light that enters a bundle of imaging fibers remains after 10 ft (3 m). Such fiber losses are acceptable for transmitting light a few feet or a couple meters, which is as long as any fiber-optic endoscope needs to be to look into the stomach. However, only 10% of the light remains after traveling 10 m (33 ft), and after 20 m only 1% is left.

Invention of the laser stimulated interest in optical communications and led to efforts to reduce light absorption in fibers, which was essential for communications.

Initially, no one thought of transmitting light any further than a few meters, so they didn't worry much about fiber loss. Theodore Maiman's demonstration of the first laser in 1960 changed that by renewing interest in optical communications. However, scientists were slow to consider optical fibers seriously, because they thought transparent solids inevitably absorbed too much light to transmit optical signals long distances. They concentrated instead on sending laser beams through the air or through new types of light pipes.

Purifying Glass Fibers

Two engineers at Standard Telecommunication Laboratories in England, Charles K. Kao and George Hockham, did take a careful look at the prospects for optical-fiber telecommunication. Instead of asking how clear the best fiber was, Kao asked what the fundamental limit on loss in glass was. He and Hockham concluded that the loss was caused mostly by impurities, not by the glass itself. In 1966, they predicted that highly purified glass should be so clear that 10% of the light would remain after passing through at least 500 m (1600 ft) of fiber. Their prediction sounded fantastic to many people then, but it proved too conservative.

Publication of Kao and Hockham's paper set off a worldwide race to make better fibers. The first to beat the theoretical prediction were Robert Maurer, Donald Keck, and Peter Schultz at the Corning Glass Works (now Corning Inc.) in 1970. Others soon followed, and losses were pushed down to even lower levels. In today's best optical fibers, 10% of the entering light remains after the light has passed through more than 50 kilometers (30 miles) of fiber. Losses are not quite that low in practical telecommunication systems, but as you will see in Chapter 5, impressive progress has been made. Because of that progress, fiber optics have become the backbones of long-distance telephone networks around the world.

The Basics of Fiber Optics

Fiber Structures

Virtually all fibers share the same fundamental structure. The center of the fiber is the core, which has a higher refractive index than the cladding that surrounds it, as shown in Figure 1.3. The difference in refractive index causes total internal reflection that guides light along the core. As we will see later, this is an oversimplified picture, but it remains the central concept of fiber optics.

The size of core and cladding can vary widely. If the goal is to transmit images or light for illumination, the cores are made large and the claddings are thin. The cores typically are much smaller and the claddings are thicker in communication fibers. The boundary between core and cladding may be abrupt or gradual, with the core glass grading into the cladding. Sometimes multiple layers are used. As we will see, adjusting these structures changes the properties of the fiber.

The standard diameter of telecommunication fibers is 125 micrometers (μm), or 0.005 in. A plastic coating increases diameter to about 250 μm, easing handling and protecting fiber surfaces from scratches and other mechanical damage. Fibers used for imaging may be as small as several micrometers; some special-purpose fibers may be more than a millimeter (0.04 in.) thick.

Fiber Materials

Most fibers are made of very pure glass, with small levels of impurities to adjust the refractive index. From a chemical standpoint, the clearest fibers used in telecommunications are essentially pure silicon dioxide, known as *silica* (SiO_2). The fibers used for medical imaging are less pure glass. Some fibers also are made from plastic, which is not as clear as glass but is more flexible and easier to handle. A few glass fibers are clad with plastic, but typically plastic is used only as an outer layer for mechanical protection.

Special-purpose fibers may be made from other types of materials. For example, fluoride compounds are transparent at longer infrared wavelengths than silica, so they are sometimes used for infrared applications. Generally, these fibers are also called glasses because they are made of materials in a glassy state, but typically they are identified by material, as, for example, fluoride glass fibers.

Fiber Properties

Mechanically, fibers are stiff but flexible and generally quite strong. Their flexibility depends on fiber diameter. Optical fibers used for communications are often compared to human hairs, but whoever thought of that comparison must have had very stiff hairs or very thin fibers. Communication fibers are stiffer than a man's coarse beard hair of the same length. A better comparison is to monofilament fishing line. Unlike wires, fibers spring back to their original straight form after being bent.

Glass fibers are surprisingly strong, but they can fail if surface cracks propagate through the fiber. Plastic coatings protect fiber surfaces from mechanical damage.

The optical properties of fibers depend on their structure and their composition. The most obvious is loss or signal attenuation, but optical pulses also suffer more subtle effects, which are described in detail in Chapter 5.

● Fibers are stiff but flexible and surprisingly strong.

Imaging and Bundled Fibers

Optical fibers were first used to transmit images. As described in more detail in Chapter 28, each fiber carries one point of an image from one end of the bundle to the other. If the fibers are arranged in the same way on both ends, this re-creates the original image on the other end of the bundle. Bundles of fibers also can carry light for illumination, in which case fiber arrangement is not as critical.

Bundles may be flexible or rigid. A flexible bundle consists of many separate fibers, with the two ends fixed together and the fibers loose in the middle (although typically encased in a protective housing). Rigid bundles are made by melting many fibers together into a single rod, which typically is bent to the desired shape during manufacture. Such rigid or fused bundles cost less than flexible bundles, and individual fibers can be thinner than loose fibers, but their inflexibility makes them unsuitable for some applications.

● Flexible and rigid bundles are used for imaging and illumination.

Communication Systems

Fiber-optic communication systems include transmitter, and receiver, as well as the fiber itself.

Most of this book covers fiber optics used for communications. It takes more than just fiber to make a communication system. The basic elements of a system are shown in Figure 1.4. The signal originates from a modulated light source, which feeds it into a fiber, which delivers it to a receiver. The receiver decodes the optical signal and converts it to electronic form for use by equipment at the receiving end.

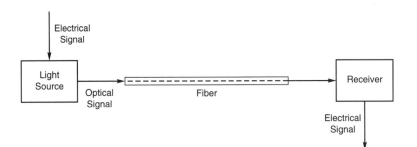

FIGURE 1.4

Fiber-optic system components.

Real-world fiber-optic systems are more complex than indicated in this simple example. Most communication travels in two directions and requires a transmitter and a receiver at each end. Usually separate fibers carry signals in each direction. The fiber or fibers are housed in a cable to simplify handling and protect them from environmental stresses. Fibers must be precisely aligned with light sources to collect their output efficiently. Likewise, if light is transferred between fibers, the two ends must be precisely aligned. Because the cores that carry light are very small, the mechanical tolerances for proper alignment are tight. Consequently, much more attention must be paid to connectors and splices than in electrical communication over wires.

Auxiliary equipment is needed for many of these tasks. Unlike metal wires, optical fibers cannot be spliced with wire cutters and a soldering iron. More elaborate fiber splicers are needed, as you will see in Chapter 14. Connector installation is also a complex task, and special measurement tools are needed to assess the quality of a fiber-optic link, as you will see in Chapter 17.

Why Fiber Optics?

Because fiber optics is a unique transmission medium, it has some unique advantages for certain types of communications.

Light Transmission

The crucial operating difference between a fiber-optic communication system and other types is that signals are transmitted as light. Conventional electronic communication relies on electrons passing through wires. Radio-frequency and microwave communications (including satellite links) rely on radio waves and microwaves traveling through open space. (I will ignore free-space optical communication systems, which send a laser beam through free space or air, because there are few such systems. To prevent confusion, I'll avoid the term "optical" communications.)

Different media are suited for different communication jobs. The choice depends on the job and the nature of the transmission medium. One important factor is how signals are to be distributed. If the same signal is to be sent from one point to many people in an area—as in broadcast television or radio—the best choice may be nondirectional radio transmission. Radio-frequency communication is the best way to avoid cables for cellular phones and to reach remote places like tropical islands or arctic bases. On the other hand, a cable system is preferable for making physical links among many fixed points, as in telephone and cable television networks. Cable is also useful for permanent connections between two fixed points. Some types of transmission are shown in Figure 1.5.

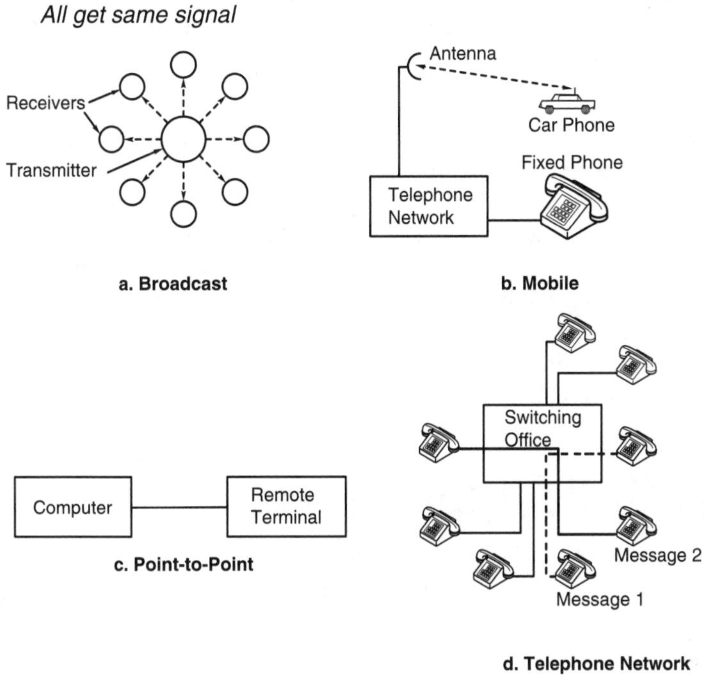

FIGURE 1.5

Types of communication transmission.

Capacity and Distance

When choosing the type of cable, key factors to consider are how far the signal must go and how much information it carries. Transmission distance depends on such effects as transmitter power, receiver sensitivity, and losses in the intervening medium. The

High transmission capacity and long transmission distance are two major advantages of fiber-optic cables.

amount of information carried is measured in the passage of signals through the system, much as we measure water volume flowing through a pipe. Some transmission media, such as simple pairs of wires, work fine for low-speed signals but cannot carry higher-speed signals very far. Others, such as coaxial cables, can carry higher-speed signals, but only over limited distances. A major attraction of optical fibers is that they can carry information at high speeds over long distances. (I'll attach some numbers to those terms in later chapters.)

Fiber optics transmit digital signals very well, an important asset because the global telecommunications network has shifted largely to digital transmission. Fibers also can transmit analog signals, still used in many video systems. An important operational advantage of fiber-optic cables is that most can be upgraded to transmit at higher speeds simply by replacing the transmitter and receiver. This is harder for copper cables but not impossible.

Secondary Factors

Secondary factors also influence the choice of transmission medium. A typical example is electromagnetic interference (EMI), which, like static on an AM radio, can sometimes block signal transmission on wires. Optical fibers cannot pick up EMI because they carry signals as light.

Different factors can dictate the choice of fiber for other applications. For example, security of the transmitted signals is a vital concern in military facilities and financial institutions. When cables must be installed in existing buildings, cable size and rigidity determine ease of installation, which is a major cost issue. The related issues of weight and bulk are major practical concerns in communication systems designed to be portable, ranging from electronic news-gathering equipment to battlefield communication systems. Avoiding sparks is a must in systems being installed in refineries and chemical plants, where the atmosphere may contain explosive gases. As you will see in Chapter 3, fiber optics can solve many of these problems.

Fiber-Optic Applications

The advantages of fiber optics have led to many applications in long-haul and short-distance communications.

The wide variety of fiber-optic systems that have come into use because of the advantages of optical fibers will be described in more detail in following chapters. They include the following:

- Long-haul telecommunication systems on land and at sea to carry many digitized signals simultaneously over long distances. These include ocean-spanning submarine cables and national backbone networks for telephone and Internet transmission.

- Interoffice trunks that carry many telephone conversations simultaneously between local and regional telephone switching facilities.

- Signal distribution from telephone switching centers to distribution nodes in residential neighborhoods and to businesses that use multiple phone lines or high-capacity digital lines.
- Connections to Internet service providers.
- Systems to carry cable television signals between microwave receivers and control facilities (called head-ends).
- Systems to transmit video and other signals (including digital data) from cable-system head-ends to neighborhood distribution nodes.
- Distribution of signals to remote interface units that convert them from optical format into electronic form suitable for transmission over twisted-wire phone lines or coaxial cables.
- Connections between the telephone network and antennas for mobile telephone service.
- Cables for remote news-gathering equipment.
- Links among computers and high-resolution video terminals used for such purposes as computer-aided design.
- Local-area networks operating at high speeds or over large areas, and backbone systems connecting slower local area networks.
- High-speed interconnections between computers and peripheral devices, between computers, or even within segments of single large computers.
- Moderate-speed transmission of computer data in places where fiber is most economical to install.
- Transmission in difficult environments, especially those plagued with severe EMI.
- Transmission of signals within ships, aircraft, and automobiles.

Meanwhile, fiber-optic technology has continued to expand into many areas outside of communications. These include fiber-optic bundles for illumination and imaging, endoscopes to view inside the body and treat diseases with light and without surgery, and optical sensors to measure rotation, pressure, sound waves, magnetic fields, and many other quantities.

These are today's fiber-optic applications. More are coming as fiber optics and other technologies develop. For example, fiber-optic systems are in development to provide a broad array of new and existing communication services to homes and businesses as described in Chapter 24. Telephone companies and cable television providers are maneuvering to corner that potentially large market. For now, however, I will concentrate on the realities of present-day technology.

What Have You Learned?

1. Light rays normally go in straight lines, but optical fibers can guide them around corners.

2. Early optical communication systems sent light through the air.

3. Optical fibers must have a cladding layer to keep light from leaking out.

4. The first applications of fiber optics were outside of communications.

5. Purification of glass reduced the loss of fibers dramatically to allow their use in communications.

6. Optical fibers are best for transmitting signals at high speeds or over long distances between fixed points.

7. Fiber optics have some special advantages, including immunity to electromagnetic interference, which can block transmission on wires.

8. Fiber optics are attractive for bringing a new generation of communication services to homes in the future.

What's Next?

In this chapter, we examined the background of fiber-optic technology. In Chapter 2, you'll learn some of the basic physics behind fiber optics before going into some specifics about fiber-optic hardware.

Quiz for Chapter 1

1. The first use of light for communication was
   a. Claude Chappe's optical telegraph.
   b. Native American smoke signals.
   c. a testbed that GTE installed in 1977.
   d. prehistoric signal fires.

2. Light can be guided around corners most efficiently in
   a. reflective pipes.
   b. hollow pipes with gas lenses.
   c. clad optical fibers.
   d. bare glass fibers.

3. The first low-loss optical fibers were made
   a. at Corning Glass Works in 1970.
   b. at Standard Telecommunication Labs in 1966.
   c. at Bell Telephone Labs in 1960.

4. Today's best optical fibers transmit light so well that 10% of the input light remains after

    a. 0.5 km.

    b. 4 km.

    c. 20 km.

    d. 50 km.

    e. 100 km.

5. Optical fibers are made of

    a. glass coated with plastic.

    b. ultrapure glass.

    c. plastic.

    d. all of these.

6. Essential components of any fiber-optic communication system are

    a. light source, fiber, and receiver.

    b. light source and cable.

    c. fiber and receiver.

    d. fiber only.

7. The small size of optical fibers makes what necessary in any device connecting them?

    a. Special glue.

    b. Tight mechanical tolerances.

    c. Low optical absorption.

    d. Small overall size.

8. What are the most important advantages of optical fibers for long-distance communications?

    a. Small fiber size.

    b. Nonmetallic.

    c. Low loss when carrying high-speed signals.

    d. Low loss only.

    e. High-speed signal capacity only.

9. Unlike wires, optical fibers are immune to

    a. electromagnetic interference.

    b. high-frequency transmission.

    c. signal losses.

10. Applications of fiber-optic communications include

    a. ocean-spanning submarine cables.

    b. long-distance telephone transmission on land.

    c. connecting telephone-company facilities.

    d. Internet backbone transmission.

    e. all of the above.

Fundamentals of Fiber Optics

About This Chapter

Fiber optics is a hybrid field that started as a branch of optics. The basic concept of a fiber is optical, and some single or bundled optical fibers are used as optical components. However, as fiber became a communication medium, the field borrowed concepts and terminology from electronic communications. Transmitters and receivers convert signals from electrical to optical format and back; they are part optics and part electronics. To understand fiber-optic communications, you need to know about three fields: optics, electronics, and communications.

This chapter is a starting point for basic concepts. In later chapters, I'll go into more detail on such topics as how light is guided in fibers and how optical fibers can serve as the basis of a communication system.

Basics of Optics

The workings of optical fibers depend on basic principles of optics and the interaction of light with matter. The first step in understanding fiber optics is to review the relevant parts of optics. The summary that follows does not cover all of optics, and some parts may seem basic, but you should read it to make sure you understand the fundamentals.

From a physical standpoint, light can be seen either as electromagnetic waves or as photons, quanta of electromagnetic energy. This is the famous wave-particle duality of modern physics. Both viewpoints are valid and valuable, but the simplest viewpoint for optics often is to consider light as rays traveling in straight lines between or within optical elements, which can reflect or refract (bend) light rays at their surfaces.

The Electromagnetic Spectrum

The light carried in fiber-optic communication systems can be viewed as either a wave or a particle.

What we call "light" is only a small part of the spectrum of electromagnetic radiation. The fundamental nature of all electromagnetic radiation is the same: it can be viewed as photons or waves and travels at the speed of light (c), which is approximately 300,000 kilometers per second (km/s), or 180,000 miles per second (mi/s). The difference between radiation in different parts of the electromagnetic spectrum is a quantity that can be measured in several ways: as the length of a wave, as the energy of a photon, or as the oscillation frequency of an electromagnetic field. These three views are compared in Figure 2.1.

Each measurement—wavelength, energy, or frequency—has its own characteristic unit.

FIGURE 2.1

Electromagnetic spectrum.

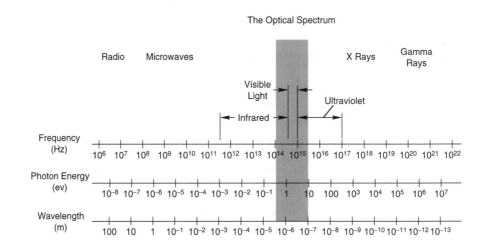

In some parts of the spectrum, frequency is used most; in others, photon energy or wavelength is. The optical world talks in wavelength, which is measured in metric units—meters, micrometers (μm or 10^{-6} m), and nanometers (nm or 10^{-9} m). Wavelength is sometimes measured in angstroms ($1\text{Å} = 10^{-10}$ m), but the angstrom is not a standard unit, so it is rarely used. Don't even think of wavelength in inches. (If you absolutely have to know, 1 μm is 1/25,000 in.) Frequency is measured in cycles per second (cps) or hertz (Hz), with megahertz (MHz) meaning a million hertz and gigahertz (GHz) meaning a billion hertz. (The metric system uses the standard prefixes listed in Table 2.1 to provide different units of length, weight, frequency, and other quantities. The prefix makes a unit a multiple of a standard unit. For example, a millimeter is a thousandth [10^{-3}] of a meter, and a kilometer is a thousand [10^3] meters.) Photon energy can be measured in many ways, but the most convenient here is in electron volts (eV)—the energy that an electron gains in moving through a 1-volt (V) electric field.

Table 2.1. Metric unit prefixes and their meanings.

Prefix	Symbol	Multiple
tera	T	10^{12} (trillion)
giga	G	10^9 (billion)
mega	M	10^6 (million)
kilo	k	10^3 (thousand)
hecto	h	10^2 (hundred)
deca	da	10^1 (ten)
deci	d	10^{-1} (tenth)
centi	c	10^{-2} (hundredth)
milli	m	10^{-3} (thousandth)
micro	μ	10^{-6} (millionth)
nano	n	10^{-9} (billionth)
pico	p	10^{-12} (trillionth)
femto	f	10^{-15} (quadrillionth)

All the measurement units shown on the spectrum chart are actually different rulers that measure the same thing. There are simple ways to convert between them. Wavelength is inversely proportional to frequency, according to the following formula:

$$\text{wavelength} = \frac{c}{\text{frequency}}$$

or

$$\lambda = \frac{c}{\nu}$$

where c is the speed of light, λ is wavelength, and ν is frequency. To get the right answer, all terms must be measured in the same units. Thus c must be in meters per second (m/s), λ must be in meters, and frequency must be in hertz (or cycles per second). Plugging in the number for c, we have a more useful formula for wavelength:

$$\lambda = \frac{3 \times 10^8 \text{ m/s}}{\nu}$$

You can also turn this around to get the frequency if you know the wavelength:

$$\nu = \frac{3 \times 10^8 \text{ m/s}}{\lambda}$$

Not many people talk about photon energy (E) in fiber optics, but a value can be gotten from Planck's law, which states:

$$E = h\nu$$

where h is Planck's constant (6.63×10^{-34} J-s, or 4.14 eV-s) and ν is the frequency. Because most interest in photon energy is in the part of the spectrum measured in wavelength, a more useful formula is

$$E\,(\text{eV}) = \frac{1.2406}{\lambda\,(\mu\text{m})}$$

which gives energy in electron volts when wavelength is measured in micrometers (μm).

Light waves that are 180° out of phase with each other can cancel each other out.

There is one practical consequence of the wave aspect of light's personality, which you will meet later on. Light waves can interfere with each other. Normally this does not show up because many different light waves are present and the effect averages out. Suppose, however, that only two identical light waves are present, as shown in Figure 2.2. The total amount of light detectable is the sum of the amplitudes of the light waves squared. If the light waves are neatly lined up, what is called "in phase," they add together and give a bright spot. However, if the two light waves are aligned so that the peaks of one coincide with the troughs of the other, they interfere destructively and cancel each other out. This happens when the two light waves are 180° out of phase with each other. If the two waves are out of phase by a different amount, they add together to give an intensity between the maximum and minimum possible.

We are mainly interested in a small part of the spectrum shown in Figure 2.1—the optical region, where optical fibers and other optical devices work. That region includes light visible to the human eye at wavelengths of 400–700 nm and nearby parts of the infrared and ultraviolet, which have similar properties. Roughly speaking, this means wavelengths of 200–20,000 nm (0.2–20 μm).

Fiber-optic communication systems transmit near-infrared light invisible to the human eye.

The wavelengths normally used for communications through silica glass optical fibers are 700–1600 nm (0.7–1.6 μm) in the near infrared, where silica is the most transparent. Glass and silica fibers can transmit visible light over shorter distances, and special grades of silica (often called fused quartz) can transmit near-ultraviolet light over short distances.

Plastic fibers typically transmit better at visible wavelengths than in the near infrared, so communications through plastic fibers typically is with visible light. However, plastic fibers are not as transparent as silica glass. Fibers made from certain other materials can transmit at longer infrared wavelengths than silica glass fibers.

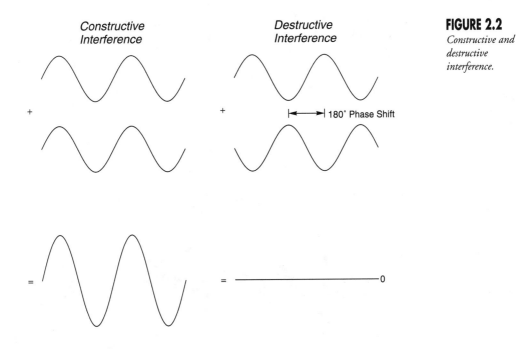

FIGURE 2.2

Constructive and destructive interference.

Refractive Index

A critical optical characteristic for any transparent material is its refractive index (n). The refractive index is the ratio of the speed of light in a vacuum to the speed of light in the medium:

$$n = \frac{c_{vac}}{c_{mat}}$$

Light always travels more slowly in a material than in a vacuum, so the refractive index is always greater than 1.0 in the optical part of the spectrum. In practice, the refractive index is measured by comparing the speed of light in the material to that in air rather than in a vacuum. The refractive index of air at atmospheric pressure and room temperature is 1.00028, so close to 1.0 that the difference is insignificant.

Although light rays travel in straight lines through optical materials, something different happens at the surface. Light is bent as it passes through a surface where the refractive index changes—for example, as it passes from air into glass, as shown in Figure 2.3. The amount of bending depends on the refractive indexes of the two media and the angle at which the light strikes the surface between them. The angles of incidence and refraction are measured not from the plane of the surface but from a line normal (perpendicular) to the surface. The relationship is known as Snell's law, which is written

$$n_i \sin I = n_r \sin R$$

The refractive index of a material is the ratio of the speed of light in a vacuum to the speed of light in the material.

Refraction occurs when light passes through a surface where the refractive index changes.

where n_i and n_r are the refractive indexes of the initial medium and the medium into which the light is refracted, and I and R are the angles of incidence and refraction, respectively, as shown in Figure 2.3.

FIGURE 2.3

Light refraction as it enters glass.

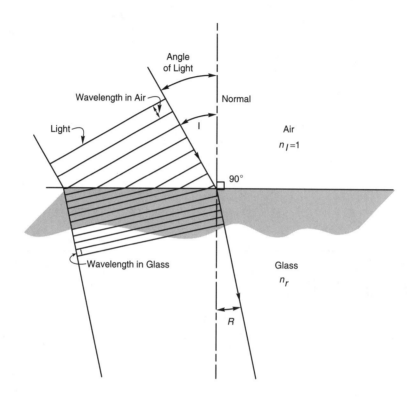

Figure 2.3 shows the standard textbook example of light going from air into glass. The frequency of the wave does not change, but because it slows down in the glass, the wavelength gets shorter, causing the light wave to bend, whether the surface is flat or curved. However, if both front and rear surfaces are flat, light emerges at the same angle that it entered, and the net refraction is zero, as when you look through a flat window. If one or both surfaces are curved, you see a net refraction or bending of the light, as if you were looking through a lens. That is, light rays emerge from the lens at a different angle than they entered. These overall refractive effects are shown in Figure 2.4.

What does this have to do with fiber optics? Stop and consider what happens when light in a medium with a high refractive index (such as glass) comes to an interface with a medium having a lower refractive index (such as air). If the glass has a refractive index of 1.5 and the air an index of 1.0, the equation becomes

$$1.5 \sin I = 1 \sin R$$

FIGURE 2.4

*Light refraction
through a window
and a lens.*

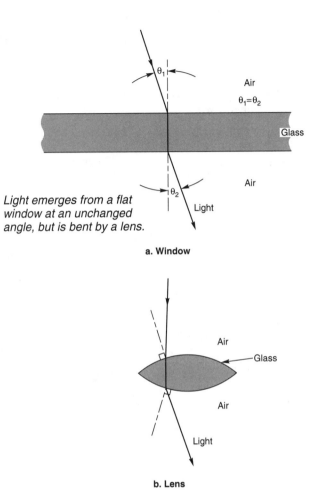

*Light emerges from a flat
window at an unchanged
angle, but is bent by a lens.*

a. Window

b. Lens

That means that instead of being bent closer to the normal, as in Figure 2.3, the light is bent farther from it, as in Figure 2.5. This isn't a problem if the angle of incidence is small. For $I = 30°$, $\sin I = 0.5$, and $\sin R = 0.75$. But a problem does occur when the angle of incidence becomes too steep. For $I = 60°$, $\sin I = 0.866$, so Snell's law says that $\sin R = 1.299$. Your pocket calculator will tell you this is an error. That angle can't exist because the sine can't be greater than 1.0.

Snell's law indicates that refraction can't take place when the angle of incidence is too large, and that's true. Light cannot get out of the glass if the angle of incidence exceeds a value called the critical angle, where the sine of the angle of refraction would equal 1.0. (Recall from trigonometry that the maximum value of the sine is 1.0 at 90°.) Instead, total internal reflection bounces the light back into the glass, obeying the law that the angle of incidence equals the angle of reflection, as shown in Figure 2.5. It is this total

If light hits a boundary with a material of lower refractive index at a steep enough (i.e., glancing) angle, it is reflected back into the high-index medium. This total internal reflection is the basic concept behind the optical fiber.

internal reflection that keeps light confined in optical fibers, at least to a first approximation. As you will see in Chapter 4, the mechanism of light guiding is more complex in most modern communication fibers.

The critical angle above which total internal reflection takes place, θ_c, can be deduced by turning Snell's law around, to give

$$\theta_c = \arcsin{(n_r/n_i)}$$

For the example given, with light trying to emerge from glass with $n = 1.5$ into air, the critical angle is arcsin (1/1.5), or 41.8°.

FIGURE 2.5

Refraction and total internal reflection.

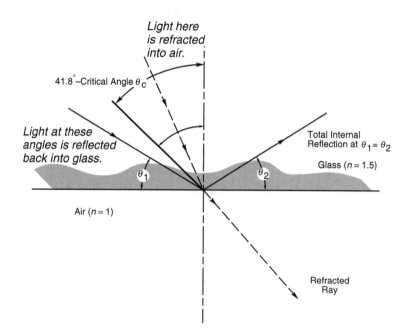

Light Guiding

Light is guided in the core of an optical fiber by total internal reflection at the boundary of the lower-index cladding.

The two key elements of an optical fiber—from an optical standpoint—are its core and cladding. The core is the inner part of the fiber, through which light is guided. The cladding surrounds it completely. The refractive index of the core is higher than that of the cladding, so light in the core that strikes the boundary with the cladding at a glancing angle is confined in the core by total internal reflection, as shown in Figure 2.6.

The difference in refractive index between core and cladding need not be large. In practice, it is only about 1%. This still allows light guiding in fibers. For $n_r/n_i = 0.99$, the critical angle, θ_c, is about 82°. Thus, light is confined in the core if it strikes the interface with

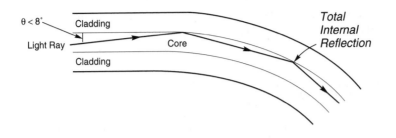

FIGURE 2.6

Light guiding in an optical fiber.

the cladding at an angle of 8°or less to the surface. The upper limit can be considered the confinement angle in the fiber.

Another way to look at light guiding in a fiber is to measure the fiber's acceptance angle— the angle over which light rays entering the fiber will be guided along its core, shown in Figure 2.7. (Because the acceptance angle is measured in air outside the fiber, it differs from the confinement angle in the glass.) The acceptance angle normally is measured as numerical aperture (NA), which for light entering a fiber from air is approximately

$$NA = \sqrt{(n_0^2 - n_1^2)}$$

where n_0 is the refractive index of the core and n_1 is the index of the cladding. For a fiber with core index of 1.50 and cladding index of 1.485 (a 1% difference), NA = 0.21. An alternative but equivalent definition is the sine of the half-angle over which the fiber can accept light rays, 12° in this example (θ in Figure 2.7). Another alternative definition is $NA = n_0 \sin \theta_c$, where θ_c is the confinement angle in the fiber core (8° in this example).

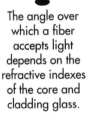

The angle over which a fiber accepts light depends on the refractive indexes of the core and cladding glass.

Note that the half acceptance angle is larger than the largest glancing angle at which light rays must strike the cladding interface to be reflected, which I said earlier was 8°. What does this mean? Go back and look at Snell's law of refraction again. The difference is the factor n_0, which is the refractive index of the core glass, or 1.5. As you can see in Figure 2.7, refraction bends a light ray entering the fiber so that it is at a smaller angle to the fiber

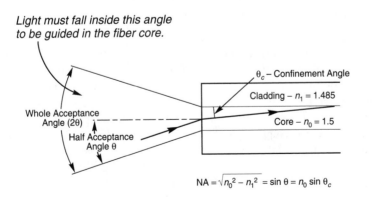

FIGURE 2.7

Measuring the acceptance angle.

axis than it was in the air. The sine of the angle inside the glass equals that of the angle outside the glass, divided by the refractive index of the core (n_0).

Light Collection

Practical applications for single fibers require ways to get light into their small cores.

Numerical aperture and acceptance angle measure a crucial concern in practical fiber-optic systems: getting light into the fiber. A century ago, British physicist Charles Vernon Boys made fine fibers of glass comparable in size to today's optical fibers, but as far as we know he didn't try to transmit light along their lengths. Even when the first practical optical fibers were developed in the 1950s, no one seemed to think that single fibers could collect much light. Instead, they grouped fibers into bundles that together could collect reasonable amounts of light. Only when lasers made highly directional beams available did researchers seriously begin to consider using single optical fibers.

Light Source and Fiber Size

A fiber will pick up some light from any source. Hold a single fiber so one end points at a lightbulb. Now look into the other end, bending the fiber so you don't look directly at the light. You can see that the fiber collects some light, but only a very small fraction of the light from the bulb.

There are two essential problems: mismatches in collection angle and between the sizes of the light source and fiber. Simple optics can focus light from an ordinary bulb down to a small angle. You can see the results in a flashlight beam or a searchlight. Look carefully, and you will see that the focusing is not perfect, but the beams are reasonably directional. Matching sizes generally proves to be more difficult. Even a bundle of fibers is small compared to most lightbulbs, and single fibers are much smaller. The largest fibers have cores about 1 mm (1000 μm), but they are rarely used in communications. Standard glass communication fibers have cladding diameter of 125 μm (0.125 mm), and their light-guiding cores are even smaller, 8–62.5 μm.

Focusing light from large sources onto such small spots is possible, but it normally leaves the light spreading at too large an angle for the fiber to collect efficiently. It's more efficient to find a light source that matches the fiber size. For small-core fibers, a good match is a semiconductor diode laser, which usually emits light from a stripe a fraction of a micrometer high and a few micrometers wide. (There are some newer types that operate differently.) Other compact lasers are alternatives, notably optical fibers doped with impurities so they can amplify light. For larger-core fibers, light-emitting diodes (LEDs) are a possible source because they are less expensive and have larger emitting areas. On the other hand, lasers and optical amplifiers generate more light and can carry signals at higher speeds. Later chapters discuss light sources in more detail.

Alignment

Transferring light between fibers requires careful alignment and tight tolerances. The greatest efficiency comes when the ends of two fibers are permanently joined in a splice (described in Chapter 14). Temporary junctions between two fiber ends, made by connectors (described in Chapter 13) typically have slightly higher losses but allow much greater flexibility in reconfiguring a fiber-optic network. Special devices called couplers (described in Chapter 15) are needed to join three or more fiber ends. One of the most important functional differences between fiber-optic and wire communications is that fiber couplers are much harder to make than their metal-wire counterparts.

Losses in transferring signals between wires are so small that they can normally be neglected. This is not so for fiber optics. As you will see in Chapter 20, system designers should account for coupling losses at each connector, coupler, splice, and light source.

Joining the ends of optical fibers requires careful alignment and tight tolerances.

Transfer losses must be considered in fiber-optic communication systems.

Transmission and Attenuation

Transmission of light by optical fibers is not 100% efficient. Some light is lost, causing attenuation of the signal. Several mechanisms are involved, including absorption by materials within the fiber, scattering of light out of the fiber core, and leakage of light out of the core caused by environmental factors. The degree of attenuation also depends on the wavelength of light transmitted, as you will see in Chapter 5. This makes operating wavelength an important feature of a fiber system.

Attenuation measures the reduction in signal strength by comparing output power with input power. Measurements are made in decibels (dB), a very useful unit, albeit a peculiar one. The decibel is a logarithmic unit measuring the ratio of output to input power. (It is actually a tenth of a unit called a *bel* after Alexander Graham Bell, but that base unit is virtually never used.) Loss in decibels is defined as

$$\text{dB loss} = -10 \times \log_{10} \left(\frac{\text{power out}}{\text{power in}} \right)$$

Thus, if output power is 0.001 of input power, the signal has experienced a 30-dB loss.

The minus sign is added to avoid negative numbers in attenuation measurements. It is not used in systems where the signal level might increase, where the sign of the logarithm indicates if the signal has decreased (minus) or increased (plus).

Each optical fiber has a characteristic attenuation that is measured in decibels per unit length, normally decibels per kilometer. The total attenuation (in decibels) in the fiber equals the characteristic attenuation times the length. To understand why, consider a simple example, with a fiber having the relatively high attenuation of 10 dB/km. That is, only 10% of the light that enters the fiber emerges from a 1-km length. If that output light was

Some light is lost in transmission through a fiber. The amount of loss depends on wavelength.

Attenuation of a fiber is the product of the length times the characteristic loss in decibels per kilometer.

sent through another kilometer of the same fiber, only 10% of it would emerge (or 1% of the original signal), for a total loss of 20 dB.

As you will see later in this chapter, the choice of operating wavelength depends not only on fiber loss but also on the available light sources and on other fiber properties. The loss of silica fibers in the near infrared is much lower than signal attenuation in other media with comparable transmission capability. Attenuation is very low at 1300 nm and even lower at 1550 nm. At the 0.4-dB/km attenuation typical near 1300 nm, 1% of the light entering the fiber remains after 50 km, for a 20-dB loss. At the 0.25-dB/km attenuation common at 1550 nm, 1% of the input light remains after 80 km. That allows signals to go through more than 100 km of fiber without amplification, an important advantage in communications. Metal coaxial cables, which have comparable information capacity, would require several dozen amplifiers over such distances (depending on transmission rate).

Bandwidth and Dispersion

Optical fibers are unique in allowing high-speed signal transmission at low attenuation.

Low attenuation alone is not enough to make optical fibers invaluable for telecommunications. The thick wires used to transmit electrical power also have very low loss, but they cannot transmit information at high speeds. Optical fibers are attractive because they combine low loss with high bandwidth to support the transmission of high-speed signals over long distances (i.e., high information capacity).

Information Capacity

Information capacity is very important in all types of communications but is measured differently in different types of systems. Where data is transmitted digitally (i.e., in digitized "bits" or units of information), transmission capacity is measured in bits per second. The more bits that can pass through a system in a given time, the more information it can carry. A 100-megabit-per-second (Mbit/s) system can carry as much information as a hundred 1-Mbit/s systems. As long as all the information is going between the same two points, it is much cheaper to build one 100-Mbit/s system than a hundred 1-Mbit/s systems. The same principle works for analog communications, like the telephone line to your home or most television signals, but we measure capacity by the frequency bandwidth in hertz.

In practice, the attenuation of copper wires increases with the frequency of the electrical signals they carry. Electrical power wires have low attenuation only at very low frequencies, including the 60-Hz variation of alternating current. Coaxial cables can transmit higher frequencies, but their loss increases sharply with frequency, as shown in Figure 2.8. However, the loss of optical fibers is essentially independent of signal frequency over their normal operating range. (The scale is measured in loss per kilometer of cable and does not take into account the transfer losses mentioned earlier.)

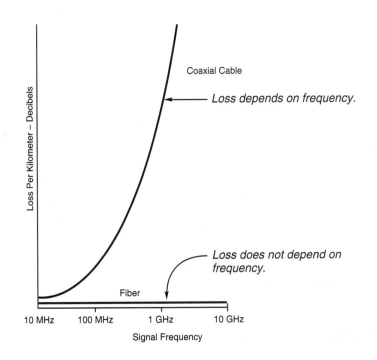

FIGURE 2.8

Loss as a function of frequency.

Transmission Speed Limits

Effects other than loss limit fiber transmission speed. They are best seen by looking at digital transmission, although they also occur for analog transmission. Consider another view of the basic optical fiber shown in Figure 2.9. As long as the fiber has a core diameter much larger than the wavelength of light (i.e., well over 10 μm), rays can enter the fiber at many different angles to its axis. A ray that bounces back and forth within the core

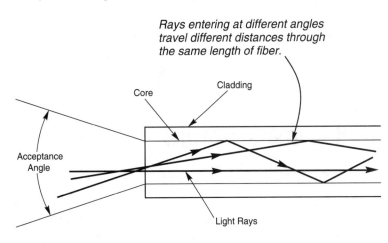

FIGURE 2.9

Light rays take different paths in a fiber core.

many times will travel a slightly greater distance than one that goes straight through. For instance, if one ray traveled straight through a 1-km fiber and another bounced back and forth at a 5° angle through a 100-μm core through the same fiber, the second ray would travel 3.8 m farther.

You can see what this means for communications by thinking about what happens to light rays that start together in an instantaneous pulse. The one that goes down the center of the fiber will reach the output end first, 19 ns before the ray that bounced back and forth at a 5° angle. Thus an instantaneous pulse at the start of the fiber would spread out to 19 ns at the end.

> **Pulse dispersion limits fiber transmission capacity.**

This phenomenon is called pulse dispersion. This example gives a rather simplified view of how light travels through the fiber in what are called different modes. As you will see in Chapter 5, other effects can also cause various degrees of pulse dispersion. Dispersion is important because, as the pulses spread, they can overlap and interfere with each other, limiting data transmission speed. In this example, if each pulse went through 1 km of fiber, it would acquire a 19-ns tail. So the time between pulses would have to be at least that long, limiting transmission to 50 Mbit/s. Because actual input pulses are not instantaneous, the real maximum pulse rate would be even slower.

Dispersion and Distance

> **Pulse dispersion increases with distance, so maximum transmission rate decreases with distance.**

Because pulses stretch out a certain amount for each kilometer of fiber, pulse dispersion—like attenuation measured in decibels—increases linearly with distance traveled. That is, pulse dispersion doubles if transmission distance doubles. Typical dispersion values for fibers that carry multiple modes are measured in nanoseconds (of dispersion) per kilometer of fiber. These can be translated into an analog bandwidth limit or a maximum data rate for digital transmission. Both bandwidth and data rate are the inverse of pulse dispersion, so they decrease as the distance of the fiber increases.

The bandwidths quoted so far are low by fiber-optic standards because they are for fibers that carry light in many modes. Dispersion is much smaller in fibers that carry light in only one mode, which will be described in more detail in Chapter 4. These single-mode fibers can carry billions of bits per second over tens of kilometers without amplification. The residual dispersion in them depends on the range of wavelengths emitted by the light source.

> **Semiconductor lasers, LEDs, and erbium-doped fiber amplifiers are the most common light sources in fiber-optic communications.**

System Considerations

Transmitters and Light Sources

Optical transmitters generate the signals carried by fiber-optic communication systems. They use light sources chosen to match the properties of optical fibers. There are several standard configurations, which are used in different circumstances.

Visible red LEDs generally are used with all-plastic fibers, which transmit visible wavelengths better than the near-infrared. Distances are short and speeds are modest.

Near-infrared LEDs and semiconductor lasers made from gallium arsenide (GaAs) and gallium aluminum arsenide (GaAlAs) emitting at 750 to 900 nm are used with glass optical fibers for relatively short links and moderate speed systems. This technology was the first developed for commercial fiber-optic systems and is relatively inexpensive, although it is limited in performance.

The most common system configuration for telecommunications is a semiconductor laser transmitting at 1300 nm through glass fibers, which have loss of 0.35 to 0.5 dB/km at that wavelength. The lasers are made from another semiconductor compound, indium gallium arsenide phosphide (InGaAsP). LEDs can be made from the same material to operate at the same wavelengths, but their power is too low and transmission speeds are too low for most applications. Solid-state crystalline lasers containing neodymium also can operate at 1300 nm, but they have not been widely used because they are much more complex—and hence more costly—to operate.

Many long-distance telecommunication systems also transmit signals at wavelengths near 1550 nm, where glass fibers have attenuation of only 0.2 to 0.3 dB/km. InGaAsP lasers operate at this wavelength (LEDs are not used because they cannot generate enough light to go long distances). Optical fibers doped with the rare earth erbium also generate light near 1550 nm, but they are used more often to amplify an optical signal that has traveled a long distance than to generate a new optical signal. Optical amplifiers are described in Chapter 12.

Signal Format and Modulation

Signals are transmitted by modulating the intensity of a carrier. For radio or television, the carrier is a single frequency transmitted steadily. For optical communication, it is a beam of light. In both cases, the modulation can be digital or analog. Digital modulation turns the carrier signal off and on; analog modulation varies the carrier intensity (or sometimes its frequency) in a way proportional to the analog input. Most fiber-optic systems use the digital transmission technology that has become common in modern telecommunications, but some use analog transmission, particularly for applications such as cable television, where signals are still transmitted in analog form.

● Signals can be transmitted in analog or digital form.

Transmitting a fiber-optic signal requires modulating the intensity of a light source. This can be done in two ways: by modulating the input power to directly change source intensity or by changing the intensity of the beam after it leaves the light source. Each approach has its advantages.

● Changing current passing through a semiconductor laser or LED directly modulates its light output.

Direct modulation is simple, which can be a compelling advantage. It works best for LEDs and semiconductor lasers, because their light output changes with the drive current passing through the semiconductor device, as shown in Figure 2.10. Turning the drive current on and off with a digital signal produces a series of light pulses. Analog modulation makes light output rise and fall continuously with variations in the drive current. The current-output curves of optical devices are not perfectly linear, so direct modulation can cause some distortion of analog signals. However, digital signals suffer little from such distortion because the intensity of the signal is less important than its presence or absence.

FIGURE 2.10
Relationship between drive current and optical output.

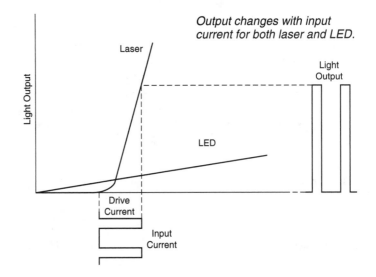

External modulation is more complex, because it requires an external modulator that changes the intensity of the light passing through it, as described in Chapter 15. External modulators offer two distinct advantages. One is their ability to modulate the output of certain types of lasers which cannot be modulated directly. A second is somewhat higher performance, because rapid modulation of a semiconductor laser can cause undesired side effects, such as small shifts in its output wavelength.

Multiplexing

Many signals can be combined or multiplexed into a single transmission in an optical fiber system.

As with other communication systems, fiber-optic systems often combine, or *multiplex*, multiple signals that follow the same route. Multiplexing is particularly valuable for fiber optics because of the huge potential capacity of individual fibers. Three main types of multiplexing can be used in fiber-optic systems: directional, time-division, and wavelength-division.

It is possible to send signals in opposite directions through the same fiber. However, this is done only rarely because the signals can interact with each other, degrading performance. Directional multiplexing works best if the signals are at different wavelengths.

Time-division multiplexing is the combining of bit streams from several different signals, as shown in Figure 2.11. For example, four signals at 10 million bits (megabits) per second can be combined to generate one 40-Mbit/s signal. As you will see later, there is a standard set of time-division multiplexing rates used in telecommunications. They were originally developed for electronic systems but have been adapted and extended for fiber-optic transmission. A demultiplexer separates them at the end for distribution.

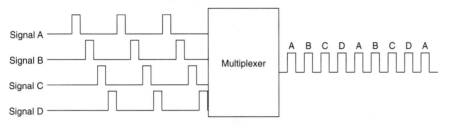

FIGURE 2.11

Time-division multiplexing combines several slow signals into a faster one.

Wavelength-division multiplexing (WDM) combines signals at different wavelengths to travel through the same fiber, as shown in Figure 2.12. Optics combine signals at several different wavelengths, which pass along the same fiber with minimal interaction to a demultiplexer, which splits them apart and routes them to their separate destinations. Wavelength-division multiplexing has become important because it can multiply the transmission capacity of a single fiber without the installation of new cable. WDM sometimes is called *frequency-division multiplexing* because the various wavelengths have different frequencies, making it analogous to frequency-division multiplexing used in radio and electronic transmission, where many television channels are sent through a coaxial cable at different carrier frequencies.

Wavelength-division multiplexing can multiply the transmission capacity of a single fiber.

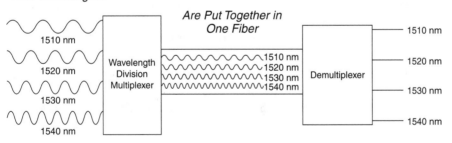

FIGURE 2.12

Wavelength-division multiplexing sends separate signals through one fiber at different wavelengths.

Switching

Switching is an integral part of telecommunication networks. Switches route signals from one point to another in the network. Historically, switching was developed for the telephone network to make temporary connections between pairs of phones so people could talk with each other. At first, local operators made temporary connections with cords on switchboards. Gradually, automated machines took over those functions and expanded

Switches are needed to route signals to separate destinations.

automatic dialing around the world. Switches direct signals from your home to a local switching center and from there to other switching centers around the world.

Electronic switching technology, using special-purpose semiconductor electronics and computers, is much better developed today than optical switching. This partly reflects the greater difficulty in manipulating photons than electrons. It also reflects the investment of much more effort in developing electronic switches over many more years than optical switches have been in development. However, optical switches do exist, and offer important advantages, such as the ability to reroute all signals carried by a single fiber in case of cable failures.

Not all systems require switches. Cables need no switches if they merely run between two points—whether from your home to the phone pole outside or from California to Hawaii. Today, most fiber-optic systems function as point-to-point links, running between nodes where electronic switches can route signals as necessary. This will change as optical switches improve.

Detection

● **A receiver converts optical signals emerging from the end of a fiber back into an electronic signal in a standard format.**

The last element in any fiber-optic link is the receiver, which detects the optical signal emerging from the end of the fiber and converts it to electronic form for further transmission or processing. Typically a receiver consists of a semiconductor photodetector and amplifying electronics. (Details are described in Chapter 11.) Further optical processing may be possible at some point in the future, but at present optical devices to process the light signals emerging from fibers are only in the laboratory stage.

How well the detector does its job depends on its sensitivity and the signal level reaching it. Sensitivity, in turn, depends on operating conditions, detector design, and how the light-sensitive detector material responds to the signal wavelength. For example, silicon photodiodes work well at 400 to 1000 nm but are not sensitive to the longer wavelengths of 1300 and 1550 nm used in most long-distance fiber systems.

● **Amplifiers, repeaters, and regenerators can stretch transmission distance beyond the point where the light signal would otherwise fade out.**

Receiver electronics process the electrical signal generated by the detector to replicate the original signal sent through the fiber. You can think of this as cleaning up the signal emerging from the optical information pipeline. The signal itself is amplified. Digital pulse edges, which grow blurred as the signal passes through the system, are sharpened by detecting when the signal strength passes a threshold level. Timing of a series of pulses is checked and corrected.

Stretching Transmission Distance

Although optical fibers can carry signals long distances because of their low loss, the signal intensity declines with distance. Eventually, it can fade to a point where the signal cannot be detected accurately or reliably. If the signal is to travel further, it must be amplified before the power becomes too low for the receivers. There are two ways to do this: by amplifying the optical signal directly or by detecting it, cleaning it up, and regenerating it.

An optical amplifier is conceptually the simplest approach. As described in Chapter 12, it takes a weak input signal and amplifies it to generate a higher power. The only type of optical amplifier now in wide use is the erbium-doped fiber amplifier, a length of fiber with the rare-earth element erbium added to its core. A separate light source illuminates the fiber, exciting the erbium atoms so they amplify light at wavelengths between about 1.5 and 1.6 µm. This strengthens the signal so it can travel through another length of fiber, but it also amplifies any noise or distortion. Semiconductor lasers also can be adapted for use as optical amplifiers, as described in Chapter 12.

A repeater or regenerator works differently. It detects a weak optical input signal and then processes it to clean it up, "regenerating" a sharp and clear signal that should accurately reproduce the original waveform. You'll see how this works in Chapter 12.

The difference between optical amplifiers and regenerators, shown in Figure 2.13, is important. Noise and distortion accumulate as a signal passes through a series of optical amplifiers, but each repeater should generate a clean signal. On the other hand, repeaters are much more complex and costly than optical amplifiers, and they have some important performance limits. In practice, this means that optical amplifiers and repeaters are used in different ways. Typically, optical amplifiers are spaced more closely together, so they amplify more signal and less noise. Regenerators are spaced further apart, because they can remove noise and because they are much more costly. We talk more about these trade-offs in Chapter 12.

Optical amplifiers simply amplify weak signals; regenerators clean them up and regenerate them.

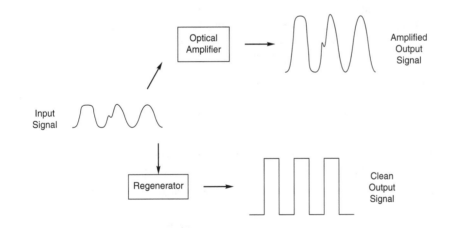

FIGURE 2.13

Optical amplification increases signal strength. Regeneration cleans up the signal.

Design Considerations

Fiber-optic communications has found a vast array of applications, as you will see in Chapter 3. System design depends largely on the application. For long-distance telecommunications—including the most demanding applications in transoceanic submarine cables—crucial factors include maximizing transmission speed and distance and minimizing fiber and splice loss. By contrast, connector loss becomes vital in local area

Design of fiber-optic systems and choice of hardware depend upon the application.

networks that distribute signals within buildings. In long-haul systems, it is important to minimize the cost of cable, while the goal is to reduce the cost of terminal equipment for local area networks (because there are many separate terminals, rather than the two required for point-to-point communications).

These system considerations make design and construction of practical fiber-optic systems a multifaceted task. Guidelines appropriate for one type of system should not be followed blindly for others, because they often lead directly to the wrong answers. Applications are diverse enough that many different components are offered.

What Have You Learned?

1. Light is part of the electromagnetic spectrum, a wave that has a distinct wavelength, frequency, and photon energy.
2. Wavelength equals the speed of light divided by the frequency.
3. Refractive index (n) is a crucial property of optical materials. It equals the speed of light in vacuum divided by the speed of light in the material, so it is always greater than 1.
4. Total internal reflection can trap light inside a material with higher refractive index than its surroundings.
5. The critical angle for total internal reflection at a surface depends on the refractive indexes of the materials on either side. The larger the difference, the larger the angle over which total internal reflection occurs.
6. The core of an optical fiber must have a higher refractive index than the cladding surrounding it.
7. Light is guided through optical fibers by total internal reflection of light entering within an acceptance angle.
8. LEDs and lasers are the light sources for fiber-optic communications.
9. Glass optical fibers transmit signals at 750–900, 1300, and 1500–1600 nm in the near infrared. Plastic optical fibers transmit visible light.
10. The small size of optical fibers makes tolerances tight for transferring light into fibers.
11. The low attenuation of optical fibers allows them to carry high-speed signals over long distances.
12. Fiber attenuation is usually measured in decibels per kilometer. Total attenuation of a length of fiber (in decibels) equals that value times the length in kilometers.
13. Transmission capacity of optical fibers depends on the dispersion of light pulses sent through them.
14. Attenuation and dispersion of an optical fiber vary with wavelength.

15. Gallium arsenide LEDs and lasers operate at 750–900 nm. InGaAsP lasers emit at 1300–1600 nm.

16. Direct modulation of drive current changes how much light a semiconductor laser or LED emits. External modulation changes power in the beam after it leaves the laser.

17. Multiplexing combines two or more signals.

18. Optical amplifiers, repeaters, and regenerators stretch transmission distance by boosting strength of weak signals.

What's Next?

In Chapter 3, we will look at the major applications for fiber optics, particularly in communications.

Quiz for Chapter 2

1. If light passes from air to glass, it is
   a. reflected.
   b. refracted.
   c. absorbed.
   d. scattered.

2. Light is confined within the core of a simple clad optical fiber by
   a. refraction.
   b. total internal reflection at the outer edge of the cladding.
   c. total internal reflection at the core-cladding boundary.
   d. reflection from the fiber's plastic coating.

3. An optical fiber has a core with refractive index of 1.52 and a cladding with index of 1.45. Its numerical aperture is
   a. 0.15.
   b. 0.20.
   c. 0.35.
   d. 0.46.
   e. 0.70.

4. The input power to a fiber-optic cable is 1 mW. The cable's loss is 20 dB. What is the output power, assuming there are no other losses?
   a. 0.10 mW.
   b. 0.05 mW.
   c. 0.01 mW.
   d. 0.001 mW.
   e. None of the above.

5. How far can an optical fiber with attenuation of 0.5 dB/km transmit a signal with initial power of 1 mW if the receiver requires an input power of 0.001 mW?
   a. 30 km.
   b. 60 km.
   c. 80 km.
   d. 90 km.
   e. 120 km.

6. The output of a 20-km fiber with attenuation of 0.5 dB/km is 0.005 mW. What is the input power to the fiber?

   a. 1 mW.

   b. 0.5 mW.

   c. 0.05 mW.

   d. 0.01 mW.

   e. None of the above.

7. What fraction of the input power remains after light travels through 100 km of fiber with attenuation of 0.3 dB/km?

   a. 10%.

   b. 5%.

   c. 1%.

   d. 0.5%.

   e. 0.1%.

8. Attenuation of glass optical fibers is lowest at

   a. 650 nm.

   b. 850 nm.

   c. 900 nm.

   d. 1300 nm.

   e. 1550 nm.

9. A pulse of light is 300 ns long when it emerges from a 20-km optical fiber. What is the fiber dispersion, assuming the pulse was instantaneous when it entered?

   a. 15 ns/km.

   b. 20 ns/km.

   c. 25 ns/km.

   d. 30 ns/km.

   e. 35 ns/km.

10. Using wavelength-division multiplexing, eight signals at 500 Mbit/s are transmitted through the same optical fiber. What is the total data rate?

   a. 500 Mbit/s.

   b. 1000 Mbit/s.

   c. 2000 Mbit/s.

   d. 4000 Mbit/s.

   e. 8000 Mbit/s.

11. A single optical fiber carries 24 signals combined by time-division multiplexing. The total data rate is 144 Mbit/s. If all 24 input signals are at the same rate, what is their data rate?

   a. 1.4 Mbit/s.

   b. 6 Mbit/s.

   c. 24 Mbit/s.

   d. 144 Mbit/s.

   e. 3456 Mbit/s.

12. What is the difference between an optical amplifier and a regenerator?

   a. No functional difference; they are different brand names.

   b. An optical amplifier amplifies a weak light signal; a regenerator processes the signal to reproduce the input signal.

   c. Regenerators work only on electrical signals; optical amplifiers work only on light.

   d. An optical amplifier is the input stage of a regenerator.

Applications of Fiber Optics

About This Chapter

The most widespread applications of fiber optics now are in communications. Optical fibers serve as flexible, low-loss "plumbing" to carry light signals in environments from climate-controlled offices to the bottom of the ocean. They span distances from across an office to across the Pacific, carrying signals at rates to tens of gigabits per second. Optical fibers also have other diverse applications, including transmitting images and delivering laser power to hard-to-reach spots, spelling out messages and images on illuminated signs, and sensing effects such as rotation and pressure.

This chapter introduces how and why fiber optics are used. I will go into more detail on applications later, but a general understanding of how fibers are used will help you better appreciate important features of fiber technology described in later chapters. The main emphasis of this chapter and this book is communications, but the final part covers sensing, imaging, and communications applications described in Chapters 27 and 28.

Types of Communications

Communication systems come in many sizes, shapes, and forms. They may send signals between two locations, link together many points, or distribute the same signals to many individual subscribers. They may carry different kinds of signals at high or low speeds. Many link only fixed points, but others can serve mobile users (like cellular telephones). Fiber optics are used to transmit signals in many such systems, but details can differ greatly.

Fiber optics can be used in many—but not all—types of communications. System designs vary widely.

At first glance, it is easy to overlook many differences among communication systems. For example, traditional telephone networks and cable television systems both distribute signals to individual homes, but their structures differ in important ways. The telephone network contains switches that make temporary two-way connections between phones in different places, whereas a traditional cable television network distributes the same signals to all homes (although not all homes have the equipment needed to decode all the signals). This approach worked fine for many years, because people were satisfied to get the same video signals—but not the same phone calls. However, it is changing rapidly as competition among providers transforms communication services. Cable-television networks are developing their own ways to provide Internet services to homes, in competition with telephone carriers. In addition, alternative carriers are starting to emerge that offer voice, video, and data services but did not begin as either a cable-TV or telephone company.

Other differences among systems are more obvious. The telephone network spans the globe, so you can call New Zealand from your home phone (although you may wish you hadn't after you get the bill). In contrast, a local area network typically links many computers in the same office or building, carrying data alongside phone lines that carry voice conversations. Some long-distance systems have capacities up to tens of gigabits per second, the equivalent of hundreds of thousands of voice circuits. Many short systems—such as the phone wires in your home—carry only a single voice circuit.

Some communication systems are dedicated to a specific job, such as a cable between a closed-circuit video camera and a security monitor in a store or a bank. Others—notably the telephone system—are "common carriers" that carry many sorts of signals for a variety of users. The entity we call the Internet is a hodgepodge of systems. Existing phone or cable-TV lines carry signals from your home to a service provider, which typically routes them through higher-capacity leased lines to a dedicated backbone network that carries digital data at very high speeds. The hardware of the Internet backbone system is essentially the same as that in telephone backbone systems, but they carry signals in different digital formats.

One common trend is a steady increase in the demand for transmission capacity. It's most visible in the speed of computer data transmission. In 1985, the fastest modems transmitted only 1200 bit/s (baud). Today, 14,400 bit/s is slow, and many modems operate at 56,000 bit/s, which is near the limit for most existing phone lines using current technology. The spread of fax machines, cellular phones, pagers, and second voice lines continues to push the demand for more and more transmission capacity. This, in turn, has pushed the growth of fiber-optic communications, because of its huge capacity. The highest speeds of commercial fiber systems likewise have grown, from 565 Mbit/s in 1985 to 40 Gbit/s in 1997.

Analog and Digital Communications

Communication signals can be transmitted in two fundamentally different forms, as shown in Figure 3.1: continuous analog signals and discrete digital signals. The level of an analog signal varies continuously. A digital signal, on the other hand, can be at only certain levels. The most common number of levels, as shown in Figure 3.1, is two, with signals coded in binary format, either off or on.

Signals can be transmitted in analog or digital formats. Each has its advantages, and both are compatible with fiber optics.

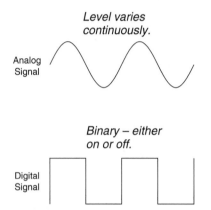

FIGURE 3.1

Analog and digital signals.

Each format has its advantages. The older analog technology is more compatible with people and much existing equipment. Our ears, for instance, detect continuous variations in the level of sound, not just the presence or absence of sound. Our eyes likewise detect levels of brightness, not simply the presence or absence of light. For that reason, audio and video communications have traditionally been in analog form. Telephone wires deliver a continuously varying signal to a standard telephone handset, which converts those electronic signals into continuously varying sound waves. Standard television sets likewise receive analog video signals, which they decode to display pictures on the screen. In the future, digital signals will go direct to home electronics, such as high-definition television (HDTV) sets, but the digital signals must be converted to sounds or pictures for our ears and eyes.

On the other hand, digital signals are easier to process with electronics and fiber optics. It is much simpler and cheaper to design a circuit to detect whether a signal is at a high or a low level (off or on) than to design and build one to accurately replicate a continuously varying signal. Digital signals are also much less prone to distortion, as shown in Figure 3.2. When an analog signal goes through a system that doesn't reproduce it exactly, the result is a garbled signal that can be unintelligible. That is exactly what happens when you get a distorted voice on the phone. However, when a digital signal is not reproduced exactly, it is still possible to tell the on from the off state, so the signal is clearer. That is one reason digital compact discs reproduce sound much better than analog cassette tapes or phonograph records.

FIGURE 3.2
*Distortion of analog
and digital signals.*

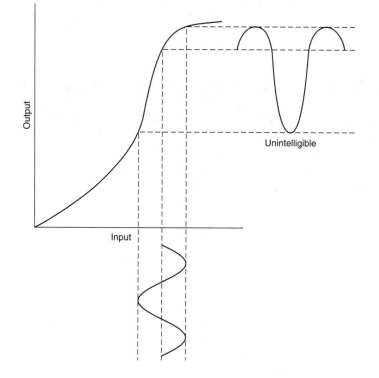

a. Analog

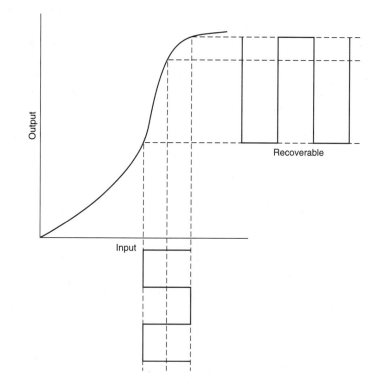

b. Digital

Converting Analog and Digital Signals

If people need analog signals, but transmission works best with digital, what about converting between the two? That is often done for audio. Compact disc players use a laser to read sound digitized as spots on a rapidly spinning disc, then use internal electronics to convert the digitized sound back to analog form. The telephone network converts the analog signals from a telephone handset into digital code for long-distance transmission, then translates the digital code back to analog form on the other end.

The idea of digitization is simple, as shown in Figure 3.3. A circuit called an analog-to-digital converter samples an analog waveform to measure its amplitude. The samples are taken at uniform intervals (8000 times per second in a telephone circuit). The converter assigns the signal amplitude to one of a predetermined number of possible levels. For a telephone circuit, that number is 128 (exactly the number of levels that can be encoded by 7 bits). This converts the 4-kHz analog telephone signal into a digital stream of sets of 7 bits sent 8000 times a second (56,000 kbits/s).

Analog telephone signals are converted to digital format by sampling them 8000 times a second.

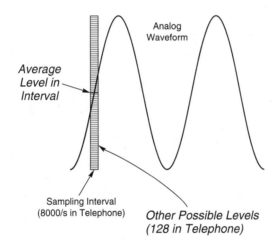

Average Level in Interval

Analog Waveform

Sampling Interval (8000/s in Telephone)

Other Possible Levels (128 in Telephone)

FIGURE 3.3
Digitization of an analog signal.

The figures in the last paragraph show one disadvantage of digital transmission. Accurate reproduction of an analog signal requires sampling at a rate faster than the highest frequency to be reproduced. In the telephone example, the sampling rate is twice the highest frequency to be reproduced (4000 Hz). Many bits (7 for telephony) have to be sent per sampling interval. This requires a large transmission bandwidth. There is no precise equivalence between analog and digital transmission capacity, but the two are comparable: a transmission line capable of handling 10 Mbit/s has an analog capacity of around 10 MHz. That means an analog signal takes only about a tenth of the transmission capacity that it needs in digital form. That is not a problem in telephony, but it led cable television carriers to stay with analog transmission for many years. That is changing with new

Signals require more transmission capacity in digital than in analog form.

technology that can compress digital video signals so that they use many fewer bits to carry the same information.

Fiber optics work well for digital signals and were initially used mainly for digital systems. They have the high transmission capacity needed for digital transmission, and many light sources suffer from nonlinearities that induce distortion in analog signals at high frequencies. However, developers have also succeeded in making highly linear analog fiber systems, which are widely used to distribute signals for cable television.

● *Fiber-optic systems handle both digital and analog signals.*

Long-Distance Telecommunications

Telephone Network Structure

The telephone network can be loosely divided into a hierarchy of systems, shown in simplified form in Figure 3.4. Your home or business telephone is part of the subscriber loop or local loop, the part between individual subscribers and telephone-company switching

● *The telephone network includes subscriber loops, trunk lines, and backbone systems. Fiber optics are widely used for trunk and backbone systems.*

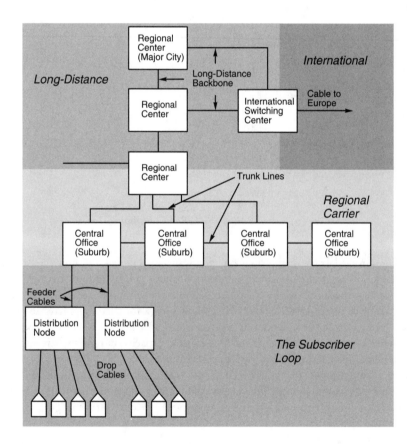

FIGURE 3.4

Parts of the fixed telephone network.

offices (called central offices in the telephone industry). Trunk lines run between central offices, for example, carrying telephone calls from one suburb to another or from suburbs to central cities. Long-distance telephone carriers operate long-haul backbone systems between regions, and these backbone systems connect with international communication systems like transatlantic cables and satellites.

In practice, the subscriber loop may be broken down into two segments—a feeder cable from the central office to a distribution node or drop-off point and individual wires from there to homes. A typical central office may serve thousands of homes, but each drop-off serves between several and several dozen. Regional telephone operating companies and long-distance carriers each have networks that reach throughout the regions where they operate, making it hard to define a boundary between trunk and backbone network.

Cellular phones, pagers, and other mobile or wireless communication services have interfaces with the fixed telephone network. You can think of the towers that send radio signals to and from mobile phones as equivalent to nodes or central offices in the fixed phone network. Instead of distributing signals through a network of wires, they send them through the air via radio waves. Pagers and new satellite-based mobile phone services work in a similar way but distribute signals from satellites and connect to the fixed network through ground stations similar to large regional telephone centers.

Optical fibers are used throughout much of the fixed phone system. Fiber-optic cables are the primary medium for international transmission, backbone systems, and trunk lines. They are common for connections to cell-phone towers and the feeder cables that serve local distribution nodes. However, the only telephone subscribers with their own fiber-optic connections are businesses that require the equivalent of many phone lines.

Telephone System Hardware

The telephone system is changing rapidly from analog to digital technology, although few telephone users see the results directly. Computer modems don't count because they take digital data from a computer and convert it to analog form for transmission through the analog phone line from your house. (Those are the whistles and warbles you hear when a modem is on a phone line.) Most homes still have analog connections to the phone system, although a few have new digital services, which I will describe in Chapter 24.

The telephone network makes extensive use of a technique called multiplexing so that cables can carry many phone circuits simultaneously. Only in the local loop, between homes and central offices or remote drop-off points, is one conversation routed over each pair of wires. At the central office or a distribution node, signals from many telephone lines are combined (multiplexed) for simultaneous transmission through a single cable. Successive levels of multiplexing raise transmission speeds and number of voice circuits carried on a single cable until the level reaches thousands in backbone systems, as you will see in Chapters 21 and 22. Initially, signals were multiplexed on analog lines by assigning them different transmission frequencies. Now multiplexers combine many signals digitized at slow speeds (e.g., 56,000 bits/s) to produce a single faster digital signal.

●
The telephone system is changing from analog to digital transmission.

●
The telephone network makes extensive use of multiplexing.

As you saw in Chapter 2, the advantages of fiber optics grow with transmission speed and distance. Thus, many early uses of fiber optics were in systems that operated at what were then high speeds. Long-distance telephone carriers (e.g., the American Telephone & Telegraph Co., Sprint, and MCI) use fiber-optic cables for their high-speed backbone systems that carry tens of thousands of voice signals between regions of the country at overall speeds to tens of gigabits per second. Microwave systems that transmit on the ground or via satellites now carry few voice telephone circuits.

Fiber-optic technology has made tremendous progress since the first fibers carried live telephone traffic in the late 1970s. First-generation fiber systems carried 45 Mbit/s several kilometers between repeaters; by the mid-1980s, a third-generation technology was operating at 565 Mbit/s, using different types of fibers that carried light tens of kilometers at a longer wavelength. The cutting edge of current commercial technology is a fifth generation that carries multiple wavelengths tens of kilometers for a total signal speed of 40 Gbit/s, and even faster speeds are in the works. These high-speed systems form the backbone networks that cross continents; they also provide high-capacity international connections through undersea cables.

The trunk cables that link central offices normally operate at somewhat lower speeds. The choice depends on the demand for service and the costs of the fiber-optic transmitters and receivers. The lowest speeds regularly used for fiber transmission in the telephone network are 1.5 Mbit/s (called T1 lines) for connections to distribution nodes that serve homes or for direct lines to businesses. (Different speeds are standard in many other countries.)

Telephone companies have found that fiber optics have many advantages besides their high transmission capacity and low signal attenuation. Fiber-optic cables are much smaller than old metal cables, so four fiber cables can fit into an underground duct that could hold only one wire cable. That means important savings because installing new ducts in urban areas costs far more than replacing old cables with new. What's more, the cables can be installed with extra fibers to leave room for future expansion—at minimal extra cost and without the need for major construction or excavation.

Fibers have other advantages that can be important for particular applications. Fiber-optic cables can be made with no electrical conductors—so they won't carry dangerous current pulses injected by lightning strikes. Signals carried in fibers cannot pick up electromagnetic interference from power lines, generating plants, or other sources. The high capacity of fibers also leaves plenty of room for future expansion—an important consideration for telecommunication planners looking for continued steady growth in demand.

Submarine Fiber Cables versus Satellites

Probably the most dramatic success of fiber optics in long-distance communications has been the development of ocean-spanning cable systems that have brought many satellite communications back to earth. A bit of history shows how much and how fast the technology has changed.

Backbone communications systems rely on fiber optics to carry tens of thousands of telephone circuits per fiber pair.

By replacing one thick metal cable with four fiber cables that can fit in the same duct, telephone companies can save much money on installation costs.

Undersea fiber-optic cables offer important advantages over satellites for intercontinental communications.

Voices first crossed the Atlantic in the 1920s, with the development of radio-telephones, which used the shortwave radio band to carry conversations. Few channels were available, their quality was poor, and the calls were expensive. In 1956, the first electronic telephone cable—a special-purpose coaxial cable called TAT-1—crossed the Atlantic, carrying 36 voice circuits. Over the next two decades, cable engineers improved the systems, until by 1976 a cable called TAT-6 carried 4000 voice circuits.

Meanwhile, communication satellites had become the first big commercial success of the space age. By the early 1970s, they promised more capacity than coaxial cables could ever offer for a lower price. Some people seriously proposed abandoning submarine cables altogether, although satellite voice links had problems, including annoying transit-time delays and echoes.

Fiber optics came to the rescue. Plans were underway for the first transatlantic fiber-optic cable, called TAT-8, by 1980. It began operation at the end of 1988, just a few months behind the original schedule—an amazing achievement for a whole new technology in an application where reliability is a primary concern (see Chapter 21). TAT-8 had a total capacity of 550 Mbit/s. By the start of 1998, submarine fiber cable capacity had reached 10 Gbit/s, with plans in the works to lay cables that would begin carrying up to 640 Gbit/s by the end of 2000. Satellites still transmit data, fax, mobile telephone, and video signals—but fiber optics have made that space-age technology obsolete for voice telephone traffic.

Submarine fiber-optic cables play a crucial role in the global telecommunications network, and they also have another important role. Their needs for long repeater spacing and high capacity have pushed the development of new generations of fiber technology that have also spread to other applications. Work on TAT-8 laid the groundwork for the fiber optic systems that now provide the backbone of the terrestrial telecommunications network. Optical amplifiers and 1.55-μm transmission, first pushed for submarine cables, are common on land.

● Submarine fiber systems push the cutting edge of high-performance fiber technology.

Cable-Television and Video Transmission

Cable-television networks are evolving to offer telephone and data transmission services in competition with the telephone network. However, cable-TV (often called CATV, from Community Antenna TeleVision) systems have fundamentally different designs, which stem from their origins. Cable-TV systems were built to offer the same set of video channels to all subscribers, so they lacked the switches that telephone networks use to route conversations to individual phones. Cable also began as purely one-way transmission, unable to carry signals originating in homes. This is changing, but the designs are based on upgrading existing equipment rather than completely rebuilding the entire network.

● Design of the cable-television network differs from that of the telephone network.

Video signals require much more bandwidth than sound, so the network that distributes cable-television signals was built with much higher capacity than the subscriber loop that distributes telephone signals. It began with coaxial cables, which can carry dozens of analog video channels, each one assigned a different transmission frequency analogous to broadcast frequencies. A central facility, called the *head-end*, sends the same video signals to all homes through cables that spread out in a "tree" architecture. (Premium services are sent to all homes in a coded form that can be viewed only through cable boxes with special decoders rented from the cable company.)

Fiber has replaced coaxial cable in much of the distribution network because it has much lower attenuation, avoiding the need for amplifiers or repeaters in most communities. However, standard television signals continue to be transmitted in analog form. Cable companies will start transmitting digital television signals after broadcasts begin in the new digital format.

Current cable systems resemble the telephone subscriber loop in some ways. Fibers and coaxial cables carry signals from the head-end to remote nodes, from which signals are distributed through coax to individual homes. In modern systems, a small fraction of the bandwidth is set aside for voice and data signals directed to and from individual homes, and some switching capacity has been added. I will describe the details in Chapter 23.

Fiber optics also carry many video signals outside of cable-TV networks. Studios and production facilities use fiber cables because they are smaller, lighter, have higher capacity, and suffer less noise than coaxial cables. Fiber cables are also widely used in temporary installations for electronic newsgathering, such as broadcasting the Olympics. The first fiber-optic Olympic system was installed as a backup for the 1980 Winter Games in Lake Placid, New York, but ended up carrying most video signals because it worked better than the then-standard coaxial cable system.

The Internet and Data Communications

Fibers are used in backbone Internet networks and in high-speed local area networks.

Fiber optics play two distinct roles in computer data communications. Fibers are widely used for Internet backbone transmission and for high-speed connections from Internet service providers to the backbone. Fibers also are used for local transmission of computer data, often as part of a network.

Backbone Internet systems are much like those for other types of telecommunications, and fibers are used for the same reason—their high capacity. The optical hardware is essentially the same; the differences come in data-transmission protocols. I will discuss protocols later, but they are not particularly important here. Think of the Internet backbone as fiber-optic telecommunication hardware owned by companies other than standard long-distance phone companies. The technology is similar, and we won't worry about the differences in ownership and traffic. The same holds for fiber connections linking Internet service providers with telephone company facilities and with the Internet backbone system.

Local data transmission is a different matter because it involves different technology. Typically data travels among computers within the same building or campus of many buildings. The data may be transmitted point-to-point, between a pair of computers, or between a computer and a separate device. Alternatively, data may travel on networks that link many computers, as shown in Figure 3.5. Networks may operate on somewhat different levels. A local-area network (LAN) may connect all the devices on one floor of an office building or belonging to one department in a company. Larger *metropolitan-area networks,* or MANs (sometimes called wide-area networks, or WANs) may provide higher-speed links between separate LANs. In a sense, they are networks of networks; a company MAN or WAN may connect separate LANs on different floors of an office building.

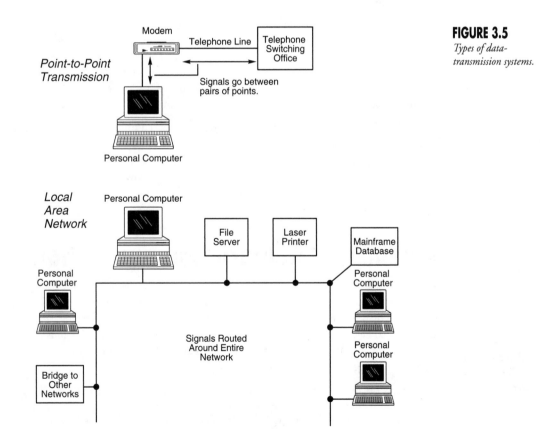

FIGURE 3.5

Types of data-transmission systems.

Fibers do not carry electric currents, so they can be used places where wire transmission would be unsafe or degraded by noise.

Data transmission to and from personal computers normally is at low speeds over short distances so it rarely requires the long-distance, high-speed capacity of fiber. However, other considerations can tilt the scales toward fiber in certain cases. Fibers do not carry electric currents, so they can be used where voltage isolation is critical, such as in power stations, or to carry signals through explosive atmospheres such as in refineries. Fibers do not pick up electromagnetic interference and power surges, so they can run alongside power cables in the elevator shafts of high-rise buildings—without picking up noise. Fibers also do not radiate electromagnetic signals and are difficult to tap, making them attractive for secure transmission at military facilities and financial institutions.

The continuing increase in data-transmission speeds is pushing growing use of fibers in networks connecting many computers, or networks linking local-area networks. A decade ago, 10-Mbit/s Ethernets seemed to promise plenty of capacity; now 100-Mbit/s and even 1-Gbit/s networks are emerging to handle the growing volume of graphic data transmission. Inexpensive *network computers,* which use networks to access files and applications stored on more powerful *server* computers, require higher-speed network connections than personal computers, which can store their own files and applications.

In the short term, fiber-optic networks can handle higher transmission speeds than wires. However, some businesses are installing fiber networks to "future-proof" their facilities. Because network installation is expensive, they can save money by starting with a fiber network—even if they don't need its capacity immediately—rather than going back in 5 years to replace wires with fibers. This trade-off is strongest for new facilities, because it's much cheaper to install extra cable during construction than to add cable later.

As I will explain later in more detail, the distinction between point-to-point transmission and networks is particularly important for computer communications. Although metal cables can connect multiple points almost as easily as they can link two points, it is harder to split and combine signals in optical fibers. As a result, fiber networks often have a different topology than metal-cable networks.

Mobile and Military Communications

Key attractions of fiber for use in ships and planes are light weight and immunity to electromagnetic interference.

The small size, light weight, and immunity to electromagnetic interference of optical fibers has attracted designers of ships, aircraft, and automobiles, as we will discuss in more detail in Chapter 26. These diverse vehicles have steadily incorporated increasingly sophisticated electronic systems, which require more internal communications capacity. Such systems are quite different from those used for long-distance communications, although the largest military ships are *big.*

Many newer planes and advanced ships already use some fiber optics to carry signals for control and communications. Electromagnetic interference is an important concern in control rooms packed with electronic equipment; in commercial aircraft, stray noise from personal stereos and laptop computers has interfered with controls. Fibers do not pick up such noise, and their small size and light weight are significant benefits in planes. Designers of military planes and ships worry even more about electromagnetic interference because an enemy could intentionally broadcast signals to knock out electronic systems. Transmitting signals over fibers can reduce system vulnerability.

Automobile designers see similar potentials in fiber optics. An important goal is to simplify the complex wire harnesses of modern cars, which are costly to build, install, and repair. Electromagnetic interference from external sources such as radio towers and internal ones such as spark plugs can affect some car electronics. However, carmakers have been slow to adopt fiber optics because of stringent requirements for low costs and concern that mechanics could not repair fiber systems.

Communication is so important on the modern battlefield that the Army carries its own systems with it to install in field headquarters. After using heavy 26-pair copper cable, the Army switched to lightweight and more durable fiber-optic cable, but is now converting to wireless communications for use in the field. Some other military communications systems also are switching to fiber.

Noncommunication Fiber Optics

Most of this book is about fiber-optic communications, but fiber optics have a variety of other applications, as you will see in Chapters 27 and 28. Many of them rely on fiber-optic bundles; others depend on the properties of single fibers.

Illumination

A light source at one end of a bundle of optical fibers illuminates whatever is at the other end. This can make a decorative lamp or a flexible illuminator for hard-to-reach places or spell out words in an illuminated sign. Short lengths of optical fibers, pressed together to make a flat plate, can concentrate light from a curved screen straight ahead, transferring faint light in low-light level military imaging tubes much more efficiently than lenses.

Single fibers or small bundles can deliver laser energy to hard-to-reach targets. For example, a fiber catheter can be threaded through the ureter to carry laser pulses powerful enough to shatter kidney stones inside the body—avoiding the need for surgery. Fiber bundles can deliver laser light for cutting or drilling objects.

Imaging and Inspection

If the fibers in a bundle are arranged in the same pattern at the ends, they can transmit images. One of the most important applications for fiber-optic image transmission is endoscopy, which lets physicians view an otherwise inaccessible part of the body. For

Optical fibers can be used for transmitting light and images and for sensing.

example, a fiber-optic endoscope can be passed down the esophagus so a physician can see into the stomach. Endoscopes can also carry laser light to treat certain conditions, such as bleeding ulcers.

Imaging fiber bundles also permit inspection of the insides of otherwise-inaccessible objects, such as the interiors of engines. Some fibers in the bundle can carry light to dark regions, and the remaining fibers collect the light and deliver it to the inspector.

Sensors

Optical fibers can also be used as sensors. Some fiber sensors use the fiber only to pick up light and bring it to a place where it can be detected. Others rely on fibers to carry light to and from a sensing element. In still others, the fiber itself is the sensing element. Examples of the latter include the sensitive acoustic detectors that the Navy hopes will keep track of the whereabouts of potentially hostile submarines and loops of optical fiber used to sense rotation, which can serve as gyroscopes in guidance systems for missiles and planes—and perhaps for land vehicles as well.

What Have You Learned?

1. Fiber optics can transmit signals in both digital and analog format. Analog transmission requires linear light transmitters.

2. The telephone system is composed of a backbone system, trunk lines, and the subscriber loop. Fiber is used mostly in the backbone system, trunk lines, and in parts of the subscriber loop where individual fiber cables carry multiplexed signals.

3. High-capacity fiber-optic cables are the backbones of national and international telecommunication networks. Submarine fiber cables have largely replaced satellite channels for telephone communication across the oceans.

4. Fibers are finding growing use in data communications and local area networks, but they are not used for short, low-speed links between personal computers and peripherals.

5. Cable television systems use fiber to deliver analog video signals to remote distribution points, where signals are split among many subscribers.

6. Cable television and telephone networks are converging toward similar architectures using fiber optics.

7. Data networks in ships and planes may use fiber.

8. Optical fibers can be used to sense, illuminate, deliver laser power, display, and image, as well as to communicate.

What's Next?

In Chapters 4–6, you will go back and take a closer look at the characteristics of optical fibers. Later on, in Chapters 18–25, you will look more closely at the variety of fiber-optic applications in communications.

Quiz for Chapter 3

1. Which of the following are true for analog signals?

    a. They vary continuously in intensity.

    b. They are transmitted in parts of the telephone network.

    c. They are compatible with human senses.

    d. They can be processed electronically.

    e. All of the above.

2. Which of the following are true for digital signals?

    a. They are used in parts of the telephone network.

    b. Their intensity can be at only certain discrete levels.

    c. They can be processed electronically.

    d. They can encode analog signals.

    e. All of the above.

3. You digitize a 10-kHz signal by sampling it at twice the highest frequency (e.g., 20,000 times a second) and encoding the intensity in 7 bits. What is the resulting data rate?

    a. 20 kbit/s.

    b. 56 kbit/s.

    c. 128 kbit/s.

    d. 140 kbit/s.

    e. 1.28 Mbit/s.

4. What part of the telephone network is connected directly to your home telephone?

    a. Subscriber loop.

    b. Feeder cable.

    c. Trunk line.

    d. Backbone system.

5. What part of the telephone network carries the highest-speed signals?

    a. Subscriber loop.

    b. Feeder cable.

    c. Trunk cable.

    d. Backbone system.

6. Which of the following features of fiber optics is least important for telephone transmission?

    a. High-quality analog transmission.

    b. Smaller size than metal cables, which allows more cables to fit into existing ducts.

    c. Immunity to electromagnetic interference.

d. Long-distance, high-speed transmission.

e. Ability to carry digitized signals.

7. What is the usual way for cable-television networks to distribute video signals to homes?

a. Via microwaves from satellites.

b. By switching digital signals to each home according to the programs requested.

c. Through pairs of twisted copper wires.

d. Transmitted from the head-end through coaxial cables to remote nodes, where fibers carry signals to individual subscribers.

e. Transmitted from the head-end through optical fiber to remote nodes, where coaxial cables carry signals to individual homes.

8. Which technical feature is shared by systems that distribute telephone and cable-television signals to homes?

a. Fibers typically carry signals to remote distribution nodes, from which wires or coaxial cables go to homes.

b. Both use extensive switching to select which

homes received which signals.

c. Both scramble signals so customers can decode only the services they pay for.

d. Both allow two-way transmission of all signals.

e. Both share an inability to carry digital data.

9. What type of communication system links many individual personal computers in a single office?

a. Cable television network.

b. The global telephone network.

c. A local-area network (LAN).

d. Point-to-point transmission.

10. Which of the following is not a likely application of fiber optics?

a. Sensing.

b. Power transmission to homes.

c. Image transmission.

d. Spelling out letters on illuminated signs.

e. Gyroscopes for measuring changes in direction.

Types of Optical Fibers

About This Chapter

Optical fibers are not all alike. There are several different types, made for different applications, which guide light in subtly different ways. This chapter describes the basic concepts behind the various types of fibers. It concentrates on fiber design and light guiding. It is closely linked to the two chapters that follow. Chapter 5 describes the important properties of optical fibers. Chapter 6 covers the materials used in fibers, which play a vital role in determining their properties. Together, these three provide an essential groundwork to understanding how most optical fibers work. Chapter 7 covers special fiber types.

Light Guiding

Chapter 2 showed how the total internal reflection of light rays could explain light guiding along optical fibers. This simple concept is a useful approximation of light guiding in many types of fiber, but it is not the whole story. The physics of light guiding is considerably more complex, because a fiber really is a waveguide and light really is an electromagnetic wave with frequency in the optical range. The theoretical basis of light guiding in fibers is the same as for the guiding of microwaves in waveguides, but this book will not go into the hairy mathematics of waveguide theory. You don't need to learn all those details to understand how fiber optics work.

You do need to understand that there are different types of fiber, which are designed using these theories to meet a variety of distinct functional requirements. For example, bundles of fibers used for imaging should collect as much of the light falling on their ends as possible, so their claddings generally are made

●
Total internal reflection of rays is a first approximation of light guiding in some fibers.

●
Core-cladding structure and material composition are the key factors in determining fiber properties.

thin compared to their cores. Over longer distances, light can leak through the thin cladding, so communication fibers have thicker cladding. Fibers used for different types of communications have distinct requirements. Fibers running short distances typically are optimized to collect as much light as possible; those carrying signals long distances are designed for high capacity and low signal loss.

There are two major design parameters for optical fibers, as well as many secondary ones. This chapter concentrates on the core-cladding structure. At its simplest, merely changing the core diameter and cladding thickness can have a profound impact on fiber properties. In addition, the core-cladding interface can be made more complex than a mere *step-index* boundary between two types of glass.

The second key parameter is fiber composition, covered in Chapter 6. The choice of materials for core and cladding controls fiber attenuation and strongly influences pulse spreading and transmission capacity.

Combined with other minor factors, these parameters determine important fiber characteristics, including

- Attenuation as a function of wavelength.
- Light-collection capacity.
- Pulse spreading and transmission capacity, as a function of wavelength.
- Tolerances for splicing and connecting fibers.
- Operating wavelengths.
- Tolerance to high temperature and environmental abuse.
- Strength and flexibility.
- Cost.

Figure 4.1 shows selected types of single fibers (as distinct from bundled fibers), along with a plot of refractive index across the core and cladding, called the *index profile*. Only the core and cladding are shown for simplicity; actual fibers have an outer plastic coating to protect them from the environment. I will start with the fiber type that is simplest to explain, called step-index multimode fiber.

Step-Index Multimode Fiber

As we saw in Chapter 2, bare, transparent filaments surrounded by air are the simplest type of optical fiber, but they don't work well in practice. Cladding the fiber with a transparent material having lower refractive index protects the light-carrying core from surface scratches, fingerprints, and contact with other cores of the same material, so the light will not escape from the surface. This simple fiber consists of two layers of material, the core and cladding, which have different refractive indexes. If you drew a cross section of the fiber and plotted the refractive index, as in Figure 4.1(a) and (b), you would see a step at the core-cladding boundary, where the index changes abruptly.

FIGURE 4.1

*Common types of
optical fiber (to scale).*

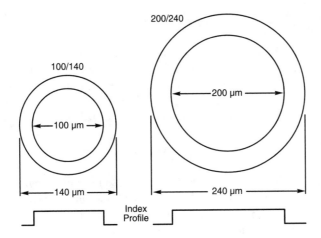

a. Step-Index Multimode Fibers

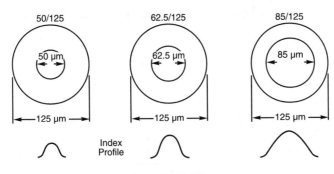

b. Graded-Index Fibers

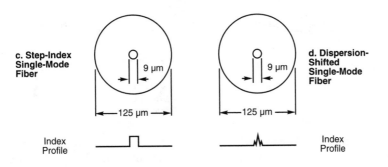

Light-Guiding Requirements

To guide light, the fiber core must have refractive index higher than the cladding.

As long as the core of a fiber has a diameter many times larger than the wavelength of light it carries, we can calculate fiber properties using the simple model of light as rays. The fundamental requirement for light guiding is that the core must have a higher refractive index than the cladding material. We saw in Chapter 2 that the critical angle for total internal reflection, θ_c, depends on the ratio of core and cladding refractive indexes.

$$\theta_c = \arcsin\left(\frac{n_{clad}}{n_{core}}\right)$$

For a typical fiber, the difference is small, about 1%, so the critical angle is arcsin (0.99), or about 82°. Because the critical angle is measured from a line perpendicular to the surface, this means that light rays that are no more than 8° from the axis of the fiber are reflected, as shown in Figure 4.2. This value is not very sensitive to the refractive index difference. If the difference is doubled to 2%, the critical angle becomes 78.5°, so light rays no more than 11.5° from the axis of the fiber are reflected. Alternatively, you can directly calculate the confinement angle measured from the core-cladding boundary ($\theta_{confinement}$) by using the arc-cosine:

$$\theta_{confinement} = \arccos\left(\frac{n_{clad}}{n_{core}}\right)$$

FIGURE 4.2

Light guiding in a large-core step-index fiber. The confinement angle measures the angle between guided light rays and the fiber axis; the acceptance angle is measured in air.

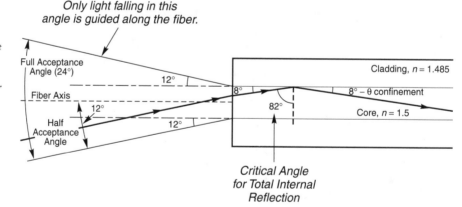

The confinement angle gives the angle at which light must strike the core-cladding boundary once it's inside the glass. However, refraction occurs when the light enters the glass from air, bending light toward the axis of the fiber. To calculate the acceptance angle, measured in air, you must account for this refraction using the standard law of refraction. As long as the light enters from air, you can simplify this to

The confinement angle is the angle at which light rays confined to a fiber core strike the core-cladding boundary.

$$\sin \theta_{half\text{-}acceptance} = n_{core} \times \sin \theta_{confinement}$$

which gives the sine of the largest possible angle from the axis of the fiber, called the half acceptance angle, $\theta_{\text{half-acceptance}}$. You can calculate the half acceptance angle directly by juggling the trigonometry a bit more:

$$\theta_{\text{half-acceptance}} = \arcsin\left(n_{\text{core}} \times \sin\theta_{\text{confinement}}\right)$$

Doubling the half acceptance angle gives the full acceptance angle. As long as the confinement angle is small, you can roughly approximate the half acceptance angle by multiplying the confinement angle by the refractive index of the core, n_{core}.

Imaging Fibers

The first clad optical fibers developed for imaging were what we now call step-index multimode fibers. Developers tested a variety of cladding materials with low refractive indexes, including margarine, beeswax, and plastics. However, the key practical development was a way to apply a cladding of glass with lower refractive index than the core.

> Step-index multimode fibers were the first fibers developed for imaging.

As we will see in Chapter 6, glass comes in many different formulations with varied refractive indexes. The simplest way to make glass-clad fibers is to slip a rod of high-index glass into a tube with lower refractive index, heat the tube so it softens onto the rod, let them fuse together, then heat the whole *preform,* and pull a fiber from the molten end. Figure 4.3 shows the process schematically.

One subtle but crucial requirement is that the core-cladding interface must be smooth and clean on the scale of the wavelength of light. That is possible if the rods are fire-polished but not if they are polished mechanically, a process that leaves grit and fine cracks on the surface. Those flaws remain when rod and tube are melted together and drawn into fiber, and they can scatter or absorb light. (A major reason Larry Curtiss succeeded in making the first good glass-clad fibers was that he used a flame-polished rod.)

The cladding of imaging fibers generally is a thin layer surrounding a thicker core. The reason for this design is that imaging fibers are assembled in bundles, with light focused on one end of the bundle to emerge at the other. Light falling on the fiber cores is transmitted from one end to the other, but light falling on the cladding is lost. Thus the cladding is made thin to increase transmission efficiency.

Reducing the size of individual fibers increases the resolution of images transmitted through a bundle, but very fine fibers are hard to handle and vulnerable to breakage. Typically, the smallest loose fibers assembled into imaging bundles are about 20 μm (0.02 mm, or 0.0008 in.). Even at this size, they remain large relative to the wavelength of visible light (0.4 to 0.7 μm in air), and you can get away with considering light guiding as determined by total internal reflection of light rays at the core-cladding boundary. (The highest-resolution fiber bundles are made by melting fibers together and stretching the whole solid block.)

FIGURE 4.3

A simple way to make step-index multimode fiber is by inserting a glass rod in a tube with lower refractive index, melting the two together to form a preform, and pulling fiber from the hot bottom of the preform.

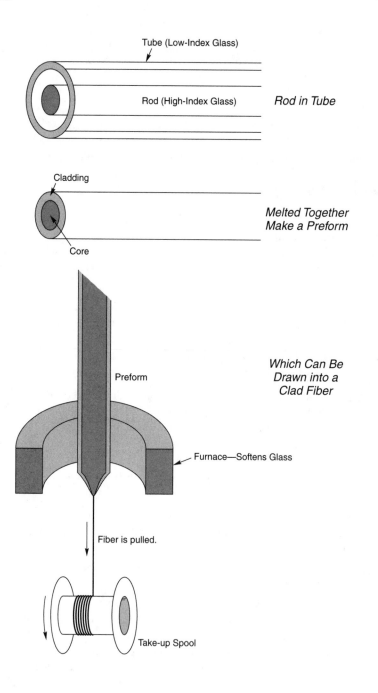

Illuminating Fiber

Single step-index fibers with large cores—typically 400 μm to 1 mm—can be used to guide a laser beam from the laser to a target or industrial workpiece. The large diameter serves two purposes. First, it can collect power from the laser more efficiently than a smaller-core fiber. In addition, it spreads the laser power over a larger area at the ends of the fiber and through a larger volume within the fiber. This is important because some laser power inevitably is lost at the surfaces and within the fiber. If the beam must be focused tightly to concentrate it in the fiber, the power density (power per unit area) may reach levels so high it can damage exposed ends of the fiber.

The design of these large-core fibers is similar to those in Figure 4.1(a). The core diameters are proportionally larger, whereas cladding thicknesses do not increase as rapidly. As the fibers become thicker, they also become less flexible.

> Large-core step-index fibers are used to deliver laser power.

Communication Fibers

Step-index fibers with cores not quite as large can be used for some types of communications. One common type, shown in Figure 4.1(a), has a 100-μm core surrounded by a cladding 20 μm thick, for total diameter of 140 μm. It is typically called 100/140 fiber, with the core diameter written before the overall diameter of the cladding. Typically an outer plastic coating covers the whole fiber, protecting it from mechanical damage and making it easier to handle. The large core is attractive for certain types of communications, because it can collect light efficiently from inexpensive light sources such as LEDs.

If you think of light in terms of rays, you can see an important limitation of large-core step-index fibers for communication in Figure 4.4. Light rays enter the fiber at a range of angles, and rays at different angles travel different paths through the same length of fiber. The larger the angle between the light ray and the axis, the longer the path. For example, a light ray that entered at 8° from the axis (the maximum confinement angle in the earlier example) of a perfectly straight 1-m length of fiber, it would travel a distance of 1.0098 m (1 m/cos 8°) before it emerged from the other end. Thus light just inside the confinement angle would emerge from the fiber very shortly after light that traveled down the middle. This pulse-dispersion effect becomes larger with distance and can limit data-transmission speed.

> Light pulses stretch out in length and time as they travel through large-core step-index fiber.

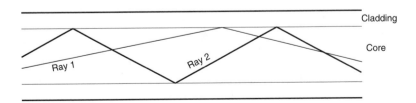

FIGURE 4.4

Light rays that enter multimode step-index fiber at different angles travel different distances through the fiber, causing pulse dispersion.

In fact, the ray model gives a greatly simplified view of light transmission down optical fibers. Strictly speaking, an optical fiber is a waveguide that carries light in one or more transmission modes. Stay tuned for the next section, and I'll explain what these modes are. The larger the fiber core, the more modes it can transmit, so a step-index fiber with a core of 20 μm or more is a multimode fiber. Light rays enter the fiber at different angles, and the various modes travel down the fiber at different speeds. What you have as a result is modal dispersion, which occurs in all step-index fibers that carry multiple modes. It is largely irrelevant for imaging and guiding illuminating beams, but it is a serious drawback for communications. To understand why, we need to take a closer look at modes.

Modes and Their Effects

●
Waves have distinct propagation modes in a waveguide. A fiber is an optical waveguide.

From a theoretical standpoint, an optical fiber is a waveguide, which confines light waves so they travel along the fiber. Modes are stable patterns in which a wave can travel along a waveguide. The wavelength of the wave and the size, shape, and nature of the waveguide determine what modes can propagate. Engineers first developed waveguide theory when they were working with microwaves, and the same theory can be applied to other electromagnetic waves. Thus an optical fiber is merely a waveguide for light or an optical waveguide.

You don't want to worry about the mathematical details of waveguide theory—and I certainly don't—but it's important to understand their consequences. One is that the number of possible modes increases with the diameter of the waveguide. For a fiber, this means the core diameter. It also depends on the wavelength. In a simple way, the larger the waveguide, measured in wavelengths, the more modes it can carry. In practice, other effects enter the picture.

Types of Waveguides

●
Optical fibers are dielectric waveguides.

In essence, the walls of a waveguide set boundary conditions for the electric and magnetic fields that make up an electromagnetic wave. Plug the nature of those boundaries into the proper differential equations, and you can calculate the theoretical properties of the waveguide. The most familiar type of microwave waveguide is a rectangular metal tube; its conductive metal walls set up boundaries for the electromagnetic fields of the microwaves passing through it. Another type of microwave waveguide is made of plastic, called a *dielectric* waveguide because the plastic is an insulator or dielectric. An optical fiber is an optical counterpart to a dielectric waveguide, made of a nonconductive material (glass or plastic) and with its size closer to the wavelength of light.

The simplest type of microwave dielectric waveguide is a plastic rod suspended in air, similar to an unclad optical fiber. In theory, the waves are guided along the surface through air, not inside the guide. Taking this view can explain some problems of unclad optical fibers. Surface waveguides work if isolated in air, but the waveguide effect is disrupted if other objects touch their surfaces. Thus an isolated plastic dielectric guide works for microwaves, but unclad glass fibers don't effectively confine light when they touch each other or have fingerprints on their surfaces.

Cladding a fiber effectively puts the waveguide surface *inside* the optical fiber, where it can't be touched. The communication theorists who first considered optical waveguides considered this a serious drawback, because it meant the light had to travel through the fiber material, which they did not think could be made as transparent as air. They later learned otherwise. Adding a cladding also changes the structure of the waveguide and the way it guides light, and this proves to have other important advantages.

Single-Mode Waveguides

One important difference between microwave waveguides and large-core step-index fibers is the number of modes they carry. Microwave guides are less than a wavelength across, and because of those dimensions microwaves can propagate through them in only one mode. In contrast, imaging fibers are many wavelengths across and can carry many modes. That was not attractive to communication researchers, who had learned the hard way that inter-actions among modes can cause problems in multimode waveguides. They wanted optical waveguides in which only a single mode could propagate, so they wouldn't have to worry about multimode effects.

The problem with that idea was size. Waveguides restrict propagation to a single mode only if their diameters are below a certain cutoff threshold, which depends on the wavelength. Bare single-mode optical waveguides, designed as scaled-down versions of dielectric microwave waveguides, would have to be less than a wavelength of light thick. That meant their diameters would have to be less than 0.5 μm, making them practically impossible to handle. The tiny fibers would inevitably have to touch surfaces, so light would leak out—if you could couple any light into something that small.

However, cladding changes the waveguide properties of fibers, because the single-mode cutoff size depends on the difference in refractive index between the core and cladding. The larger the difference, the smaller the fiber must be. The difference is large for a glass fiber (with $n = 1.5$) in air ($n = 1.00028$). It is small—typically less than 1%—for a clad fiber. Although a bare fiber could be no larger than about half the wavelength of light to transmit only a single mode, a clad fiber could have a core diameter several times the wavelength. The larger the core, the more easily it can collect light. The cladding increases fiber diameter, making it easier to handle. (In theory, the cladding could be infinitely thick.) In addition, the cladding prevents anything from contacting the boundary between core and cladding, which serves a vital function in the waveguide structure.

Clad fibers with larger core diameters can carry multiple modes. The number of possible modes increases rapidly with fiber core diameter.

Small-diameter waveguides carry waves in only a single mode.

Clad single-mode fibers have core diameters several times the wavelength.

Modal Properties

Propagation modes are standing waves that travel through the fiber. The details of mode propagation theory are far too complex to discuss here and generally have little relevance to most day-to-day concerns of fiber-optic users. However, there are some exceptions.

Some light penetrates slightly into the fiber cladding.

We saw earlier that waves travel along the surface of an unclad dielectric waveguide. In clad fibers, the core-cladding boundary becomes the "surface" that guides the waves. The cladding changes the structure of the waveguide so much that light travels within the fiber core, but some does penetrate into the cladding, despite the fact that it nominally undergoes total internal reflection. This occurs both in single-mode and multimode fibers. The effect is significant enough for single-mode fibers that in practice they are characterized by mode-field diameter rather than core diameter, which is slightly less. The effect is easier to show graphically in step-index multimode fibers, as in Figure 4.5.

FIGURE 4.5

Light penetrates slightly into the cladding of a step-index multimode fiber.

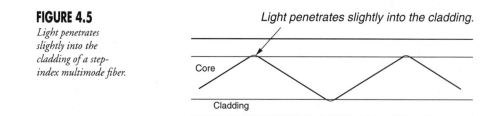

Light penetrates slightly into the cladding.

This leakage of some light into the cladding means that transparency of the cladding material is important, although not as crucial as for the core material. Some modes may propagate partly in the cladding of a multimode fiber, where their energy can leak out more readily than from the core.

Modes are sometimes characterized by numbers. Single-mode fibers carry only the lowest-order mode, assigned the number 0. Multimode fibers also carry higher-order modes. The number of modes that can propagate in a fiber depends on the fiber's numerical aperture (or acceptance angle) as well as on its core diameter and the wavelength of the light. For a step-index multimode fiber, the number of such modes, N_m, is defined by

$$\text{Modes} = 0.5 \left(\frac{\text{core diameter} \times \text{NA} \times \pi}{\text{wavelength}} \right)^2$$

or

$$N_m = 0.5 \left(\frac{\pi D \times \text{NA}}{\lambda} \right)^2$$

where λ is the wavelength and D is the core diameter. To plug in some representative numbers, a 100-μm core step-index fiber with NA = 0.29 (a typical value) would transmit thousands of modes at 850 nm.

Leaky Modes

The difference between the highest-order modes guided in a multimode fiber and the lowest-order modes that are not guided is quite small. Modes that are just beyond the threshold for propagating in a multimode fiber can travel for short distances in the fiber cladding. In this case, the cladding itself acts as an unclad optical fiber to guide those cladding modes.

Because the difference between guided and unguided modes is small, slight changes in conditions may allow light in a normally guided mode to leak out of the core. Likewise, some light in a cladding mode may be recaptured. Slight bends of a multimode fiber are enough to allow escape of these leaky modes.

Modal-Dispersion Effects

Each mode has its own characteristic velocity through a step-index optical fiber, as if it were a light ray entering the fiber at a distinct angle. This causes pulses to spread out as they travel along the fiber, in what is called *modal dispersion*. The more modes the fiber transmits, the more pulses spread out.

Later we will see that there are other kinds of dispersion, but modal dispersion is the strongest. Precise calculations of how many modes cause how much dispersion are rarely meaningful. However, you can make useful approximations by using the ray model (which works for multimode step index fibers) to calculate the difference between the travel times of light rays passing straight through a fiber and bouncing along at the confinement angle. For the typical confinement angle of 8° mentioned earlier, the difference in propagation time is about 1%. That means that an instantaneous pulse would stretch out to about 30 ns (30 billionths of a second) after passing through a kilometer of fiber.

That doesn't sound like much, but it becomes a serious restriction on transmission speed, because pulses that overlap can interfere with each other, making it impossible to receive the signal. Thus pulses have to be separated by more than 30 ns. You can estimate the maximum data rate for a given dispersion from the equation

$$\text{Data rate} = \frac{1}{\text{dispersion}}$$

Plug in a dispersion of 30 ns, and you find the maximum data rate is 33 Mbits/s. In practice, the maximum data rate also depends on other factors.

Dispersion also depends on distance. The total dispersion is the product of the fiber's characteristic dispersion per unit length, D_0, multiplied by the fiber length, L:

$$D = D_0 \times L$$

Some modes can propagate short distances in the cladding of a multimode fiber.

Modal dispersion in multimode step-index fibers is the largest type of pulse dispersion.

Thus a pulse that spreads to 30 ns over 1 km will spread to 60 ns over 2 km and 300 ns over 10 km. (For very accurate calculations, you should replace L with L^γ, where γ is a factor close to one that depends on the fiber type. However, γ normally is so close to one that it doesn't matter.)

Because total dispersion increases with transmission speed, the maximum transmission speed decreases. If the maximum data rate for a 1-km length of fiber is DR_0, the maximum data rate for L kilometers is roughly

$$DR = \frac{DR_0}{L}$$

We will learn more about dispersion in Chapter 5. For now, the important thing to remember is that modal dispersion seriously limits transmission speed in step-index multimode fiber.

Graded-Index Multimode Fiber

Replacing the sharp boundary between core and cladding with a refractive index gradient nearly eliminates modal dispersion.

As communication engineers began seriously investigating fiber optics in the early 1970s, they recognized modal dispersion limited the capacity of large-core step-index fiber. Single-mode fibers promised much more capacity, but many engineers doubted they could get enough light into the tiny cores. As an alternative, they developed multimode fiber in which the refractive index grades slowly from core into cladding. Careful control of the refractive-index gradient nearly eliminates modal dispersion in fibers with cores tens of micrometers in diameter, giving them much greater transmission capacity than step-index multimode fibers.

Optically, graded-index fibers guide light by refraction instead of total internal reflection. The fiber's refractive index decreases gradually away from its center, finally dropping to the same value as the cladding at the edge of the core, as shown in Figure 4.6. The change in refractive index causes refraction, bending light rays back toward the axis as they pass through layers with lower refractive indexes, as shown in Figure 4.7. The refractive index does not change abruptly at the core-cladding boundary, so there is no total internal reflection. However, it isn't needed because refraction bends guided light rays back into the center of the core before they reach the cladding boundary. (The refractive index gradient cannot confine all light entering the fiber, only rays that fall within a limited confinement angle, as in step-index fiber. The refractive-index gradient determines that angle.)

As in a step-index fiber, light rays follow different paths in a graded-index fiber. However, their speeds differ because the speed of light in the fiber core changes with its refractive index. Recall that the speed of light in a material, c_{mat}, is the velocity of light in a vacuum, c, divided by refractive index:

$$c_{mat} = \frac{c_{vacuum}}{n_{mat}}$$

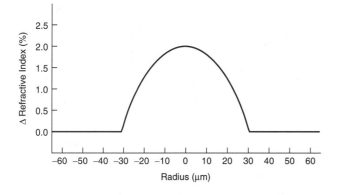

FIGURE 4.6
Refractive-index profile of a graded-index fiber with 62.5-μm core.

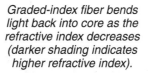

Graded-index fiber bends light back into core as the refractive index decreases (darker shading indicates higher refractive index).

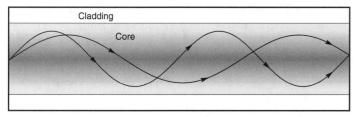

FIGURE 4.7
The refractive-index gradient in a graded-index fiber bends light rays back toward the center of the fiber.

Thus the further the light goes from the axis of the fiber, the faster its velocity. The difference isn't great, but it's enough to compensate for the longer paths followed by the light rays that go furthest from the axis of the fiber. Careful adjustment of the refractive-index profile—the variation in refractive index with distance from the fiber axis—can virtually eliminate modal dispersion by equalizing the transit times of different modes.

Practical Graded-Index Fiber

Graded-index fibers were developed especially for communications. The long-time standard types have core diameters of 50 or 62.5 μm and cladding diameters of 125 μm; some are made with 85-μm cores and 125-μm cladding diameter. The core diameters are large enough to collect light efficiently from a variety of light sources. The cladding must be at least 20 μm thick to keep light from leaking out.

The graded-index fiber is a compromise, which has much higher transmission capacity than large-core step-index fibers while retaining a core large enough to collect light easily. It was used for some telecommunications until the mid-1980s but gradually faded from

Standard graded-index fibers have 50- or 62.5-μm cores.

use in telephone systems because single-mode fibers worked much better. Graded-index fibers remain in use, mostly for data communications and networks carrying signals moderate distances—typically no more than a couple of kilometers.

Limitations of Graded-Index Fiber

Residual dispersion and modal noise limit performance of graded-index fibers.

Graded-index fibers suffer some serious limitations that ultimately made them impractical for high-performance communications.

Modal dispersion is not the only effect that spreads out pulses going through optical fibers. Other types of dispersion arise from the slight variation of refractive index with the wavelength of light. These remain present in graded-index fibers and became increasingly important as transmission moved to higher speeds. Chapter 5 will describe these dispersion effects.

Multimode transmission itself proved a serious problem. Different modes can interfere with each other, generating what is called *modal noise.* This appears as an uneven distribution of light across the end of the fiber, which continually changes in response to very minor fluctuations, generating noise. Such modal effects also made it impossible to control precisely how fibers behaved when several were spliced together, because the light in some modes can shift into other modes or leak into the cladding at joints.

In addition, ideal refractive-index profiles are very difficult to realize in practice. The refractive-index gradient must be fabricated by depositing many thin layers of slightly different composition in a precisely controlled sequence. This is expensive, and some fluctuations from the ideal are inevitable.

These limitations do not prevent graded-index fibers from being used in short-distance, moderate-speed systems. However, various types of single-mode fibers now are used for long-distance, high-performance systems.

Single-Mode Fiber

The simplest type of single-mode fiber has a step-index profile, with an abrupt boundary between a high-index core and a lower-index cladding.

The basic requirement for single-mode fiber is that the core be small enough to restrict transmission to a single mode. This lowest-order mode can propagate in all fibers with smaller cores (as long as light can physically enter the fiber). Because single-mode transmission avoids modal dispersion, modal noise, and other effects that come with multimode transmission, single-mode fibers can carry signals at much higher speeds than multimode fibers. They are the standard choice for virtually all kinds of telecommunications that involve high data rates or span distances longer than about a kilometer and are often used at slower speeds and shorter distances as well.

The simplest type of single-mode fiber, often called *standard* single mode, has a step-index profile, with an abrupt boundary separating a high-index core and a lower index cladding.

The refractive-index differential usually is less than 1%. Figure 4.8 shows cross sections of the two principal types of step-index single-mode fiber made from fused silica.

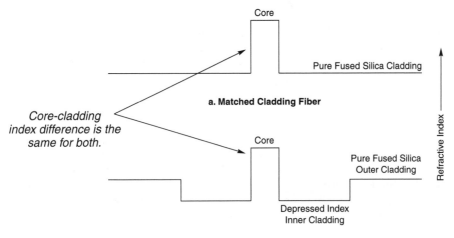

FIGURE 4.8

Two types of step-index single-mode fiber. The difference between core and cladding refractive index is the same, but in the depressed cladding fiber at the bottom, the inner cladding is doped with fluorine to reduce its refractive index.

The simplest design is the matched-cladding fiber shown at the top of Figure 4.8. The cladding is pure fused silica; germanium oxide (GeO_2) is added to the core to increase its refractive index.

An alternative design is the depressed cladding fiber shown at the bottom. In this case, the core is fused silica doped with less germanium oxide than is needed for a matched cladding fiber. The inner part of the cladding surrounding the core is doped with fluorine, which *reduces* its refractive index below that of pure fused silica. The outermost part of the core is pure fused silica, without the fluorine dopant.

Both these designs typically are used for 1.31-µm transmission; core diameters are around 9 µm.

Conditions for Single-Mode Transmission

Earlier in this chapter, you saw that the number of modes, N_m, transmitted by a step-index fiber depends on the fiber core diameter, D, the refractive indexes of core (n_0) and cladding (n_1), and the wavelength of light λ. You can write the formula in terms of numerical aperture (NA):

$$N_m = 0.5 \left(\frac{\pi D \times \text{NA}}{\lambda} \right)^2$$

Fiber with a small enough core transmits only a single mode of light.

You also can replace NA with the core and cladding indexes—useful because NA as acceptance angle isn't very meaningful for single-mode fibers—and reformulate the equation:

$$N_m = 0.5 \left(\frac{\pi D}{\lambda}\right)^2 \left(n_0^2 - n_1^2\right)$$

It would be convenient to solve the equation for the core diameter needed for single-mode transmission. Unfortunately, you can't do that. To properly arrange the equation, you have to use Bessel functions, which are taught in third-year advanced calculus classes. We will skip the gory details and go directly to the formula that gives the conditions required for single-mode transmission in a step-index fiber.

$$D < \frac{2.4\lambda}{\pi \sqrt{n_0^2 - n_1^2}}$$

where D is the core diameter. If the core is any larger, the fiber can carry two modes. (The equation can also be written to give the single-mode diameter in terms of numerical aperture, but the standard definition of NA as a measurement of acceptance angle does not apply to single-mode fibers.)

Note that D is the *maximum* allowable core diameter for single-mode transmission. To allow for the inevitable margin of error, single-mode fibers normally have core diameters somewhat smaller than this maximum value. In practice, the refractive-index difference in step-index single-mode fiber typically is less than 1%, and the core diameter is roughly five or six times the wavelength the fiber is designed to transmit.

Note that this makes core size quite sensitive to operating wavelength. Because the core area increases as the square of the diameter, the core of a fiber designed to operate at 1.55 μm has an area more than three times as large as a single-mode fiber for use at 0.85 μm.

Although core diameter is the physical parameter that enters the equations for single-mode transmission, remember that a single-mode fiber is a dielectric waveguide. That means that some of the light it guides extends into the cladding. This light-guiding area is measured as the *mode field diameter,* which is cited in fiber specifications because it is important for light coupling. Typically the difference between mode-field diameter and core diameter in step-index single-mode fiber is about 10% to 15%. A typical mode-field diameter for step-index single-mode fiber is 9.3 μm at 1.31 μm and 10.5 μm at 1.55 μm.

> The cutoff wavelength of a single-mode fiber is the shortest wavelength at which it carries only one mode. At shorter wavelengths it carries two or more modes.

Cutoff Wavelength

We saw before that the maximum core diameter for single-mode transmission depends on the wavelength. If you solve the equation for wavelength, you find that a fiber with a specific core diameter transmits light in a single mode only at wavelengths longer than a value called the *cutoff wavelength,* λ_c, given by

$$\lambda_c = \frac{\pi D \sqrt{n_0^2 - n_1^2}}{2.4}$$

A fiber with diameter D is single-mode at wavelengths longer than λ_c, but as wavelength decreases, it begins to carry two modes at λ_c.

Although core diameter is an important consideration in fiber *design,* cutoff wavelength is important in fiber *use.* If you want a fiber to carry signals in only one mode for a high-performance communication system, you must be sure that all wavelengths transmitted are longer than the cutoff wavelength. In practice, fibers are designed with a cutoff wavelength significantly shorter than the wavelength where they will operate. For example, a single-mode fiber for use at 1.3 μm probably has a cutoff wavelength shorter than 1.25 μm.

Single-mode fibers always remain single-mode longer than the cutoff wavelength. Thus a single-mode fiber specified for transmission at 1.3 μm also is single-mode at 1.55 μm. However, a 1.55-μm fiber *may* not be single-mode at 1.3 μm, and neither 1.3- nor 1.55-μm fibers are likely to be single-mode at 0.85 μm.

What happens at wavelengths shorter than the cutoff? As the wavelength decreases, you first get a second mode and then additional modes. The extra modes can interfere with each other and with the primary mode, and causing serious performance problems. As with any multimode fiber, minor perturbations can affect mode propagation, so the more modes, the less predictable the fiber's characteristics.

Trade-offs with Single-Mode Fiber

The sheer simplicity of single-mode transmission is one of its primary attractions for fiber-optic communications. By confining light to a single mode, it greatly reduces pulse dispersion due to the waveguide itself. Some dispersion remains, but it depends primarily on the range of wavelengths transmitted in the signal. The smaller the dispersion, the faster pulses can be turned off and on.

Charles Kao recognized the advantages of single-mode fiber in the mid-1960s, but other early developers pointed to a trade-off that seemed inevitable. The smaller the core diameter, the harder it was to couple light into the fiber. Coupling light into single-mode fiber inevitably requires much tighter tolerances than coupling light into the larger cores of multimode fiber. However, those tighter tolerances have proved achievable, and single-mode fibers are widely used. The main applications of multimode fibers today are in systems where connections must be made inexpensively and transmission distances and speeds are modest.

On the other hand, the properties of step-index single-mode fiber are not ideal. Its dispersion is at a minimum at 1.31 μm, but its attenuation has a minimum at 1.55 μm. The best available optical amplifiers, erbium-doped fibers, operate at 1.5 to 1.6 μm,

> Single-mode fiber is a clean and simple transmission system.

where dispersion of step-index single-mode fibers is relatively large. These and other limitations have led to development of other single-mode fibers with different structures, which alter their dispersion.

Dispersion-Shifted Single-Mode Fiber

Step-index single-mode fibers have much better properties than developers dreamed were possible 30 years ago. However, they are not ideal. As we will see in Chapter 6, the attenuation of glass fiber has been reduced close to the theoretical minimum, and little improvement is possible without shifting to a new family of materials.

Pulse dispersion is another matter. The major concern in single-mode fiber is spectral or chromatic dispersion, caused by the variation in the speed of light through the fiber with wavelength. Chromatic dispersion is the sum of two quantities, dispersion inherent to the material and dispersion arising from the structure of the waveguide. These two can have opposite signs, depending on whether the speed of light increases or decreases with wavelength. (See Chapter 5 for a more thorough explanation.) Fortuitously, the two cancel each other out near 1.31 μm in standard step-index single-mode fiber.

This is a useful wavelength, but it is not ideal. The loss of glass fibers is lowest at 1.55 μm, and erbium-doped fiber amplifiers operate in that range. Material dispersion is an inherent characteristic of silica fiber that cannot be readily changed without altering glass composition in ways that increase attenuation. However, it is possible to shift the dispersion minimum by changing waveguide dispersion.

Waveguide dispersion arises because light propagation in a waveguide depends on wavelength as well as the waveguide dimensions. The important number is the diameter divided by wavelength. Measured that way, decreasing the wavelength serves to increase the waveguide diameter, whereas increasing wavelength effectively shrinks the waveguide. Thus the distribution of light between core and cladding changes with wavelength.

That change in light distribution affects how fast the light travels through the fiber. The core and cladding have different refractive indexes, which determine the speed of light through them. Because light spends time in both core and cladding, its effective speed through the whole fiber is an average that depends on the distribution of light between core and cladding. A change in wavelength changes that distribution, and thus the average speed, causing waveguide dispersion.

Both chromatic and waveguide dispersion depend on the range of wavelengths in the signal. Fortunately, dispersion can have different signs, depending on whether the speed of light through the fiber increases or decreases with wavelength. It turns out that waveguide and chromatic dispersion neatly cancel each other out at 1.31 μm in step-index single-mode fibers, as shown in Figure 4.9. Changing the design of the core-cladding interface can alter waveguide dispersion so it cancels chromatic dispersion at other wavelengths.

More complex core-cladding designs can enhance performance of single-mode fiber by reducing dispersion near 1.55 μm.

There are two types of dispersion-shifted fiber, with subtle differences that have become important as fiber-optic technology has evolved.

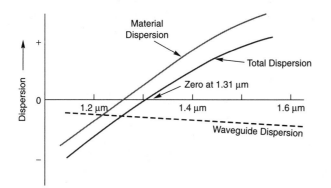

FIGURE 4.9

Waveguide dispersion offsets chromatic dispersion to produce zero dispersion at 1.31 μm in step-index single-mode fiber.

Zero-Dispersion-Shifted Fiber

The first dispersion-shifted fibers were designed with zero-dispersion wavelength shifted to 1.55 μm to match the minimum absorption wavelength. This was done by increasing the magnitude of waveguide dispersion, as shown in Figure 4.10. They were introduced in the mid-1980s and remain in use, although they have never been as common as standard step-index single-mode fibers.

Some dispersion-shifted fibers have zero dispersion at 1.55 μm.

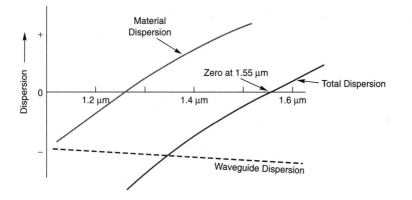

FIGURE 4.10

A fiber designed with more waveguide dispersion shifts the zero-dispersion wavelength to 1.55 μm.

Figure 4.11 shows one design for a commercial zero-dispersion-shifted fiber. The central core has peak refractive index in the center, dropping gradually to the same value as the outer cladding, made of pure silica. A thin inner cladding of pure silica surrounds the inner core, and it, in turn, is surrounded by an outer core. The refractive index of the inner core increases with distance from the core until it reaches a peak about halfway between the index of pure silica and the inner peak. Then it drops smoothly to the level of an outer cladding of pure silica. This design increases waveguide dispersion, as required for dispersion-shifted fiber. The design also affects mode-field diameter, reducing it to about 8.1 μm at 1.55 μm, compared to 10.5 μm for typical step-index single-mode fiber operated at 1.55 μm.

FIGURE 4.11

Zero-dispersion-shifted fiber with segmented core gives zero dispersion at 1.55 μm.

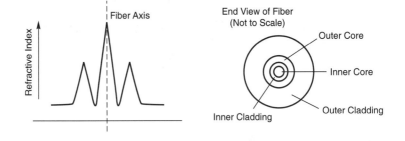

This design works well for systems transmitting signals only at the zero-dispersion wavelength. However, if the fiber transmits multiple wavelengths in the 1.55-μm region, signals at the different wavelengths can mix with each other, generating noise that degrades system performance. (The problem is called four-wave mixing, and I will cover it later.)

Nonzero-Dispersion-Shifted Fiber

Fibers with zero-dispersion wavelength just outside the range of erbium-doped fiber amplifiers work better for wavelength-division multiplexing.

The design of dispersion-shifted fibers can be modified to shift the zero-dispersion wavelength beyond the range of erbium-doped amplifiers, thus avoiding four-wave mixing that could cause problems in wavelength-division-multiplexed systems. For example, a further increase of waveguide dispersion could shift the zero-dispersion wavelength to 1.6 μm. These fibers are called nonzero-dispersion-shifted fibers because the low-dispersion range is shifted, but the zero-dispersion point is outside the range used for signal transmission.

The difference in fiber design is subtle; the refractive index profile shown in Figure 4.12 resembles that of the zero-dispersion-shifted fiber shown in Figure 4.10. Note, however, the differences in relative magnitude of the peaks in the curve.

The overall change in dispersion is also subtle, but significant, taking the zero-dispersion point *outside* the range of erbium-doped fiber amplifiers, as shown in Figure 4.13. The dispersion remains relatively low through the 1.55-μm window, where signals are transmitted. Although the difference between these types of dispersion-shifted fibers is subtle, it can strongly affect performance of systems using wavelength-division multiplexing.

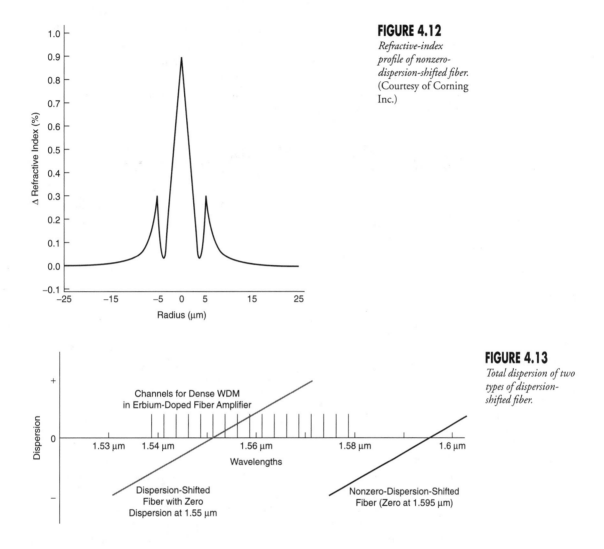

FIGURE 4.12
Refractive-index profile of nonzero-dispersion-shifted fiber. (Courtesy of Corning Inc.)

FIGURE 4.13
Total dispersion of two types of dispersion-shifted fiber.

Special Dispersion-Tailored Single-Mode Fiber

As we will see later, one way to limit total dispersion in a fiber system is to add segments of a different type of fiber that can compensate for the dispersion in the transmission fiber. This is possible because the total chromatic dispersion can have positive or negative signs, depending on whether the refractive index increases or decreases with wavelength. Just as waveguide dispersion offsets material dispersion to produce zero dispersion at one wavelength, so dispersion of one length of fiber can offset that in another length.

Fibers can be made with special dispersion profiles to compensate for dispersion in other parts of a fiber system.

In general, dispersion compensation requires lengths of fiber with dispersion that is much higher than standard fiber but of the opposite sign. It also is possible to make fiber with alternating portions having dispersion of the opposite sign. The design and use of these dispersion-compensating fibers is evolving rapidly and is beyond the scope of this chapter, but you should realize that they exist and may be used in high-performance systems, and to upgrade step-index single-mode fiber systems for operation at 1.55 µm.

Polarization in Single-Mode Fiber

Light has two orthogonal polarizations.

One final complication in fiber structure comes from a property of light that I so far have ignored: polarization. In Chapter 2, we saw that light waves consist of oscillating electric and magnetic fields. The fields are perpendicular to each other and to the direction light travels, as shown in Figure 4.14.

FIGURE 4.14

Electric and magnetic fields in a light wave.

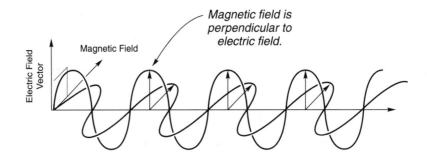

Ordinary unpolarized light is made up of many waves, with their electric and magnetic fields oriented randomly (although always perpendicular to each other for each wave). If all the electric fields (and hence the magnetic fields as well) were aligned parallel to one another, the light would be linearly polarized, which is the simplest type of polarization. Normal light is considered a combination of two polarizations, vertical and horizontal (determined by the direction of the electric field). A single light wave with its electric field oriented at a different angle is viewed as a combination of waves, one vertically polarized, the other horizontally polarized. Light can also be polarized circularly or elliptically, depending on how electric and magnetic fields oscillate with respect to each other's phase, but that is a matter beyond the scope of this chapter.

A "single-mode" fiber actually carries two modes with different polarizations.

Polarization doesn't matter in multimode fibers, but it can be important in single-mode fibers. The reason is that what we call single-mode fibers actually carry two modes with orthogonal polarization. Fibers with circularly symmetric cores can't differentiate between the two linear polarizations. From the standpoint of waveguide theory, the two modes are *degenerate,* meaning they're functionally identical and can't be told apart.

If the circular symmetry of fibers were perfect, polarization would have little practical impact for communications. However, fiber symmetry is never absolutely perfect. Nor are the forces affecting the fiber applied in perfect symmetry around it. As a result, the two polarization modes may experience slightly different conditions and travel along the fiber at slightly different speeds. This effect is called polarization mode dispersion, and it can cause problems in high-performance systems, such as those transmitting time-division multiplexed signals faster than about 2.5 Gbit/s.

Special single-mode fibers can control the polarization of light they transmit. There are two types: true single-polarization fiber and polarization-maintaining fiber. Both intentionally avoid circular symmetry, so they transmit vertically and horizontally polarized light differently. Their cores are asymmetric, and the fiber material may be strained in ways that affect light propagation. The two types have crucial differences in operation.

Single-polarization fiber has different attenuation for light of different polarizations. It transmits light of one polarization well but strongly attenuates light with the orthogonal polarization. Under the proper conditions, a single-polarization fiber attenuates the undesired polarization by a factor of 1000 to 10,000 within a few meters but transmits the desired polarization almost as well as standard single-mode fiber. Thus, only the desired polarization remains at the end.

Polarization-maintaining fiber has internal strain or asymmetry, which effectively splits the input light into two separate polarization modes. This property is called birefringence, which means that the refractive index of the fiber differs for the two polarizations. This prevents the light from shifting between polarizations, as it can while passing through a standard single-mode fiber. Attenuation of the two polarization modes is similar, but because of the difference in refractive index, they travel at different speeds. Polarization-maintaining fiber will transmit light in a single polarization if the input light is polarized and properly aligned with the polarization direction of the fiber, but otherwise it transmits both polarizations.

What Have You Learned?

1. There are several different types of optical fibers, with distinct properties.
2. Total internal reflection of light rays only approximates the actual process of light guiding. An optical fiber actually is a dielectric optical waveguide, which propagates light in distinct modes.
3. Fiber properties depend on the core-cladding structure and the materials from which the fiber is made.
4. To guide light, a fiber must have a core with higher refractive index than the cladding.
5. Step-index multimode fibers have a core diameter tens of wavelengths of the light they are guiding. They are used for imaging and illumination, but modal dispersion limits their transmission speed for communications.

6. The number of modes carried by a fiber depends on its core diameter, the refractive indexes of core and cladding, and the wavelength.

7. As dielectric optical waveguides, optical fibers carry light along the core-cladding boundary, with some light in the cladding.

8. Fibers with core diameters only a few wavelengths transmit a single mode of light.

9. Grading the refractive-index differential between core and cladding can nearly eliminate modal dispersion in a multimode fiber.

10. Graded-index fibers have standard core diameters of 50 or 62.5 μm. They are used for short-distance communications, but chromatic dispersion and modal noise limit their performance, so they are rarely used to transmit much beyond a kilometer.

11. Single-mode fibers are used for most communications at high speeds or more than 1 km.

12. Standard single-mode fibers have a step-index profile.

13. The cutoff wavelength is the shortest wavelength at which a single-mode fiber carries only one mode.

14. Single-mode fibers experience chromatic dispersion, which depends on wavelength and is the sum of two terms. One is material dispersion, arising from the variation of the refractive index of glass with wavelength. The other is waveguide dispersion, arising from the effects of changing wavelength on a fiber's properties as a waveguide.

15. Standard single-mode fiber has zero dispersion at 1.31 μm, where material dispersion and waveguide dispersion cancel each other.

16. Dispersion-shifted fiber has waveguide dispersion adjusted so it cancels material dispersion at a longer wavelength. Zero-dispersion-shifted fiber has zero dispersion at 1.55 μm; nonzero-dispersion-shifted fiber has zero dispersion at a longer wavelength, outside the range of erbium-doped fiber amplifiers.

17. Light can be polarized in vertical or horizontal directions. Normal single-mode fiber carries both polarizations and can suffer polarization-mode dispersion.

18. Single-polarization fibers transmit light in only one polarization. Polarization-maintaining fibers keep light in the same polarization that it had when it entered the fiber.

What's Next?

In Chapter 5, you will learn about the most important properties of optical fibers. Chapter 6 will cover fiber materials and fabrication.

Quiz for Chapter 4

1. What is the half acceptance angle for a large-core step-index fiber with core index of 1.5 and cladding index of 1.495?

   a. 4.7°

   b. 7.0°

   c. 9.4°

   d. 11°

   e. 14°

2. Modal dispersion is largest in what type of fiber?

   a. Step-index multimode.

   b. Graded-index multimode.

   c. Step-index single-mode.

   d. Dispersion-shifted single-mode.

   e. Polarization-maintaining.

3. A fiber has modal dispersion of 20 ns/km. If an instantaneous light pulse traveled through 8 km of such fiber, what would the pulse length be at the end?

   a. 8 ns.

   b. 20 ns.

   c. 40 ns.

   d. 80 ns.

   e. 160 ns.

4. What is the maximum data rate that the 8-km length of fiber in Problem 3 could carry?

   a. 160 Mbit/s.

   b. 100 Mbit/s.

   c. 20 Mbit/s.

   d. 8 Mbit/s.

   e. 6 Mbit/s.

5. What guides light in multimode graded-index fibers?

   a. Total internal reflection.

   b. Mode confinement in the cladding.

   c. Refraction in the region where core grades into the cladding.

   d. The optics that couple light into the fiber.

6. What is the maximum allowable core diameter for a step-index single-mode fiber operating at 1.3 μm, with core index of 1.5 and cladding index of 1.0003 (air)?

   a. 0.34 μm.

   b. 0.89 μm.

   c. 3.0 μm.

   d. 4.8 μm.

   e. 5.5 μm.

7. What is the maximum allowable core diameter for a step-index single-mode fiber operating at 1.3 μm, with core index of 1.5 and cladding index of 1.495?

   a. 0.89 μm.

   b. 3.0 μm.

   c. 4.1 μm.

   d. 8.1 μm.

   e. 10.3 μm.

8. What is the cutoff wavelength of a single-mode step-index fiber with core diameter of 8 μm, core index of 1.5, and cladding index of 1.495?

a. 0.89 μm.

b. 1.15 μm.

c. 1.28 μm.

d. 1.31 μm.

e. 1.495 μm.

9. What is the cutoff wavelength of a single-mode step-index fiber with core diameter of 8 μm, core index of 1.5, and cladding index of 1.496?

a. 0.89 μm.

b. 1.15 μm.

c. 1.28 μm.

d. 1.31 μm.

e. 1.495 μm.

10. What is done to design a dispersion-shifted fiber?

a. Waveguide dispersion is increased to offset material dispersion near 1.55 μm.

b. Material dispersion is reduced at 1.31 μm.

c. Material dispersion is increased to offset waveguide dispersion near 1.55 μm.

d. Core diameter is increased to allow multimode transmission.

e. The fiber core is made asymmetrical to control polarization.

11. For what applications are nonzero-dispersion-shifted fiber better than zero-dispersion-shifted fiber?

a. Single-wavelength transmission at 1.55 μm.

b. Short-distance data communications.

c. Single-wavelength transmission at 1.31 μm.

d. Dense wavelength-division multiplexing around 1.55 μm.

e. Dense wavelength-division multiplexing around 1.31 μm.

12. Does single-polarization fiber transmit more or fewer modes than standard step-index single-mode fiber?

a. Both transmit the same number.

b. Single-mode fiber transmits fewer because polarization-sensitive fibers distinguish between the two orthogonal polarizations.

c. Single-polarization fiber carries fewer because standard step-index fibers do not distinguish between the two orthogonal polarizations.

d. Need more information to answer the question.

Properties of Optical Fibers

About This Chapter

Now that you have learned about the basic designs of optical fibers, the next step is to understand the properties of fibers important for light transmission. I have already touched upon many properties in Chapter 4; this chapter examines them more carefully.

The most important properties for communications are attenuation, light collection and propagation, fiber dispersion, and mechanical strength. Nonlinear effects can be important in some cases, particularly for sensing and high-performance systems. I will start with the property usually at the top of the list—attenuation.

Fiber Attenuation

The attenuation of an optical fiber measures the amount of light lost between input and output. Total attenuation is the sum of all losses. It usually is dominated by imperfect light coupling into the fiber and absorption and scattering within the fiber. Sometimes other effects can cause important losses, such as light leakage from fibers that suffer severe microbending. Attenuation limits how far a signal can travel through a fiber before it becomes too weak to detect.

Absorption and scattering are both cumulative, with their effects increasing with fiber length. In contrast, coupling losses occur only at the ends of the fiber. The

●
Loss during fiber transmission is the sum of scattering, absorption, and light-coupling losses.

longer the fiber, the more important are absorption and scattering losses, and the less important coupling losses. Conversely, attenuation and scattering may be much smaller than end losses for short fibers. If you deliver an input power P_0 to a fiber, you can write the power at a distance D along the fiber as

$$P(D) = (P_0 - \Delta P)(1 - \alpha)^D (1 - S)^D$$

where ΔP is the input coupling loss, α is the absorption per unit length, and S is the scattering per unit length.

This chapter will concentrate on the characteristics of bulk fiber, absorption, and scattering; later chapters will cover coupling losses.

Absorption

●
Absorption of a material depends on wavelength. It is cumulative with distance.

Every material absorbs some light energy. The amount of absorption depends on the wavelength and the material. Ordinary glass absorbs relatively little visible light, so it looks transparent; the paper this book is printed on absorbs much more visible light, so it looks opaque. (You can read these words because the paper reflects more light than the ink, which absorbs most light striking it and reflects little.) The amount of absorption can vary widely with wavelength. The clearest glass is quite opaque at an infrared wavelength of 10 μm. Air absorbs so much light in part of the ultraviolet that scientists call wavelengths shorter than about 0.2 μm the *vacuum ultraviolet* because they don't go through air.

Absorption depends very strongly on the composition of a substance. Some materials absorb light very strongly at wavelengths where others are quite transparent. For glass, this means that small amounts of certain impurities can dramatically increase absorption at wavelengths where glass is otherwise transparent. Removing those impurities was a crucial step to making the extremely transparent fibers used for communications. Typically, absorption is plotted as a function of wavelength. Some absorption peaks can be quite sharp because the material absorbs only a narrow range of wavelengths; others are spread over a wider range.

Absorption is cumulative, so it also depends on the amount of material that the light passes through. Suppose you have a long glass rod made of glass that in each 1-cm length absorbs 1% of the light passing through it. It will absorb 1% of the *remaining* light in the next centimeter, and so on. If the only thing affecting light is absorption, the fraction of light absorbed per unit length is α and the total length is D, the fraction of light remaining after a distance D is

$$(1 - \alpha)^D$$

In our example, this means that after passing through 1 m (100 cm) of glass, the fraction of light remaining would be

$$(1 - 0.01)^{100} = 0.366, \qquad \text{or } 36.6\%$$

Scattering

Atoms and other particles inevitably scatter some of the light that hits them. The light isn't absorbed, just sent in another direction in a process called Rayleigh scattering, after the British physicist Lord Rayleigh, as shown in Figure 5.1. However, the distinction between scattering and absorption doesn't matter much if you are trying to send light through a fiber, because the light is lost from the fiber in either case.

Atoms scatter a small fraction of passing light.

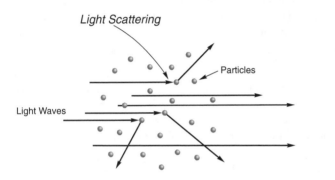

Light Scattering

Particles

Light Waves

FIGURE 5.1

Light scattering.

Like absorption, scattering is cumulative. The further the light travels through a material, the more likely scattering is to occur. The relationship is the same as for light absorption, but the fraction of scattered light is written S.

$$\text{Remaining light} = (1 - S)^D$$

Scattering depends not on the specific type of material but on the size of the particles relative to the wavelength of light. The closer the wavelength is to the particle size, the more scattering. In fact, the amount of scattering increases quite rapidly as the wavelength λ decreases. For a transparent solid, the scattering loss in decibels per kilometer is given by

$$\text{Scattering} = A\lambda^{-4}$$

where A is a constant depending on the material. This means that dividing the wavelength by 2 multiples scattering loss (in dB/km) by a factor of 16.

Total Loss or Attenuation

Scattering and absorption combine to give total loss, or attenuation. Figure 5.2 plots their contributions across the range of wavelengths used for communications. Attenuation normally is measured in decibels per unit length, typically decibels per kilometer for communication fibers. The plot shows small absorption peaks from traces of metal impurities remaining in the glass and other absorption arising from bonds that residual hydrogen atoms form with oxygen in the glass. (I picked this example to show the peak, which is

Total attenuation, or loss, is the sum of scattering and attenuation; it normally is measured in decibels per kilometer.

much lower in state-of-the-art communication fibers.) The absorption at wavelengths longer than 1.6 μm comes from silicon-oxygen bonds in the glass; as the plot shows, the absorption increases rapidly at longer wavelengths. As a result, silica-based fibers are rarely used at wavelengths much longer than 1.6 μm.

Rayleigh scattering accounts for most attenuation at shorter wavelengths. As you can see in Figure 5.2, it increases sharply as wavelength decreases. The space between measured total attenuation and the theoretical scattering curve represents the absorption loss. The closer the two lines, the larger the fraction of total attenuation that arises from scattering. The rapid decrease in scattering at longer wavelengths makes loss lowest in the "valley" around 1.55 μm, where both Rayleigh scattering and infrared absorption are low. Except for the infrared absorption of silica, fiber loss would decrease even more at longer wavelengths.

Total attenuation is what matters for system performance.

It's hard to separate absorption from scattering in practical measurements. Note that the plot compares *theoretical* scattering with total measured attenuation and does not isolate absorption. You can consider the difference between the two curves as the net absorption, but from a practical standpoint total attenuation is what matters for system performance, not absorption or scattering. Thus it's more useful to think of the power (P) at a distance D along the fiber as defined by

$$P(D) = (P_0 - \Delta P)(1 - A)^D$$

where A is attenuation per unit length, P_0 is initial power, and ΔP is the coupling loss, as before. In practice, it is simpler to make calculations if you first separate fiber attenuation from coupling losses by starting with the power that *enters* the fiber rather than the input power you *attempt* to couple into the fiber.

Calculating Attenuation in Decibels

Attenuation normally is calculated on the logarithmic decibel scale.

As we saw in Chapter 2, attenuation measures the ratio of input to output power: P_{out}/P_{in}. It normally is measured in decibels, as defined by the equation

$$\text{dB (attenuation)} = -10 \log_{10}\left(\frac{P_{out}}{P_{in}}\right)$$

Output power is less than input power, so the result would be a negative number if the equation didn't include a minus sign. You should remember that in some publications decibels are defined so that a negative number indicates loss.

Decibels may seem to be rather peculiar units, which appear to understate high attenuation. For example, a 3-dB loss leaves about half the original light, a 10-dB loss leaves 10%, and a 20-dB loss leaves 1%. However, a 100-dB loss leaves only 10^{-10} of the original light, and a 1000-dB loss leaves 10^{-100}—a ratio smaller than one atom in the whole known universe. Table 5.1 translates some representative decibel measurements into ratios. You can also use the simple conversion

$$\text{Remaining power} = 10^{(-dB/10)}$$

FIGURE 5.2

*Total attenuation in a
fiber is the sum of
absorption and
scattering losses.*

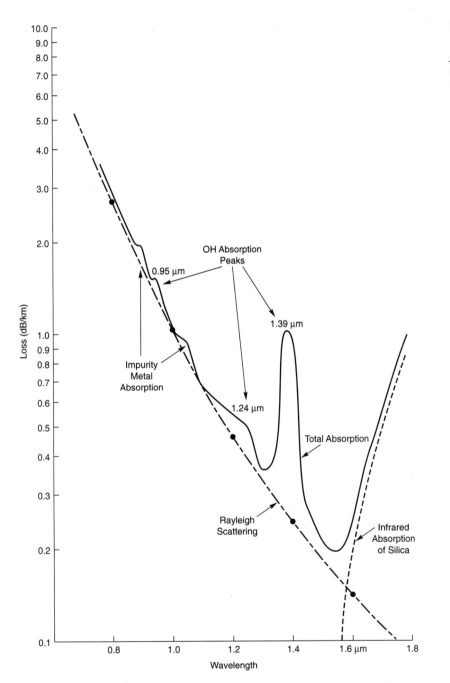

Table 5.1 Decibels and equivalent power ratios.

Loss in Decibels	Power Ratio
0.1	0.9772
0.2	0.9550
0.3	0.9333
0.4	0.9120
0.5	0.8913
0.6	0.8710
0.7	0.8511
0.8	0.8318
0.9	0.8128
1	0.7943
2	0.6310
3	0.5012
4	0.3981
5	0.3162
6	0.2512
7	0.1995
8	0.1585
9	0.1259
10	0.1
20	0.01
30	0.001
40	0.0001
50	0.00001
60	0.000001
70	0.0000001
80	0.00000001
90	10^{-09}
100	10^{-10}
200	10^{-20}
300	10^{-30}
400	10^{-40}
500	10^{-50}
600	10^{-60}
700	10^{-70}
800	10^{-80}
900	10^{-90}
1000	10^{-100}

Decibels are very convenient units for calculating signal power and attenuation. Suppose you want to calculate the effects of two successive attenuations. One blocks 80% of the input signal, and the second blocks 30%. To calculate total attenuation using fractions, you must convert both absorption figures to the fractions of power transmitted, then multiply them, and convert that number from the fraction of light transmitted to the fraction attenuated. If you use decibels, you merely add attenuations to get total loss.

$$\text{Total loss (dB)} = \text{loss (dB)}_1 + \text{loss (dB)}_2 + \text{loss (dB)}_3 + \ldots$$

The calculations are even simpler if you know the loss per unit length and want to know total loss of a longer (or shorter) piece of fiber. Instead of using the exponential formula mentioned previously, you simply multiply loss per unit length times the distance:

$$\text{Total loss} = \text{dB/km} \times \text{distance}$$

You can also measure power in decibels relative to some particular level. In fiber optics, the two most common decibel scales for power are decibels relative to 1 mW (dBm) and relative to 1μW (dBμ). Powers above those levels have positive signs; those below have negative signs. Thus 10 mW is 10 dBm, and 0.1 mW is −10 dBm, or 100 dBμ.

If everything is in decibels, simple addition and subtraction suffice to calculate output power from input power and attenuation. You also can write the equation in other ways:

$$P_{\text{out}} = P_{\text{in}} - \text{loss (dB)}$$
$$\text{Loss (dB)} = P_{\text{in}} - P_{\text{out}}$$
$$P_{\text{in}} = P_{\text{out}} + \text{loss (dB)}$$

Note that it is vital to keep track of the plus and minus signs. In this case, we give loss in decibels a positive sign, as we did earlier. If you ever feel confused, you can do a simple truth test, by checking to see if the output power is less than the input. (The only way output can be more than input is if you have an optical amplifier or regenerator somewhere in the system.)

As an example of how the calculations work, consider a fiber system in which 3 dB is lost at the input end and that contains 5 km of fiber with loss of 0.6 dB/km. If the input power is 0 dBm (exactly 1mW), the output is

$$P_{\text{out}} = 0 \text{ dBm} - 3 \text{ dB (input loss)} - (5 \text{ km} \times 0.6 \text{ dB/km}) = -6.0 \text{ dBm}$$

If you rewrite this as milliwatts, you have 0.25 mW.

Spectral Variation

As we saw before, fiber attenuation is the sum of absorption and scattering, both of which vary with wavelength. The spectral variation depends largely on the fiber composition. The overall variation shown in Figure 5.2 is fairly typical for fibers made of highly purified fused silica, but the "water" peaks near 1.4 μm are higher than for most high-performance single-mode communication fibers.

The decibel scale simplifies calculations of power and attenuation.

Attenuation varies with wavelength, depending on the material.

In practice, optical fibers are designed for use at specific wavelengths. The choice depends largely on the fiber material and is also influenced by the available light sources. If you look at the plot in Figure 5.2, you can see why the regions around 1.3 and 1.55 μm are used as fiber-transmission windows. Both are in regions where attenuation is relatively low. That is not true for the 0.8–0.85-μm window, used in some moderate-performance systems, which was chosen to match the wavelength of low-cost gallium-arsenide light sources.

Other materials are used in fibers for other wavelengths. Special grades of quartz are used for ultraviolet-transmitting fibers. Some plastics have relatively even transmission across the visible spectrum. Fluoride compounds are transparent at longer infrared wavelengths than glass. Chapter 6 will cover various materials in more detail.

Light Collection and Propagation

Several factors enter into how fibers collect light and propagate it. Most arise from the structure of fibers, described in Chapter 4. This section examines the impact of those structures.

Core Size and Mode-Field Diameter

The larger the core diameter, the easier it is to align with a light source.

Core size is important in coupling light into a fiber. The core must be aligned with the light-emitting region, which can be a laser or LED light source or the output end of another fiber. To collect light efficiently, the core should be at least as large as the light source. As shown in Figure 5.3, if the light source is larger than the fiber, much of its light goes right into the cladding and quickly escapes from the fiber. The larger the core diameter, the easier it is to align with the light source to collect light. This is purely a matter of geometry, matching the light source to the collecting aperture. Core size does not directly affect the acceptance angle of a fiber, the range of angles over which it collects light.

Core size is the physical dimension of the core. In single-mode fibers, the light spreads through a slightly larger volume, including the inner edge of the cladding. This *mode-field diameter* is the critical dimension for transferring light between single-mode fibers.

Transferring light between fibers is the business of splices and connectors; details will be provided in Chapters 13 and 14.

Numerical Aperture

Numerical aperture (NA) measures the fiber's acceptance angle.

A second factor in determining how much light a fiber collects is its acceptance angle, the range of angles over which a light ray can enter the fiber and be trapped in its core. The full acceptance angle is the range of angles at which light is trapped; it extends both above and below the axis of the fiber. The half acceptance angle is the angle measured from the fiber axis to the edge of the cone of light rays trapped in the core; it is shown in Figure 5.4.

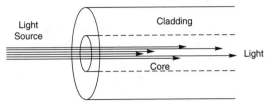

FIGURE 5.3

The match between light-source dimensions and core diameter helps determine light transfer.

Light Source Well Matched to Fiber

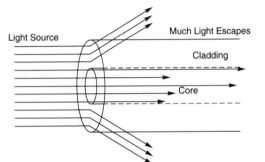

Light Source Poorly Matched to Fiber

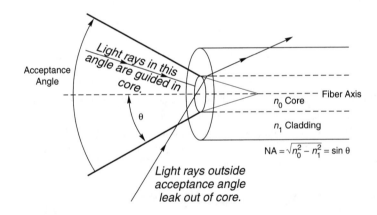

FIGURE 5.4

Light rays have to fall within a fiber's acceptance angle, measured by NA, to be guided in the core.

$$NA = \sqrt{n_0^2 - n_1^2} = \sin \theta$$

The standard measure of acceptance angle is the numerical aperture, NA, which is the sine of the half acceptance angle, θ, for reasonably small angles. It is defined as

$$NA = \sqrt{(n_0^2 - n_1^2)} = \sin \theta$$

where n_0 is the core index and n_1 is the cladding index.

Core diameter does not enter directly into the equation, but in order to be guided within the core, light rays must both enter the core and fall within the fiber's acceptance angle. Light is not guided within the core if it enters the core but is outside the acceptance angle or if it falls within the acceptance angle but enters the fiber outside the core. Large core size and large NA do not have to go together, but in practice larger-core fibers tend to have larger NA. Generally, large-core step-index multimode fibers have NA 0.3 or larger; NA is largest in fibers used for imaging or light guiding, where collecting light from a large angle is important. Graded-index multimode fibers have NA of 0.2–0.3, and a typical single-mode fiber NA is 0.1 to 0.15.

It is impractical to calculate NA from measurements of the core and cladding indexes, but NA can be measured directly by looking at the output of a multimode fiber. The light-guiding properties of fibers are symmetrical, so light emerging from a multimode fiber spreads over an angle equal to its acceptance angle. For practical measurements, care must be taken to eliminate modes guided along the cladding, and the *edge* of the beam is defined as the angle where intensity drops to 5% that in the center, as shown in Figure 5.5.

FIGURE 5.5

Intensity of light emerging from a multimode fiber falls to about 5% of peak value at the edge of its acceptance angle.

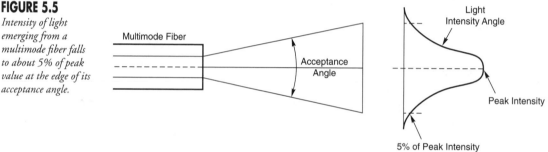

The numerical aperture of single-mode fibers is defined by the same equation as for multimode fibers, but light does not spread out from them in the same way. (They carry only a single mode, and their cores are so small that another wave effect called *diffraction* controls how light spreads out from the end.) NA generally is not as important for single-mode fibers as it is for multimode fibers.

Cladding Modes and Leaky Modes

Light entering a fiber can be guided along the cladding.

As we have seen earlier, not all light aimed into a fiber is guided along the core. Some enters the cladding at the end of the fiber; other light escapes from the core by hitting the core-cladding boundary at greater than the confinement angle. This light excites *cladding modes,* which can propagate in the cladding.

Total internal reflection at the boundary between cladding and the surrounding material can guide light in the cladding just as it guides light along an unclad fiber. This can happen as long as the surrounding material—air or a plastic coating—has a lower refractive index than the cladding. This might sound like a good way to maximize light transmission, but it's usually undesirable. It can introduce noise in communication fibers and crosstalk between adjacent fibers in an imaging bundle. To prevent this, manufacturers often coat fibers with a plastic having a higher refractive index than the cladding, so light striking the cladding-coating boundary leaks out. The fibers in rigid bundles sometimes are separated by "dark" glass, which absorbs light so it can't pass between claddings.

In multimode fibers, the boundary between modes guided in the core and modes confined to the cladding is not sharp. Some light falls into intermediate *leaky* modes, which propagate partly in both core and cladding. These modes travel much further than cladding modes but also are prone to leakage and loss.

Both cladding and leaky modes can lead to spurious results in fiber measurements, so mode strippers have been developed to remove them. These devices work by surrounding part of the fiber with a material having a refractive index equal to or larger than that of the cladding, preventing total internal reflection at the outer boundary of the cladding. Light that leaks into this material is absorbed and lost from the fiber. A long length of fiber also can serve as a mode stripper if the cladding attenuation is much higher than that of the core.

● Leaky modes are not perfectly confined to the core.

Microbending Losses

Optical fibers are not totally isolated from the outside world. A variety of outside influences can change their physical characteristics and affect how they guide light. Typically these effects are modest and must be enhanced or accumulated over long distances to make the type of sensors described in Chapter 27. However, significant losses can arise from microbending—the formation of many tiny kinks in a fiber, which can occur if there is a bit of excess fiber or a cable shrinks.

● Microbends can cause excess fiber loss.

The cause of bending loss is easiest to see using the ray model of light in a multimode fiber. If the fiber is straight, it falls within the confinement angle of a fiber. However, as shown in Figure 5.6, a bend changes the angle at which the light hits the core-cladding boundary. If the bend is sharp enough, the light strikes the boundary at an angle outside the confinement angle θ_c, so it is refracted into the cladding, where it can leak out. Microbending can be useful in sensors, but it can cause problems elsewhere.

Dispersion

Dispersion is the spreading out of light pulses as they travel along a fiber. It occurs because the speed of light through a fiber depends on its wavelength and the propagation mode. The differences in speed are slight, but like attenuation, they accumulate with distance. The four main types of dispersion arise from multimode transmission, the dependence of refractive index on wavelength, variations in waveguide properties with wavelength, and transmission of two different polarizations of light through single-mode fiber.

● The principal types of dispersion are modal, material, waveguide, and polarization.

FIGURE 5.6

Light can leak out of a bent fiber.

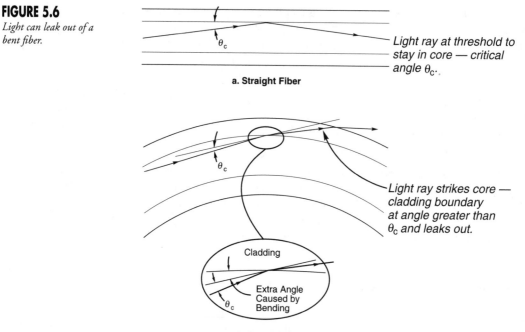

Light ray at threshold to stay in core — critical angle θ_c.

a. Straight Fiber

Light ray strikes core — cladding boundary at angle greater than θ_c and leaks out.

Cladding

Extra Angle Caused by Bending

b. Bent Fiber

Like attenuation, dispersion can limit the distance a signal can travel through an optical fiber, but it does so in a different way. Dispersion does not weaken a signal; it blurs it. If you send one pulse every nanosecond but the pulses spread to 10 ns at the end of the fiber, they blur together. The signal is present, but it's so blurred in time that it is unintelligible.

In its simplest sense, dispersion measures pulse spreading per unit distance in nanoseconds or picoseconds per kilometer. Total pulse spreading, Δt, is

$$\Delta t = \text{dispersion (ns/km)} \times \text{distance (km)}$$

This is the case for modal dispersion, which is most important for step-index single-mode fibers, where modes travel through the fiber at different speeds. Graded-index fibers nominally equalize the speeds of all modes transmitted by the fiber, but things don't work that nicely in the real world. It's functionally impossible to match the ideal refractive-index profile needed to make all modes travel at the same speed, particularly because that profile depends on wavelength, and the fibers may carry signals at different wavelengths. In practice, you have to rely on manufacturer specifications for total dispersion of graded-index fibers, although they often specify in units of bandwidth, which are described shortly.

However, both material and waveguide dispersion also depend on the range of wavelengths in the signal. They are properly measured in units of picoseconds per kilometer (of fiber length) per nanometer (of light-source spectral width). Material and waveguide dispersion typically are added together to give chromatic dispersion, $\Delta t_{\text{chromatic}}$, which is given by

$$\Delta t_{\text{chromatic}} = \text{dispersion (ps/nm-km)} \times \text{distance (km)} \times \text{spectral width (nm)}$$

This means that although chromatic dispersion is a characteristic of the fiber used, the amount of chromatic dispersion also depends on the light source. Spend the extra money for a narrow-line laser source, and you can greatly reduce pulse spreading in a system limited by chromatic dispersion.

As we saw in Chapter 4, modal dispersion occurs because different modes follow distinct paths in multimode fibers. In multimode fibers, modal dispersion normally is larger than chromatic dispersion, but you have to consider the two together. (Polarization-mode dispersion is technically a subcategory of modal dispersion, but it is observable by itself only in single-mode fibers.) They are independent effects but not cumulative, so to be accurate, you need to add them quadratically:

$$\Delta t_{\text{total}} = \sqrt{(\Delta t_{\text{modal}})^2 + (\Delta\lambda\, \Delta t_{\text{chromatic}})^2}$$

where $\Delta\lambda$ is the range of wavelengths in the pulse.

For single-mode fibers, the only modal dispersion remaining is the small effect of polarization-mode dispersion, so total dispersion is

$$\Delta t_{\text{total(SM)}} = \sqrt{(\Delta\lambda\, \Delta t_{\text{chromatic}})^2 + (\Delta t_{\text{polarization mode}})^2}$$

In practice, polarization-mode dispersion is a concern only in the highest-speed systems, where chromatic dispersion has been reduced by using narrow-line sources and low-dispersion fibers. Polarization dispersion depends on coupling between polarization modes as well as on total fiber length, so it is expressed in units of $\text{ps}/\sqrt{\text{km}}$.

Dispersion and Digital Transmission Capacity

Dispersion limits digital-transmission speed by causing pulses to overlap, so they cannot be distinguished. The degree of overlap at which the signal becomes obscured by dispersion depends on the system design. As a rough guideline, you can estimate maximum bit rate by multiplying the dispersed pulse length by 4 and dividing it into 1.

$$\text{Bit rate} = \frac{1}{4\,\Delta t}$$

Thus, if pulses experience 1 ns (10^{-9} s) of dispersion, the maximum bit rate is about 250 Mbit/s. In practice, it isn't quite this simple, because performance depends on how much power reaches the receiver as well as pulse spreading, but this is a useful guideline.

Material and waveguide dispersion, which combine to give chromatic dispersion, are measured in picoseconds per kilometer per nanometer.

Dispersion limits digital-transmission capacity.

Dispersion and Wavelength

Material
dispersion
depends strongly
on wavelength.

Material dispersion arises from the change in refractive index with wavelength. Dispersion, like absorption, is a complex function of the individual material that depends on wavelength. Communication fibers are nearly pure silica (SiO_2), so their material dispersion is close to that of pure silica. Figure 5.7 shows a plot of refractive index and material dispersion of silica against wavelength.

FIGURE 5.7

Material dispersion and refractive index of silica as a function of wavelength.

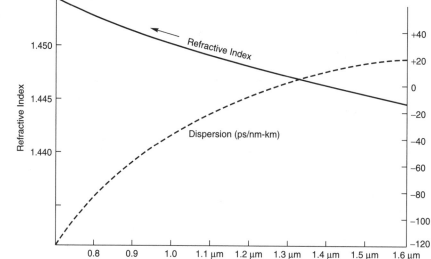

Note that material dispersion has a positive or negative sign, unlike modal dispersion. This sign indicates how the pulses spread—that is, whether longer or shorter wavelengths travel faster in the fiber. These signs are important in adding material and waveguide dispersion to calculate total chromatic dispersion, as we will see. However, the sign does not matter when calculating total dispersion because chromatic dispersion is squared in the formula for total dispersion.

As Figure 5.7 shows, the magnitude of material dispersion is large at wavelengths shorter than 1.1 μm. High material dispersion at 0.85 μm limits transmission speeds possible at that wavelength even in single-mode fiber, so little work has been done on single-mode transmission at 0.85 μm. The real benefits of single-mode fiber come from operating at a wavelength where material dispersion is small.

Waveguide dispersion is a separate effect. Recall that waveguide properties are a function of the wavelength of light. As a result, changing the wavelength affects how light is guided in a single-mode fiber. For a simple step-index single-mode fiber, the resulting waveguide dispersion is small, but it still can be important. More complex refractive index profiles can increase waveguide dispersion. As in the case of material dispersion, it has a sign that indicates how pulse travel time changes with wavelength.

Chromatic dispersion is the sum of material and waveguide dispersion:

$$\Delta t_{\text{chromatic}} = \Delta t_{\text{material}} + \Delta t_{\text{waveguide}}$$

In this formula, the signs of the two elements of chromatic dispersion are important. Material dispersion that makes short wavelengths travel slower than long wavelengths can be offset by waveguide dispersion that makes the longer wavelengths travel slower, and vice versa. This results in low chromatic dispersion at certain wavelengths. Figure 5.8 shows how this works for standard step-index single-mode fiber and dispersion-shifted fiber.

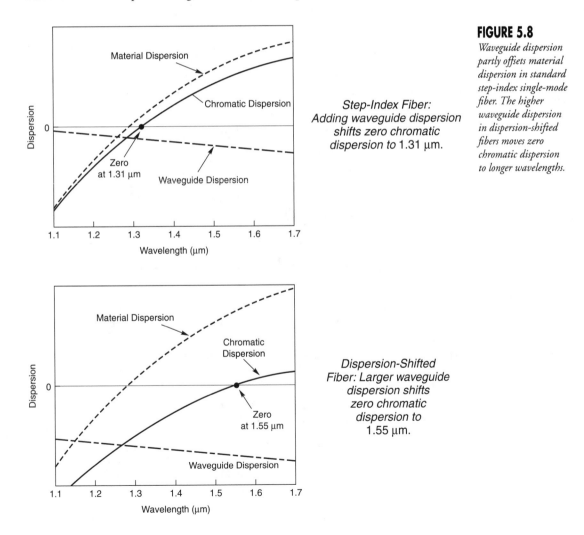

FIGURE 5.8

Waveguide dispersion partly offsets material dispersion in standard step-index single-mode fiber. The higher waveguide dispersion in dispersion-shifted fibers moves zero chromatic dispersion to longer wavelengths.

Step-Index Fiber: Adding waveguide dispersion shifts zero chromatic dispersion to 1.31 μm.

Dispersion-Shifted Fiber: Larger waveguide dispersion shifts zero chromatic dispersion to 1.55 μm.

Waveguide dispersion changes less with wavelength than material dispersion, but the amount of waveguide dispersion can be changed by altering fiber design. Material dispersion is essentially the same in all silica fibers; adding dopants causes only slight changes. Silica has zero material dispersion at 1.27 to 1.29 μm, depending on dopants; a typical value is 1.28 μm. Adding the waveguide dispersion of a step-index single-mode fiber gives zero chromatic dispersion at 1.31 μm. The higher waveguide dispersion of dispersion-shifted fiber offsets zero chromatic dispersion to 1.55 μm or longer, depending on the design. Especially at longer wavelengths, dispersion usually is low in a range around the point of zero chromatic dispersion.

If you know the zero-dispersion wavelength, λ_0, and the slope of the chromatic dispersion at that wavelength, S_0, you can approximate chromatic dispersion as a function of wavelength, $D(\lambda)$, using the formula

$$D(\lambda) = \frac{S_0}{4}\left(\lambda - \frac{\lambda_0^4}{\lambda^3}\right)$$

This formula gives chromatic dispersion over a fiber's normal operating range, typically 1.2 to 1.6 μm for standard single-mode fiber, 1.5 to 1.6 μm for dispersion-shifted single-mode fiber, and 0.75 to 1.45 μm for graded-index multimode fiber.

Total pulse spreading caused by chromatic dispersion in a communication system depends on the range of wavelengths, $\Delta\lambda$, as well as the amount of dispersion:

$$\Delta t_{\text{spreading}} = \Delta\lambda \times \Delta t_{\text{chromatic}} \times \text{distance}$$

This result means that the effects of chromatic dispersion depend not only on the fiber, but also on the range of wavelengths in the source. Narrow-line sources can limit pulse spreading as effectively as low-dispersion fibers.

Dispersion Compensation and Tailoring

Fibers with opposite signs of chromatic dispersion can be combined in sequence to yield low overall dispersion.

We saw before that pulse dispersion is cumulative, adding up over the entire length of a fiber system. In general, that fact means that adding more fiber only makes things worse. However, it is possible to cancel *chromatic* dispersion if you have fibers with chromatic dispersion of opposite signs. If you have a fiber where the shorter wavelengths tend to fall behind the longer ones, you could add a fiber with chromatic dispersion in the opposite direction, which slows the longer wavelengths and allows the shorter ones to catch up. The idea is similar to having waveguide dispersion offset material dispersion to give zero dispersion at the desired wavelength. In this case, it is two separate fibers, spliced together, that offset each other's dispersion, as shown in Figure 5.9.

The dispersion-compensating fiber is designed so its dispersion offsets that of standard fibers at the transmission wavelength. Because it is optimized for dispersion rather than attenuation, it typically has higher loss than standard fiber, so it is used in shorter

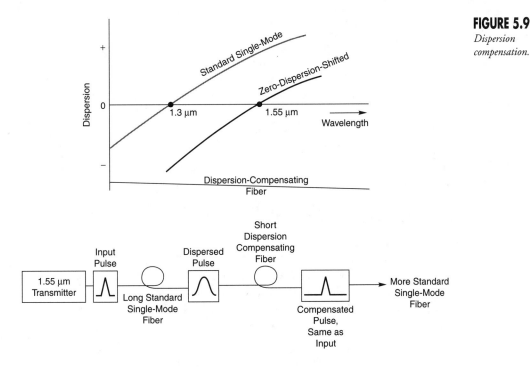

FIGURE 5.9
*Dispersion
compensation.*

lengths. However, dispersion compensation is an attractive concept because adding segments of dispersion-compensating fiber can reduce dispersion of existing cables so they can be upgraded to higher transmission capacity. The concept can be used to compensate for dispersion at one wavelength or at a range of wavelengths, typically in the range near 1.55 μm, where erbium-doped fiber amplifiers operate.

Suppose, for example, you want to use a fiber with dispersion of +10 ps/nm-km at 1.55 μm in a communication system. You can buy dispersion-compensating fiber with dispersion of −100 ps/nm-km at 1.55 μm. You can figure out how to combine the two to get net pulse spreading of zero by using the formula

$$\Delta t_{\text{spreading}} = \Delta\lambda\Delta t_{\text{chrom1}}L_1 + \Delta\lambda\Delta t_{\text{chrom2}}L_2$$

where Δt_{chrom} and L are chromatic dispersions and lengths for fiber types 1 and 2, and $\Delta\lambda$ is the range of wavelengths in the signal. If we want zero pulse spreading, $\Delta t_{\text{spreading}}$ should equal zero. We can ignore the wavelength range because the same signal travels through both fibers. This leaves us with

$$\Delta t_{\text{chrom1}} \text{ dist}_1 = -\Delta t_{\text{chrom2}} \text{ dist}_2$$

Plug in the values for chromatic dispersion, and you find

$$10 \text{ dist}_1 = -(100)\text{dist}_2$$

Thus for every 10 km of fiber with +10 ps/nm-km, you need 1 km of dispersion-compensating fiber to offset its chromatic dispersion.

Other optical components can compensate for fiber dispersion.

You can also design other optical components to compensate for chromatic dispersion in other ways. For example, you could build an optical delay line that routed optical signals different distances depending on their wavelengths. If fiber dispersion left the short wavelengths lagging behind, the delay line could make the longer wavelengths travel further, so the shorter wavelengths could catch up.

At this writing, various technologies are in development for dispersion compensation in high-performance fiber-optic systems. You will learn about another approach, fiber gratings, in Chapter 7. The field is moving fast. Stay tuned for further progress.

Dispersion and Analog Bandwidth

So far I have concentrated on the effects of dispersion on digital pulses, because dispersion is easy to explain for the example of an instantaneous pulse. Even digital transmission isn't really this simple. Signals don't start as instantaneous pulses or even neatly trimmed square waves; they begin as analog waveforms, which take a certain time to rise and a certain time to drop back to zero. If the initial pulse is Δt_{in} and the total dispersion is Δt_{total}, the output pulse duration Δt_{out} is

$$\Delta t_{out} = \sqrt{\Delta t_{in}^2 + \Delta t_{total}^2}$$

It is this output pulse length, rather than only the dispersion, that limits bit rate of a digital system.

Dispersion effects on analog bandwidth are similar to those on digital pulses.

Dispersion also affects analog transmission, in roughly the same way as it limits digital bit rate. Instead of lengthening digital pulses, dispersion stretches out the whole analog waveform. This limits the analog bandwidth, the frequency at which the detectable signal has dropped 3 dB (50%) compared to lower frequencies.

The transmission capacities of graded-index and step-index multimode fiber are often specified in terms of bandwidth, typically megahertz-kilometers, rather than dispersion (ns/km). You can roughly convert between the two using the formula

$$BW = \frac{350}{\Delta t_{total}}$$

Typical bandwidths of step-index multimode are around 20 MHz-km. Bandwidths of graded-index fibers are sensitive to manufacturing processes; typical values at 0.85 μm are 150 to 200 MHz-km for 62.5/125 fiber at 400 to 600 MHz-km for 50/125 fiber. At 1.3 μm, graded-index fiber bandwidths range from 200 to 1000 MHz-km, with the higher values for 50/125 fiber and the lower for 62.5/125.

Nonlinear Effects

Normally, light waves or photons transmitted through a fiber have little interaction with each other, and are not changed by their passage through the fiber (except for absorption and scattering effects). However, there are some exceptions, which in certain cases can affect signal transmission. They generally are called *nonlinear* effects, because their strength generally depends on the square (or some higher power) of intensity rather than simply on the amount of light present. Thus, they are weak at low powers but can become much stronger when light is concentrated in a small area or is present at high powers.

Nonlinear optical devices have become common in some applications, such as doubling the frequency (halving the wavelength) of laser light to generate shorter wavelengths than readily available from commercial lasers. Most of them use exotic materials not present in fiber-optic systems, and you normally would not see nonlinear effects in glass at the power levels used for communications. However, the glass used in optical fibers has some small nonlinearities, and these accumulate when light passes through many kilometers of fiber.

I will describe some effects that can significantly limit the performance of fiber-optic communications systems. Note that these nonlinear effects depend on power density, the amount of power passing through a unit area in the fiber core. This means that they are much more likely in a single-mode fiber with 8-μm core than in a multimode fiber with 50- or 62.5-μm core, which has a cross section 40 to 60 times as large.

> Nonlinear effects are weak at low powers but can become significant at high powers. They are most likely in single-mode fibers.

Brillouin Scattering

The nonlinear effect that occurs at the lowest powers is *stimulated Brillouin scattering*. It occurs when signal power reaches a level that can generate acoustic vibrations in the glass, corresponding to powers as low as a few milliwatts in the small cores of single-mode fiber. Acoustic waves change the density of a material and thus alter its refractive index. The resulting fluctuations in refractive index can scatter light; this effect is called Brillouin scattering. Because the light wave being scattered itself generates the acoustic waves, the process in fibers is called stimulated Brillouin scattering.

> Stimulated Brillouin scattering can occur at powers as low as a few milliwatts in single-mode fibers.

In fibers, stimulated Brillouin scattering takes the form of a light wave shifted slightly in frequency from the original light wave. (The change is 11 GHz, or slightly under 0.0001 μm for a wavelength of 1.5 μm.) The scattered wave goes back toward the transmitter. The effect is strongest when the light pulse is long (allowing a long interaction between light and the acoustic wave), and the laser linewidth is very small, around 100 MHz. Under such conditions, it can occur at power levels as little as 3 mW in single-mode fibers. However, the power level needed to trigger stimulated Brillouin scattering increases as pulse length decreases, so the effect becomes less severe at higher data rates.

Brillouin scattering reduces signal strength by directing part of the light back toward the transmitter, effectively increasing attenuation. Careful design can reduce the impact of Brillouin scattering, but it does set an upper limit for power levels in systems using narrow-linewidth laser sources. The strength of the effect can increase with the number of optical amplifiers in a system, but adding optical isolators to block light from going toward the transmitter blocks that increase.

Raman Scattering

Stimulated Raman scattering occurs when light waves interact with vibrations of atoms in a crystalline lattice. In essence, the atom absorbs the light and then quickly reemits a photon with energy equal to the original photon plus or minus the energy of a vibration characteristic of the atom. This has the effect of both scattering light and shifting its wavelength.

> **Stimulated Raman scattering transfers power between signals at different wavelengths.**

It takes more laser power to stimulate Raman scattering than Brillouin scattering, and the results are different. Raman scattering goes both forward and backward along the fiber. By shifting the wavelength a much larger amount than Brillouin scattering, Raman scattering can cause crosstalk between two separate wavelengths going through the same fiber.

Careful choice of wavelengths can reduce the interference between Raman scattering and other channels. Nonetheless, Raman scattering does impose limits on wavelength-division multiplexed systems with many optical amplifiers. Its effects are more serious on the shorter wavelengths in a multiwavelength system.

Four-Wave Mixing

When multiple wavelengths pass through the same fiber, they interact weakly with each other. The effect is weak in silica, but light waves that travel through long lengths of fiber can combine to generate waves at new wavelengths. The most important of these effects in fiber systems is called *four-wave mixing,* with three wavelengths interacting to generate a fourth. The interaction is easiest to explain if we identify the light waves by their frequencies, ν:

> **Light at three different wavelengths can combine to generate a fourth wavelength.**

$$\nu_{new} = \nu_1 + \nu_2 - \nu_3$$

The generated wavelength is close to the three input wavelengths. In a wavelength-division multiplexed system with channels separated by equal *frequency* increments, the new wave falls on top of an existing channel—adding crosstalk. If the frequency spacing is not equal, it produces noise between channels, which poses other problems.

Four-wave mixing becomes a serious problem for wavelength-division multiplexing through fibers operating near their zero-dispersion wavelengths. It led to development of nonzero-dispersion-shifted fiber, with zero-dispersion wavelength outside the normal operating range of erbium-doped fiber amplifiers.

Mechanical Properties

So far, I have concentrated on the optical properties of fibers. However, you also need to understand the most important mechanical properties that affect fiber optics.

In practice, bare glass fibers are coated with plastic as they are manufactured. The plastic coating eases handling and protects the outer surface of the glass from physical damage. The standard diameter of most communication fibers is 125 μm, or 0.125 mm (0.005 inch), thin enough to be difficult to handle. Plastic coating doubles this diameter to 250 μm, or 0.01 inch, making them easier to pick up and process. (Although factory automation reduces the need for people to handle individual fibers in the plant, installation often requires handling single fibers.)

Optical fibers are flexible. Standard communication fibers can be bent into a loop with a 5-cm (2-in.) diameter without damage and left that way indefinitely. Standard installation equipment is designed to accommodate that degree of bending. You usually can get away with bending such fiber somewhat more, but don't count on it. In general, thicker fibers with larger diameters cannot be bent as tightly.

In theory, a mechanically perfect optical fiber can withstand a force of 2 million pounds per square inch pulling along its length. In practice, inevitable minor surface flaws typically reduce this to about 600,000 lb/in.^{2}. Manufacturers typically proof-test fibers under a load of 100,000 lb/in.^{2}, so weaker fibers don't make it out of the plant because they break at any weaker point during the proof test. This doesn't mean you can hold an elephant in the air on a single fiber—fibers are small, and pounds per square inch measures the load applied to a solid square inch of glass, not a thin fiber. (Figure it out yourself, and you'll be surprised.) But the numbers do show that fibers can withstand reasonable handling.

Fibers withstand tension well, but they do not stretch like copper wires when pulled too hard. After stretching only a small amount, a fiber will snap. Release the fiber before you break it, and it will return to its original length.

> Bare glass fibers are coated with plastic to ease handling and protect their surfaces.

What Have You Learned?

1. Loss in fiber transmission is the sum of scattering, absorption, and light-coupling losses.

2. Material absorption depends on wavelength and is cumulative with distance.

3. Scattering also depends on wavelength and is cumulative with distance.

4. Fiber attenuation is the sum of scattering and absorption; it usually is measured in decibels per kilometer.

5. The logarithmic decibel scale is preferred for calculating attenuation and transmission losses. Total attenuation of a length of fiber is the loss in decibels per kilometer times its length in kilometers.

6. The larger the fiber core, the easier it is to align with a light source.

7. Numerical aperture measures a fiber's acceptance angle.

8. Some light is guided short distances along the cladding in cladding modes. Leaky modes are only partly confined in the fiber core.

9. The main types of dispersion are modal, material, waveguide, and polarization. Dispersion can limit transmission capacity in both analog and digital systems.

10. Material and waveguide dispersion depend on the range of wavelengths being transmitted. They can have positive or negative signs and add together to give chromatic dispersion.

11. Material dispersion is a characteristic of the fiber material; it varies strongly with wavelength.

12. Waveguide dispersion does not vary as much with wavelength; it occurs because waveguide properties depend on wavelength.

13. Material and waveguide dispersion can cancel each other to give zero chromatic dispersion at one wavelength.

14. Fibers with opposite signs of chromatic dispersion can be combined in sequence to give low total chromatic dispersion.

15. Nonlinear effects become stronger at higher powers. They are most likely in single-mode fibers.

16. Stimulated Brillouin scattering can occur at powers as low as a few milliwatts in single-mode fibers.

17. Four-wave mixing can become a problem when using wavelength-division multiplexing.

18. Bare glass fibers are coated with plastic to protect their surfaces and ease handling. Fiber strength depends on surface flaws; without them, glass fibers are quite strong.

What's Next?

Now that we've talked about fiber structures and characteristics, we will turn to the materials used to make fibers.

Quiz for Chapter 5

1. A 1-m length of fiber transmits 99.9% of the light entering it. How much light will remain after 10 km of fiber?
   a. 90%.
   b. 10%.
   c. 1%.
   d. 0.1%.
   e. 0.0045%.

2. A fiber has attenuation of 0.00435 dB/m. What is the total attenuation of a 10-km length?
   a. 0.0435 dB.
   b. 1.01 dB.
   c. 4.35 dB.
   d. 43.5 dB.
   e. Cannot tell without knowing wavelength.

3. If 10 mW of light enters the 10-km fiber in Problem 2, how much light remains at the output end?
   a. 0.00045 mW.
   b. −33.5 dBm.
   c. −3.5 dBμ.
   d. All the above are equivalent.
   e. None of the above.

4. You lose 1.0 dB coupling a 1-mW light source into an optical fiber. You need a signal of 0.1 mW at the other end. How far can you send a signal through fiber with attenuation of 0.5 dB/km?

   a. 1.8 km.
   b. 10 km.
   c. 18 km.
   d. 20 km.
   e. 40 km.

5. You transmit an instantaneous pulse through a 20-km multimode fiber with total dispersion of 10 ns/km at the signal wavelength. What will the pulse length be at the end?
   a. 200 ns.
   b. 100 ns.
   c. 50 ns.
   d. 20 ns.
   e. 10 ns.

6. You transmit a 100-ns pulse through the same fiber used in Problem 5. What will the pulse length be at the end?
   a. 300 ns.
   b. 224 ns.
   c. 200 ns.
   d. 150 ns.
   e. 100 ns.

7. You transmit an instantaneous pulse through a 20-km single-mode fiber with chromatic dispersion of 10 ps/nm-km at the signal wavelength. The spectral width of the input pulse is 2 nm. What is the pulse length at the end of the fiber?
   a. 400 ps.
   b. 250 ps.

   c. 200 ps.

   d. 100 ps.

   e. 32 ps.

8. You transmit an instantaneous pulse through a 20-km single-mode fiber with chromatic dispersion of 10 ps/nm-km at the signal wavelength. This time you've spent an extra $2000 for a super-duper laser with spectral width of only 0.002 nm. What is the pulse length at the end of the fiber?

   a. 30 ps.

   b. 20 ps.

   c. 4 ps.

   d. 1 ps.

   e. 0.4 ps.

9. A single-mode fiber has material dispersion of 20 ps/nm-km and waveguide dispersion of −15 ps/nm-km at the signal wavelength. What is the total chromatic dispersion?

   a. 35 ps/nm-km.

   b. 25 ps/nm-km.

   c. 5 ps/nm-km.

   d. 0 ps/nm-km.

   e. −35 ps/nm-km.

10. You send 200-ps pulses through a 100-km length of the fiber in Problem 9, using a laser with spectral width of 0.002 nm. What is the width of the output pulse?

   a. 1 ps.

   b. 200 ps.

   c. 250 ps.

   d. 400 ps.

   e. 500 ps.

11. Your boss says you can't have the extra $2000 for the super-duper narrow-bandwidth laser, so you have to use the cheap model with 2-nm spectral linewidth in the system in Problem 10. What's the width of the output pulse?

   a. 200 ps.

   b. 250 ps.

   c. 500 ps.

   d. 1000 ps.

   e. 1020 ps.

12. An optical fiber 125 μm in diameter can withstand a force of 600,000 lb/in.^{2}. What's the heaviest load it could support?

   a. A 4-ton elephant.

   b. A 1/2-ton cow.

   c. A 95-lb weakling.

   d. A 10-pound concrete block.

   e. A 5-oz. hamster.

Fiber Materials and Manufacture

About This Chapter

Materials are the heart of optical fibers. Without ultratransparent materials, fiber-optic communications would be impractical. This chapter describes requirements for fiber-optic materials, the types of materials used, and how they are made into fibers.

Requirements for Making Optical Fibers

The fundamental requirements for making optical fibers sound deceptively simple. You need a material that is transparent and can be drawn into thin fibers with a distinct core-cladding structure that is uniform along the length of the fibers and will survive in the desired working environment. Meeting those requirements turns out to be a challenge, particularly achieving the extreme transparency needed for communications.

Look around and you're sure to see many transparent objects but comparatively few different transparent materials. Ice is transparent, but it doesn't count; it melts at room temperature. Salt and sugar crystals are transparent, but both dissolve too easily in water to be used at normal humidity levels. Virtually all other transparent solids are glass or plastic.

●
Optical fibers are made by stretching transparent materials into thin filaments.

Making thin, uniform fibers is another problem. The usual approach is to heat a material until it softens into a very thick or viscous liquid and then stretch the thick fluid into thin filaments. You can test this for yourself with a glass rod and a flame. Hold both ends, heat the middle until it softens, and then pull the ends apart. The thick liquid holds together as you stretch it finer and finer; it cools rapidly to make a thin filament, although that simple stretching doesn't make it very uniform. You can do something similar with thick sugar syrup, spinning and pulling it to make cotton candy. Some plastics also work well, but thin liquids don't make fibers, because they tend to fall apart, like water.

Durability is vital. Common sodium chloride is very transparent, but it also soaks up moisture from the atmosphere, so optics made of salt have a distressing tendency to turn into salty puddles unless they are sealed in a dry environment. Some materials are too fragile to survive as long, thin fibers. Plastics and many other materials can't withstand extreme temperatures.

Over the years, silica-based glass and plastic have proven the best materials for optical fibers, although you need special glasses and plastics to make low-loss communication fibers. They are most transparent at a limited range of wavelengths in the visible spectrum (0.4 to 0.7 μm) and the near infrared (0.7 to about 2 μm). The clearest windows for glass fibers are at 1.3 and 1.55 μm; plastic fibers have a window at 0.65 μm and also are reasonably transparent to other visible light.

If you need to transmit wavelengths longer than about 2 μm, you need one of the few exotic compounds that can be made into reasonably transparent fibers, which are described at the end of this chapter.

Glass Fibers

What is Glass?

●
Ordinary glass is a noncrystalline compound of silica and other oxides. Many different variations have been developed.

Glass is by far the most common material used in optical fibers, but glass takes many forms, so we should define our terms carefully.

From a scientific standpoint, a glass is a noncrystalline solid—that is, a solid in which the atoms are arranged randomly, not lined up in the neat arrangements of a crystal. You can think of a glass as a sort of liquid with atoms frozen in place by very fast cooling, but it does not flow like a liquid, even over hundreds of years. Typically glasses are compounds such as oxides, but many compounds do not form glasses because they always crystallize. Even compounds such as silica (SiO_2), which readily form good glasses, will crystalize when cooled slowly. Quartz is natural crystalline silica.

The stuff we think of as glass in everyday life is made by melting sand with lime, soda, and some other materials and then cooling the melt quickly. Chemically, the main constituents of ordinary window glass are silica, calcium oxide (CaO), and sodium oxide (Na_2O). Silica accounts for the bulk of the compound. Calcium and sodium compounds improve its properties for glassmaking, notably by reducing its melting temperature. You can make many other types of glass by mixing in other materials. Lead compounds make fine crystal; a dash of cobalt turns the glass a striking deep blue. The glass industry has developed a vast array of glass recipes for different purposes, many going back generations.

These ordinary glasses look transparent in a window because you don't look through very much glass. Look into the edge of a pane of window glass and you find a strong green color; the wider the pane, the darker the green. The color comes from impurities in the glass. You don't notice their effects when light passes through a few millimeters of window glass, but they add up if you look through the side of a pane.

Since the 1800s, the optics industry has developed a large family of optical glasses, made of materials which are purer, clearer, and freer of tiny flaws than window glass. Compounds are blended to give glasses with different refractive indexes, important for designers of optical devices. Standard optical glasses have indexes between about 1.44 and 1.8 at visible wavelengths, with pure silica having nearly the lowest refractive index.

Early fiber-optic developers turned to optical glasses after finding that ordinary glasses absorbed too much light for use in optical fibers. They initially tried coating glass fibers with low-index plastic to serve as the cladding, but when results were poor, they turned to glass cladding.

Rod-in-Tube Glass Fibers

The simplest way to make a glass-clad fiber is by inserting a rod of high-index glass into a tube with lower refractive index. The two are heated so the tube melts onto the rod, forming a thicker solid rod. Then this rod (called a *preform*) is heated at one end and a thin fiber is drawn from the soft tip. The process is shown in Figure 4.3. It is used for image-transmission and illuminating fibers but not for communication fibers.

For the fiber to transmit light well, the core-cladding interface must be very clean and smooth. This requires that the rod inserted into the tube must have its surface fire-polished, *not* mechanically polished. Although mechanical polishing gives a surface that looks very smooth to the eye, tiny cracks and debris remain, and if that surface becomes the core-cladding boundary, they can scatter light, degrading transmission.

Another way to draw glass fibers is to pull them from the bottom of a pair of nested crucibles with small holes at their bottoms. Raw glass is fed into the tops of the crucibles, with core glass going into the inner one and cladding going into the outer one. The fiber is pulled continuously from the bottom, with the cladding glass covering the core glass from the inner crucible. The double-crucible process is very rare today, but it has been used in the past and may be used with some special materials.

> Refractive indexes of most optical glasses are between 1.44 and 1.8.

> Simple glass-clad fibers are made by collapsing a low-index tube onto a higher-index rod.

Limitations of Standard Glasses

Impurities limit transmission of standard glasses.

Fibers made from conventional optical glasses typically have attenuation of about 1 dB/m, or 1000 dB/km. This is adequate for noncommunication applications but not for communications.

The main cause of this high loss is absorption by impurities in the glass. Traces of metals such as iron and copper inevitably contaminate the raw materials used in glass manufacture, and those metals absorb visible light. To make extremely clear glass, you need to start with extremely pure silica, which has virtually no absorption at wavelengths from the visible to about 1.6 μm in the near infrared. The concentrations of critical impurities that absorb light at 0.6 to 1.6 μm—including iron, copper, cobalt, nickel, manganese, and chromium—must be reduced to a part per billion (1 atom in 10^9). That level is impractical with standard glass-processing techniques.

Fused Silica Fibers

Fused silica is the basis for modern communication fibers.

The starting point for modern communication fibers is fused silica, an extremely pure form of SiO_2. It is made synthetically by burning silicon tetrachloride ($SiCl_4$) in an oxyhydrogen flame, yielding chloride vapors and SiO_2, which settles out as a white, fluffy soot. The process generates extremely pure material, because $SiCl_4$ is a liquid at room temperature and boils at 58° C (136° F). Chlorides of troublesome impurities, such as iron and copper, evaporate at much higher temperatures than $SiCl_4$, so they remain behind in the liquid when $SiCl_4$ evaporates and reacts with oxygen. The result is much better purification than you can get with wet chemistry, reducing impurities to the part-per-billion level required for extremely transparent glass fibers.

Dopants, Cores, and Claddings

Silica must be doped to change the refractive index for core and/or cladding.

You cannot make optical fibers from pure silica alone. Optical fibers require a high-index cladding and a low-index core, but all pure silica has a uniform refractive index, which declines from 1.46 at 0.550 μm to 1.444 at 1.81 μm. You need to add dopants to change the refractive index of the silica, but they must be chosen carefully to avoid materials that absorb light or have other harmful effects on the fiber quality and transparency.

Cladding index may be matched to pure silica or depressed by the addition of fluorine.

Most glasses have higher refractive index than fused silica, and most potential dopants tend to increase silica's refractive index. This allows them to be used for the high-index core of the fiber, with a pure silica cladding having a lower refractive index. The most common core dopant is germanium, which is chemically similar to silicon. Germanium has very low absorption, and germania (GeO_2), like silica, forms a glass.

Only a few materials reduce the refractive index of silica. The most widely used is fluorine, which can reduce the refractive index of the cladding, allowing use of pure silica cores.

In practice, most step-index silica fibers fall into the three broad categories shown in Figure 6.1. The fiber core may be doped to raise its refractive index above that of pure silica, which is used for the entire cladding. Alternatively, a smaller level of dopant may raise the core index less, but the surrounding inner part of the cladding may be doped—generally with fluorine—to reduce its refractive index. This design is called a *depressed-clad* fiber; normally the fluorine-doped zone is surrounded by a pure silica outer cladding. (Doping at the proper levels complicates processing, so manufacturers prefer to make as much as possible of the fiber from pure silica.) Both designs are used for single-mode fiber. An alternative used for multimode step-index fiber is a pure silica core clad with a lower-index plastic.

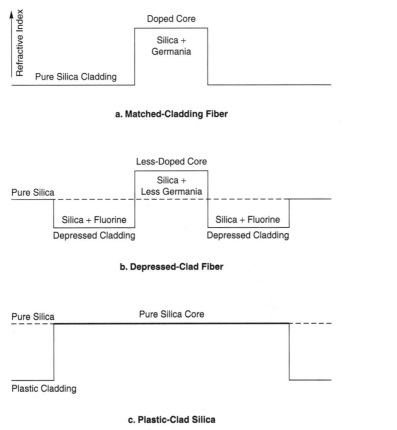

a. Matched-Cladding Fiber

b. Depressed-Clad Fiber

c. Plastic-Clad Silica
(Not Used for Single-Mode Fiber)

FIGURE 6.1

Refractive-index profiles of matched-clad and depressed-clad single-mode fibers and plastic-clad silica multimode fibers.

As you learned in Chapter 4, the refractive-index profiles of dispersion-shifted fibers are considerably more complex, to provide the extra waveguide dispersion needed to shift the zero-dispersion point to longer wavelengths. So are the profiles of graded-index multimode fibers. The same dopants are used in these more complex fibers as in simple step-index fibers.

Silica Fiber Manufacture

The trickiest stage in manufacture of fused-silica optical fibers is making the preform from which the fibers are drawn. Several processes have been developed, which share some common features but have important differences.

The crucial common feature is formation of fluffy fused-silica soot by reacting $SiCl_4$ (and $GeCl_4$, when it is used as a dopant) with oxygen to generate SiO_2 (and GeO_2 if the silica is doped). The crucial variations are in how the soot is deposited and melted into the final preform.

One approach is to deposit the soot on the inside wall of a fused-silica tube, as shown in Figure 6.2. Typically, the tube serves as the outer cladding, onto which an inner cladding layer and the core material are deposited. Variations on the approach are called inside vapor deposition, modified chemical vapor deposition, plasma chemical vapor deposition, and plasma-enhanced chemical vapor deposition. The major differences center on how the reaction zone is heated.

●
Fused-silica
preforms can be
made by
depositing glass
soot inside a tube
of fused silica,
which becomes the
cladding.

FIGURE 6.2

*Soot deposition inside
a fused silica tube.*

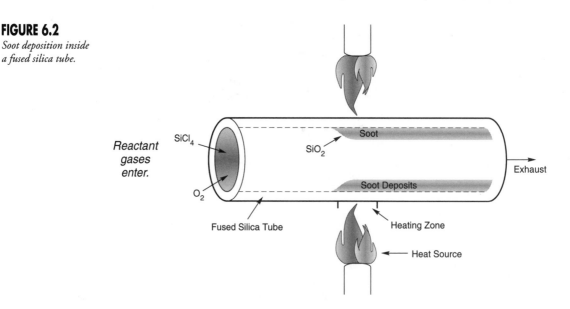

The chemicals react to deposit a fine glass soot, and the waste gas is pumped out. To spread soot along the length of the tube, the reaction zone is moved along the tube. Heating melts the soot, and it condenses into a glass.

The process can be repeated over and over to deposit many fine layers of slightly different composition, which are needed to grade the refractive index from core to cladding in graded-index fibers. The doping of input gases is changed slightly for each deposition step, producing a series of layers with small steps in the refractive index. Step-index profiles are easier to fabricate, because the whole core has the same doping. A final heating step collapses the tube into a preform.

Another important approach is the outside vapor-deposition process, which deposits soot on the outside of a rotating ceramic rod, as shown in Figure 6.3. The ceramic rod does not become part of the fiber; it is merely a substrate. The glass soot that will become the fiber core is deposited first, then the cladding layers are deposited. The ceramic core has a different thermal expansion coefficient than the glass layers deposited on top of it, so it slips out easily when the finished assembly is sintered to form a preform. Typically the central hole remains, but this disappears when a fiber is drawn from the preform.

Preforms also can be made by depositing soot on the outside or on the end of a rod.

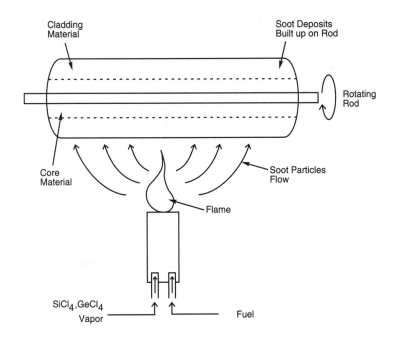

FIGURE 6.3
Outside vapor deposition to make a preform.

The third main approach is vapor axial deposition, shown in Figure 6.4. In this case, a rod of pure silica serves as a "seed" for deposition of glass soot on its end rather than on its surface. The initial soot deposited becomes the core. Then more soot is deposited radially outward to become the cladding, and new core material is grown on the end of the preform. Vapor axial deposition does not use a central ceramic rod that must be removed, so it leaves no central hole.

FIGURE 6.4

Vapor axial deposition to make a preform.

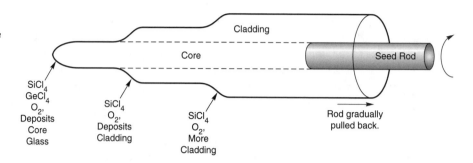

SiCl$_4$
GeCl$_4$
O$_2$,
Deposits
Core
Glass

SiCl$_4$
O$_2$,
Deposits
Cladding

SiCl$_4$
O$_2$,
More
Cladding

Rod gradually
pulled back.

All three processes yield rods called *preforms*, essentially fat versions of fibers, which are heated and drawn into thin fibers.

Drawing Towers

● **Fibers are drawn from the bottom of a hot preform.**

To make fiber, you mount the preform vertically, heat its bottom, and then pull soft hot glass from the lower end, as shown in Figure 6.5. The drawing process stretches the thick rod into a thin fiber, with the same refractive index profile as the preform. As it is exposed to air, the hot glass thread emerging from the furnace solidifies almost instantaneously. The manufacturer monitors fiber diameter, applies a protective plastic coating, and winds it onto a spool.

The equipment used is called a drawing tower. Drawing towers typically are a couple of stories tall and loom above everything else on the floor of a fiber factory. The towers accommodate large preforms, which can yield long continuous runs of fiber, as well as stages for fiber-diameter measurement, coating, and winding.

Types of Silica Fiber

● **All-silica fibers are used for communications. Hard-clad silica fibers are used for illumination and beam delivery.**

Silica is the standard material for all long-distance communication fibers and for most other fibers used in communications. Except in a few special cases described later, both core and cladding are made of silica, differentiated by different levels of doping. Typically, the cores contain dopants; the claddings may be pure silica (match clad) or doped with index-depressing materials such as fluorine (depressed-clad). This basic design is used for single-mode and graded-index multimode fibers used for communications.

Figure 6.6 shows typical attenuation curves for high-quality dispersion-shifted single-mode fiber and graded-index multimode fiber. The attenuation curve for step-index single-mode fiber is just slightly lower than for dispersion-shifted fiber.

An alternative approach is to clad a pure silica core with silica doped to have a lower refractive index or with a plastic having a lower refractive index. This is mainly done for large-core, step-index multimode fibers. Advantages include simplifying fiber manufacture and avoiding the need for dopants in a large core. (Some large-core step-index fibers are used to deliver high-power laser beams.) Claddings generally are thin compared to the core, with a protective plastic coating 50 to 100 μm thick over the cladding.

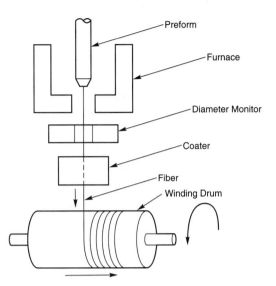

FIGURE 6.5

Drawing glass fibers from preforms. (Courtesy of Corning Inc.)

Large-core step-index silica fibers are specialty products, which come in a variety of configurations. The oldest type is *plastic-clad silica* (PCS), in which the cladding is a silicone plastic. The silicone cladding is fairly easy to strip from the silica core, which is a problem for many applications but an advantage for some uses. *Hard-clad* silica fibers have a tougher plastic cladding, which makes the fibers more durable. Silica-clad fibers can handle higher power levels, important where fibers deliver significant laser powers. The selection of cladding affects attenuation as a function of wavelength, as shown in Figure 6.7.

Large-core silica fibers may be clad with doped silica, hard plastic, or soft plastic; they are used mostly for power transmission.

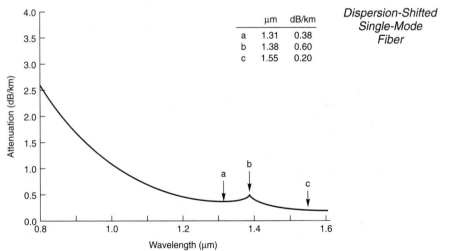

	μm	dB/km
a	1.31	0.38
b	1.38	0.60
c	1.55	0.20

Dispersion-Shifted Single-Mode Fiber

FIGURE 6.6

Attenuation of non-zero-dispersion-shifted fiber (left) and graded-index multimode fiber (next page). (Courtesy of Corning Inc.)

FIGURE 6.6

Continued

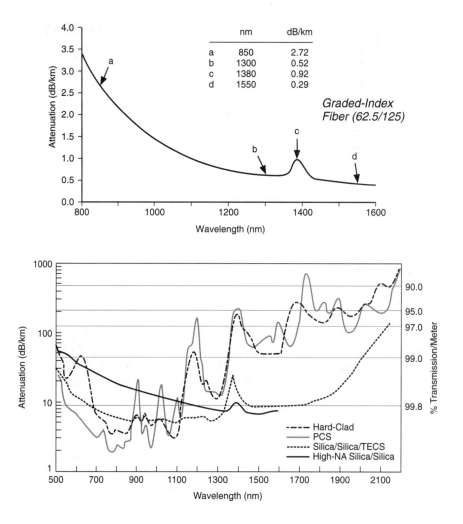

	nm	dB/km
a	850	2.72
b	1300	0.52
c	1380	0.92
d	1550	0.29

Graded-Index Fiber (62.5/125)

FIGURE 6.7

Spectral attenuation of various large-core silica fibers. (Courtesy of 3M Specialty Optical Fibers.)

Legend:
- - - Hard-Clad
— PCS
····· Silica/Silica/TECS
── High-NA Silica/Silica

Composition of the silica core is another important variable. Fibers made in a low-water environment contain little OH and are more transparent in the near infrared, but those with high OH levels are more transparent in the ultraviolet. (The fibers in Figure 6.7 are all low-OH fibers.)

Typical core diameters of large-core step-index fibers range from 100 to 1000 μm. The smaller fibers may be used for short-distance communication, but the larger fibers are used mostly for illumination. The largest-core fibers can carry considerable power, making them useful for laser-beam delivery, but they are significantly stiffer. For example, the rated continuous power capacity of one family of silica-clad fibers increases from 0.2 kW for 200-μm core fibers to 1.5 kW for 550-μm core fibers, but the rated minimum bend radius increases by a factor of 2.5. Table 6.1 summarizes important optical characteristics of selected fibers.

Table 6.1 Characteristics of large-core step-index silica fibers. Bandwidths of fibers with cores over 200 μm generally are unrated because they are very rarely used in communications.

Fiber Type	Core/Clad Diameter (μm)	Attenuation at 0.82 μm	Bandwidth at 0.82 μm	NA
Silica clad	100/120	5 dB/km	20 MHz-km	0.22
Hard clad	125/140	20 dB/km	20 MHz-km	0.48
Plastic-clad, low OH	200/380	6 dB/km	20 MHz-km	0.40
Plastic-clad, high OH	200/380	12 dB/km	20 MHz-km	0.40
Silica clad	400/500	12 dB/km	—	0.16
Hard clad	550/600	12 dB/km	—	0.22
Silica clad	1000/1250	14 dB/km	—	0.16
Plastic-clad, low OH	1000/1400	8 dB/km	—	0.40

Although most large-core silica fibers have step-index profiles, some are made with a graded-index core, surrounded by a thin silica cladding and typically a plastic coating and outer buffer layer. Their main application is in delivering high-power laser beams.

Plastic Fibers

Plastic optical fibers have long been a poor relation of glass. Light, inexpensive, flexible, and easy to handle, plastic has some important attractions. However, these advantages have long been outweighed—especially for communications—by the much higher attenuation of plastic. Years of research have reduced plastic loss considerably, but it still remains much higher than glass. The best laboratory plastic fibers have loss around 50 dB/km. At the 650-nm wavelength preferred for communications using red LEDs, commercial plastic fibers have loss as low as about 150 dB/km. Unlike glass fibers, the loss of plastic fibers is somewhat lower at shorter wavelengths and is much higher in the near-infrared, as shown in Figure 6.8.

Multimode fibers made entirely of plastic have higher loss than silica fibers.

For this reason, plastic optical fibers have found only limited applications. They are used in some flexible bundles for image transmission and illumination, where the light does not have to go far and where lower cost can be important. In communications, plastic fibers are usable only for short links, such as those within an office building or automobile.

Another important concern with plastic optical fibers is long-term degradation at high operating temperature. Typically plastic fibers cannot be used above 85° C (185° F). This may sound safely above normal room temperature, but it leaves little margin in many environments. The engine compartments of cars, for example, can get considerably hotter. Newer plastics can withstand temperatures to 125° C (257° F), but their optical properties are not as good.

FIGURE 6.8

Attenuation versus wavelength for one commercial PMMA step-index fiber. (Courtesy of Toray Industries Ltd.)

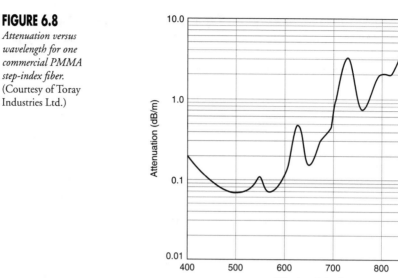

Plastic fibers are designed using the same principles as glass fibers. A low-index core surrounds a higher-index cladding. The refractive-index difference can be large, so many plastic fibers have large numerical apertures. Commercial plastic fibers are multimode types with large cores and step-index profiles, but graded-index fibers have been made in the laboratory. There is little interest in single-mode plastic fibers because the material's high loss makes long-distance transmission impossible.

Step-Index Plastic Fibers

Standard step-index plastic fibers have a core of polymethyl methacrylate (PMMA) and a cladding of a lower-index polymer, which usually contains fluorine. The differences in refractive index typically are larger than in silica or glass fibers, leading to a large numerical aperture. For example, one commercial plastic fiber designed for short-distance communication has a PMMA core with refractive index of 1.492 and a cladding with index of 1.402, giving an NA of 0.47.

Plastic fibers typically have core diameters from about 85 μm to more than 3 mm (3000 μm). You can find larger light-guiding rods of flexible plastic, which sometimes are called fibers, but it's hard to think of something as thick as a pencil as a "fiber." The smaller fibers typically are used only in bundles, but larger fibers are used individually. Typically the claddings are thin, only a small fraction of overall fiber diameter. Large-core plastic fibers cannot carry optical powers as high as those carried by large-core silica fibers, but they are more flexible and less expensive. Plastic fibers with diameters up to around a millimeter are used for some short-distance communication because they are much easier to handle than glass fibers. For example, technicians can splice and connect plastic fibers on site with minimal equipment, instead of the expensive precision equipment required for glass fibers.

Traditional plastic fibers are made of PMMA, with large step-index cores. They are used in bundles and for short data links.

Figure 6.8 plots attenuation of one PMMA fiber against wavelength, on a scale of decibels per *meter*. The minimum loss, near 500 nm, is equivalent to 70 dB/km, but for communications transmission normally is at the 650-nm wavelength of inexpensive red LEDs. The step-index profile also limits bandwidth, so signals normally are limited to traveling within a building or between adjacent structures.

Graded-Index Plastic Fibers

Recently, graded-index plastic fibers with losses below 50 dB/km have been fabricated in the laboratory. The graded-index profile promises higher transmission bandwidth but has been difficult to achieve in plastics. In the developmental fibers, the gradient is produced by diffusion of high-index materials from a fluorinated plastic in the core into a lower-index plastic in the cladding. This requires heat-treating of a preform, which then is drawn into a fiber, as with glass fibers.

Graded-index plastic fibers have been developed but are not yet readily available.

The ability to make graded-index plastic fibers is important for communications. Step-index plastic fibers are unlikely to suffice for the next generation of local area networks, as bandwidth requirements continue to escalate to gigabit speeds.

Reducing Plastic Attenuation

Glass fibers are extremely transparent because they absorb very little light at the wavelengths that have come to be used for communications. This is not true for plastics. Bonds between atoms commonly found in plastics—notably carbon-hydrogen and carbon-oxygen bonds—absorb light at visible and near-infrared wavelengths, even in plastics that look transparent in small blocks.

Developers are experimenting with novel plastics to reduce attenuation.

The only way to avoid these losses is to change the chemical composition of the plastic. Adding fluorine to the compound reduces loss somewhat. Researchers have pushed loss to as low as 50 dB/km by replacing normal hydrogen with the heavier (stable) isotope deuterium, which shifts the material's characteristic absorption wavelength. Figure 6.9 compares attenuation for plastics of various composition. It is not yet clear if this will be a cost-effective commercial process.

Liquid-Core Fibers

In the early days of fiber-optic communication, developers desperately seeking low-loss materials made fibers with liquid cores. They filled thin silica tubes with tetrachloroethylene, a dry-cleaning fluid that is extremely clear. The heavy liquid has a refractive index higher than silica, so it met the requirements for guiding light. Developers eventually reduced loss to several decibels per kilometer, very good for the time and respectable even today.

A liquid can be the core of an optical fiber as long as it is contained in a tube of material with lower refractive index.

FIGURE 6.9

Attenuation spectra of graded-index plastic fibers made with regular PMMA, a fluorinated plastic, and deuterated PMMA. (Courtesy of Takaaki Ishigure.)

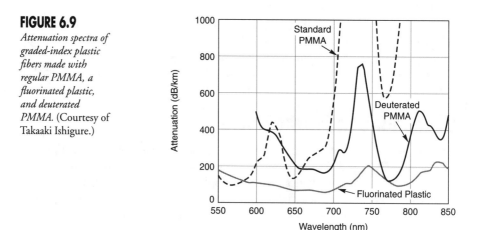

However, liquid-core fibers were far from a practical technology for communications. It took a long time to fill the tiny capillary tubes with the liquid, but the real problem was thermal expansion. The liquid expanded at a different rate than the tube that held it, so the liquid-core fiber acted as a thermometer, with liquid rising and falling with temperature. If you weren't careful, the liquid might squirt out the ends.

Now larger-diameter liquid-core light guides are finding a new life transmitting visible light short distances for illumination. Single liquid-core light guides 2 to 8 mm thick are an alternative to standard illuminating bundles. Using suitable fluids, they have lower attenuation than standard bundle fibers, particularly at green and blue wavelengths. The liquid is housed in a plastic tube rather than glass, so the liquid waveguide is flexible. Because lengths are modest—at most 20 m and typically only a few meters—thermal expansion poses little problem.

Liquid-core fibers also are used in scientific research. Although most liquids have a low refractive index, some fluorine polymers are available with indexes as low as 1.29, so they can serve as a "cladding" for water and many other liquids with refractive indexes lower than that of silica.

Infrared Transmission

Midinfrared Fibers

Fibers made of fluoride and chalcogenide glasses transmit infrared wavelengths which silica absorbs.

The extremely low scattering losses expected at wavelengths longer than 1.55 μm prompted interest in those wavelengths for long-distance communications in the 1980s. The absorption of silica rises rapidly at longer wavelengths, so developers looked to other materials that are transparent in that region. Theorists hoped that extremely low-loss glass fibers could be made from some of those materials. (Recall that glass is a disordered material, not necessarily made from silica.) If other losses could be avoided, the floor set by scattering loss suggested attenuation might be as low as 0.001 dB/km. Such incredibly low loss would allow extremely long transmission distances without amplifiers or repeaters.

Unfortunately, very low-loss infrared fibers have proven exceedingly difficult to make. Purification of the materials is difficult. The raw materials are far more expensive than those for silica fibers. (Despite occasional jokes about desert nations cornering the market on raw materials, silica fibers can't be made from raw sand, as can some glass products.) Infrared materials are harder to pull into fibers because they are much less viscous than silicate glass when molten. The fibers that can be produced are weaker mechanically than silica and suffer other environmental limitation. In short, infrared fibers have been a bust for ultra-long-distance communications.

On the other hand, fibers made from nonsilicate glasses can transmit infrared wavelengths that do not pass through silica fibers. This makes them useful in specialized applications such as infrared instrumentation, although their losses are much larger than the minimum loss of silica fibers at shorter wavelengths.

Fluorozirconate fibers transmit light between 0.4 and 5 μm. They are made primarily of zirconium fluoride (ZrF_4) and barium fluoride (BaF_2), with some other components added to form a glass compound. The lowest losses for commercial fluorozirconate fibers are about 25 dB/km at 2.6 μm, but loss as low as about 1 dB/km has been reported in the laboratory. A typical transmission curve is shown in Figure 6.10. Fluoride fibers are vulnerable to excess humidity, so they should be stored and used in low-humidity environments. In addition to guiding light, fluoride fibers are used in some optical amplifiers.

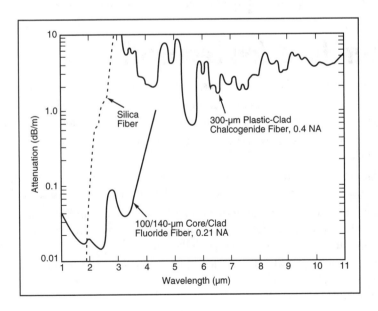

FIGURE 6.10

Attenuation of midinfrared fibers. (Reprinted from *Laser Focus World,* June 1991, p. 149, by permission of PennWell Publishing Co., Copyright 1991 PennWell Publishing Co. Also courtesy of Galileo Corp.)

Fibers made from sulfur and selenium compounds, called chalcogenide glasses, transmit over a broader range, from 3.3 to 11 μm, but their overall loss is much higher. Attenuation is more than 1 dB/m for most of their range, with a minimum of 0.7 dB/m at 5.5 μm. The compounds resist water but are attacked by strong bases.

Hollow Optical Waveguides

Hollow waveguides can transmit longer infrared wavelengths.

Although they are not true conventional optical fibers, hollow waveguides can serve a similar purpose at infrared wavelengths longer than a few micrometers. I list them here because they serve the same purpose as infrared optical fibers and compete successfully with infrared fibers in certain infrared applications. There are two basic types of hollow optical waveguides—metal and hollow glass.

Hollow metal waveguides are coated inside with a nonconductive dielectric material to make them more reflective. The infrared light bounces along the shiny walls, with very high reflectivity limiting loss to about 500 dB/km. That isn't bad considering how many reflections the light undergoes.

Hollow glass waveguides work on a different principle. At certain wavelengths, some materials have an effective refractive index less than 1. Functionally, that means they absorb those wavelengths strongly, but it also means they can serve as a low-index cladding surrounding a hollow core of air. Silica glass meets these conditions at wavelengths of 7 to 9.4 μm; synthetic sapphire (Al_2O_3) does at 10 to 17 μm. These waveguides are called *attenuating total internal reflection* guides because the fraction of the wave in the cladding is absorbed, so loss is 1000 dB/km or more. However, hollow sapphire guides can be used at the important 10.6-μm wavelength of carbon dioxide lasers.

What Have You Learned?

1. Fiber-optic materials must be transparent and drawable into thin fibers.

2. Glass is a noncrystalline solid. Most glasses are compounds of silica and other oxides. A wide variety of compositions have been developed for various uses.

3. Silica-based glasses have refractive indexes of 1.44 to 1.8, with pure silica among the lowest.

4. Simple glass-clad fibers are made by collapsing a low-index tube onto a high-index rod, called a preform, heating the tip, and drawing fiber from the soft, hot end.

5. Impurities are the main limit to transmission in standard silica glasses. Synthetic fused silica is the base for communication fibers; it is very clear because impurities are reduced to a part per billion or less.

6. Silica must be doped to form either a high-index core or a low-index cladding for an all-glass fiber. Fluorine can reduce the index of silica; germanium can increase its index.

7. Fused silica preforms are formed by depositing glass soot inside a fused silica tube, on a ceramic rod that is later removed, or on the end of a preform. This soot is melted to make the preform. Fiber is drawn from the bottom of a preform mounted in a drawing tower.

8. Large-core silica fibers are used for illumination and beam delivery. They may be clad with doped silica, hard plastic, or soft plastic.

9. All-plastic fibers have attenuation much higher than silica fibers. They are used for image transmission or short-distance communications.

10. Standard plastic fibers are made from PMMA and have step-index profiles. Graded-index plastic fibers have been made in the laboratory but are not readily available. Lower-loss plastics are in development, but there are no prospects for reaching the low losses of silica fibers.

11. Fibers made of exotic glasses transmit infrared wavelengths absorbed by silica. Fluorozirconate fibers transmit 0.4 to 5 μm. Fibers made of sulfur and selenium compounds transmit at 3.3 to 11 μm. Both types have loss much higher than silica fibers.

12. Hollow metal or glass waveguides transmit infrared wavelengths from 7 to 17 μm, but their losses are much higher than silica.

What's Next?

In Chapter 7 you will learn about special types of fibers used in optical amplifiers and as optical components that select the wavelengths to be transmitted.

Quiz for Chapter 6

1. What is the most essential property of all glass?

    a. It is a noncrystalline solid.

    b. It is a crystalline solid.

    c. It must be transparent.

    d. It must be made of pure silica.

    e. It must have a refractive index of 1.5.

2. What type of fiber is drawn from a preform made by fusing a low-index tube onto a higher-index rod?

    a. Step-index single-mode.

    b. Graded-index multimode.

    c. Dispersion-shifted.

    d. Short-distance imaging and illumination.

    e. All the above.

3. What impurity levels are required in fused silica for communications fibers?

    a. Less than 0.1%.

    b. Less than 0.001%.

    c. One part per million.

    d. Ten parts per billion.

    e. One part per billion.

4. What is done to make a depressed-clad fiber?

    a. The fiber is flattened by rollers to depress it before the cladding is applied.

    b. The refractive index in the core is depressed by adding germanium.

    c. The refractive index in the inner part of the cladding is depressed by adding fluorine.

    d. The fiber is clad with a low-index plastic.

    e. The entire fiber is made of pure silica because it has the lowest refractive of any glass.

5. How are preforms for communications fibers made?

    a. By the rod-in-tube method.

    b. By soot deposition in a fused silica tube.

    c. By soot deposition on the outside of a ceramic rod.

    d. By vapor axial deposition on the end of a rod.

    e. By methods b, c, and d.

6. What is not used as a cladding for silica fiber?

    a. Silica with refractive index depressed by adding fluorine.

    b. Silica with refractive index increased by adding germanium.

    c. Hard plastic.

    d. Soft plastic.

    e. Pure silica cladding on a core doped to have higher refractive index.

7. What type of fiber could transmit the highest laser power?

    a. Step-index silica fiber with a 550-μm core.

    b. Hard-clad silica fiber with a 100-μm core.

    c. All-plastic fiber with a 1000-μm core.

    d. Single-mode fiber.

    e. Plastic-clad silica fiber with a 200-μm core.

8. What is the lowest loss of laboratory all-plastic fibers?

    a. 1 dB/km.

    b. 50 dB/km.

    c. 150 dB/km.

    d. 500 dB/km.

    e. 1 dB/m.

9. At what wavelength does PMMA plastic fiber have lowest loss?

    a. 500 nm.

    b. 650 nm.

    c. 850 nm.

    d. 1.3 μm.

    e. 1.55 μm.

10. Why would you use fluorozirconate fibers?

    a. You couldn't find any other fibers.

    b. Because their attenuation is 0.001 dB/km.

    c. To transmit near-infrared wavelengths of 2–5 μm where silica fibers have high loss.

    d. To transmit infrared wavelengths near 10 μm.

    e. To compensate for losses in plastic fibers.

Special-Purpose Fibers

About This Chapter

Chapters 4 through 6 covered standard optical fibers whose main function is to guide light, whether for communications or imaging. This chapter covers special-purpose fibers designed for other purposes, primarily fiber amplifiers and fiber gratings. Polarizing fibers were described earlier. Fiber sensors are described in Chapter 27.

Fiber amplifiers have become important components in high-performance fiber-optic communication systems. This chapter concentrates on the fibers used to make them; their performance as optical amplifiers is covered in Chapter 12. Fiber gratings are becoming important components for wavelength selection and wavelength-sensitive applications such as dispersion compensation. I will close by briefly mentioning special-purpose illuminating fibers.

Fiber Amplifiers and Lasers

Fiber amplifiers and fiber lasers are descendants of some of the very earliest lasers. Their operation depends on two fundamental principles—the guiding of light in an optical fiber and the laser principle, light amplification by the stimulated emission of radiation. You've already learned about light guiding. Now we need to introduce stimulated emission and describe how it applies to fiber lasers. You'll learn more about other lasers in Chapter 9.

The Laser Principle

Lasers generate light by a process called *stimulated emission,* which differs from the normal "spontaneous" emission we see from everyday light emitters, such as the sun or lightbulbs.

Fiber amplifiers and fiber lasers depend on light guiding and laser physics.

Lasers depend on light amplification by the stimulated emission of radiation.

Normally, atoms or molecules absorb energy and then quickly release it by themselves, in what is called *spontaneous emission*. Spontaneous emission requires no outside intervention and generates light going in all different directions at many different wavelengths, such as a candle or lightbulb. However, in certain cases the atoms or molecules trap some energy for a tiny fraction of a second that is incredibly short in human terms but very long on an atomic time scale—much longer than they normally hold extra energy. During the time they hold onto that trapped energy, they can be stimulated to emit it under certain conditions.

Stimulated emission occurs only when the atom or molecule drops from one excited energy state to a state with less energy, releasing the excess. The best way to understand this is to think of light as tiny chunks of energy, called *photons*. When an atom drops from one energy to a lower one, it normally releases a photon with exactly the energy difference between the two states. If an atom is stuck in the upper energy level, you can stimulate it to emit light by hitting it with a photon of exactly that transition energy (or, equivalently, light of the same wavelength). Once you stimulate the emission of one photon, that photon can stimulate the emission of others, increasing the strength of the stimulated emission. All the waves are emitted in phase with each other, so they are coherent and all have the same energy.

You also need more atoms or molecules in the excited state than in the lower energy state. Normally, conditions are the other way around, with more atoms in lower energy states. However, if you zap the laser medium with the right pulse of energy, you can excite more atoms or molecules into higher energy states, producing a population inversion which is the inverse of the normal situation. This requires both the right kind of excitation, to put enough atoms into the excited state, and an excited state that doesn't decay spontaneously very fast. Physicists call these long-lived states *metastable*, but they are long-lived only on an atomic scale, where a millionth of a second is a *very* long time. Once you begin stimulating emission in a material with a population inversion, you can amplify light at the right wavelength or generate a laser beam.

Figure 7.1 shows how stimulated emission works for atoms of erbium, a rare-earth element used in most fiber amplifiers. Photons with wavelengths of 0.98 and 1.48 μm have enough energy to boost erbium atoms from their normal *ground state* to one of two excited states. The atoms then settle into a *lower excited level*, where they get stuck, unable to release their excess energy promptly. However, light at wavelengths near 1.55 μm can stimulate the excited erbium atom to release its excess energy—as a second photon at exactly the same energy—and drop back to the ground state. This second photon is stimulated emission; it can stimulate more emission from other erbium atoms. So can the first photon, which continues along with the one it stimulated. Energy is conserved because the photon that excited the erbium atom had more energy than the photon released by stimulated emission.

Stimulated emission occurs in many crystals, glassy solids, and many other materials. In most cases, only a few atoms actually take part in stimulated emission. Those atoms are

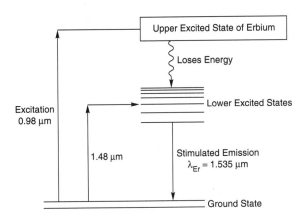

FIGURE 7.1
*Stimulated emission
from erbium atoms.*

dopants added to a material such as glass, which forms a host matrix containing the active atoms but do not take part in stimulated emission. In fiber amplifiers, a small amount of erbium (or another atom generating stimulated emission) is added to the glass that makes up the fiber.

The Fiber Amplifier Concept

Stimulated emission amplifies light. Start with a weak light signal at the right wavelength, and stimulated emission can give you a strong signal. In fiber amplifiers, an optical fiber is the amplifying medium where stimulated emission takes place, yielding a stronger optical signal.

Figure 7.2 shows the workings of a typical fiber amplifier, which uses erbium atoms to amplify a light signal. Only the core of the fiber contains erbium atoms. Light from an external laser excites the erbium atoms, typically at a wavelength of 0.98 or 1.48 μm. This laser operates continuously, so it maintains a population inversion of the erbium atoms. When a weak signal beam at the erbium emission wavelength (λ_{Er}) enters the fiber core, it stimulates emission, which amplifies its strength. In the figure, a single initial photon stimulates emission of a second photon, and each of those two stimulate emission from other erbium atoms. The result is higher power at the erbium wavelength, which the communication system sees as amplification.

The same principle works for any kind of fiber amplifier. Erbium amplifies light at a range of wavelengths from about 1.53 μm to as long as 1.6 μm, depending on the material used for the fiber. (The fluoride materials described in Chapter 6 may be used as well as glass, because they interact with the erbium atoms in different ways better for certain types of amplifier.) In theory, you can substitute other materials for erbium to amplify other wavelengths. In practice, erbium-doped fiber amplifiers are the best available, so system designers have turned increasingly to the 1.55-μm region compatible with erbium amplifiers.

Fiber amplifiers are crucial components for high-performance fiber-optic systems. Their ability to directly amplify optical signals, without having to convert them to some other

> Stimulated emission amplifies light, yielding stronger optical signals.

FIGURE 7.2
*Signal amplification
in an erbium-doped
fiber amplifier.*

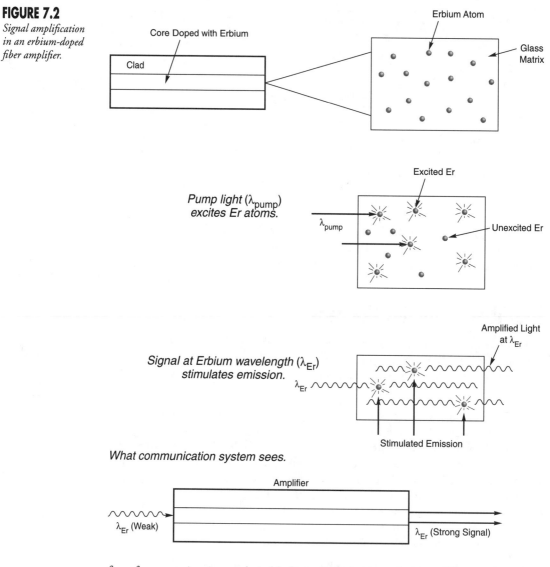

form for processing, is very desirable for communications. As you will learn in later chapters, fiber amplifiers are widely used to extend transmission distances.

Fiber Amplifier Structure

Fiber amplifier
cores are doped
with erbium.

Simple fiber amplifiers have the same core-cladding structure as standard step-index fibers, but the core is doped with erbium (or another light-amplifying species) as well as with dopants that change its refractive index.

In fiber amplifiers designed for communication systems, the fiber generally has a small core and transmits only a single mode. Both the pump light at λ_{pump} and the signal to be amplified at λ_{Er} are coupled into the core of the fiber, as shown in Figure 7.3. Amplifiers are used exclusively with single-mode communication systems, so using single-mode fiber for amplification helps couple light efficiently into and out of the rest of the communication system. In addition, concentrating both pump light and stimulated emission in a small area increases efficiency of light amplification.

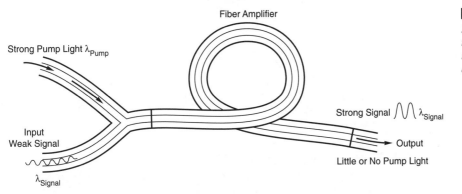

FIGURE 7.3

Both pump light and the amplified signal travel through the core of a fiber amplifier.

As the signal travels along the segment of amplifying fiber, its strength increases. Meanwhile, the pump light is absorbed, so it becomes weaker as the signal grows. In practice, as we will see in Chapter 12, fiber amplifiers include additional elements to make them work better in a communication system.

Other types of fiber structures can be used for applications where fiber amplifiers (or lasers) must generate more power than required for communications. For example, the light to be amplified can be confined in a high-index inner core, and the pump light can be inserted in a larger outer core with refractive index higher than the cladding but lower than the inner core. This guides the pump light along what is in effect a larger waveguide than the guide containing the amplified light. The pump light also passes through the core, so it can excite the light-amplifying atoms there, as shown in Figure 7.4.

Fibers as Amplifiers

Several factors enter into how a fiber amplifier performs as an optical amplifier. You'll learn more about some details in Chapter 12, but you should be aware of the general principles.

- The degree of amplification depends on the amount of pump energy, dopant levels, length of fiber, and the wavelength. (The relationships are complex, so we won't bother with the details.)

Amplification depends on pump energy, dopant level, fiber length, and wavelength.

FIGURE 7.4

Dual-core fiber for amplifiers and fiber lasers, based on a design patented by Polaroid.

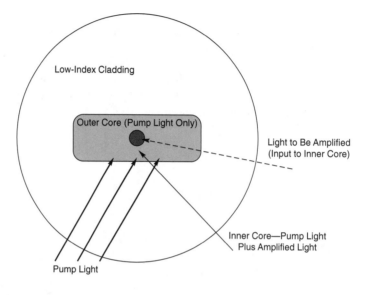

- The range of wavelengths amplified depends primarily on the dopant chosen for the amplifier and secondarily on the fiber material. Erbium works very well, and its amplification band lies in the 1.55-μm window of minimum fiber attenuation, so it is the standard type of fiber amplifier. The exact range of wavelengths amplified and the strength of the amplification depend on whether the erbium atoms are in silica or fluoride glass. Other dopants generate other wavelengths.

> **Fiber amplifiers can simultaneously amplify signals at two or more wavelengths.**

- Fiber amplifiers boost any wavelength within their range, so they can simultaneously amplify many wavelength-division-multiplexed channels in the same fiber.

- The degree of gain naturally varies with wavelength across the amplification band of any dopant. The gain spectrum also depends on the type of glass in the fiber. If signals at two or more wavelengths pass through the same amplifier, you may need special optical tricks to assure that the gain is the same at all wavelengths. Variations in gain with wavelength can cause serious problems in communication systems.

- Fiber amplifiers are analog, not digital, devices. They amplify the input, noise and all, without cleaning it up. They also have their own low-level internal noise.

Fiber Lasers

> **Adding mirrors to the ends makes a fiber amplifier into a fiber laser.**

A fiber amplifier amplifies light by the stimulated emission of radiation. All you need to make it into a laser is to put mirrors on the ends and figure out how to transfer energy into and out of the fiber. Figure 7.5 shows a simplified example, in which a length of fiber amplifier is coated at both ends. The pump light, λ_{pump}, enters at one end through a coating that transmits it but reflects the laser wavelength, λ_{laser}. A coating on the other end reflects all light at the pump wavelength, λ_{pump}, but transmits much of the laser wavelength, λ_{laser}, which becomes the laser beam. (Normally the coating reflects some light at the laser wavelength back inside the fiber to optimize the power level.)

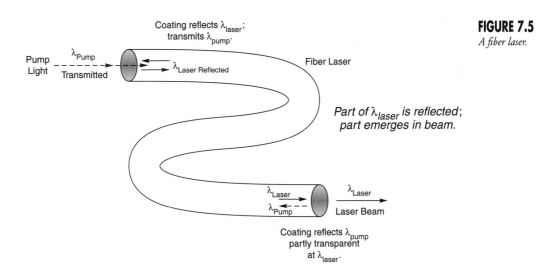

FIGURE 7.5
A fiber laser.

A fiber laser is not necessarily designed for use with fiber-optic communications systems. It is merely another type of compact laser and differs in some crucial ways from a fiber amplifier:

- A fiber laser is an *oscillator,* which generates its own signal with no external input other than the pump energy. A fiber amplifier requires an input signal to produce an output signal, although it may generate low levels of noise without an input signal.

- The operating wavelength of a fiber laser is set by its optical cavity; it may span a broad or narrow range of wavelengths. The output wavelengths of a fiber amplifier identical to those of the input signals; they can cover a broader range.

- The output of a fiber laser is either continuous or repetitively pulsed and carries no information unless it is modulated externally. The output of a fiber amplifier reproduces the input signal and carries the same information as the input.

- Fiber amplifiers are optimized for transmitting a communication signal through fiber-optic cable, so their output typically is limited in power. Fiber lasers can generate much higher powers if they are needed. Present fiber lasers can reach powers of tens of watts, with the limit coming from optical damage to the small-surface regions through which the light must pass.

Erbium-Doped Fiber Amplifiers

The best-developed fiber amplifiers are the erbium-doped fiber amplifiers (EDFAs) that operate in the 1.55-μm window. The major variants are types using silica and fluorozirconate fibers. Their availability has played an important role in the growth of 1.55-μm systems for long-distance transmission. Chapter 12 covers their operation as optical amplifiers in detail.

Other Fiber-Amplifier/Laser Materials

The principles of fiber amplifiers and fiber lasers can be applied broadly. Fiber cores can be doped with many other materials that amplify light at a variety of wavelengths. Indeed, the first glass laser that Eli Snitzer made back in 1961 actually was a fiber laser, with a thick core doped with neodymium.

Unfortunately, most materials don't make very good fiber lasers or amplifiers. The best materials are rare-earth elements in the same family as erbium, which happens to be among the best materials. Nothing as good as erbium is available at the older 1.3-μm fiber window; the best material for that wavelength is praseodymium.

It is possible to enhance fiber laser or amplifier performance by doping fibers with two elements, with one absorbing pump energy and transferring the energy to the other element to emit light. This can be done by combining erbium (to absorb pump light) and ytterbium (to emit light at a different wavelength, around 1.1 μm).

Fiber Gratings

Normal optical fibers are uniform along their lengths. If you took a slice from any one point of the fiber, it would look very much like a slice taken anywhere else along the fiber, disregarding tiny imperfections. However, it is possible to make fibers in which the refractive index varies regularly along their length. These fibers are called *fiber gratings* because they interact with light, much like optical devices called *diffraction gratings*. Their effects on light passing through them depend very strongly on the wavelength.

A diffraction grating is a row of fine parallel lines, usually on a reflective surface. Light waves bounce off the lines at an angle that depends on their wavelength, so light reflected from a diffraction grating spreads out in a spectrum. You can see the same effect if you reflect light from a CD, where the lines spiral very tightly around the reflective disk.

In a fiber grating, the "lines" are not grooves etched on the surface; instead, they are variations in the refractive index of the fiber material. The variations scatter light by what is called the *Bragg effect*. Bragg scattering isn't exactly the same as scattering from a diffraction grating, but the overall effect is similar. In the case of fiber gratings, Bragg scattering reflects certain wavelengths of light with wavelengths that resonate with the grating spacing while transmitting other light.

Fabrication of Fiber Gratings

Ultraviolet light creates fiber gratings by breaking atomic bonds in the germania-doped silica glass of the fiber. (A special glass composition is used to maximize the effect.) Typically, an external ultraviolet laser illuminates the fiber through a thin flat slab of silica with a pattern of fine parallel troughs etched on its bottom, as shown in Figure 7.6. The slab is called a *phase mask*. It diffracts most of the light in two directions, as shown, where they generate an interference pattern covering the fiber. Regions of high and low intensity alternate. In the regions of high intensity, the ultraviolet light breaks bonds in the glass, changing its refractive index and forming a grating. Because of the geometry, the grating lines in the fiber are half as far apart as the parallel lines in the phase mask. If the phase mask spacing is D, the spacing of the fiber grating is $D/2$. The laser wavelength does not affect line spacing, but it does affect the strength of the grating.

Ultraviolet light
forms gratings
by affecting bonds
in a fiber.

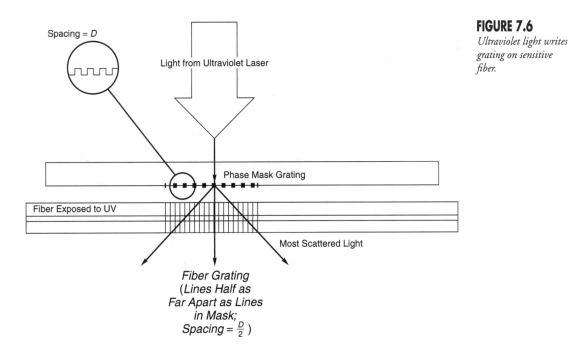

FIGURE 7.6
Ultraviolet light writes grating on sensitive fiber.

The amount of change in the refractive index depends on the extent of ultraviolet irradiation, the glass composition, and any special processing before treatment. Typically, pulsed ultraviolet lasers illuminate the fibers for a few minutes at high intensities. This can increase the refractive index of germania-doped silica fibers by a factor of 0.00001 to 0.001. Treating the fiber with hydrogen before illuminating it can increase the sensitivity, so the refractive index increases up to 1%. The higher levels of change are comparable to the difference in refractive index between core and cladding, which typically does not reach 1% in single-mode fiber.

Reflection and Transmission in Fiber Gratings

●

The wavelength reflected by a fiber grating depends on line spacing and refractive index. Other wavelengths pass through it.

What happens to light traveling through the fiber depends on its wavelength. If the wavelength in the glass happens to match the spacing of the lines written into the fiber, each line reflects a little bit of the light. The more lines, the more uniform the spacing, and the more strongly they are written, the stronger the reflection.

The wavelength selected is not equal to the line spacing, because in glass the speed of light is divided by the refractive index, making the wavelength shorter than in air. The selected wavelength λ_g is

$$\lambda_g = 2nD$$

where n is the refractive index of the glass and D is the grating spacing. If the grating spacing is 0.44 µm and the refractive index 1.5, the selected wavelength is 1.32 µm.

Wavelengths that don't match this criteria pass through the grating essentially unaffected. The result is a simple line-reflection filter, which reflects the selected wavelength and transmits other wavelengths. No optical device behaves perfectly, and in practice reflection increases strongly over a range of wavelengths, with peak reflection at the selected wavelength, as shown in Figure 7.7 for a grating with peak reflection at 1.5525 µm.

FIGURE 7.7

Reflection and transmission in a fiber grating.

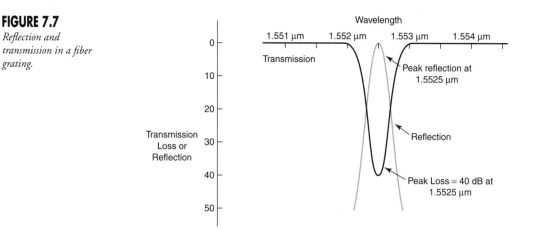

Reflection at that wavelength is 40 dB, meaning that the grating reflects all but 10^{-4} (-40 dB) of the light at the selected wavelength. Reflection affects wavelengths spanning about 0.8 nm (0.0008 μm) around the peak. Other wavelengths pass through unaffected.

The variation of the reflectivity with the wavelength depends on the nature of the grating. Fine, thin, evenly spaced lines tend to concentrate reflection at a narrow range of wavelengths. Turning up exposures to make a stronger grating tends to increase reflectivity and broaden the range of reflected wavelengths. Commercial devices using this simple standard design select a range of wavelengths as narrow as a few tenths of a nanometer and ranging up to several nanometers wide. The narrow ranges are well matched to the requirements of wavelength-division-multiplexed transmission in the 1.55-μm band.

Complex and Graded Gratings

Fiber gratings also can be made in which the regions with high refractive index are not uniformly spaced or are not perpendicular to the length of the fiber. For example, a grating can be "chirped," so the spacing changes along the length of the fiber.

The details of these designs are worthy of a (rather complicated) book of their own, and you need not worry about them. The technology for them is still evolving. What you do need to remember is that fiber gratings can be made into a range of optical devices that have different effects on different wavelengths. We'll talk about the most important examples later, but more devices are likely to emerge from the laboratory in coming years.

Wavelength Selection by Fiber Gratings

The ability of fiber gratings to select one or more wavelengths is important in systems that carry signals at multiple wavelengths or where pump and signal wavelengths must be combined or separated. Other optical devices can do the same thing, but fiber gratings select a narrow range of wavelengths and fit naturally into fiber-optic systems. To see the uses of a fiber grating, consider a system carrying signals at eight separate wavelengths, 1546 nm, 1548 nm, 1550 nm, 1552 nm, 1554 nm, 1556 nm, 1558 nm, and 1560 nm.

Fiber gratings can select one wavelength from many carried by a fiber.

You already saw how a fiber grating selectively reflects one wavelength. Suppose you want to pick out one of the eight wavelengths, 1552 nm, and deliver that signal to an individual customer. The simplest approach is to aim the signal down a short stub of fiber ending in a fiber grating that reflects 1552 nm and collect the reflected light in another fiber, as shown in Figure 7.8. This is called a narrow-pass filter, which selects *reflected* instead of transmitted light. It's essentially a reflective filter turned on its head.

The fiber gratings in the narrow-pass filter transmit light like other fiber gratings, but they essentially dump it into the fiber at the top of Figure 7.8. The light they reflect, at 1552 nm, goes out the output fiber at right.

The other wavelengths are not lost and don't have to be thrown away. The light going out the top fiber can be routed to another narrow-pass filter that picks off another wavelength,

FIGURE 7.8

A narrow-pass filter made with fiber gratings.

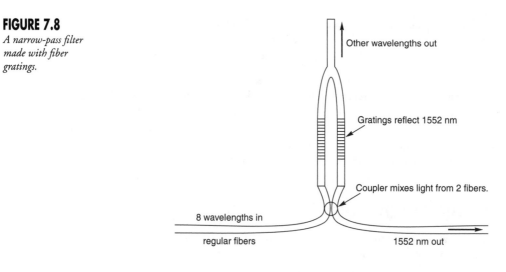

Other wavelengths out

Gratings reflect 1552 nm

Coupler mixes light from 2 fibers.

8 wavelengths in

regular fibers

1552 nm out

such as 1554 nm; then the remaining wavelengths can go to yet another narrow-pass filter. In the end, a series of seven narrow-pass filters can split out all eight wavelengths carried by the fiber. This is a function called wavelength-division demultiplexing, and as you'll see later it is essential in systems that carry signals through fibers at more than one wavelength.

●

Fiber gratings can serve as add or drop multiplexers.

Fiber grating devices can do fairly complex functions, such as shown in Figure 7.9, where a communication system carries four wavelengths, 1550, 1552, 1554, and 1556 nm. The three shorter wavelengths go from town A to C, but separate 1556-nm signals go from A to B and from B to C. You need to extract the A-B 1556-nm signal at the midpoint and replace it with the B-C signal. A pair of fiber gratings that reflect light at 1556 nm can do the job, as shown, functioning as an add-drop multiplexer. They divert that wavelength to its destination and pick up another signal at the same wavelength to send to a different destination.

FIGURE 7.9

A fiber grating module to add and drop one wavelength at point B while other signals go from A to C.

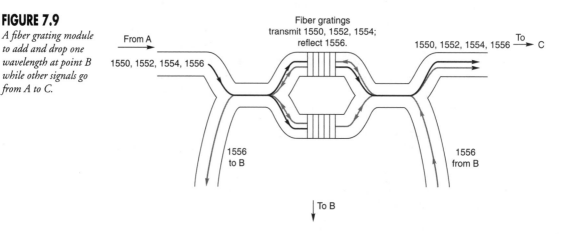

Fiber gratings transmit 1550, 1552, 1554; reflect 1556.

From A

1550, 1552, 1554, 1556

1550, 1552, 1554, 1556 →To→ C

1556 to B

1556 from B

To B

Dispersion Compensation

Another use of fiber gratings is to compensate for chromatic dispersion in an optical fiber. The gratings serve as a selective delay line, which delays the wavelengths that travel fastest through the fiber until the other wavelengths catch up. The spacing of the grating is chirped, increasing along its length, so it reflects different wavelengths at different points along the fiber.

Suppose, for example, that the longer wavelengths in a pulse arrived first and the slower wavelengths arrived last. You could stack a series of gratings along a fiber so that the longer wavelengths would travel furthest and shorter wavelengths less far, as shown in simplified form in Figure 7.10. If there were 100 ps of dispersion, the longest wavelengths would have to be reflected after spending 50 ps going through the fiber. They would need another 50 ps to return, so they would get back to the end of the grating just as the shorter wavelengths arrived and were reflected. This delay would compensate for dispersion, cleaning up the input pulse.

A series of gratings with different spacings can serve as a delay line to compensate for dispersion.

$\lambda_1 < \lambda_2 < \lambda_3 < \lambda_4$

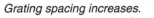
Grating spacing increases.

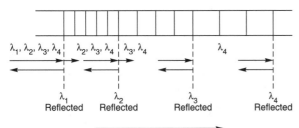

Longer wavelengths delayed more.

FIGURE 7.10

Fiber grating works as a delay line.

This picture is oversimplified, because a dispersed pulse includes a range of wavelengths, not several separate wavelengths. But the idea is the same—the distance the light travels along the grating depends on its wavelength. Design the grating right, and you have a handy little module to compensate for a certain amount of dispersion at particular wavelengths. This means you can't just plug in one standard compensation module for any amount of dispersion at any wavelength; you'd need different modules for different amounts of dispersion. However, fiber gratings are simple and compact, and they're designed so you don't need much fiber to compensate for dispersion.

Other Fiber Grating Functions

Many other types of fiber gratings have been demonstrated or are in development. They can be designed for sensing, to convert light between modes, or to alter polarization. There is intense development in the field now, so expect more advances in the coming years.

Sensing Fibers

Fibers can be designed to be particularly sensitive to certain effects, so they can function as sensors. The most important fiber sensors at this writing are fiber-optic gyroscopes, which sense rotation by comparing two beams of light passing in opposite directions through a coil of optical fiber. Special fibers for fiber gyros and other sensors are covered in Chapter 27.

Special-Purpose Illuminating Fibers

Fibers containing scattering material glow along their lengths like neon tubes.

In normal optical fibers, most light emerges from the end or is lost within the fiber. When used in displays, these kind of fibers glitter at their ends but do not emit significant light from their sides.

It is possible to make fibers that scatter light to the sides. Figure 7.11 shows the basic idea. Special light-scattering materials are added to the core of a large-core plastic fiber, so much of the light directed down the fiber scatters out the sides. The fiber, the scattering, or the illuminating light may be colored; you could even add fluorescent materials. The fibers look like glowing neon tubes.

FIGURE 7.11
Side-glowing fiber contains material in the core that scatters light out the side, so the fiber glows along its length like a neon tube.

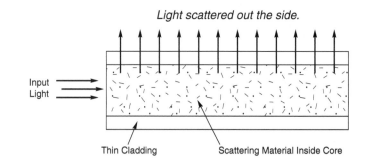

Light scattered out the side.

Input Light

Thin Cladding   Scattering Material Inside Core

These liner fiber optic lights typically are thick by fiber standards, a few millimeters to over a centimeter in diameter. It might be fairer to call them flexible rods. However, they share the core-cladding structure of conventional optical fibers.

What Have You Learned?

1. Fiber amplifiers and fiber lasers depend on both light guiding in a fiber and light amplification by the stimulated emission of radiation, better known as the laser principle. Their cores are doped with light-amplifying materials such as erbium.

2. In a fiber amplifier, a weak input light signal stimulates excited atoms to emit light at the same wavelength in phase with the input. This amplifies the light signal.

3. Erbium is widely used in fiber amplifiers because it amplifies light at a range of wavelengths near 1.55 μm. Erbium-doped fiber amplifiers are the most widely used type.

4. The degree of amplification depends on pump energy, dopant levels, length of fiber, and wavelength.

5. Fiber lasers are similar to amplifiers, but lasers have mirrors on both ends so they function as oscillators, generating their own signal instead of amplifying light from an external source.

6. Fiber gratings are periodic variations in refractive index along the length of a fiber, produced by illuminating the fiber with ultraviolet light.

7. A uniformly spaced fiber grating selectively reflects light at a narrow range of wavelengths selected by the grating spacing. It transmits other wavelengths.

8. Suitable arrangements of fiber gratings can select one wavelength from among several in an optical fiber and route different wavelengths to various destinations.

9. Fiber gratings can be designed to compensate for chromatic dispersion.

10. Fibers with scattering material included in their cores glow along their lengths like neon tubes.

What's Next?

In Chapter 8, we move on to learn about the cables that contain optical fibers for communication systems.

Quiz for Chapter 7

1. Which of the following phrases describes laser emission?

   a. Light amplification by the stimulated emission of radiation.

   b. Light amplification by the spontaneous emission of radiation.

   c. Light emission by the spontaneous amplification of radiation.

   d. Spontaneous amplification of light emission.

   e. Stimulated amplification of light emission.

2. Which of the following conditions are necessary for laser emission?

   a. Erbium atoms must be present.

   b. Light must be guided along an optical fiber.

c. A population inversion, with more atoms or molecules in excited state than ground state, must occur.

d. Ground state must be completely populated.

e. Atoms must have lost all their energy.

3. What supplies energy to power an erbium-doped fiber amplifier?

a. Light in the optical signal.

b. Electric current passing through the fiber.

c. No external energy is needed.

d. Light from an external pump laser at 0.98 or 1.48 μm.

e. Heat energy from the environment.

4. Amplification in an erbium-doped fiber amplifier depends on which of the following?

a. Length of the erbium-doped fiber.

b. Amount of erbium dopant in the fiber.

c. Wavelength of the transmitted light.

d. Pump power present.

e. All the above.

5. How does a fiber laser differ from a fiber amplifier?

a. A fiber laser has totally reflecting mirrors on both ends.

b. Only a fiber amplifier requires external energy.

c. A fiber laser is an oscillator that can generate its own light.

d. A fiber amplifier generates much more power.

e. They are the same thing, with different brand names.

6. An erbium-doped fiber amplifier can amplify which of the following signals?

a. 2.5 Gbit/s at 1.3 μm.

b. 2.5 Gbit/s at 1.551, 1.553, 1.555, and 1.557 μm.

c. 2.5 Gbit/s at 1.3 μm and 1.551 μm.

d. 1 Gbit/s at 1.3 μm and 2.5 Gbit/s at 1.551 μm.

e. All the above

7. What creates the grating effect in a fiber grating?

a. Lines etched on the fiber surface by high-power ultraviolet pulses.

b. Changes in the refractive index induced by ultraviolet light.

c. Interference between light in different modes in a multimode fiber.

d. Variations in glass composition caused by changes in doping during preform fabrication.

e. Optical white magic.

8. A grating with period of 0.5 μm is made in a glass fiber with refractive index of 1.5. What is the wavelength of light it reflects most strongly?

a. 0.5 μm.

b. 0.75 μm.

c. 1.0 μm.

d. 1.5 μm.

e. 1.6 μm.

9. Which wavelengths are transmitted by the grating in Problem 8?

a. None.

b. 0.5, 0.75, 1.0, 1.5, 1.6 μm.

c. 0.5, 0.75, 1.0, 1.6 μm.

d. 1.6 μm.

e. 0.5, 0.75, 1.0 μm.

10. Which are applications for fiber gratings?

a. Sensors.

b. Narrow-line reflectors.

c. Dispersion compensators.

d. Add-drop wavelength division multiplexers.

e. All the above.

Cabling

About This Chapter

Cabling is not glamorous, but it is a necessity for virtually all communication uses of fiber optics. A cable structure protects optical fibers from mechanical damage and environmental degradation, eases handling of the small fibers, and isolates them from mechanical stresses that could occur in installation or operation. The cable makes the critical difference in determining whether optical fibers can transmit signals under the ocean or just within the confines of an environmentally controlled office building.

This chapter discusses the major types of fiber-optic cable you are likely to encounter. You will see what cables do, where and why different types are installed, what cables look like on the inside, how cables are installed, and what happens to fibers in cables.

Cabling Basics

Fiber-optic cables resemble conventional metal cables externally, and they use some materials and jacketing technology borrowed from copper wire cables. Polyvinyl chloride (PVC) sheaths are common on both fiber-optic cables and coaxial cables used inside buildings, but fiber cables are sometimes brightly colored, whereas coax usually has a black jacket. Polyethylene (PE) is used on both metal and fiber outdoor cables to protect against the environmental rigors of underground burial or aerial installation.

Some important differences can be subtle. Because optical fibers are not conductive, they do not require electrical insulation to isolate circuits from each

Fiber-optic cables resemble metal-wire cables but differ because signals are transmitted as light, not electricity.

other. Optical cables can be made nonconductive by avoiding use of metals in their construction, which produces all-dielectric cables that are immune to ground-loop problems and resistant to lightning strikes. Fiber-optic cables tend to be smaller because one fiber has the same capacity as many wire pairs and because fibers themselves are small.

Some major differences in cable design are necessary because glass fibers react differently to tension than copper wires. Pull on a fiber and it will stretch slightly and then spring back to its original length. Pull a fiber hard enough and it will break (starting at a weak point or surface flaw) after stretching about 5%. Pull a copper wire, applying less stress than you did to break the fiber, and it will stretch by up to about 30% and not spring back to its original length. In mechanical engineering terminology, fiber is elastic (because it contracts back to its original length), and copper is inelastic (because it stays stretched out).

Fibers must be isolated from tension, which can cause breakage or long-term reliability problems.

Fibers are strong. They can withstand tensions of hundreds of thousands of pounds per square inch of cross-sectional area, or over a giganewton per square meter. (The usual units are thousands of pounds per square inch, kpsi.) Theoretically, fiber strength should reach 2000 kpsi, stronger than steel, but in practice fibers break at lower tensions, with cracks starting from small surface defects. Applying tension to a fiber can cause formation of tiny surface defects that later lead to fiber failure. Although the strength per unit area is high for fibers, you should keep in mind that a strong tug applies a large force per unit area across the small diameter of a fiber. A standard 125-μm fiber has a cross-sectional area of only 0.000019 in.^{2}, so a 10-lb force applied to the fiber alone corresponds to 500 kpsi.

The fact that fibers tend to break at surface flaws has an important consequence. The longer the fiber, the more likely it is to contain a flaw that will cause breakage at a certain tension. Fiber manufacturers have a simple test to weed out the weakest points in the fiber; they apply a weight to the fiber, which applies a certain tension (called the proof test) along its length. The fiber breaks if it contains any flaws that cannot withstand that tension. Normally all cabled fibers have been plastic-coated for environmental protection and then have undergone proof testing.

Cables are designed to isolate the fibers from tension, both during installation and afterwards (such as when they are hanging from poles). Most do so by applying tension to strength members that run the length of the cable, either at the center or in another layer. The strength members may be metallic or nonmetallic, as described later.

Reasons for Cabling

Cabling is the packaging of optical fibers for easier handling and protection. Uncabled fibers work fine in the laboratory and in certain applications such as sensors and a fiber-optic system for guiding missiles, which I will describe later. However, like wires, fibers must be cabled for most communications uses.

Ease of Handling

One reason for cabling fibers is to make them easier to handle. Physically, single glass optical fibers resemble monofilament fishing line, except the fibers are stiffer. Protective plastic coatings raise the outer diameter of communication fibers to 250–900 μm, but they are still so small that they are hard to handle. They are also transparent enough to be hard to see on many surfaces. Try to pick up one loose fiber with your fingers and you'll soon appreciate one of the virtues of cable.

Cabling also makes multiple fibers easy to handle. Most communication systems require at least two fibers, one carrying signals in each direction. Some require many fibers, and some cables contain hundreds of fibers. Cabling puts the fibers in a single easy-to-see and easy-to-handle structure.

Cables also serve as mounting points for connectors and other equipment used to interconnect fibers. If you take that function too much for granted, try butting two bare fibers together with your hands and finding some way to hold them together permanently.

Cables make fibers easier to handle.

Protection

STRESS ALONG FIBERS

Another goal of cabling is to prevent physical damage to the fiber during installation and use. The most severe stresses along cables normally come when they are pulled or laid in place. Aerial cables always experience some static stress after installation because they hang from supports. Dynamic stresses applied for short periods can be the most severe, and the most damaging to cables. The worst problems come from contractors with backhoes and other earth-moving equipment, who dig up buried cables, applying sharp forces and snapping the cables. Falling branches can break aerial cables. Cables can isolate the fibers from static stresses by applying the force to strength members. As you saw earlier, fibers are much more vulnerable to excess force than are copper wires, so strength members in fiber cables must resist stretching. However, the cable designer cannot provide absolute protection against careless contractors or heavy falling branches.

Cables prevent physical damage to fibers during installation and use.

CRUSH-RESISTANCE

Cables must also withstand force applied from the sides. Requirements for crush-resistance differ greatly. Ordinary intrabuilding cables are not made to be walked on, but a few are made for installation under carpets, and military field cables must survive being driven over, requiring that the fibers be embedded in sturdy materials. Submarine cables must be capable of withstanding high static pressures underwater—and deep-sea cables must be capable of withstanding the pressure of several kilometers of seawater. Internal structures typically protect cables against forces they must withstand continually. For example, the fibers and the internal structure of submarine cables are encased in a thick polyethylene coating.

Cables are armored to withstand unusual stresses. For example, the portions of submarine cables near shore are armored to protect them against damage from fishing trawlers and boat anchors. Buried cables must withstand a different type of crushing force applied in a small area: the teeth of gophers, who gnaw anything they can get their teeth around. The front teeth of gophers and other rodents grow continually, so they instinctively gnaw on objects they find underground. This is one case where the small size of fiber cables is undesirable, because it makes them just bite-sized for gophers. To prevent such damage, cables buried in areas where burrowing rodents live typically are sheathed in steel armor and built to larger sizes than gophers like to munch.

Cables are made stiff to keep fibers from being bent too tightly. This practice also helps prevent fibers from developing tiny microcracks, caused by surface nicks, which can lead to fiber breakage.

Figure 8.1 gives a sampling of cable cross sections and shows their applications. The light-duty office cable at top looks like electric zip cord for a lamp; the indoor-outdoor cable resembles indoor coaxial cable; and the armored cable is lighter than armored electrical cable. The deep-sea cable is about an inch thick and feels as hefty as a policeman's nightstick, but in shallow water it requires extra layers of heavy steel armor to prevent damage from shipping and fishing operations.

DEGRADATION

●
Cabling helps
protect fibers
against
degradation
caused by
moisture.

Cabling also protects fibers from more gradual degradation. Long-term exposure to moisture can degrade fiber strength and optical properties. Most cables designed for use in uncontrolled (i.e., outdoor or underground) environments include barriers to keep moisture out. Aerial cables must withstand extremes of temperature—from heating to high temperatures on a hot, sunny day in the summer to freezing in the winter. The combination of cold and moisture presents an added danger—freezing of moisture in the cable. Because water expands when it freezes, it can apply forces on the fiber that produce microbends and increase losses. Cables are designed to prevent the types of degradation important in the environments where they are used; for example, water-blocking materials are used to prevent water from entering loose-tube cables.

A significant long-term concern in some cables that transmit at 1300 or (particularly) 1550 nm is the possible influx of molecular hydrogen into the fiber. If a fiber is kept in an atmosphere with a large hydrogen content, the tiny hydrogen molecules diffuse throughout the fiber, adding significantly to losses at long wavelengths in some types of fiber. Hydrogen is rare in open air, but it can accumulate in some cable structures; for example, by diffusion from or decomposition of certain plastics or by electrolytic breakdown of moisture by electrical currents in the cable (e.g., the power delivered to repeaters in undersea cables). Hydrogen effects were not discovered until some early systems had gone into use, and they gave fiber developers a big scare. However, after the problem was recognized, engineers redesigned cables to keep hydrogen out, and fiber manufacturers largely abandoned doping glasses with phosphorus, which made fibers much more vulnerable to hydrogen. With modern designs, hydrogen loss should not be an issue.

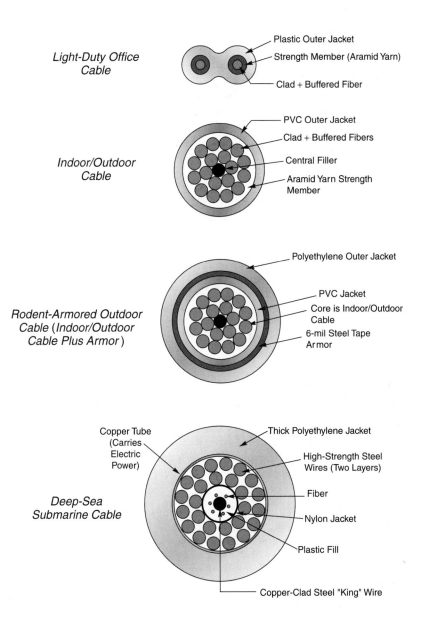

Light-Duty Office Cable

Plastic Outer Jacket
Strength Member (Aramid Yarn)
Clad + Buffered Fiber

Indoor/Outdoor Cable

PVC Outer Jacket
Clad + Buffered Fibers
Central Filler
Aramid Yarn Strength Member

Rodent-Armored Outdoor Cable (Indoor/Outdoor Cable Plus Armor)

Polyethylene Outer Jacket
PVC Jacket
Core is Indoor/Outdoor Cable
6-mil Steel Tape Armor

Deep-Sea Submarine Cable

Copper Tube (Carries Electric Power)
Thick Polyethylene Jacket
High-Strength Steel Wires (Two Layers)
Fiber
Nylon Jacket
Plastic Fill
Copper-Clad Steel "King" Wire

FIGURE 8.1

Cross sections of four grades of cable, from light-duty indoor to deep-sea submarine cable (not to scale).

More than 20 years have passed since the first fiber-optic systems were installed. Although the technology has changed greatly, manufacturers have gone back and checked some of their early systems after they have been operating for a decade or more. They have reported no signs of serious degradation in normal operating conditions since the great hydrogen scare was resolved in the mid-1980s.

Types of Cable

The same optical fiber may be used in many different environments, but this is not so for cable. Cables are designed to provide a controlled environment for the fibers they contain under particular conditions. They must meet fire and electrical safety codes, which ban indoor installation of materials that produce toxins or catch fire easily. Thus, choice of a cable design depends on the environment in which it is to be installed.

Cable manufacturers use modular designs, which they adapt and assemble into cables for particular needs. They have families of cables, which can include all the major types of fiber used for communications, including single-mode, graded-index multimode, and even step-index multimode. They often assemble cables from subunits, which can contain various numbers of fibers. They may adapt an indoor/outdoor cable for direct burial in the ground by adding metal armor and a waterproof plastic jacket to a product normally used indoors. In short, they build to fit customer requirements.

A variety of factors enter into their choices. We'll start by looking at environmental considerations.

Types of Environments

The major types of environments for optical cable can be loosely classified as follows:

- Inside devices (e.g., inside a telephone switching system or computer).
- Intraoffice or horizontal (e.g., across a room, usually to individual terminals or work groups).
- Intrabuilding or riser (e.g., up wiring risers or along elevator shafts between floors in a structure; typically between distribution nodes on each floor that serve multiple users).
- Plenum installations (i.e., through air spaces in a building; must meet special codes).
- Interbuilding or campus links (short exterior connections; link distribution nodes in separate buildings).
- Temporary light-duty cables (e.g., remote news gathering at sports events).
- Temporary heavy-duty cables (e.g., military battlefield communications).
- Aerial cables (e.g., strung from utility poles outdoors). May be supported by lashing to support wires or other cables.
- All-dielectric self-supporting cables.
- Cables installed in plastic ducts buried underground.
- Direct-burial cables (i.e., laid directly in a trench or plowed into the ground).

- Submarine cables (i.e., submerged in ocean water or sometimes fresh water).

- Instrumentation cables, which may have to meet special requirements (e.g., withstand high temperatures, corrosive vapors, or nuclear radiation).

- Composite cables, which include fibers and copper wires that carry signals (used in buildings). Note the differences from hybrid cables, as follows.

- Hybrid power-fiber cables, which carry electric power (or serve as the ground wire for an electric power system) as well as optical signals.

These categories are not exhaustive or exclusive, and some are deliberately broad and vague. Instrumentation, for example, covers cables used to log data collected while drilling to explore for oil or other minerals. Special cables are needed to withstand the high temperatures and severe physical stresses experienced within deep wells. There is some overlap among categories; composite cables, for example, may also be classed as intraoffice cables.

Cable Design Considerations

Cables are designed to meet the special requirements of particular environments. A variety of considerations go into cable design, starting with the physical environment and the services being provided. They lead to a wide variety of cable types on the market. The most important considerations are summarized next.

●
Cables used inside buildings must meet fire and electrical codes.

- Intradevice cables should be small, simple, and low in cost, because the device containing them protects the cables.

- Intraoffice and intrabuilding cables must meet the appropriate fire and electrical codes. The National Electric Code (issued by the National Fire Protection Association) covers fiber cables that contain only fibers and cables that contain both fibers and copper wires. The primary concern is fire safety, because many cable materials are flammable, and some release toxic gases when they burn. Table 8.1 lists cable types and fire-safety tests specified by Underwriters Laboratories. Outdoor cables that do not meet these requirements can run no more than 50 ft (15 m) within a building before terminating in a cable box or being spliced to an approved indoor cable. Indoor/outdoor cables are available that meet indoor requirements and can withstand outdoor conditions, although they are not as rugged as outdoor cables.

- Plenum cables are special intrabuilding cables made for use within air-handling spaces, including the spaces above suspended ceilings, as well as heating and ventilation ducts. They are made of materials that retard the spread of flame, produce little smoke, and protect electronic equipment from damage in fires, called "little smoke, no halogen" (LSNH) materials. (Halogens produce toxins.) Cables meeting the UL 910 specification can

Table 8.1 Cable specifications under U.S. National Electric Code.

Cable Type	Description	Designation	UL Test
General-purpose (horizontal)—fiber only	Nonconductive optical fiber cable	OFN	Tray/1581
General-purpose (horizontal)—hybrid (fiber/wire)	Conductive optical fiber cable	OFC	Tray/1581
Riser/backbone—fiber only	Nonconductive riser	OFNR	Riser/1666
Riser/backbone—hybrid	Conductive riser	OFCR	Riser/1666
Plenum/overhead—fiber only	Nonconductive plenum	OFNP	Plenum/910
Plenum/overhead—hybrid	Conductive plenum	OFCP	Plenum/910

be run through air spaces without special conduits. The special materials are expensive and are less flexible and less abrasion-resistant than other cable materials, but installation savings and added safety offset the extra cost.

● Fiber count depends on the number of terminals served. Individual terminals may be served by a two-fiber duplex cable that looks like the zip cord used for electric lamps. Other types are round or oval in cross section and may contain up to hundreds of fibers. Multifiber cables often terminate at patch panels or communications "closets" where they connect to cables serving individual terminals.

● Breakout or fanout cables are intrabuilding cables in which the fibers are packaged as single- or multifiber subcables. This allows users to divide the cable to serve users with individual fibers, without the need for patch panels. Figure 8.2 shows an example.

● Composite or hybrid cables include both fibers and copper wires to deliver different communication services or communication and power to the same point. For example, the fiber may connect a workstation to a local area network while the wires carry voice telephone service to the same user. Figure 8.3 shows an example.

● Temporary light-duty cables are portable and rugged enough to withstand reasonable wear and tear. They may contain only a single fiber (e.g., to carry a video feed from a camera) and should be durable enough to be laid and reused a few times.

● **Breakout cables are intrabuilding cables with fibers packaged into subcables.**

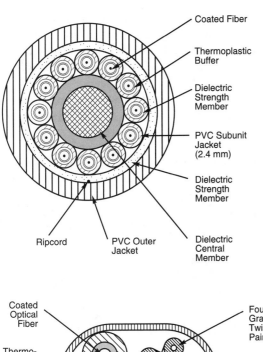

FIGURE 8.2

Breakout cable.
(Courtesy of Siecor
Corp., Hickory, NC)

Labels: Coated Fiber; Thermoplastic Buffer; Dielectric Strength Member; PVC Subunit Jacket (2.4 mm); Dielectric Strength Member; Dielectric Central Member; PVC Outer Jacket; Ripcord

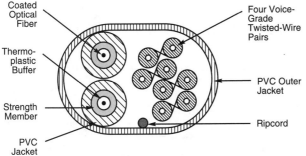

FIGURE 8.3

*Composite cable
contains both copper
wires and fibers.*
(Courtesy of Siecor
Corp., Hickory, NC)

Labels: Coated Optical Fiber; Thermoplastic Buffer; Strength Member; PVC Jacket; Four Voice-Grade Twisted-Wire Pairs; PVC Outer Jacket; Ripcord

● Temporary military cables are made rugged for military use in a field camp, where they must survive considerable abuse, such as being walked and driven across while laid in mud. They are special-purpose cables made to withstand both hostile conditions and unskilled users. Because they are used only in military equipment, they will not be covered in detail.

● Outdoor cables are designed to survive harsh outdoor conditions. Most are strung from overhead poles, buried directly in the ground, or pulled through underground tubes called ducts, but a few in protected areas are exposed to surface conditions. Most have polyethylene jackets, which keep out moisture and withstand temperature extremes and intense sunlight. However, polyethylene does not meet indoor fire codes, so such cables can run only short distances indoors, typically to equipment bays from which indoor cables fan out.

●
Outdoor cables
can withstand
harsher
environments than
intrabuilding
cables but do not
meet the same fire
and building
codes.

● Aerial cables are made to be strung from poles outdoors and typically also can be installed in underground ducts. They normally contain multiple fibers, with internal stress members of steel or synthetic yarn that protect the fibers from stress. Figure 8.4 shows two types of aerial installations, which normally use different types of cables. One suspends the cable between adjacent poles, supported by internal strength members or by a strength member packaged parallel to the fiber unit, which hangs below in what is called a "figure-8" cable. The other approach is to run a strong "messenger wire" between poles and lash the fiber cable to it by winding a supporting filament around both. Lashing supports the fiber cable at more frequent intervals and reduces the stress applied along its length, which can be large if the only supports are at the poles. Many aerial fiber cables are designed only for lashing, not to withstand the high stress of suspension between poles.

FIGURE 8.4

Aerial cable installations.

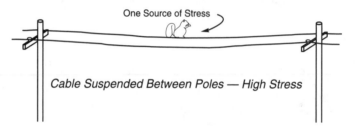

Cable Suspended Between Poles — High Stress

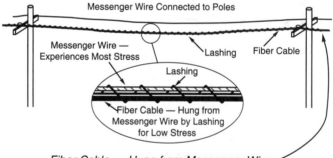

Fiber Cable — Hung from Messenger Wire by Lashing — Low Stress

● All-dielectric cables contain no metal elements, either to conduct electricity or serve as strength members. These cables use nonconductive strength members, such as aramid yarns or Kevlar. The all-dielectric construction prevents lightning surges and ground-loop problems, so they are widely used outdoors, particularly in lightning-prone areas.

● Armored cables are similar to outdoor cables but include an outer armor layer for mechanical protection and to prevent rodent damage. Steel or all-dielectric central members may be used. They can be installed in ducts or aerially, or directly buried underground (which requires extra protection against the demanding environment of dirt). Normally, the armor is surrounded inside and out with polyethylene layers that protect it from corrosion and cushion the inside from bending damage.

● Submarine cables can operate while submerged in fresh or salt water. Those intended to operate over relatively short distances—no more than a few kilometers—are essentially ruggedized and waterproof versions of direct-burial cables. Cables for long-distance submarine use are much more elaborate, as I will describe in Chapter 21. Some parts of submarine cables are buried under the floor of the river, lake, or ocean, largely to protect them from damage by fishing trawlers and boat anchors. The multilayer design shown in Figure 8.5 can withstand ocean floor pressures; the outer armor is not needed on the deep-sea bed, where no protection is necessary against fishing trawlers and other boat damage.

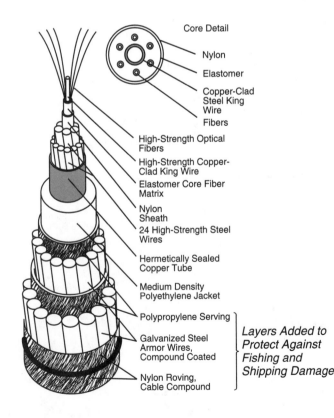

Core Detail

Nylon

Elastomer

Copper-Clad Steel King Wire

Fibers

High-Strength Optical Fibers

High-Strength Copper-Clad King Wire

Elastomer Core Fiber Matrix

Nylon Sheath

24 High-Strength Steel Wires

Hermetically Sealed Copper Tube

Medium Density Polyethylene Jacket

Polypropylene Serving

Galvanized Steel Armor Wires, Compound Coated

Nylon Roving, Cable Compound

Layers Added to Protect Against Fishing and Shipping Damage

Outside Diameter 51mm (2.010 in.)

FIGURE 8.5

Fiber-optic submarine cable. (Courtesy of AT&T and Simplex Wire & Cable Co.)

Elements of Cable Structure

As indicated previously, fiber-optic cables are diverse in nature, reflecting the diverse environments cables encounter. However, the same basic elements are used in those different cables.

> All fiber-optic cables are made up of common elements.

Fiber Housing

> Fibers can be housed in a loose tube, tightly jacketed with a plastic material, or placed in a plastic ribbon structure.

One critical concern is the structure that houses individual fibers. Two basic approaches are the loose-tube structure and the tightly jacketed structure, both shown in Figure 8.6. Each has distinct advantages and has earned its own niche—in general, the loose-tube cables outdoors and the tightly buffered design indoors. A third approach is encasing parallel fibers in a plastic ribbon, shown in Figure 8.7. All three structures are made from fibers with protective plastic coatings, applied by the manufacturer.

FIGURE 8.6

Fiber housings.

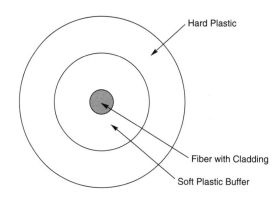

Hard Plastic

Fiber with Cladding

Soft Plastic Buffer

a. Tightly Buffered Fiber — Fiber Encased in Plastic

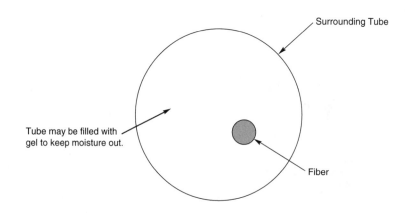

Surrounding Tube

Tube may be filled with gel to keep moisture out.

Fiber

b. Loose-Tube — Fiber Inside a Hollow Tube

LOOSE-TUBE CABLE

In the simplest loose-tube design, a single plastic-coated fiber is contained in a long tube, with inner diameter much larger than the fiber diameter. The fiber is installed in a loose helix inside the tube, so it can move freely with respect to the tube walls. This design protects the fiber from stresses applied to the cable in installation or service, including effects of changing temperature. Such stresses can cause bending losses as well as damage the fiber.

There are several variations on the loose-tube approach. Multiple fibers can run through the same tube. The tube does not have to be a physically distinct cylinder running the length of the cable. It can be formed by running grooves along the length of a solid cylindrical structure encased in a larger tube, or by pressing corrugated structures together and running fibers through the interstices. The end result is the same: the fiber is isolated from stresses applied to the surrounding cable structure.

Loose tubes can be used without any filling. However, if they are to be used outdoors, they are normally filled with a jellylike material. The gel acts as a buffer, keeping out moisture and letting the fibers move in the tube.

Loose-tube cables are used outdoors because they effectively isolate the fibers from external stresses such as changes in temperature, preventing damage and resulting in lower fiber loss. They can be installed from poles, in ducts, or by direct burial. A single tube can contain up to a dozen fibers, making it possible to achieve high fiber densities in a compact cable. The cables can be made of flame-retardant materials to meet codes for indoor use, especially where high fiber counts are needed.

> Loose-tube cables are filled with a gel for use outdoors.

TIGHTLY BUFFERED FIBER

A tightly buffered fiber is encased (after coating) in a plastic layer. The coating is a soft plastic that allows deformation and reduces forces applied to the fiber. The surrounding buffer is a harder plastic, to provide physical protection. Tightly buffered fibers may be stranded in conventional cables.

Tight buffering tolerances assure that the fibers are in precisely predictable positions, making it easier to install connectors. The tight-buffer structure creates subunits that can be divided among many terminals, without using patch panels. Tight-buffer cables are smaller for small fiber counts than loose-tube cables, but the ability to pack many fibers into a single loose tube makes that advantage disappear as the fiber count increases. Above about 36 fibers, loose-tube cables are smaller.

A major advantage of tight-buffered cable for indoor use is its compatibility with materials that meet fire and electrical codes. (Loose-tube cables may require enclosure in metal tubing.) Although losses may be somewhat higher than in loose-tube cables, indoor transmission distances are short enough that it's not a problem.

> Tightly buffered fibers are typically used indoors.

RIBBON CABLE

Many parallel fibers can be encased in plastic to form a ribbon, around which cables can be built.

The ribbon cable shown in Figure 8.7 is in some ways a variation on the tight-buffered cable. A group of coated fibers is arranged in parallel, then coated with plastic to form a multifiber ribbon. This differs from tightly buffered cables in that one plastic layer encases many parallel fibers. The flat ribbon looks something like flat 4-wire cables used for household telephones. Typical ribbons contain 5 to 12 fibers. Up to 12 ribbons can be stacked together to form the core of a cable.

The simple structure makes a ribbon cable easy to splice in the field; a single splice can connect multiple fibers. Multifiber connectors can also be installed readily. Ribbon cables offer very dense packing of fibers, important for some applications. However, installation can cause uneven strain on different fibers in the ribbon, leading to unequal losses and potential problems with some fibers. Like loose-tube and tight-buffered cables, ribbon cables have their advocates but are not the solution to every fiber-optic cabling problem.

FIGURE 8.7

Core of a ribbon cable.

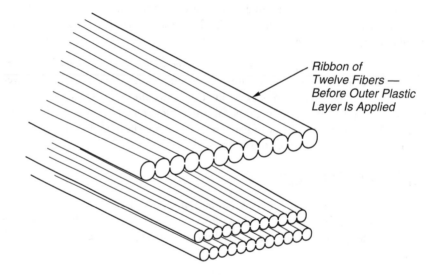

Ribbon of
Twelve Fibers —
Before Outer Plastic
Layer Is Applied

Fiber Arrangements in Cable

Fibers can be arranged in a cable in many different ways. The simplest cables are round with a single fiber at their center. Duplex (two-fiber) cables may either be circular or oval in cross section or be made like electrical zip cord, with two single-fiber structures bonded together along their length, as in Figure 8.1.

The more fibers in the cable, the more complex the structure. One common cable structure has six buffered fibers wound loosely around a central member. The buffered fibers are wound so that they don't experience torsion in the cable. In loose-tube cables, the fiber count can be raised by putting multiple fibers in each tube. Groups of 8 or 12 fibers may also be wound around a central member.

Cables with more fibers are built up of modular structures. For example, a 36-fiber cable can be made from six loose-tube modules containing six fibers each, or from three 12-fiber ribbons. A dozen 12-fiber ribbons make a 144-fiber cable. Putting 12 fibers in each loose tube and adding a second ring of 12 loose tubes gives a 216-fiber cable, as shown in Figure 8.8. Design details depend on the manufacturer.

> 216-fiber cables are in use, and cables with many more fibers are in development.

High fiber counts were rare in early installations, but they are becoming popular as fibers are used to distribute signals to many subscribers in metropolitan areas and large buildings or campuses. Cables with several hundred fibers are in use, and developers are working on cables containing thousands of fibers.

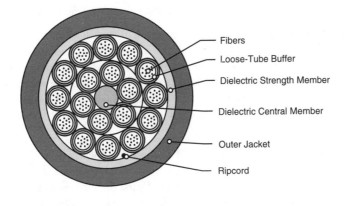

- Fibers
- Loose-Tube Buffer
- Dielectric Strength Member
- Dielectric Central Member
- Outer Jacket
- Ripcord

FIGURE 8.8
Modular cable containing 216 fibers, with 12 in each of 18 loose tubes. (Courtesy of Siecor Corp., Hickory, NC)

Cabling Materials

The choice of materials plays a crucial role in determining characteristics of a cable. Designers usually face trade-offs among several factors. Fire safety is crucial for indoor cables, particularly those that run through air spaces, because some compounds used in outdoor cables produce toxins or catch fire easily. Moisture resistance and temperature tolerance is critical in most outdoor environments. Aerial cables must survive severe temperature extremes, sunlight, and wind loading; cable pulled through ducts must withstand surface abrasion as well as tension along its length. The major materials used in cabling are as follows:

> Materials play an important role in cable properties.

- Polyethylene: Standard for outdoor cables because it resists moisture, it is stable over a wide temperature range, and resists abrasion. It does not meet indoor fire-safety rules.

- Polyvinyl chloride (PVC): The most common material for indoor cables, it is available in different grades for various requirements. It is flexible, fire-retardant, and can be extruded easily during cabling, but it is not as durable or moisture-resistant as polyethylene.

- Polyvinyl difluoride (PVDF): A plastic used for plenum cables, it retards fire better than polyethylene and produces less smoke. It is less flexible and harder to extrude.

- Low smoke–no halogen (LSNH) plastics: Produce little smoke and no toxic halogen compounds, they are safest for use in enclosed spaces. They also protect electronic equipment from corrosion damage during fires but are costly and less durable than PVC.

- Aramid yarn: Dielectric strength members, they are known by the trade name Kevlar.

Other Structural Elements

Fibers and their buffers are not the only structural elements of cables. Many—but not all—fiber-optic cables include other components to provide strength and rigidity.

Many cables contain central members to make them rigid and strength members to withstand tensile forces.

Many cables are built around central members made of steel, fiberglass, or other materials. These run along the center of the cable and provide the rigidity needed to keep it from buckling, as well as a core to build the cable structure around. A central member may be overcoated with plastic or other material to match cable size requirements and to prevent friction with other parts of the cable. Small indoor cables containing few fibers generally lack central members, but they are common in outdoor cables, and in indoor cables with high fiber counts.

Strength members in general are distinct from central members. Their role is to provide tensile strength along the length of the cable during and after installation. The usual strength members are strands of dielectric aramid yarn (better known under the trademark Kevlar) wound around the core of the cable. In some cases, tight-buffered fibers may be wound around them to form subunits of the cable. When a cable is pulled into a duct, the tension is applied directly to the strength member.

The structure containing the fibers normally surrounds the central member and, in turn, is surrounded by the strength member and one or more outer jacketing layers of plastic. The composition depends on the application.

Buried and underwater cables require armor.

Underwater and buried cables are among the types that require one or more layers of protecting armor. Typically for buried cables, steel is wound around an inner plastic sheath. An outer plastic sheath is then applied over the armor to prevent corrosion. The metal armor helps protect against crushing damage, rocks, and rodents. Underwater cables in shallow waters may have multiple layers to protect against damage from shipping and fishing operations, as shown in Figure 8.5.

Blown-in Fibers

Traditionally, cables are installed as finished units, containing both fibers and protective structures. An alternate approach is to install hollow microducts—typically about 5 mm in diameter—then to blow fibers through them. Forcing air through the microduct carries the fiber along with it.

The process uses conventional single- or multimode fibers coated with a blowable coating, designed to be dragged along by air forced through the microducts. The air can carry the coated fibers around bends, and over distances of more than 1000 feet (300 meters), usually within a building or between adjacent buildings.

The use of blown fibers is a two-stage process. The flexible microducts which carry the fibers must be installed first, then the fiber is blown through them. The major attraction is that the fibers need not be blown in at once, and that fibers can be replaced easily, like cables in underground ducts. Thus you could install the microducts when renovating a building, and blow in the fibers later, when you knew transmission requirements. If a fiber was damaged, you could pull it out and blow in a replacement. With the proper equipment, fibers can be blown into place very quickly.

From a functional standpoint, blow-in fibers behave like loose-tube cables without a filler in the tubes. Materials used in the plastic tubes are chosen to meet the appropriate fire and electrical codes. While blown fibers are not widely used, the technology is available.

> Fibers can be blown through microducts instead of installing normal cables.

Cable Installation

Cable installation is not as simple as it sounds, but reliable methods developed for conventional metal cables have been successfully adapted for optical cables. The methods chosen depend on the type of installation.

> Special techniques are used to install different types of cable.

- Submarine cables are laid from special ships built for that purpose.
- Buried cables are normally installed by digging a deep, narrow trench with a cable plow, laying the cable in the trench, and filling the trench with dirt, or by plowing the cable directly into the ground.
- Cables are installed in ducts by threading a pull line through the duct, attaching it to the cable, then pulling the cable through the ductwork. Manholes or other access points are normally available along the duct route, so the cable need not be pulled all at once through a long route.
- Self-supporting aerial cables may be suspended directly from overhead poles. Other aerial cables can be suspended from messenger wires, strong steel wires strung between poles. If a messenger wire is used, the cable is lashed to it with a special lashing wire running around both the cable and the messenger wire, or sometimes wound around it. This is a common installation for many overhead fiber cables because it minimizes strength requirements.
- Plenum cables are strung through interior air spaces.

- Interior cables may be installed within walls, through cable risers, or elsewhere in buildings. Installation is easiest in new construction. Only special cables designed for installation under carpets should be laid on the floor where people walk.

- Temporary light-duty cables are laid by people carrying mobile equipment that requires a broadband (typically video) connection to a fixed installation.

- Temporary military cables may be laid by helicopters from the air or by soldiers on the ground, during field exercises, in preparation for engagements, or in actual battle. Typically they are unreeled from cable spools.

Changes in Cabled Fiber

Microbending can cause fiber loss to change after cabling.

Ideally, characteristics of optical fibers should not change when they are cabled, but in practice some changes do occur, particularly in attenuation. A major cause of these changes is microbending, which depends on the fiber's local environment and the stresses applied to it. Tight buffering affects single-mode fiber more than multimode fiber, but in properly made cables the increase in loss is small.

Cabled fibers rarely suffer physical damage unless the entire cable is damaged. Fiber manufacturers apply a stress test to fibers before they leave the factory. The test is a simple one in which a series of pulleys and wheels apply a given stress to the fiber. If the fiber fails the test, it breaks and, thus, cannot be used. These proof tests assure levels of fiber strength that meet normal cable requirements.

Causes of Cable Failure

Most cable failures are a result of physical abuse.

Telephone companies were very cautious before beginning their massive switchover to fiber-optic cables and conducted extensive tests and field trials to evaluate the reliability of optical cables. These studies have shown that optical fibers have excellent reliability. Proof testing of fibers before they are cabled assures that mechanical strength is high, and proper splicing produces splices about as strong as unspliced fiber. Poor installation can damage fibers, but failures of properly installed fiber-optic cables are extremely rare.

Virtually all fiber-optic cable failures are due to physical abuse. The archetypical problem is a backhoe digging up and breaking a buried cable. Aerial cables are broken by falling branches or errant cranes. High-capacity cables have been cut mistakenly. Fibers in light-duty indoor cables could be broken by slamming doors or windows on the cable, although the cable might not show serious damage. Applying a sharp stress along a short indoor cable (e.g., tripping over it) is not likely to break the cable. However, it could jerk the cable out of a connector at one end. In general, connector junctions are the physical weak points of short-distance cables.

If the cable itself breaks, the fibers in it will also break. Because fibers tend to break at weak points, they may not break at precisely the point of the cable break but should break close to it. However, fibers can remain intact despite evident physical damage that does not completely sever the cable.

What Have You Learned?

1. Fibers can break at inherent flaws and develop microcracks under tension, so they must be protected from stretching forces.

2. Cabling packages fibers for protection and easier handling.

3. Cables must resist crushing as well as isolate the fiber from tension along its length.

4. Cables protect fibers from heat, cold, and moisture. The designs chosen vary widely, depending on environmental conditions.

5. Indoor cables must meet fire and electrical safety codes. The major impact of these codes is on composition of the plastics used in the cable structure.

6. Cables can carry from one to hundreds of fibers.

7. Important structural elements in a cable are the housing for the fiber, strength members, jacketing, and armor. Armor is used only in certain environments where physical damage is a threat.

8. Outdoor cables may be hung from poles, pulled through ducts, or buried directly in the ground.

9. Fibers can be enclosed in a loose tube, a tight plastic buffer, or a ribbon.

10. The physical arrangement of fibers in the cable depends on the number of fibers and how they are to be distributed in the installation.

11. Most cable damage occurs when a sudden force is applied, such as when a backhoe digs up a buried cable.

What's Next?

In Chapter 9, we will examine the light sources used with fiber-optic cables.

Quiz for Chapter 8

1. What happens if an optical fiber is pulled along its length?

   a. It stretches out and does not return to its original length.

   b. It can stretch by about 5% before breaking.

   c. Its length is unchanged until it breaks.

   d. It breaks if any force is applied to it.

2. Cables cannot protect fibers effectively against

   a. gnawing rodents.

   b. stresses during cable installation.

   c. careless excavation.

   d. static stresses.

   e. crushing.

3. Light-duty cables are intended for use

   a. within office buildings.

   b. in underground ducts.

   c. deep underground where safe from contractors.

   d. on aerial poles where temperatures are not extreme.

4. The special advantages of plenum cables are what?

   a. They are small enough to fit in air ducts.

   b. They meet stringent fire codes for running through air spaces.

   c. They are crush-resistant and can run under carpets.

   d. They have special armor to keep rodents from damaging them.

5. Outdoor cables are not used in which of the following situations?

   a. Suspended overhead between telephone poles.

   b. Tied to a separate messenger wire suspended between overhead poles.

   c. Inside air space in office buildings.

   d. Pulled through underground ducts.

6. A loose-tube cable is

   a. a cable in which fibers are housed in hollow tubes in the cable structure.

   b. a cable for installation in hollow tubes (ducts) underground.

   c. cable for installation in indoor air ducts.

   d. none of the above.

7. Which of the following are usually present in direct-burial cables but not in aerial cables?

   a. Strength members.

   b. Outer jacket.

   c. Armor.

   d. Fiber housing.

8. Which type of cable installation requires pulling the cable into place?

a. Direct burial.

b. Underground duct.

c. Military field systems.

d. Submarine cable.

9. The main cause of differences in properties of a fiber before and after cabling is

a. microbending.

b. temperature within the cable.

c. application of forces to the fiber.

d. damage during cabling.

10. The major reason for failure of cabled fiber is

a. hydrogen-induced increases in attenuation.

b. corrosion of the fiber by moisture trapped within the cable.

c. severe microbending losses.

d. physical damage to the cable.

Light Sources

About This Chapter

Many types of light sources are used in fiber-optic systems, from cheap LEDs directly driven by signal sources to sophisticated narrow-line lasers with external modulators. Some operate at telephone-like speeds and bandwidths over several meters; others send thousands of megabits per second through tens of kilometers of fiber. All these light sources generate the signals transmitted through the fibers.

Light sources are actually parts of transmitters, but to approach the subject systematically I am dividing the two. This chapter covers the various light sources used in fiber-optic transmitters, which are covered in more detail in Chapter 10. In Chapter 11, you will look at receivers, which convert the optical signals back into electronic form at the other end of the fiber.

Light Source Considerations

Several important factors enter into selecting a light source for a fiber-optic system. The light must be at a wavelength transmitted effectively by the optical fiber, usually the 780-850, 1300, or 1550 nm windows for glass fibers or the 650 nm window for plastic fibers. The range of wavelengths is also important, because the larger the range, the larger the potential chromatic dispersion. The light source must also generate adequate power to send the signal through the fiber, but not so much power that it causes nonlinear effects or distortion in the fiber or receiver. The output light must be modulated so that it carries the signal. The light source must also transfer its output effectively into the fiber.

The main light sources used with fiber-optic systems are semiconductor devices—light-emitting diodes (LEDs) and semiconductor lasers (often called

Light source
wavelength,
modulation,
spectral width,
size, and power
are all important
for fiber-optic
systems.

Source wavelength
affects signal
attenuation and
pulse dispersion.

diode lasers). As semiconductor devices, they fit well with standard electronic circuitry used in communication systems. Fiber lasers and other compact solid-state lasers are used in some systems. I'll look more closely at the light sources after a quick overview of key operational characteristics important for fiber-optic communications.

Operating Wavelength

Source wavelength affects both the attenuation and pulse dispersion that signals experience in fibers. As you saw earlier, both attenuation and pulse dispersion are functions of wavelength. The usual transmission windows are 780–850, 1300, and 1550 nm in silica fibers and around 650 nm in plastic fibers, although other wavelengths can be used.

Chromatic dispersion increases with the spectral width, or range of wavelengths, in an optical signal. Spectral width is a major difference between LEDs and lasers, as shown in Figure 9.1. Standard LEDs have spectral widths of 30 to 50 nm, compared to 1 to 3 nm for modest-priced diode lasers. High-performance fiber systems operating at gigabit speeds require narrow-line or *single-frequency* lasers with spectral widths a small fraction of a nanometer. (Their spectral widths often are measured in frequency units rather than wavelength. Because a 1300-nm wavelength corresponds to a frequency of 230,000 GHz, 1 nm at that wavelength is about 178 GHz. Thus, a 1300-nm laser with 1-GHz bandwidth has a spectral width of 0.0056 nm.)

FIGURE 9.1

Comparison of LED and laser spectral widths.

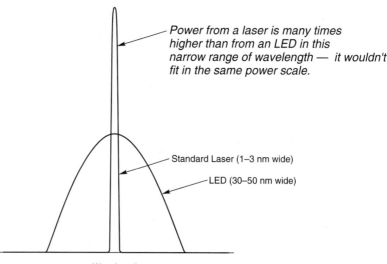

Power from a laser is many times higher than from an LED in this narrow range of wavelength — it wouldn't fit in the same power scale.

Standard Laser (1–3 nm wide)

LED (30–50 nm wide)

Wavelength

The emitted wavelength and the spectral width depend on different factors. The emitted wavelength depends on the semiconductor material from which the light source is made, as described later. The spectral width depends on device structure. A laser and LED made of the same material have the same center wavelength, but the LED has a much broader spectral width. Two lasers with the same structure made of different materials have comparable spectral widths but different center wavelengths.

Output Power and Light Coupling

Power from communication light sources can range from more than 100 mW for certain lasers to tens of microwatts for LEDs. Not all that power is useful. For fiber-optic systems, the relevant value is the power delivered into an optical fiber. That power depends on the angle over which light is emitted, the size of the light-emitting area, the alignment of the source and fiber, and the light-collection characteristics of the fiber, as shown in Figure 9.2. The light intensity is not uniform over the entire angle at which light is emitted but rather falls off with distance from the center. Typical semiconductor lasers emit light that spreads at an angle of 10–20°; the light from LEDs spreads out at larger angles.

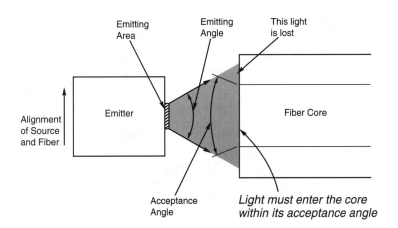

FIGURE 9.2

Light transfer from an emitter into a fiber.

Losses of many decibels can easily occur in coupling light from an emitter into a fiber, especially for LEDs with broad emitting areas and wide emitting angles. This makes it important to be sure you know what power is specified.

Modulation

One important advantage of semiconductor lasers and LEDs is that their output power varies directly with the input current. This is called *direct modulation*. Other lasers generate steady beams or fire a series of evenly timed pulses. To carry signals, these beams must pass through external modulators, which modulate the beam by changing their transparency in response to an applied signal.

Diode lasers and LEDs are modulated directly.

Several variables are important in modulation. One is speed; lasers are faster than LEDs. Another is how modulation affects the light signal; as you will see later, direct modulation can increase the spectral width of diode lasers. The linearity of the modulation is also important, especially for analog communications. Depth of modulation and modulation format are also important. Although I will cover some of these topics later in this chapter, many details of modulation belong in the realm of transmitters in Chapter 10.

Cost/Performance Trade-offs

As any student of engineering reality would expect, light sources with the most desirable characteristics cost the most. The cheapest light sources are LEDs with slow rise times, large emitting areas, and relatively low output power. Diode lasers with narrow bandwidths that emit the 1300- and 1550-nm wavelengths where optical fibers have their lowest losses are the most expensive. The higher-power and narrower-line emission of lasers comes at a marked price premium, with the narrowest-line lasers costing the most. The only real performance advantage of LEDs is generally longer lifetime than some lasers.

LED Sources

An LED emits light when a current flows through it.

LEDs that emit red or near-infrared light are common light sources for short-fiber systems. The basic concept of a light-emitting diode is shown in Figure 9.3. A small voltage applied across a semiconductor diode causes a current to flow across the junction. The diode is made up of two regions, each doped with impurities to give it the desired electrical characteristics. The p region is doped with impurities having fewer electrons than atoms they replace in the semiconductor compound, which create "holes" where there is room for electrons in the crystalline lattice. The n region is doped with impurities that donate electrons, so extra electrons are left floating in the crystalline matrix. Applying a positive voltage to the p region and a negative voltage to the n region causes the electrons and holes to flow toward the junction of the two regions, where the electrons drop into the holes in a process called recombination. As long as the voltage is applied, electrons keep flowing through the diode and recombination continues at the junction.

In many semiconductors, notably silicon and germanium, the released energy is dissipated as heat—vibrations of the crystalline lattice. (The recent discovery of light emission from porous silicon appears to be a special case that depends on the microstructure of the silicon crystal.) However, in other materials, usable in LEDs, the recombination energy is released as a photon of light, which can emerge from the semiconductor material. The most important of these semiconductors, gallium arsenide and related materials, are made up of elements from the IIIa and Va columns of the periodic table:

IIIa	Va
Aluminum (Al)	Nitrogen (N)
Gallium (Ga)	Phosphorus (P)
Indium (In)	Arsenic (As)
	Antimony (Sb)

FIGURE 9.3
LED operation.

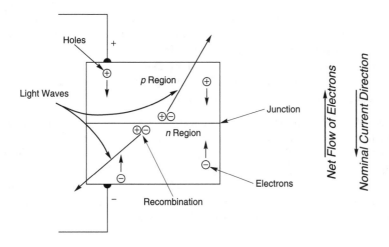

a. **Basic Idea of LED**

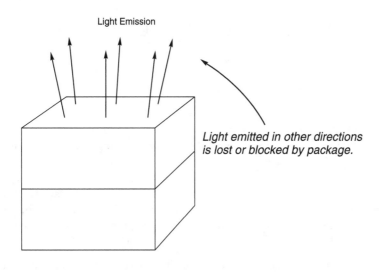

b. **LED as Packaged (Surface-Emitting)**

A new technology is developing around semiconducting polymers. These are plastics that have the electrical characteristics of semiconductors. (Conventional plastics are insulators, because they bond electrons tightly.) As with their crystalline counterparts, semiconducting plastics can be doped to make *p* and *n* materials, and electrical devices, including LEDs, can be made from them.

The wavelength emitted by a semiconductor depends on its internal energy levels. In a pure semiconductor at low temperature, all the electrons are bonded within the crystalline lattice. As temperature rises, some electrons in this valence band jump to a higher-energy conduction level, where they are free to move about in the crystal. The valence and conductor bands are separated by a void where no energy levels exist—the band gap that gives semiconductors many of their special properties.

Conduction-band electrons leave behind a hole in the valence band, which is considered to have a positive charge. This hole can move about, as electrons from other spots in the crystalline lattice move to fill in the hole and leave behind their own hole (i.e., the hole moves from where the electron came to where the electron was). Impurity doping of semiconductors can also generate free electrons and holes. When an electron drops from the conduction level to the valence level (i.e., when it recombines with a hole), it releases the difference in energy between the two levels, as shown in Figure 9.4.

FIGURE 9.4

Semiconductor energy levels.

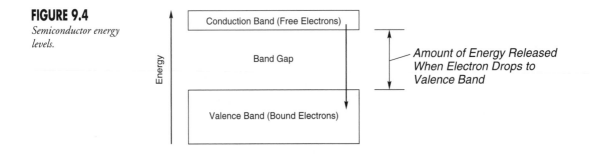

The band-gap difference between the energy levels—and hence the amount of energy released and the emitted wavelength—depends on the composition of the semiconductor. The usual near-infrared LEDs used in fiber-optic systems are made of gallium aluminum arsenide or gallium arsenide. Gallium arsenide LEDs emit near 930 nm. Adding aluminum decreases the threshold current to improve lifetime and can also increase the energy gap and shift emission to shorter wavelengths of 750 to 900 nm. The usual LED wavelengths for fiber-optic applications are 820 or 850 nm. At room temperature, the typical 3-dB bandwidth of an 820-nm LED is about 40 nm.

> The usual LED wavelengths for glass fibers are 820 or 850 nm.

Other semiconductor compounds can be used to make LEDs that emit different wavelengths. Gallium arsenide phosphide (GaAsP) LEDs emitting visible red light around 650 nm are used with plastic fibers, which are most transparent in the red and transmit poorly at GaAlAs wavelengths. GaAsP LEDs are lower in performance than GaAlAs LEDs, but they cost less and are fine for short, low-speed plastic fiber links.

> Visible LEDs are used with plastic fibers, which transmit poorly in the infrared.

The most important compound for high-performance fiber optics is InGaAsP, made of indium, gallium, arsenic, and phosphorus mixed so the number of indium plus gallium atoms equals the number of arsenic plus phosphorous atoms. The resulting compound is written as $In_xGa_{1-x}As_yP_{1-y}$, where x is the fraction of indium and y is the fraction of arsenic. These so-called quaternary (four-element) compounds are more complex than ternary (three-element) compounds such as GaAlAs but are needed to produce output at 1300 and 1550 nm. In practice, LEDs are sometimes used for short systems at 1300 nm, where conventional fibers have low chromatic dispersion, but never at 1550 nm.

InGaAsP LEDs emit at 1300 nm.

Other LED characteristics depend on device geometry and internal structure. The description of LEDs so far hasn't indicated in which direction they emit light. In fact, simple LEDs emit light in all directions, as shown in Figure 9.3, and are packaged so most emission comes from their surfaces. The light is emitted in a broad cone, with intensity falling off roughly with the cosine of the angle from the normal to the semiconductor junction. (This is called a Lambertian distribution.)

More complex internal structures can concentrate output of surface-emitting LEDs in a narrower angle, by means such as confining drive current to a small region of the LED. Such designs typically require that the light emerge through the substrate, which can lead to transmission losses. One way to enhance output and make emission more directional is to etch a hole in the substrate to produce what is called a Burrus diode, after its inventor Charles A. Burrus of Bell Laboratories. A fiber can be inserted into the hole to collect light.

A fundamentally different configuration is the edge-emitting diode, shown in Figure 9.5. Electrical contacts cover the top and bottom of an edge emitter, so light cannot emerge there. The LED confines light in a thin, narrow stripe in the plane of the *p-n* junction. This is done by surrounding that stripe with regions of lower refractive index, creating a waveguide that functions like an optical fiber, and channeling light out both ends where it can be coupled into a fiber. One disadvantage is that this increases the amount of heat the LED must dissipate.

An edge-emitting diode emits light from its ends.

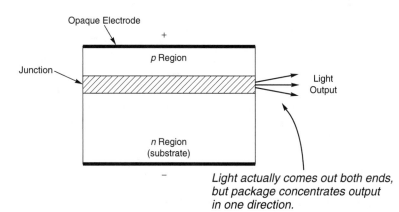

FIGURE 9.5

An edge-emitting LED.

In general, the more complex the LED structure, the brighter and more tightly collimated is the emitted light. Concentration of the emitting area and the region through which current passes also decreases rise time and, thus, enhances possible modulation bandwidth. Of course, as with other devices, the greater complexity comes at higher cost.

Semiconductor Laser Sources

Semiconductor lasers are superficially like LEDs, but they produce light in a different way that results in higher output powers, much narrower spectral widths, and more directional beams. Understanding their operation requires a quick review of laser physics. I will concentrate initially on the semiconductor diode lasers that are most widely used in fiber-optic communications and then describe other lasers sometimes used in fiber-optic systems later in this chapter. Some LED materials are not suitable for use in semiconductor lasers, but all semiconductor laser materials can work as LEDs.

Stimulated Emission

Laser emission is
stimulated.

Light is emitted when something (e.g., an electron in a semiconductor) drops from a high energy level to a lower one, releasing the extra energy. Normally, it emits light without outside influence, in what is called spontaneous emission, but it does not do so the instant it is first able to. It takes its time to get around to spontaneous emission. Suppose, however, that the electron is sitting in the upper energy level waiting to emit its extra energy and another photon comes along, with just the amount of energy the electron needs to emit. That external photon can stimulate the electron in the upper energy level to drop to the lower one and emit its energy as light of the same wavelength. The result is a second identical photon. The process is called Light Amplification by the Stimulated Emission of Radiation, and the acronym spells *Laser.* Recall that this is the process that amplifies light in a fiber amplifier and generates light in a fiber laser.

Population Inversion

Special conditions are needed for laser emission. One requirement is that there be more electrons (or atoms or molecules) in the upper energy level than in the lower one. Specialists call this a population inversion because normally more electrons are in lower levels. This is necessary because whatever is in the lower energy level can absorb the emitted light. If more things are in the lower level than in the upper level, they would absorb the light faster than it could be emitted. However, if only that condition is met, the stimulated emission will go off in every direction, more like a lightbulb than what we think of as a laser.

Light Confinement

Stripe geometry in
a laser confines
light in a
waveguide similar
to the core of an
optical fiber.

You need some way to trap some of the stimulated emission to generate a laser beam. The more efficiently you can trap the light, the more efficient you can make your laser.

One example of light trapping is the core-cladding boundary in a fiber amplifier or fiber laser, which traps stimulated emission and guides it along the core of the fiber. Conventional semiconductor lasers do something similar. The active layer at the *p-n* junction is made of a semiconductor compound with refractive index slightly higher than that of the surrounding material, as shown in Figure 9.6. Typically, the semiconductors do not differ much in composition, so they can be grown on top of each other with minimal difficulty. The junctions of different-composition semiconductors are called *heterojunctions,* and lasers with them on top and bottom of the active layer are called *double-heterojunction* (or double-heterostructure) lasers.

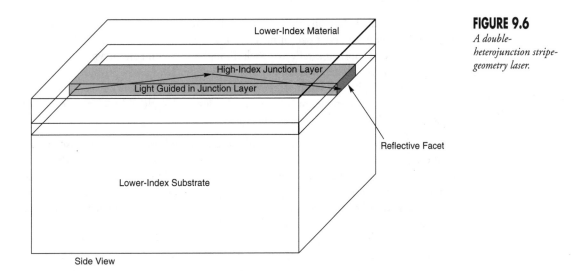

FIGURE 9.6

A double-heterojunction stripe-geometry laser.

Look closely at Figure 9.6, and you can see that the whole junction plane is not made of the same high-index material. Only a narrow stripe is; the rest of the material in the junction plane is made of lower-index material. This is called a *stripe-geometry laser,* and the stripe serves as a rectangular waveguide similar in concept to the high-index core of an optical fiber. Typically the stripe is only a few micrometers wide and a fraction of a micrometer high and limits the laser to generating light in a single waveguide mode. Light emerges from a spot at the edge of the wafer the same size as the waveguide, nicely matched to the core of a single-mode fiber. This extra confinement improves laser performance, and in general semiconductor lasers benefit from the tightest possible confinement of the beam within the semiconductor. (The figure does not show *electrical* confinement in the junction plane, which typically confines current flow through the narrow stripe portion of the junction.)

The beam emerging from the laser is oblong in cross section. Because the emitting area is so narrow, the light waves diffract from it and spread more rapidly in the direction perpendicular to the junction (initially the thin dimension of the beam) than in the junction plane. Once you get a little way from the chip, the beam becomes a flattened cone.

A further refinement in light confinement is the use of quantum wells, extremely thin layers that further constrain where electrons and holes can recombine to emit light by differences in their internal energy states. We'll avoid the details of their operation, but you can think of quantum wells as a technique to improve confinement and performance of semiconductor lasers.

Laser Beam Generation

●

A laser beam is formed by a resonator that reflects light back and forth through the laser medium.

Merely guiding the light along the laser stripe does not itself generate a laser beam. As in a fiber laser, you must add a pair of mirrors, one at each end, to form a resonator. Light emitted toward one mirror is reflected back through the laser medium, where it can stimulate more emission. Then it hits the other mirror and bounces back through the laser medium again. Light emitted in other directions leaks away if it is not confined. Thus stimulated emission amplifies only light aimed along the length of the laser, so it bounces back and forth between the resonator mirrors.

Figure 9.7 shows the process in more detail. In all lasers, at least one mirror must let some light escape through or around it to form the laser beam. The laser shown in Figure 9.7 is a conventional design called an *edge emitter,* because the "mirrors" are the cleaved edges of the semiconductor wafer, called *facets,* and light emerges from the edges of the wafer. The GaAs and InP compounds used in standard semiconductor lasers have high refractive indexes, so even uncoated facets reflect much of the light back into the wafer. In practice, the rear facet usually lets some light escape (which is often collected by a detector that monitors laser output power), but it may be coated to reflect most light back into the laser. In practice, the front facet is left uncoated so most light escapes, but some is reflected back into the semiconductor. Semiconductors generate such strong stimulated emission that this is all the feedback needed to produce laser action.

Functional Differences

There are two important functional differences between LEDs and diode lasers. One is that LEDs lack reflective facets and, in fact, may be designed to minimize reflection back into the semiconductor. The other is that lasers must operate at higher drive currents to get the high density of ready-to-recombine electrons needed at the *p-n* junction.

The output of a semiconductor laser depends on the drive current passing through it, as long as the bias voltage is above the minimum required (the band-gap energy). At low currents, the laser emits feeble spontaneous emission, operating as an inefficient LED. However, as drive current passes a threshold value, the device shifts over to laser emission, and output rises steeply, as shown in Figure 9.8. For most diode lasers, LED emission is so weak it can be ignored.

These internal differences lead to some important functional differences. Lasers convert electrical input power to light more efficiently than LEDs and also have higher drive cur-

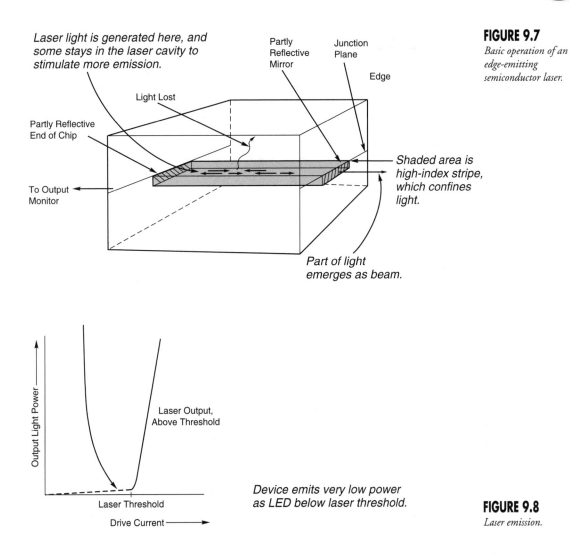

FIGURE 9.7

Basic operation of an edge-emitting semiconductor laser.

Laser light is generated here, and some stays in the laser cavity to stimulate more emission.

Partly Reflective Mirror

Junction Plane

Edge

Light Lost

Partly Reflective End of Chip

To Output Monitor

Shaded area is high-index stripe, which confines light.

Part of light emerges as beam.

Laser Output, Above Threshold

Output Light Power

Laser Threshold

Drive Current

Device emits very low power as LED below laser threshold.

FIGURE 9.8

Laser emission.

rents, so lasers are much more powerful than LEDs. The concentration of stimulated emission leads to a beam narrower than from an LED (although semiconductor laser beams are broad by laser standards). The higher drive currents and optical power levels make laser lifetimes shorter than LEDs, although this usually is not an important limitation except where temperatures of GaAlAs lasers cannot be controlled. The amplification inherent in laser action tends to concentrate emission in a much narrower spectral width than LED output, about a couple of nanometers in the design of Figure 9.7. In essence, the center of the emission curve is amplified much more than the fringes, making the laser curve much more steeply peaked, as shown in Figure 9.1.

Lasers are much more powerful than LEDs and emit a narrower range of wavelengths.

Vertical Cavity Semiconductor Lasers

A VCSEL emits
from its surface
instead of its edge.

An alternative design for semiconductor lasers is to have the resonator mirrors above and below the active layer. This is called a *vertical-cavity surface-emitting laser* (VCSEL) because the light resonates vertically in the wafer, perpendicular to the junction, and emerges from the surface, as shown in Figure 9.9.

FIGURE 9.9

*A vertical-cavity
surface-emitting laser.*

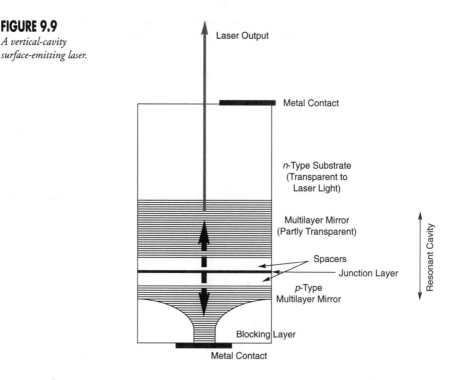

The mirrors in VCSELs are formed by depositing a series of layers with alternating compositions, so they selectively reflect a narrow range of wavelengths, depending upon their thickness and refractive indexes. This multilayer reflector uses an effect similar to a fiber grating, but the concept of selective reflection by multilayer films coated on optics came before either fiber gratings or VCSELs. A VCSEL emits from a round spot on the surface of the wafer that is larger than the core of a single-mode fiber. Because the emitting area is circular and larger than an edge-emitting laser, a VCSEL beam is circular and does not spread out as rapidly. (The differences arise from diffraction effects.)

VCSELs have a number of attractions. They have low threshold currents and are quite efficient in converting electrical input into light. This means they consume little power and have to dissipate less heat than edge-emitting lasers, giving them a longer lifetime than standard lasers. They are easy to manufacture and package. Like other semiconductor lasers, they can be directly modulated at high speeds—so they can generate signals faster than 1 Gbit/s.

At this writing, most VCSELs are made from GaAs semiconductor materials, which meet the requirements for making multilayer mirrors much better than InP-based compounds. The present strength of single VCSELs is as inexpensive light sources at wavelengths of 750 to 1000 nm, where they offer better lifetimes than edge-emitting GaAs lasers and serious competition for LED sources. A crucial advantage of VCSELs is their ability to generate higher-speed signals than LEDs. Although their present short wavelengths can't go far enough through fiber to be useful for telecommunications, VCSELs are quite attractive for gigabit networks that transmit signals within a building or complex.

Unlike other diode lasers, VCSELs can be fabricated in two-dimensional arrays covering the surface of a wafer, which can generate separately modulated outputs that emerge from the chip surface. Such arrays of independent emitters are attractive for optical switching and signal processing, with beams going through free space as well as through fibers.

Wavelengths

The output wavelengths of diode lasers depend on composition of the junction layer, like those of LEDs. The primary compositions used in diode laser light sources for fiber optics are variations on the standard III-V semiconductor compounds that can be fabricated on substrates of gallium arsenide or indium phosphide:

- $Ga_{(1-x)}Al_xAs$ on GaAs for 780 to 850 nm
- $In_{0.73}Ga_{0.27}As_{0.58}P_{0.42}$ on InP for 1310 nm
- $In_{0.58}Ga_{0.42}As_{0.9}P_{0.1}$ on InP for 1550 nm

Other InGaAsP mixtures are used for other wavelengths between about 1100 and 1600 nm. InGaAs on GaAs can generate 980 nm, a wavelength used to pump erbium-doped fiber amplifiers and lasers. The major constraints are the need for the proper band-gap in the active layer and for interatomic spacings reasonably close to those of readily available substrates (a restriction that has been relaxed recently with the development of strained-layer structures).

OUTPUT SPECTRUM

Diode lasers have a much narrower spectral width than LEDs, allowing the use of standard diode lasers to carry signals at reasonable speeds through single-mode fiber. However, the linewidth of 1 to 3 nm is large enough to cause dispersion problems if transmission speed is high or if the laser output does not match the fiber's zero-dispersion wavelength. High-speed systems require lasers with a much narrower spectral width, which have a more elaborate design.

Single-frequency lasers are needed for high-speed transmission.

The simple edge-emitting laser design we've talked about so far is called a Fabry-Perot laser, because it's based on an optical interferometer devised many years ago by Fabry and Perot. Figure 9.10 provides a close look at the output spectrum of a typical narrow-stripe Fabry-Perot laser. Although much power is concentrated at one wavelength, the laser can oscillate simultaneously at several discrete lines. This occurs because the cavity limits oscillation to lines for which the round-trip distance between the two mirrors is an integral number *(N)* of wavelengths, λ:

$$2Dn = N\lambda$$

where D is the spacing between mirrors and n is the refractive index. Oscillation also is limited to wavelengths that fall within the range where stimulated emission can occur in the material.

Each narrow spike in Figure 9.10 is a longitudinal mode of the laser. For typical semiconductor lasers, these modes together span a range of 1 to 3 nm, the peak of the gain curve for the material. As you can see, an individual longitudinal mode spans a much narrower range, a small fraction of 1 nm. The spacing between longitudinal modes depends on the cavity length and wavelength; the longer the cavity length (measured in wavelength), the closer the modes are spaced. Fabry-Perot semiconductor lasers are short, only about half a millimeter long, so the spacing between longitudinal modes is wide compared to other lasers. (VCSEL cavities are even shorter.)

Minor fluctuations during operation can cause Fabry-Perot lasers to "hop" between modes, shifting the emission wavelength. The easiest way to envision this is by looking at Figure 9.10 and imagining the peak emission shifting to one of the weaker modes.

FIGURE 9.10

Wavelengths in multiple longitudinal modes.

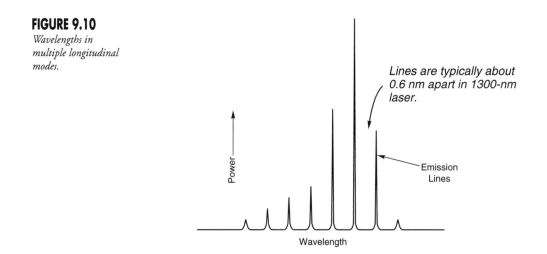

Lines are typically about 0.6 nm apart in 1300-nm laser.

Emission Lines

Power

Wavelength

For high performance and low dispersion, laser emission must be limited to a single longitudinal mode or, equivalently, to a single frequency.

SINGLE-FREQUENCY LASERS

To restrict oscillation to a single longitudinal mode, researchers have developed laser resonators more elaborate than simple facets on the ends of a semiconductor chip. Three leading approaches are shown in Figure 9.11. One is the distributed feedback laser, in which a series of corrugated ridges on the semiconductor substrate (replacing the mirrored end facts) reflect only certain wavelengths of light back into the laser, and light at only one resonant wavelength is amplified. The distributed Bragg reflection laser works in much the same way, but the grating is etched outside the part of the laser that is pumped by electric current.

The approaches shown in Figure 9.11(a) and 9.11(b) are quite similar and generate light at a fixed narrow range of wavelengths. In the distributed feedback (DFB) laser, a series of corrugated ridges on the semiconductor substrate reflect certain wavelengths of light back into the laser, providing the feedback otherwise generated by the laser cavity mirrors. This design chooses a single wavelength for feedback and amplification, which depends on the spacing of lines in the grating and the refractive index of the laser material. The distributed Bragg reflection laser in Figure 9.11(b) works much the same way, but the grating is etched outside the part of the laser that is pumped by electric current.

A different way to stabilize laser wavelength is by placing a semiconductor laser within an external cavity which selects the emission wavelength. This requires coating one or both facets of an edge-emitting laser to suppress reflection back into the semiconductor, and adding one or two external mirrors to extend the resonator cavity beyond the laser chip. In addition, a wavelength-selective element is added to the laser cavity. In the simple design of Figure 9.11(c), the tuning element is a diffraction grating which serves as one external mirror, reflecting light at an angle which depends on its wavelength. Normally, a simple edge-emitting diode laser will emit a range of wavelengths, but when these wavelengths strike the diffraction grating, most are reflected at angles which take them away from the laser chip. Only a narrow range of wavelengths return to the laser junction to be amplified. Turning the grating changes those wavelengths reflected back to the chip, and thus tunes the output wavelength of the laser. (You also can get the same effect by inserting a prism or other wavelength-selective element into the laser cavity, but diffraction gratings generally are the simplest components to use.)

You should not confuse tunability with spectral width. Over a brief interval, such as 50 ms, an external-cavity laser can emit light stabilized to span a frequency range of 1 MHz or less (less than 0.001 nm at 1.5 μm). By adjusting the grating, you can tune the laser to emit a much larger range of wavelengths—for example, from about 1490 to 1570 nm. However, the laser is not emitting all those wavelengths at once, only a narrow range. If the grating is fixed in position, an external-cavity laser emits a fixed wavelength.

Distributed feedback lasers emit only a single frequency.

External-cavity lasers emit a single frequency that can be tuned in wavelength.

FIGURE 9.11

Three single-frequency lasers.

Grating limits emission to one frequency.

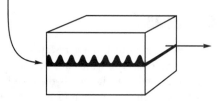

a. Distributed Feedback Laser

Drive current only through this region

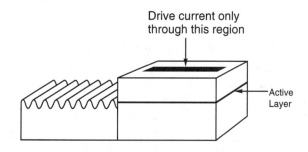

Active Layer

b. Distributed Bragg Reflection Laser

Facet coated to prevent reflection Diode Laser (Size Exaggerated)

Reflective Grating

Selected λ

Output Beam

Output Facet

Other Wavelengths

Length of Laser Cavity

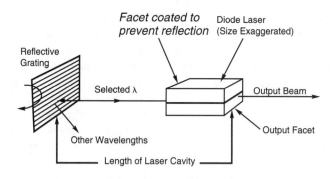

c. External Cavity Tunable Laser

External modulation of lasers avoids wavelength chip, which causes dispersion.

EXTERNAL MODULATION

Turning the drive current off and on is the simplest way to modulate a diode laser with a signal. However, it has the side effect of subtly shifting the wavelength during a pulse of light. As the electron density in the semiconductor changes, so does the refractive index of the material. That effectively changes the optical length of the laser cavity ($D = nL$, where n is the refractive index and L is the physical separation of the cavity mirrors). From the earlier equation for the wavelength at which the laser resonates, you can see that this means the wavelength λ changes by an amount $\Delta\lambda$:

$$\Delta\lambda = \frac{2(\Delta n \times L)}{N}$$

where Δn is the change in refractive index and N is an integer, the number of wavelengths in a round-trip of the cavity. Although that change is small, it occurs during the laser pulse, causing each pulse to contain a range of wavelengths. The different wavelengths travel at slightly different velocities, limiting performance.

Reliability

Reliability was a big problem with early GaAs lasers, but great improvements have been made in the technology. Nonetheless, LEDs are inherently more reliable than semiconductor lasers, particularly edge-emitters, because lasers have much higher current densities and optical power outputs. InGaAsP lasers and LEDs are inherently more reliable than similar devices made from GaAs, partly because longer-wavelength photons carry less energy and partly because InGaAsP is less sensitive to temperature.

Operating temperature is a key factor in reliability. The threshold current of a semiconductor laser tends to increase with temperature, increasing the amount of waste heat generated within the laser. The excess heat can further increase temperature, degrading efficiency even further. Gallium arsenide is more vulnerable to this problem, which can lead to thermal runaway if laser temperature is not controlled. In addition, laser lifetime decreases as temperature increases, so accelerated aging tests are conducted at high temperatures. To control these problems, many laser transmitters are operated with active temperature stabilization, such as thermoelectric coolers. Most lasers are packaged with heat sinks, even if active cooling is not required.

An important cause of failure in semiconductor lasers is a slow decline in output power with age. To compensate for this, transmitter circuits can be designed to slowly increase drive current to maintain a constant power. In this case, failure is defined as the point at which a laser can no longer deliver the required power.

Semiconductor lasers are particularly vulnerable to damage by electrostatic discharges during handling. This problem can be overcome by care in packaging and handling, but you should be aware of its potential to damage lasers.

Semiconductor Laser Amplifiers

If you remove the mirrors from the ends of any laser, it can amplify light passing through it. This is true for semiconductor lasers as well as for fiber lasers, although semiconductor laser amplifiers have not gained wide acceptance.

LEDs are more reliable than lasers; InGaAsP devices are more reliable than GaAs devices.

A semiconductor laser without a resonant cavity can function as an optical amplifier.

A mirrorless semiconductor laser can amplify light passing along the junction layer, guided in the active stripe. The weak light signal stimulates recombining electrons and holes to emit light at the same wavelength. The amplification per unit length—"gain" in laser terminology—is high for semiconductor lasers, so a relatively short length of semiconductor laser can amplify light many times.

I mentioned earlier that semiconductor lasers generally do not have external mirrors but rely on light reflection from the cleaved facets on the edges of the wafer. This presents a problem in designing semiconductor laser amplifiers, because such reflection could generate undesirable noise. To overcome this, the facets of semiconductor laser amplifiers used as separate devices are coated with an antireflective material. An alternative is to make the semiconductor laser amplifier part of a larger monolithic semiconductor device, as shown in Figure 9.12. In this case, a waveguide fabricated in the semiconductor layer delivers light to the amplifier stage, and another waveguide collects the light. (Again, some form of isolator is needed to prevent reflection back into the laser-amplifier stripe.) Because there are no facets at the ends of the laser, there is no reflective feedback.

Chapter 12 will describe more about both fiber and semiconductor laser amplifiers and their uses in fiber-optic systems.

FIGURE 9.12

Semiconductor laser amplifier integrated with waveguide.

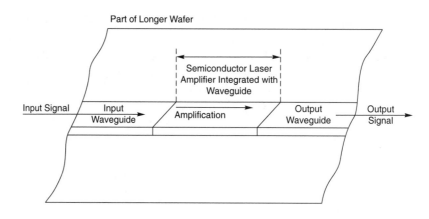

Fiber Lasers and Amplifiers

You learned in Chapter 7 that optical fibers doped with erbium or some other rare-earth elements could be used in lasers and amplifiers. Let's look at the structures of amplifiers and lasers made with these fibers, starting with amplifiers.

Fiber Amplifiers

Fiber amplifiers require pump light to amplify an input signal.

Fiber amplifiers require two separate inputs of light. One is the optical signal to be amplified, which must be at a wavelength the fiber can amplify. As an example, we'll consider the erbium-doped fiber amplifier, which can amplify signals at wavelengths between about 1.53 and 1.62 μm. Erbium-doped fibers are the best-developed and most widely used fiber amplifiers.

The second input is light to excite the erbium atoms into the proper excited state, which can amplify the input signal by stimulated emission. For erbium, this usually is one of two wavelengths, 0.98 or 1.48 μm. The usual pump sources are semiconductor lasers emitting those wavelengths.

Figure 9.13 shows one possible structure for a fiber amplifier. For simplicity, I show it amplifying only one wavelength, although it can amplify multiple signals. A weak signal at 1.55 μm enters from a fiber on the left. It passes through an optical isolator, a device that transmits light only in one direction, and through a filter that transmits the 1.55-μm signal but not the pump light. Then it passes through a length of amplifying fiber, where it is amplified. Light from the pump laser enters the fiber in the other direction, through a coupler that transmits the pump beam but directs the amplified signal through the output fiber. Another optical isolator keeps light from being scattered the wrong direction through the fiber amplifier.

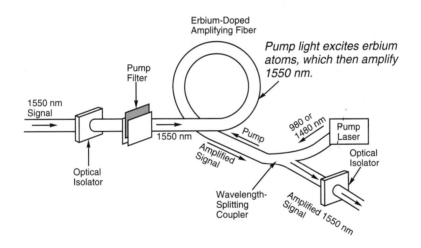

FIGURE 9.13

An erbium-doped fiber amplifier.

The light being amplified makes only a single pass through the fiber, from left to right in Figure 9.13. Total amplification typically is 10 to 40 dB, a factor of 10 to 10,000. Output powers can exceed 100 mW. These and other properties make the erbium-doped fiber amplifier nearly an ideal optical amplifier. As single-mode fibers, they are easy to couple to communication fiber. They have very low signal distortion; the pulses that come out are very similar to those that go in. Noise and crosstalk also are low, and fiber amplifiers are not sensitive to the polarization of the input light. They respond very rapidly to changes in input. Signals can pass through many of them in series—separated by tens of kilometers of fiber—and still be recognizable at the end of the chain. We'll look more at these considerations in Chapter 12.

Fiber amplifiers
are insensitive
to signal speed
and format.

All types of fiber amplifiers are analog devices that amplify the input signal regardless of its speed and format. Their operating wavelengths depend on the range of wavelengths where the active element such as erbium has gain, which is a function both of the element and of the fiber material. Erbium ions in silica glass fibers have slightly different gain spectra than those in fluoride-glass fiber or other materials, such as a recently developed glass containing tellurium. A fiber amplifier can simultaneously amplify signals at multiple wavelengths within its operating band without causing overlap or crosstalk. However, inherent gain is not uniform over the entire amplification band, so measures must be taken to balance the strengths of the signals at different wavelengths. I will discuss this more in Chapter 12.

No technology is ever completely ideal for any purpose, and fiber amplifiers are no exception. If the pump laser burns out, a doped fiber strongly absorbs the light it's supposed to amplify. As analog devices, fiber amplifiers can amplify noise as well as signal. However, they have done very well and gained widespread acceptance.

Fiber Lasers

Erbium-doped
fibers can be
made into lasers
that generate a
continuous beam
or a train of
ultrashort pulses at
1550 nm.

Put mirrors on both ends of an erbium-doped fiber and it can become a laser. The mirrors provide the resonant cavity needed for the laser to generate its own light, or *oscillate*. As in a diode laser, a few of the excited atoms release their excess energy as light, and this light can stimulate the emission of more photons, building up a beam. The fiber laser may be arranged with mirrors at each end, or in a loop, with couplers bringing light from the pump laser and splitting off the output beam, as shown in Figure 9.14. As with external-cavity lasers, adding a diffraction grating to the cavity of a fiber laser makes it possible to tune its output wavelength.

FIGURE 9.14

Erbium-fiber ring laser.

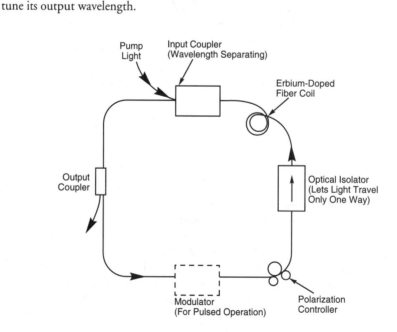

An erbium-fiber laser cannot be directly modulated with an electrical signal like a diode laser. Instead, it must be modulated externally in one of two ways. The fiber laser can be made to generate a steady or continuous beam at a narrow range of wavelengths. This stable single-wavelength output does not suffer the chirp that comes when a diode laser is directly modulated, so modulating it produces signals that suffer little dispersion in a fiber with high dispersion at 1550 nm. Erbium fiber lasers can also generate higher power than standard diode lasers, so a single erbium fiber laser could send signals to more terminals.

Alternatively, an erbium-fiber laser can be operated in a mode that generates a series of pulses shorter than 1 ps (10^{-12}s), separated by the time light takes to make a round-trip of the fiber laser. An optional modulator (shown dashed in Figure 9.14) controls generation of the pulses by a technique called *modelocking*. The pulses are spaced uniformly in time, like a series of 1s in digital code, so an external modulator is needed to convert them into a signal. However, the shortness of the pulses makes them useful for high-speed transmission.

Other Solid-State Laser Sources

Other solid-state lasers also can be signal sources in fiber-optic systems. From a physical standpoint, they function as fiber lasers, with light from an external source exciting a solid material between a pair of mirrors. As with the core of a fiber laser, the laser material is a glass or crystal host doped with atoms that emit light by stimulated emission. However, the laser material is usually shaped as a rod, is much shorter than a typical fiber laser, and lacks an internal light-guiding structure.

Diode-pumped neodymium lasers can generate more than a watt near 1300 nm.

The most important of these are crystalline neodynium lasers, in which the rare earth neodyMium is doped into crystals called YAG (for yttrium aluminum garnet) or YLF (for yttrium lithium fluoride). These lasers can be excited by semiconductor lasers of gallium arsenide emitting near 800 nm. The primary neodymium line is near 1060 nm, but there are secondary lines at 1313 and 1321 nm in YLF and 1319 nm in YAG. Those fall right in the 1300-nm fiber window.

Like erbium-fiber lasers, solid-state neodymium lasers cannot be modulated directly; they require external modulators. Their big attraction is their ability to generate high power—more than a watt near 1300 nm. That's much more than you want to send signals through a single length of fiber, but it can be split among many fibers to carry the same signals to many terminals, for network communications or cable television signal distribution.

What Have You Learned?

1. The most common light sources for short silica fiber-optic systems are GaAlAs LEDs operating at 820 or 850 nm. InGaAsP lasers and LEDs emit at 1300 and 1550 nm.

2. Red LEDs are the usual signal sources for plastic fibers.

3. LEDs and semiconductor lasers are both semiconductor diodes that emit light when forward biasing causes current carriers to recombine at the junction between *p*- and *n*-doped materials.

4. The wavelength emitted by an LED or diode laser depends on the material from which the diode is made.

5. Laser light is produced by the amplification of stimulated emission, which can occur at a semiconductor diode junction when there is a population inversion. A resonant cavity creates a laser beam.

6. Edge-emitting semiconductor lasers are more complex in structure than LEDs and can emit higher powers. Unlike LEDs, they do not operate below a certain threshold current. Above that threshold, lasers are much more efficient than LEDs.

7. A narrow stripe in the junction layer of an edge-emitting double-heterojunction diode laser confines light using a waveguide effect. Current flow also is concentrated through the stripe.

8. Laser light oscillates between a pair of mirrors in a reflective cavity. One mirror transmits some light that becomes the laser beam.

9. Vertical-cavity surface-emitting lasers (VCSELs) have mirror layers above and below the junction layer and emit light from their surfaces.

10. LEDs are longer-lived and less expensive than most diode lasers and do not require as careful control of operating conditions.

11. Special narrow-line lasers are needed to generate the single-frequency light needed for high-speed transmission. The most common designs are DFB (distributed feedback), DBR (distributed Bragg reflection), and tunable external-cavity lasers.

12. Single-frequency lasers can be driven with a steady current, and modulated externally to limit linewidth and reduce dispersion effects.

13. Erbium-doped fiber amplifiers can amplify signals at 1.53 to 1.62 μm. With the addition of resonator mirrors, erbium-doped fibers become lasers that generate their own signals.

14. A semiconductor laser without mirrors can amplify light passing through it.

15. Solid-state neodymium lasers can generate high powers at 1.3 μm but require external modulation to transmit a signal.

What's Next?

Now that I have discussed light sources, Chapter 10 will examine how they are incorporated into fiber-optic transmitters.

Quiz for Chapter 9

1. Operating wavelengths of GaAlAs LEDs and lasers are
   a. 820 and 850 nm.
   b. 665 nm.
   c. 1300 nm.
   d. 1550 nm.
   e. none of the above.

2. Light emission from an LED is modulated by
   a. voltage applied across the diode.
   b. current passing through the diode.
   c. illumination of the diode.
   d. all the above.

3. Which of the following statements about the difference between semiconductor lasers and LEDs are true?
   a. Lasers emit higher power at the same drive current.
   b. Lasers emit light only if drive current is above a threshold value.
   c. Output from LEDs spreads out over a broader angle.
   d. LEDs do not have reflective end facets.
   e. All the above.

4. Laser light is produced by
   a. stimulated emission.
   b. spontaneous emission.
   c. black magic.
   d. electricity.

5. The spectral width of a Fabry-Perot semiconductor laser is about
   a. 2 nm.
   b. 30 nm.
   c. 40 nm.
   d. 850 nm.
   e. 1300 nm.

6. A distributed-feedback laser is
   a. a laser that emits multiple longitudinal modes from a narrow stripe.
   b. a laser with a corrugated substrate that oscillates on a single longitudinal mode.
   c. a laser made of two segments that are optically coupled but electrically separated.
   d. a laser that requires liquid-nitrogen cooling to operate.

7. Which of the following is an important advantage of external modulation of lasers?
   a. Simpler operation.
   b. Does not require electrical power.
   c. More precise control over output.
   d. Avoids wavelength chirp that could cause dispersion.

8. Which of the following is not an advantage of erbium-doped fiber amplifiers?
   a. High gain.

b. Insensitive to signal speed.

c. Operation near 1300 nm.

d. Broad amplification bandwidth at 1550 nm.

9. What is the power source for erbium-doped fiber amplifiers?

a. Electric current passing through the fiber.

b. They require no power.

c. Diode lasers emitting at 980 or 1480 nm.

d. Power is drawn from the optical signal.

10. What guides light in a narrow-stripe edge-emitting laser?

a. Reflective layers on the edges of the laser wafer.

b. The stripe has higher refractive index than surrounding material, so it functions as a waveguide.

c. Coatings applied above and below the junction.

d. Light entering it from an external optical fiber.

11. Which of the following is *not* true for VCSELs?

a. VCSELs emit light from their surfaces.

b. VCSEL beams are rounder than those from edge-emitting lasers.

c. VCSELs can be made easily from GaAs or InGaAsP compounds.

d. VCSELs have low threshold currents.

e. VCSELs have multilayer coatings as their resonator mirrors.

12. A Fabry-Perot diode laser operating at 1.3 μm has a cavity length of 500 μm and a refractive index of 3.2. How far apart are its longitudinal modes? (*Hint:* First estimate the number of waves that could fit into the cavity; then calculate the wavelengths of modes N and $N + 1$.)

a. 0.013 nm.

b. 0.053 nm.

c. 0.53 nm.

d. 5.3 nm.

e. 0.13 μm.

Transmitters

About This Chapter

Optical transmitters generate the signals sent through fiber-optic cables. They come in many types—from cheap LEDs directly driven by signal sources to sophisticated transmitters using externally modulated distributed-feedback lasers. Some operate at telephone-like speeds and bandwidths over several meters; others send tens of thousands of megabits per second through tens of kilometers of fiber. All are based on the light sources described in Chapter 9.

This chapter examines transmitters and how they work. It begins by describing the major functional considerations for transmitters, then outlines how they generate signals. Because my emphasis is on optics, I don't go into detail about the electronics. I will cover signal amplifiers and regenerators later, in Chapter 12.

A Few Words About Terminology

Strictly speaking, transmitters are the devices that generate the signal sent through optical fibers. However, the terminology and packaging of commercial equipment can be confusing and deserves more explanation.

Fiber-optic transmitters are often packaged with receivers and cables and sold as systems. For short-distance digital transmission between two points, these systems are labeled data links. A transmitter may be packaged with a receiver as a "transceiver" to provide two-way service to a single terminal or node. Local area networks interconnect multiple terminals spread over relatively small distances (typically no more than a few kilometers); only a small fraction use fiber optics. MANs (metropolitan area networks) and WANs (wide area networks) cover wider areas than LANs, from a campus-sized area to an entire city; more of them use fibers.

Performance of a
fiber-optic
transmitter is
affected by signal
type, speed,
operating
wavelength, and
light source.

Industry terminology is vague, and more than one short analog system has been called a data link. Details of how transmitter, receiver, cable, and other components come together to make fiber-optic systems, and the specialized terminology of different applications, will be described in later chapters on system design and applications.

Transmitter Performance

Several factors enter into the performance of a fiber-optic transmitter, including the type of signal being sent, the speed, the operating wavelength, the type of light source, and the cost. Each of these deserves a brief explanation.

Analog versus Digital Transmission

Fiber-optic systems
can transmit
analog or digital
signals.

Although much of the communications world has shifted from analog to digital transmission, not everyone has. Some applications require continuous analog waveforms; others operate best with discrete digital pulses. In theory, a simple LED source could be modulated by either an analog or digital signal, but in practice, transmitters are designed for one or the other type of modulation.

As you saw in Chapter 3, digital signals can withstand distortion better than analog signals. Figure 10.1 shows how the inherently analog process of signal transmission can distort signals by not precisely reproducing the input waveform. Distortion presents a problem for analog signals because the output should be a linear reproduction of the

FIGURE 10.1

Effects of distortion on analog and digital signals.

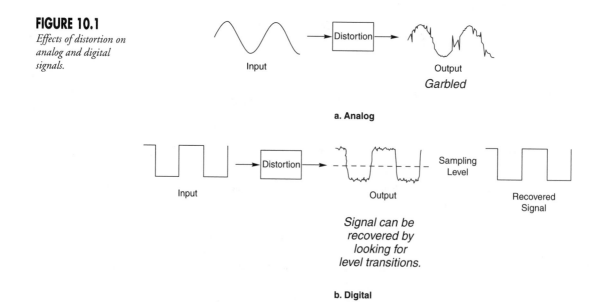

input. That is, if the input signal is F(t), the output should be cF(t), where c is a constant. Digital systems can tolerate distortion because they need to detect only the presence or absence of a pulse—not its shape.

Digital transmission, on the other hand, demands faster response than analog to follow the rapid rise of signals. Breaking a digital signal down into its component frequencies shows that the sharp edge of a digital pulse is made up of high frequencies. However, the system need detect only the difference between off and on, so the sharp edges can be somewhat blurred without introducing errors.

Thus, analog systems must accurately reproduce inputs, but speed is not as crucial as in digital systems, which must be fast but need not be accurate. These differences mean that analog and digital transmitters use different designs. They may be capable of using the same light source but with different electronics.

Bandwidth and Data Rate

The operating speed of a fiber-optic transmitter is measured in two ways: bandwidth for analog signals and data rate for digital signals. Both refer to the amplitude modulation of light from the source, which is shown in Figure 10.2. (Light waves are actually much

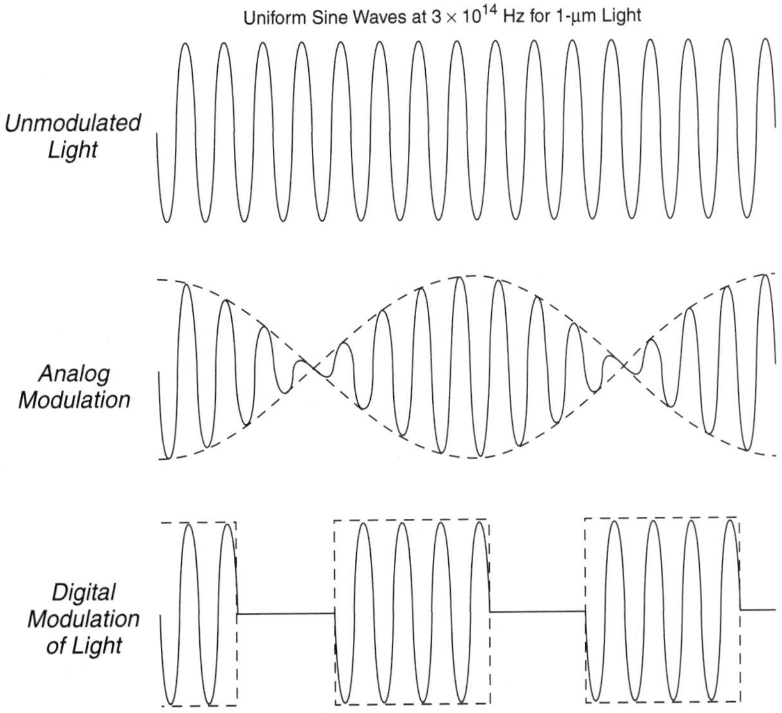

> Bandwidth usually defines the capacity of an analog system. Digital capacity is measured as data rate.

Uniform Sine Waves at 3×10^{14} Hz for 1-µm Light

Unmodulated Light

Analog Modulation

Digital Modulation of Light

FIGURE 10.2

Light modulation by digital and analog signals.

smaller than shown. If each digital pulse was 1 ns [10^{-9} s] long, it would contain 300,000 waves of 1-μm light.) Analog bandwidth is normally defined as the modulation frequency where the modulated signal amplitude drops 3 dB below the low-frequency modulated signal (a reduction of 50% in power). The digital data rate is the maximum number of bits per second that can be transmitted with an error rate below a specified level (often one error in 10^{12}, or a bit error rate of 10^{-12}).

Neither of these quantities actually measures the limiting characteristic of transmitters: their response time. The rise time is how long it takes light output to rise from 10% to 90% of the steady-state level; fall time is the inverse. If rise and fall times are equal (they aren't always), this can be used to approximate the bandwidth:

$$BW = \frac{0.35}{\text{rise time}}$$

where BW is in megahertz if rise time is in microseconds. The precise relationship between bandwidth and rise time differs among light sources and transmitters. Rise time is an important variable in selecting a light source and a way of modulating it. LED sources respond more slowly to changes in drive current than lasers; LED rise times range from a few nanoseconds to a few hundred nanoseconds. Semiconductor lasers modulated directly by changing their drive current typically have rise times of a fraction of a nanosecond.

Extremely high transmission speeds—several gigabits per second and above—generally require external modulation. The problem is not that the lasers cannot respond that fast; some can. However, direct modulation of the laser induces a slight variation, or chirp, in wavelength, which leads to dispersion that limits the capacity of optical fibers. External modulators can be made with very sharp rise times, so they turn the laser beam off and on at speeds to 10 Gbits/s or more without causing such chirp.

Operating Wavelengths

Wavelength-division multiplexing sends signals at multiple wavelengths through one fiber.

A single optical fiber can transmit signals at one, two, or more wavelengths. Sending multiple signals down the same fiber at different wavelengths is called *wavelength-division multiplexing* (WDM). It has great practical importance because it can multiply the capacity of an individual fiber. (In practice, as with most fiber systems, signals go through pairs of fibers, one carrying signals in each direction.) Figure 10.3 shows how four wavelengths can be combined. Most WDM is done at wavelengths near 1.55 μm, but some older systems transmit one channel at 1.3 μm and a second at 1.55 μm. *Dense wavelength-division multiplexing* (DWDM) involves multiple wavelengths, usually less than a few nanometers apart near 1.55 μm.

There are some limitations on wavelength-division multiplexing. The signals cannot be so close in wavelength that they interfere with each other. How close this is depends on system design, particularly on the type of optical amplification (if any), and on the optics

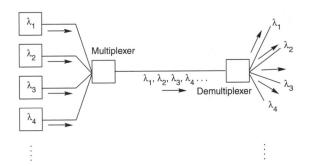

FIGURE 10.3
Wavelength-division multiplexing.

used to combine and separate signals at the different wavelengths. The International Telecommunications Union standardized on a frequency grid with spacing of 100 GHz or multiples of that value (e.g, 200 GHz) between adjacent wavelengths in DWDM systems. At 1550 nm, a 100-GHz frequency spacing corresponds to wavelength spacing of about 0.8 nm. For example, five successive wavelengths separated by 100-GHz steps would be 1550.0, 1549.2, 1548.4, 1547.6, and 1546.8 nm.

Another practical WDM requirement is that the overall signal strength should not differ greatly among wavelengths. Signal strength is affected both by fiber attenuation and by the degree of amplification in the system, both of which depend on wavelength. Normally the wavelengths multiplexed are closely spaced, so attenuation differs little among them. In present systems, all wavelengths must fall within the range of any optical amplifiers used, and care must be taken to balance the extent of amplification across the whole range. (In the past, a few systems were built with wavelength multiplexing in different fiber "windows," such as the 1.3- and 1.55-μm wavelengths, but this is no longer done.)

Each wavelength in a WDM system is modulated separately, with its own signal. Thus you can think of a system carrying eight separate wavelengths as containing eight transmitters and eight receivers, which happen to send their signals through the same fiber. To simplify things in the descriptions that follow, I will consider a "transmitter" as a device that generates a signal at only one wavelength, except where I explicitly describe wavelength-division multiplexing. Remember, however, that you can package many transmitters operating at separate wavelengths into a single WDM transmitter that sends signals through one fiber.

The wavelength of light from an individual transmitter affects system performance in other important ways, because light transmission in fibers and gain in amplifiers depends on wavelength.

As you learned earlier, fiber attenuation depends on wavelength. This limits transmission distance directly by reducing power available at the receiver.

You also saw that pulse spreading, or dispersion, in a fiber puts an upper limit on bandwidth or data rate by causing successive pulses to interfere with each other. Chromatic

Standard spacing in dense WDM is 100 GHz between adjacent channels.

Operating wavelength affects both transmission distance and speed.

dispersion depends on wavelength in two ways—the magnitude of dispersion depends on wavelength and on the range of wavelengths in the signal. (Recall that chromatic dispersion is measured in picoseconds per nanometer of source spectral width per kilometer of fiber length. This quantity varies with wavelength but increases directly with the spectral width. Double the wavelength range, and you double the pulse spreading.) Chromatic dispersion accounts for most dispersion in single-mode fibers and much of the dispersion in graded-index multimode fibers.

Output Power

Output power also is critical to transmitter performance. Some light is inevitably lost between the light source and the transmitter output. It is possible to boost this output power by adding an optical amplifier between the transmitter output and the fiber input. However, care must be taken not to deliver too much light, which can cause nonlinear effects in a single-mode fiber. The power reaching the receiver must be adequate for it to detect the light signal but not so high that it overwhelms the detector. I will cover basic receiver characteristics in Chapter 11.

Transmitter Design

A transmitter includes housing, drive circuitry, and monitoring equipment, as well as a light source.

The light source is important, but it's not the only part of the transmitter. A housing is required to mount and protect the light source and to interface with the electronic signal source and the transmitting optical fiber. Internal components may be needed to optimize coupling to the fiber. Drive circuitry is usually needed, and temperature control and output monitoring can be crucial for sophisticated lasers.

The practical boundaries between transmitters and light sources can be vague. Simple LED sources can be mounted in a case with optical and electronic connections and little or no drive circuitry. On the other hand, a high-performance laser may be packaged as a transmitter in a case that also houses an output monitor and thermoelectric cooler, and perhaps an external modulator. Then that whole package may be incorporated into a larger transmission system that performs electronic functions such as time-division multiplexing, and several of these units can be combined for wavelength-division multiplexing. Thus you can say that some transmitters can contain transmitters.

Elements of Transmitters

Several elements make up fiber-optic transmitters.

The basic elements that may be found in transmitters, as shown in Figure 10.4, are as follows:

-  Housing
- Electronic interfaces
-  Optical interfaces

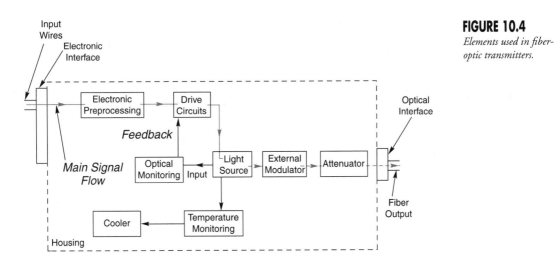

FIGURE 10.4
Elements used in fiber-optic transmitters.

- Drive circuitry
- Temperature sensing and control
- Optical output sensing
- Electronic signal preprocessing (e.g., data buffers)
- External modulator (if the light source is not modulated directly)
- Attenuator (for short systems)

Note that the figure does not show an actual physical arrangement, only the relationships of the elements. Neither does it show wavelength-division multiplexing. Many transmitters do not contain all these elements.

HOUSING

The housing for a fiber-optic transmitter, in its simplest form, is just a box designed to be mounted conveniently. Screws or other mounting equipment attach it mechanically to printed circuit boards or other electrical components. Some are quite compact, only an inch or two long, including integral optical connectors. Others are packaged to mount on standard equipment racks.

ELECTRONIC INTERFACES

Electronic interfaces may be wires, standard electronic connectors, or pins emerging from packages. Some simple transmitters can be driven directly by electronic input signals. More complex transmitters may require power and may accept multiple electronic inputs (and provide one or more electronic outputs as well).

OPTICAL INTERFACES

Common optical interfaces are connectors and fiber pigtails.

The optical interface between light source and fiber can take various forms, as shown in Figure 10.5. One of the most common is integration of a fiber-optic connector in the housing. Light is delivered to that connector by internal optics, including a collimating lens and sometimes a short fiber segment. Another approach is a short fiber pigtail that collects light from the emitting area and delivers it outside the case, where it can be spliced to an external fiber. The choice between these types depends on factors including cost, whether connections are to be temporary or permanent, type of fiber, importance of minimizing interconnection losses, and operating environment.

FIGURE 10.5

Transmitter optical interfaces.

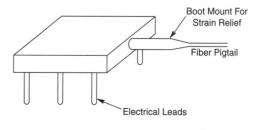

a. Transmitter with Fiber Pigtail

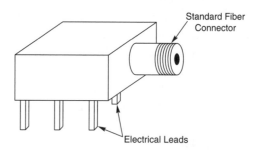

b. Transmitter with Integral Connector

DRIVE CIRCUITRY

Drive circuitry depends on application requirements, data format, and the light source.

The drive circuitry depends on application requirements, data format, and the light source. LEDs can be directly driven by a suitable current source (although most signals are in the form of voltage and must be converted to current). However, semiconductor lasers must be biased to a current level near laser threshold. Some LEDs work better with drive circuitry to tailor electrical input. For example, the proper drive waveform can effectively reduce the rise time of an inexpensive LED and allow its use at higher-than-specified bandwidths.

ELECTRONIC PREPROCESSING

The drive circuitry of some transmitters electronically preprocesses the input electrical signals to put them into a form suitable for driving the light sources. A simple example is the conversion of signals from the voltage variations that drive electronic circuitry to the current variations that modulate lasers and LEDs. Other preprocessing may change signal formats to types better suited for fiber transmission, or provide a buffer that holds input data until it is transmitted (necessary in local area networks where data is not sent as fast as it arrives).

OUTPUT SENSING AND STABILIZATION

Laser transmitters typically include output-stabilization circuits. A photodetector monitors light emitted from the rear facet of the laser and drives a feedback circuit that adjusts drive current so total output power remains stable, avoiding age-induced drops in laser output.

TEMPERATURE SENSING AND CONTROL

Operating characteristics of a laser diode, notably threshold current, output power, and wavelength, change with temperature. The threshold current, I_{thresh}, increases roughly exponentially:

$$I_{\text{thresh}}(T) = I_0 \exp\left(\frac{T}{T_0}\right)$$

where I_0 is a constant and T_0 is a characteristic temperature of the particular material. The characteristic temperature for InGaAsP is typically 50 to 70 K, much lower than the 120 K or more for GaAs, so threshold currents of InGaAsP lasers increase more rapidly with temperature than GaAs lasers. The higher the threshold current, the lower the overall laser efficiency, so the more power is used in the laser. Unless drive current is increased to compensate for the rising threshold, laser output power will decline as temperature increases. Higher temperatures also tend to decrease laser lifetime.

The change in wavelength is more subtle, arising from a change in the refractive index of the semiconductor with temperature. This change in refractive index alters the effective length of the laser cavity (the length of the laser times the refractive index) and, thus, the resonant wavelength. Thus as temperature changes, laser wavelength tends to drift.

The extent of cooling required depends on the system; heat sinks often suffice. Thermoelectric coolers can keep high-performance transmitters at a stable temperature, reducing temperature-induced changes in output power. Stable output is important for proper receiver operation. As detected power decreases, the signal-to-noise ratio decreases in analog systems and the bit error rate increases in digital systems. Wavelength drift generally is not a problem in systems operating at a single wavelength but could cause serious problems

Characteristics of a semiconductor laser change with temperature.

in wavelength-division multiplexing by shifting one laser to a wavelength where another is supposed to be operating.

Attenuators

Transmitters are made to produce standard power levels, but in some cases those levels may be higher than desired. This is most likely in networks that have legs of much different lengths or that contain many more fiber junctions than others. Because receivers can handle only limited input powers, attenuators are sometimes used to reduce transmitter output to safe levels for the receiver. Note, however, that they are comparatively rare; they may also be used at the receiver.

External Modulators

An external modulator imposes a signal on a steady light beam passing through it. You can think of it as turning the laser beam off and on, chopping the beam into a series of pulses that carry the signal. What it really does is to rely on some complicated optical physics to vary the amount of light it transmits at the laser wavelength. In other words, it switches between transparent and opaque modes, sometimes blocking the beam and sometimes transmitting it. You will learn more about modulators in Chapter 16.

External modulators work very fast. They can operate at well over 10 Gbit/s, switching a signal off or on more than 10 billion times a second. That's faster than standard diode lasers. Letting the laser generate a steady beam also avoids the problem of wavelength chirp I mentioned before, reducing the effect of dispersion on signals transmitted long distances. Think of external modulators as high-end devices, used in high-performance systems but not where simple direct modulation will suffice.

Types of Transmitters

The block diagrams may look similar, but fiber-optic transmitters can differ greatly in detail, depending on performance requirements, particularly data rate, power level, and (for analog systems) noise level. First I will look at major differences among transmitters, and then I will look more closely at some factors that cause these differences, such as modulation format.

Transmitters differ in modulation scheme and speed.

Functional Differences

Most major functional differences are in the modulation scheme and speed. Analog modulation is typically for audio, video, or radar signals. Audio signals require bandwidths measured in tens of kilohertz at most, whereas each standard analog (NTSC) video signal requires 6 MHz. Much higher bandwidths are needed for multichannel cable television systems or for transmitting radar signals.

Digital transmitter circuits must have fast response to produce fast rise-time digital pulses. Again, the speed depends on the application. Some simple computer data links may require no more than tens of thousands of bits per second, but long-haul telephone systems now operate at 2.5 or 10 Gbit/s on each wavelength channel.

The choice of light source depends mainly upon transmission speed, type of signal, and operating distance. In rough order of increasing performance, both for speed and distance, choices are red LEDs, infrared LEDs, GaAs lasers, 1.3-μm lasers, and 1.55-μm lasers. The light source should have linear response for analog transmission, but linearity is not critical in digital systems.

Important differences lie in the transmitter electronics. Suitable circuitry can increase the effective speed of transmitters, for example. Logic circuits can change digitally encoded signals from one format to another. Drive circuits can compensate for nonlinearities in light source analog response.

The design of transmitter and receiver circuitry is a specialized realm of electronics, which I will not explore deeply because this book is concentrating on optics. Sophisticated transmitters and receivers are typically manufactured and sold to users, who see them as complete, functional black boxes, or as fiber-optic links that mate on each end with electronic devices and are linked by a fiber-optic cable.

Intensity Modulation

Most fiber-optic transmitters send optical signals in a form called *intensity modulation.* Simply put, the signal is proportional to the intensity of the light sent down the fiber, as in Figure 10.1. Intensity modulation works for both analog and digital transmission. It is implemented simply by converting the input electrical signal to a drive current applied to a diode laser or external modulator.

Most fiber-optic transmitters use intensity modulation.

Multiplexing

Multiplexing is the combination of multiple signals into a single signal for transmission. Various techniques can be used, but all serve the same fundamental purpose. They are implemented in different ways for fiber-optic transmission.

Signals can be combined by time-division, frequency-division, or wavelength-division multiplexing.

- **Time-division multiplexing** combines two or more digital signals, essentially by interleaving the bits from separate data streams to give one higher-speed signal, as shown in Figure 10.6. For example, 24 voice phone lines, digitized at 56,000 bit/s, can be combined into one 1.5-Mbit/s digital signal, which carries all the bits from all the digitized voice signals, plus extra data needed to organize and route the signals. There are standard hierarchies of digital transmission rates, each one feeding to the next level. Normally, time-division multiplexing is done before signals get to the transmitter, but sometimes the circuits are packaged together. A demultiplexer sorts them out on the other end of the receiver.

FIGURE 10.6

Time-division multiplexing.

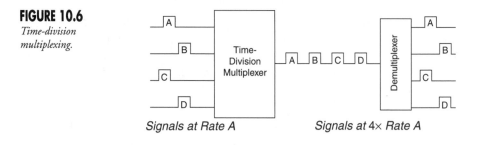

● **Frequency-division multiplexing** combines two or more analog signals by using them to modulate different frequency signals in a broad-bandwidth analog signal. Broadcast radio stations do this; each one is assigned a discrete frequency, which it modulates with its own signal. Your radio receiver can pick up the whole spectrum of stations, but you tune it to select only one. An analog cable-television system does the same thing when it assigns television stations to cable "channels" which it transmits in different frequency slots. Each channel has a specific bandwidth; 6 MHz in American analog video systems. Then the modulated channels are combined to generate a composite signal covering the whole range of frequencies carried by the cable system. As with time-division multiplexing, frequency-division multiplexing is normally done before a signal reaches the transmitter. A demultiplexer may sort the channels out at the other end of the receiver, or the receiver may be tuned to pick up only one channel at a time, like your radio.

● **Wavelength-division multiplexing** is similar in concept to frequency-division multiplexing, but is the most visible from the fiber-optic system standpoint because it involves sending multiple signals at different wavelengths through the same optical fiber. The idea is to send multiple signals through the same fiber by using them to modulate lasers transmitting at different wavelengths. As with different radio frequencies broadcast through the air, the different wavelengths in a WDM system normally do not interfere with each other. In fact, if you start from fundamental engineering principles, you could consider wavelength-division multiplexing as just another example of frequency-division multiplexing, because different wavelengths have different frequencies. However, you'd only confuse yourself, because frequency-division multiplexing has a distinct meaning in practice.

Although all multiplexing ultimately serves the same purpose, wavelength-division multiplexing is an optical technology rather than an electronic one, which makes it our problem because our topic is fiber optics. Time- and frequency-division multiplexing are done to signals before they're fed into optical transmitters; wavelength-division multiplexing is done optically. You need optics to combine and split the signals; you can use optics to separate one wavelength from the rest and route it to a different location. WDM technology isn't easy, and it requires expensive, high-performance transmitters. However, it is spreading rapidly because it can pay tremendous dividends where that high performance is necessary.

Soliton Transmission

Certain optical transmitters can generate special pulses called *solitons,* which retain their shapes as they travel through optical fibers. Technically speaking, a soliton is a special solution of a complex equation for wave propagation, the sort of thing that normally belongs to esoteric theory. However, solitons have a special property that makes them attractive for fiber-optic transmission: they conserve their shapes, although their intensity drops because of attenuation.

Solitons are pulses that retain their shapes as they pass through optical fibers.

Solitons work because two effects occur in optical fibers that serve to offset each other. One is the pulse dispersion you learned about earlier, which causes pulses containing a range of wavelengths to spread out as they travel along a fiber. The other is called *self-phase modulation,* which spreads the pulse out over a range of wavelengths. The two balance each other out, so once the pulse comes to equilibrium in the fiber, it retains its shape. Attenuation does weaken the pulse, but optical amplifiers can restore its strength. The self-restoring nature of solitons makes them attractive for high-speed transmission over tremendous distances.

Coherent Transmission

Over the years, there has been extensive work on another approach called coherent or heterodyne transmission. The form shown in Figure 10.7 operates like a heterodyne radio system and requires two lasers, one at the transmitter and a second (a local oscillator) at the receiver. The two lasers transmit at slightly different frequencies, v_1 and v_2. At the receiver, the two beams are mixed together to obtain the difference frequency, $v_1 - v_2$, in the microwave region. That microwave signal—at about 1 GHz in many experiments—is amplified and demodulated to give the desired signal.

Why go through all that trouble? Because coherent receivers can pick out weaker signals from a noisy background than conventional direct-detection receivers, just as in radio sets. The idea is elegant and some experiments have been encouraging, but other systems are now far ahead in performance.

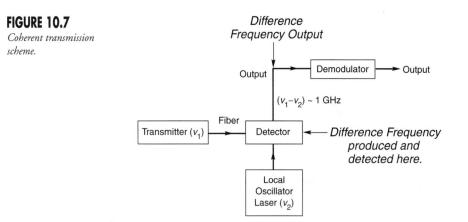

FIGURE 10.7

Coherent transmission scheme.

Sample Transmitters

Although I won't go into detail on transmitter design, it is useful to have a general idea of what is inside the black boxes you're likely to encounter. The best way to get a feeling for the internal workings of transmitters is to look at some simple circuits. As you would expect, the complexity of transmitters increases rapidly with their performance level, but the basic concepts remain the same.

An LED or laser emits light when it is forward biased at a voltage higher than the band-gap voltage, about 1.5 V for GaAlAs LEDs emitting at 800–900 nm and around 1 V for 1300 and 1550-nm InGaAsp lasers. As with other forward-biased semiconductor diodes, you can consider the voltage drop across the diode constant regardless of current. To modulate the light output, you modulate the drive current, not the voltage.

●

Modulation of a voltage fed into a transistor causes current passing through the LED—and its light output—to vary.

A very simple drive circuit for an LED is shown in Figure 10.8. A modulated voltage is fed into the base of a transistor, causing variations in the current passing through the LED and current-limiting resistor. The LED can be on either side of the transistor, but the transistor or some other circuit element must be there to modulate the current. The resistor is needed to limit LED current. The auxiliary drive circuitry (not shown) becomes increasingly complex in more sophisticated transmitters as it is called upon to perform more functions (e.g., converting digital signal encoding format). However, the basic idea remains the same.

Simple commercial transmitters come in simple packages, such as the one shown in Figure 10.9, along with a block diagram of the circuit. Note that the transmitter includes a buffer to hold input data until it can be transmitted. The whole package is about 2 in. (5 cm) long, including an integral ST-type connector.

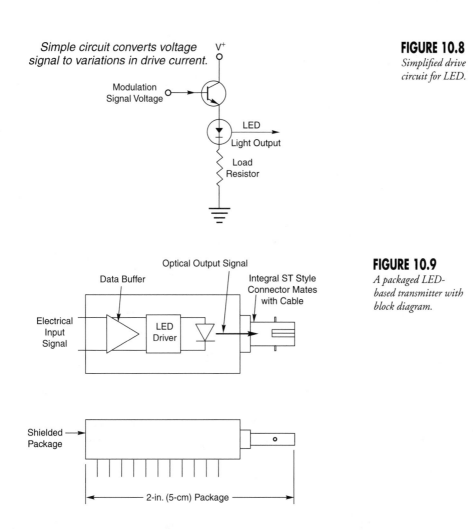

Simple circuit converts voltage signal to variations in drive current.

FIGURE 10.8
Simplified drive circuit for LED.

FIGURE 10.9
A packaged LED-based transmitter with block diagram.

Laser Transmitters

The electrical characteristics of a semiconductor laser are similar to those of an LED because both are semiconductor diodes. However, the laser does not emit much light until drive current passes a threshold value well above zero. Also, because lasers need much higher drive currents than LEDs, their current-limiting resistors are usually smaller.

Laser diodes are often packaged in modules like the 14-pin dual-in-line package shown in Figure 10.10. The package includes only components that must be physically mounted in the same case as the laser diode. One is a thermoelectric cooler, needed to maintain stable operating temperature. Another is a thermistor, which monitors temperature inside

Laser drive circuits must deliver higher currents than those for LEDs.

the case. Also included is a photodiode, which detects light from the rear facet of the laser to monitor power levels. Pins on the package carry signals to the rest of the transmitter circuitry.

FIGURE 10.10

Laser diode packaged for mounting on a transmitter board.

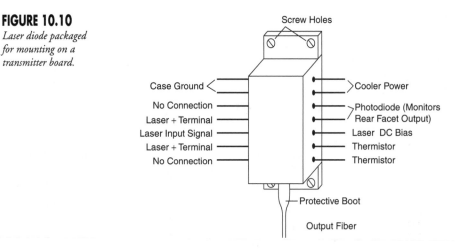

The circuit in Figure 10.11 is an example of the type used in laser transmitters. The drive signal is applied as a voltage to the base of a transistor, so it modulates the drive current through the laser diode. The detector packaged with the laser monitors output, providing feedback to an amplifier (at right), which adjusts the bias applied to the laser diode, thus controlling average power level. The circuitry can get considerably more complex. Simple circuits can be used to drive lasers that emit continuous beams that are modulated externally.

Typically, the drive circuit prebiases the laser with a current close to, but still below, the threshold. The modulated drive signal raises it above the threshold. This approach enhances speed by avoiding the delay needed to raise drive current above the threshold. At high speeds, it may be useful to bias the laser so that it emits a little light in the off state but a much higher power when turned on. One concern with prebiasing is that the small amount of light emitted in the off state could confuse the receiver if transmission losses are too low. However, careful design can minimize the cost in receiver sensitivity.

Transmitter and receiver can be packaged in parallel as a transceiver.

Transceivers, Repeaters, and Regenerators

Transmitters may be packed with other equipment for some applications. A transceiver is a package that includes both transmitter and receiver, which send and receive signals to and from a single attached source, like a computer terminal. Normally, the signals are sent

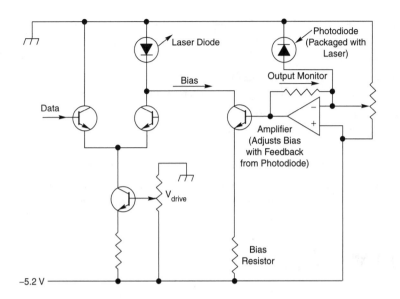

FIGURE 10.11
Laser diode drive circuitry. (Adapted with permission from a figure by Paul Shumate, Bellcore)

over one fiber and received over a second fiber. Circuitry for the transmitter and receiver are separate, as are the electrical signal input and output. In fact, in most cases the transceiver is simply a way to package a separate transmitter and receiver when two-directional transmission is required.

In Chapter 12, I will talk about how transmitters can be packaged in series with receivers to serve as repeaters and regenerators.

What Have You Learned?

1. Both digital and analog transmitters rely on direct amplitude modulation of light intensity. Changes in drive current change the light output of LEDs and semiconductor lasers.

2. The most common light sources for short fiber-optic systems are GaAlAs LEDs operating at 820 or 850 nm. Red LEDs are used with plastic fibers. Laser sources are used at high speeds and long distances.

3. Performance of a fiber-optic transmitter is affected by signal type, speed, operating wavelength, and light source.

4. Bandwidth is capacity of an analog transmitter. Data rate is capacity of a digital transmitter. Both depend on transmitter response time.

5. Wavelength-division multiplexing sends multiple signals through the same fiber at different wavelengths near 1.55 µm. Dense WDM packs closely spaced wavelengths through the same fiber.

6. Time-division multiplexing and frequency-division multiplexing are done electronically on signals *before* they reach the fiber-optic transmitter.

7. A transmitter includes housing, drive circuitry, monitoring electronics, and a light source. It may include temperature stabilization circuits, attenuators, and external modulators.

8. Common optical interfaces are connectors and fiber pigtails.

9. Modulation of a voltage fed into a transistor causes variations in current passing through an LED or laser diode—and in its light output. Lasers require higher drive currents than LEDs.

What's Next?

Now that I have discussed fiber-optic transmitters, Chapter 11 will examine the other end of the system, the receiver, and Chapter 12 will describe the roles of repeaters, regenerators, and optical amplifiers.

Quiz for Chapter 10

1. Digital transmission capacity is measured as
    a. bandwidth in megahertz.
    b. rise time in microseconds.
    c. frequency of 3-dB point.
    d. number of bits transmitted per second.

2. Analog transmission capacity is measured as
    a. bandwidth in megahertz.
    b. rise time in microseconds.
    c. frequency of 3-dB point.
    d. number of bits transmitted per second.

3. If the rise time of a transmitter is 1 nanosecond, what is its theoretical bandwidth?
    a. 1 Gbit/s.
    b. 100 MHz.
    c. 350 MHz.
    d. 350 kHz.
    e. None of the above.

4. Which of the following is not found in fiber-optic transmitters?
    a. Electronic drive circuitry.
    b. Helium-neon gas laser.
    c. Photodiode to sense laser output.
    d. Temperature sensor.

5. Which of the following is not a standard optical interface with transmitters?

    a. An integral fiber-optic connector.

    b. An output window.

    c. A fiber-optic pigtail.

6. What provides feedback to help stabilize laser intensity in a transmitter?

    a. A signal relayed from the receiver.

    b. Changes in input impedance.

    c. Output from the rear face of the laser monitored by a photodiode.

    d. Light scattered from the optical interface with the output fiber.

    e. No feedback is used.

7. What is the usual modulation method for fiber-optic transmitters?

    a. Intensity modulation.

    b. Frequency modulation.

    c. Wavelength modulation.

    d. Voltage modulation.

8. What does time-division multiplexing do?

    a. Transmits different signals at different wavelengths.

    b. Shifts the frequencies of several analog signals to combine them into a single output.

    c. Encrypts signals for secure transmission.

    d. Interleaves several digital signals into a single stream of bits.

9. To allow a margin for safety, you decide to separate the eight wavelengths in a WDM system by twice the standard spacing set by the International Telecommunications Union. The longest wavelength is 1570 nm. What is the shortest wavelength? (*Hint:* You should use the exact speed of light, 299,792,458 m/s, if you want to convert frequency to wavelength precisely.)

    a. 1550.02 nm.

    b. 1556.95 nm.

    c. 1558.57 nm.

    d. 1564.27 nm.

    e. 1581.60 nm.

10. What is the total data rate of a WDM system carrying 2.5-Gbit/s signals at 1550, 1552, 1554, 1556, 1558, 1560, 1562, and 1564 nm?

    a. 2.5 Gbit/s.

    b. 10 Gbit/s.

    c. 12.5 Gbit/s.

    d. 20 Gbit/s.

    e. 40 Gbit/s.

11. With wavelength-division multiplexing, how many fibers do you need for two-way transmission of 2.5-Gbit/s signals at 1550, 1552, 1554, 1556, 1558, 1560, 1562, and 1564 nm?

    a. One.

    b. Two.

    c. Four.

d. Eight.

e. 16.

12. Which of the following is an example of time-division multiplexing?

a. Combining 4 2.5-Gbit/s signals into one 10-Gbit/s signal.

b. Transmitting 4 2.5-Gbit/s signals at different wavelengths through the same fiber.

c. Transmitting 70 analog video signals on a cable-television network.

d. Digitizing a single-voice telephone signal to 56 kbit/s.

e. Converting an analog video signal to digital HDTV format.

Receivers

About This Chapter

The receiver is as essential an element of any fiber-optic system as the optical fiber or the light source. The receiver's job is to convert the optical signal transmitted through the fiber into electronic form, which can serve as input for other devices or communication systems, including repeaters.

This chapter discusses the basic types of receivers, important performance considerations, and how they work. It focuses particularly on the types of detectors and to a lesser extent on the electronics.

Basic Elements of Receivers

Fiber-optic receivers detect light signals and convert them into electrical form. They come in many varieties, from simple types that are little more than packaged photodetectors to sophisticated systems that do considerable processing to extract a signal. The simple ones essentially plug onto the end of a fiber, but more complex receivers may be integrated with optical amplifiers and wavelength-division demultiplexers. Not all receivers have all the pieces described here.

Note that I define a receiver as a device that converts light signals into electronic form. By this definition, optical amplifiers and optical demultiplexers are *not* considered parts of a receiver. However, as shown in Figure 11.1, they may sit between the end of the fiber and the receiver. An optical amplifier (sometimes called a preamplifier) can be placed in front of the receiver to increase strength of the optical signal. This amplification can improve the bit error rate or signal-to-noise ratio of the receiver as well as compensate for any losses in wavelength-division demultiplexing. An optical amplifier can increase the strength of all wavelengths in a WDM signal, so it should precede the demultiplexing stage.

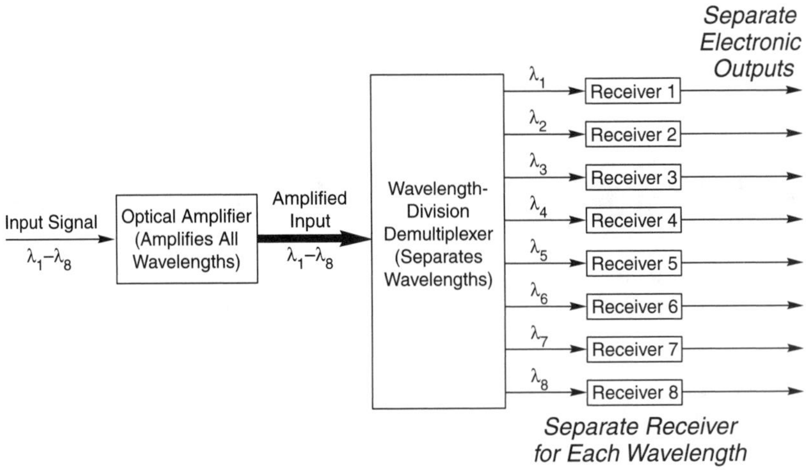

FIGURE 11.1

Splitting a WDM signal among separate receivers for each wavelength.

Separate Electronic Outputs

Input Signal λ_1–λ_8 → Optical Amplifier (Amplifies All Wavelengths) → Amplified Input λ_1–λ_8 → Wavelength-Division Demultiplexer (Separates Wavelengths)

λ_1 → Receiver 1
λ_2 → Receiver 2
λ_3 → Receiver 3
λ_4 → Receiver 4
λ_5 → Receiver 5
λ_6 → Receiver 6
λ_7 → Receiver 7
λ_8 → Receiver 8

Separate Receiver for Each Wavelength

If the fiber carries multiple wavelengths, they must be separated (demultiplexed) before the optical signals are converted to electronic form. You need optics to separate the wavelengths; photodetectors can't tell the difference between signals at 1550 and 1552 nm, so they add the two and generate a garbled signal. As shown in Figure 11.1, each wavelength from the wavelength-division demultiplexer goes to a separate receiver, which decodes the optical signal to produce its own electrical output.

The block diagram of Figure 11.2 shows the basic functional elements of digital and analog receivers:

1. The photodetector or detector (to convert the received optical signal into electrical form).

2. Amplification stages (to amplify the signal and convert it into a form ready for processing).

3. Demodulation or decision circuits (to reproduce the original electronic signal).

In practice, the functional distinctions can be hazy, because some detectors (e.g., avalanche photodiodes) have internal amplification. Some receivers do not have separate demodulation or decision circuits because the electrical signal from the amplification stages is good enough for use by other electronic equipment. The entire receiver is packaged in a housing designed to meet user requirements, which provides interfaces with the optical fiber and with whatever is to receive the signal.

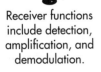

Receiver functions include detection, amplification, and demodulation.

The similarities between analog and digital receivers are striking. The initial stages are the same in the two types of receivers; the differences come where the signal is converted into final form for output to other equipment. Why is there an analog receiver at the front end of a digital receiver? Because the real world is analog. The signal reaching the detector may start in digital form, but by the time it reaches the receiver it varies continuously in level like an analog signal. It must be converted to electrical form and amplified as an analog signal before electronic decision circuits can convert it back to digital form.

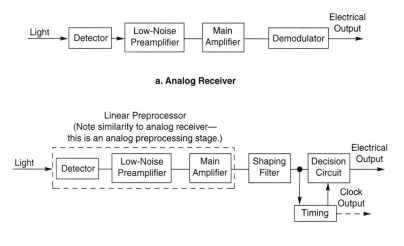

a. Analog Receiver

b. Digital Receiver

FIGURE 11.2

Basic elements of analog and digital receivers.

Then why bother with digital transmission and receivers? Because analog transmission requires precise replication of the original waveform. Any changes are distortion. Once distortion is added, the electronics don't know what is distortion and what is signal. Digital transmission, on the other hand, does not require precise replication of the waveform. Instead, it requires only the ability to decide whether the signal is off or on, which can be done even in the presence of distortion (although severe distortion can lead to bit-interpreting errors).

● Analog and digital receivers use similar detectors and amplifiers; the differences are in the demodulation or decision circuits.

Detector Basics

The detectors used in fiber-optic communications are semiconductor photodiodes or photodetectors, which get their name from their ability to detect light. The simplest semiconductor detectors are solar cells, where incident light energy raises electrons from the valence band to the conduction band, generating an electric voltage. Unfortunately, such photovoltaic detectors are slow and insensitive.

Photodiodes are much faster and more sensitive if electrically reverse-biased, as shown in Figure 11.3. (This is the opposite of LEDs and lasers, which are forward-biased to emit light.) The reverse bias draws current-carrying electrons and holes out of the junction region, creating a depleted region, which stops current from passing through the diode. Light of a suitable wavelength can create electron-hole pairs in this region by raising an electron from the valence band to the conduction band, leaving a hole behind. The bias voltage causes these current carriers to drift quickly away from the junction region, so a

● Semiconductor photodiodes are reverse-biased to detect light; they produce a current proportional to the illumination level.

current flows proportional to the light illuminating the detector. Several types of detectors can be used in fiber-optic systems, as described below.

FIGURE 11.3

Photodetector operation.

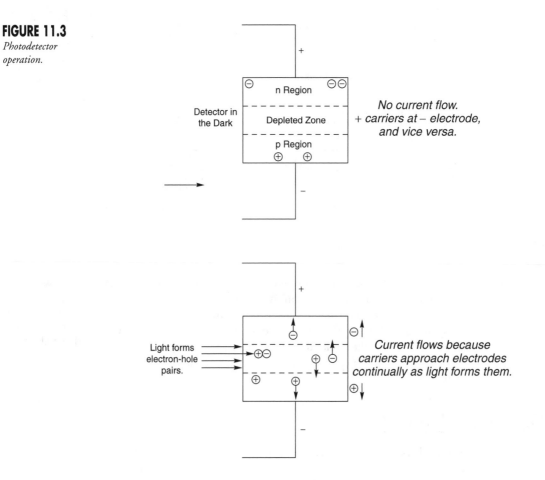

Photodetectors can be made of silicon, gallium arsenide, germanium, indium phosphide, or other semiconductors. The wavelengths to which they respond depend on their composition. To produce a photocurrent, photons must have enough energy to raise an electron across the band gap from the valence band to the conduction band. This gives most photodetectors a fairly sharp cut-off at long wavelengths; the sensitivity of silicon, for example, drops sharply between 1000 and 1100 nm. Other effects, such as absorption in other parts of the device, cause response to drop more gradually at shorter wavelengths. The approximate operating ranges for the most important detector materials are shown in Table 11.1.

Wavelength sensitivity of photodetectors depends on the materials from which they are made.

Table 11.1 Detector operating ranges.

Material	Wavelength (nm)
Silicon	400–1100
Germanium	800–1600
GaAs	400–1000
InGaAs	400–1700
InGaAsP	1100–1600 (doping dependent)

Some detectors can be integrated with electronic circuits. Silicon, germanium, and GaAs are usable both as detectors and in electronic circuits. Detectors can also be combined with electronic components in hybrid circuits. I'll look at the details later.

Performance Considerations

The factors influencing receiver performance are complex and often interrelated. At first glance, they might seem to be sensitivity, speed, and cost. In practice, these factors often depend on other factors, including operating wavelength, choice of fiber and transmitter, dark current, noise-equivalent power, and nature of transmission coding. They depend upon both the response of the detector itself and the processing performed by the electronics. Let's look at the most important receiver parameters.

Sensitivity

Sensitivity measures response to a signal as a function of its intensity. Although sensitivity sounds like a simple concept, it is actually a conceptual umbrella covering how detectors and receivers respond to signal intensity. To help you understand the nature of the problem, let's look briefly at how a receiver handles a weak signal.

SIGNAL QUALITY

The role of a receiver is to accurately reproduce the signal it receives through an optical fiber. Two fundamental characteristics affect how well this can be done: signal strength and the noise level, which tends to obscure or degrade the signal. For analog systems, the signal-to-noise (S/N) ratio (the signal power divided by noise power, normally expressed in decibels) measures quality. The higher the signal-to-noise ratio, the better the received signal. High noise, like scratches on an old-fashioned phonograph record, can overwhelm the signal. The practical definition of a good S/N ratio depends on the application. In many fiber-optic systems, 40–50 dB is considered good to excellent, but S/N ratios in the 30 dB range are acceptable for some applications.

Sensitivity measures how well a receiver responds to a signal as a function of its intensity.

Signal strength and noise affect how well a receiver can reproduce a signal.

In digital systems, where the received information is either 1 or 0, quality is measured as the probability of incorrect transmission, the bit error rate. That tells how accurately the receiver can tell 0s from 1s, which in turn depends on factors such as received power, sensitivity, noise, and transmission speed. For a given receiver, the dependence on received power is striking, as shown in Figure 11.4. In certain ranges, a 5-dB decrease in received power can make the error rate soar from 10^{-12} to 10^{-3}. The bit error rate also depends on data rate; the slower the data rate, the lower the error rate. A common goal for telecommunications is a maximum bit error rate of 10^{-9}, or one error per billion bits, but even lower rates (10^{-12}) are needed for computer data transmission.

FIGURE 11.4

Bit error rate as a function of power. (Courtesy of AMP Inc.)

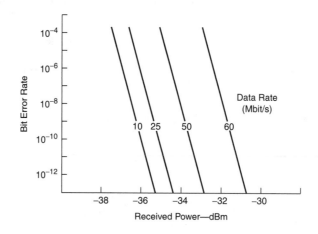

Signal-to-noise ratio and bit error rate are introduced here because they become important at the receiver. However, they really measure overall system performance. Receiver performance enters the picture because of the importance of sensitivity, but overall performance also depends on transmitter output and losses in transmission. The effect on overall system design will be described later.

WAVELENGTH

Sensitivity of a receiver depends on the wavelength of light reaching the detector.

Receiver sensitivity generally refers only to how well a receiver responds to a signal of a given amplitude—not to its time response or bandwidth. The sensitivity depends on the detector itself and the circuits in the receiver that amplify and process the electrical signal from the detector. The detector parameters themselves depend on wavelength of the light and operating conditions.

DETECTOR MATERIALS

The main factor controlling how receivers respond at different wavelengths is the composition of the detector. As you saw earlier, each type of semiconductor responds to a distinct range of wavelengths. They generally are most efficient at certain wavelengths but respond less efficiently at the edges of their ranges, as shown in Figure 11.5. Silicon responds best at wavelengths shorter than about 1 μm, whereas germanium, InGaAs, and InGaAsP respond better at longer wavelengths. Control of device structure and composition can fine-tune response curves, making devices more sensitive at certain wavelengths, but the overall response is inherent in the material.

Note different curves for different materials.

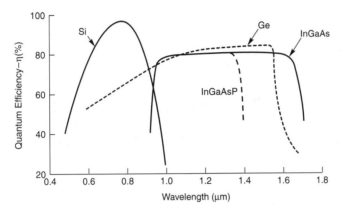

FIGURE 11.5

Typical wavelength response of photodiodes. (Courtesy of Tran V. Muoi)

RESPONSIVITY AND QUANTUM EFFICIENCY

One measure of photodetector sensitivity is responsivity, the ratio of electrical output from the detector to the input optical power. Most fiber-optic detectors generate signals as current, so this is normally measured as amperes per watt (A/W). (Because input optical powers are in the microwatt range, responsivity might be more properly given as microamperes per microwatt [μA/μW] and sometimes is, but the two measurements are equivalent.) If electrical output signals are voltages, response can be measured in volts per watt (V/W).

● Responsivity is the ratio of a detector's electrical output to the input optical power.

A closely related quantity for detectors is quantum efficiency. This measures the fraction of incoming photons that generate electrons in the output signal:

$$\text{Quantum efficiency} = \frac{\text{Electrons}}{\text{Photons}}$$

● Quantum efficiency is the fraction of incoming photons that generate electrons.

This and responsivity both depend on wavelength, as can be seen in the plots of quantum efficiency in Figure 11.5. Like responsivity, quantum efficiency depends on the detector material and structure. Shape of a quantum efficiency curve differs from that of a responsivity curve, because photon energy changes with wavelength. A 400-nm photon carries twice as much energy as an 800-nm photon, so only half as many 400-nm photons are needed to generate a given power.

Quantum efficiency cannot be larger than 1.0 by that formal definition for a simple detector. However, values larger than 1.0 are possible if quantum efficiency is defined as the ratio of output electrons to incoming photons. That can be greater than 1.0 in detectors (or receivers) with internal amplification, which can generate multiple electrons from a single electron generated by light at the p/n junction.

AMPLIFICATION

A final factor that enters into sensitivity is internal amplification of electrons within certain detectors, such as phototransistors or avalanche photodiodes. This amplification of current flow can multiply receiver responsivity. However, amplification is indiscriminate; it multiplies noise as well as signal and can add some of its own noise. I'll explain more about these devices later in this chapter.

Dark Current and Noise-Equivalent Power

Detector output includes noise as well as signal.

The electrical signal emerging from a detector includes noise as well as signal. Some noise comes with the input optical signal (optical noise), and some is generated within the detector. Other noise is added by the amplifier. Electromagnetic interference causes noise when stray electromagnetic fields induce currents in conductors in the receiver. Noise mechanisms are complex enough to be a field in themselves, and the details are beyond the scope of this book. However, it is important to understand two key concepts: dark current and noise-equivalent power.

Dark current is the noise current a detector produces when it is not illuminated.

Any detector will produce some current when it is operated in the normal manner but not exposed to light (i.e., kept in the dark). This dark current measures inherent electrical noise within the detector, which will also be present when the detector is exposed to light. It sets a floor on the minimum detectable signal, because for a signal to be detected it must produce measurably more current than the dark current. Dark current depends on operating temperature, bias voltage, and the type of detector.

Noise-equivalent power is optical power needed to generate output current equal to root-mean-square noise.

Noise-equivalent power (NEP) is the input power needed to generate an electrical current equal to the root-mean-square noise of the detector (or receiver). This is a more direct measurement of the minimum detectable signal because it compares noise level directly to optical power. NEP depends on frequency of the modulated signal, the bandwidth over which noise was measured, area of the detector, and operating temperature. Its units are the peculiar ones of watts divided by the square root of frequency (in hertz) or $W/Hz^{1/2}$. Specified values are normally measured with a 1-kHz modulation frequency and a 1 Hz bandwidth.

Operating Wavelength and Materials

As you saw earlier, the sensitivity of a detector—and hence of the entire receiver—depends strongly on wavelength, because of differences among materials. Individual photodiodes are often designed to work best in part of the material's range. For fiber optics, silicon may be optimized for either the red region, where plastic fibers transmit best, or the 800–900-nm region of GaAlAs emitters. Germanium, InGaAs, and InGaAsP are typically designed for use at 1300 to 1600 nm, although they may be optimized for one wavelength. The spectral response of InGaAs and InGaAsP depends on the fractions of indium, gallium, arsenide, and phosphorous they contain, which affects their band gaps and other properties, as in diode lasers.

Photodetector sensitivity also depends on temperature. The effect is not pronounced at the wavelengths used in present fiber-optic systems, but detector sensitivity at wavelengths much longer than 2 or 3 μm is generally improved by cooling.

The choice of material affects more than the wavelengths that can be detected. Electrical characteristics, such as speed and dark current, also differ among materials. Germanium detectors tend to be noisier and slower than those made of silicon or the III-V materials such as GaAs and InGaAs, and InGaAs is often preferred for use at 1300 and 1550 nm.

> Each photodiode material has a unique response as a function of wavelength.

Speed and Bandwidth

Detectors take finite times to respond to changes in input. That is, there is a delay between when light hits a detector and when the detector produces an electrical current. The delay depends on the material and the device design.

> Detectors do not respond instantly to changes in input.

A second internal speed limit affects fiber-optic systems more directly: the time it takes the electrical output signal to rise from low to high levels and the corresponding fall time. The rise time is normally defined as the time the output signal takes to rise from 10% to 90% of the final level after the input is turned on abruptly. Analogously, fall time is how long the output takes to drop from 90% to 10% after the input is turned off. Device geometry, material composition, electrical bias, and other factors all combine to determine rise and fall times, which may not be equal. Generally the longer of these two quantities is considered the device response time. (The fall times of some detectors are much slower than their rise times.)

Although internal delay does not directly affect bandwidth or bit rate of a fiber-optic receiver, the rise and fall times do. Propagation delays shift the signal in time, but rise and fall times spread it out. A 10-ns delay, for example, means that a 10-ns pulse arrives at the output 10 ns late, but it is still only 10 ns long. However, a 10-ns response time doubles the pulse length to 20 ns, in effect halving the maximum bit rate.

> Rise and fall times limit receiver bandwidth and bit rate.

The speed of a detector also can be defined as a bandwidth, or the maximum modulation frequency of an optical signal it can process properly. Detector bandwidth typically is defined as the frequency where response has dropped 3 dB below the response at a low frequency. In essence, this is the point where the detector output cannot change as fast as the input light is changing. If rise and fall times are equal, it is roughly equal to

$$\text{Bandwidth}_{3\text{-dB}} = \frac{0.35}{\text{rise time}}$$

Thus our detector with 10-ns rise time has a 3-dB bandwidth of 35 MHz. Conversely, you can flip the formula to calculate the detector rise time needed for a certain bandwidth:

$$\text{Rise time} = \frac{0.35}{\text{bandwidth}_{3\text{-dB}}}$$

Thus for a 5-GHz bandwidth, you need detector rise time of 70 ps.

For relatively slow devices, response time is proportional to the RC time constant—the photodiode capacitance multiplied by the sum of the load resistance and the diode series resistance. Speed can be increased by reducing equivalent capacitance. As speeds increase, two other factors can limit response time: diffusion of current carriers in the photodiode and time needed for carriers to cross the depletion region.

There are wide differences among detector response times. The slowest are photodarlingtons, with response times measured in microseconds. With avalanche photodiodes and fast *pin* photodiodes, response time can be well under a nanosecond. (The fastest commercial detectors have response times in the 5-ps range.) I'll get into these characteristics when I examine the different types of detectors.

Signal Coding, Analog and Digital Modulation

Signal format also affects performance of a fiber-optic receiver. The simplest type is straightforward analog intensity modulation. In this case, it is the job of the receiver to reconstruct the transmitted waveform with as little distortion as possible. Accuracy of the reproduced waveform depends on intensity of the received signal, linearity and speed of the receiver, and noise levels in the input signal and the receiver.

Coding format is important for digital signals.

The detection of digital signals is strongly influenced by the coding scheme. Bit rates in digital fiber-optic systems are so much slower than the frequency of the light waves that digital modulation schemes can be considered as being superimposed on a steady optical carrier. The modulation is strictly binary; the light is either off or on. (However, in some high-speed systems, off may actually be a very low-level light signal when a laser light source is prebiased.)

The two most common ways of optically encoding this kind of modulation are shown in Figure 11.6. One is return-to-zero (RZ) coding, where the signal level returns to a nominal zero level between bits. The other is no-return-to-zero (NRZ) coding, in which the signal does not return to zero but remains at one if two successive 1 bits are transmitted. The two differ in their effective speed, because RZ signals have twice as many pulses. Each modulation scheme has its own advantages.

Device Geometry

As mentioned earlier, detector geometry can influence detector speed and sensitivity. You should also be aware of another geometrical factor: detector active area.

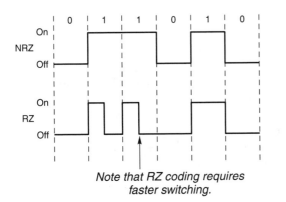

FIGURE 11.6

Signal levels for digital coding.

Note that RZ coding requires faster switching.

For a detector to operate efficiently, all light emerging from the fiber should fall onto its light-sensitive (active) area. This means that the detector's active area should be larger than the fiber core (how much larger depends on how light is transferred to the detector). If the output fiber has core diameter d and half-acceptance angle θ and is a distance S from the detector, then it will project onto the detector a spot with diameter D:

$$D = d + 2S \tan \theta$$

If that spot size is larger than the active area of the detector, some light is lost and sensitivity is reduced.

Most detectors have active areas larger than fiber cores, so normally little light misses them. However, losses can occur if the fiber is far from the detector, if the fiber core is large, or if the fiber end and detector are misaligned.

On the other hand, detector speed is limited by its area—the larger the device, the longer it takes to respond. For simple *pin* detectors, bandwidth decreases with increasing device width, according to

$$\text{Bandwidth} = \frac{\text{Constant}}{\text{device width}}$$

The fastest detectors have active areas only a little wider than the core of a single-mode fiber.

Dynamic Range

Another concern in detectors and receivers is dynamic range—the range of input power over which they produce the desired output. At first glance, it might seem that the higher the input power, the better the response would be. However, that isn't the case, because any detector or receiver responds linearly to light input over only a limited range. Once input power exceeds the upper limit of that range, signals are distorted, leading to high noise in analog systems and errors in digital transmission.

All light emerging from a fiber should fall onto a detector's light-sensitive area.

Input signals must be within a detector's dynamic range to avoid distortion.

The basic problem can be seen in Figure 11.7, which shows detector output as a function of input light power. In the lower part of the curve, the response is linear. An increase in input power by an amount Δp produces an increase in output current Δi, where $\Delta i / \Delta p$ is the slope of that part of the curve. Typically, the response is nearly linear at low levels, although noise overwhelms the signal at the lowest powers. However, if the input power is too high, the detector or receiver response saturates and output power falls short of the expected level. The result is distortion, much as when an audio speaker is driven with more power than it can handle. Exceeding the dynamic range in a digital receiver can likewise increase the bit-error rate. In either case, inserting attenuators can reduce average signal intensity to a level within the device's dynamic range.

FIGURE 11.7

Receiver output as a function of input light power. Both the detector and the receiver electronics affect dynamic range.

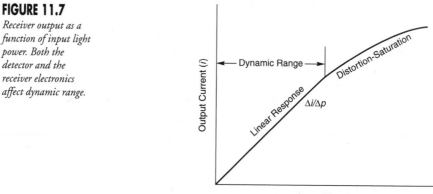

The dynamic ranges of receivers vary widely, with those intended for short-distance communication often having the widest ranges because they may be used with different lengths of fiber. Some receivers used in long-distance systems have much more limited dynamic ranges and may be limited to input powers below 100 μW. However, some receivers include automatic gain-control circuits to prevent high input signals from overloading the output. Important limits on dynamic range come from the receiver circuitry; as load resistance rises, nonlinear response begins to occur at lower input powers.

Detector Types

The detectors used in fiber-optic receivers are more complex than the simple photodiodes described earlier in this chapter. More sensitive detectors, with higher current outputs, are normally used. Some provide enough output current to serve as receivers by themselves (when packaged), whereas others require external electronics to amplify and process electrical signals. The same basic structures can be used in any semiconductor, but in practice the lowest-cost types (phototransistors and photodarlingtons) are used only in silicon detectors for short, low-speed data links.

pn and *pin* Photodiodes

You saw earlier that fiber-optic photodiodes are reverse-biased so the electrical signal is a current passing through the diode. Such a detector is said to be operating in the photoconductive mode because it produces signals by changing its effective resistance. However, it is not strictly a resistive device, because it includes a semiconductor junction, forming a *pn* photodiode. (True "photoconductive" detectors exist, in which light produces current carriers that increase the conductivity of a bulk semiconductor that lacks a junction layer, but they are not used in fiber-optic systems.)

Reverse biasing draws current carriers out of the central depleted region, blocking current flow unless light frees electrons and holes to carry current. The amount of current increases with the amount of light absorbed, and the light absorption increases with the thickness of the depleted region. Depletion need not rely entirely on the bias voltage. The same effect can be obtained if a lightly doped or undoped intrinsic semiconductor region is between the *p*- and *n*-doped regions shown in Figure 11.8. In a sense, such *pin* (*p*-intrinsic-*n*) photodiodes come predepleted because the intrinsic region lacks the impurities that can generate current carriers in the dark. This design has other practical advantages. By concentrating absorption in the intrinsic region, it avoids the noise and slow response that occur when the p region of ordinary *pn* photodiodes absorbs some light. The bias voltage is concentrated across the intrinsic semiconducting region because it has higher resistivity than the rest of the device, helping raise speed and reduce noise.

> Photodiode sensitivity is improved by sandwiching an undoped intrinsic region between the *p* and *n* regions.

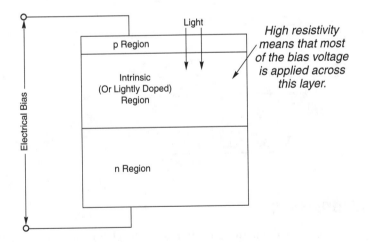

FIGURE 11.8
A simple pin *photodiode.*

The speed of *pin* photodiodes is limited by variations in the time it takes electrons to pass through the device. This time spread can be reduced in two ways—by increasing the bias voltage and/or by decreasing the thickness (and width) of the intrinsic layer. Reducing intrinsic layer thickness must be traded off against detector sensitivity because *pin detectors can have response times well under 1 ns and dynamic ranges of 50 dB.*

this reduces the fraction of the incident light absorbed. Typical biases are 5–20 V, although some devices have specified maximum bias above 100 V. Typical response times range from a few nanoseconds to about 5 ps. Sensitivity of silicon *pin* detectors is about 0.7 A/W at 800 nm; InGaAs is somewhat more sensitive at longer wavelengths. An important attraction of *pin* photodiodes is a large dynamic range; their output-current characteristics can be linear over 50 dB.

pin photodiodes are widely used because of their high speed and good sensitivity.

The speed and sensitivity of *pin* photodiodes are more than adequate for most fiber-optic applications, and they are widely used even in high-performance systems. Sending their electrical output directly to an electronic preamplifier can boost sensitivity.

The designs of actual *pin* photodiodes are more complex than this simple example, particularly in fast devices, like the multigigahertz detector in Figure 11.9. Light signals at 1200 to 1600 nm pass through the antireflection coating and upper layer of InP (which are transparent at those wavelengths) and are absorbed in the intrinsic InGaAs layer. Other designs direct light through the InP substrate, which is also transparent to the signal wavelengths.

FIGURE 11.9
Structure of a multigigahertz pin *detector.* (Copyright 1993 Hewlett-Packard Company. Reproduced with permission.)

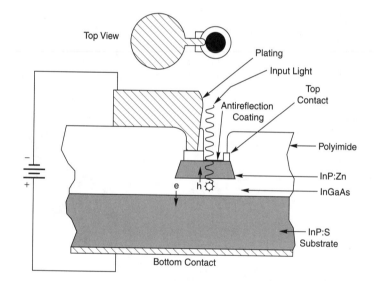

Phototransistors

Phototransistors both sense light and amplify light-generated current; they are used only in low-cost, low-speed systems.

The simplest detector with internal amplification is the phototransistor. Those familiar with transistors can view it as a transistor in which light generates the base current. An alternative is to see a phototransistor as a *pn* photodiode within a transistor. In practice, light normally reaches the base through or around the emitter, which has a wide band gap so it is transparent to the wavelengths detected. Most commercial phototransistors are made of silicon; their most common uses are in inexpensive sensors, but the same devices can be adapted for low-cost, low-speed fiber-optic systems.

The photocurrent generated in the base-emitter junction is amplified, like base current in a conventional transistor, giving much higher responsivity than a simple photodiode. However, this increase comes at a steep price in response time and linearity and at some cost in noise. You can see this by looking at Table 11.2, which compares several photodetectors. In practice, phototransistors are limited to systems operating below the megahertz range.

Table 11.2 Typical detector characteristics.

Device	Responsivity	Rise Time	Dark Current
Phototransistor (Si)	18 A/W	2.5 µs	25 nA
Photodarlington (Si)	500 A/W	40 µs	100 nA
pin photodiode (Si)	0.5 A/W	0.1–5 ns	10 nA
pin photodiode (InGaAs)	0.8 A/W	0.005–5 ns	0.1–3 nA
Avalanche photodiode (Ge)	0.6 A/W	0.3–1 ns	400 nA
Avalanche photodiode (InGaAs)	0.75 A/W	0.3 ns	30 nA
Si *pin*-FET (detector-amp)	15,000 V/W	10 ns	NA (output is V)
InGaAs *pin*-FET (detector-amp)	5,000 V/W	1–10 ns	NA (output is V)

Photodarlingtons

The photodarlington is a simple integrated darlington amplifier in which the emitter output of a phototransistor is fed to the base of a second transistor for amplification. Adding the second transistor increases responsivity but lowers speed and increases noise. Thus, the photodarlington's uses are even more narrowly constrained than the phototransistor's, but it offers higher responsivity for low-cost, slow-speed applications.

Avalanche Photodiodes

A different approach to providing internal amplification within a detector is the avalanche photodiode (APD). It relies on avalanche multiplication, in which a strong electric field accelerates current carriers so much that they can knock valence electrons out of the semiconductor lattice. The result at high enough bias voltage is a veritable avalanche of carriers—thus the name.

The avalanche photodiode gets high sensitivity from internal multiplication of light-generated electrons.

Multiplication factors—the degree to which an initial electron is multiplied—typically range from 30 to about 100. The multiplication factor M is

$$M = \frac{1}{1 - (V/V_B)^n}$$

where V is the operating voltage, V_B is the voltage at which the diode would break down electrically, and n is a number between 3 and 6 dependent on device characteristics. Care must be taken in operation because exceeding the breakdown voltage could fatally damage the device. A representative plot of this characteristic as bias voltage approaches breakdown is shown in Figure 11.10. (Note that to reach multiplication factors of 100, bias must approach within a few percent of breakdown.) Breakdown voltages normally are well over 100 V and in some devices can range up to a few hundred volts.

FIGURE 11.10

Increase of multiplication factor in APD.

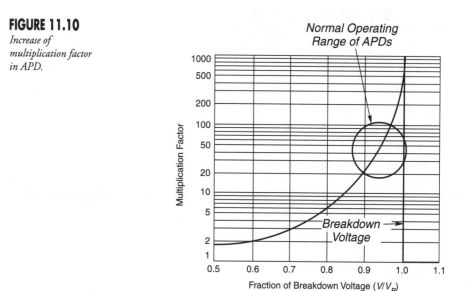

APDs are fast, but the uneven nature of multiplication introduces noise. Avalanche gain is an average; not all photons are multiplied by the same factor. Signal power increases roughly with the square of the multiplication factor M; for moderate values of M, it increases faster than noise. However, as M increases to high levels, noise increases faster than the square of M (approximately as $M^{2.1}$). As a result, avalanche photodiodes have an optimum multiplication value, typically between 30 and 100.

The biases used for avalanche photodiodes are much higher than the few volts normally used in semiconductor electronics. The need for special circuits to provide this drive voltage, and to compensate for the temperature sensitivity of APD characteristics, makes APD receivers more complex than *pin* types and has limited their applications.

pin-FET and Integrated Receivers

A *pin* photodiode can be integrated with an amplifier.

As mentioned earlier, external electronics can amplify the electrical signal from a photodetector. Some receivers integrate the functions of detector and amplifier (or preamplifier) in a single hybrid or integrated circuit that serves as a detector-(pre)amplifier. These devices are called integrated detector-amplifiers, detector-amplifiers, or *pin*-FETs (the last because the preamplifier uses field-effect transistor, or FET, circuitry).

Figure 11.11 shows the type of circuit used in a hybrid receiver with *pin* photodiode and low-noise FET preamplifier. This circuit amplifies the electrical signal before it encounters the noise associated with the load resistor, increasing S/N ratio and output power. The amplifier circuit also converts the current signal from the photodiode into a voltage signal, as used by most electronic devices. The voltage level depends on the circuitry. Often, the circuit includes automatic gain control so the voltage level will be compatible with later amplification stages. However, some *pin*-FET circuits do not limit gain; their responsivity can vary widely, but a typical value is around 10,000 V/W.

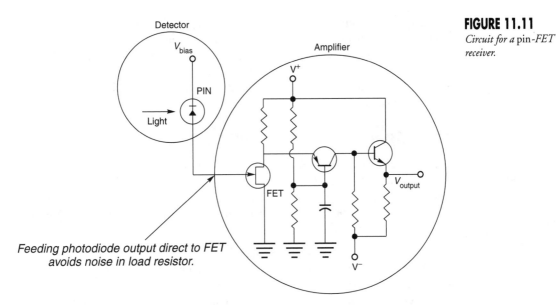

FIGURE 11.11

Circuit for a pin-*FET receiver.*

Integrated detector-preamplifiers have become popular for many moderate-speed fiber-optic applications because of their simplicity and reasonable cost. Unlike avalanche photodiodes, they do not require voltages above the 5-V levels normally needed by semiconductor electronics. Their rise times tend to be slower than the fastest discrete *pin* photodiodes or avalanche photodiodes, but they are adequate for transmitting hundreds of megabits per second.

● Integrated detector-preamplifiers are used in many moderate-speed applications.

Electronic Functions

Converting an optical signal into electrical form is only the first part of a receiver's job. The raw electrical signal generally requires some further processing before it can serve as input to a terminal device at the receiver end. Typically, photodiode signals are weak currents that require amplification and conversion to voltage. In addition, they may require such cleaning up as squaring off digital pulses, regenerating clock signals for digital transmission, or filtering out noise introduced in transmission. The major electronic functions are as follows:

1. Preamplification
2. Amplification
3. Equalization
4. Filtering
5. Discrimination
6. Timing

If you're familiar with audio or other electronics, you will recognize some of these functions. Not all are required in every receiver, and even some of those included may not be performed by separate, identifiable devices. A phototransistor, for example, both detects and amplifies. And many moderate-performance digital systems don't need special timing circuits. Nonetheless, each of these functions may appear on block diagrams. Their operation is described briefly below.

Preamplification and Amplification

Typical optical signals reaching a fiber-optic receiver are 1–10 μW and sometimes lower. If a *pin* photodiode with 0.6 to 0.8 A/W responsivity detects such signals, its output current is in the microampere range and must be amplified for most uses. In addition, most electronics require input signals as voltage, not current. Thus, detector output must be amplified and converted.

Receivers may include one or more amplification stages. Often the first is called preamplification because it is a special low-noise amplifier designed for weak input. (An optical amplifier placed in front of a detector also may be called a preamplifier.) In some cases, as mentioned earlier, the preamplifier may be packaged with the detector. The preamplifier output often goes into an amplifier, much as the output of a tape-deck preamplifier goes to a stereo amplifier that can produce the power needed to drive speakers.

Equalization

Detection and amplification can distort the received signal. For example, high and low frequencies may not be amplified by the same factor. The equalization circuit evens out these differences, so the amplified signal is closer to the original. Much the same is done in analog high-fidelity equipment, where standard equalization circuits process signals from tape heads and phonograph cartridges so they more accurately represent the original music.

Filtering

Filtering helps increase the S/N ratio by selectively attenuating noise. This can be important when noise is at particular frequencies (e.g., a high-frequency hiss on analog audio tapes). It is most likely to be used in fiber optics to remove undesired frequencies close to the desired signal, such as harmonics.

Filtering blocks noise while transmitting the signal.

Discrimination

So far, the functions you've looked at are needed to regenerate the original waveform for both analog and digital receivers. However, a further stage is needed to turn a received analog signal back into a series of digital pulses—decoding and discrimination. Rectangular pulses that started with sharp turn-on and turn-off edges have been degraded into unboxy humps, as shown in Figure 11.12. Dispersion may have blurred the boundaries between pulses.

Discrimination circuits generate digital pulses from an analog input.

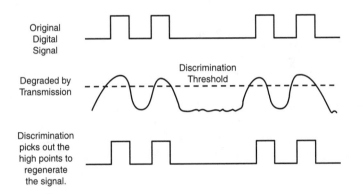

FIGURE 11.12
Discrimination cleans up noise to regenerate digital pulses.

From a theoretical standpoint, this rounding of square pulses represents loss of high frequencies in the signal. Mathematically, a square-wave pulse is the sum of many sine waves of different frequency, the first with frequency equal to the square-wave frequency and others with frequencies that are integral multiples (harmonics) of the square-wave frequency. The highest frequencies (the highest-order harmonics) make up the sharp rising and falling edges of the pulse, so if they are lost, the pulses lose their square edges.

The remaining low-frequency components contain most of the information needed, but they are not clean enough to serve as input to other electronic devices. Regeneration of clean pulses requires circuitry that decides whether or not the input is in the on or off state by comparing it to an intermediate threshold level. The decision circuit generates an "on" pulse if the power is above the threshold; otherwise it produces an "off" signal. Care must be taken in selecting this threshold level to avoid misinterpreting input; too low a threshold, for example, could turn noise spikes in the off state into signal pulses.

Pulse regeneration requires circuitry to decide if the input is on or off.

Timing

Another essential task in many receivers, particularly in high-performance systems, is resynchronizing the signal. Digital signals are generated at a characteristic clock rate, such as once every nanosecond for a 1-Gbit/s data stream. If you look carefully at Figure 11.12, you can see that discrimination circuits do not necessarily spot the precise times the pulses started and ended. These random errors, called *jitter,* can cause the signal to drift from the clock rate, introducing errors.

Timing synchronization recreates the clock signal and puts the regenerated pulses in the right time slots. It is an essential part of cleaning up signals at a sophisticated receiver.

Packaging Considerations

As with transmitters, packaging is important for receivers. The basic requirements are electronic, mechanical, and optical interfaces that are simple and easy to use. The main mechanical issues are mounts. Electronic interfaces must allow for input of bias voltage and amplifier power (where needed) and for output of signals in the required format. Details can vary significantly.

Optical interface requirements are simpler than for transmitters because mechanical tolerances for aligning fibers with detectors generally are looser. The active areas of detectors are larger than the cores of single-mode fibers. Larger-core multimode fibers transmit signals at slower speeds, so they normally are used only with slower detectors with larger active areas. In practice, receivers are assembled with integral fiber pigtails or connectors which collect light from the input fiber and deliver it to the detector.

In general, packaged receivers look very much like transmitters, and packaged detectors look like light sources. You may have to read the labels to tell them apart. Detector modules are packaged inside receivers just as light-source modules are put inside transmitters. Internal design constraints become increasingly severe at high frequencies because of the problems inherent in high-frequency electronic transmission.

Sample Receiver Circuits

Details of receiver circuitry vary widely with the type of detector used and with the purpose of the receiver. For purposes of this book, I will cover only a few simple circuits for important devices and avoid detailed circuit diagrams.

Photoconductive Photodiodes

The typical *pin* or *pn* photodiode used in a fiber-optic receiver is used in a circuit with a reverse-bias voltage applied across the photodiode and a series load resistor, such as that shown in Figure 11.13. In this mode, the photodiode is photoconductive because the photocurrent flowing is proportional to the nominal resistance of the illuminated photodiode. This simple circuit converts the current signal from a photodiode to a voltage signal.

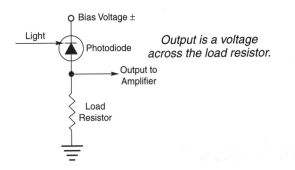

FIGURE 11.13

Basic circuit for photoconductive pin *or* pn *photodiode.*

The division of the bias voltage between the photodiode and the fixed resistor depends on illumination level. The higher the illumination of the photodiode, the more current it will conduct and, thus, the larger the voltage drop across the load resistor. In the simple circuit shown, the signal voltage is the drop across the load resistor. Most circuits are more complex, with amplification stages beyond the load resistor, as in *pin*-FET and detector-preamplifier circuits. Figure 11.14 is an example that includes automatic gain control to increase dynamic range.

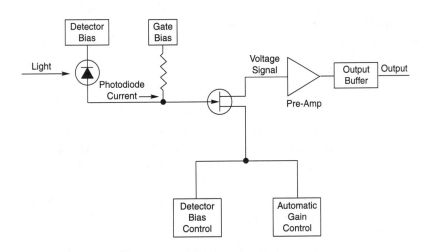

FIGURE 11.14

Block diagram of pin-*FET receiver circuit.*

Avalanche Photodiode Circuits

The circuits used for avalanche photodiodes are conceptually similar to those used for photoconductive *pin* photodiodes. However, because of the high bias voltages required and the sensitivity of the photodiode to bias voltage, care must be taken to assure stable bias voltage. This adds to circuit complexity, as shown in the block diagram of Figure 11.15.

FIGURE 11.15

Basic receiver circuit for avalanche photodiode.

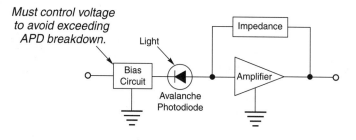

What Have You Learned?

1. Basic elements of a receiver are the detector, amplification stages, and demodulation or decision circuits. Optical amplifiers and wavelength-division demultiplexers come before the receiver.

2. Many fiber-optic detectors are reverse-biased semiconductor photodiodes. Light striking the depleted region near the junction generates free electrons and holes, so a current flows through the diode; this current is the signal. Simple circuits can convert the current signal into a voltage needed for electronic processing.

3. Other fiber-optic detectors use avalanche photodiodes, with an internal amplification stage that requires high bias voltage.

4. Different detectors are needed for different wavelengths. Silicon is used at 600 to 1000 nm. Germanium can be used at 1300 nm, and InGaAs is usable between 1200 and 1600 nm.

5. Phototransistors and photodarlingtons have internal amplification that gives them high responsivity, but they are too slow for most fiber-optic applications.

6. Detectors operate best over a limited dynamic range. At higher powers, they distort received signals, whereas at lower powers the signal can be lost in the noise. Automatic gain control can extend the dynamic range of *pin*-FET detectors.

7. *pin* photodiodes are often packaged with FET preamplifiers in *pin*-FETs that are common fiber-optic detectors. That packaging avoids load-resistor noise but slows response time.

8. The input stages of analog and digital receivers are similar because by the time the signals reach the receivers they are weak and rounded. The difference in those receivers is in the electronic processing after amplification.

9. Digital receivers include a discrimination stage to regenerate digital pulses from analog waveforms. They may also include retiming circuits.

What's Next?

In Chapter 12, I move on to optical amplifiers and to electro-optic repeaters and regenerators, which combine transmitters and receivers.

Quiz for Chapter 11

1. What is the main difference between an analog and a digital receiver?

   a. Special amplification circuitry.

   b. The presence of decision circuitry to distinguish between on and off signal levels.

   c. The two are completely different.

   d. Digital receivers are free from distortion.

2. Photodiodes used as fiber-optic detectors normally are

   a. reverse-biased.

   b. thermoelectrically cooled.

   c. forward-biased.

   d. unbiased to generate a voltage like a solar cell.

3. What bit-error rate is most often specified for digital telecommunication systems?

   a. 40 dB.

   b. 10^{-4}.

   c. 10^{-6}.

   d. 10^{-9}.

   e. 10^{-15}.

4. Silicon detectors are usable at wavelengths of

   a. 800–900 nm.

   b. 1300 nm.

   c. 1550 nm.

   d. all the above.

5. The fastest photodetectors have response times of

   a. a microsecond.

   b. hundreds of nanoseconds.

   c. tens of nanoseconds.

   d. a few nanoseconds.

   e. around 5 ps.

6. A *pin* photodiode is

   a. a point-contact diode detector.

   b. a detector with an undoped intrinsic region between *p* and *n* materials.

   c. a circuit element used in receiver amplification.

   d. a photovoltaic detector.

7. Match the characteristics listed below with the type of detector.

   a. *pin* photodiode

   b. avalanche photodiode

   c. *pin*-FET receiver

   d. photodarlington

   e. phototransistor

   A. Response time can be less that 1 ns; responsivity under 1 A/W.

B. Rise time a few microseconds; responsivity about 20 A/W.

C. Rise time about 10 ns; responsivity thousands of volts per watt.

D. Response time 1 ns or less; responsivity tens of amperes per watt.

E. Rise time tens of microseconds; responsivity hundreds of amperes per watt.

8. Which of the following does not include an amplification stage?

a. Photodarlington.

b. Phototransistor.

c. Avalanche photodiode.

d. *pin*-FET.

e. *pin* photodiode.

9. A receiver's bandwidth is limited by

a. dynamic range.

b. rise time.

c. responsivity.

d. quantum efficiency.

e. bias voltage.

10. A discrimination or decision circuit

a. filters out noise in analog receivers.

b. tells "off" from "on" states.

c. decides which pulses to amplify.

d. controls input level to avoid exceeding a receiver's dynamic range.

Repeaters, Regenerators, and Optical Amplifiers

About This Chapter

In the last three chapters, I have talked about the components on the ends of fiber-optic systems: light sources, transmitters, and receivers. However, if you look carefully you will find some components in the middle.

Repeaters, regenerators, and optical amplifiers all serve to stretch transmission distances. Inserted into a fiber system at a point where the original signal is becoming weak, they generate a stronger signal, letting the system operate over much longer distances. Repeaters and regenerators convert the signal into electronic form before amplifying it; optical amplifiers work directly on light.

The Distance Problem

Signals fade away with distance when traveling through any type of cable. The further you go, the fainter they become, until they become too faint to detect reliably. As you saw in the last chapter, when a digital signal fades below a certain level, the bit error rate rises rapidly. Likewise, an analog signal becomes noisy or distorted, like a distant radio station.

Communication systems avoid this problem by amplifying signals. As shown in Figure 12.1, a repeater or amplifier is inserted into the system at a point where the signal has become weak, where it boosts the strength of the signal so it can be transmitted through another length of cable. Many amplifiers or repeaters can be placed in sequence, each one taking a weak signal and generating a strong one. However, care must be taken to install them at a point where the signal has not become too weak, distorted, or corrupted by noise because noise and distortion are also amplified.

FIGURE 12.1
Amplification in a fiber-optic system.

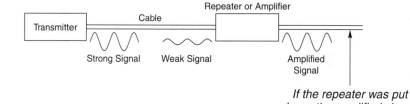

Regenerators clean up signals as well as amplify them.

Regenerators serve a related but distinct function, because they *regenerate* signals, removing noise and distortion. Normally this is only possible in digital systems. The first step is to amplify the weak signal, noise and all. Then the regenerator examines the time-varying signal, deciding which changes in signal strength represent data bits. This is the same function as the discrimination circuit in a receiver, shown in Figure 11.12, and often is performed by similar electronics. Retiming circuits make sure the pulses fall into the right time slots, and don't drift away to be mistaken for a pulse in an earlier or later time slot. The result is a series of clean digital pulses, ready to be transmitted through the next length of cable.

Fibers can transmit high-speed signals much farther than wires before amplification is needed.

Signals need amplification or regeneration if they travel far enough through either metal or fiber-optic cables. However, as you saw earlier, optical fibers attenuate high-speed signals much less than coaxial cables, so they can carry signals much further between amplification stages. Exactly how far depends on the system design, but in general it is many times farther. For example, coaxial cables need repeaters every few thousand feet (roughly 1 km) to carry hundreds of megabits per second, while fiber systems can carry signals at the same speed for 50 to 150 km (30 to 90 mi). It's no wonder telecommunications companies prefer fibers if signals have to go far.

To be fair, it isn't always that simple because of other differences between metal cables and fibers. Optical signals do not divide the same way electrical signals do, so a fiber system in general can drive fewer terminals. Thus, if you're trying to split signals among many terminals that aren't very far away, fiber systems may need more amplification. However, the basic idea remains the same.

Types of Amplification

So far I've been deliberately vague in talking about what goes on in the amplification stage. This is because two different types of amplification are possible—electronic and optical. Electronic amplification came first, in the form of repeaters. They first convert the input signal into electronic form (in a receiver) and then amplify it to drive another optical transmitter. In general, they also clean up, or regenerate, the signal before sending it to the transmitter. You can think of an electro-optic repeater as a receiver and transmitter placed back to back, so the receiver output drives the transmitter, as shown in Figure 12.2(a). Their function is very similar to the electronic repeaters used in copper cable and radio-frequency communication systems.

Electro-optic repeaters must convert an optical signal into electronic form for amplification. Optical amplifiers directly amplify the optical signal.

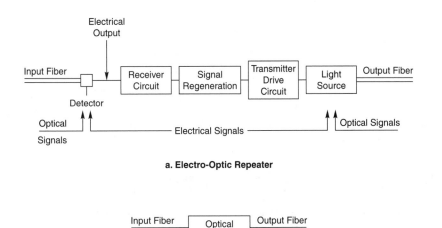

a. Electro-Optic Repeater

b. Optical Amplifier

FIGURE 12.2
Electro-optic and optical amplifiers.

In contrast, an optical amplifier takes a weak optical input and amplifies it to generate a strong optical output signal, as shown in Figure 12.2(b). It never converts the signal into electronic form at all. (The wires attached to an optical amplifier provide it with electrical power.) Present optical amplifiers do not regenerate signals; they merely increase their amplitude, noise and all.

Optical amplifiers are simple both in concept and in practice. They contain far fewer components than electro-optic repeaters and generally are far more reliable. They also offer two important operational advantages over electro-optic repeaters. A single optical amplifier can simultaneously amplify many wavelength-division multiplexed signals carried in the same fiber, without causing them to interfere with each other; because receivers cannot discriminate between closely spaced wavelengths, WDM signals must be

Optical amplifiers are simpler than electro-optic repeaters, but they cannot clean up signals.

demultiplexed and amplified separately by electro-optic repeaters. Optical amplifiers also are not sensitive to signal format; if you change signal speeds, you must replace electro-optic repeaters (which are designed for particular frequencies or data rates), but you can use the same optical amplifier.

A major operational disadvantage of present optical amplifiers is that they cannot regenerate input signals. This means they cannot clean up noise or compensate for dispersion that has accumulated during fiber transmission. However, optical amplifier spacing can be limited to reduce noise, and as you learned earlier, other means can be taken to compensate for fiber dispersion.

There are two types of optical amplifiers, doped fiber amplifiers and semiconductor amplifiers, which you learned about in Chapter 9. Both work on the principle of stimulated emission that is basic to the laser, but in optical amplifiers the light being amplified comes from an outside source and makes a single pass through the medium, which lacks the mirrors present in lasers. The two families of optical amplifiers have quite distinct characteristics, so I will describe them separately in this chapter.

Over the past few years, optical amplifiers have largely replaced electro-optic repeaters in new telecommunication systems. The most widely used are erbium-doped fiber amplifiers, but other types remain in development and have some limited application. First, however, we should look at the applications for amplifiers and then learn about electro-optic repeaters and regenerators, because they still have some applications and many remain in service.

Requirements for Amplification

Optical amplification is needed in-line, after transmitters, before receivers, and after lossy components.

Optical signals may require amplification at different points in communication systems. Figure 12.3 shows some places where optical amplifiers may be used. Repeaters and regenerators can serve some of these functions, as noted:

- **Postamplifiers** are placed immediately after a transmitter to increase strength of a signal being sent through a length of fiber. It might seem easier just to crank up the transmitter output, but that can degrade the quality of the output signal. External amplification of a lower-power transmitter output gives a cleaner signal. Postamplifiers also can generate powerful signals that can be split among many separate outputs.

- **In-line amplifiers** compensate for signal attenuation in long stretches of fiber. This is the traditional role of electro-optic repeaters, which also serve the function of regenerating the input signal. The goal is to amplify a weak signal sufficiently to send it through the next segment of fiber. These generally are required in long telecommunication systems but may be used in some networks where many branching points reduce transmitted power.

- **Preamplifiers** amplify a weak optical signal just before it enters a receiver, in effect increasing the sensitivity of the receiver and stretching transmission distances.

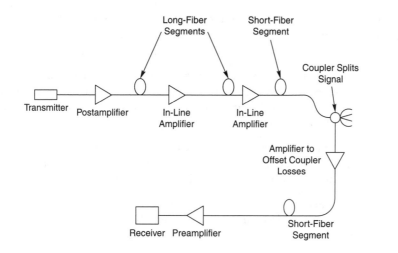

FIGURE 12.3
Roles for optical amplifiers.

● **Offsetting component losses** that otherwise would reduce signals to unacceptably low levels is done mainly with couplers that split signals among multiple outputs. Optical couplers must physically divide the signal among different terminals, which reduces the signal strength arriving at each one. For example, splitting a signal in half reduces each output to a level 3 dB below the input. Dividing a signal among 20 terminals reduces signal strength by 13 dB—assuming every output gets exactly $\frac{1}{20}$ of the input. Placing an optical amplifier after the lossy component can raise the signal strength to compensate for the loss.

Electro-Optic Repeaters and Regenerators

You saw earlier that electro-optic repeaters and regenerators are essentially a receiver and transmitter placed back to back and packaged in a single unit. The input end performs the usual receiver functions; the output end performs standard transmitter functions. If necessary, the receiver electronics can regenerate the signal. Essentially they join two separate fiber-optic systems together end to end, and virtually their only use was for in-line amplification at a point where the signal became too weak to transmit further.

Few new repeaters are being installed in telecommunications systems because optical amplifiers better meet most system requirements. Today, they are used only where the signal must be regenerated before it can be transmitted further, to compensate for noise or dispersion that has accumulated through several amplification stages. This situation is rare in practice. Submarine cables are engineered to avoid electro-optic repeaters and regenerators. On land, most "long-haul" systems connect large urban

●
Electro-optic repeaters consist of a receiver and transmitter back to back.

centers or concentration points but do not cross whole continents. Most such systems do not go through enough optical amplification stages for the signals to require regeneration. Instead, receivers at the ends of the cables regenerate signals.

The nodes in some types of local-area networks have an architecture similar to electro-optic repeaters, because they convert optical signals into electronic form and then drive one or more transmitters with that signal. However, their function is different, and they are covered briefly in Chapter 25.

Because they contain sensitive electronics, repeaters and regenerators must be housed in controlled conditions, usually in buildings. The few that have been installed elsewhere require sealed cases for environmental control.

I won't go through the details of repeater and regenerator operation, because they are covered under transmitters and repeaters in Chapters 10 and 11. However, a few points deserve special emphasis:

- Repeaters and regenerators are designed to operate at a specific transmission speed and format. They may contain timing circuits that generate clock signals at a specific rate, and their electronics may be optimized to operate at that rate. Circuits made to operate at 45 Mbit/s may contain components too slow to operate at 150 Mbit/s or 400 Mbit/s. Likewise, circuits may require specific signals. In short, repeaters and regenerators are not "transparent" to signal format.

- Regeneration can be useful in long systems where noise and pulse dispersion can accumulate to obscure the signal. Pulse dispersion is the more important problem in many cases, but dispersion compensation and careful design allow the use of optical amplifiers.

- True regeneration is usually limited to digital systems, where the digital structure of pulses makes it possible to discriminate between signals and noise. As long as the pulses can be recognized as pulses, the regenerator can produce new ones with the same timing and signal information. However, receivers have no way to remove noise from analog signals, so repeaters merely amplify it and pass it along. (Because they generate a new signal, repeaters can control the accumulation of pulse dispersion that can limit transmission bandwidth of a long analog system.)

Erbium-Doped Fiber Amplifiers

Erbium-doped fiber amplifiers are the most widely used optical amplifiers.

The most widely used optical amplifiers are erbium-doped fiber amplifiers (EDFAs). You have already learned about the basic concept of their operation as a light source in Chapter 9. They operate at wavelengths from 1520 to 1630 nm, although the longer part of that range is not well developed. Their success has led to interest in other types of fiber amplifiers for use at other wavelengths, which at this writing are not as well developed.

Function

Erbium-doped fiber amplifiers can simultaneously amplify weak light signals at wavelengths across their entire operating range. As you will see shortly, this range varies with amplifier design, but this capability is crucial for wavelength-division multiplexing. Fiber amplifiers respond very rapidly to variations in strength of the input signal, so they can amplify signals over a wide range of modulation speeds, although the response is not unlimited.

Fiber amplifiers are used to boost signal strength wherever necessary. In addition to being in the middle of a system, fiber amplifiers may follow the transmitter and wavelength-division multiplexer to boost output into the fiber system, or they may precede the receiver as a preamplifier.

Gain and Power Levels

There are three basic optical performance figures to watch for: input power requirement, gain, and output power delivered. Each of these have some nuances.

- **Input power** must be above a minimum value and below a maximum. The minimum is important to provide a strong-enough signal to amplify, because the fiber amplifier also boosts the strength of background noise. If the input signal is too low, it may be overwhelmed by noise, particularly after a few amplification cycles. On the other hand, excess input power can lead to saturation effects, which cause their own distortion, such as when you turn up an audio amplifier to deliver more power than your speaker can handle.

> Input power, gain, and output power are key performance parameters for fiber amplifiers.

- **Gain** measures the amplification in decibels. The higher the gain, the fewer amplifiers you need but the more risk you run of noise problems. Gain depends on the input power. At small input levels, you get maximum gain. At higher input levels, the gain can saturate. Saturation means that you have run out of gain or, equivalently, that you can't extract any more light energy from the amplifier. This means that you get less gain, in decibels, when you have a high input signal than when you have a lower input. It doesn't mean that you get less power, although once you reach saturation, you can't increase the output power by adding more input. If you are working with analog signals, hitting saturation means you get distortion. Depending on the design, net small-signal gain can be 10 to more than 40 dB.

> Gain is highest for small input signals; it saturates at high inputs.

- **Output power** is what you get out, measured in mW or dBm. If you're measuring in dBm and dB, it equals input plus gain:

$$P_{out} = P_{in} + \text{gain}$$

Maximum outputs range from 10 dBm to more than 20 dBm and represent the level where saturation occurs.

This all gets more complicated when the fiber amplifier is handling many wavelengths simultaneously. The saturation effects that limit output power occur when the amplifier runs out of excited erbium atoms that can be stimulated to emit light. Individual erbium atoms can be stimulated to emit light at any of the wavelengths within erbium's gain curve; they're not reserved for amplifying particular wavelengths. Thus you can saturate the amplifier by generating 100 mW at one wavelength or by generating 12.5 mW at each of eight wavelengths. Thus the more wavelengths, the less power that is available at each one.

In addition, erbium does not have uniform gain over its entire wavelength range, and the differences vary with power levels. This requires equalization, which we'll talk about later, along with other complications of transmitting multiple wavelengths.

Structure of Fiber Amplifiers

Figure 12.4 schematically shows the structure of a typical fiber amplifier. A weak optical signal enters from the left, passing through an optical isolator, which prevents light scattered within the optical amplifier from heading back down the input fiber and potentially generating noise. The input signal also passes through a filter, which transmits the signal wavelength but blocks the shorter wavelengths of the pump laser. It then enters a coil of doped fiber, typically several meters long. Light from a pump laser operating at 980 or 1480 nm illuminates the doped fiber from the other end, exciting erbium atoms along its length. The signal light then stimulates the excited atoms to emit light at the signal wavelength and in phase with the signal. A coupler at the end of the doped fiber separates the output signal from the pump wavelength. Another optical isolator keeps scattered light from the output fiber from going back into the fiber amplifier.

FIGURE 12.4
A fiber amplifier.

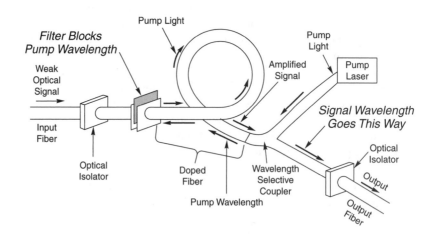

This is a generic diagram, so it doesn't show whether the input signal includes one or many wavelengths. If you ignore the specific mentions of erbium and pump wavelengths in the last paragraph, the description can be made general to all types of fiber amplifiers.

The structure of individual fiber amplifiers depends on the intended applications. Some applications require amplifiers to be spaced relatively closely and have low gain to minimize noise amplified with the signal. Others may require high gain so repeaters can be spaced far apart, thus minimizing their number and reducing costs. These lead to differences in design, such as doping of the fiber, amplifier length, and the arrangement of pump lasers.

Operating Wavelengths

Many lasers emit light at only a narrow range of wavelengths, but erbium-doped fiber amplifiers have a surprisingly wide range. Figure 12.5 gives an indication of this range by plotting the cross section for stimulated emission as a function of wavelengths. This cross section measures the likelihood that a photon of that wavelength can stimulate emission from an excited erbium atom. The cross section depends on the glass "host" as well as the erbium atom; it is highest for a special glass formulation containing tellurium and is somewhat lower for fluoride and silica-based glass. (The silica glass shown has extra aluminum and phosphorous to enhance erbium emission.)

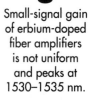

Small-signal gain of erbium-doped fiber amplifiers is not uniform and peaks at 1530–1535 nm.

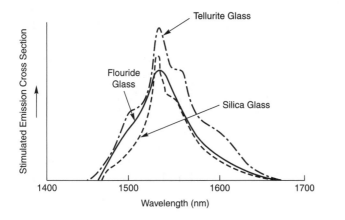

FIGURE 12.5

Stimulated emission cross section for erbium-doped fibers of various compositions.

You can't actually realize amplification across this entire range. Erbium atoms tend to absorb light at the shorter wavelengths, damping the possible amplification. In addition, the amplification process concentrates gain at the wavelengths where the probability of stimulated emission is highest. For relatively short lengths of fiber—a few meters—the gain is highest at 1520 to 1560 nm, as shown in Figure 12.6. This figure shows gain at various wavelengths for different amounts of input power. Recall that the gain is highest for small input signals. As the figure shows, for small inputs, gain varies significantly with wavelength—by more than 10 dB from the peak between 1530 and 1535 nm to the plateau at 1540 to 1560 nm. However, for high inputs, where gain saturates, gain is more uniform across that wavelength range.

FIGURE 12.6

Erbium-fiber amplifier gain versus wavelength at different input powers. (Courtesy of Corning Inc.)

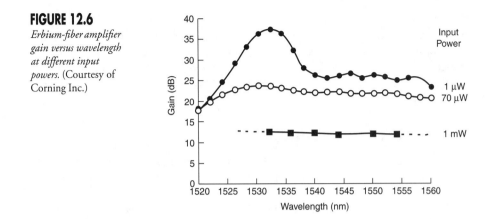

● Long-fiber amplifiers can operate at 1560 to 1620 nm.

Developers recently have started exploring the longer end of the erbium-doped fiber range, from 1560 to 1620 nm. Gain is much lower at those wavelengths, but there still is a net gain—that is, stimulated emission is higher than absorption, so more light at the signal wavelength emerges from the fiber than entered it. Some developers are testing doped tellurite fibers, which have higher gain at the longer wavelength. Others are using much longer lengths of erbium-doped silica fiber, up to several hundred meters. That may seem cumbersome, but laser designers have grown expert at extracting laser light from materials with low gain, and those skills can be adapted to fiber amplifiers.

Using such techniques, developers have doubled the operating range of erbium-doped fiber amplifiers to span wavelengths from 1530 to 1605 nm. These amplifiers have begun to appear on the market, although they are not yet standard. They can be used by themselves, or long-wave band amplifiers can be run in parallel with amplifiers for the shorter erbium band. In that approach, a coupler divides input signals by wavelength, routing the shorter wavelengths to the short-wave amplifier and the longer ones to the long-band amplifier.

Multiwavelength Operation

● Erbium-doped fiber amplifiers can amplify multiple wavelengths in a WDM signal.

Erbium-doped fiber amplifiers were first developed to amplify only a single wavelength near the 1550-nm loss minimum of silica fibers. With the advent of wavelength-division multiplexing, they now amplify multiple wavelengths in that band.

Multiwavelength operation adds some complications to the use of fiber amplifiers. One important requirement is that the various wavelengths should be amplified equally. Differences can accumulate, causing problems if signals at the strongest wavelength exceed the receiver's dynamic range, but those at the weakest wavelength are below the threshold of detection. This requires equalization of gain across the spectrum.

Draft recommendations from the International Telecommunications Union recommend creating a "grid" of possible fiber wavelengths, which are defined in frequency terms. The base of the grid is 193.1 THz (193,100 GHz, or about 1552.52 nm), and the spacing is 100 GHz (about 0.8 nm at 1550 nm). Wavelength channels need not be separated by 100 GHz, but they should be separated by a multiple of that frequency. For example, they could be every 400 GHz or unevenly spaced. Many developers seem sympathetic to this standard, but it is not mandatory, and some new systems use 50 GHz spacing.

Draft recommendations specify WDM channel spacing of 100 GHz, about 0.8 nm.

The downside of even spacing is that it can generate noise from nonlinear four-wave mixing in a fiber amplifier. Four-wave mixing is the combination of three frequencies to generate a fourth:

$$v_1 + v_2 - v_3 = v_4$$

If this happens with signals nicely spaced 100 GHz apart, adding three frequencies can easily generate a fourth. One example is

$$v + (v + 300 \text{ GHz}) - (v - 200 \text{ GHz}) = v + 100 \text{ GHz}$$

This generates a frequency 100 GHz above the base frequency v, which is one of the standard channels. This means that a bit of three other channels are added to this frequency, which becomes noise. The more wavelengths, the more possible combinations that can add up to noise. Nonzero dispersion-shifted fibers can avoid this problem, as you learned earlier, but if you have a different type of fiber installed, you may need to try spacing wavelengths at unequal multiples of 100 GHz, such as 300 and 500.

Equalization

If your fiber amplifier is carrying multiple wavelengths, it needs some kind of equalization scheme to maintain uniform gain at all wavelengths. This generally is done by adding optical filters to reduce the intensity of the wavelengths that are amplified most strongly. These filters often are packaged with the amplifier, so what you see is an amplifier with uniform gain, although the gain in the fiber itself is not uniform.

Equalization is needed to keep gain uniform at multiple wavelengths.

Look back at Figure 12.6, and you can see another equalization issue. The shape of the gain curve changes with power level. If you add filters to filter the gain at one power level, it won't be flat at another. Normally changes in operating power at the amplifier are modest, but new technology will let you switch one or more wavelengths to other places, and this can change the power enough to offset equalization. Special equipment will be needed to keep this from becoming a problem.

Noise

By their nature, fiber amplifiers can't help but amplify any noise that comes along with the input signal. They also generate a certain level of background noise that arises from the nature of the optical amplification process.

Amplified spontaneous emission spreads across the whole operating range of a fiber amplifier.

Remember that optical amplification occurs when the input signal stimulates emission from excited erbium atoms in the fiber. A small fraction of the erbium atoms spontaneously drop from the excited state, releasing their extra energy as light in the form of spontaneous emission. If this is directed along the fiber, it can be amplified, generating noise by *amplified spontaneous emission*.

Amplified spontaneous emission noise is spread across the whole operating range of a fiber amplifier, as shown in Figure 12.7. In contrast, amplified signals appear as spikes against that low-level background. For good performance, the signals should be at least 30 dB higher than the amplifier noise.

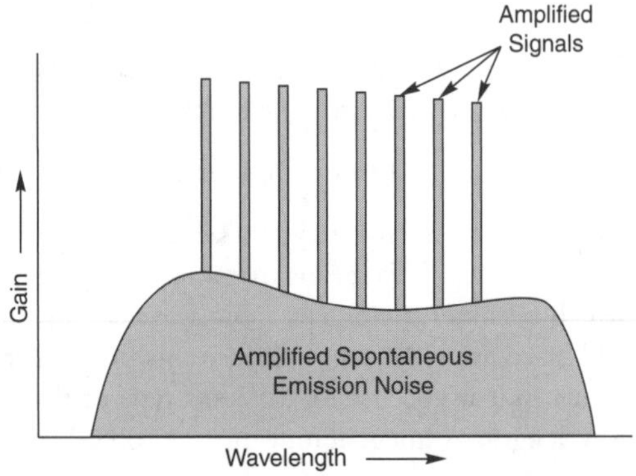

FIGURE 12.7

Amplified spontaneous emission noise in a fiber amplifier.

Other Fiber Amplifiers

Other types of fiber amplifiers are in development.

The success of the erbium-doped fiber amplifier and its compatibility with wavelength-division multiplexing have led the telecommunications industry to shift fiber-optic transmission from 1.3 to 1.55 μm in new systems. However, there's still room for other types of fiber amplifiers. Many existing systems transmit at 1.3 μm, and large amounts of standard single-mode fiber, with zero dispersion at 1.3 μm, have been installed around the world. That creates continuing interest in amplifiers for 1.3 μm. In addition, steady increases in demand for transmission capacity is fueling interest in amplifying more wavelengths in the 1.55-μm window.

The most promising candidate for 1.3 μm remains the praseodymium- (Pr) doped fiber. However, the performance of Pr-doped fiber amplifiers falls short of erbium-doped fiber amplifiers.

Neodymium received strong attention because it has a strong laser line nearby, but it turned out to be a poor match with the 1.31-μm zero-dispersion wavelength of step-index single-mode fibers. Other rare-earth dopants also have been tried, including dysprosium (Dy). So far, none of those technologies has gone beyond the laboratory stage.

Raman Amplification in Fibers

In Chapter 5, you learned about Raman scattering, which can be an undesirable nonlinear effect in a transmitting fiber. In different circumstances, the same physical phenomenon can amplify weak optical signals. It's just a matter of what beam you want.

Stimulated Raman scattering is an undesirable loss mechanism when it steals energy away from the signal wavelength and transfers it to other wavelengths. Suppose, however, that you are transmitting a strong pump beam through the fiber along with a weak signal beam. The strong pump beam excites vibrational modes in atoms in the fiber; the weak signal beam stimulates those excited atoms to emit light at the *signal* wavelength. The result is to amplify the signal wavelength at the cost of the pump beam, which is exactly what you want in a Raman amplifier.

Like an erbium-doped fiber amplifier, a Raman fiber amplifier requires a pump beam. The process of Raman amplification can occur in ordinary silica fibers, so you don't need special doping. However, the pump energy must be considerably higher to get reasonable Raman gain. Even with high power, the Raman gain per unit length is very low, so Raman fiber amplifiers are not attractive as discrete devices. However, you can create Raman amplification in ordinary telecommunications fiber and thus distribute Raman gain along the length of a communication system. This would make the fiber itself the amplification medium. You need enough gain to offset losses in the fiber as well as other losses in the communication system.

Raman gain occurs over a fairly wide bandwidth, so it could amplify multiple wavelengths. It is not limited to as narrow a range of wavelengths, so it can amplify signals at either 1.3 or 1.55 μm, as long as you have a pump source offset by a suitable amount, to about 1.24 or 1.48 μm, respectively.

The main problem with Raman amplification is that it takes a lot of power in the pump beam—around 1 W. Recent experiments with specially designed fibers have reduced this level below 700 mW, but it remains high. Raman amplification is a promising idea, but like many other promising ideas, it isn't ready yet and may never be used in commercial systems.

> Raman amplification can extract energy from a pump beam to amplify a weak optical signal at another wavelength.

Semiconductor Optical Amplifiers

In principle, any laser can serve as an optical amplifier. Just remove the mirrors and send a signal through it, as you send a signal through a fiber amplifier. Semiconductor diode lasers are logical candidates for this approach, particularly because they are the primary light sources for most fiber-optic transmitters used in applications that require amplification. Diode lasers can amplify light over a range of wavelengths and are available for the 1300- and 1550-nm regions. They have very high gain per unit length, so compact devices can provide the required amplification. They can be integrated on a semiconductor substrate with other optical components, with planar waveguides transporting the

> Semiconductor optical amplifiers are semiconductor lasers without reflective cavities.

light between components (an important concept described in Chapters 15 and 16). They also can switch and control optical signals and convert them to other forms. However, they are not as well developed as for erbium-doped fiber amplifiers.

Characteristics of Semiconductor Optical Amplifiers

Semiconductor optical amplifiers can switch signals off and on and be integrated with other optical components.

Semiconductor optical amplifiers share some operating characteristics with other optical amplifiers. They have a characteristic gain that is high for small input signal levels but that saturates at high powers. They also have a peak output power and can amplify light across a range of wavelengths.

A crucial difference comes from their mode of operation. Like semiconductor lasers, they get their power from a current flowing through the junction layer, causing carrier recombination. This current can be modulated rapidly to control the gain of the amplifier and thus switch signals off and on. In principle, you could do this with fiber amplifiers by switching the pump laser off and on, but the response time would be too slow to be of any practical use. However, semiconductor optical amplifiers respond very fast, making them useful as fast optical switches.

A second crucial difference is structural. Fiber amplifiers are fibers, discrete devices that are physically separate from fibers that carry signals. Semiconductor optical amplifiers can be integrated with other semiconductor optical devices on a monolithic wafer. This makes it possible to combine multiple functions on the same chip, an important attraction.

Limitations of Semiconductor Optical Amplifiers

The basic concept of a semiconductor amplifier as a discrete device is shown in Figure 12.8. Light from a single-mode fiber is focused onto the active stripe at one edge of the chip, is amplified as it travels through the laser, and emerges more intense from the other side, where it is coupled to another fiber.

One obvious problem with this approach is the geometry. Light emerges from a single-mode fiber in a circular spot roughly 10 μm across, but it has to be focused onto a narrow stripe a fraction of a micrometer thick. Some light is inevitably lost in this process.

Semiconductor optical amplifiers can respond very quickly to changes in the input signal, but this is a mixed blessing. The response is so fast that the output changes as intensity of analog input signals changes—and the gain changes with it as a function of input power. Signal gain might be 30 dB when signal intensity is low but only 20 dB when intensity is high, leading to serious distortion of analog signals.

A more subtle problem is light reflection from the ends of the laser cavity. The high refractive index of semiconductor materials makes it difficult to completely suppress reflection from the facets at the edges of the wafer. Such reflections can introduce instabilities and noise into an optical amplifier; semiconductor optical amplifiers are particularly vulnerable to this effect because of their high gain.

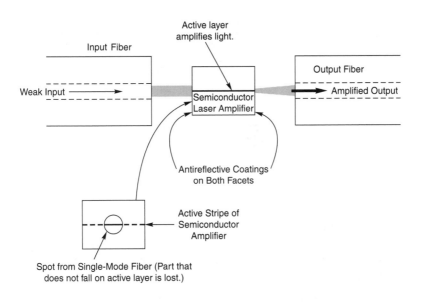

FIGURE 12.8

Semiconductor laser amplifier.

An additional problem is that semiconductor optical amplifiers may be sensitive to the polarization of input light, so they amplify light of different polarizations by different amounts. Standard fibers do not control the polarization of light they transmit, so uncontrolled fluctuations in polarization—normally not an issue with fiber-optic systems—can affect the amount of amplification, so the gain depends on an uncontrollable factor. Engineers don't like that sort of thing, because it can introduce noise.

Developers have made progress in solving some of these problems, at least for some applications. But they remain obstacles for others. These effects are prime reasons why semiconductor optical amplifiers are not serious challengers to erbium-doped fiber amplifiers for the most important uses of EDFAs as in-line amplifiers in telecommunication systems. However, semiconductor optical amplifiers have strengths that offset their weaknesses for other applications.

Integrated Semiconductor Optical Amplifiers

You can make planar semiconductor waveguides and other components from the same materials as semiconductor optical amplifiers, so you can integrate various components on the same substrate. They are essentially all portions of the same planar waveguide, as shown in Figure 12.9. The optical amplifier portion of the waveguide differs in two ways: it has a junction layer, and a voltage is applied across it so a drive current flows through the junction, causing recombination so the input can stimulate emission. Because the optical amplifier is integrated with the waveguide, there are no reflections at the ends of the amplifier zone. This also avoids coupling losses—if you already have the light in the waveguide.

For convenience, I show only a simple waveguide delivering the weak optical signal to the amplifier and a coupler that divides the output between two outputs on the right.

Semiconductor optical amplifiers can be integrated with other planar optical devices on a wafer.

FIGURE 12.9

Integrated semiconductor optical amplifier.

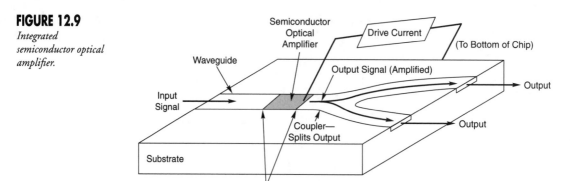

Note: No reflections at ends of amplifier.

However, you can add more components if you have the real estate on the wafer and if they're compatible with semiconductor waveguide technology. Usable components include switches, couplers, and modulators, although semiconductor optical amplifiers themselves can serve some of these functions.

Figure 12.10 shows how this capability might be used in practice. You need to multiplex the outputs of six diode lasers emitting at different wavelengths and then distribute the signals to six locations. A simple approach is to mix the signals in a single device called a *star coupler,* shown at the middle, but the coupler and dividing the signals among the six identical outputs causes a 20-dB loss, leaving only a weak signal at each output. In this example, an initial 1-mW output from each output drops 20 dB as it passes through the coupler and then is amplified another 20 dB by the semiconductor optical amplifier, so each output includes 1 mW of light at each wavelength.

FIGURE 12.10

Semiconductor amplifier integrated with laser array and waveguide coupler.

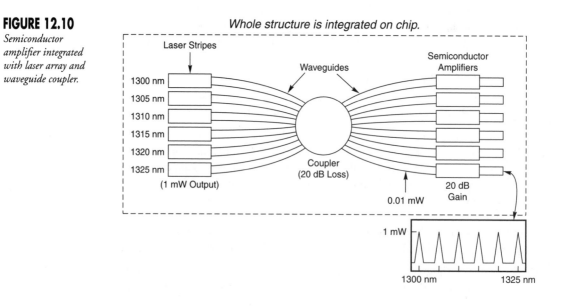

Switching, Modulation, and Signal Control

Semiconductor optical amplifiers respond to changes in drive current as quickly as diode lasers. This means that you can modulate the gain and hence the output signal by changing the drive current passing through the optical amplifier. This is a degree of signal control impractical with erbium-doped fiber amplifiers.

You can use this modulation capability to switch signals between a pair of waveguides, as shown in Figure 12.11. The input signal is divided between two waveguides, each leading to an optical amplifier. You switch signals between the two outputs by turning one semiconductor amplifier on and the other off. More refined schemes are also possible.

● Semiconductor optical amplifiers can modulate and switch signals.

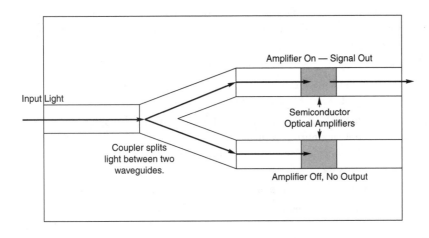

FIGURE 12.11
Semiconductor optical amplifiers used as switches.

Regeneration in Optical Amplifiers

The current generation of optical amplifiers cannot regenerate signals. However, researchers are working on ways to adapt the technology for regeneration and have performed some interesting laboratory demonstrations. The goal is to develop devices that—like electro-optic regenerators—can clean up weak input signals, regenerating sharp, correctly timed digital pulses to eliminate dispersion and distortion effects. At this writing, it's hard to say what will prove the best approach.

What Have You Learned?

1. Signals require amplification because they fade with distance.
2. Amplification increases the strength of a signal. Regeneration cleans up a signal as well as amplifying it.

3. Electro-optic repeaters convert a weak optical signal to electronic form, amplify it, regenerate it, and use the electronic output to drive another optical transmitter. They consist of a receiver and transmitter back to back.

4. Optical amplifiers directly increase the strength of an optical signal, using the laser principle of stimulated emission. The two major types are doped fiber amplifiers and semiconductor optical amplifiers.

5. Erbium-doped fiber amplifiers are the only kind in common use. Their operating range is from 1520 to 1620 nm, although most are limited to 1520 to 1570 nm.

6. Input power, gain, and output power are key parameters for fiber amplifiers. Gain saturates as input power increases and the fiber runs out of excited erbium atoms to amplify the signal.

7. Energy for fiber amplifiers comes from pump lasers, which excite atoms of erbium (or another dopant) to a state that can be stimulated to emit the signal wavelength.

8. Gain must be equalized at different wavelengths in fiber amplifiers.

9. Raman amplification can extract energy from a pump beam to amplify a weak optical signal at another wavelength.

10. Semiconductor optical amplifiers amplify light passing through a semiconductor junction but lack mirrors to make laser light oscillate. They are not as well developed as fiber amplifiers but can be integrated with other semiconductor optics such as waveguides and couplers on a wafer.

11. Semiconductor optical amplifiers can serve as modulators and switches.

12. Practical optical regenerators are not yet available.

What's Next?

In Chapter 13, I move on to the connectors that bridge the gaps among optical fibers, transmitters, receivers, and other components.

Quiz for Chapter 12

1. Amplifiers are needed
   a. to overcome the threshold for driving an optical fiber.
   b. to compensate for fiber attenuation.
   c. only with copper-wire systems.
   d. to convert optical signals into electronic form.

2. What is the difference between amplification and regeneration?
   a. Regeneration retimes and cleans up the signal as well as amplifying it.

b. Regeneration does not increase signal power.

c. There is no difference.

d. Regeneration is done optically; amplification is electronic.

3. What can optical amplifiers do that electro-optic repeaters cannot?

a. Compensate for fiber dispersion.

b. Retime signals.

c. Operate at a wide range of signal speeds without adjustment.

d. Convert signal wavelengths.

4. What can electro-optical repeaters do that optical amplifiers cannot?

a. Compensate for fiber dispersion.

b. Retime signals.

c. Operate at a wide range of signal speeds without adjustment.

d. Both a and b.

e. None of the above.

5. Erbium-doped fiber amplifiers operate at which of the following wavelengths?

a. 1520 to 1620 nm.

b. 1280 to 1330 nm.

c. 750 to 900 nm.

d. At all important fiber windows.

e. Only at exactly 1550 nm.

6. How many different wavelengths can you transmit using a fiber amplifier with operating range 1540 to 1565 nm if your signals are spaced at the 100-GHz spacing recommended by the International Telecommunications Union? (Remember the speed of light is 299,792,458 m/s.)

a. 8.

b. 16.

c. 25.

d. 31.

e. 32.

7. The gain of an erbium-doped fiber amplifier is 5 dB higher at 1535 nm than at the other wavelengths between 1540 and 1560 nm that it transmits. What do you need to do to equalize gain?

a. Nothing, gain will saturate eventually.

b. Add a filter that attenuates 1535-nm light by 5 dB and transmits the other wavelengths without loss.

c. Add a filter that attenuates all wavelengths but 1535 by 5 dB.

d. Add a separate amplifier that does not affect 1535-nm light but amplifies the other wavelengths by 5 dB.

e. Replace the amplifier; it's defective.

8. Fiber amplifiers and semiconductor optical amplifiers both increase signal strength by

   a. spontaneous emission of light at the signal wavelength.

   b. stimulated emission of light at the signal wavelength.

   c. Raman amplification of the signal light.

   d. converting the light into electrical form and amplifying the current.

   e. They share no common mechanism.

9. How does a semiconductor optical amplifier differ from a semiconductor laser?

   a. Only a laser can generate stimulated emission.

   b. Only an amplifier can generate stimulated emission.

   c. An amplifier does not require an electric drive current.

   d. An amplifier has nonreflective ends.

   e. There is no difference.

10. How does a semiconductor optical amplifier differ from a fiber amplifier?

   a. A semiconductor amplifier can modulate the light it amplifies more easily.

   b. A semiconductor amplifier can be integrated on a wafer with other planar optical components.

   c. Gain per unit length is higher in a semiconductor amplifier.

   d. Semiconductor amplifiers are not widely used as in-line amplifiers.

   e. All the above.

Connectors

About This Chapter

In the world of fiber optics, connectors are not the only way to make connections. The term "connector" has a specific meaning: a device that can be mated (and unmated) repeatedly with similar devices to transfer light between two fiber ends or between a fiber end and a transmitter or receiver. The connector is mounted on the end of a cable or on a device package. A permanent junction between two fibers is called a splice, which you'll learn about in Chapter 14. A device to interconnect three or more fiber ends or devices is called a *coupler,* which I will describe in Chapter 15, along with other possive components.

This chapter first explains connectors and how they work, starting with the basic concepts behind fiber-optic connectors and the mechanisms causing their inherent loss or attenuation. Then it discusses important types of connectors.

Why Connectors Are Needed

Electrical connectors are common in modular electronic, audio, or telephone equipment, although you may think of them as plugs and jacks. Their purpose is to connect two devices electrically and mechanically, such as a cable and a stereo receiver. A plug on the cable goes into a socket in the back of the receiver, making electrical contact and holding the cable in place. Both the electrical and mechanical junctions are important. If the cable falls out, it can't carry signals; if the electrical connection is bad, the mechanical connection doesn't do any good. (You'll understand the problem all too well if you've ever tried to find an intermittent fault in electronic connectors.)

●
Connectors make temporary connections among equipment that may need to be rearranged.

Fiber-optic connectors are intended to do the same job, but the signal being transmitted is light through an optical fiber, not electricity through a wire. That's an important difference because, as you learned in Chapter 4, the way light is guided through a fiber is fundamentally different from the way current travels in a wire. Electrons can follow a convoluted path through electrical conductors (wires) if the wires make good electric contact somewhere. However, fiber cores must be precisely aligned with each other—just how precisely you'll see later.

Electrical connectors are used for audio equipment and telephones because the connections are not supposed to be permanent. You use fiber connectors for the same reason. For permanent connections, you splice or solder wires, and you splice optical fibers. Permanent connections have some advantages, including better mechanical stability and—especially for fiber optics—lower signal loss. However, those advantages come at a cost in flexibility; you don't want to cut apart a splice each time you move a computer terminal or telephone.

●
Splices and connectors are used in different places.

Fiber-optic connectors and splices are far from interchangeable. Connectors are normally used at the ends of systems to join cables to transmitters and receivers. Connectors are used in patch panels where outdoor cables enter a building and have their junctions with cables that distribute signals within the building. They are used where configurations are likely to be changed, such as at telecommunication closets, equipment rooms, and telecommunication outlets. Examples include the following:

- Interfaces between devices and local area networks
- Connections with short intrabuilding data links
- Patch panels where signals are routed in a building
- The point where a telecommunication system enters a building
- Connections between networks and terminal equipment
- Temporary connections between remote mobile video cameras and recording equipment or temporary studios
- Portable military systems

Splices are used where junctions are permanent or where the lower loss of splices is critical. For example, splices are made in long cable runs because there is no need to disconnect the cable segments and because connector losses would reduce maximum transmission distance. (Splices offer better mechanical characteristics for outdoor locations.)

●
Distinctions between splices and connectors are not always sharp.

The distinctions between connectors and splices are not always as sharp as they might seem. The most common fiber connectors, which superficially resemble those for metal coaxial cables, differ obviously from the most common splices—the welding, fusion, or gluing of two fiber ends together. However, between these extremes are such hybrids as demountable splices, which nominally bond fibers together permanently but can be removed. Some of these approaches will be covered in Chapter 14. In addition, some connectors are installed by splicing them to the cable.

Connector Attenuation

The key optical parameter of fiber connectors is attenuation—the fraction of the signal lost within the connector. This loss is measured in decibels for a mated pair—that is, the loss in going from one fiber (or other device) to the other. (Light actually passes through two connectors, but the loss of one connector is not meaningful because the signal isn't going anywhere.) Typical attenuation is a fraction of a decibel. Manufacturers specify loss for specific fiber types; as you will see in the next section, mismatched fibers almost always have higher loss. Note that in most of the discussion that follows I assume that a connector is joining the ends of two fibers. Connectors can be mounted on transmitters and receivers as well, and although details differ, the principles are the same.

Connector attenuation is the sum of losses caused by several factors, which are easier to isolate in theory than in practice. These factors stem from the way light is guided in fibers. The major ones are as follows:

- Overlap of fiber cores
- Alignment of fiber axes
- Fiber numerical aperture
- Fiber spacing
- Reflection at fiber ends

These factors interact to some degree. One—overlap of fiber cores—really is the sum of many different effects, including variation in core diameter, concentricity of the core within the cladding, eccentricity of the core, and lateral alignment of the two fibers. The fiber geometry can affect not only loss but also the internal structure of the connector.

> The most important optical characteristic of connectors is loss.

Overlap of Fiber Cores

To see how core overlap affects loss, look at Figure 13.1, where the end of one fiber is offset from the end of the other. For simplicity, assume that light is distributed uniformly in the cores of identical fibers and that the two fiber ends are next to each other and are otherwise well aligned. The loss then equals the fraction of the input-fiber core area that does not overlap with that of the output fiber. If the offset is 10% of the core diameter, the excess loss is about 0.6 dB.

Mismatches of emitting and collecting areas also occur if core diameters differ. Suppose that the fibers were perfectly aligned but that the 50-μm nominal fiber core diameter varied within tolerance of ± 3 μm, as specified on a typical commercial graded-index fiber. With simple geometry, you can calculate the loss for going from a fiber with core diameter d_1 to one with core diameter d_2. (You also can use radius if

> Offset of fiber cores by 10% of their diameter can cause a 0.6-dB loss.

Understanding Fiber Optics

you want—the factor of two differences from diameter cancels out—but usually core diameter is what's specified.) The relative difference in area is

$$Loss = \frac{(d_1^2 - d_2^2)}{d_1^2}$$

FIGURE 13.1

Offset fibers can cause loss.

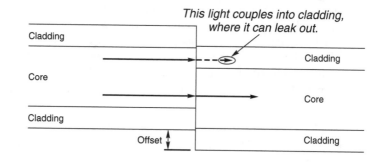

For the worst case of going from a fiber with a 53-µm core to one with a 47-µm core, this is a factor of 0.21. If light was distributed uniformly through the core, that fraction of the light, about 1 dB, would be lost. Fortunately things are rarely that bad, because light is not distributed uniformly through the core, and core diameter rarely varies as much as the maximum allowed by the specifications.

The same principles apply for single-mode fiber, but in that case the critical dimension is mode-field diameter, which is typically slightly larger than core diameter. The formula for relative loss is the same, but the tolerances are much tighter because single-mode fibers have much smaller cores. For example, a nonzero dispersion-shifted fiber has mode-field diameter of 8.4 ± 0.5 µm at 1550 nm. Although the diameter tolerance is very small, going from the largest fiber that meets these tolerances to the smallest can be costly in loss:

$$Loss = \frac{(8.9^2 - 7.9^2)}{(8.9)^2}$$

The result is essentially the same as for the maximum variation in core diameter of 50-µm fiber, 0.21, or 1 dB. As with multimode fiber, things are rarely this bad in practice, and most specified single-mode connector losses are 0.5 dB or less.

You can get into trouble if the fiber types are mismatched, so signals go from a multimode fiber into a single-mode fiber. This makes it vital for you to know the fiber type. Going from a 62.5-µm graded-index fiber to a single-mode fiber with a 9-µm core results in 97.9% of the light being lost, a 17-dB loss. Even going between 62.5- and 50-µm multimode fibers causes a 1.9-dB loss, 36% of the light.

Mismatches in area also can arise from other factors. The fiber core may be slightly elliptical, or the core might be slightly off center in the fiber. Figure 13.2 shows these problems in exaggerated scale. Variations in cladding or coating dimensions can throw off alignment in connectors that hold the fiber in position by gripping its outside.

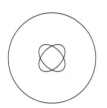
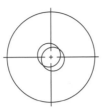

a. Elliptical Cores   **b. Off-Center Cores**

FIGURE 13.2

Losses arise when cores are elliptical or off center.

Alignment of Fiber Axes

The importance of aligning fiber axes is shown in Figure 13.3. As the fibers tilt out of alignment and the angle θ increases, the light enters the second fiber at increasingly steeper angles, so some rays are not confined. The severity of this loss decreases as numerical aperture increases because the larger the NA, the larger the collection angle.

> ● Angular misalignment of fiber ends can cause significant losses.

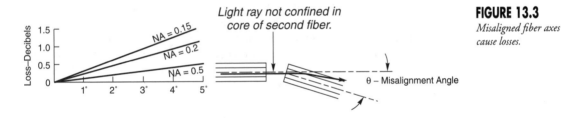

Light ray not confined in core of second fiber.

θ – Misalignment Angle

FIGURE 13.3

Misaligned fiber axes cause losses.

Fiber Numerical Aperture

Differences in NA between fibers can also contribute to connector losses. If the fiber receiving the light has a smaller NA than the one delivering the light, some light will enter it in modes that are not confined in the core. That light will quickly leak out of the fiber, as shown in Figure 13.4. In this case, the loss can be defined with a simple formula:

> ● Differences in NA can contribute to connector losses.

$$\text{Loss (dB)} = 10 \log_{10} \left(\frac{NA_2}{NA_1} \right)^2$$

where NA_2 is the numerical aperture of the fiber receiving the signal and NA_1 is the NA of the fiber from which light is transmitted. The NA must be the measured value for the segment of fiber used (which for multimode fibers is a function of length, light sources, and other factors), rather than the theoretical NA. Note also that there is no NA-related loss if the fiber receiving the light has a larger NA than the transmitting fiber.

FIGURE 13.4

Mating fibers with different NAs can cause losses.

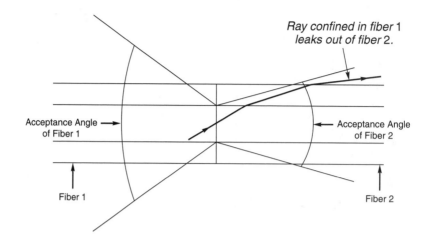

Spacing Between Fibers

Numerical aperture also influences the loss caused by separation of fiber ends in a connector. Light exits a fiber in a cone, with the spreading angle—like the acceptance angle—dependent on numerical aperture. The more the cone of light spreads out, the less light the other fiber can collect, as shown in Figure 13.5. This is one case where transfer losses increase with numerical aperture because the larger the NA of the output fiber, the faster the light spreads out. The formula for the end-separation loss is rather involved, even assuming the transmitting and receiving fibers are identical:

$$\text{Loss (dB)} = 10 \log_{10} \left(\frac{d/2}{\frac{d}{2} + S \tan \left(\arcsin \right) \left(\frac{\text{NA}}{n_0} \right)} \right)$$

FIGURE 13.5

End-separation loss.

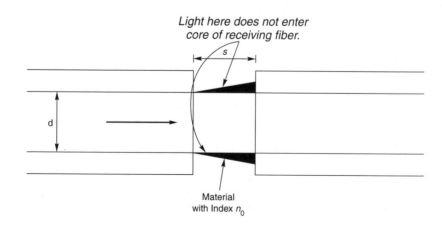

where d is core diameter, S is the fiber spacing, NA is the numerical aperture, and n_0 is the refractive index of the material between the two fibers. Figure 13.6 shows a plot of the loss for three different fibers, two with 50-µm cores and NAs of 0.2 and 0.4 and one single-mode fiber with 0.15 NA; the material between the fibers is air, which has a refractive index almost equal to 1.

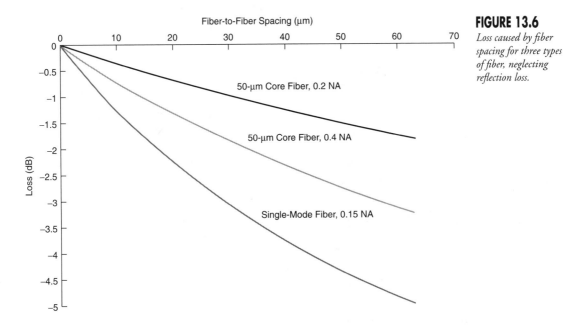

FIGURE 13.6
Loss caused by fiber spacing for three types of fiber, neglecting reflection loss.

An additional spacing loss is Fresnel reflection, which occurs whenever light passes between two materials with different refractive indexes. It occurs for all transparent optical materials, even ordinary window glass. (It causes the reflections you see on windows when looking from a lighted room out into darkness.) Fresnel loss depends on the difference in refractive index between the fiber core and the material in the gap. For uncoated glass fiber ends in air, it is about 0.32 dB. This loss can be reduced by putting the fiber ends together (carefully, to avoid damage), by adding antireflective coatings, which have a refractive index between that of glass and air, or by filling the gap with a transparent index-matching gel, which has a refractive index closer to that of glass.

Fresnel reflection losses occur when light enters material of a different refractive index.

Other End Losses

Other effects can add to connector loss. So far, I have assumed that the fiber ends are cut and polished cleanly and perfectly perpendicular to the fiber axis. However, extra losses can occur if the ends are cut and polished at a slight angle and the angles do not match in the connector. Other losses can arise if the ends are not smooth or if dirt gets into the connector.

With all these loss mechanisms, it is no wonder early fiber-optic developers were very worried about connectors. Tremendous progress has been made, but connector losses can still be significant in designing fiber-optic systems, as you will see in Chapter 20. Typical losses of good single or multimode connectors are 0.2 to 0.5 dB, with some inexpensive connectors around 1 dB. In practice all the factors discussed earlier can cause considerable variation. Connector installation is a critical variable. Repeated matings and unmatings of the connector can change attenuation. Generally a typical connector loss is specified, along with changes that both mechanical and environmental factors are expected to cause during use.

Internal Reflections

Internal connector reflections can cause spurious modulation and noise in laser light sources.

Index-matching fluids reduce reflections in connectors.

Losses are not the only potentially harmful things that happen within connectors. Strong back-reflections from fiber ends can cause problems with laser light sources. As mentioned in Chapter 9, the operation of a semiconductor laser relies on optical feedback, reflection from front and rear facets of the semiconductor cavity. Reflection from fiber ends in a connector can provide additional feedback that in some cases effectively modulates the laser with a spurious signal, increasing noise levels.

Internal reflections can be suppressed by reducing refractive-index differences at fiber ends. One possibility is to butt fiber ends together, so they appear (to the light) to be a single continuous piece of glass. Another is to fill the inside of the connector with an index-matching fluid or gel having a refractive index close to that of the glass. However, wet connectors are subject to contamination or leakage that can increase losses.

Optical isolators and directional couplers suppress back-reflection in a different way, by allowing light transmission in only one direction (forward). They are among components described in Chapter 15.

Reflection noise is an important concern for analog cable-television systems, which are inherently more vulnerable than digital systems. Some cable systems use angled-fiber connectors, in which the fiber ends are cut at an angle so any reflected light is lost from the fiber (as in the case of misaligned fibers, described earlier). However, angled connectors must be mated carefully to avoid excess losses if the angles don't match.

Mechanical Considerations

So far, I have concentrated on the optical characteristics of a fiber connector. However, mechanical characteristics are also important, and in some cases critical. Virtually all fiber connectors are designed well enough that they will stay in place under normal conditions. However, connectors must withstand physical stress applied during their use, from the normal forces in mating and unmating them to the sudden stress applied by a person tripping over a cable. Connectors must also prevent contamination of the optical interface, with dirt and moisture the main threats.

Durability

Durability is a concern with any kind of connector. Repeated mating and unmating of fiber connectors can wear mechanical components, introduce dirt into the optics, strain the fiber and other cable components, and even damage exposed fiber ends. Typical connectors for indoor use are specified for 500 to 1000 mating cycles, which should be adequate for most use. Few types of equipment are connected and disconnected daily. Specifications typically call for attenuation to change no more than 0.2 dB over that lifetime.

Connectors are attached to cables by forming mechanical and/or epoxy bonds to the fiber, cable sheath, and strength members. (Usually the fiber is epoxied, and the other bonds are crimped.) That physical connection is adequate for normal wear and tear but not for sudden sharp forces, such as those produced when someone trips over an indoor cable. That sharp tug can detach a cable from a mounted connector, because the bond between connector and fiber is the weakest point. The same is true for electrical cords, and the best way to address the problem is to be careful with the cables.

Because sharp bends can increase losses and damage fibers, care should be taken to avoid sharp kinks in cables at the connector (e.g., when a cable mates with a connector on a patch panel). Fibers are particularly vulnerable if they have been nicked during connector installation. Care should also be taken to be certain that fiber ends do not protrude from the ends of connectors. If fiber ends hit each other or other objects, they can easily be damaged, increasing attenuation.

Environmental Considerations

Most fiber-optic connectors are designed for use indoors, protected from environmental extremes. Keeping them free from contaminants is even more important than it is for electrical connectors. Dirt or dust on fiber ends or within the connector can scatter or absorb light, causing excessive connector loss and poor system performance. This makes it unwise to leave fiber-optic connectors open to the air, even inside. Many connectors and patch panels come with protective caps for use when they are not mated. These caps are the sort of things that are easily lost, but they should not be.

Special hermetically sealed connectors are required for outdoor use. As you might expect, those designed for military field use are by far the most durable. Military field connectors are bulky and expensive, but when sealed they can be left on the ground, exposed to mud and moisture. They are designed to operate even after having one end stuck in mud and wiped out with a rag! Normally, nonmilitary users will avoid outdoor connectors or house them in enclosures that are sealed against dirt and moisture.

● Typical fiber connectors are specified for 500 to 1000 matings. Most can be torn from cable ends by a sharp tug.

● Fiber ends must be kept free of contaminants to avoid excess losses.

Connector Structures

I have talked about fiber connectors in fairly general terms so far for an important practical reason—many different types have been developed. This was a logical response to the difficult technical problems faced in developing durable, low-loss optical connectors. However, order has emerged from the chaos as users insisted on standard types to simplify their logistics.

● Connectors have common elements, including ferrules, bodies, and strain-relief boots.

Most connectors in common use today have some common elements, shown in simplified form in Figure 13.7. The fiber is mounted in a long, thin cylinder called a *ferrule,* with a hole sized to match the fiber cladding diameter. The ferrule centers and aligns the fiber and protects it from mechanical damage. The end of the fiber is at the end of the ferrule. The ferrule is mounted in the connector body, which is attached to the cable structure. A strain-relief boot shields the junction of the connector body and the cable.

FIGURE 13.7

A simplified generic fiber connector with coupling receptacle or adapter.

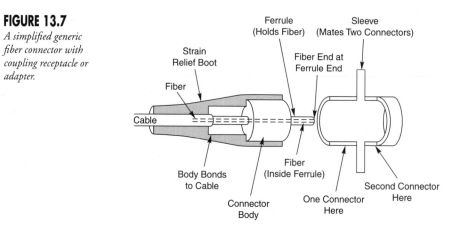

● Most fiber connectors are mated through coupling receptacles between connector pairs.

Standard fiber connectors lack the male-female polarity common in electronic connectors. Instead, fiber connectors mate in adapters (often called *coupling receptacles,* or *sleeves*) that fit between two fiber connectors. Similar adapters are mounted on devices such as transmitters and receivers, to mate with fiber connectors. Although this approach requires the use of separate adapters, which must be kept in stock to link cables, it otherwise reduces inventory requirements. The adapters can also be designed to mate different types of connectors.

Ferrules are typically made of metal or ceramic, but some are made of plastics. Normally, the protective plastic coating is stripped from the fiber before it is inserted in the ferrule. The hole through the ferrule must be large enough to fit the clad fiber and tight enough to hold it in a fixed position. Standard bore diameters are 126 + 1/−0 μm for single-mode connectors and 127 + 2/−0 μm for multimode connectors, but some manufacturers supply a range of sizes (e.g., 124, 125, 126, and 127 μm) to accommodate the natural variation in fiber diameter. Adhesive is typically put in the hole before the fiber is pushed in to hold the fiber in place. The fiber end may be pushed slightly past the end of the ferrule and then polished to a smooth face.

The ferrule may be slipped inside another hollow cylinder (also called a sleeve) before it is mounted in the connector body. The body, typically made of metal or plastic, includes one or more pieces that are assembled to hold the cable and fiber in place. Details of assembly vary among connectors; cable bonding is usually to strength members and the jacket. The end of the ferrule protrudes beyond the connector body to slip into the mating receptacle. A strain-relief boot is slipped over the cable end of the connector to protect the cable-connector junction.

Many connectors are attached to transmitters, receivers, or junction boxes. Look carefully, and you find these are the same standard connectors; the difference is in how they are attached. For transmitters, the light source couples light directly into the connector inside the box, and the cable is plugged into an adapter on the outside. For receivers, the detector is attached to the connector so it collects light from a cable attached to an adapter on the outside of the box. In a junction box or patch panel, you are likely to find an array of connector adapters, ready for you to plug an input cable in one side and an output in the other, such as the panel shown in Figure 13.8. Fiber connectors also can be mounted in wall outlets, comparable to wall outlets for telephone wiring; as in junction boxes, what you see are the adapters that fit between two connectors.

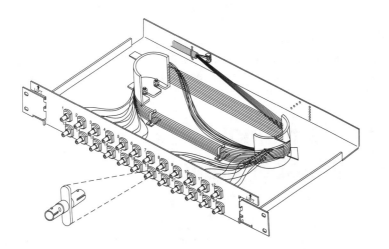

FIGURE 13.8
Connector panel.
(Courtesy of Siecor, Hickory, N.C.)

Connector Installation

Fiber users face important trade-offs in deciding where and how to install connectors. The tight tolerances needed for low loss are easier to reproduce in a factor environment. However, field installation gives much more flexibility in meeting system requirements and

Fiber connectors may be installed in the factory or in the field.

allows on-the-spot repairs. Each approach has its advantages, and connector manufacturers have taken some steps to offer users the best of both worlds.

A big advantage of factory installation is that it's the cable supplier's responsibility to do it right. Trained technicians mount and test the connectors, with all the equipment they need in a controlled environment. Generally, they can mass-produce standard lengths of connectorized cable economically. That's fine for short jumper cables used in patch panels, but it's more difficult to supply the many different lengths needed for intrabuilding cable.

An intermediate step is to supply cable segments with factory-mounted connectors on one end and fiber pigtails on the other. These pigtails can be spliced to cables in the field, using mechanical or fusion splices (described in Chapter 14). This is a quick and easy approach using splicing equipment that many field technicians already have. Factory polishing makes connector losses low, and many types of connectors can be used. However, it requires additional splicing hardware and can add to costs. It works best for many-fiber loose-tube cables.

Field installation of the complete connector enhances flexibility and has low consumable costs. Labor costs may be low, depending on the location, but installation results depend on both the skill of the technician and the forgivingness of the connector design. It generally takes more time and skill on the part of the technician than splicing a premounted connector, and it requires some special tools. It works best for tight-buffered cables. Some manufacturers supply field connectorization kits with some of the most sensitive alignments already done.

Connector manufacturers continue efforts to simplify connector installation. One example is a field-installable connector with a built-in mechanical splice. This allows the incoming fiber to be spliced to a factory-polished and -installed fiber stub only an inch long—an extremely short pigtail.

Connecting Single- and Multifiber Cables

Connector installation is simplest for single-fiber cables. However, most cables contain two or more fibers, complicating matters.

The simplest case is the duplex connector, connecting a cable with two fibers. It is often made from two single-fiber connectors arranged side by side in a single housing. This is not quite enough for most practical applications, because fiber polarity is important. To ensure that the proper fibers are connected, most duplex connectors are keyed, so they can be inserted in only one way.

Multifiber cables are often broken out into separate fibers at patch panels or junction boxes, with single connectors on each fiber, as shown in Figure 13.8. This is often the sim-

Connectors for multifiber cables are more complex than those for single-fiber cables. Often multifiber cables may be broken out at each end into many single-fiber connectors.

plest approach for multifiber cables, especially where they come into buildings and must be split to distribute signals to different areas. It is also the usual approach for multifiber cables within buildings.

An alternative is multifiber connectors, which simultaneously connect many fibers, greatly simplifying installation and reducing space requirements. The basic idea is to arrange a set of fibers in a fixed format and mate them to the corresponding fibers from a different cable arranged in the same format. Such connectors require precision alignment to avoid the loss problems I described earlier and tend to have somewhat higher loss than single-fiber connectors.

Standard Connector Types

During the 1980s, almost every manufacturer of fiber-optic connectors seemed to have its own designs. Some remain in production, but much of the industry has shifted to standardized connector types, with details specified by standards organizations such as the Telecommunications Industry Association, the International Electrotechnical Commission, and the Electronic Industries Association. Standards groups, in turn, have developed standards for about two dozen connector types, most of them widely used types and some of them new types developed for emerging needs.

Many connector designs have been standardized by the IEC and other organizations.

I can't hope to cover the whole variety of connectors in any detail; that's best done by consulting catalogs and product specifications. However, I will discuss a few examples of important types used for single- and multimode glass fibers. Other types of connectors may be used for plastic fibers and large-core fibers. I divide them loosely into families: single-fiber connectors that snap or twist in place, special-purpose connectors, polarizing connectors, and multifiber connectors.

Snap-in Single-Fiber Connectors (SC)

Figure 13.9 shows a widely used snap-in connector, the SC connector developed by Nippon Telegraph and Telephone of Japan. Like most fiber connectors, it is built around a cylindrical ferrule that holds the fiber, and it mates with an interconnection adapter or coupling receptacle. Pushing the connector latches it into place, without any need to turn it in a tight space, so a simple tug will not unplug it. It has a square cross section that allows high packing density on patch panels and makes it easy to package in a polarized duplex form that assures the fibers are matched to the proper fibers in the mated connector.

The SC is a widely used snap-in single-fiber connector.

Twist-on Single-Fiber Connectors (ST and FC)

Figure 13.10 shows a widely used twist-on connector, the ST connector long used in data communications. It may look familiar because it is one of several fiber connectors that evolved from designs originally used for copper coaxial cables. Like the SC, it is built

FIGURE 13.9

SC connector, expanded and assembled. (Courtesy of AMP Inc.)

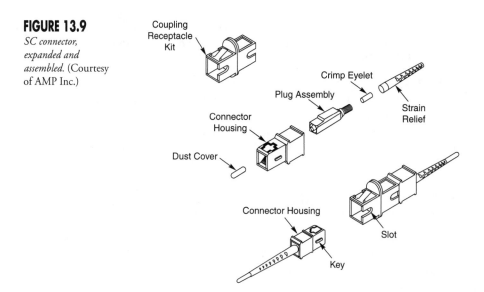

around a cylindrical ferrule and mates with an interconnection adapter or coupling receptacle. However, it has a round cross section and is latched into place by twisting it to engage a spring-loaded bayonet socket.

FIGURE 13.10

ST connector, expanded and assembled. (Courtesy of Siecor Corp., Hickory, N.C.)

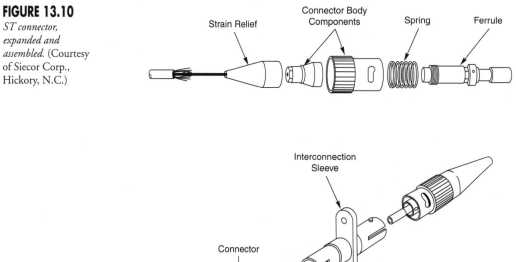

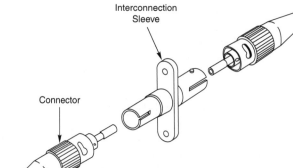

Another design for a twist-on connector is the FC (sometimes called FC-PC). Its structure is similar to that of the ST, but it is threaded and screws in place rather than twisting to latch. One drawback of such twist-on connectors is that they generally cannot be mounted in pairs as a duplex connector.

Duplex Connectors

Duplex connectors include a pair of fibers and generally have an internal key so they can be mated in only one orientation. *Polarizing* the connector in this way is important because most systems use separate fibers to carry signals in each direction, so it matters which fibers are connected. Attach the connector the wrong way and you have one transmitter sending signals to the other transmitter while the two receivers stare at each other through a dark fiber, each waiting forever for the other to send a signal.

One simple type of duplex connector is a pair of SC connectors, mounted side by side in a single case. This takes advantage of their plug-in-lock design.

Other duplex connectors have been developed for specific types of networks, as part of comprehensive standards. One example is the fixed shroud duplex (FSD) connector specified by the Fiber Distributed Data Interface (FDDI) standard, shown in Figure 13.11. Another is the retractable shroud duplex (RSD) connector developed for the Fibre Channel system. Both superficially resemble long, flat wall plugs for electric lamps but are designed to meet fiber-optic network standards.

Duplex connectors are keyed to mate in only one orientation.

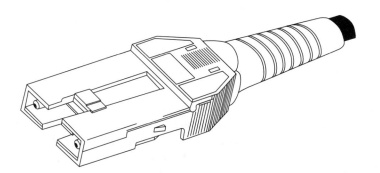

FIGURE 13.11
Fixed shroud duplex (FSD) connector for FDDI network. (Courtesy of Siecor Corp., Hickory, N.C.)

Polarizing Connectors

In addition to duplex connectors, which are polarized so they can be mated in only one orientation, special connectors are made for use with single fibers that transmit polarized light. Their role is to orient polarizing fibers so the orientation of polarized light is the same in both input and output fibers.

MT Multifiber Connectors

The MT ferrule can align up to a dozen fibers in a multifiber connector.

A family of multifiber connectors is built around the MT ferrule, which aligns up to a dozen fibers parallel to each other, as shown in Figure 13.12. As you may suspect from this arrangement, the MT connector was developed for use with multifiber ribbon cable. Coatings are removed before the fibers are mounted in the ferrule, leaving 125-μm fibers mounted on 250-μm centers. The ferrules also include a pair of 0.7-mm holes, running parallel to the fibers on the outer sides of the ferrule. These holes accommodate precision metal guide pins, which align mated ferrules with tight tolerances so the fibers match up properly.

FIGURE 13.12

MT ferrule holds a dozen fibers in parallel grooves.

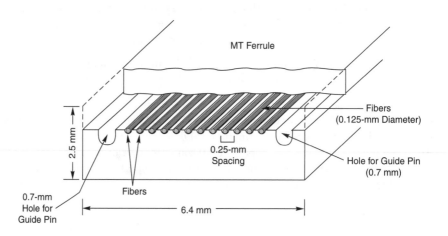

Pairs of MT ferrules can be mated together with guide pins and held in place with metal clips. Alternatively, the MT ferrules can be mounted within connector bodies, which mate together, usually with an adapter, while the guide pins align the ferrules precisely with each other.

Depending on details of the design, the guide pins may be supplied separately for insertion when the connectors are mated or may be installed permanently in one ferrule (typically one that is permanently mounted in a case rather than on a cable). It is the guide pins that assure the precise alignment of fiber ends. The connector bodies provide the mechanical force holding the ferrules in place; typically they are spring-loaded and snap into position, like SC connectors. There are a variety of connectors built around MT ferrules.

One such new design is the rectangular-format MPO connector, shown in Figure 13.13. A pair of connectors mate in an adapter, connecting up to 12 fibers. The male connector (shown in the figure) has the guide pins; the female connector does not. Some companies have modified designs with minor differences, such as allowing two plugs to mate with each other without an adapter between them. These connectors are intended for installations that require many fiber connections.

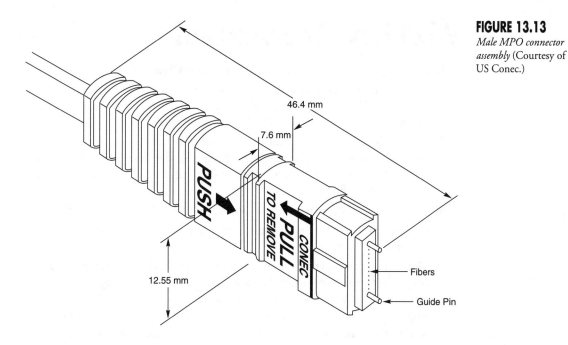

FIGURE 13.13
*Male MPO connector
assembly* (Courtesy of
US Conec.)

Another spinoff of the MT connector is the MT-RJ, which uses a two-fiber ferrule based on the MT design and a small connector about the same size as the RJ45 connector used in telephone jacks. It's intended to be installed in buildings in much the same way as telephone wires, and the connector can even fit in the same slot in a wall plate as the socket for a telephone jack. The MT-RJ connectors can be installed like other connectors, with two plugs mating in an adapter. However, another possibility is to insert bare fibers directly into one end of a wall jack, as telephone wires in the wall are mounted to wall plates. A plug can then be snapped into the jack.

Trying to align many fibers at once stresses mechanical tolerances, so typical losses of multifiber connectors can be higher than those of single-fiber connectors, up to about 1 dB. (Duplex connectors typically have about the same loss as single-fiber connectors.) However, multifiber connectors greatly reduce installation costs for multifiber systems.

Adapters for Different Connector Types

As you can imagine, with all these connector types it's easy to end up with equipment that uses different types. As with electronic cables, the solution is to install adapters, which allow the mating of different connector types. Such adapters are readily available for single-fiber connectors but may not be available for multifiber connectors.

What Have You Learned?

1. Connectors make temporary connections between fiber ends.

2. The most important specification of connectors is attenuation, which is always given for a pair of connectors, measuring the loss in transferring a signal between two fibers.

3. Causes of connector loss include mismatch of fiber cores, misalignment of fiber axes, differences in numerical aperture, spacing between fibers, and reflection at fiber ends. Tolerances are tighter for small-core single-mode fibers than for larger-core multimode fibers.

4. Typical single-fiber connector losses are 0.2 to 0.5 dB, but some have higher loss.

5. Connector back-reflection is an important parameter because it can cause noise in laser transmitters.

6. Most connectors contain cylindrical ferrules that hold the fiber inside a connector body. Most connectors lack male-female polarity and mate through interconnection adapters or coupling receptacles.

7. Many types of connectors have been marketed, and many remain available. Standards groups have written specifications for more than two dozen types.

8. Fiber connectors can be installed in the field or in the factory. Some field-installable connectors are factory-mounted on cable segments that are spliced into place in the field.

9. Duplex connectors are used for pairs of fibers. Multifiber cables may be broken out to individual single-fiber connector or attached to multifiber connectors.

What's Next?

In Chapter 14, I will look at splices—the permanent connections between two fiber ends.

Quiz for Chapter 13

1. Connectors are used

    a. to permanently join two fiber ends.

    b. to make temporary connections between two fiber ends or devices.

    c. to transmit light in only one direction.

    d. to merge signals coming from many devices.

2. Which of the following effects affect connector attenuation?

    a. Fiber core overlap.

    b. Alignment of fiber axes.

    c. Numerical apertures.

    d. End-to-end spacing of fibers.

    e. All the above.

3. What does index-matching gel do in a connector?

    a. Holds the fibers in place.

    b. Keeps dirt out of the space between fiber ends.

    c. Prevents reflections at fiber ends.

    d. Eliminates effects of numerical aperture mismatch.

4. What will be the excess loss caused by the mismatch in core diameters when a connector transmits light from a 62.5/125 multimode fiber into a 50/125 fiber?

    a. 0 dB.

    b. 0.1 dB.

    c. 1 dB.

    d. 1.9 dB.

    e. 12.5 dB.

5. The largest excess loss will occur in which of the following cases?

    a. Transfer of light from a single-mode to a multimode fiber.

    b. Transfer of light from a fiber with a high NA to one with a low NA.

    c. Transfer of light from a fiber with a low NA to one with a high NA.

    d. Transfer of light through a connector filled with index-matching gel.

6. Back-reflections from fiber ends

    a. can cause laser noise in analog systems.

    b. are lower in high-loss connectors.

    c. are not a significant problem in practical systems.

    d. do not occur if fiber ends are separated in connectors.

7. Which of the following factors tends to favor field installation of connectors?

    a. Ease of measuring connector performance.

    b. Ease of matching precise cabling requirements.

    c. Installation is more accurate and repeatable.

    d. Minimizing time required to mount each connector.

8. What are functions of coupling adapters?

    a. To provide an interface between two connectors.

    b. To allow mating of two different connector types.

    c. To attach connectorized cables to terminal equipment.

    d. The same as interconnection adapters.

    e. All the above.

9. Ferrules do what in a fiber-optic connector?

    a. Relieve strain on the cable.

    b. Allow adjustment of attenuation.

    c. Hold the fiber precisely in place.

    d. Prevent back-reflection.

e. Screw the connector into place.

10. What are the major trade-offs with multifiber connectors?

a. Lower loss but too new to be sure of reliability.

b. Smaller, lower cost, and easier to use, but loss may be higher because

tolerances are hard to achieve.

c. Smaller but cost much more.

d. Lower cost but much bulkier.

e. Easier cable installation but higher cost.

Splicing

About This Chapter

Splices, unlike the connectors discussed in the last chapter, are permanent connections between fibers. Splices weld, glue, or otherwise bond together the ends of two fibers. Like fiber-optic connectors, fiber-optic splices are functionally similar to their wire counterparts. However, as with connectors, there are important differences between splicing wires and optical fibers.

In this chapter you will learn when and why optical fibers are spliced, the major considerations in fiber splicing, the types of splices, and the special equipment used in splicing.

Applications of Fiber Splices

Splices and connectors both join fiber ends, but they do so in different ways, so they are used for different purposes. (If you're familiar with electronics, you can compare splicing to soldering and connectors to plugs.) Splices have lower loss, and they bond fibers together permanently. You use them in places where you never expect to make any more changes. Connectors have higher loss, but you can move them around, changing the way they connect fibers. To complicate things somewhat, there are different types of splices, although they are more similar to each other than to connectors.

Typically, splices are used to join lengths of cable outside buildings, whereas connectors are used at the ends of cables inside buildings. Splices may be incorporated in lengths of cable or housed in indoor or outdoor splice boxes; connectors are typically in patch panels or attached to equipment at cable interfaces. The decision isn't always that simple; it depends on the advantages of splices and connectors, listed in Table 14.1.

● Splices are low-loss, permanent connections between fiber ends.

Table 14.1 Comparison of splice and connector advantages.

Connectors	Splices
Nonpermanent	Permanent
Simple to use once mounted	Lower attenuation
Factory installable on cables	Lower back-reflection
Allow easy reconfiguration	Easier to seal hermetically
Provide standard interfaces	Usually less expensive per splice
	More compact

● Permanent and nonpermanent junctions are needed in different situations.

● The lower loss of splices allows long-haul cables to be spliced together as the cable is installed.

● Enclosures are needed to protect splices.

It might seem strange to see "Permanent" listed as an advantage of splices and "Nonpermanent" as an advantage of connectors. However, each characteristic is desirable in certain applications. For example, splices to fix a broken underground cable should be permanent. However, you don't want to make permanent junctions between a local area network and terminals that may be moved about within a building.

The lower attenuation of splices simplifies installation of long-haul fiber-optic systems. Bare fiber normally comes on reels in standard lengths from 1 to 25 km. Cables are much bulkier than fibers—particularly the heavy-duty types intended for outdoor use—and normally come in lengths of 12 km or less.

Longer cable runs are made by splicing cable segments together. If the cables are installed in underground ducts, the splices are made and installed in manholes, with cable-segment length dependent on manhole spacing. Overhead cables are spliced in the field from segments with lengths that depend on the cable configuration.

The physical characteristics of splices are important in many long-distance applications. The spliced cables must be capable of withstanding the hostile outdoor environment, so splices are housed in protective enclosures. Although many splice enclosures are designed to be re-opened if repairs or changes are needed, they can be hermetically sealed to protect against moisture and temperature extremes. This combines with the low loss of splices to make them the preferred way to join lengths of fiber in long-haul telecommunication systems. These considerations are less important in shorter systems and systems in more controlled environments, where connectors are often used.

Types of Splicing

There are two basic approaches to fiber splicing: fusion and mechanical. Fusion splicing melts the ends of two fibers together so they fuse, like welding metal. Mechanical splicing holds two fiber ends together without welding them, using a mechanical clamp and/or glue. Each approach has its distinct advantages. Fusion splicers are expensive, but they require almost no consumable costs, and fusion splices have better optical characteristics. Mechanical splicing requires less equipment (and no costly fusion splicer), but consumable costs per splice are much higher. I'll discuss each approach in turn before looking at considerations of splice performance.

Fusion Splicing

Fusion splicing is performed by butting the tips of two fibers together and heating them so they melt together. This is normally done with a fusion splicer, which mechanically aligns the two fiber ends, then applies a spark across the tips to fuse them together. Typical splicers also include instruments to test splice quality and optics to help the technician align the fibers for splicing. Typical splice losses are 0.05 to 0.2 dB, with more than half below 0.1 dB. The basic arrangement of a fiber splicer is shown in Figure 14.1.

Fusion splicing welds fiber ends together.

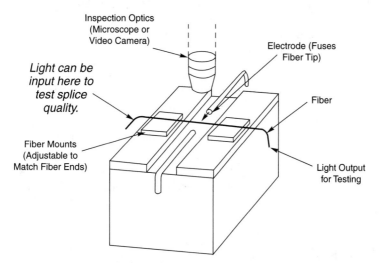

FIGURE 14.1

Key components of a fusion splicer.

Individual fiber splicers are designed differently, but all have the common goal of producing good splices reliably. Many are automated to assist the operator. They are expensive instruments, with prices starting at thousands of dollars and reaching tens of thousands of dollars for the most sophisticated models. Major differences center on the degree of automation and the amount of instrumentation included. Most models share the following key elements and functions:

- A fusion welder, typically an electric arc, with electrode spacing and timing of the arc adjustable by the user. The discharge heats the fiber junction. Portable versions are operated by batteries that carry enough charge for a few hundred splices before recharging. Factory versions operate from power lines or batteries.

● Mechanisms for mechanically aligning fibers with respect to the arc and each other. These include mounts that hold the fibers in place, as well as adjust their position. More expensive splicers automate alignment and measurement functions.

● A video camera or microscope (generally a binocular model) with magnification of 50 power or more so the operator can see the fibers while aligning them.

● Instruments to check optical power transmitted through the fibers both before and after splicing. Typically, light is coupled into a bent portion of the fiber on one side of the splice and coupled out of a bent portion on the other side. With proper calibration, this can measure the excess loss caused by the splice. (This may be missing from inexpensive field splicers.)

●

Before fusion splicing, plastic coatings must be removed from the fiber, and the end must be cleaved perpendicular to the fiber axis.

Fusion splicing involves a series of steps. First, the fiber must be exposed by cutting open the cable. Then the protective plastic coating or jacket must be stripped from a few millimeters to a few centimeters of fiber at the ends to be spliced. The fiber ends must be cleaved to produce faces that are within 1°–3° of being perpendicular to the fiber axis. The ends must be kept clean until they are fused.

The next step is alignment of the fibers, which may be done manually or automatically. After preliminary alignment, the ends may be "prefused" for about a second with a moderate arc that cleans their ends and rounds their edges. These ends are then pushed together, allowing power transmission to be tested to see how accurately they are aligned. After results are satisfactory, the arc is fired to weld the two fiber ends together. Care must be taken to ensure proper timing of the arc so the fiber ends are heated to the right temperature. After the joint cools, it can be recoated with a plastic material to protect against environmental degradation. The spliced area can also be enclosed in a plastic jacket. The entire splice assembly is then enclosed mechanically for protection, which in turn is mounted in a splice enclosure. The case around the individual splice provides strain relief.

Mechanical Splicing

●

Mechanical splicing gives higher losses but requires simpler equipment than fusion splicing.

Mechanical splices join two fiber ends either by clamping them within a structure or by gluing them together. A variety of approaches have been used in the past, and many are still in use. The extremely tight tolerances in splicing single-mode fiber often require special equipment not needed for splicing multimode fiber. Those extra requirements typically make single-mode splicing more expensive.

In general, mechanical splicing requires less costly capital equipment but has higher consumable costs than fusion splicing. This can tilt the balance toward mechanical splicing for organizations that don't perform much splicing, or for emergency on-site kits for temporary repairs. Mechanical splices tend to have slightly higher loss than fusion splices, but the difference is not dramatic. Back-reflections can occur in mechanical splices, but they can be reduced by using epoxy to connect the fibers, or by inserting into the splice a fluid or gel with a refractive index close to that of glass. This index-matching gel suppresses the reflections that can occur at a glass-air interface.

We will look briefly at important types of mechanical splices.

CAPILLARY SPLICE

One of the simplest types of splices relies on inserting two fiber ends into a thin capillary tube, as shown in Figure 14.2. The plastic coating is stripped from the fiber to expose the cladding, which is inserted into a tube with an inner diameter that matches the outer diameter of the clad fiber. The two fiber ends are then pushed into the capillary until they meet (often with index-matching gel inserted to reduce reflections). Compression or friction usually holds the fiber in place, although epoxy may also be used.

A capillary splice holds two fiber ends in a thin tube.

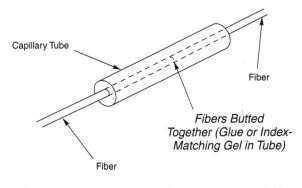

Capillary Tube

Fiber

Fibers Butted Together (Glue or Index-Matching Gel in Tube)

Fiber

FIGURE 14.2
Capillary splice joins two fibers.

Alignment of the fiber ends depends on mechanical alignment of the outside of the fibers. The result is a simple splice that is easy to install and can compensate for differences in the outer diameters of fibers. However, it is not designed to compensate for other differences between the fibers being joined.

ROTARY OR POLISHED-FERRULE SPLICE

A more elaborate arrangement is needed to compensate for subtle differences in the fibers being spliced. An older approach is the polished-ferrule splice, often called a rotary splice, shown in Figure 14.3. As with other splices, the plastic coating is first removed from the fiber. Then each fiber end is inserted into a separate ferrule, and its end is cleaved and polished to a smooth surface. The two polished ferrules then are mated within a jacket or tube.

The ferrules are designed to mount the fibers slightly off-center. After they are inserted into the tube, the ferrules are rotated while splice loss is monitored. The ferrules are fixed in place at the angle where splice loss is at a minimum. Although this technique is more complex and time-consuming than capillary splicing, it offers a more precise way of mating fibers. Its sensitivity to rotation of the fiber around its axis makes it suitable for splicing polarization-sensitive fibers.

FIGURE 14.3

Rotary or polished-ferrule splice.

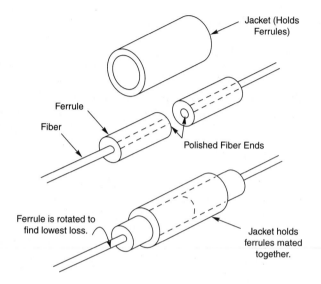

V-GROOVE SPLICE

• V-groove splices are valuable for multifiber splicing.

Fibers can also be held in V-shaped grooves in a plate like those used in multifiber connectors. V-groove splices can take various forms. The two fiber ends can be slipped into the same groove and a matching plate applied on top. The fiber ends can be put into separate grooved plates, and the ends polished before they are mated and aligned with another plate.

The V-groove splice is particularly useful for multifiber splicing, as shown in Figure 14.4 for ribbon cable. Each fiber in the cable slips into a separate groove, and mating the top and bottom plates automatically aligns all fibers with respect to one another. A practical limitation is the need for tight tolerances in the grooves. Field splicing of multifiber ribbon cables is aided by assembling end mounts on each cable in the factory and mating them in the field.

ELASTOMERIC SPLICE

• Elastomeric splices align fibers in a hole in a flexible plastic.

Another type of mechanical splice is the elastomeric splice shown in Figure 14.5. The internal structure is similar to the V-groove splice, but the plates are made of a flexible plastic material. An index-matching gel or epoxy is first inserted into the hole through the splice. Then one fiber end is inserted until it reaches about halfway through the splice.

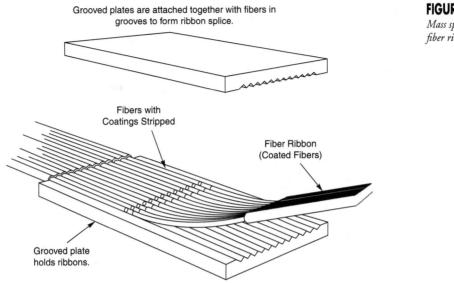

Grooved plates are attached together with fibers in grooves to form ribbon splice.

Fibers with Coatings Stripped

Fiber Ribbon (Coated Fibers)

Grooved plate holds ribbons.

FIGURE 14.4

Mass splicing of 12-fiber ribbons.

Finally, the second fiber end is inserted from the other end until it can be felt pushing against the first.

The elastomeric splice is often used in field kits for emergency restoration of service over a broken cable. Typical losses are about 0.25 dB, good for such applications.

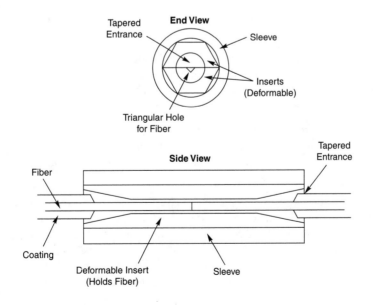

End View

Tapered Entrance

Sleeve

Inserts (Deformable)

Triangular Hole for Fiber

Side View

Tapered Entrance

Fiber

Coating

Deformable Insert (Holds Fiber)

Sleeve

FIGURE 14.5

Elastomeric splice developed for field use. (Courtesy of GTE)

The Connector-Splice Borderline

As you saw in the last chapter, the borderline between connectors and splices can be hazy. Some splices can be opened and reused a few times, but they are not designed for use as connectors. The factory-mounted splice elements on ribbon cables resemble multifiber connectors, and the splices can be opened and remated a few times, but these devices are not true connectors.

Splicing Issues

●

Loss, durability, and ease of operation are major concerns in splicing.

There are three principal concerns in splicing: the optical characteristics of the finished splice, its physical durability, and ease of splicing. Trade-offs among them enter into the choice of splice technology.

Attenuation

The attenuation mechanisms described for connectors in the last chapter also affect fiber-optic splices. However, splicing tends to align fibers more accurately, giving lower attenuation. Some sources of connection loss are essentially eliminated in splices; others are greatly reduced.

●

Fiber ends are fused, glued, or mechanically held together.

In a splice, the two fiber ends are bonded together by melting (fusing) them, gluing them, or mechanically holding them in a tightly confined structure. Bonding the two fiber ends together with no intervening air space reduces or eliminates losses from fiber spacing, as well as back-reflections.

Splice losses fall into two categories: intrinsic and extrinsic. Many are analogous to those encountered in connectors.

Intrinsic losses arise from differences in the fibers being connected. Mechanisms include variations in fiber core and outer diameter, differences in index profile and in ellipticity and eccentricity of the core. They can occur even in fibers with nominally identical specifications, because of inevitable variations in the manufacturing process.

Extrinsic losses arise from the nature of the splice itself. They depend on fiber end alignment, end quality, contamination, refractive-index matching between ends, spacing between ends, waveguide imperfections at the junction, and angular misalignment of bonded fibers.

●

Average splice loss is comparable for multimode and single-mode fibers.

Typically these two loss mechanisms are comparable in magnitude for well-made splices. Fortunately, the two types of loss combine to give a total splice loss that may be less than their arithmetic sum. (Note, however, that modal distribution effects can give misleading results in multimode fibers). Losses can be very low—near 0.05 dB—in properly made splices, but imperfect junctions can suffer from high loss. A single 10 μm dust particle in the wrong place can block the entire core of a single-mode fiber. With proper tools and procedures, splice attenuation is comparable for single-mode and multimode fibers.

Fiber Curl

If you've ever tried to splice together broken cassette tape, you've discovered the phenomenon of end curl. The ragged ends refuse to lie flat and straight, but instead curl, making splicing a frustrating task. Optical fibers suffer from a much smaller degree of end curl, but even a few micrometers can cause problems in splicing single-mode fibers. This makes it vital to design fibers and splicers to control fiber end curl.

Mismatched Fibers

All specifications are written with the implicit assumption that the two fibers being spliced are identical. If they are not, losses can be significant. For single-mode fibers, the most important losses come from mismatches in mode field diameter—the effective size of the mode transmitted by the fiber—and offset of the fiber cores. Slight variations occur in these characteristics even for fibers with nominally identical specifications, contributing to average splice loss of 0.05 to 0.1 dB. Note, however, that individual splices may have higher losses because of natural variations in fiber characteristics.

Most telecommunication fibers have the same 125-μm cladding diameter, making it physically possible to splice different fiber types. The loss of such splices depends on transmission direction. It would be negligibly small in going from a 10-μm-core single-mode fiber to a 62.5/125 multimode fiber but about 20 dB in the opposite direction. The mechanism involved, the difference in core areas, is the same as for connectors.

Back-Reflection

Reflections from within a splice can also affect optical performance. A good fusion or mechanical splice should have low reflection, but high reflections could occur if the splice is not made properly. Problems are more likely in mechanical splices because the ends can be physically separated, allowing reflection.

Strength

If you pull hard on a spliced metal wire, you expect it to part at the splice long before the wire itself fails. Optical fibers likewise are more vulnerable at splices. Different mechanisms affect fusion and mechanical splices.

Stripping the coating from fibers can damage them before splicing, causing microcracks that can cause failure later. In fusion splicing, contaminants can weaken the fusion zone itself, and thermal cycling can weaken the surrounding area. When fusion splices fail, they typically do so close to, but not at, the splice interface. The lifetime of the splice can be enhanced by claddings or jackets that protect the spliced zone from mechanical and environmental stresses.

Mechanical splices likewise can fail because the fibers were damaged in preparation. Other failures can occur in bonding the splice to the two fibers.

Ease of Splicing

Because splices are often installed in the field, the ease with which they can be made is an important concern. This has led to development of specialized equipment for field as well as factory use.

The need for a fusion splicer is the main practical limitation on fusion splicing. Standard factory splicers are boxes that measure up to a foot (30 cm) on all three sides, weigh 20 lb (10 kg) and up, and may cost as much as $50,000. The most expensive units are highly automated, able to prepare and align fibers precisely for splicing and estimate the loss *before* splicing. Some can perform multifiber ribbon splices, usually one fiber at a time.

Field splicing equipment that comes in for heavy use, such as in a van that a regional phone company equips specifically for fiber work, also may be quite sophisticated. Lighter-duty portable models that lack the most sophisticated features may weigh only a few pounds and cost several thousand dollars.

Installation of mechanical splices requires special splice housings and tools. However, the housings are small, and the tools are smaller and less expensive than those needed for fusion splicing. This makes mechanical splicing practical on a smaller scale than fusion splicing, so it's a common choice for emergency cable repair kits that are unlikely to be used often.

Mass versus Individual Splicing

So far I've implicitly assumed that fibers are spliced one at a time. However, cables generally contain two or more fibers that must be spliced. Often the simplest approach is to splice the fibers individually and house the splices in a splice enclosure of the sort described in the next section. However, this approach becomes time-consuming and costly for many-fiber cables.

An alternative is mass splicing many fibers at once. This can be done simply for ribbon cables, which contain many fibers in a flat line. Figure 14.4 showed mechanical splicing of a 12-fiber ribbon by aligning the fibers in parallel grooves. Similar alignment methods can be used to arrange fibers for mass fusion splicers. Mass splicing of multifiber cables can be considerably faster than individual splicing, and developers claim that losses are comparable or only slightly higher.

Splice Housings

Fiber-optic splices require protection from the environment, whether they are indoors or outdoors. Splice enclosures help organize spliced fibers in multifiber cables. They also protect the splices from strain and contamination.

Splice housings typically contain a rack such as the one shown in Figure 14.6, which contains an array of individual splices. This rack is mounted inside a case that provides environmental protection. Individual fibers broken out from a cable lead to and from the splices. To provide a safety margin in case further splices are needed, an excess length of fiber is left in the splice case. Like splice enclosures for telephone wires, fiber-optic splice cases are placed in strategic locations where splices are necessary (e.g., in manholes, on utility poles, or at points where fiber cables enter buildings).

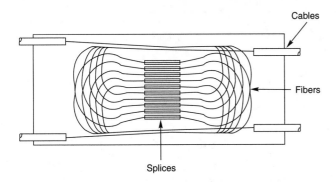

Cables

Fibers

Splices

FIGURE 14.6

Splices arrayed inside housing.

Fiber splice enclosures should be designed to

- Hold cable strength member tightly
- Block entrance of water
- Provide redundant seals in case one level fails
- Electrically bond and ground any metal elements in the cable (e.g., strength members and armor)
- Be re-enterable if the splice must be changed or repaired
- Organize splices and fibers so they can be readily identified
- Provide room for initial splicing and future modifications
- Leave large enough bend radii for fibers and cables to avoid losses and physical damage

Splice Testing

Where high performance is crucial, attenuation can be measured as the splice is being made. Many fusion splicers come with equipment that measures loss as the fibers are being aligned, then test loss after the splice is completed. As will be described in more detail in Chapter 17, precise measurement requires passing light through the splice from the remote end of one fiber being spliced to the remote end of the other—in the same direction that light will travel in the system. This is awkward in the field, where the remote ends may be several kilometers away.

A simpler approach is possible as long as the person making a splice needs to know only relative attenuation as the fibers are aligned. In practice, this is the needed information, because a peak in transmitted power indicates that the fiber alignment is best and the fibers are ready to be spliced. Such relative measurements can be made by bending the fibers near the splice point so light can be coupled into (and out of) them. Although this does not measure actual splice loss, it can make field fiber splicing a one-person job.

What Have You Learned?

1. Splices are permanent connections between fibers. They have lower attenuation than connectors.

2. Major issues in splices are attenuation, physical durability, and ease of installation.

3. Splices are normally made in the field.

4. Fusion splicing melts two fiber ends together; typical loss of fusion splices is less than 0.1 dB. It requires an expensive fusion splicer.

5. Mechanical splices hold fiber ends together mechanically or with glue. Losses tend to be slightly higher than with fusion splices, but they do not require expensive equipment to install.

6. The factors influencing attenuation of splices are very similar to those influencing connector attenuation. Mismatched fibers can cause high attenuation.

7. Splices are mounted in enclosures for protection against stress and the environment. The enclosures may be indoors or outdoors.

8. Fibers in multifiber cables may be spliced individually or in mass splices.

What's Next?

In Chapter 15, I will look at fiber-optic couplers, which transfer light between fibers, as well as other passive components.

Quiz for Chapter 14

1. Which of the following is not an advantage of a splice?

    a. Permanent junction between two fibers.

    b. Ease of making changes.

    c. Low attenuation

    d. Ease of installing in the field.

    e. Strength.

2. Which place is a splice most likely to be used?

a. In the middle of a long-distance cable.

b. To connect a computer terminal with a local area network.

c. To couple light from an LED to a short-distance fiber system.

d. To join an intrabuilding cable to a patch panel.

3. Splice loss typically is around

a. 0.01 dB.

b. 0.1 dB.

c. 0.5 dB.

d. 1.0 dB.

e. 0 dB.

4. Which of the following mechanisms could not cause loss in a fusion splice?

a. Differences in fiber core diameter.

b. Dirt in the splice zone.

c. Misalignment of fiber ends.

d. Separation between fiber ends.

5. What would happen in a splice between fibers of identical outer diameters but different size cores?

a. The splice would fail mechanically.

b. Loss would be high in both directions.

c. Loss would be high going from one large-core fiber to the small-core fibers, and low in the opposite direction.

d. Loss would be high going from the small-core fiber to the large-core fibers, and low in the opposite direction.

6. Where is a fusion splice most likely to fail under mechanical stress?

a. At the exact splice point.

b. About a millimeter from the splice point.

c. Far from the spliced point.

d. At the end being pulled.

e. Failure is unpredictable.

7. What is the major advantage of mechanical splices over fusion splices?

a. Lower attenuation.

b. Higher mechanical strength.

c. Elaborate fusion-splicing system not required.

d. Physically smaller.

8. Which of the following is not required in a fusion splicer?

a. A welder to heat fiber ends.

b. A microscope to view fiber ends.

c. A mechanical alignment system.

d. A device to cut fibers.

e. A glue-delivery system.

9. What is the primary advantage of mass splicing?

a. Lower attenuation.

b. Requires less costly splicing equipment.

   c. Reduces labor requirements and installation costs for multifiber cables.

   d. Reduces operator errors in matching fiber ends.

10. Splice housings are important because they

   a. reduce splice attenuation.

   b. protect splices from physical and environmental stresses.

   c. prevent hydrogen from escaping from splices.

   d. allow measurement of splice attenuation.

Passive Components

About This Chapter

Components in fiber-optic systems fall into two basic categories—passive and active. Passive components require no input power to operate on an optical signal. You have already learned about three important types, connectors, splices, and fibers. In this chapter, you will learn about other important passive components.

We will concentrate largely on couplers, which split signals from one fiber into two or more output fibers or combine two or more inputs into one output. As you will see, optical coupling is more involved than its electronic counterpart. Other important passive components include wavelength-division multiplexers and demultiplexers, filters, attenuators, planar waveguides, and optical isolators. There is some overlap among these categories; for example, couplers may be made using planar waveguide technology.

In this chapter, you will learn about these components and their structures and functions and examine some of their strengths and weaknesses.

Couplers and Taps

Defining Couplers

Connectors and splices join two fiber ends together. That's fine for sending signals between two devices, but many applications require connecting more than two devices. Connecting three or more points is a job for a coupler. (*Taps* usually connect three points, by taking part of a signal passing through

Couplers connect three or more points.

a communication line.) Couplers differ from switches in that couplers make unchanging connections, but switches can alter the connections. (Switches are active devices, covered in Chapter 16.)

Couplers are used in many places that you may not notice. For example, you need a coupler to connect both a telephone and an answering machine to the same telephone line. It may plug into the wall and give you two adjacent sockets, one for the phone and the other for the answering machine. It may be attached to the back of the answering machine, so you see two sockets, one for the line to the wall, the other for the line to the phone. Or it may be inside a single unit that contains both a phone and answering machine, dividing the signals between the two units in the same box. But the coupler must be there.

Couplers and taps are easy to make for electronic equipment. Electric current flows as long as you have physical contact between conductors; you don't have to line them up carefully, as you must with fiber cores. In addition, electronic signals usually are in the form of voltage. If you hook 1, 2, or 20 identical resistors across an ideal voltage source, each will see the same voltage signal. In reality, that's only a rough approximation of what happens in a telecommunication system. Putting more resistors in parallel across the signal source lowers the total resistance, so the voltage across the load will drop, depending on transmission-line resistance and other source characteristics. However, if the system is carefully designed, many loads in parallel will all have voltages close to what they would see individually. Thus electronic coupling can be as simple as hooking up wires to a signal source.

An optical signal must be divided among output ports, reducing its strength.

Optical signals are transmitted and coupled differently than electrical signals. First, you have to direct light into fiber cores, not merely make physical contact anywhere on the conductor. In addition, the nature of the optical signal is different. An optical signal is not a potential, like an electrical voltage, but a flow of signal carriers (photons), similar in some ways to an electrical current. Unlike a current, an optical signal does not flow *through* a receiver on its way to ground. The optical signal *stops* in the detector, which absorbs the light. That means you cannot put multiple fiber-optic receivers in series optically, because the first would absorb all the signal (except in certain special circumstances). If you want to divide an optical signal between two or more output ports, they must be in parallel. However, because the signal is not a potential, you cannot send the whole signal to all the ports. You must divide it between them in some way, so no terminal receives a signal as strong as the input.

The need to divide an optical signal limits the number of terminals that can be connected to a passive coupler, which merely splits up the input signal. With more ports, less signal reaches each one if the signal is divided equally, as shown in Table 15.1. Each doubling of the number of outputs reduces signal strength by 3 dB. Add too many outputs, and the signal grows too weak to detect reliably. The maximum number of ports depends on receiver sensitivity and other elements of system design.

Table 15.1 Loss from splitting signals equally in passive couplers with no excess loss.

Number of Output Ports	Fraction of Input in Each Output	Loss in dB
2	0.5	3.01
4	0.25	6.02
5	0.2	6.99
8	0.125	9.03
10	0.1	10
15	0.067	11.76
20	0.05	13.01
25	0.04	13.98
50	0.02	16.99
100	0.01	20
200	0.005	23.01
400	0.0025	26.02
1000	0.001	30

The loss shown in Table 15.1 is the best case possible, assuming all the input light emerges from one of the outputs. In practice, things aren't that good, particularly if the coupler has more output ports. You can divide a signal in half efficiently, but dividing it into 50 or 100 equal parts is harder; some inevitably gets lost, reducing output signal strength. The difference between input signal and the sum of all the outputs (P_1 to P_n) is called *excess loss*.

$$\text{Excess loss (dB)} = -10 \log\left(\frac{(P_1 + P_2 + \cdots + P_n)}{P_{\text{input}}}\right)$$

Note that Table 15.1 assumes the input signal is divided equally among the output ports. This does not have to be the case; you can design couplers that send 90% to one output and 10% to a second. It also assumes that the couplers are passive devices, which draw no input power and merely divide the input power among output ports. Most couplers fall into that category, but there are a few exceptions, which I will explain later.

Coupler Applications

Couplers have many different applications, so many types have been developed, which divide signals in different ways. Dividing signals between two outputs is the simplest example. As shown in Figure 15.1, couplers may need to split off a small fraction of the signal for each of several terminals, deliver identical signals to many different terminals,

Coupler choice and design depend on applications.

or direct different wavelengths to different places. Each of these applications requires a different type of coupler.

FIGURE 15.1

Different coupler applications: (a) tapping signals in a local area network; (b) delivering cable television to many subscribers; and (c) splitting wavelengths.

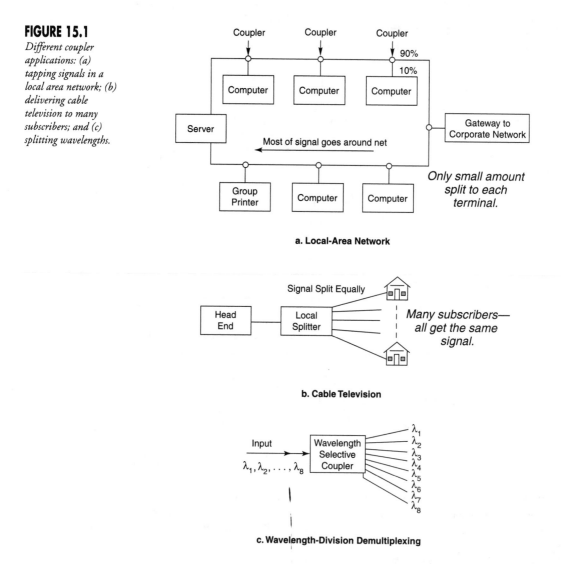

a. Local-Area Network

b. Cable Television

c. Wavelength-Division Demultiplexing

In the local area network of Figure 15.1(a), you need to direct a small fraction of the optical signal from the server to each terminal. Thus you might use a coupler that transmits 90% of the signal through the network and diverts only 10% to each terminal. (This turns out to be rather inefficient, because coupler losses accumulate around the ring, so real local-area networks usually use different architectures.)

For cable-television distribution, shown in Figure 15.1(b), you want to divide the same signal into many equal portions, one for each subscriber. For this application, you use a simple 1-to-n splitter, which divides the signal equally among *n* outputs.

For wavelength-division demultiplexing, shown in Figure 15.1(c), you want to separate several wavelengths carried in the same fiber and distribute them to different places. For example, a telephone company might want to send signals at different wavelengths to each of eight towns. You need a wavelength-selective coupler, which will direct all the signal at each wavelength to the proper destination. Thus, 100% of the input at λ_1 should go to the first town, 100% of the input at λ_2 should go to the second town, and so on. Wavelength-selective couplers can be used in a different way to *combine* signals; imagine the signals are going from right to left instead of from left to right across the page. In this case, the coupler serves as a wavelength-division *multiplexer*. You'll learn more about wavelength-selective couplers later.

These examples highlight some functions couplers can serve in fiber-optic systems. They can combine signals from different sources, separate signals carried at different wavelengths and route them to different destinations, or split signals among two or more receivers. Note that the couplers do not change the signals; they merely combine, divide, or separate them.

> WDM systems require wavelength-selective couplers.

Coupler Characteristics

You can look at couplers in a variety of ways, but we'll start with their functional characteristics and then consider specific types and technologies.

Several characteristics are important in determining their use and function:

- Directionality of light transmission: which way light goes through the coupler
- Number of input and output ports, which may or may not be distinct
- Wavelength selectivity
- Type of transmission: single- or multimode, or sensitive to polarization
- Signal attenuation and splitting
- Polarization-dependent loss

DIRECTIONALITY

The transmission of many couplers depends on which way light goes through them. Figure 15.2(a) shows an example of one such directional coupler, where light branches between two diverging guides, such as a pair of fibers. Light entering from the left port is split between the two outputs to the left. However, if light enters the upper right port, virtually all of it will emerge from the left port because of the coupler geometry. (A tiny fraction will emerge from the lower right port, but not enough emerges to be useful.)

> The transmission of directional couplers depends on which way the light is going.

FIGURE 15.2

*Directional and
nondirectional
couplers.*

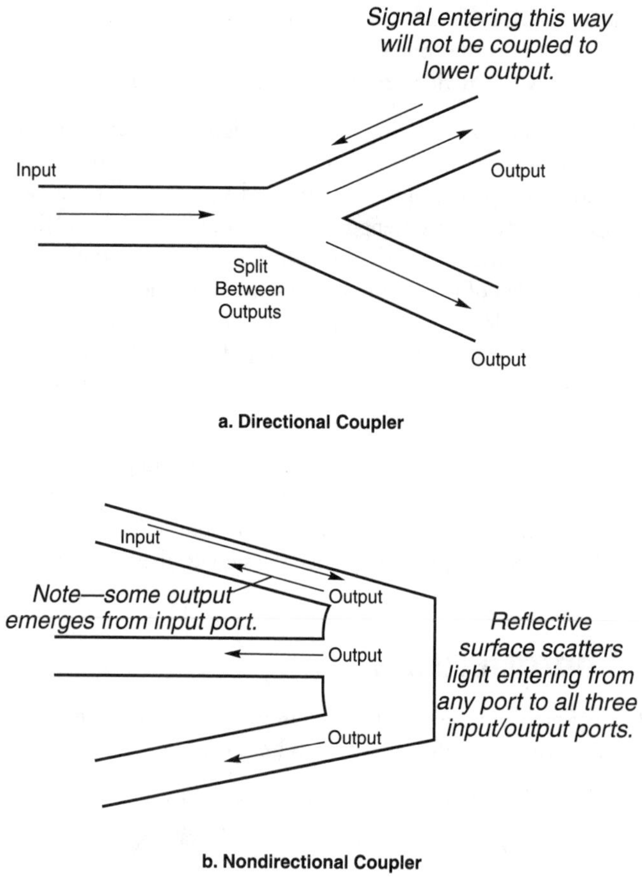

Signal entering this way
will not be coupled to
lower output.

Input

Output

Split
Between
Outputs

Output

a. Directional Coupler

Input

Note—some output
emerges from input port.

Output

Output

Reflective
surface scatters
light entering from
any port to all three
input/output ports.

Output

b. Nondirectional Coupler

Other couplers show little or no sensitivity to light direction. Figure 15.2(b) is one example, where light entering from the three ports on the left is reflected from a mirror on the right, which scatters light to all three ports. It doesn't matter which port the light enters; reflected light emerges from all three—including the input port. Such a coupler mixes the light from all inputs and delivers it to all outputs.

Most directional couplers are really bidirectional devices. That is, they can transmit light in either direction, but the light keeps going in that direction. The 1-by-2 coupler in Figure 15.2(a) is such a device. If you direct light through the upper-right port, it will keep going in the same direction and emerge through the single port at the left. Note the difference from a *nondirectional* coupler. In a bidirectional coupler, light going in a port on either side emerges only from the ports on the other. In a nondirectional coupler, light going in any one port emerges from all the ports, including the input. There isn't much demand for truly nondirectional couplers, but they can be made if you need them.

Generally, directionality or bidirectionality is an advantage in couplers, because it sends the signal in the direction you want it. Light headed in the wrong direction—back toward the transmitter in an input fiber, for example—can cause problems such as generating noise in laser transmitters.

Directionality or suppression of reflection back toward the source generally is measured in decibels. If a 1-mW (0-dBm) signal goes through a coupler with 50-dB directionality, only 0.01 μW (−50 dBm) will go in the wrong direction.

INPUT AND OUTPUT PORTS

The number of input and output ports must be matched to the application. To split one input between two outputs, you need a 1-by-2 (1 input, 2 output) coupler. To divide the signal between 20 outputs, you need a 1-by-20 coupler. And if you want to combine the signals from 10 terminals and distribute the outputs among the same 10 terminals, you need a 10-by-10 coupler.

In practice, different coupler technologies are best suited to particular types of couplers. We'll sort them out when we consider coupler technologies.

WAVELENGTH SELECTIVITY

Light transmission by a coupler, like that of any optical device, may vary with wavelength. Some couplers are made to be independent of wavelength, so the variation should be small over their normal operating range. (Be aware, however, that their transmission may not be specified at all wavelengths used for fiber transmission.) Alternatively, the variation can be made large so the coupler can separate light of different wavelengths. Typically this is done using layered thin films, fiber gratings, or other layered materials that selectively reflect certain wavelengths.

Suppose, for example, you are pumping an erbium-doped fiber amplifier with a 1480-nm diode laser and want the amplified output at 1550 nm to go a different path, as shown in Figure 15.3(a). You could direct the light at a mirror coated with many thin layers designed to reflect light at 1550 nm but transmit 1480 nm, as shown in Figure 15.3(b). The straight-through path sends light between the pump laser and the fiber amplifier. The reflected 1550 nm output from the fiber amplifier exits through the output fiber at lower right.

Couplers can be made with very high wavelength selectivity. Virtually all the light supposed to be reflected is reflected; virtually all the light supposed to be transmitted goes through. Couplers can be made to select a very narrow range of wavelengths for use in wavelength-division-multiplexing systems.

> ● Wavelength-selective couplers are needed for WDM systems.

FIGURE 15.3

Wavelength-selective coupler transmits wavelengths shorter than 1500 nm and reflects longer wavelengths.

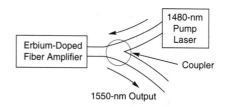

a. Coupler transmits 1480-nm pump through top port and 1550-nm amplifier output through bottom port.

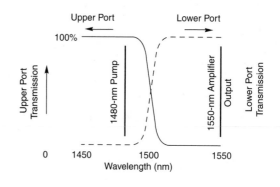

b. Coupler Transmission

TYPES OF FIBER

Depending on the technology used, couplers may work only for single-mode fiber, only for multimode fiber, or for both. This should be clear from device specifications. You should also watch for input and output interfaces because of potential losses when transferring light between different types of fibers.

EXCESS LOSS AND SIGNAL SPLITTING

Insertion loss combines signal splitting and excess loss.

Two effects contribute to port-to-port signal attenuation within couplers. One is the normal attenuation inevitable when dividing an optical signal between two or more outputs. With one input and a pair of equal outputs, this is 3 dB. The other is excess loss, essentially the light wasted within the coupler that doesn't get divided among the outputs. Generally excess loss is small, but it is not safe to ignore it. Specifications for port-to-port loss usually combine both types of loss as insertion loss.

Most couplers divide signals equally among all output ports, but some divide signals unequally. One example is a coupler that directs 90% of the light out one port and 10%

out a second; another is a splitter that divides output among three ports in a 90:5:5 ratio. These couplers generally have special uses, but their existence means you can't assume all couplers divide signals equally among outputs.

Port-to-port attenuation also may be specified for light going the wrong way in a directional coupler. In this case, the higher the loss, the better, because this is stray light.

POLARIZATION-DEPENDENT LOSS

Light transmission in some couplers depends on polarization, leading to an effect called *polarization-dependent loss.* This is a significant concern because most fiber-optic systems do not constrain polarization. If coupler loss depends on polarization, random variations in polarization of the input light can essentially modulate the signal with polarization noise, which is not a good thing because it degrades transmission quality. The larger the polarization-dependent loss, the larger this noise can be.

Types of Couplers

There are several distinct families of couplers and splitters. The names vary to some extent among manufacturers, but the basic families shown in Figure 15.4 are 3-port T couplers, "tree," or 1-to-*n*, port splitters, star couplers, and wavelength-selective couplers. The names often come from their geometry.

T AND Y COUPLERS

T and Y couplers, sometimes called *taps,* are three-port devices, which split one input between two outputs. They may divide the signal equally between the two outputs or split it in some other ratio. Some T couplers are analogous to electrical taps that take part of a signal from a passing cable and relay it to a terminal; they are often shown as one fiber coming off a cable in a T configuration. Others have a Y-shaped geometry, with two outputs branching at an angle from one input, and are called Y couplers. They are often—but not always—directional.

T couplers are
three-port devices.

1-TO-*N* OR TREE, COUPLERS

Tree, or 1-to-*n*, couplers generally take a single input signal and split it among multiple outputs. Some have a pair of inputs that are each divided among multiple outputs; some may combine multiple inputs to one or two outputs. They are generally directional.

STAR COUPLERS

Star couplers get their name from the geometry used to show their operation in diagrams such as in Figure 15.4, a central mixing element with fibers radiating outward like a star. They have multiple inputs and outputs, often (but not always) equal in number. There are two basic types. One type is directional, mixing signals from all input fibers and distributing them among all outputs, like the upper star coupler in Figure 15.4, often made by fusing fibers together. These are bidirectional devices because they also can transmit light in the opposite direction. A second is nondirectional, instead taking inputs from all fibers and distributing them among all fibers—both input and output—as with the lower star coupler shown in Figure 15.4.

FIGURE 15.4

Important coupler types.

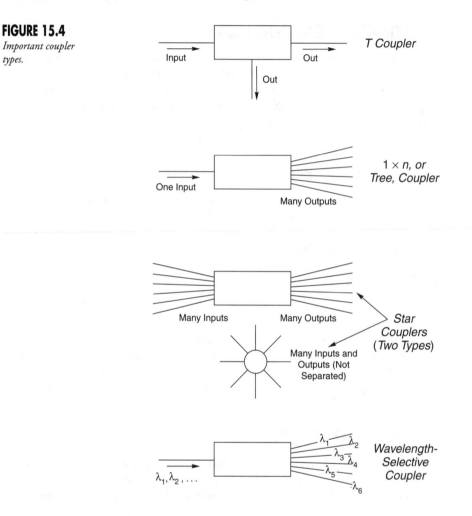

WAVELENGTH-SELECTIVE COUPLERS

Wavelength-selective couplers distribute signals according to their wavelength.

Wavelength-selective couplers distribute signals according to their wavelengths. Their main uses are to route WDM signals to their proper destinations and to separate wavelengths transmitted for different purposes through the same fiber, such as separating the light pumping an optical amplifier from the amplified signal. Wavelength-selective couplers are supposed to block other wavelengths from reaching the wrong destination. They may be directional or nondirectional.

Types of wavelength-selective couplers include the following:

- Demultiplexers for WDM systems, which route different wavelengths to different points.
- Add-drop multiplexers, which separate a single wavelength to route that signal to a particular destination while sending other wavelengths elsewhere. They also may add a new signal at that wavelength.
- Pump-wavelength separators, which divert the pump wavelength for an optical amplifier on a path different than the amplified signal.
- Wavelength combiners or multiplexers, which merge multiple wavelengths into one WDM signal. 1-by-n couplers can serve the same role, functioning as n-by-1 couplers when inputs enter through the multiple-port side of the coupler.

Coupler Technologies

Couplers can be made using several different technologies. Some approaches require taking light out of a fiber and dividing it before delivering it to other fibers; others transfer light energy directly between fibers. The choice of a technology depends on the type of coupler and the cost and performance requirements. Important approaches include bulk or micro optics, GRIN (graded-index) rods, fiber segments fused together, fiber gratings, and planar waveguides.

BULK AND MICRO OPTICS

In the world of fiber optics, *bulk optics* are conventional lenses, mirrors, and diffraction gratings, the sort of things you can hold in your hands. Bulk optics do not have to be large; they may be made quite small to match the dimensions of optical fibers and light sources. Such *micro optics* may be tiny, but they are still based on the same optical principles as larger bulk optics, so I will cover them together.

Bulk optics were the basis of many early types of couplers, and they still work. Figure 15.5 shows a simple example, the use of a device called a *beamsplitter* to split one input signal into two outputs. Like a one-way mirror, the beamsplitter transmits some light that hits it and reflects the rest. Collect the light from the two outputs in fibers, and you have a T coupler.

Bulk optical couplers often include lenses that expand, collimate, or focus light. The simple coupler of Figure 15.5 generally works better if a lens expands the light emerging from a fiber and focuses it onto a large area of the beamsplitter. Then additional lenses focus the output beams into output fibers. Standard lenses with curved surfaces may be used; generally they are tiny, to match the sizes of fibers.

Micro optics are tiny versions of conventional lenses and other optical components, shrunk in size to work with fibers.

GRIN lenses are rods or fibers with refractive index graded so they act like ordinary lenses.

FIGURE 15.5

Bulk optical coupler: A beamsplitter splits a signal in half.

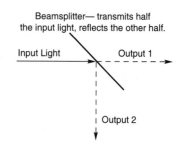

Alternatively, gradient-index (GRIN) lenses (or rods) may be used. These are rods or fibers in which the refractive index of the glass changes either with distance along the rod or with distance from the axis. The refractive-index gradient makes GRIN lenses focus light in a way functionally equivalent to ordinary lenses, but GRIN lenses are smaller and easier to adapt to fiber systems.

Another application of bulk optics is the use of a diffraction grating to separate wavelengths. A diffraction grating is an array of closely spaced parallel grooves, which act together to scatter light at an angle that depends on its wavelength, generating a rainbow of colors. You can see the same effect in light reflected at an angle from the circular grooves in a CD. A diffraction grating will scatter each wavelength in a WDM signal at a different angle, so you can use this effect to demultiplex WDM signals. The main practical problem is that gratings often cannot completely separate wavelengths that are closely spaced, such as those in dense WDM systems.

FUSED-FIBER COUPLERS

Fused fiber couplers are the most widely used type.

Normally you can't transfer light between fibers just by touching them together. The light-guiding cores are covered by claddings which keep light from leaking out. If you want to couple light between fibers, you have to transfer it between the cores. That means you have to remove the claddings so the cores can touch. That is the basis of fused-fiber couplers, made by melting together fibers, usually with claddings removed partly or totally from one side, as shown in Figure 15.6. Fused-fiber couplers sometimes are called *biconic* couplers, which should not be confused with biconic connectors, an early type in only limited use today. They are the most common technology used to make couplers.

Although Figure 15.6 shows the cores merged, they don't have to merge completely in the middle zone. A phenomenon called evanescent wave coupling lets light pass through a thin zone of lower refractive index—say, a few micrometers—between the lower-index fiber cores. This is possible because some light actually travels in the inner portion of the cladding, as you learned in Chapter 4.

Fusing two fibers produces a 2 × 2 coupler with two inputs and two outputs. In practice, these are often turned into 1 × 2 couplers by terminating one fiber end inside the case. This design is inherently directional, although it is bidirectional in the sense that light can go through it in either direction. If light enters the fiber end at upper left in Figure 15.6, the only way light can reach the fiber end at lower right is by reflection or scattering. Directivity is measured by comparing the input power, P_1, to the power reflected back through the other fiber end on the input side, P_4:

$$\text{Directivity (dB)} = -10 \log\left(\frac{P_4}{P_1}\right)$$

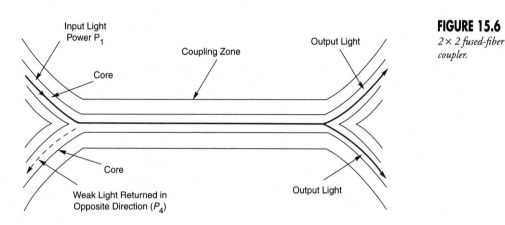

FIGURE 15.6

2 × 2 fused-fiber coupler.

For a typical fused-fiber coupler, the directivity is 40 to 45 dB.

The fused-fiber coupler design can be extended to multiple fibers using the same basic principles. The important change is adding more fibers, so signals from all the input fibers mix in the coupling zone and emerge out all the output fibers. This approach can be used to make star couplers with many distinct inputs and outputs, as shown in Figure 15.4. Multifiber fused couplers also are bidirectional.

PLANAR WAVEGUIDES

Optical fibers are not the only type of optical waveguides. Planar waveguides are based on the same idea of confining light in a region of high refractive index by surrounding it with material having a smaller refractive index. However, a planar waveguide is flat instead of cylindrical. Generally, a planar waveguide is a thin stripe of high-index material embedded in the surface of a flat substrate, as shown in Figure 15.7. It also can be a stripe deposited on top of the surface.

Typically, the stripe is made by diffusing a dopant into the substrate, which raises the refractive index of the material. The lower-index substrate material forms three walls of the waveguide, confining light in it. The top is exposed to air, which also has a lower refractive index, so the whole stripe serves as a waveguide for light. Planar waveguides are a versatile technology, also used in active devices described in Chapter 16, but here we will concentrate on planar waveguide couplers.

Planar waveguides work like fibers, confining light to a zone with higher refractive index.

FIGURE 15.7

*Cross section of a
planar waveguide.*

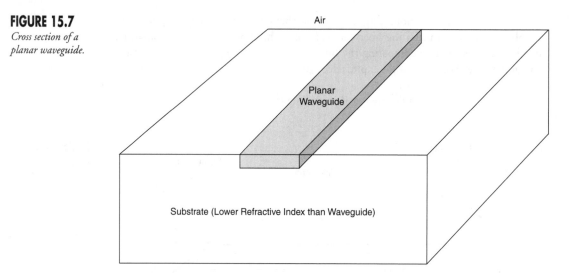

Waveguides don't have to be straight lines. They are written using standard semiconductor techniques, so you can make them in a variety of patterns, including structures that branch and merge—the planar waveguide equivalents of fused fiber couplers.

● Simple waveguide couplers are branched planar waveguides.

The simplest type of waveguide coupler is a Y-shaped structure like the directional coupler in Figure 15.2(a). The actual split angle is much smaller than shown. If the output waveguides go off at equal angles, the light splits evenly between them. This approach can be extended to more than two outputs either by making more than two output branches or by putting two or more Y junctions in series, one after the other, to split the signal among multiple outputs. The division of power among the outputs depends on the junction angles and how successive junctions are arranged.

● Light can leak between two closely spaced waveguides, forming a coupler.

Another approach is to use evanescent-wave coupling between two closely spaced waveguides, as shown in Figure 15.8. As with optical fibers, waveguides generate evanescent waves in the surrounding low-index material, and these evanescent waves can leak into adjacent waveguides.

In the evanescent wave coupler, the power in each waveguide varies along the length of the region where they are close enough for light to leak between them. As light travels along the upper waveguide in Figure 15.8, more and more of it transfers to the lower waveguide. This continues until all the light shifts to the lower waveguide at a point called the *transfer length,* which depends on the optical characteristics of the waveguide. Then the light starts shifting back from the lower waveguide to the upper one. Thus the distribution of light energy between the two waveguides oscillates back and forth between them with distance, as shown in the lower part of Figure 15.8. The oscillation stops at the end of the coupling region, determining the final distribution of light. Designers select lengths and optical properties of the two parallel guides to give the desired distribution of light (e.g., 50–50 or 75–25). In practice, some light is lost within the waveguide and in transferring between the two guides.

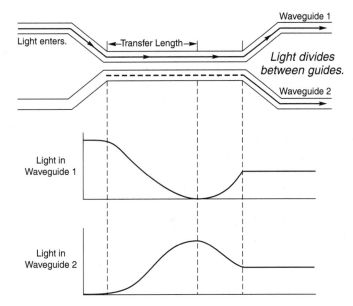

FIGURE 15.8

Light transfer between two evanescently coupled waveguides.

Surface waveguides can be fabricated in complex patterns on a variety of materials. When they are made on the same substrate with many other devices, they are often called integrated optics, but then they usually contain active devices such as lasers, switches, or modulators. Chapter 16 covers such devices.

Planar waveguides can be made in a variety of materials. They include glass, semiconductors such as gallium arsenide, and materials such as lithium niobate with properties that change when an electric field is applied to them.

One important practical issue with planar waveguides is transferring light between them and fibers. The thin, flat profile of a planar waveguide is a poor match for the cylindrical core of a single-mode fiber and presents some problems for the larger cores of multimode fibers. You need lenses and other optics to couple light efficiently from a fiber into a waveguide or from a waveguide into a fiber. In practice, this has been a major limitation on the use of planar waveguide components.

FIBER-GRATING COUPLERS

The Bragg fiber gratings described in Chapter 7 often serve as the basis of wavelength-selective couplers. Recall that the fiber grating selectively reflects light at a narrow range of wavelengths while transmitting other light. As shown in Figures 7.8 and 7.9, fiber gratings can be arranged in various ways to separate wavelengths for wavelength-division multiplexing. Because they are strongly selective, they are widely used for dense WDM systems.

Fiber gratings are used in wavelength-selective couplers.

Active Couplers

Another way to split signals from a fiber-optic transmission line is with a device called an *active coupler*. This is essentially a dedicated repeater that produces two (or more) output signals, which can be optical and/or electronic. Strictly speaking it isn't a passive device, but it belongs here because it serves the same function as passive couplers.

The main uses of active couplers are in local-area networks. For example, the fiber running to a network node may end at a receiver that generates two electronic outputs. One goes to an optical transmitter, which generates a signal to send through the next length of fiber. The other goes directly to the terminal attached to that network node. Alternatively, the receiver can generate electronic signals to drive a pair of optical transmitters.

WDM COMPONENTS

Couplers are not the only passive components used in wavelength-division multiplexing. The rapid growth of WDM systems demands a closer look at all passive wavelength-selective components.

WDM components have a variety of names, sometimes confusing and sometimes synonymous. The important ones are

- Multiplexers, or combiners, which combine signals of different wavelengths so they all pass through a single optical fiber.

- Demultiplexers, or splitters, which separate signals of different wavelengths so they emerge through different fibers.

- Routers, which direct signals of certain wavelengths to specified points but may not separate all signals carried by one fiber. Thus a router might direct one wavelength through one fiber and all others through a separate fiber. WDM routers as demonstrated to date are passive devices which always direct the same wavelength along the same path; switches are active devices, described in Chapter 16. (Note that routers have a different function in telecommunications, as explained in more detail later.)

- Add/drop multiplexers, or combiners, which drop one (or more) wavelengths at one point and pick up one (or more) signals for transmission through the next length of fiber. They transmit other wavelengths unchanged.

- Filters, which reflect or transmit one wavelength, usually doing the opposite for other wavelengths, although some filters absorb undesired wavelengths.

Just to confuse things, the terminology is hazy. Some people use the term *splitters* for devices that combine multiple signals. Other types of routers direct data packets in digital telecommunicaton systems. However, you generally can tell the meaning from the context.

The performance required of WDM components depends on the spacing between the wavelengths being used. It's relatively easy to separate light in the 1300- and 1550-nm windows or to separate the 980-nm pump band from the 1550-nm emission band of an erbium-doped fiber amplifier. The 1480-nm pump band is a bit harder. WDM systems that combine four or eight channels in the erbium-doped fiber amplifier window are harder. Most demanding are dense-WDM (D-WDM) systems, where adjacent wavelengths may be less than a nanometer apart.

Several technologies are used for WDM components, with the choice depending on the usual cost-performance trade-offs. You will find that some manufacturers may not clearly identify the technology used in their components. I will briefly describe major competing technologies, but the field is moving fast, and the choices are likely to change.

Interference Filters

Interference filters are among the simpler approaches. An interference filter is a coating made by depositing a series of thin alternating layers of two materials with different refractive indexes. This structure generates interference effects that depend on the thickness of the layers, their refractive indexes, the wavelength of light, and the angle at which it strikes the coating. These are the same type of interference effects that cause fiber gratings to strongly reflect selected wavelengths while transmitting other wavelengths very well. The optical characteristics of interference filters are fixed, but the wavelengths selected depend on the angle at which light strikes the coating.

The technology of thin-film interference coatings is well established for conventional bulk optics, particularly those for use with laser systems. They absorb little light, reflecting or transmitting virtually all the light that strikes them. This is an important asset for wavelength separation. However, conventional interference filters generally lack the extremely fine wavelength resolution needed for D-WDM.

Bulk Optical Gratings

I mentioned earlier that a diffraction grating—a series of parallel grooves—diffracts light, scattering it at an angle that depends on the wavelength. You can see the same rainbow effect if you tilt a CD, because the pits that record music form rings that are essentially parallel to each other. Interference of waves reflected from the parallel grooves is what causes the scattering angle to vary with wavelength. You can use this effect to separate wavelengths. In practice, lenses focus the input light, collect the reflected light, and focus it onto the output fibers.

Figure 15.9 gives an example of a grating coupler, combined with a gradient-index (GRIN) rod lens. The lowest fiber delivers light at three wavelengths, λ_1, λ_2, and λ_3. The GRIN rod lens focuses the light onto a diffraction grating at the back end of the rod, which is cut at an angle. The grating diffracts the three wavelengths at different angles, and the GRIN rod focuses them back to the three output fibers. When everything is properly aligned (which, of course, is a big part of the job), λ_1 emerges from the top output fiber, λ_2 emerges from the middle output fiber, and λ_3 emerges from the lowest output fiber.

FIGURE 15.9

A grating coupler with GRIN rod separates three wavelengths

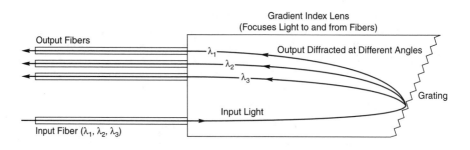

You can make grating couplers with tiny conventional lenses, but the GRIN rod serves the same function in a small device that is easier to align. Grating couplers are good for separating several wavelengths in WDM systems but are hard to make for the many closely spaced wavelengths in D-WDM systems.

Arrayed Waveguides

● A waveguide array can separate wavelengths.

Another way to separate wavelengths is to pass them through an array of planar wave-guides, as shown in Figure 15.10. The multiwavelength signal enters through the wave-guide at left. The light from the input waveguide spreads out in the coupler at left and exits through the multiple curved waveguides. The waveguides have slightly different lengths, so light takes different times to pass through each waveguide.

FIGURE 15.10

Arrayed waveguides separate wavelengths for WDM system.

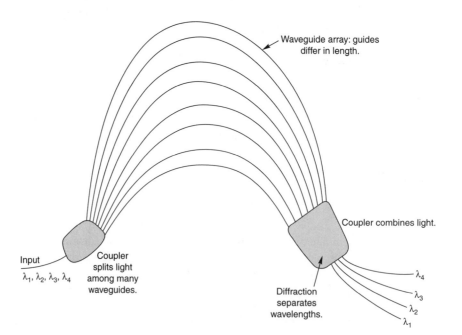

This regular delay of the light in the separate waveguides causes interference and diffraction when they mix in the coupler at the right. As a result, each wavelength emerges on the other side of the coupler at a different angle. The waveguides collecting the light from the combining coupler are spaced to collect the desired wavelengths.

Although the theory behind these devices is complex, their operation is fairly simple. Arrayed waveguides are particularly useful for separating the many closely spaced wavelengths in D-WDM systems.

Fiber Gratings

As fiber components, fiber gratings also are attractive for WDM. As you learned in Chapter 7, they can select a narrow range of wavelengths, depending on how they are made. Figure 7.7 showed how narrow the wavelength range can be.

By combining fiber gratings in various arrangements, you can sort many closely spaced wavelengths and direct them to different output fibers. Typically, each fiber grating isolates a single wavelength, as shown in Figures 7.8 and 7.9; assembling many gratings can separate all the wavelengths in a D-WDM signal. Fiber gratings that reflect one wavelength but transmit others can split that wavelength off at a transfer point, deliver it to a local terminal, collect another signal at the same wavelength, and combine that with the wavelengths that were transmitted by the grating. Thus they act as add-drop multiplexers.

Fiber gratings have high resolution, so they can separate many closely spaced wavelengths. An additional advantage is the ease of connecting fibers to fiber gratings, which are better matched to their dimensions than waveguide arrays.

> Fiber gratings can separate closely spaced dense-WDM signals.

Fused-Fiber Couplers

Fused-fiber couplers are inherently sensitive to wavelength. As with waveguide couplers, the transfer of light between fused fibers changes with the length of the coupling region. In this case, the length is measured not in an absolute number of micrometers or millimeters, but as a number of waves. Thus, the distance looks longer to shorter wavelengths, because more of the shorter waves span the same distance.

You can use this effect to separate wavelengths, as shown in Figure 15.11. For each wavelength, the division of light between top and bottom outputs changes with the length of the fused region. The pattern is a sine wave, and the distribution varies from all light emerging from the top to all light emerging from the bottom. You need only pick the length so that all the light at one wavelength emerges from one output, whereas all the light at the other wavelength emerges from the other. In the example, the wavelengths are 980 and 1550 nm. The process works best for two wavelengths that are not closely spaced, so fused-fiber couplers are not used for isolating one wavelength from several others that differ by only a few nanometers.

> Fused-fiber couplers are wavelength-sensitive, but their selectivity is limited.

FIGURE 15.11

Fused-fiber coupler splits two wavelengths.

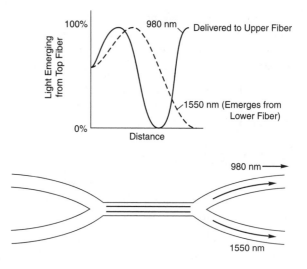

The physics of waveguide couplers works the same way, so they are sensitive to the wavelength of light transmitted through them in the same way as fused fiber couplers. However, they are more complex and are rarely used for separating two wavelengths.

Attenuators and Other Filters

Attenuators and filters are a broad family of optical devices that block some input light from reaching a particular point. For WDM systems, the goal is to separate signals at different wavelengths and route them to different destinations. In other cases, the goal is to reduce signal intensity, which might otherwise overload the receiver, to block extraneous signals at other wavelengths or to balance signals transmitted through the same system at different wavelengths.

Attenuators and filters block some input light as well as separating wavelengths.

You have already learned about some types of filters used in WDM couplers, particularly interference filters for demultiplexing. Fiber gratings really are special-purpose filters, made in fiber form. I won't go back over WDM filters, but you should realize that they are specialized filters, which distribute signals at different wavelengths to separate outputs. Instead, we will look at other types of filters.

Attenuators

Attenuators block some input light.

There can be such a thing as too much light in a fiber-optic communication system, because excess input power can overload a receiver. You can reduce the input signal to the level required by the receiver by inserting an attenuator, a filter that transmits only a certain fraction of the input light. Attenuators are like sunglasses which protect your eyes from being dazzled by bright lights. They generally absorb the extra light energy, which in general is too little to heat the attenuator noticeably. You generally don't want attenuators to reflect the unwanted light, because it could return through the fiber system to introduce noise into a laser transmitter.

Ideally attenuators should block the same fraction of light at all wavelengths. Most come with a fixed value of attenuation in decibels; put a 5-dB attenuator in the path of an optical signal, and its intensity drops 5 dB.

Variable attenuators also are available, which you can adjust to obtain attenuation within a specified range. These generally are precision instruments used in making measurements.

Line and Band Filters

Some filters selectively block light or, alternatively, transmit only selected wavelengths. Functionally this sounds like the same thing, but different types of filters can serve the same purpose. Line and band filters can be used in some types of wavelength-division multiplexing, but more often they serve to block undesired wavelengths rather than to separate signals.

The main function of line and band filters is to restrict light transmission so only certain wavelengths pass through, blocking other wavelengths that might generate noise or other problems. For example, you might need to remove 1480-nm pump light from the output of an erbium-doped fiber amplifier. A simple way to do this is by adding a filter that blocks the undesired wavelength. In practice, you can do this either with a filter that transmits only the desired wavelengths (e.g., 1520–1570 nm from a fiber amplifier) or that specifically blocks the undesired wavelength (1480 nm in the example). Another approach that works for this example is a filter that blocks all light at wavelengths less than 1500 nm.

Equalizing Filters

In Chapter 12, you learned that fiber amplifiers do not amplify all wavelengths equally, because their gain varies with wavelength. This can lead to some wavelengths in a WDM signal becoming stronger than others. For example, if a 1535-nm signal is amplified to a level 5 dB higher than one at 1550 nm, the shorter wavelength will be 25 dB stronger after a series of 5 amplifiers. This means that the weaker signals may get lost in the noise.

Equalizing filters balance the degree of amplification of signals at different wavelengths.

Figure 15.12 shows how an equalizing filter can compensate for this difference. If you know how the gain of an amplifier varies with wavelength, you can make a filter that transmits more light at wavelengths where gain is weakest and blocks some light at wavelengths where gain is strongest. The idea is to have the gain of the amplifier and the loss of the equalizing filter add up to the same number at all wavelengths used in the system.

For example, if the amplifier gain at 1535 nm is 2 dB higher than at 1550 nm, the filter should absorb 2 dB more light at 1535 nm.

FIGURE 15.12

Equalizing filter balances uneven gain in a fiber amplifier.

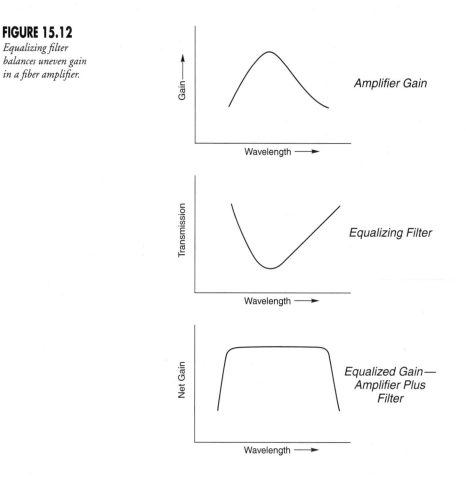

Equalization becomes more important the longer the system is. You can live with a 0.5-dB difference in each of a series of five amplifiers, because that builds up to a modest 2.5-dB difference. But that's not acceptable in a submarine cable that has 100 amplifiers spaced over 5000 km, where the difference would build up to 50 dB.

Filter Designs and Variations

Filter designs can vary widely. Wavelength-separation filters typically have sharp cutoffs, particularly for dense-WDM systems, because the goal is to transmit all the light at one wavelength and reflect all the light at another wavelength. On the other hand, attenuators generally should reduce light intensity uniformly at all wavelengths; a 5-dB attenuator should reduce intensity 5 dB at 1300 nm as well as at 1550 nm. An equalization filter should have properties that vary with wavelength in a precisely controlled way. Special-purpose filters called *beamsplitters* may be used in couplers to divide light beams in half, with part reflected and the rest transmitted.

Both conventional filters and fiber gratings can be designed to meet these criteria by adjusting the spacing and composition of a series of layers.

Fixed and Tunable Filters

Standard filters always transmit light in the same way unless subjected to environmental abuse. Changing temperatures and environments can affect transmission slightly, but the results are not very controllable.

However, it is possible to make tunable filters, which can be adjusted to select different wavelengths. Like active couplers, they aren't completely passive devices, but they belong in this chapter with other types of filters. There are two major types in use today.

One type is the Fabry-Perot interferometer, which is essentially an optical cavity similar to those used as laser resonators, but without the laser medium inside. It consists of two partially reflecting mirrors aligned parallel to each other, so light bounces back and forth between them. Both mirrors are partly transparent, so light can enter the cavity, but once it enters it generally bounces back and forth many times, because the mirrors reflect most of the light. Interference effects select light with wavelengths that resonate in the cavity; that is, the round-trip distance within the cavity, $2L$, equals an integral number (N) of wavelengths λ:

$$2L = \frac{N\lambda}{n}$$

where n is the refractive index of the material between the mirrors (needed to account for the difference in wavelength between the medium and empty space).

The cavity transmits light at wavelengths that match the resonant condition. Normally the cavity is short so the spacing between wavelengths will be large. Adjusting the length of the cavity changes the selected wavelength, tuning the filter.

A second type is the tunable acousto-optic filter, in which acoustic waves travel through a transparent material such as glass. The acoustic waves are atomic vibrations, which create regions of higher and lower density within the glass. The denser regions have higher refractive index, so this creates a layered effect within the filter, which selects certain wavelengths the same way that a fiber grating does. However, in the tunable acousto-optic filter, the grating spacing—and, hence, the selected wavelength—can be chosen by tuning the frequency of the acoustic signal.

Tunable filters offer precise adjustment of wavelength, so they are used in WDM systems, as well as in laboratory experiments. They are considerably more complex and costly than fixed filters.

Some filters can be tuned to select different wavelengths.

Optical Isolators

Optical isolators
transmit light only
in one direction.

Optical isolators are devices that transmit light only in one direction. They play an important role in fiber-optic systems by stopping back-reflection and scattered light from reaching sensitive components, particularly lasers. You can think of them as optical one-way streets with their own traffic cops or as the optical equivalent of an electronic rectifier (which conducts current only in one direction).

The inside workings of optical isolators depend on polarization. An optical isolator includes a pair of linear polarizers, oriented so the planes in which they polarize light are 45° apart. Between them is a device called a Faraday rotator, which rotates the plane of polarization of light by 45°. As shown in Figure 15.13, what happens to the light passing through an optical isolator depends on the direction it is going.

FIGURE 15.13

*An optical isolator
transmits light in only
one direction.*

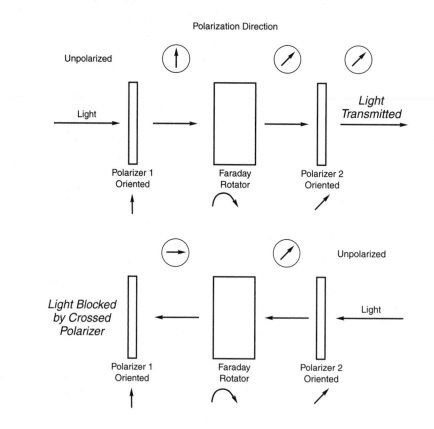

First consider light going from left to right. The input light is unpolarized, but the first polarizer transmits light only if it is polarized vertically. The Faraday rotator twists the plane of polarization 45° to the right. The second polarizer transmits light if its plane of polarization is 45° to the right of vertical, which in this case is all the light that passed through the first polarizer and the Faraday rotator. The signal goes through unimpeded.

Now consider light going in the opposite direction, from right to left. The polarizer on the right transmits only light polarized at 45° to the vertical. The Faraday rotator turns it another 45° to the right, so the plane of polarization is horizontal. That horizontally polarized light is blocked by the polarizer on the left, which transmits only light polarized vertically.

Light blocking is never perfect, but with good polarizers an optical isolator can attenuate light headed in the wrong direction by 40 dB or more, protecting lasers from noise that might affect their performance.

Dispersion Compensators

In Chapter 5, you learned about the importance of dispersion in fiber transmission. As you recall, dispersion has a sign, which indicates how the refractive index changes with wavelength. Because of this sign, it is possible to compensate for dispersion. The long wavelengths usually get ahead of the short ones because the refractive index of glass decreases with increasing wavelength, but you can compensate by adding components to slow down the long wavelengths so the short ones can catch up. I mentioned the concept earlier; now let's look at the types of dispersion compensation.

One approach is to balance the types of fiber in the system so their net dispersion is small. You can alternate lengths of fiber that transmit longer and shorter wavelengths faster. The fibers need not be of equal length, but the net dispersions should add to zero.

Another approach is to add short lengths of special fiber designed to have high dispersion of the opposite sign as normal fiber. For example, 10 m of dispersion-compensating fiber might offset the dispersion in 1 km of normal fiber.

A third approach is to insert a fiber grating that functions as a differential delay line. The spacing of the grating is graded, so different parts of the grating reflect different wavelengths. If the spacing of the high-index zones increases with distance along the grating, the shortest wavelengths are reflected first; then longer and longer wavelengths are reflected. As a result, the longest wavelengths go furthest down the fiber grating before being reflected. This delays them so the shorter wavelengths can catch up. Only modest lengths of grating are required.

Dispersion compensation is important mainly in enhancing performance of systems already installed with fiber having relatively high dispersion at 1550 nm. Gratings tend to work better with systems that transmit a smaller range of wavelengths; dispersion-compensating fibers work better for broader wavelength ranges.

> Dispersion compensators use special fibers or fiber gratings to reduce overall system dispersion.

Special Optical Accessories

Fiber-optic systems often include other optical components and accessories. Many are used in other optical systems, but a couple deserve mention because they have particular uses in fiber optics that require explanation.

Index-Matching Materials

Stray reflections can be a problem in fiber-optic systems, and they can occur in many places. One troublesome area is at interfaces between glass and air, such as at gaps between fibers in mated connectors or mechanical splices. You can suppress these reflections almost completely by filling the gaps with index-matching materials, which have refractive indexes close to that of glass.

Reflection at the interface between two optical materials depends on the difference in their refractive indexes and the angle at which light strikes the interface. This is called *Fresnel reflection,* and the larger the difference in refractive index, the larger the amount of reflection and the range of angles over which it occurs. The formula is complex if you consider the angle, but if you simplify things by assuming the light is going straight through—as it is at a connector—you get

$$\text{Loss (dB)} = 10 \log_{10}\left[1 - \left(\frac{n_1 - n_0}{n_1 + n_0}\right)^2\right]$$

where n_1 and n_0 are the refractive indexes of the fiber and the surrounding material.

The formula gives loss per surface. Where two surfaces are involved (as in light passing from glass to air to glass through a gap between fibers in a connector), total loss is the sum of the reflections at the two interfaces. If the two interfaces are between the same materials, the total loss is double the loss at one. The signs and direction of travel don't matter because the difference in refractive index is squared.

The glass used in fibers has a refractive index of about 1.5, much higher than air (1.00), so the loss at an air-glass interface is about 0.3 dB. That light does not vanish; some becomes undesired back-reflections that can cause noise. To reduce the loss, you can fill the space between fiber ends with a transparent gel or solid with refractive index close to 1.5. Transparent epoxies fill that role in glued joints. Thick, viscous liquids such as glycerine or silicone grease are sometimes used as index-matching materials in unglued joints, where they fill the interior of a connector so no air space remains between fiber ends. An index-matching material with index of 1.4 can reduce Fresnel reflection to 0.005 dB per surface, or 0.01 dB overall.

The big practical drawbacks of gels are the mess they make if a connector is demounted and the dirt they accumulate, which can block the light. As a result, they are used only rarely, and the fiber ends in connectors are usually polished so they contact precisely without scratching each other.

Index-matching materials reduce reflections at joints where there is space between fibers.

Mounting and Positioning Equipment

Single fibers are so small that you often need special equipment to manipulate them. Equipment for installing splices and connnectors include accessories that hold fibers in place. However, in a laboratory environment you generally need special equipment to mount and position fibers.

Mounts hold a fiber in place. Typically, they include precision adjustments for aligning the fiber precisely; motion may be manual or computer-controlled. Mounts may be attached to positioning equipment, so the mount holds the fiber while the positioner moves it. Typically motion is along three linear axes (*x*, *y*, and *z*) and two angles.

Note that mounts and positioning equipment for fibers normally are designed to work with a variety of general-purpose optical equipment on an optical bench or table. An optical table has a precisely flat surface and is often mounted on legs, which isolate it from vibration. An optical bench is a linear rail-like structure that holds optical mounts. They're also used with lenses, lasers, detectors, and a wide variety of other optical equipment.

> You need special equipment to manipulate single fibers.

Fiber Reels

Optical fibers fresh from the factory come on reels, just as you would expect. However, the reels are not simply pieces of throw-away packaging for everyone but the janitor to ignore. Reels can have a surprisingly large effect on the characteristics of fibers wound on them, and fibers often are left on reels for experiments and measurements. Winding can induce microbending losses that affect fiber attenuation, and if you're doing serious fiber measurements you need to pay attention to the reels.

Passive Optical Networks

The term *passive optical network* (PON) is often used to describe certain systems that distribute signals to many terminals. The design goal is to avoid installing expensive components at every terminal, but the networks are not strictly speaking completely passive. I will talk about them in Chapter 24.

What Have You Learned?

1. Couplers connect three or more points. Dividing an optical signal among two or more ports reduces its strength.

2. Couplers have specific applications. Wavelength-selective couplers are needed for WDM systems.

3. Directional couplers transmit light primarily in one direction, from inputs to outputs. Most couplers are bidirectional, with different channels for inputs and outputs, which could be reversed if necessary.

4. Loss of some couplers depends on polarization of the light they transmit.

5. T couplers are three-port devices. Tree, or 1-to-*n*, couplers divide one input among *n* ports. Star couplers have multiple inputs and outputs.

6. Many couplers are made from bulk or micro optics, such as beamsplitters.

7. GRIN lenses are rods or fibers with refractive index graded so they refract light like ordinary lenses.

8. Fused fiber couplers transfer light between the cores of two fused fibers. They are sensitive to wavelength.

9. Planar waveguides work on the same principles as optical fibers, guiding light through a region with higher refractive index than the surrounding material. Light can leak between two adjacent planar waveguides.

10. Fiber gratings are used as wavelength-selective couplers; they can provide high wavelength resolution.

11. Active couplers are dedicated repeaters with two or more outputs.

12. Requirements for WDM components depend on wavelength spacing in the system.

13. Diffraction gratings can separate wavelengths.

14. Arrayed waveguides separate wavelengths by transmitting light through an array of parallel waveguides of different lengths. They offer high resolution.

15. Attenuators and filters block some light to control signal strength or remove unwanted wavelengths.

16. Equalizing filters balance the degree of optical amplification at different wavelengths.

17. Filters can be made with fixed or tunable wavelength ranges.

18. Optical isolators transmit light in only one direction.

What's Next?

In Chapter 16, you will learn about other active optical components used in fiber-optic systems.

Quiz for Chapter 15

1. You have a coupler that divides an input signal equally among 16 outputs. It has no excess loss. If the input signal is -10 dBm, what is the output at any port?

   a. −12 dBm.

   b. −20 dBm.

   c. −22 dBm.

   d. −26 dBm.

   e. −30 dBm.

2. You have a 1 × 20 coupler with an input signal of −10 dBm and output signals at each port of −30 dBm. What is its excess loss?

    a. 0 dB.

    b. 1 dB.

    c. 2 dB.

    d. 4.2 dB.

    e. 7 dB.

3. A WDM system delivers an input of −20 dBm at each of four wavelengths to a demultiplexer. Assuming no excess loss, what is the output power at each of the four output ports?

    a. −26 dbm.

    b. −25 dBm.

    c. −23 dBm.

    d. −20 dBm.

    e. −16 dBm.

4. A coupler splits an input signal between two ports with a 90:10 ratio. If the input signal is −20 dBm and the coupler has no excess loss, what is the output at the port receiving the smaller signal?

    a. −21 dBm.

    b. −29 dBm.

    c. −30 dBm.

    d. −31 dBm.

    e. −110 dBm.

5. Which type of coupler would be the best choice for distributing identical signals to 20 different points?

    a. T coupler.

    b. Tree coupler.

    c. Star coupler.

    d. $M \times N$ coupler.

    e. WDM coupler.

6. Which of the following technologies can be used in wavelength-selective couplers?

    a. Micro optics.

    b. Fused fibers.

    c. Arrayed waveguides.

    d. Fiber gratings.

    e. All the above.

7. Which of the following technologies can be used in a tunable filter?

    a. Planar waveguides.

    b. Acousto-optic devices.

    c. Fused fibers.

    d. Fiber gratings.

    e. All the above.

8. Which of the following technologies is best suited for dense-WDM systems?

    a. Arrayed waveguides.

    b. Fused fiber couplers.

    c. Bulk optical gratings.

    d. Bulk interference filters.

    e. None of the above.

9. At the receiver end of your fiber-optic system, a −5-dBm signal enters a 1 × 10 tree coupler that divides signals equally. The receiver at each port can accept a maximum input signal of −18 dBm. What attenuator do you need to put in front of the coupler (that is, between the input signal and the coupler) to avoid overloading the receivers?

a. None.

b. 3 dB.

c. 5 dB.

d. 10 dB.

e. 13 dB.

10. You have the same system as in Problem 9, but you cannot install an attenuator in front of the coupler, so you have to install separate attenuators after each output port. What attenuator do you need for each receiver?

a. None.

b. 0.3 dB.

c. 0.5 dB.

d. 1 dB.

e. 3 dB.

Active Components

About This Chapter

Active components require some input of power to operate upon signals in a fiber-optic system. In addition to the lasers and optical amplifiers you learned about earlier, they include devices such as switches, modulators, and a few other devices to perform functions such as converting signals to different wavelengths.

In this chapter, you will learn the roles of these active components and how they work. You also will learn about active integrated optics.

Modulators and Modulation

Light must be modulated to carry information. If a fiber system is operating at moderate speeds, the simplest approach is to directly modulate the light source by varying the current passing through a semiconductor laser or LED. However, this approach has limitations, which become significant at data rates above about 1 Gbit/s:

- Limited output power possible
- Limited modulation speed
- Limited extinction (off-on) ratio
- Nonlinearities in modulation
- Wavelength "chirp" arising from changes in semiconductor refractive index as drive current rises and falls

The more you push system performance, the more serious these limitations become. Output power limits spacing between amplifiers. Modulation speed

●

External modulation is attractive for high-performance systems.

limits the transmission capacity. Extinction ratio—the ratio between power when the signal is on and off—affects transmission distance and receiver performance. Nonlinearities can distort analog signals, important in cable-television systems. Wavelength chirp increases the dispersion penalty. In short, if you want a high-performance system, you look at external modulation.

Unfortunately, optical modulation is not easy, because it requires changing the transparency of the modulator, and few physical processes do that fast enough and completely enough to be useful. Fiber-optic systems are particularly demanding because they require modulators that can switch off and on billions of times a second or respond very accurately to changes in the input signal.

Over the years, a host of technologies have been developed for modulating laser beams, but few are in practical use, and fewer of them meet fiber-optic requirements. For example, liquid crystals do modulate light, but they're not fast enough. Two main families of modulators are used in modern fiber-optic systems. Electro-optic modulators rely on changes in the way certain thin-film waveguides carry light. Electro-absorption modulators are semiconductor diodes that in some ways resemble lasers but absorb light instead of generating it. Their operation differs greatly, so we will look at them separately.

Electro-Optic Modulators

●

Electro-optic modulators rely on changes in refractive index caused by an electric field.

Electro-optic modulation depends on what is called the electro-optic effect, a change in the refractive index of certain materials when an electric field is applied to them. The change affects light passing through the material virtually instantaneously. Increasing the refractive index slows down the light; reducing it speeds up the light. The change is proportional to the voltage applied to the material.

Normally, you measure this change in degrees by comparing the phase of the modulated light wave to the position it would otherwise have:

$$\text{Phase shift } (\Delta\Phi) = 180° \times \frac{V}{V_{180}}$$

where V is the voltage applied to the modulator and V_{180} is the voltage needed to shift the phase a half-wavelength, or 180°.

Merely delaying the light does not modulate it. Electro-optic modulators for fiber optics split the input light equally between a pair of parallel waveguides. In the example shown in Figure 16.1, a modulated voltage is applied to one waveguide but not to the other. You see the modulation of light only where the two waveguides merge at the right. If the waveguides are equal lengths and the voltage is zero, the light waves are in phase at the end, so the waves add, producing a signal. The light is on. However, if you apply the voltage needed to delay the signal by 180°, the light in the two waveguides is out of phase when it merges at right. The two waves interfere destructively, canceling each other out and generating an off signal.

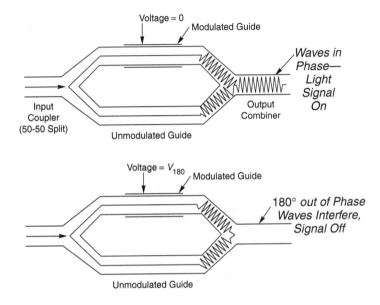

FIGURE 16.1
Simple electro-optic waveguide modulator.

The same approach works for analog modulation, but in this case you adjust the voltage so the delay varies continuously between 0 and 180°. The result is a continuous variation in output intensity, shown in Figure 16.2. (Note that the peak power is lower than the laser output by an amount that equals the insertion loss of the modulator, even when there is no voltage applied.)

Of course, it isn't really this simple in practice. In many electro-optic modulators, voltages are applied across *both* waveguides, but with the opposite polarities, so the voltage increases the speed of one wave at the same time it decreases the speed of the other. This gives you the same modulation with lower voltage. Typically two voltage signals are applied to each channel—one a bias that sets the operating level, and the other the modulating signal. For example the bias may set the modulator to normally transmit the average power, with the modulation signal varying voltage incrementally to change the transmitted power above and below that level.

A further complication is that refractive index actually depends on the polarization of light. In glass and many other materials, the refractive index is essentially the same for light of different polarizations, but in other materials it depends on the orientation of the polarization relative to the crystal axes. Materials with noticeable differences in refractive index for the vertically and horizontally polarized light are called *birefringent* materials.

Delaying the light phase causes interference effects that modulate the output intensity.

FIGURE 16.2

Variation in modulator output with voltage.

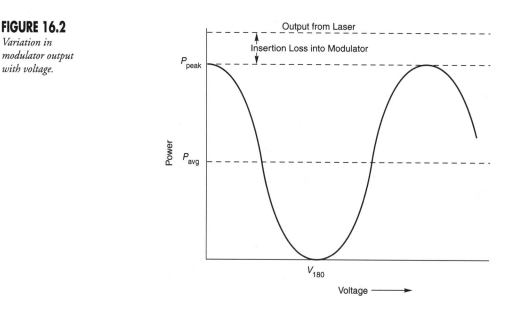

The electro-optic effect tends to be different for light of different polarizations. That means that light with different polarizations are not delayed the same amount. An electric field that delays vertically polarized light by 180° may delay horizontally polarized light only 120°, so the horizontally polarized component of the light does not cancel itself out. To avoid this problem, a filter blocks light of the undesired polarization before the light goes through an electro-optic modulator, so only one polarization is transmitted.

In theory, electro-optic modulators can be made of any material that displays the electro-optic effect and is transparent at the signal wavelength. In practice, the only material in practical use at 1.3 and 1.55 μm is lithium niobate ($LiNbO_3$). Waveguides are made by diffusing titanium or hydrogen into the lithium niobate, raising the refractive index of a narrow stripe that forms a waveguide. One process raises the refractive index for one polarization but depresses it for the other, so only one polarization stays in the guide, whereas the other diffuses into the substrate. The goal is to eliminate the need to polarize light before sending it through the modulator.

> Electro-optic modulators are made of lithium niobate.

> An electro-absorption modulator is similar to a semiconductor laser, but it is reverse-biased, so modulation makes it absorb rather than emit light.

Lithium niobate modulators are well developed and widely used today. They can be modulated at 10 Gbit/s or more for digital transmission or at high speeds in analog systems.

Electro-Absorption Semiconductor Modulators

An electro-absorption semiconductor modulator has a structure similar to that of a semiconductor laser, and the two can be integrated on the same chip, as shown in Figure 16.3. The most important difference is in their modes of operation. The laser is forward-biased so current tends to flow through it, but the modulator is operated with a reverse bias, like a *pin* photodetector. When the modulator is unbiased, it is transparent, but when the bias voltage is applied, it absorbs light at the laser wavelength.

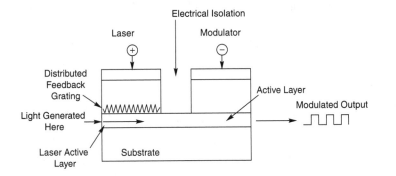

FIGURE 16.3

An electro-absorption modulator integrated with a semiconductor laser.

The laser and modulator are electrically isolated from each other. A steady current drives the laser, while the input signal drives the modulator. In this case, the active layer is transparent at the laser wavelength with no voltage applied. Applying a drive voltage to the modulator increases light absorption.

The structures of the laser and modulator are not identical, nor is the structure of the active layer that carries light between them. For best performance, there are slight differences in layer thickness as well as in the doping that differentiates between the laser and modulator sections. However, the two devices can be fabricated on the same substrate.

Like electro-optic modulators, electro-absorption modulators are polarization-sensitive, although integrating them on the laser chip simplifies packaging. They are made of the usual III-V semiconductors, including InGaAsP and InP, so they can readily match laser wavelengths. They are used in some communication systems, but they are not as common as lithium-niobate electro-optic modulators.

Switches

Switches let you redirect optical signals. This is important because communication systems need to adapt to changing conditions, whether the change is sending signals around a cable break, accommodating a customer's move to another location, or simply making temporary point-to-point connections through a network, as you would during a telephone call.

In practice, most switching is still done electronically. Individual telephone calls are just tiny drops in a torrent of information passing through fiber-optic lines; they are separated at telephone switching offices and directed electronically. Most other switching is done

Switches redirect signals. Most switching today is electronic.

electronically because electronic switching technology is much better developed and less expensive. However, optical switching is improving steadily, and the need for it is growing as transmission rates increase. Once signals are converted to optical form, system operators would prefer to keep them in that form until they reach their destination, without having to convert them to electronic form for switching.

To understand switching, you need to look both at its functions and at the technologies used. I will start with functions and then move to technologies.

Switching Functions

Switches can serve several distinct functions. One important role is emergency-route restoration, in case of a cable break or failure. Modern fiber-optic systems typically have at least two paths to any important location, so if one cable goes down, the signals can be redirected through a second. This should be done automatically, in a fraction of a second. However, it need not be done extremely fast (e.g., in a microsecond or less) because the main goal is to avoid breaking connections and disrupting human users, who respond much more slowly than communication systems. Any break will inevitably lose a few bits in a high-speed system.

A second function is changing configurations, either in instruments or at customer sites, which can range from individual moves to resetting a whole corporate division in a new building. Switching time is not a significant consideration.

A third function is dynamically switching large blocks of traffic or reconfiguration of loads. This typically is done automatically, for example, when a system recognizes it needs more transmission capacity between Chicago and Detroit and redirects signals so they go through Indianapolis, where there is extra capacity. It's functionally comparable to switching individual phone calls, but if the loads are large enough, it needs to be done optically rather than electronically.

A closely related function is wavelength management in WDM systems. The goal here is to direct individual wavelengths to particular destinations as uses change. The wavelengths sent to each destination may need to change.

Electronic switches also serve more-general purposes, particularly routing of signals to particular destinations. Individual phone calls pass through banks of electronic circuits that direct them from a local telephone exchange through regional and long-distance circuits to their eventual destination. This switching now is done by special-purpose electronic computers.

You should note that switches can work on different levels of signals. For example, the switches that connect an individual phone call from you to your cousin in Toronto operate on one voice circuit. Switches that bypass a cable break in Buffalo operate on a much higher level, simultaneously switching thousands of calls in a single data stream.

- Switches serve several distinct functions.

- Switches work on different levels of signals.

This is true for optical switches as well as electronic ones. In a WDM system the switch may transfer all wavelengths in the system or only one individual wavelength. Engineers speak of this as working on the optical multiplex layer (all channels) or on the optical channel layer (individual wavelengths). The important functional difference is where the switch goes relative to the multiplexer and demultiplexer. Typically you might adjust the system load by switching on the optical channel level. If you had to restore service around a broken cable, you would switch all wavelengths on the optical multiplex layer.

Routers and Switches

Routers may sound like the same things as switches, but they are not identical in fiber optics or in telecommunications, and confusingly have somewhat different meanings in each field.

In fiber optics, a WDM router is a passive device that separates the multiple wavelengths transmitted in a fiber system, and directs one (or more) of them in a different direction. You already read about them in Chapter 15. They always send the same wavelengths to the same points. Thus, for example, 1548-nm signals passing through Toledo would always go to Detroit, while all other wavelengths would be routed to Chicago. This differs from fiber-optic switches, active devices which direct optical signals through different fibers.

In telecommunications, both switches and routers are active devices which direct signals to various destinations. Telecommunication switches are special-purpose computers which make temporary connections between circuits and devices, such as connecting telephone calls. Routers direct data packets to their destinations, based on information contained in packet headers. This means that routers must read some of the data they transmit, but this allows them to transmit more efficiently. I'll explain more about these distinctions in Chapter 18.

Eventually, some confusion between the two types of routers is likely, because fiber-optic developers want to develop optical systems that perform the same functions as electronic routers. Unlike the current generation of WDM routers, such optical routers would be active devices that could analyze optical signals and direct them to their destinations. These devices do not exist yet, but they may in a few years.

Switch Terminology

Many terms used to describe optical switches were borrowed from electronic switching. If you understand electronic switches, you have a good head start; if you don't, I'll give you a quick introduction.

The major specifications for most switches are the numbers of inputs and outputs. You often see this abbreviated as a pair of numbers, such as 2×2 or 2 by 2, for a switch with two inputs and two outputs. Thus a 1×8 switch has one input and eight potential outputs.

Some switches are described by the number of *poles* and *throws,* such as a single-pole, double-throw (SPDT) switch. This is a switch that routes one input signal into one of two possible outputs. (The words *pole* and *throw* come from the way old-fashioned electrical switches were built.) A double-pole, double-throw switch simultaneously switches two input signals between two possible outputs for each signal (a total of four outputs). The goal for electronic systems was to build a switch to handle a pair of circuits simultaneously. For fiber optics, a DPDT switch can simultaneously switch signals on a pair of fibers handling signals going in opposite directions.

Note that DPDT switches do not reverse connections between a pair of possible outputs but send signals to different outputs. Reversing connections is the job of a 2 × 2 switch, which can direct the two inputs out either of two outputs.

Another important feature of switches is whether they stay in place until changed (like wall switches for overhead lights) or whether they return to a default position when the power goes off.

Cross-Connects

A cross-connect makes connections among many possible inputs and outputs.

In one sense, a cross-connect is just a fancy term for a big, complex switch. However, it has a more specific meaning, a way of connecting any of *N* inputs to any of *M* outputs, as shown in Figure 16.4. It's called a cross-connect because it can make any connection you want among the inputs and outputs. It's also sometimes called a switching fabric or a digital cross-connect, because most switching involves digitized signals. Note that any input can be routed to any output; the two heavy arrows show two possible paths.

FIGURE 16.4

A cross-connect.

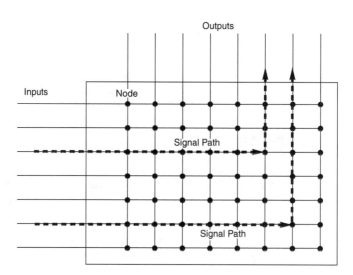

The idea of a cross-connect should look familiar. It is the function performed by your local telephone exchange, which can make temporary connections between any pair of phones it serves. You will find lots of articles that are rather vague about the technology used for cross-connects because they are talking about the concept rather than specific devices. A generation or two ago, cross-connections were monstrous banks of electro-magnetic switches that you could sometimes hear clicking as they switched your calls. Modern cross-connects use electronic technology.

Research engineers are developing optical cross-connects, but so far they remain small. Large cross-connects in practical use today use electronic switching, which is much better developed than optical switching.

Opto-Mechanical Switches

Opto-mechanical switches redirect signals by moving fibers or optical components so they transfer light into different fibers. Figure 16.5 shows a simple example. The input signal comes through the fiber on the left. A mechanical slider moves that fiber up and down, latching into one of three positions. Each position directs light from the input fiber into a different output fiber. In this design, the slider flexes a short length of the fiber.

Opto-mechanical switches move fibers or optics to redirect signals.

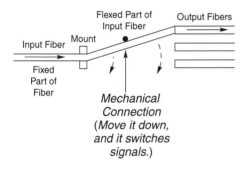

FIGURE 16.5

An opto-mechanical switch.

A variety of other designs are possible. Instead of moving a fiber, a switch could move a mirror or lens so it focuses light into different output fibers. The switch could be toggled manually or electronically. With precise optics, you can use this approach to make a switch that functions as an optical cross-connect by focusing light from one of several input fibers onto one of several output fibers. The common element in all opto-mechanical switches is that switching depends on mechanical motion of something in the switch. Precise motion is important. Opto-mechanical switches must align fiber cores with the same precision as connectors, which—as you learned in Chapter 13—is far more demanding than making electrical connections. Although they are simple in concept, opto-mechanical switches have moving parts, a disadvantage that communications companies try to avoid in this solid-state age.

Nonetheless, opto-mechanical switches have come into wide use because they are the cheapest and simplest optical switches available. They are used mainly in places where it is vital to be able to switch signals, but you hope you won't have to do it very often. Important examples are protection switches to route signals around cable breaks and in fiber-optic instruments.

Electro-Optical Switches

●
Lithium-niobate switches adapt electro-optic modulator technology.

Switches with no moving parts can be made by adapting the lithium-niobate waveguide technology used in electro-optic modulators. You replace the one output with two branching waveguides, arranged like a 3-dB coupler, to switch one input between two outputs. If you want two inputs, you can replace the one input with two parallel inputs coupled to the pair of switching waveguides by a combining coupler, as shown in Figure 16.6. By selecting voltages so you induce the proper delay between the signals in the parallel waveguides, you can direct the output into one or the other output waveguide.

FIGURE 16.6

A 2 × 2 electro-optic switch.

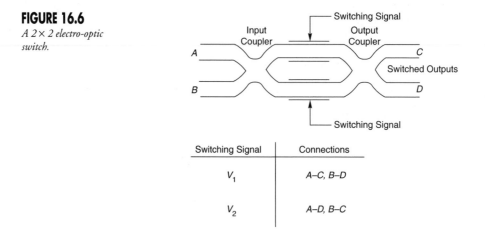

Switching Signal	Connections
V_1	A–C, B–D
V_2	A–D, B–C

The result is a solid-state switch with no moving parts. All that changes is the drive voltage, raised or lowered to shift the delay between waveguides by 180°. This switches the output light from one waveguide on the right side to the other. Because interference depends on phase, you can also turn up the voltage further to switch the signal back to the other output. You can use other techniques to change the effective lengths of the pair of switching waveguides, but electro-optic switching is the most common approach. Lithium niobate also is not the only waveguide material; polymers and semiconductors are other possibilities.

The waveguide-switching mechanism works well to divide one or two inputs between one or two outputs, but other configurations are more difficult. The simplest way to build more complex switches is by cascading a series of waveguides. For example, you could make a 1 × 4 waveguide switch by arranging three waveguide switches, so the two outputs of the first each feed into one of the others, giving a total of four possible outputs.

At this writing, electro-optical switches are the most important solid-state optical switch in use. Electro-optical switching is the subject of intense laboratory development using a variety of technologies. Most involve integrated optics in some form, but lithium niobate is only one of many materials. Its main advantage is that it is well developed and is considered to be the most "mature" technology.

Free-Space Optical Switching

An alternative still in development is optical switching by directing signals through free space. You earlier saw that some opto-mechanical switches work this way, by moving lenses or mirrors to direct beams of light. Another conceptual approach is modulating individual VSCELs in a two-dimensional array spread out on the surface of a chip. Directing the signals to the right places remains a problem.

Integrated Optics

The concept of integrated optics emerged in the late 1960s, when integrated electronic circuits were becoming common. As with integrated electronics, the idea of integrated optics was to combine many elements on a single monolithic substrate to reduce size and cost and to make a simple, durable device. However, it's taken a very long time for integrated optics to get anywhere, and with a few exceptions the technology remains mostly in the laboratory.

In practice, integrated-optic devices are fabricated on a single monolithic substrate, connected by planar waveguides, which you learned about in Chapter 15. One family of integrated-optic devices is made from semiconductors and in some ways resembles integrated electronic circuits. The other leading family is made on other substrates, particularly lithium niobate, which change their refractive index under conditions you can control. For lithium niobate, you control the refractive index by applying a voltage across the waveguide. Both major families of integrated-optic devices remain largely research technologies. Pick up a research journal, and you'll find it full of papers on integrated optics, but look in a catalog and you'll find very few integrated-optic devices you can buy.

Integrated optics on a monolithic substrate are linked by planar waveguides.

The most notable exceptions to this picture are devices often called integrated opto-electronics. They are essentially light sources or detectors integrated on the same substrate with signal-processing or driving electronics. This is possible because you can make electronic components from the III-V semiconductors used in lasers, LEDs and detectors, and optical detectors with the silicon technology widely used for most semiconductor electronics. Components made from the different semiconductors also can

Integrated opto-electronics combine light sources or detectors with signal processing or drive electronics.

be bonded together in what is called a hybrid circuit. (It is not a monolithic circuit on a single substrate.)

Why are integrated opto-electronics considered separate from integrated optics? The functions performed by integrated opto-electronic devices are all electronic, except for emitting or detecting light. They contain no waveguides to carry light from place to place on the circuit, only electrical conductors. In contrast, true integrated optics include passive waveguides that transfer light between devices. That means they can process information in the form of light, not merely convert electrical signals into light or vice versa.

You may wonder why integrated optics have not been as successful as their electronic counterparts. In large part, the technology is not as easy. Interactions with light are not as strong as those with electrons. You can make transistors into microscopic dots on an electronic integrated circuit, but optical modulators and switches typically must be a few centimeters long to change the direction of light. Planar waveguides attenuate light signals much more than optical fibers, and you lose light going back and forth between fibers and waveguides. No optical material is very good at everything, as must be the case if you want to make monolithic integrated circuits. Finally, government agencies and corporations have invested far more money in developing electronic technology than anyone has spent on integrated-optic research.

Semiconductor Integrated Optics

A laser can be integrated with an electro-absorption modulator.

A major attraction of semiconductor integrated optics is that semiconductor devices can emit, detect, and amplify light, as well as serve as waveguides, modulators, and switches. Lithium niobate cannot detect or emit light. The trade-off is that lithium niobate technology is better developed for modulation and switching, so the devices are better than their semiconductor counterparts.

At this writing, the most important practical example of semiconductor integrated optics is the integration of a distributed-feedback laser on the same chip with an electro-absorption modulator, as shown in Figure 16.3. The laser emits a steady beam, which a waveguide directs to an external modulator on the same wafer. Integrating the two components on the same wafer both simplifies fabrication and avoids losses from coupling light among lasers, waveguides, and fibers.

Many other semiconductor integrated optic devices have been demonstrated. For example, a waveguide-array demultiplexer can be integrated on a wafer with a series of detectors (one for each output wavelength). Semiconductor optical amplifiers can be added to boost signal strength before or after couplers that split signals. Development continues in a wide variety of areas.

So far, however, semiconductor integrated optics have found few applications outside of integrating lasers with electro-absorption modulators.

Lithium Niobate Integrated Optics

The big advantage of lithium niobate is that it makes good modulators, switches, and waveguides and that the technology is well developed. The big disadvantage is that lithium niobate itself cannot emit, detect, or amplify light. Researchers have shown that erbium can emit and amplify light when it is added to lithium niobate, but so far that technology remains in the laboratory.

You've already learned about lithium niobate modulators, switches and waveguides. Integration merely involves making them on the same substrate. Because the interaction lengths are fairly long, the substrates normally must be centimeters or inches long—tiny chips are not possible. However, lithium niobate integrated optics have found some uses, where combining functions improves performance.

> Lithium niobate is well developed but can't emit or detect light.

Wavelength Converters

As multiwavelength fiber-optic systems spread, interest is growing in converting signals from one wavelength to another. Suppose, for example, you had signals coming in from two nearby cities at λ_1, λ_2, λ_3, and λ_4 and you needed to drop one wavelength from each at your local town, and then route the remaining three from each—a total of six wavelengths—to a third city, as shown in Figure 16.7. Because city A and city B both deliver λ_1 and λ_2, you have to find some way to convert one pair of signals at those wavelengths to λ_5 and λ_6. You need a wavelength converter.

> Optical wavelength converters are being developed for WDM systems.

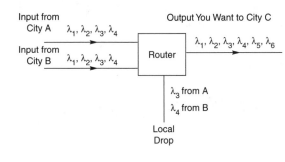

FIGURE 16.7
The need for wavelength conversion.

In a few special cases, optical wavelength conversion can be fairly simple. Focus a reasonably powerful laser beam onto certain materials, and the light interacts with the material to generate the second harmonic at twice the frequency or, equivalently, half the wavelength. At high enough powers, you learned earlier that nonlinear interactions could generate extra wavelengths in optical fibers. However, such interactions are not very useful for fiber-optic communications, where powers tend to be modest and you need specific wavelengths.

The easiest way to convert wavelengths today is opto-electronically. You detect the input signal with a receiver, convert it to electronic form, and then use the electronic signal to modulate a transmitter operating at the desired wavelength. This straightforward technology is used today wherever wavelengths must be converted, but like electro-optical repeaters, it's cumbersome. To change the wavelength, you need a complete receiver-transmitter pair. It would seem better to convert wavelengths by purely optical means, but that is difficult in practice.

One approach is to use a process like four-wave mixing. In this case, you combine the input signal with light at another wavelength to generate a different wavelength. For example, if you had an input signal at a frequency v_1, you could add a strong pump signal at $v_1 + 100$ GHz. By four-wave mixing, this would generate a signal at

$$v_{out} = (v_1 + 100 \text{ GHz}) + (v_1 + 100 \text{ Ghz}) - v_1 = v_1 + 200 \text{ GHz}$$

You also could use other wavelength-mixing effects, such as difference-frequency generation. However, although the concepts are simple, you need considerable input power to get useful output power, as well as a pump source that can be tuned to generate different wavelength outputs, which is difficult to build.

A second approach is to use light at one wavelength to control a semiconductor laser operating at another wavelength. The input light changes the population of current carriers in the laser, modulating its output. Although simple in concept, it turns out to be difficult in practice.

A third approach is to build an optically controlled gate. Essentially, this is a modulator controlled by the input of light rather than by a voltage signal. It directly modulates a laser output or controls an external modulator that modulates another laser. Developers have demonstrated several variations on this approach, some of them quite complex.

So far, purely optical wavelength converters remain in development, but progress has been encouraging.

Optically Controlled Modulation and Switching

All-optical control is attractive but hard to achieve.

So far, I have said very little about direct optical control of active devices. Electronics control electronic logic and switching devices, but light does not control the current generation of optical modulators and switches. Electronic circuits remain in control of the optics, except for a few research devices like the wavelength converters I just described.

All-optical switching and modulation would be ideal for many applications. Instead of having to convert signals into electronic form, light could modulate an optical signal passing through a modulator or throw an optical switch to direct signals. You could use such components as the basis of optical logic circuits, which could perform the same functions as electronic logic circuits—if, that is, you could build practical devices.

In practice, all-optical control is difficult to achieve. A major reason is that light generally interacts only weakly with other light waves. There are a few exceptions such as interference, but they aren't particularly useful for optical control. The idea would be a material that modulated light passing through it when another light beam hit it but not in response to the signal passing through it. Materials specialists call such stuff "unobtainium"—so far as we know, it doesn't exist. Research continues on all-optical logic, and some progress has been made, but the concept remains at the laboratory stage.

What Have You Learned?

1. External modulation works better than direct modulation of laser sources in high-performance systems.

2. Electro-optic external modulators rely on the electro-optic effect in planar lithium niobate waveguides.

3. Electro-absorption semiconductor modulators have structures like semiconductor lasers but are reverse-biased. Driving them causes them to absorb light at the laser wavelength. Laser and modulator can be integrated on the same chip.

4. Optical switches are needed to route signals around cable breaks, make changes at patch panels, and switch large blocks of traffic in WDM systems. Electronic switches now route individual phone calls.

5. Cross-connects can connect any of multiple inputs to any of multiple outputs. A telephone switch is a good example.

6. Opto-mechanical switches move a fiber or optical element to redirect signals.

7. Electro-optical switches are solid-state devices based on lithium niobate waveguides; they work best as 2×2 switches.

8. Integrated opto-electronics combine light sources or detectors with electronic circuitry, but they handle optical signals rather than electronic ones.

9. The two leading types of integrated optics are semiconductor waveguides and lithium niobate waveguides.

10. Wavelength converters are being developed for WDM systems. So far the most practical way to convert wavelengths is by converting signals to electronic form and using the electronic signal to drive a transmitter at the desired wavelength. Other approaches are in development.

11. Optical control of modulation and switching is difficult because optical interactions are weak.

What's Next?

In Chapter 17, you will learn about optical and fiber-optic measurement techniques.

Quiz for Chapter 16

1. Which of the following are advantages of direct modulation over external modulation? (More than one answer is possible.)

    a. Simpler.

    b. Can handle higher powers.

    c. Less signal distortion.

    d. Can operate at higher frequencies.

    e. No wavelength chirp.

2. Which of the following are advantages of external modulation over direct modulation? (More than one answer is possible.)

    a. Simpler.

    b. Can handle higher powers.

    c. Less signal distortion.

    d. Can operate at higher frequencies.

    e. No wavelength chirp.

3. How do electro-optic waveguide modulators work?

    a. They rotate polarization so a polarizer blocks light.

    b. They become opaque as voltage increases.

    c. A phase delay between two waveguides cases interference.

    d. A phase delay causes one waveguide to absorb light.

    e. They alter the magnitude of laser gain.

4. What phase shift do you need to cause destructive interference between two coherent light beams?

    a. 0°.

    b. 45°.

    c. 90°.

    d. 180°.

    e. 360°.

5. Which of the following can be integrated on the same chip with a semiconductor laser to externally modulate it?

    a. Semiconductor electro-absorption modulator.

    b. Semiconductor photodetector.

    c. Electro-optic modulator.

    d. Acousto-optic modulator.

    e. Electronic drive circuitry.

6. Where would you not want to use an opto-mechanical switch?

    a. For protection routing to an alternate cable in case of cable failure.

    b. To rearrange connections in a building patch panel.

    c. To route telephone calls in your local central office.

d. To switch large blocks of traffic at multiple wavelengths.

7. An opto-mechanical switch

    a. uses light to mechanically throw an electrical switch.

    b. mechanically moves a fiber to redirect optical signals.

    c. mechanically moves an electronic switch to redirect optical signals.

    d. uses light to mechanically throw an optical switch

    e. none of the above.

8. How could you assemble a 1×8 electro-optical switch?

    a. By dividing one input waveguide into eight output waveguides.

    b. By moving one input fiber to connect with one of eight output fibers.

    c. By arranging a series of seven 2×2 switches so the two outputs of the first were inputs to two separate 2×2 switches and each of

the four outputs of those two switches was the input to a separate 2×2 switch.

    d. None of the above.

9. Integrated optics consist of

    a. planar waveguides and optical elements on semiconductor substrates.

    b. planar waveguides and optical elements on lithium niobate.

    c. optical fibers fused together.

    d. a and b.

    e. a, b, and c.

10. An effective way to control an optical modulator with an optical signal would

    a. be physically impossible.

    b. solve many problems in future optical networks.

    c. be a good way to get seriously rich.

    d. require unobtainium.

    e. b, c, and maybe d.

Measurements

About This Chapter

Measurement capability is as vital for fiber optics as it is for other technologies, but optical measurements differ in important ways from other ones. As with electronic systems, some measurements are done in the factory or laboratory, and others are done in the field, to monitor system performance or make repairs. However, the quantities being measured are different, as are the techniques and (often) the terminology.

In this chapter, I discuss the basics of optical and fiber-optic measurements, the quantities that are measured, and the capabilities of some important measurement tools. I also examine some pitfalls of fiber-optic measurements and discuss misconceptions that you might carry over from other fields. I emphasize optical measurements because they are what make fiber optics different from other fields. This is only an overview of the field; so many specialized instruments are available that I cannot cover them all.

About Measurement

You can't start making measurements by pulling out the fiber-optic version of a yardstick and measuring away. Proper measurements require careful definition and control so that everyone knows exactly what's being measured and what it means. Otherwise, you end up with units like the cubit. Although the word "cubit" recurs throughout the Bible and other ancient literature, nobody is sure how long a cubit was. In fact, scholars believe that the cubit had many different definitions, just as the foot would if each of you defined the unit as the length of your own foot. To avoid such problems, specialists develop standard techniques and definitions so measurements made in one place yield the same results as those made elsewhere.

●
Measurement terms and techniques must be defined carefully so everyone knows what's being measured.

Specialists at organizations such as the National Institute of Standards and Technology devote their lives to developing, perfecting, and standardizing measurement techniques. The Department of Defense and industrial groups such as the Electronic Industries Association, the International Electrotechnical Commission, and the American National Standards Institute have programs to establish standard measurement techniques. To outsiders, much of this work may seem like the splitting of technological hairs. Indeed, the level of detail involved is far more than you need to know at this stage of your involvement in fiber optics; I won't delve into it deeply in this chapter.

Nonetheless, such exhaustive standardization does have practical importance. Without precise and generally accepted measurement standards, you can't be sure what performance specifications and other quantities mean, or that they are measured in the same way. If you get involved in fiber measurements, you will find that many have highly detailed and specific procedures. However, I will concentrate on basic concepts here.

Basics of Optical Measurement

●
Fiber-optic measurements involve light and other quantities, such as the variation of light with time.

Most important fiber-optic measurements involve light, in the same way that important electronic measurements involve electric fields and currents. There are some exceptions, such as the length and diameter of optical fibers and cables, the sizes of other components, and the electrical characteristics of transmitter and receiver components. Because this is a book about fiber optics, I will mention such measurements only in passing. However, I will talk about measuring things other than light, because you cannot qualify the properties of optical fibers if you consider only light. For example, to measure the dispersion of light pulses traveling through an optical fiber, you must observe how light intensity varies as a function of time, which requires measuring time as well as light.

When you're working with light, you need to know what can be measured. The most obvious quantity is optical power, which like electrical voltage is a fundamental measuring stick. However, power alone is rarely enough; it usually must be measured as a function of other things, such as time, position, and wavelength. Wavelength itself is important because optical properties of optical components, materials, light sources, and detectors all depend on wavelength. Other quantities that are sometimes important are the phase and polarization of the light wave. You need to learn a little more about these concepts before getting into more detail on measurement types and procedures.

Optical Power

●
Specialized terminology makes fine distinctions about quantities related to optical power.

DEFINED

People have an intuitive feeling for the idea of optical power (measured in watts) as the intensity of light. However, a closer look shows that optical power and light intensity are rather complex quantities and that you need to be careful what you talk about.

Table 17.1 lists the most important quantities, which are described in more detail in the following section.

Table 17.1 Measurable quantities related to optical power.

Quantity and Symbol	Meaning	Units
Energy (Q)	Amount of light energy	joules
Optical power (P or ϕ)	Flow of light energy past a point at a particular time (dQ/dt)	watts
Intensity (I)	Power per unit solid angle	watts per steradian
Irradiance (E)	Power incident per unit area	W/cm^2
Radiance (L)	Power per unit solid angle per unit projected area	W/steradian-m^2
Average power	Power averaged over time	watts
Peak power	Peak power in a pulse	watts

Power (P or ϕ) measures the rate at which electromagnetic waves transfer light energy. It is a function of time, because this rate can vary with time. Mathematically, it is expressed as

$$P = \frac{dQ}{dt}$$

or

$$\text{Power} = \frac{d(\text{energy})}{d(\text{time})}$$

Sometimes called radiant flux, this optical power is measured in watts, which is equivalent to joules (a measure of energy) per second. It is the same type of power that you measure electrically or thermally in watts. (Note, however, that the power ratings of lightbulbs measure how much electrical power they use—not the amount of light output, which is much lower.)

Like electrical power, optical power is a measurable manifestation of more fundamental quantities. In the case of electrical power, those are voltage (V) and current (I):

$$P = VI$$

or power = volts × amperes. This relationship can also take other forms, using the relationship $V = IR$ (voltage = current × resistance):

$$\text{Power} = I^2 R = VI = \frac{V^2}{R}$$

Power measures the rate of flow of light energy.

As you saw earlier, light and other electromagnetic radiation can be described as a wave comprising oscillating electric and magnetic fields. The wave has a characteristic amplitude (A) and oscillates with a particular period or frequency ν, as shown in Figure 17.1. The frequency, in turn, determines the wavelength, λ, which equals the speed of light, c, divided by the frequency, ν:

$$\lambda = \frac{c}{\nu}$$

FIGURE 17.1

Properties of an electromagnetic wave.

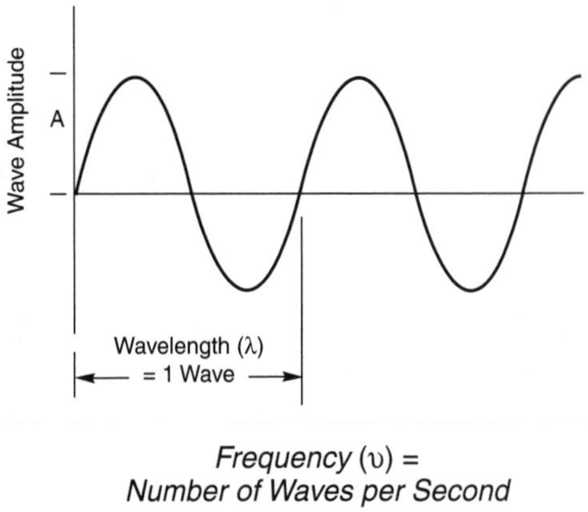

Frequency (υ) =
Number of Waves per Second

COMPARED TO ELECTRICAL POWER

Optical power is proportional to the square of the light wave amplitude.

For light and other forms of electromagnetic radiation, the power is proportional to the square of the electromagnetic wave amplitude (A). The amplitude measures the electrical field in the wave. Recall that the electrical power is proportional to the square of the amplitude of the voltage across a resistance (R). That similarity should not surprise you, because optical and electrical power are just different versions of the same thing.

You also can view the number of photons (quanta of light energy) passing a given point as analogous to the flow of electrons in an electrical current. However, the energy of each electron depends on voltage, but the energy of each photon depends on its frequency. Planck's law states that the energy of a photon is

$$E = h\nu$$

where h is Planck's constant and ν is the frequency of the light wave. Recalling that the frequency equals the speed of light divided by wavelength λ, you can rewrite the equation:

$$E = \frac{hc}{\lambda}$$

Thus the higher the frequency, or the shorter the wavelength, the higher the photon energy. The total energy is the number of photons passing a given point times the energy per photon, and power is the energy divided by the time.

In practice, you generally don't worry about those details; you just measure optical power directly. That is not the case with electricity, where voltage and current can be measured directly and multiplied to give power.

MEASUREMENT QUIRKS

Before I go deeper into measuring various forms of optical power, I'll warn you about a few potentially confusing measurement quirks. In electrical measurements, the decibel power ratio can be defined in terms of voltage and current. These are in the form

$$\text{Power ratio (dB)} = 20 \log\left(\frac{V_1}{V_2}\right) = 20 \log\left(\frac{I_1}{I_2}\right)$$

where the Vs and Is are voltages and currents, respectively.

That definition differs from the definition of power ratio in decibels for powers P_1 and P_2:

$$\text{Power ratio (dB)} = 10 \log\left(\frac{P_1}{P_2}\right)$$

Why the different factor preceding the log of the power ratio? Because electrical power is proportional to the square of voltage or current. If you measure the ratio of voltage or current, you have to square it to get the power ratio, which is the same as multiplying the log of the ratio by 2. You don't have to do that if you measure power directly, either optically or electrically. Electrical measurements are usually in voltage or current, but optical measurements are in power, so it may seem that the difference is between optical and electrical. However, the real difference is between measuring power directly or indirectly. Both formulas are correct, but be careful to use the proper one for power measurements.

A second potentially confusing point is measurement of optical power in some peculiar-seeming units. Normally, power is measured in watts or one of the metric subdivisions of the watt—milliwatts, microwatts, or nanowatts. Sometimes, however, it is convenient to measure power in decibels to simplify calculations of power level using attenuation measured in decibels. The decibel is a dimensionless ratio, so it can't measure power directly. However, power can be measured in decibels relative to a defined power level. In fiber optics, the usual choices are decibels relative to 1 mW (dBm) or to 1 μW (dBμ). Negative numbers mean powers below the reference level; positive numbers mean higher powers. Thus, +10 dBm means 10 mW, but −10 dBm means 0.1 mW.

Such measurements will come in very handy when I talk about system design in later chapters. Suppose, for instance, that you start with a 1-mW source, lose 3 dB coupling its output into a fiber, lose another 10 dB in the fiber, and lose 1 dB in each of three

The definition of the decibel power ratio is different when power and voltage are measured.

Optical power can be measured in decibels relative to 1 mW (dBm) or 1 μW (dBμ).

connectors. You can calculate that simply by converting 1 mW to 0 dBm and subtracting the losses:

Initial power	0. dBm
Fiber coupling loss	−3. dB
Fiber loss	−10. dB
Connector loss	−3. dB
Final Power	−16. dBm

Convert the −16 dBm back to power, and you find that the signal is 0.025 mW; however, that often isn't necessary because many specifications are given in dBm. This ease of calculation and comparison is a major virtue of the decibel-based units.

Types of Power Measurement

As Table 17.1 indicates, optical power can be measured not just by itself but also in terms of its distribution angle or space. In many cases (e.g., measuring the brightness of illumination), it is important to know not just total power but also power per unit area. The main concern of fiber-optic measurements is with total power (in the fiber or emerging from it) or power as a function of time, but you should be aware of other light-measurement units to make sure you know what you're measuring.

LIGHT DETECTORS

Light detectors measure total power incident on their active (light-sensitive) areas—a value often given on data sheets. Fortunately, the light-carrying cores of most fibers are smaller than the active areas of most detectors. As long as the fiber is close enough to the detector, and the detector's active area is large enough, virtually all the light will reach the active region and generate an electrical output signal.

The response of light detectors depends on wavelength. As you learned in Chapter 11, silicon detectors respond strongly to 650 and 850 nm but not to the 1300 and 1550 nm wavelengths used in long-distance systems. On the other hand, InGaAs detectors respond strongly to 1300 and 1550 nm but not to the shorter wavelengths. In addition, detector response is not perfectly uniform across their entire operating region. You have to consider the wavelength response of detectors to obtain accurate measurements.

Detectors cannot distinguish between different wavelengths within their operating regions. If eight WDM channels all reach the same detector, it will measure their total average power, not the power of one channel.

In addition, individual detectors give linear response over only a limited range. Powers in fiber-optic systems can range from over 100 mW near powerful transmitters used to drive many terminals to below 1 μW at the receiver ends of other systems. Special detectors are needed for accurate measurements at the high end of the power range.

IRRADIANCE AND INTENSITY

Things are more complicated when measuring optical power distributed over a large area; all the power may not be collected by the detector. Then another parameter becomes important, irradiance (E), the power density per unit area (e.g., watts per square centimeter). You cannot assume that irradiance is evenly distributed over a given area unless the light source meets certain conditions (e.g., that it is a distant point source such as the sun and that the entire area is at the same angle relative to the source). Total power (P) from a light source is the irradiance (E) collected over area (A). This can be expressed as an integral:

$$P = \int E \, dA$$

over the entire illuminated surface. If the irradiance (E) is uniform over the entire area, this becomes

$$P = EA$$

where A is the area.

The term intensity (I) has a special meaning in light measurement—the power per unit solid angle (steradian), with the light source defined as being at the center of the solid angle. This is a measure of how rapidly light is spreading out from its source. Unfortunately, the term is often misused (used in place of "irradiance") to indicate power per unit area or power at a point, so it is wise to be certain what is intended.

> Irradiance (E) is power per unit area. Intensity (I) is power per unit solid angle.

PEAK AND AVERAGE POWER

When output of a light source or optical fiber varies with time, measured power can differ with time. Power is an instantaneous measurement. The highest power level reached in an optical pulse is called the peak power, as shown in Figure 17.2. The average level of optical power received over a comparatively long period (say over a minute), is average power. For digitally modulated fiber optic light sources operating at a 50% duty cycle (i.e., on half the time), average power is half peak power. However, the peak power may be thousands of times the average power for a laser that emits only a few very short (but quite powerful) pulses per second. Most meters made specifically for fiber optics measure average power.

> Power is an instantaneous measurement that varies with time.

ENERGY

At the beginning of this section, you saw that power measures the flow of energy (which in light measurement is usually symbolized by the letter Q, not E). Most fiber-optic measurements are of power rather than energy, but you should recognize the relationship of

> Energy of a pulse is the product of average power in the pulse multiplied by the pulse duration.

the two quantities. Energy can be measured in joules or (equivalently) watt-seconds. Total energy (Q) delivered is the area under the power curve in Figure 17.2, or mathematically the integral of power P over time:

$$Q = \int P(t) \, dt$$

FIGURE 17.2
Peak and average power, and total pulse energy.

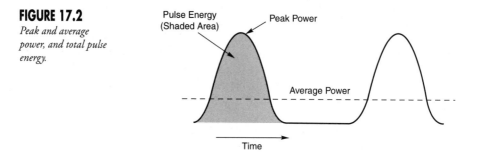

where $P(t)$ is in general a function that varies with time. If the average power over an interval t is P, this can be simplified to

$$Q = P \times t$$

Thus, if average power in a pulse that lasts t seconds is P watts, the pulse energy is $Q = Pt$ joules. This approximation is useful for digital signals, for which the power is roughly constant while a pulse is on.

As this formula indicates, each light pulse contains an amount of energy (Q). If you go deeply into communication theory, you will find that the ultimate limits on detection of pulses and communication capacity are stated as the minimum pulse energy required to deliver a bit of information. Energy per pulse is measured in some experiments with ultra-high performance laboratory systems. However, in practical fiber-optic systems, the emphasis is on measuring power.

Radiometry and Photometry

Fiber-optic measurements are only a small part of light measurement. I have only skimmed the surface of that broader field because not much of it is critical if you're working only with fiber optics. However, you should appreciate the critical difference between the related fields of radiometry and photometry.

The words *radiometry* and *photometry* are often used interchangeably, but they are not synonyms. Strictly speaking, photometry is the science of measuring light visible to the human eye. If the light isn't visible by the human eye, it doesn't count in photometric measurements. Radiometry, in contrast, is measurement of light in the whole electromagnetic spectrum, whether or not people can see it. Radiometry measures power in watts. The corre-

Radiometry measures light in the whole electromagnetic spectrum. Photometry measures only light visible to the human eye.

sponding unit in photometry (power visible to the human eye) is the lumen, and the output of lightbulbs is given in lumens. Radiometric measurements give equal weight to light at visible and invisible wavelengths. Photometric measurements weigh the contributions of different wavelengths according to eye sensitivity. Thus, 550-nm light, where the eye is most sensitive, counts much more on a photometric scale than light of equal power at a wavelength where the eye is less sensitive (e.g., 450 nm in the blue or 650 nm in the red). Photometry ignores invisible ultraviolet and infrared light.

Fiber-optic measurements are made on a radiometric scale. The only time to use a photometric scale is when measuring light visible to the human eye. Some people in the industry are inexcusably sloppy in their terminology and call instruments photometers even though they measure radiometric units. Perhaps they'll learn better if you insist you want only radiometers. (A radiometer-photometer is a common instrument calibrated in both radiometric and photometric units.)

So far I've talked about ideal photometers and radiometers, but the real world doesn't work quite that nicely. Detectors do not have uniform response across the electromagnetic spectrum. As shown in Figure 17.3, their response varies markedly with wavelength and is limited in range. This makes it essential to calibrate radiometers to account for detector response at the wavelengths being measured.

> Fiber-optic power meters are calibrated for wavelengths used in fiber systems. Power meters measure average power.

FIGURE 17.3

Detector response at different wavelengths.

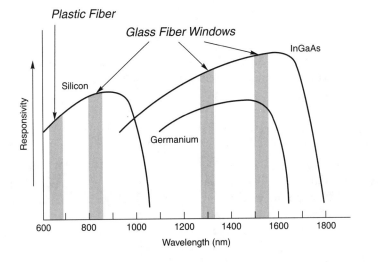

In practice, fiber-optic power meters are calibrated specifically for the wavelengths used in fiber systems, at 650, 850, 1300, and 1550 nm. (This means that in the strict sense, they are not true radiometers because they work only at certain wavelengths.) You should also recognize that fiber-optic power meters, radiometers, and photometers all measure average power. Their response times are much slower than signal speeds, and their displays cannot track instantaneous power fluctuations.

Wavelength

Wavelength-measurement requirements vary widely, depending on the application. Precise knowledge of source wavelengths is critical in dense WDM systems, where the transmission channels are closely spaced and must be matched to the transmission of demultiplexing components. Knowledge of the spectral response of system components also is vital in WDM systems, particularly for filters used in demultiplexing signals. On the other hand, wavelength need not be known precisely in systems carrying only one wavelength.

WAVELENGTH AND FREQUENCY PRECISION

So far, I have usually described wavelengths in nice round numbers, such as 1550 nm. That's common in optics; engineers who work with light think in terms of wavelength. However, wavelength is not as fundamental a characteristic of a light wave as its frequency. The wavelength depends on the refractive index of the medium transmitting the light; the frequency is constant. This is why standard channels and spacing for WDM systems are specified in terms of frequency.

Earlier, you learned that the wavelength in vacuum equals the speed of light divided by frequency, v:

$$\lambda = \frac{c}{v}$$

However, this equation holds only in vacuum. When the light is passing through a medium with refractive index n, the equation becomes

$$\lambda = \frac{c}{nv}$$

which means the wavelength decreases by a factor $1/n$.

I have used round numbers in much of this book because they're usually good enough. Why punch 10 digits into your calculator when you can learn the same concept by punching only 2 or 3? Those approximations don't work for WDM systems. You have to use exact numbers or you get into trouble. To understand why, run through a set of calculations first using the approximations of 1 for the refractive index of air and 300,000 km/s for the speed of light; then use the real values. Let's calculate the wavelength corresponding to the base of the ITU standard for WDM systems, 193.1 THz.

Using round numbers,

$$\lambda = \frac{3 \times 10^8}{1 \,(193.1 \times 10^{12})} = 1553.6 \text{ nm}$$

Using the exact values, the wavelength is

$$\lambda = \frac{2.997925 \times 10^8}{1.000273 \times (193.1 \times 10^{12})} = 1552.1 \text{ nm}$$

The difference is only 0.1%, but that's enough to shift the wavelength by nearly two whole 100-GHz frequency slots in the ITU standard. In short, the wavelength tolerances in dense-WDM systems are too tight to get away with approximations. You have to be precise.

Because of the importance of precision, frequency units may be used in measurements rather than the more familiar wavelength units. You should be ready to convert between the two when necessary, always using the precise formulas.

WAVELENGTH-MEASURING INSTRUMENTS

Precise wavelength measurements are not easy; they require sophisticated instruments and carefully controlled conditions. The spread of WDM systems has led manufacturers to develop some very sophisticated commercial instruments, which are beyond the scope of this chapter. However, you should understand a few key concepts.

The measurements can be absolute or relative. Absolute measurements tell you the precise wavelength (or frequency) of a light source. Relative measurements tell you the difference between two light sources, usually in frequency units, and tend to be easier to make.

Absolute measurements have to be calibrated against some standard wavelength source. In practice, there may be levels of calibration, where the source in an instrument is calibrated against a primary or secondary standard. In any case, the calibration sources are important.

Operating conditions are critical for proper measurements. Refractive index, in particular, varies with wavelength, so careful control is important.

LINEWIDTH MEASUREMENTS

In addition to measuring the central wavelength of a laser source, you often need to measure the *linewidth,* or range of wavelengths in the signal. Where fiber dispersion is an issue or where the system carries several closely spaced wavelengths, the linewidth should be small and often is measured in frequency units—e.g., 150 MHz for a DFB laser emitting continuously that is modulated externally. On this scale, frequency units are more convenient than wavelength; at 1550 nm, 100 GHz is about 0.8 nm, so 150 MHz is about 0.0012 nm.

At lower speeds, where dispersion is not a critical concern, such as where a simple diode laser is modulated directly, the linewidth is much larger and is generally measured in wavelength units. In this case, wavelength units are more convenient.

> Sophisticated commercial instruments measure wavelength precisely.

SPECTRAL RESPONSE MEASUREMENTS

Spectral response measures how systems and components respond to different wavelengths.

In addition to knowing the wavelength of the transmitter, you need to know how a fiber-optic system and its components respond to different wavelengths. This is called *spectral response*. For most components, the most important response is loss or attenuation as a function of wavelength. In the case of filters, multiplexers, and demultiplexers, you need to know how light is divided as a function of wavelength. That is, you need to know how much light is routed in different directions at various wavelengths. For optical amplifiers, the important feature is gain as a function of wavelength.

Spectral response measurements require a properly calibrated light source that emits a suitably narrow range of wavelengths. Figure 17.4 illustrates the problem by comparing two light sources with the transmission of a fiber Bragg grating that selectively reflects at 1555 nm for wavelength-division demultiplexing. A narrow-line source such as a tunable laser can accurately measure the response of the fiber grating, but a broadband source cannot, because its light contains a range of wavelengths much broader than the range of wavelengths the grating reflects.

FIGURE 17.4

Only a narrowband source can measure transmission of a narrow-line demultiplexer.

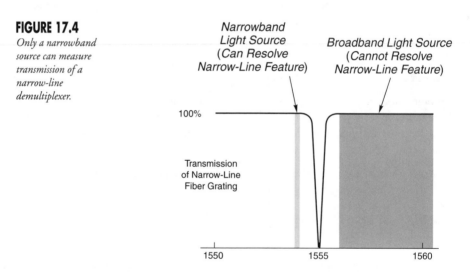

Conventional monochromators do not have the fine spectral resolution needed for WDM measurements; you need special instruments built for the purpose, which use tunable lasers or other narrow-line sources. However, monochromators may suffice for undemanding measurements.

LESS PRECISE MEASUREMENTS

Although WDM systems demand extreme precision in wavelength measurement—to five or six significant figures—other fiber-optic applications do not require such stringent controls. In fact, it's very difficult to make lasers repeatedly with exactly the same wavelength, and for many years manufacturers didn't worry about it. If you're transmitting a single wavelength through a fiber system, it doesn't matter very much if it is 1550 or 1560 nm. The characteristics of optical fibers, optical amplifiers, and detectors do not vary much over that range. You should remember that you may encounter such systems and that they are a legitimate cost-saving design choice for many applications.

Phase

Like other types of waves, electromagnetic waves have a property called *phase*. Envision a light wave as a sine wave, which goes through a cycle of 360° or 2π radians before repeating itself, as shown in Figure 17.5. The phase of a light wave is a measure of its progress in its oscillation cycle.

Phase measures a light wave's progress in its oscillation cycle.

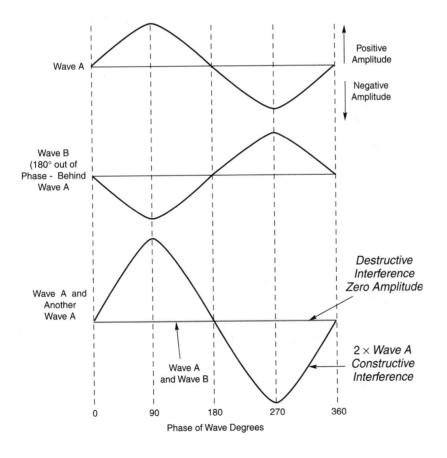

FIGURE 17.5

Phase and interference of light waves.

Phase of a light wave can be measured only by comparing it to other light waves of the same wavelength. This measurement relies on the interference of two waves, a phenomenon shown in Figure 17.5. When two light waves come together at a point, their net amplitude at any instant is the sum of their amplitudes, which can be either positive or negative. If the peak of one wave arrives at the same time as the valley of an equal-amplitude wave, the two cancel and the net amplitude is zero. However, if the peaks arrive at the same time, the two waves add.

Normally, many light waves arrive at once, and their different phases and wavelengths overwhelm interference effects. However, you can see interference if coherent light (initially in phase and with the same wavelength) travels different paths to reach the same point, causing a delay or phase shift. This does not occur in single-mode fibers, because they transmit only a single mode. However, it is a problem with multimode fibers carrying laser light, because the phases of the modes shift randomly, generating an effect called *modal noise*. This is an interference effect that would show up as a pattern of shifting bright and dark zones if you projected a laser spot onto a flat surface. In a fiber-optic system, this effect creates a similar pattern at the fiber end and detector. Even slight disturbances of the fiber can change this pattern, adding noise to the system and increasing the bit error rate for digital transmission. The problem of modal noise was one major impetus for the use of single-mode fiber for telecommunications.

Polarization

●

Polarization is the alignment of the electric fields that make up light waves.

You saw earlier that light waves are made up of electric and magnetic fields oscillating perpendicular to each other and to the direction the light wave is traveling. The polarization direction is defined as the alignment of the electric field, which automatically sets the direction of the perpendicular magnetic field. Light waves with their electric fields in the same plane are linearly polarized. If the field direction changes regularly along the light wave, it is elliptically or circularly polarized. And if the fields are not aligned with each other, the light is unpolarized.

Polarization is measured by passing light through a polarizer, which transmits light only if its electric field is aligned in a particular direction. The fraction of light transmitted by the polarizer indicates the degree of polarization in the direction of the polarizer.

Polarization has taken on increasing importance in high-performance fiber-optic systems and in certain fiber-optic sensors. Some fibers are sensitive to polarization. In addition, a number of components are sensitive to polarization, including optical amplifiers, optical isolators, couplers, waveguides, multiplexers, and demultiplexers. This makes it important to measure polarization dependance of such quantities as loss, gain, and dispersion.

POLARIZATION-DEPENDENT LOSS AND GAIN

Polarization-dependent loss measures the maximum difference in attenuation for light with various degrees of polarization. For example, if loss is 3 dB when transferring horizontally polarized light from a fiber to a waveguide but 6 dB for vertically polarized light at the same junction, the polarization-dependent loss is 3 dB (assuming that those are the minimum and maximum losses). This is measured by adding polarization analyzers to conventional loss measurement instruments.

Polarization-dependent gain is the inverse; it measures the maximum difference in gain for light of various polarization states. This is an important quantity for optical amplifiers.

Polarization-dependent loss and gain can introduce noise into a fiber-optic system because polarization fluctuates randomly in some components, such as nonpolarizing fibers. For example, suppose a waveguide has loss of 10 dB for vertically polarized light but only 3 dB for horizontally polarized light. If the polarization of the input light changes from horizontal to vertical, the extra attenuation reduces output 7 dB. Since the input fiber does not control polarization, this means that the output power can vary randomly with input polarization over a range of 7 dB, an undesirable level of noise.

> Polarization-dependent loss is the maximum difference in loss for different polarizations.

POLARIZATION-MODE DISPERSION

Polarization-mode dispersion is important in high-speed, single-mode fiber systems, where it may be the largest residual type of dispersion. It arises from slight differences in the propagation of the two orthogonal polarization modes transmitted by a single-mode fiber. Measurements require a polarization analyzer and tunable laser source.

Timing

As you learned in Chapter 11, the electrical output of a detector reproduces the input optical signal. Monitoring this electrical output lets you measure how an optical signal varies in time. Important pulse timing characteristics include the pulse duration, the rise time, the fall time, and the pulse spacing or repetition rate. Figure 17.6 illustrates these. An additional consideration is jitter, or the uncertainty in pulse timing.

> Timing is measured electronically by monitoring detector output.

- *Rise time* is defined as how long the signal takes to rise from 10% to 90% of peak power.
- *Pulse duration* is typically defined as the time from when the signal reaches half its maximum strength to when it drops below that value.
- *Fall time* is defined as how long the signal takes to drop from 90% to 10% of peak power.
- *Pulse spacing* is the time between the start of one pulse and the start of the next. Thus if the signal is on for 1 ns and off for 2 ns, the spacing is 3 ns. This usually assumes that pulses repeat steadily, ignoring coding that might "skip" some pulses.

FIGURE 17.6

Pulse timing.

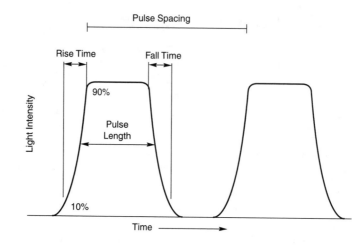

- *Repetition rate, signal speed,* and *clock rate* all refer to the number of pulses per second.
- *Jitter* is the uncertainty in timing of pulses, typically measured from the start of the pulses.

In practice, the detector output takes time to rise and fall, even in response to an instantaneous change in the optical signal. Thus the rise and fall times of the detector output depend both on the rise and fall times of the optical pulse itself and on the response time of the detector. This effect can become significant at high speeds.

Note that pulse repetition rates in even the slowest fiber-optic systems are extremely fast on a human scale—tens of thousands per second—so you cannot see variations in signal level in real time. They are recorded on an oscilloscope or other display in a way that lets people see events too fast to perceive otherwise.

Position

> ●
> Optical detectors can measure distribution of light, but high resolution is needed for precise measurements.

Optical power varies with position as well as time, and suitable optical detectors can sense this differential. The cells in the retina of your eye can tell light regions from dark spots—otherwise, you couldn't read this page. Retinal cells have small areas, giving your eye a very fine resolution. Electro-optic light detectors can be made with large or small active areas. The detectors used with fiber-optic systems have a single active cell wider than the fiber core. Other detectors, used to record images, may have many discrete active cells, like the retina of your eye. Some special types have electrical output that varies with the position of a spot of light on the sensitive area.

As mentioned previously, a single-element detector measures the total power incident on its active area. It can measure the distribution of optical power by scanning an illuminated surface. Alternatively, a multielement array of detectors can measure power distribution over its surface. Use of either technique allows measurement of light distribution, for example, as it emerges from an optical fiber. However, you should realize that assumptions made about the pattern of light distribution can have an impact on the results. The coarser the resolution relative to the size of the measured structure, the larger the effect of the assumptions. And as you would expect, measurements with a detector with 500 μm active area can tell nothing about light distribution in a 50-μm fiber core.

Measurements Specific to Fiber-Optic Systems

So far I have talked about measuring optical quantities that are relevant in fiber-optic systems. Optical power level and polarization are examples. You also will encounter other types of measurements designed specifically to assess the performance of fiber-optic systems. These include quantities such as transmission bandwidth and bit error rate. Some are derived directly from the usual optical measurements; others require special measurements. We will start by looking at important conventions of fiber-optic measurement.

> Some measurements are specific to fiber-optic systems.

Measurement Standards

When you start digging seriously into fiber-optic measurements, you quickly find references to cryptic-seeming codes, such as EIA/TIA-455A. These codes identify standards that specify how certain measurements should be made and which organizations have written them. They may sound befuddling, but they serve the vital function of making sure that measurements performed by different people in different places are comparable.

> The use of standard measurement techniques assures that results are comparable.

Measurement standards specify the techniques and equipment that should be used to measure various quantities. They often go into excruciating detail, but that detail is important. Seemingly small differences in measurement techniques can lead to large differences in results. As a simple example, output power from an optical fiber cannot be measured accurately if some light from the fiber misses the active area of the detector. Likewise, calculated results can be thrown off if pulse width is measured one way at the light source and another way at the output of a fiber. Standards make sure that measurements are repeatable.

This is not the place to go into detail on standards. As a starting point, you should check with manufacturers of test equipment, or with suppliers of other equipment. Table 17.2 lists major organizations that write standards for fiber measurements.

Table 17.2 Standards organizations.

ANSI	American National Standards Institute
ASTM	American Society for Testing and Materials
Bellcore	Bell Communications Research
CCITT	International Consultative Commission on Telephone and Telegraph
EIA	Electronic Industries Association
ICEA	Insulated Cable Engineers Association
IEC	International Electrotechnical Commission
IEEE	Institute of Electrical and Electronics Engineers
NEC	National Electrical Code
REA	Rural Electrification Administration
TIA	Telecommunications Industry Association
UL	Underwriters Laboratories

Measurement Assumptions

● Unwarranted assumptions can cause you to discard essential data.

Making such indirect measurements requires some implicit and explicit assumptions, and unless you're careful, those assumptions can lead to the wrong results. The assumptions you think are absolutely essential to make a measurement task manageable may oversimplify the task so you throw away vital data.

● Modal distribution changes along the length of a multimode fiber.

One example is assumptions about light distribution in a fiber. It is reasonable to assume that light is distributed in the same way along the length of a single-mode fiber, but not in a multimode fiber. Light may take a kilometer or more to distribute itself stably among the modes a multimode fiber can transmit, and that mode distribution can be rearranged by a splice or connector. This mode distribution affects many things, including loss within the fiber, numerical aperture and light-acceptance angle, transfer of light between fibers, and the distribution of light emerging from the fiber. Standard test methods and techniques such as mode scrambling can control mode distribution to produce consistent results.

● Loss of a connector or splice can depend on the direction light is traveling.

Another logical (but sometimes false) assumption is that loss of a connector or splice is the same for light going in either direction. Suppose that light distribution in the cores is uniform, and the only difference between fibers is that one has a 49-μm core and the other has a core 51 μm across—within normal manufacturing tolerances. When light goes from the smaller fiber into the larger one, there are no geometrical losses caused by the difference in core size. However, if light were going in the opposite direction, the core-diameter difference would cause an added 0.3-dB loss.

Pitfalls become subtle in more sophisticated measurements. I can't go through them all here, but the important point to remember is to think measurement techniques through carefully and exercise care in making assumptions. Using standard measurement techniques is one way to minimize the risk.

Fiber Continuity

A major concern in installing and maintaining fiber-optic cables is system continuity. If something has gone wrong with the system, you need to check to see if the cable can transmit signals. If it can, you know you have another problem. If it can't, you need to find out where the break or discontinuity is. In some cases, the break may be obvious—a cable snapped by a falling tree limb or a hole dug by a careless contractor. However, such damage is not always obvious, and the cable route may not be readily accessible.

Early fiber technicians developed a quick-and-dirty test of fiber continuity that required no elaborate equipment. One shined a flashlight into the fiber, and a second on the other end looked to see if any light emerged. However, that simple approach has a number of problems. Flashlight beams do not couple efficiently into optical fibers, especially single-mode types, and faint light emerging from a fiber is hard to see in a brightly lit area. The measurement is hardly quantitative. Furthermore, it requires people at both ends of the fiber—one to send the light and the other to look for the transmitted light—and those people must be able to communicate with each other.

Other instruments are available that can do a much better job, often without requiring people on both ends. Optical fault indicators send pulses of light down the fiber and look for reflections that indicate a fault. They work somewhat like simplified versions of the optical time domain reflectometer (OTDR) described later, which can also locate faults. Optical test sets measure power transmission. Fiber identifiers can tell if exposed fibers are carrying signals (they work by bending the fiber and observing light that leaks out at the bend). Visible fault identifiers send visible red light through the fiber, and visual inspections show if any is leaking out.

In practice, these instruments may be used in different places. Visible fault indicators are best for tests where fibers are exposed in a small area close to the fiber end, but they are of little use in searching for faults in buried exterior cables. Conversely, fault indicators and OTDRs excel at finding faults in buried or aerial cables but may not detect breaks close to the fiber end.

Optical Power

Optical power is the quantity most often measured in fiber-optic systems. I described the basic principles earlier. The power may be output from a light source, power emerging from a length of optical fiber, or power in some part of a system. The wavelength must be known so that the detector can be calibrated for that wavelength. Duty cycle—the fraction of the time the light source is on—should also be known to interpret properly measurements of

> Fiber continuity checks can verify system function. The simplest test is to see if light can pass through the fiber.

> Measurements of optical power require knowing the wavelength and duty cycle.

average power. The usual assumption is 50% (half on, half off) for digital modulation, but under certain circumstances that may be far off (e.g., if a series of 1s are being transmitted in NRZ code so the transmitter is continually sending at its high level).

Normally, power is measured where the light emerges from a light source or fiber. Fiber-optic power meters collect the light from the fiber through an optical connector, which directs the light to a detector. Electronics process the detector output and drive a digital display that shows the power level in linear units (nanowatts to milliwatts) or in dB referenced to either 1 mW or 1 μW. Measurement ranges are automatically switched across the dynamic range, which is typically a factor of one million. Typical measurement accuracy is ±5%.

Measuring optical power stops the beam, because it's absorbed by the detector. If you want to sample the power level in a transmitted signal, you need a beamsplitter that will divert a calibrated fraction of the light to a detector and transmit the rest.

It is important to keep input power within the dynamic range of the power meter. Excessive powers won't be measured correctly, and in extreme cases, long-term exposure to excess power can damage some detectors.

Attenuation

Attenuation is $-10 \log\left(\dfrac{P_{out}}{P_{in}}\right)$.

Attenuation is the most important property of passive optical components, because it determines what part of an optical signal is lost within the component and how much passes through. It is always a function of wavelength, although the wavelength sensitivity varies widely. In fibers, the variation with wavelength is significant; in some other components, it is negligibly small.

Attenuation is measured by comparing input and output levels, P_{in} and P_{out} respectively. It is given in decibels by

$$\text{Attenuation (dB)} = -10 \log\left(\frac{P_{out}}{P_{in}}\right)$$

The negative sign is added to give attenuation a positive value, because the output power is always lower than the input power for passive devices.

The standard way to measure cable loss with an optical test set—which includes a light source and transmitter—is shown in Figure 17.7. First the light source is connected to the power, meter through a short launch cable, and the power is adjusted to a convenient level (−10 dBm in this case). Then a short receive cable is added between the launch cable and the power meter; a power change no more than 0.5 dB verifies the receive cable is good. The meter is again adjusted to the desired level. Then the cable to be tested is connected between launch and receive cables and the power it transmits is read (−14.2 dBm in this case). The difference, 4.2 dBm, is taken as the total attenuation of the cable being tested, including fiber, connectors, and splices. For more precise measurements, the loss should be measured in both directions through the test cable. As I mentioned earlier, attenuation typically differs slightly in the two directions because of differences in light coupling at the connectors.

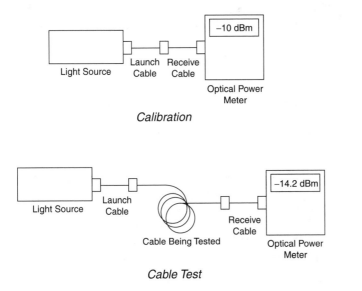

FIGURE 17.7
Cable loss measurement.

The same principles can be used to measure the attenuation of other components, such as couplers, or of segments of cable installed in a system. If cable ends are located at different places, the tests can be performed by technicians working at both ends, one with a light source and the other with a power meter, or by temporarily installing a "loop-back" cable to send the signal back to the origination point through a second fiber. Inevitably, small losses are measured less accurately than large ones.

Optical time domain reflectometers can also measure attenuation, as described later.

This simple comparison technique is adequate for most purposes, but it does not precisely measure pure fiber loss, because it includes loss within the connectors at each end. More precise measurements of fiber loss alone require the cut-back technique. First, power transmission is measured through the desired length of fiber. Then the fiber is cut to a short length (about a meter) and the power emerging from that segment is measured with the same light source and power meter. Taking the ratio of those power measurements eliminates input coupling losses (which occur in both measurements), while leaving the intrinsic fiber transmission loss (which is present only in the long-fiber measurement).

Precise measurements of fiber attenuation rely on cutting back fibers to compare power emerging from short and long lengths.

The cut-back method can be more accurate for single-mode fibers than for multimode fibers because of the way mode distribution changes along the fiber. Accurate measurement of long-distance attenuation of multimode fibers requires use of a mode filter to remove the higher-order modes that gradually leak out of the fiber. However, this won't accurately measure the loss of short multimode fibers, which depends on propagation of the high-order modes.

One special problem with single-mode fibers is that light can propagate short distances in the cladding, throwing off measurement results by systematically underestimating input coupling losses. To measure true single-mode transmission and coupling, fiber lengths should be at least 20 or 30 m.

Dispersion

Pulse dispersion measures changes in pulse length along a fiber.

As you learned earlier, pulse dispersion can limit the bandwidth and data rate of optical fibers. There are four elements of dispersion: modal dispersion (present only in multimode fibers), material dispersion, waveguide dispersion, and polarization-mode dispersion. They are measured in somewhat different ways.

Modal dispersion is measured in units of nanoseconds per kilometer of fiber length, because it is not affected by the range of wavelengths emitted by the source. It does depend weakly and indirectly on the source wavelength, so it should be measured at the operating wavelength by comparing input and output pulse widths. For precise measurements, you need to know the distribution of modes launched into the fiber. Modal dispersion is not present in single-mode fibers.

Material and waveguide dispersion add together to give chromatic dispersion, which is measured in picoseconds per kilometer of fiber length per nanometer of source bandwidth. Commercial instruments can measure chromatic dispersion of a system and plot it as a function of wavelength. Note that the actual chromatic dispersion in the system depends on source bandwidth as well as fiber length. Chromatic dispersion is the largest dispersion for single-mode fibers, but it can be kept low by operating near the zero-dispersion wavelength or by using a source with very narrow linewidth.

Polarization-mode dispersion is the difference in arrival times of light in the two orthogonal polarizations. It is normalized for distance by measuring in units of picoseconds per square root of distance in kilometers (ps/$\sqrt{}$km). It is most important in high-speed, single-mode systems, where other types of dispersion have been reduced to low levels. You measure polarization-mode dispersion separately from chromatic dispersion at a single wavelength or over a range of wavelengths; it does vary with wavelength, although not as regularly or uniformly as chromatic dispersion.

Bandwidth and Data Rate

Bandwidth and data rate can be measured directly or calculated from dispersion.

Bandwidth in analog systems and data rate in digital systems are essentially the inverse of pulse dispersion in a fiber. Although these quantities can be measured indirectly as dispersion, they can also be measured directly. Frequency measurements can be made by comparing the strengths of signals at various frequencies. The result is a plot of signal strength versus frequency, such as the one shown in Figure 17.8 for a multimode fiber.

This plot, with level response over a broad range of frequencies, then a rapid decline past a certain level, is characteristic of fiber-optic systems. Typically, the upper limit on bandwidth is specified as the point at which signal strength has dropped by 3 dB.

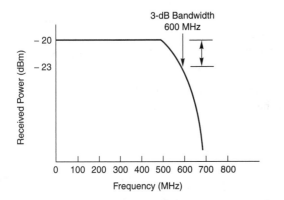

FIGURE 17.8

Received signal strength as a function of frequency.

Maximum digital data rate can be extrapolated from analog bandwidth or pulse dispersion characteristics, or it can be estimated in other ways. One method is to study the shapes of output pulses in the eye pattern described later. Another is to define the maximum data rate as the highest possible with bit error rate no more than a certain acceptable level, which is also described later.

Signal-to-Noise Ratio

A standard way to assess the quality of an analog communication system is by measuring the ratio of signal power to background noise. The higher the signal-to-noise ratio (sometimes written S/N ratio), the higher the transmission quality. The cable-television industry, the primary user of analog fiber systems, has standards for signal-to-noise ratios in various parts of its network.

The signal-to-noise ratio also assesses performance of some individual components. Such measurements are important for optical amplifiers, where the "noise" is amplified spontaneous emission generated within the fiber amplifier. The signal wavelength normally stands as a peak above the amplified spontaneous emission, which is spread across the gain range of erbium-doped fibers, as shown in Figure 12.7.

Bit Error Rate

The bit error rate is a straightforward concept used in assessing the performance of many digital systems, including fiber-optic as well as other types. It is based on generating a randomized bit pattern and comparing the original pattern with the signal emerging from the system being tested. Counting both total bits and the number of errors detected gives

Digital transmission is evaluated by measuring the fraction of bits received incorrectly, the bit-error rate.

the bit error rate—the fraction of bits received incorrectly. This gives a convenient and quantitative assessment of the performance of a digital communication system.

As might be expected, the bit error rate increases as received power drops, as well as when the system approaches other performance limits, such as maximum transmission rate. The drop is generally quite steep and can be more than a factor of 100 for a 1-dB increase in received power in certain power ranges. Other factors generally set a minimum bit error rate when the receiver gets adequate output power. If too much power reaches the detector, the bit error rate again increases because the receiver is saturated.

Different users have their own standards for bit error rate. The limit is typically 10^{-9} (one bit in a billion) for a telephone voice transmission system and 10^{-12} for data transmission.

Eye Pattern Analysis

An eye pattern is the superposition of the waveforms of successive bits; open eyes indicate good quality transmission.

One popular way to assess performance of a digital fiber-optic link is to superimpose the waveforms of a series of pulses on an oscilloscope display. This produces the "eye pattern" shown in Figure 17.9. Each pulse trace draws its own pattern on the screen, with noise added to the signal. If there weren't any noise, each trace would follow exactly the same line. The more noise, the more the signal varies, and the thicker the line is vertically. Likewise, the larger the jitter (difference in pulse arrival times), the thicker the lines are horizontally.

FIGURE 17.9

An eye pattern.

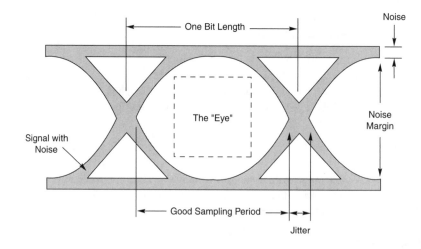

In essence, the eye pattern measures the repeatability of pulses reaching the instrument. The better the transmission quality and the more uniform the received signal, the more open the eye will appear. If the eye starts to close, it indicates that transmission errors are likely as successive bits interfere with each other.

Careful interpretation of the eye pattern can yield important data on fiber link performance. Data signals can be sampled at any point within the eye, but the best point is in the middle. Some important points for interpreting eye patterns are as follows:

- Height of the central eye opening measures noise margin in receiver output.
- Width of the signal band at the corner of the eye measures the jitter (or variation in pulse timing) in the system.
- Thickness of the signal line at top and bottom of the eye is proportional to noise and distortion in the receiver output.
- Transitions between top and bottom of the eye pattern show the rise and fall times of the signal that can be measured on the eye pattern.

Mode-Field and Core Diameter

As you learned earlier, fiber core diameter can vary because of manufacturing tolerances. In addition, mode-field diameter—the diameter of the region occupied by light propagating in a single-mode fiber—is somewhat larger than the core diameter. These quantities can be measured.

Practical interest in the mode-field and core diameters depends on the distribution of light, and measurements are, therefore, based on light distribution. One approach is to scan across the end of the fiber with another fiber of known small core diameter, observing variations in light power collected by the scanning fiber. Other approaches rely on observing the spatial distribution of light near to or far from the fiber—the near-field and far-field intensity patterns. Those distributions of optical power can be used to calculate the core diameter.

A related quantity important for both single- and multimode fibers is the refractive-index profile, the change in refractive index with distance from the center of the fiber. This also is measured by examining the light distribution across the fiber.

Numerical Aperture and Acceptance Angle

The numerical aperture measures how light is collected by an optical fiber and how it spreads out after leaving the fiber. It measures angles, but not directly in degrees or radians. Although NA is widely used to characterize fiber, it isn't NA that is measured, but the fiber acceptance angle, from which NA can be deduced.

Numerical aperture and acceptance angle are most important for multimode fibers. As mentioned earlier, measured numerical aperture depends on how far light has traveled through the fiber, because high-order modes gradually leak out as light passes through a fiber. The measured numerical aperture can be larger for shorter fibers, which carry a larger complement of high-order modes, than it will be for long fiber segments. Measurements are made by observing the spread of light emerging from the fiber.

Mode field diameter is the region occupied by light in a single-mode fiber.

Numerical aperture is not measured directly; it is calculated from the acceptance angle.

Cutoff Wavelength

Cutoff wavelength, the wavelength at which the fiber begins to carry a second waveguide mode, is an important feature of single-mode fibers. The measured effective cutoff wavelength differs slightly from the theoretical cutoff wavelength calculated from the core diameter and refractive-index profile. As with core and mode-field diameter, cutoff wavelength is a laboratory rather than a field measurement.

Normally, the cutoff wavelength is measured by arranging the fiber in a test bed that bends the fiber a standard amount. Fiber attenuation as a function of wavelength is measured twice. First, the fiber is bent in a manner that causes the second-order mode to leak out almost completely. Second, the fiber is arranged so it transmits both first- and second-order modes. These two measurements are compared, giving a curve such as the one in Figure 17.10, which shows excess loss as a function of wavelength. In this case, λ_c is the effective cut-off wavelength, which is defined as the wavelength above which second-order mode power is at least a certain amount below the power in the fundamental mode. The measurement finds this value by locating the point where excess loss caused by stripping out the second-order mode is no more than 0.1 dB.

FIGURE 17.10

Measurement of effective cutoff wavelength. (Courtesy of Douglas Franzen, National Institute of Standards and Technology)

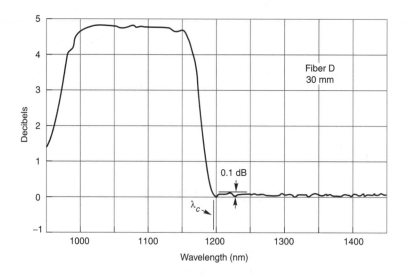

Measurement Instruments

I started by describing fiber-optic measurements in general terms and by specifying the quantities that you needed to measure. Specialized instruments have been developed to perform the most important of these measurements. Many are analogous to instruments used for other optical or telecommunication systems. I'll look at the most important of these instruments in the following section.

Optical Power Meters

The simplest optical measurement instruments are optical power meters, which include a fiber connector, calibrated detectors, electronics to process the signal, and a digital display. Most are compact and portable, with autoranging digital readouts that show power on either decibel or watt scales. Priced at a few hundred dollars and up, they are invaluable tools that can be adapted for many measurements.

Power meters are calibrated for use at one or more of three standard wavelengths: 850, 1300, and 1550 nm. (Some are calibrated at extra, nonstandard wavelengths, such as 660 nm for plastic fiber transmission and 780 nm for CD laser systems.) Be careful that you find a meter usable at the wavelength you want. Many are calibrated for only one wavelength, and detectors used at 850 nm do not respond to light at 1300 and 1550 nm (and vice versa).

All measurements should be made at the calibrated wavelengths because they are the nominal transmission wavelengths of fiber systems. Most instruments can store measurements, and many come with computer interfaces.

> Optical power meters are calibrated for wavelengths used in fiber-optic systems.

Test Sources

Fiber-optic test sources provide light to measure attenuation and other optical characteristics of fiber components and systems. A variety of sources are available, designed for different applications, and you must match the source to the measurement task. The output wavelength in simpler instruments is fixed, but it is tuned in more sophisticated (and more expensive) sources.

> Test sources provide output at fiber system wavelengths.

Important source types include the following:

- Broadband sources, often called *white-light sources,* although they usually emit in the near-infrared rather than at visible wavelengths. These are tungsten bulbs or other sources that generate a wide range of wavelengths but only a limited power at any one wavelength. Typically a prism or diffraction grating selects one wavelength at a time while sweeping through the instrument's operating range to measure spectral characteristics. These instruments are essentially special-purpose versions of instruments called *monochromators,* which have long been used for optical measurements.

- LEDs, which generate more power at a given wavelength than broadband sources, but emit over a more limited range, 50 to 100 nm in the 1200- to 1700-nm region. Untuned LEDs are used in simple instruments; more elaborate instruments select certain wavelengths from the LED emission and may contain several LEDs to cover the whole range. Untuned LEDs emitting at 850 nm or 660 nm are test sources for short systems.

● Erbium-doped fibers operated in broadband mode, generating amplified spontaneous emission. These fibers can deliver higher powers than LEDs at 1530 to 1570 nm. Typically they are tuned to select a limited range of wavelengths and can be used for WDM and optical-amplifier measurements.

● Fixed-wavelength semiconductor laser sources can operate at any of the standard semiconductor laser windows, 850, 1310, or 1550 nm. They provide high power at a comparatively modest cost because they do not include tuning optics.

● Tunable semiconductor laser sources can be tuned to generate light at a narrow range of wavelengths within their operating bands. They can be used for WDM and optical amplifier measurements.

These sources normally emit continuous beams, but their output can be modulated for certain tests. Their output power can be stabilized during tests.

Test sources normally come with a variety of connectors and adapters so they can be mated to various types of fiber and cable. It's important to match the light source properly to the fiber or device being tested. Some sources are designed specifically for single- or multimode fiber.

Optical Loss Test Sets

●

An optical loss test set includes a light source and an optical power meter calibrated to work together.

You can combine an optical power meter with a calibrated light source as an optical loss test set. The power meter measures how much optical power is reduced from the level emitted by the source. Source and power meter wavelength must be matched for accurate results. Test sets often are packaged for specific applications, such as testing local-area networks.

Optical loss test sets measure attenuation by comparing power levels with and without the component being tested. Figure 17.7 shows a typical arrangement to test a length of fiber. In practice, the source and power meter may be calibrated together but used at separate field sites, with the source at one end of the cable and the power meter at the other.

Back-Reflection Testers

The reflection of light back toward the source can seriously affect system performance, so special test sets have been developed to accurately measure low levels of back-reflection.

Oscilloscopes

Oscilloscopes are useful in measuring waveforms transmitted through optical fibers, as they are in other waveform measurements. They are often used in measuring the eye pattern shown in Figure 17.9. They can also display the variations of optical power with time. However, optical probes are needed to convert the optical signals to electronic form.

Bit Error Rate Meters

Specialized instruments are made for the bit error rate measurements I discussed earlier. Some models are portable; others are designed for laboratory use. They are generally similar to instruments made for use in nonoptical systems, although they have been adapted for use specifically with fiber optics.

Fiber-Optic Talk Sets

Strictly speaking, fiber-optic talk sets are simple communication systems, not measurement instruments. However, they are used by technicians performing measurements. The talk set includes a simple transmitter and receiver that lets it send voice signals through optical fibers. It lets pairs of technicians at opposite ends of an installed cable talk with each other to coordinate their activities.

Optical Time-Domain Reflectometers

The optical time-domain reflectometer (OTDR) is one of the most powerful fiber-optic measurement instruments. It is a sort of optical radar that sends a short light pulse down a fiber and monitors the small fraction of that light scattered back to it. Plotting the returned light as a function of time can identify places where the fiber has excess loss, such as connectors, splices, or fiber breaks. Its slope indicates the loss of the fiber. Figure 17.11 shows typical features on an OTDR plot.

The distance scale at the bottom is calculated from the time the light takes to return. Although the optical pulse is fast and the electronics respond rapidly, the signal received from the several meters to several tens of meters of fiber closest to the instrument is not useful; this is called the dead zone. The signal strength declines gradually through uninterrupted lengths of fiber. The slope of the decline indicates fiber loss.

Peaks in the slope indicate points where light is reflected back to the source. The largest peak in the plot in Figure 17.11 is reflection from the end of the fiber. The next largest peak is reflection from a connector. Look carefully and you can see that the signal just after the connector is slightly lower than it was before; this drop measures the connector loss. Mechanical splices likewise reflect some light back to the instrument and have some loss, although both loss and reflection are smaller in this example. The other discontinuity shows the loss from a fusion splice (or from a sharp fiber bend), which does not reflect light back to the OTDR. Breaks or other fiber flaws also appear in OTDR plots, much as connectors or the end of the fiber in this example.

> The optical time-domain reflectometer sends pulses down a fiber to measure its characteristics from one end.

FIGURE 17.11
OTDR plot.

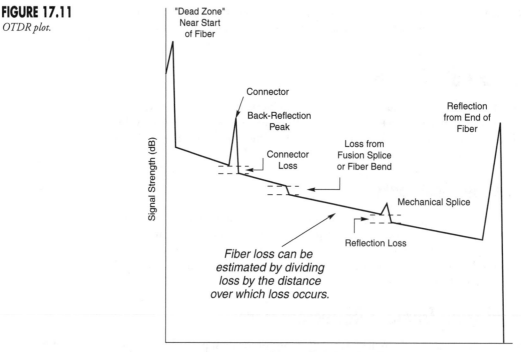

"Dead Zone" Near Start of Fiber

Connector

Back-Reflection Peak

Connector Loss

Loss from Fusion Splice or Fiber Bend

Reflection from End of Fiber

Mechanical Splice

Reflection Loss

Fiber loss can be estimated by dividing loss by the distance over which loss occurs.

Signal Strength (dB)

Distance (Calculated from Return Time)

The major attraction of the OTDR is its convenience and ability to spot cable faults remotely. It requires access to only one end of the fiber in cable segments up to tens of kilometers long. Timing how long it takes light to travel from the instrument to a point in the fiber and back can locate flaws and junctions in the fiber. That's invaluable if you have to play detective and find where a fiber is broken in a long cable. Just plug your OTDR into one end of the cable and send a pulse of light down it. If you see a smoothly declining curve, the cable is okay. But if there is a large, sharp drop in the curve, the fiber is damaged. The instrument can locate a break to within a matter of meters, except in the dead zone. Because they are widely used in field measurements, OTDRs are normally packaged for field use. They also come with some internal computer power, which can add considerable information to the display and let you zoom in on areas of interest and measure losses directly. Many can interface directly with personal computers.

Care must be taken in interpreting OTDR loss measurements because they are not as accurate as direct measurements of attenuation. One problem is variations in the fraction of light backscattered toward the instrument. Splicing two fibers with different degrees of backscatter can give spurious results. In one direction, the splice becomes a "gainer," with the excess backscatter making it appear to have increased signal strength. In the other, the splice appears to have excess loss, because less of the signal is being returned to the instrument. OTDRs should also be matched to the fiber being tested, both in wavelength and core diameter, to enhance their accuracy.

OTDRs have proved invaluable for spotting fiber faults, optimizing splices, or inspecting fibers and cables for manufacturing flaws. However, it is important to understand their limitations.

Other Instruments

Look through any catalog of fiber-optic test equipment, and you will find even more instruments than I have listed here. If you look carefully, you will find some of them serve the same functions I described previously but are packaged differently. Some instruments might be modules that plug into a general-purpose instrument or special-purpose instruments, such as OTDRs optimized to spot "features" where attenuation changes.

Other instruments perform other tests or analysis. Examples are component analyzers, spectrum analyzers, polarization analyzers, and calibration sources.

It's impossible to cover all fiber measurement instruments and measurement procedures in a general text. For that, you'll need a separate course.

What Have You Learned?

1. Standards define what is to be measured so everyone makes comparable measurements.

2. The basic quantity measured in fiber optics is light. Measurements give information such as how optical power varies in time and space. Optical power is the rate of change in light energy with time.

3. Like electrical power, optical power is the square of a field amplitude, but unlike voltage, the light wave field is not easy to measure directly.

4. Optical power can be measured in decibels relative to 1 mW (dBm) or 1 μm (dBμ).

5. Photon energy equals $h\nu$ (where h is Plank's constant and ν is the frequency) or, equivalently, hc/λ, where c is the speed of light and λ is the wavelength.

6. Pulse energy is the average power in the pulse multiplied by the duration of the pulse.

7. Fiber-optic power meters are calibrated for the wavelengths used in fiber systems; they measure average power.

8. Wavelength is critically important in WDM systems, and for that application it must be measured and calculated precisely. Always use the exact values for the speed of light in a vacuum (2.997925×10^8 m/s) and the refractive index of air when calculating WDM system properties.

9. Phase measures a light wave's progress in its 360° oscillation cycle; it can be measured only relative to the phase of other light waves with the same wavelength.

10. Polarization measures the alignment of electric fields in light waves. Polarization-dependent loss can affect performance of single-mode fiber systems.

11. Attenuation is measured by comparing input and output power levels. Specific procedures are needed to assure accuracy.

12. Modal dispersion affects only multimode fibers. Chromatic dispersion affects single- and multimode fibers. When chromatic dispersion is low, polarization mode dispersion can limit performance of single-mode systems.

13. Bandwidth in analog systems and data rate in digital systems are essentially the inverse of pulse dispersion. They can be measured directly or indirectly.

14. An eye pattern is the superposition of the wave forms of a series of received bits. The clearer the eye, the more uniform the pulses and the better the transmission quality.

15. Various test sources are available for fiber-optic measurements, including broadband sources, LEDs, erbium-doped fiber sources, fixed-wavelength lasers, and tunable lasers.

16. An optical loss test set includes light source and optical power meter calibrated to work together.

17. An optical time-domain reflectometer sends a short light pulse down a fiber and measures the light reflected back to it. In this way, it can spot discontinuities from one end of the fiber and indicate their magnitude.

What's Next?

Now that you understand the nuts and bolts of fiber optics and the basics of measurement, the next several chapters will delve into fiber-optic systems and applications.

Quiz for Chapter 17

1. Optical power is
   a. The light intensity per square centimeter.
   b. The flow of energy past a point.
   c. A unique form of energy.
   d. A constant quantity for each light source.
   c. Average power.
   d. Radiant flux.
   e. Energy.

2. What measures power per unit area?
   a. Irradiance.
   b. Intensity.

3. A digitally modulated light source is on 25% of the time and off 75% of the time. Its rise and fall times are instantaneous. If its average power is 0.2 mW, what is its peak power?
   a. 0.2 mW.
   b. 0.4 mW.
   c. 0.8 mW

d. 1.0 mW

e. Impossible to calculate with information given.

4. The light source in Problem 3 is left on for 10 s. How much energy does it deliver over that period?

  a. 0.2 mW.

  b. 0.2 mJ.

  c. 0.8 mJ.

  d. 2 mJ.

  e. 8 mJ.

5. Light input to a 10-km-long fiber is 1 mW. Light output at the end of the fiber is 0.5 mW. What is the fiber attenuation, measured in dB/km?

  a. 0.3 dB/km.

  b. 0.5 dB/km.

  c. 1 dB/km.

  d. 3 dB/km.

  e. 5 dB/km.

6. The base of the ITU frequency standard for WDM systems is 193.1 THz. What is the wavelength in air of the eleventh 100-GHz frequency step on the ladder of WDM frequencies?

  a. 1.5434 μm.

  b. 1.5441 μm.

  c. 1.54453 μm.

  d. 1.5449 μm.

  e. 1.5541 μm.

7. How many photons do you need at the 193.1-THz frequency (1552.1 nm) to make a millijoule of energy equivalent to a 1-mW

signal for 1 s? Planck's constant is $h = 6.626 \times 10^{-34}$ J/Hz.

  a. 10^9 photons.

  b. 193.1×10^9 photons.

  c. 7.816×10^{12} photons.

  d. 193.1×10^{12} photons.

  e. 7.816×10^{15} photons.

8. Why is the bit error rate measured?

  a. To calculate attenuation of an optical fiber.

  b. To measure pulse dispersion.

  c. To assess quality of digital transmission.

  d. To locate broken fibers.

  e. To evaluate analog transmission quality.

9. What does jitter measure?

  a. Rise time of a digital pulse.

  b. Uncertainty in pulse timing.

  c. Duration of a digital pulse.

  d. Uncertainty in bit error rate.

  e. Uncertainty in signal frequency.

10. What does an open eye pattern indicate?

  a. Good-quality digital transmission.

  b. Only that the signal is reaching the receiver.

  c. That no signal is reaching the receiver.

  d. Poor-quality analog transmission.

  e. A broken fiber.

11. An optical time-domain reflectometer can

    a. measure fiber attenuation.

    b. locate faults.

    c. measure connector loss.

    d. identify sites of back-reflection.

    e. All the above.

12. Tunable laser sources are most likely to be used for what sort of measurements?

    a. Bit error rate.

    b. WDM system tests.

    c. Signal-to-noise ratio.

    d. Numerical aperture.

    e. Fiber fault location.

Introduction to System Concepts

About This Chapter

The last several chapters have concentrated on specific elements of fiber-optic systems, from the fibers and light sources to measurement techniques. This chapter teaches you about the ways these components can be put together to make various types of fiber-optic systems. It concentrates specifically on the concepts used in fiber-optic systems. Chapter 19 will cover standards, Chapter 20 will go into design details, and later chapters will cover specific applications.

Types of Transmission Systems

So far I've talked much more about fiber-optic components than about how they are put together to make systems. To understand system concepts, I will start by looking at the ways that communication systems are connected.

You can divide fiber systems into a few basic categories, according to how they transmit signals. You can think of these categories as the basic building blocks of communication systems:

 Point-to-point systems, which simply carry signals back and forth between two points.

 Point-to-multipoint, or broadcast, systems, which distribute identical signals from a central facility to multiple terminals, which may (or may not) be able to send signals back.

● **Networked systems,** which transmit signals among many terminal points somehow linked to each other.

● **Switched systems,** which make temporary connections between pairs of terminals or subscribers attached to the system.

Figure 18.1 shows each of these building blocks. You can find variations on most of these concepts, such as broadcast systems that include networking or switched elements. Practical systems are assembled from these elements to meet particular needs. For example, an office building may have a hierarchy of networks, with local-area networks in each department, each local-area network connected to a node in a network that serves the whole floor, and each of those floor-wide networks, in turn, linked to a building-wide network. Similarly, the telephone network employs levels of switched systems, which route calls first to large cities, then to districts within the cities, to neighborhoods, and finally to individual homes.

Let's look briefly at each of these building blocks and their uses.

Point to Point

● Point-to-point transmission links pairs of terminals.

Point-to-point transmission is the simplest type of fiber-optic system. It provides two-way communication between a pair of terminals, each with a transmitter and receiver, that are permanently linked together.

Conceptually, the distance between terminals doesn't matter. The two could be on opposite sides of the room or on opposite sides of the ocean. If the link is too long for the transmitter to send signals through the entire length of fiber, optical amplifiers or repeaters can be added to boost signal strength. Examples of point-to-point links range from a cable linking a personal computer and a dedicated printer to a transatlantic submarine cable.

If you look closely enough, you can break other types of fiber-optic systems into point-to-point links. That reflects the reality that any fiber system has a transmitter on one end and a receiver on the other, although couplers in between may split the signals among multiple fibers. It also reflects the fact that point-to-point fiber links generally are easy to build.

Point to Multipoint (Broadcast)

● Point-to-multipoint transmission uses one transmitter to serve many terminals.

Another family of transmission systems sends the signal from one transmitter to many terminals. This is sometimes called broadcasting, because it is analogous to the way a radio or television transmitter sends signals to many home sets within its transmission range. In a fiber-optic system, the terminals may or may not return signals to the central transmitter. If there is a return signal it is often at a lower speed than the broadcast transmission.

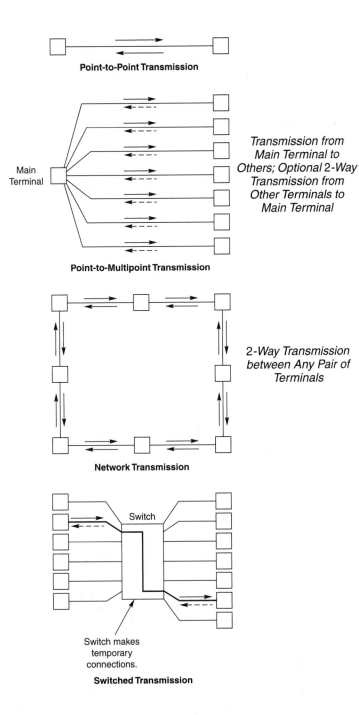

FIGURE 18.1

Types of transmission systems.

Point-to-Point Transmission

Main Terminal

Transmission from Main Terminal to Others; Optional 2-Way Transmission from Other Terminals to Main Terminal

Point-to-Multipoint Transmission

2-Way Transmission between Any Pair of Terminals

Network Transmission

Switch

Switch makes temporary connections.

Switched Transmission

Because they serve many terminals, point-to-multipoint transmitters generally send higher-power signals than those in point-to-point systems. The basic design can vary considerably, as shown in Figure 18.2. A tree or star coupler can split the signal from one transmitter to drive many terminals. Or the split signals can drive relay transmitters, which amplify and repeat the signal from the main transmitter and send it to terminals (or another stage of relay transmitters in a multilevel system). Optical amplifiers may be used as relay transmitters or to boost the output of the main transmitter.

FIGURE 18.2

Point-to-multipoint transmission.

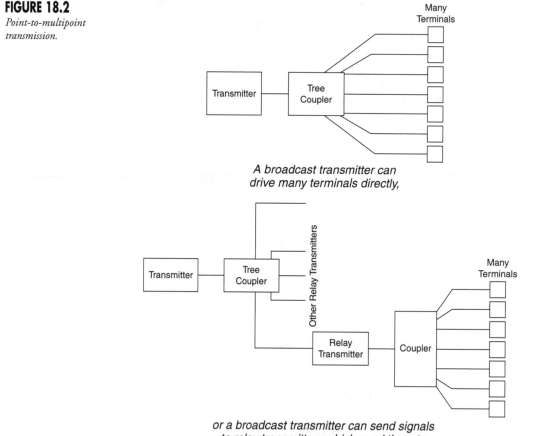

A broadcast transmitter can
drive many terminals directly,

or a broadcast transmitter can send signals
to relay transmitters which send them to
terminals (or other relay terminals) in a multilevel system.

Like a point-to-point transmission system, a point-to-multipoint system is fixed, with permanent connections between transmitters and receivers. Typically, point-to-point systems include multiple levels of signal distribution. For example, the head end of a cable-television system sends signals to local distribution nodes, which in turn send signals to neighborhood nodes, which distribute signals to individual homes. Typically these signals send relatively few signals "upstream" from home terminals to the head end where signals originate. A *pure* point-to-multipoint system distributes identical signals to all terminals, but modern cable-television systems can distribute some unique signals to individual homes, in ways that I will cover later.

You should realize that the main transmitter in a point-to-multipoint system is more "important" than the terminals it serves. Even in a two-way system, it sends most information handled by the system, and is essentially an information provider (whatever you think of the offerings of your local cable system). Individual terminals provide little or no information, and that can go only to the main transmitter; they generally cannot communicate directly with each other. If the main transmitter dies, a point-to-multipoint system is off the air.

Networks

A network system differs fundamentally from a point-to-multipoint system because all terminals are treated (more or less) equally. All terminals can both send and receive signals, and all can send signals to any other terminal on the network. Figure 18.3 shows a few simple variations. Small networks are often called local-area networks; larger ones may be called metropolitan-area or wide-area networks.

Networks allow many terminals to talk with each other.

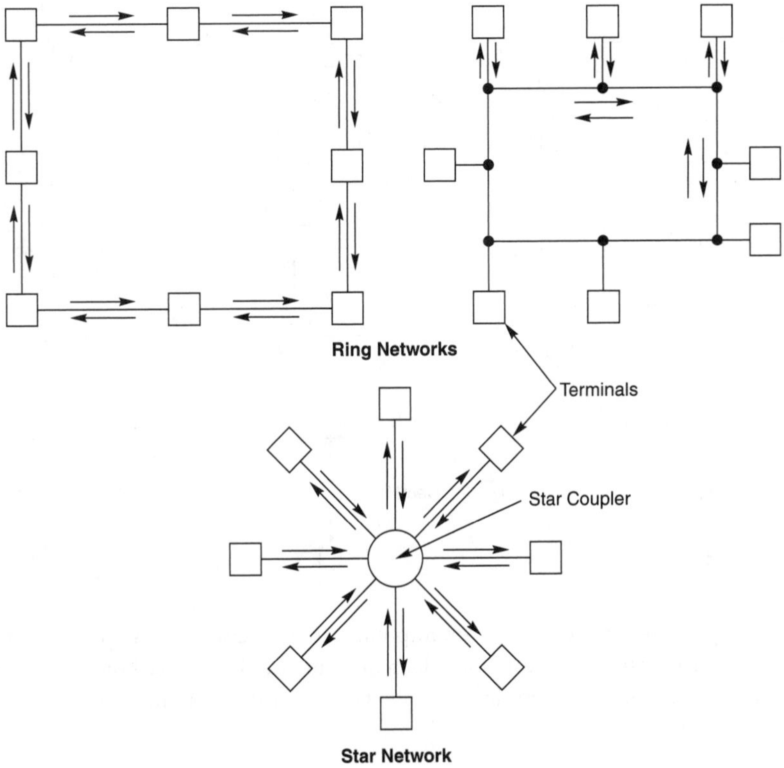

FIGURE 18.3
Network transmission.

Ring Networks

Terminals

Star Coupler

Star Network

Terminals can be connected to the network in various ways. One approach is to put them all around a ring or loop. Signals may be split or tapped from the loop to serve each terminal, or they may pass through each terminal, where they can be modified. Because fiber couplers have high attenuation, it is often easier to build networks as a collection of point-to-point links that are regenerated, with some modifications possible, at each terminal. That approach is used in some standard fiber networks, including FDDI. Another design is the star network, shown in Figure 18.3, where signals to and from each terminal pass through a central point, either a passive coupler that divides input light or an active coupler that receives and retransmits the signal. This approach is most often used with Ethernet and certain other networks where one node connects many terminals to the network backbone.

Networks can be linked together with other networks, so you can have a network of networks, as shown in Figure 18.4. In this case, each small-scale (department) network interfaces with a larger-scale (floor-wide) network, which in turn interfaces with an even larger (building-wide) network.

FIGURE 18.4

A hierarchy of networks, interconnected to larger-scale networks.

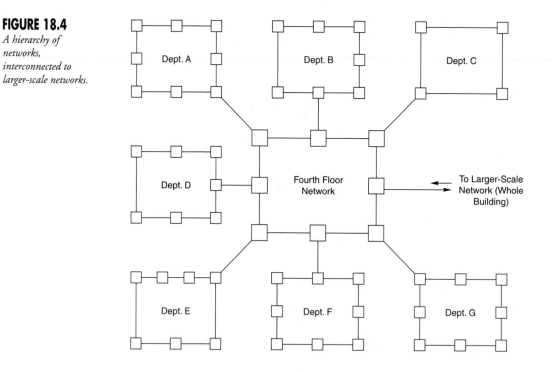

As with point-to-point and point-to-multipoint systems, networks have permanent connections to each terminal, and the overall architecture can be changed only by rewiring. This means that the same terminals always talk to each other unless the network is changed. In practice, reconfiguration is simplified by designing the network with patch panels for attaching and removing terminals. A typical example is a local area network (LAN) for personal computers in an office. Note that the terminals do not all have to be identical devices but require only a common protocol to talk with one another. Thus a local-area network may include a group printer, a group server, a scanner, an Internet connection node, and different types of computers.

Switched Transmission

Adding switches to a communication network makes it more flexible. Switches allow any pair of terminals to send and receive signals directly to and from each other. The connections are inherently temporary, so each terminal can talk—at different times—to any other terminal, as shown in Figure 18.1. Depending on the system design, multiple terminals may be linked together at once. The telephone network is the standard example.

Switching adds a level of complexity to the system in the form of switches, which make and break connections. Switch technology is complex, but it adds tremendous power to the system by making temporary connections to send signals between any pair of terminals linked to the switch. You can assemble switches in series, so each one directs signals at a different level. This allows the global telephone network to send calls around the world. To give a simplified example, one switch might direct a long-distance call to your state, another to the city where you live, a third to your part of town, a fourth to your block, and a fifth to your home. In practice, several of these switches may be in the same place—typically those serving your part of town, your block, and your home all are installed in a telephone-company switching office.

As you learned in Chapter 16, optical switching is difficult. However, signals do not have to be switched optically. In practice, most switching in the telephone network is done electronically. In effect, the fiber-optic elements of the telephone network are point-to-point systems linking electronic switches. That will change as optical switching technology develops, but it highlights an important aspect of system design: the choice of components is a pragmatic one. If electronic switches are the most cost-effective type, you use them, even if you are designing what is nominally a fiber-optic system.

Switching and Routing

Switching and routing are different operations in telecommunication systems, although they serve similar functions in directing signals to their destinations. A detailed comparison of the two is beyond the scope of this book, but I can give you a general idea of the distinction between them.

Switches are relatively simple-minded hardware. A switch makes connections that create a circuit linking two points, using simple rules based on information like the area

Switching allows temporary connections between pairs of terminals.

Switching and routing are different operations.

code of a telephone number. The connections may be physical connections that carry electrons from the power lines through a lamp in your home or direct light through optical fibers to a receiver somewhere in the telephone system. Switching creates a path for the signals. Switches in the telephone system create a temporary path from your phone to your grandmother's when you call her and maintain that path until you finish your conversation.

Routers are more complex devices which direct signals that are transmitted in a different way, by breaking them up into blocks of digital data called *packets*. Each packet carries a header that specifies its destination, as well as a block of data. The router reads the address header and determines the best route for the data packet to follow. Two successive data packets need not follow the same path between two points. If you're sending packets from New York to Chicago, routers may send the first through Cleveland and the second through Cincinnati. Both should reach the same destination, but they need not follow the same path. Note that although routing can replace switching in some ways, it does not create temporary circuits, or maintain open pathways for additional packets.

As an analogy, you can think of a switch as a robot, programmed to send every car going from Chicago to New York along the same set of highways. A router is a traffic officer who asks you your destination, checks traffic conditions on the roads you might take, then hands you a map giving you the best route at the moment. Each has their advantages. The robotic switch is faster and cheaper; the traffic-officer router takes more time to decide the best route and has to be paid more, but will help you avoid traffic jams, and efficiently allocates limited highway space.

Broadcasting, Networking, and Switching

●
Broadcasting, networking, and switching are distinct architectures.

The distinction among broadcasting, networking, and switching is important because it determines how signals are distributed to terminals attached to the system.

Broadcasting sends the same signals to everybody. You and your neighbors receive the same cable-television channels, although the neighborhood sports fanatic may pay extra for a decoder that unscrambles every sports channel.

Networking routes the same signals to all terminals, but each terminal collects only the signals directed to it. All the terminals share the network. A network works a bit like a mail carrier, lugging the mail around the block, reading the addresses, dropping incoming mail in the proper boxes, and collecting outgoing mail. Old-fashioned party-line phones worked on similar principles. Several homes shared a single phone line, but each home had a different ring, and you were only supposed to pick up the phone when you heard your ring. (As you will learn later, details of signal distribution differ among networks.)

Switching sends signals only between a pair of terminals, so the other terminals never see or hear that signal. Unlike a network, you get a dedicated private line, although only a temporary one. With modern private-line phones, every home on the block has a separate phone line, so your neighbors can't tie up your line or hear your calls. (Exceptions can happen when you and your neighbor buy cordless phones that operate on the same frequency, but those are supposed to be exceptions, like the mail carrier who misreads an address and misdelivers a letter.)

Although this book covers fiber optics, these basic principles of signal distribution also hold for wires and for wireless transmission. In practice, modern telecommunication systems include a mixture of fibers, wires, and wireless (radio or microwave) transmission.

Transmission Formats

Signals are transmitted through optical fibers by modulating light with a signal. Different systems use different modulation techniques, depending on application requirements. Analog and digital signals can each be modulated in different ways. We will first review the differences between analog and digital signals and then consider variations on the two approaches.

Digital and Analog Signals

In Chapter 3, you learned that signals could be transmitted as continuous analog variations in intensity (or some other parameter) or as a series of digital pulses. Analog transmission was used for many years and remains common in cable-television systems and some other applications. It can pack more information into less bandwidth than digital signals but is much more vulnerable to noise and distortion, and analog signals cannot be manipulated as easy as digital signals.

Digital transmission has grown much more popular for most telecommunications applications. It requires simpler electronics and can encode any form of information, making it possible to merge digital data streams from many different sources and transmit them with little worry about interfaces. Although your home telephone line carries analog signals, the telephone network converts them to digital form for easier switching and processing. Thanks to the low noise of digital telephony, a transatlantic telephone call usually sounds no different than one across the street.

Note that there is a subtle distinction between signal formats and modulation schemes that often gets lost because the terminology is not very clear. Digital and analog signals are ways of representing information. An analog signal varies in a continuous way analogous to, for example, the variations in air pressure we sense as sound. A digital signal encodes these variations as numbers, which can be used to reconstruct the original vibrations our ears hear as sound.

Modulation schemes describe how the digital or analog signal is carried. In fiber optics, the carrier is a beam of light, with a frequency much higher than the signal. (Radio

> Digital signals are used more widely than analog signals.

> Analog and digital are signal types; modulation is the transmission format for those signals.

carriers likewise have frequencies much higher than the audio or video signals that modulate them for broadcast transmission.) The simplest type of modulation varies the carrier amplitude in proportion to the strength of the signal. If you use amplitude modulation for digital signals, the pulses turn the carrier off and on. If you use amplitude modulation for analog signals, the carrier intensity varies continuously with analog signal strength. You can also use other modulation schemes; frequency modulation is common for radio transmission, for example.

Although the terminology is not very clear, you should remember there is a difference. Analog and digital are types of signals. Modulation is the format used to transmit the signals, and the same type of modulation may be used for either analog or digital signals. We will look at a few important modulation formats to understand how they work.

Amplitude Modulation

Analog and digital fiber-optic systems use amplitude modulation.

Virtually all fiber-optic systems use amplitude modulation, in which the light intensity varies in proportion to the instantaneous signal strength. You can see the basic idea if you look again at Figure 10.2. The signal varies much more slowly than the light waves (you couldn't see the light waves if they were drawn to true scale). The stronger the signal, the more light from the transmitter.

Amplitude-modulated analog signals vary continuously in strength, in direct proportion to the continuously changing input signal. The signal format depends on the source. It's possible to have an analog voice signal as the source, but typically analog fiber-optic systems carry video signals in standard formats used for cable television. I will talk a little more about them later, in Chapter 23 on video transmission, but the details belong in the cable-television world.

Digital Coding Schemes

Digital bit strings can be coded in several different ways.

Nominally, amplitude-modulated digital signals are a series of bits. However, there are several distinct coding techniques, shown in Figure 18.5. Each has its own distinct characteristics, and you should understand the differences among them:

- NRZ (no-return-to-zero) coding—Signal level is low for a 0 bit and high for a 1 bit and does not return to zero between successive 1 bits.

- RZ (return-to-zero) coding—Signal level during the first half of a bit interval is low for a 0 bit and high for a 1 bit. Then it returns to zero for either a 0 or 1 in the second half of the bit interval.

- Manchester coding—Signal level always changes in the middle of a bit interval. For a 0 bit, the signal starts out low and changes to high. For a 1 bit, the signal starts out high and changes to low. This means that the signal level changes at the end of a bit interval only when two successive bits are identical (e.g., between two zeros).

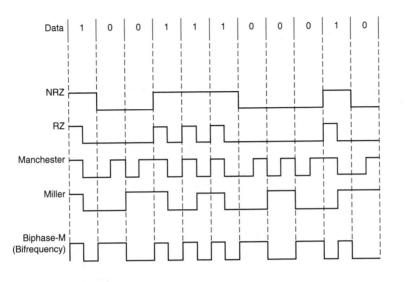

FIGURE 18.5
Digital data codes.

● Miller coding—For a 1 bit, the signal changes in the middle of a bit interval but not at the beginning or end. For a 0 bit, the signal level remains constant through a bit interval, changing at the end of it if followed by another 0 but not if it is followed by a 1.

● Biphase-M or bifrequency coding—For a 0 bit, the signal level changes at the start of an interval. For a 1 bit, the signal level changes at the start and at the middle of a bit interval.

NRZ coding is probably the most common in fiber systems, but each scheme has its advantages and disadvantages. Some, including RZ, Manchester, and bifrequency coding, can make two transitions during a bit interval. This requires more system bandwidth, but improves performance. For instance, the frequently switched Manchester code generates its own clock, whereas NRZ-coded signals can suffer loss of timing or signal-level drift during a long string of 0 or 1 bits.

Soliton Transmission

Soliton transmission is an alternative to the usual methods of transmitting a series of amplitude-modulated digital pulses through a fiber-optic system. Solitons are pulses that rise and fall in intensity in a specific pattern, which allows them to regenerate themselves as they travel along a fiber.

You can think of solitons as doing a delicate balancing act between two competing effects that degrade the transmission of other pulses. One is chromatic dispersion, which stretches out pulses carrying a range of wavelengths as they travel along a fiber. The other is self-phase modulation, which spreads out the range of wavelengths as pulses pass through an optical fiber. The details depend on some rather abstruse mathematics that

●
Solitons are self-regenerating pulses that do not change shape along a fiber.

you don't want to worry about, but if a pulse of the correct shape is sent through fiber with the proper characteristics, the two types of stretching offset each other. This means that the shape of the pulse—how its intensity changes with time—is not affected by the chromatic dispersion that normally makes pulses spread out. Solitons can exist in places other than fibers—the first were waves spotted in nineteenth-century canals—but their only use in communications is for fiber-optic transmission.

Although the pulse shape survives unchanged, the light is attenuated as it travels down the fiber. However, optical amplifiers can compensate for that loss, so systems with optical amplifiers can transmit soliton pulses extremely long distances.

Soliton pulses have proved surprisingly robust in optical fibers. The input pulses don't have to match the ideal soliton shape exactly, because fiber transmission gives them the proper soliton shape. A laser source can generate a series of soliton pulses, and an external modulator can generate a signal by blocking certain pulses, as shown in Figure 18.6. Thus the presence of a pulse can mean a 1, and the absence can indicate a 0. Note that solitons must be spaced a certain distance apart to keep them from interfering with each other and that their return to zero at the end of the pulse makes this signal RZ coded.

FIGURE 18.6

Soliton pulses modulated with a digital signal.

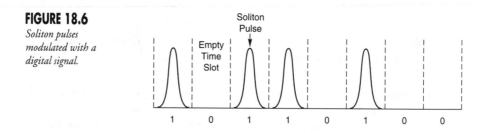

Soliton systems have demonstrated very high transmission speeds in the laboratory. However, they have not kept up with the rapid increases in speed achieved by wavelength-division multiplexing. Research continues, and soliton systems may eventually find some applications.

Frequency Modulation

You may be familiar with the idea of frequency modulation from radio and television. Instead of modulating the amplitude or strength of the carrier, frequency modulation changes the frequency. Amplitude modulation was developed first for radio and is simpler to implement, but you can hear the difference in performance when you switch between AM and FM bands on your radio. Frequency modulation works better for broadcast signals because it does not pick up noise caused by random fading of signal amplitude. It's widely used to broadcast analog signals.

The digital counterpart of frequency modulation is called frequency-shift keying (FSK). It shifts the frequency a detectable amount when the signal shifts from on to off. For example, the transmitter might jump between 998.3 MHz for off and 998.4 MHz for on.

Frequency modulation is more difficult to implement optically than it is electronically, but systems have been demonstrated. They rely on the principle of coherent, or heterodyne, transmission, which is adapted from heterodyne radio transmission. Figure 18.7 shows the basic idea. The laser transmitter emits a frequency v_1, which is modulated by the signal. At the receiver, that light is mixed with light from a second laser at a nearby frequency v_0, giving an intermediate frequency signal at the difference frequency, $v_1 - v_0$ (or, strictly speaking, the absolute value of that difference). That intermediate frequency signal can then be processed by the receiver electronics to give an output signal.

Coherent fiber-optic systems have been demonstrated but are not in practical use.

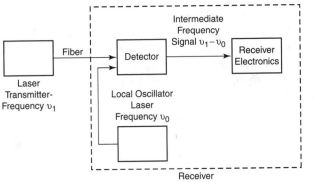

FIGURE 18.7

Coherent, or heterodyne, transmission.

The major attraction of coherent detection is that it avoids noise encountered in direct detection, making the receiver sensitive to fainter signals and allowing more loss between transmitter and receiver. It also allows the use of frequency-shift modulation, which won't work with direct detection. The greater sensitivity would let signals travel further between transmitter and receiver. Alternatively, that higher sensitivity could allow higher transmission speed, because the detector would need to see fewer photons to detect a bit. Another theoretical advantage of coherent transmission is that it might let system designers pack channels closer together in frequency than would otherwise be possible.

However, the attractions of coherent transmission and frequency modulation remain largely theoretical for fiber optics. Advances in those areas have not kept up with the rapid progress in WDM systems, which are now considered much more practical.

Phase-Shift Modulation

Another approach to modulation is to vary the phase of the transmitted wave continuously in proportion to the signal. In principle, you can extract the phase-shift information by combining the transmitted wave with another identical wave in a system such as the coherent transmitter of Figure 18.7. The digital counterpart of phase modulation is phase-shift keying, which alters the phase shift by a fixed amount between on and off states.

The idea sounds good and has been demonstrated in the laboratory. However, it has not yet proven practical.

Transmission Capacity

Transmission capacity is the amount of information a fiber can carry.

The transmission capacity of a communication system measures how much information it can carry. For digital systems this is the number of bits per second passing a given point. For analog systems, it is the transmission bandwidth, usually measured in megahertz or gigahertz. Typically it is specified for individual fibers, with a pair of fibers needed to carry two-way communications—one transmitting in each direction. The total capacity is the sum of the capacity of all the fiber pairs. (It is possible for fibers to carry signals simultaneously in two directions, but there are significant performance drawbacks, so it generally is not done at high speeds, and generally the wavelengths should be well separated. For example, a single fiber might carry signals at 1300 and 1550 nm, with the 1550-nm signals at a much lower speed.)

You can achieve high speed in various ways. One is to modulate the transmitter at higher and higher speeds. Another is to add other transmitters, and send multiple signals through the fiber at different wavelengths. A third is to add more fibers to the cable or transmission route.

Conversely, various factors can limit transmission speed. You need a light source that can be modulated rapidly. You need low dispersion at the transmitted wavelengths—meaning both low dispersion in the fiber and a narrow spectral width from the laser source. Because total fiber dispersion increases with distance, you may need to limit transmission distance to achieve high speed. You also need fast, sensitive receivers.

Multiplexing

Multiplexing is the transmission of two or more signals at once through the same fiber.

The combining of multiple signals to send through the same transmission channel is called *multiplexing*. Multiplexing is used throughout communications, because it greatly increases transmission capacity, reducing system costs. Telephone calls are multiplexed so one fiber or wire can carry multiple conversations. Dozens of video channels are multiplexed on a cable-television network, so a single fiber or coaxial cable carries all the video channels delivered to homes.

Two fundamentally different types of multiplexing are used in fiber-optic systems. One is the combination of multiple signals into a single combined signal that modulates an optical transmitter. This is called time-division multiplexing for digital signals and frequency-division multiplexing for analog signals. The other is simultaneously transmitting signals at two or more wavelengths through the same optical fiber, wavelength-division multiplexing.

Electronic and Time-Division Multiplexing

Electronic multiplexing began long before optical fibers were first used in telecommunications. Electronic equipment combines two or more separate input signals into a single output signal. That combined signal is transmitted through a communication system and then "demultiplexed" to break it into its original components. Multiplexing takes different forms in digital and analog systems.

Digital systems use time-division multiplexing (TDM), which combines several input signals into a single bit stream, as shown in Figure 18.8. In the example shown, four separate 1.5-Mbit/s inputs feed into a multiplexer. The multiplexer combines the signals, selecting first one pulse from input 1, then a pulse from input 2, and so on in sequence. Essentially, the multiplexer shuffles the pulses together and retimes them because the lower-speed pulses are too long to stuff into a faster stream of bits. At the other end of the system, a demultiplexer sorts the bits out, putting bit 1 into channel 1, bit 2 into channel 2, and so forth.

> Electronic multiplexers combine two or more signals to produce a signal that drives a fiber-optic transmitter.

> Time-division multiplexers generate a single bit stream.

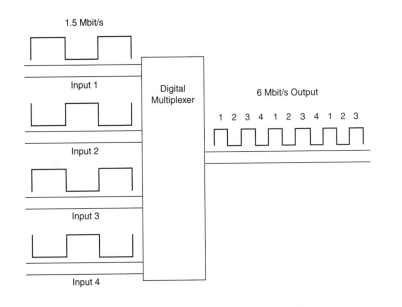

FIGURE 18.8

Time-division digital multiplexing.

Analog multiplexers work differently, by shifting the frequencies of the input signals so each is at a separate frequency and does not interfere with the others. Then the signals are combined to generate a signal covering a wider range of frequencies. In Figure 18.9, each input signal covers a frequency range of 0–1 MHz. The first signal modulates a 10-MHz carrier, generating signals varying in frequency from 10 to 11 MHz. The second modulates a 12-MHz carrier, generating a signal from 12 to 13 MHz. The third and fourth signals modulate carriers at 14 and 16 MHz, respectively, to generate signals at 14–15 and 16–17 MHz. This is called frequency-division multiplexing. Note that some dead space may be left between channels to avoid interference and that the carrier frequency is much higher than the signal frequency. The signals are sorted out by a demultiplexer at the other end of the system. Electronic bandpass filters separate the multiplexed signals that are mixed with the carrier frequencies to regenerate the original signals.

FIGURE 18.9

Analog electronic
frequency-division
multiplexing.

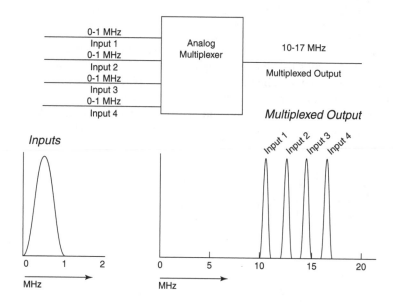

The outputs of both analog and digital electronic multiplexers behave like complete signals of that bandwidth or bit rate. A fiber-optic system can carry them without any special provisions because all the signal combining is done electronically. All the fiber-optic system has to do is carry the signal that drives its transmitter—whether or not the input is a composite of many different signals.

Wavelength-Division Multiplexing

You've already learned something about optical multiplexing, in the form of wavelength-division multiplexing (WDM). You're going to hear a lot more about it because it's one of the hottest topics in fiber optics. With current technology, time-division multiplexing becomes impractical at speeds much above 10 Gbit/s. To squeeze more bits per second through a fiber, you need to send more high-speed TDM signals at separate wavelengths.

Conceptually, wavelength-division multiplexing is much like electronic frequency-division multiplexing. The difference is that optical frequencies are much higher than radio frequencies. Instead of separate signals modulating frequencies of 10, 12, 14, and 16 MHz, you have separate signals modulating frequencies of 193.1, 193.2, 193.3, and 193.4 THz. Although the lasers almost always are modulated with digital signals, the separate wavelengths function like analog channels at separate frequencies. (Remember that while signals are in digital format, the real world is an analog place, with light intensity varying continuously, not simply switching between off and on states.)

It is possible to use WDM to send signals at two different wavelengths in opposite directions through the same fiber. Wavelength-selective couplers at each end separate the signals going in opposite directions. This is not done in high-performance systems because it invites noise problems. However, it does work if wavelengths are widely separated, so it's attractive for applications such as allowing low-speed transmission in one direction and high-speed transmission in the other.

More typically, wavelength-division multiplexing carries multiple signals at different wavelengths in the same direction. Early systems typically carried just two wavelengths, typically at 1300 and 1550 nm, doubling the transmission capacity of a fiber at the cost of extra transmitters, receivers, and couplers. Newer systems combine many closely spaced wavelengths in the 1550-nm region, where erbium-doped fiber amplifiers can boost signal strength. Systems with carrying signals spaced more than 200 GHz or 1.6 nm apart normally are called simply *WDM,* while those with channels spaced 200 GHz (1.6 nm) or less generally are called dense-WDM, or D-WDM. The more wavelengths, the more closely they must be packed. At this writing, the most offered in a commercial system are 80 wavelengths, spaced 50 GHz (roughly 0.4 nm) apart. With current technology, the spacing between channels normally must be larger when each channel carries 10 Gbit/s than when channels carry 2.5 Gbit/s.

Do the multiplication, and you find that these systems can pack up to 400 Gbit/s through a single fiber. Most fibers do not operate at that speed, but it is, nonetheless, an impressive achievement.

> WDM systems promise tremendous capacity.

Cost and Reliability

If you pick up research journals, you will find descriptions of impressive demonstrations. Some of them foreshadow dramatic technological advances such as wavelength-division multiplexing, which quickly find a place in the real world. Others are elegant achievements but never prove practical. Two crucial factors that determine practicality are cost and reliability.

> Cost and reliability are crucial parameters in real-world communications.

Telecommunication companies are in business to provide services, which means they need equipment that is cost-effective and reliable. The special narrow-line lasers needed for dense-WDM systems are expensive, but they save money by sending more signals through fibers already installed. The extra cost of the special lasers is more than offset by the savings in not having to install new cables.

Equipment is not the only cost they face. The costs of installation are often much higher than the price of the equipment being installed. Digging up city streets to lay new underground cables costs many times the price paid for the cable. It's expensive to send an emergency crew to repair a failed cable, and the more remote the cable, the higher the cost. That's why submarine cables laid across the Atlantic have to meet much higher reliability standards than cables buried beside rural interstate highways.

In the competitive telecommunications market, reliability is important in itself. If your long-distance phone company can't give you a decent connection to your uncle Phil in Moose Jaw, Saskatchewan, you can go find another carrier that will do a better job. As I write these words, my phone service has been out for a day because a careless technician cut a major cable a mile from my house, and you can bet I'm rather annoyed at the local phone company.

I can't go into all the factors that influence costs and reliability, but I will briefly describe a few examples.

Environmental and Service Requirements

The great outdoors is not a friendly place for sensitive equipment. You don't want to put anything sensitive to moisture in a manhole, or anything that has to operate in a narrow temperature range in a box on a telephone pole. It's well worth the extra expense to avoid environmental problems with equipment, such as stretching transmission distances to avoid having to install repeaters or optical amplifiers at remote sites.

Telecommunications companies do not want equipment that requires constant adjustments. Research laboratories achieve spectacular results by having a small army of specialists fine-tuning delicate apparatus, but you don't want to send a person with a Ph.D. up a telephone pole every week to adjust an optical interface unit.

Amplifier and Repeater Spacing

You need amplifiers or repeaters for long-distance transmission, but you don't want many of them. A traditional design goal is to stretch spacing as long as possible without degrading speed or signal quality. Not only are amplifiers and repeaters expensive, but they require controlled environments.

Ring networks offer backup paths in case of cable breaks.

Network Topology

The connection of nodes is another important consideration in fiber-optic network design because it can have a large impact on reliability.

Figure 18.10 shows two possible configurations for a telecommunication system: a branching network and a network made up of multiple rings. The branching network seems a logical approach, because it makes direct connections and minimizes the amount of cable used. With the tremendous capacity of modern systems, single cables could carry the traffic between most points.

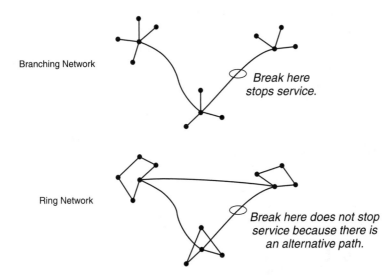

FIGURE 18.10

Branch and ring topologies for connecting network nodes.

Unfortunately, branching networks are very sensitive to single-point failures. If someone breaks the main cable serving your neighborhood, it knocks out all service to the area because no other cable makes that connection. The ring topology avoids that problem by offering two routes to any node on the system. If the cable fails at any point on the ring, signals can be sent in the opposite direction around the loop, maintaining service until the break can be repaired. Rings can be nested, as shown in Figure 18.10, to serve local nodes as well as regional nodes.

What Have You Learned?

1. Point-to-point transmission links pairs of terminals permanently. Point-to-multipoint transmission serves many terminals with one transmitter.

2. Networks connect many terminals with each other.

3. Switching makes temporary connections between pairs of terminals, as in the phone system.

4. Broadcasting, networking, and switching are distinct architectures with their own applications.

5. Digital and analog signals can be transmitted by amplitude modulation of a light beam.

6. There are several different digital coding schemes. NRZ (no return to zero) is used most widely in fiber-optic systems.

7. Solitons are self-regenerating pulses that do not change their shape along a fiber.

8. Coherent fiber-optic transmission and optical frequency modulation have been demonstrated in the laboratory but are not yet practical.

9. Transmission capacity is the amount of information a fiber can carry.

10. Multiplexing is transmitting two or more signals simultaneously through the same fiber. Time-division multiplexing electronically assembles a series of digital pulses for transmission in a single bit stream. Analog signals also can be multiplexed electronically using different carrier frequencies.

11. Wavelength-division multiplexing sends signals through the same fiber at different wavelengths. It's generally called dense-WDM if channel spacing is 200 GHz or less.

12. Cost and reliability are critical practical concerns for telecommunication companies. Important considerations include environmental requirements, labor costs, repeater or amplifier spacing, and network topology.

What's Next?

In Chapter 19, I will cover important standards affecting fiber-optic communications.

Quiz for Chapter 18

1. What type of fiber-optic system is used to distribute cable-television signals?

    a. Point to multipoint.

    b. Local-area network.

    c. Switched.

    d. Point to point.

2. What type of system is used for telephone transmission?

    a. Point to multipoint.

    b. Local-area network.

    c. Switched.

    d. Point to point.

3. What type of multiplexing is used to combine the 60 video channels transmitted at different frequencies in an analog cable-television system?

    a. Pulse-code modulation.

    b. Return-to-zero coding.

    c. Electronic frequency-division multiplexing.

    d. Optical wavelength-division multiplexing.

    e. Time-division multiplexing.

4. Which of the following relies on amplitude modulation?

    a. Digital transmission of 2.5-Gbit/s fiber signals.

    b. Analog transmission of cable-television signals.

    c. Wavelength-division multiplexing of 8 2.5-Gbit/s signals.

    d. AM radio broadcasting.

    e. All the above.

5. What is the proper name for the digital coding used in most fiber-optic systems, in which a strong signal means a 1 and a zero signal means a 0?

    a. No return to zero (NRZ).

    b. Return to zero (RZ).

    c. Manchester coding.

    d. Frequency-division multiplexing.

    e. Phase modulation.

6. What unique characteristic makes solitons attractive for long-distance communications?

    a. Soliton pulses are immune to attenuation.

    b. Soliton pulses can be amplified.

    c. Soliton pulses can carry digital signals.

    d. Soliton pulses retain their original shapes after passing through a fiber.

    e. Soliton pulses can be frequency-modulated.

7. How are digital signals multiplexed electronically for transmission at a higher speed?

    a. They are transmitted at different frequencies.

    b. The bits are interleaved.

    c. The signals are transmitted at different wavelengths.

    d. They are converted to analog signals.

    e. None of the above.

8. Wavelength-division multiplexing does which of the following?

    a. Separates signals at different wavelengths to pass through separate fibers in the same cable.

    b. Allows transmission at high speeds in opposite directions through a single fiber.

    c. Combines signals at different wavelengths to pass through a single fiber in the same direction.

    d. Reduces transmission speed because the wavelengths interfere with each other.

9. Wavelength-division multiplexing is similar to which of the following?

    a. Frequency-division multiplexing for radio-frequency transmission.

    b. Frequency modulation.

    c. Point-to-multipoint transmission.

    d. Time-division multiplexing.

    e. All the above.

10. What is the most important advantage of a ring topology for a telecommunication system?

a. Reduces the amount of cable needed.

b. Reduces installation costs.

c. Reduces the number of transmitters needed.

d. Can continue serving all nodes after a single cable break.

e. It has no advantages.

Fiber System Standards

About This Chapter

For two people to communicate, they must speak the same language. Communication systems likewise work only if transmitters and receivers attached to them speak the same language. Communication engineers have devised standards to assure that equipment from different companies will be able to interface properly.

This chapter will introduce you to the system-level standards most important for fiber-optic systems. Some of these are specific to fiber optics, but others are not and cover other kinds of communications systems as well. The topic of standards is complex and continually evolving, so I can't cover all standards and will not go into much depth, especially for standards with little direct impact on fiber-optic systems. However, you should at least learn to recognize the most important standards and their functions.

Why Standards Are Needed

As you learned earlier, signals can be transmitted in a variety of ways, with different types of digital and analog coding. However, those differences only scratch the surface of the immense potential for variations. You can think of those physical differences as being similar to the distinctions between the media you use to communicate with other people—speech, the written word, sign language, pictures, and so on.

There are many other levels of variations in signal formats, just as people speak many different languages or computer programs store data in different formats. Unlike human languages, signal formats are designed by engineers to transmit signals efficiently and economically. Their choices depend on the types of signals being carried, the distances and types of terminals involved, and the hardware and software they have available. The results can vary widely with factors such as time and network scale.

These differences become a problem when you want networks to connect to each other or when you want to combine two or more generations of equipment, such as existing telephones with new digital switches and transmission lines. Then you need common languages and ways of translating signals between formats. That's when you need standards.

Standards establish the languages spoken by communications systems as well as the medium they use to transmit signals. Groups of engineers from various organizations work on committees that develop the standards, usually sponsored by industry groups and organizations responsible for standards, such as the International Telecommunications Union, the American National Standards Institute, and the Telecommunications Industry Association. The standards they write are intended to make sure that communications systems can understand each other.

The importance of standards increases with the scale of the system, the degree of interconnection, and the variety of services it carries. For a simple fiber-optic link connecting two points, all that is really needed is for the transmitters and receivers at the two terminals to speak the same language. However, fiber-optic links that use a unique format cannot be connected to other equipment. If you want to make that link part of a network, it has to speak a language the other terminals understand.

Some formats are proprietary, meaning they were devised by one company (or a group of companies) for use on its own equipment. Typically those standards are optimized for that equipment. Other companies may or may not use those proprietary formats. Standard formats, on the other hand, are used by many companies making similar equipment, so you can attach Company A's terminal to Company B's transmitter and send signals to Company C's receiver. You can think of standards as agreements for everyone to speak English at a technical meeting or for everyone sending electronic mail to send messages in text-only format.

Standards have evolved considerably over the years, changing with both the marketplace and the technology. In the 1970s, AT&T was effectively America's telephone monopoly, so it set the standards for telecommunication systems. Since the 1984 breakup of AT&T, industry groups have come to set the standards. Many standards have become international as the telecommunications industry has become increasingly global. This assures that you can make phone calls to Brazil, send faxes to India, and dispatch e-mail to Indonesia.

Changing standards have accommodated changes in industry practice. In the 1960s, telephone lines carried only analog voice telephone conversations. By the 1970s, the telephone network started to convert to digital transmission between switching centers. In the 1980s, the telephone network started to handle more computer data and video transmission, plus fax signals. Today, the high-speed lines operated by long-distance carriers are digital data highways that transmit a wide variety of signals, all digitized into a common form that can be reconverted to other formats at the receiving end. Standards make this multipurpose system possible.

Standards are crucial to the function of an open, deregulated market for equipment that must interconnect. You need to be sure you can plug any phone you buy today into the telephone jack in your wall and use it with any local or long-distance carrier. Most standards take into account the existence of old equipment and can accommodate much of it. You can use your digital PCS cell phone to call your grandmother on the heavy black dial phone she has used since 1952. Neither you nor your grandmother should notice the automatic electronic conversion between the two formats. You should remember, however, that some new standards do not accommodate old equipment, such as standards for digital television transmission, which make no effort to talk with the "old" analog set you bought brand new in 1998.

> Standards are crucial in an open, deregulated market.

Layers of Standards

Modern standards have been developed in *layers,* each of which serves a different function. One layer specifies particular services seen by customers, such as voice, fax, and data transmission. Another layer specifies the data format for digital interchange of information—essentially the packaging of data bits representing those signals. Yet another layer specifies how the signals are physically transported, on fibers, through metal cables, or via radio transmission. Various conversion stages exist between each of these layers, as shown in Figure 19.1.

> Modern standards are arranged in layers, which serve different functions.

The diagram may look complex, but it really is an oversimplification of a far more complex process involved in connecting networks with different transmission formats. There are many more standards, generally described by cryptic acronyms. In addition, it is impossible to show on a single page the many alternative ways in which signals can be routed. Nor does this attempt to cover standards being developed for optical networking and wavelength-division multiplexing.

The top layer of Figure 19.1 shows the services seen by end users, such as voice, data, and video services. Typically these are in standard formats, which in themselves may cover more than one service. What we call standard analog voice telephone lines actually can carry fax signals and computer modem signals as well. The fax machines and modems generate analog signals (which you hear as sounds when you listen to them), which carry digital data over a line that the telephone company treats as if it were a phone call, or a "voice channel." If you had a digital (ISDN) phone line, the telephone company would instead see digital data in a standard format. If your company has a dedicated high-capacity line, it also transmits digital data to the phone company.

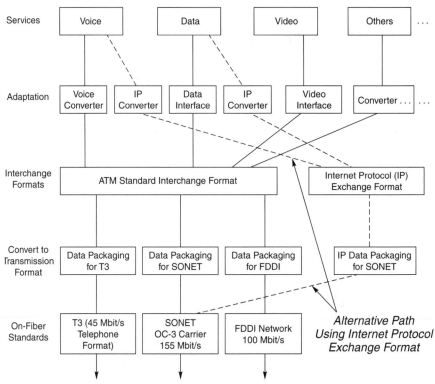

FIGURE 19.1

*Relationships of
standard layers of
communications for
services, data
interchange, and
transmission.*

The second layer is the adaptation layer, which converts these signals into a standard format for data interchange. The adapters convert these signals into digital form and then assemble the raw bits into a standard format used by whatever organization is carrying the data.

The third layer shows two of the most common interchange formats. ATM stands for asynchronous transfer mode, widely used in the telephone industry. IP is the Internet Protocol, generally used for long-haul data transmission on Internet backbone systems. These are ways of packaging bits that I will describe later in this chapter. Note that they say nothing about the transmission medium. They are simply logical packages of bits, such as the 8-bit *bytes* used in a computer. All the signals generated by the various services can be intermingled here; the data packages include labels for sorting them out at the other end. (ATM and IP formats do not serve identical purposes, and sometimes signals in IP format are repackaged into ATM format, although this is not shown in Figure 19.1. As I warned you, this can get complicated.)

That raw interchange format data must be repackaged into forms that match the transmission requirements of particular media. This is the fourth layer in Figure 19.1, a second set of conversions that generate signals in the proper form for transmission.

The bottom layer of Figure 19.1 shows three standard formats for fiber transmission. You can think of this as a physical layer, because it is how bits follow one another through an optical fiber. The figures show three possible fiber standards, the old but still widely used 45-Mbit/s T3 standard in the North American digital telephone hierarchy, the 155-Mbit/s OC-3 standard for SONET transmission, and the 100-Mbit/s FDDI standard for local-area networks. Eventually these signals are reconverted through the same stages on the other end.

If you follow the solid flow lines from top to bottom, you will see that everything on those paths is put into the ATM standard interchange format. That's what you would expect in dealing with many long-distance telephone carriers. However, if you were communicating over the Internet, signals would be more likely to follow the dashed lines and be converted into the Internet Protocol (IP) interchange format, which is different. Then those signals could be repackaged into SONET form for transmission through fibers. The resulting IP on SONET is not the same as ATM on SONET and has to be unpackaged differently.

Note also that the need for interchange formats arises when signals pass through two or more networks with different formats. It's often simpler to leave signals that travel only within a single network in the native format for that network. For example, data from terminals hooked directly to an FDDI network could be converted directly into FDDI format. Voice phone lines hooked to a digital switch at your local switching offices need not be converted into ATM interchange format if they are being routed to other local phones. If you call the local pizza parlor, your call will be digitized for switching but not converted to ATM for long-distance routing.

Trying to make sense of all these formats and protocols would take a book in itself, so I'll concentrate here on the standards that are most important for fiber optics. The goal is not to make you an expert, but to help you understand enough to get along.

Transmission Format Concepts

What we call transmission format is a way of coding and packaging information. Although some analog systems remain important, I will concentrate on digital systems to explain basic concepts.

In addition to transmitting the signal you are sending, the system must transmit routing and decoding information. That means that the transmitted data must identify its destination and how it should be interpreted (e.g., as voice, video, or a particular kind of data). This information can be encoded in various ways, often as *headers* in the first bytes of data, depending on the type of system. As one network passes its data to another, the headers of one can become part of the data transmitted by the network making the interconnection. Networks may also transmit other *overhead* information, such as priority of a transmission or check bits to verify the signal was received correctly.

Transmission formats are ways of coding and packaging information.

Networks developed for different purposes have taken different approaches in transmitting signals. We can view them in two different ways—the choice of data-packaging methods and the task of linking networks.

Time-Division Multiplexing and Packet Switching

• Digital signals can be assigned fixed transmission slots or switched as data packets.

There are two fundamental approaches to breaking down digital signals for transmission. One is to allocate fixed slots for each incoming data stream. Time-division multiplexing works that way, as shown at the top of Figure 19.2. The system reserves successive slots for three input signals. In the example, the high-speed data of input A always fills its slot, the slower data of input B fills only part of the slot some of the time, and the system keeps a slot for input C even when it's off.

FIGURE 19.2

Time-division multiplexing compared with packet switching.

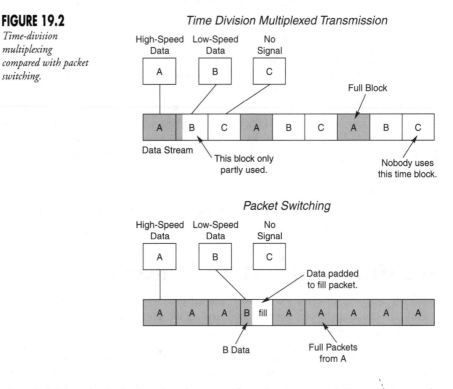

Time-division multiplexing has the advantage of guaranteeing service, but as the example shows, it may do so at the expense of efficiency. When input C doesn't supply any signal, its slots go unused. When B generates slow input, most of its slots go unused.

A more efficient alternative is to break down the input signals into a series of packets, and then drop them into slots as they become available. As shown at the bottom of Figure 19.2, this approach makes more efficient use of limited resources. As long as input A keeps feeding data at a high speed, it will fill all the available slots. In practice, you also need to assign some sort of priority so the fastest input won't hog all the slots; the details can become complex.

The two types of systems handle routing information in different ways. If a signal is dropped into a fixed slot—e.g., byte 16 in a series of 32—the system knows where to route it. In practice, the signal includes a header identifying its type and ultimate destination. That header information can be transmitted first, but it does not need to be repeated as long as the signal occupies the same slot. (A signal may leave the slot when, for example, you finish one phone call and dial another number.) Packet switching works differently; every packet must have a header, because otherwise the system has no way of knowing which packet is which, what it is, and where it goes. This adds to the overhead, but in practice that loss of efficiency is more than offset by avoiding empty time slots.

Packet switching was originally developed for data transmission, where input is inherently "bursty"—high at some times and slow or zero at others. The flexibility of allocating packets works well for this purpose and pays big dividends in efficiency. The down side of packet switching is that the data-flow rate varies with time. That variation can be annoying when it makes the Internet into the World Wide Wait, but you can live with the delays for data transmission.

On the other hand, delays can cause serious problems with voice or video channels, which need to be guaranteed transmission at a constant speed. Time-division multiplexing better fits their needs, but it is still not efficient. A compromise is to develop protocols that give voice and video channels priority so they are routed at the proper rate, while other signals with lower priority can be delayed if necessary. This is done in some packet-switching systems but not in others.

> ● Packet-switched signals must include headers.

Internetworking

Another way to look at the telecommunications network is as an interconnection of networks. What we call the Internet evolved from systems developed to interconnect computer networks at large organizations, or "internetwork" connections.

This viewpoint is based on the assumption that individual networks already exist, with their own transmission standards. The function of the Internet or internetworking protocols is to make connections among these networks. Thus the Internet has its own transmission protocols, and naturally enough they're different from those developed for telephone systems, which carry different types of signals with different priorities.

Internetworking protocols are essentially standards for the interchange of data among networks that can have different architecture. Local-area networks typically carry signals at moderate speeds—tens to hundreds of megabits per second are common. Internetworking links typically operate at somewhat higher speeds, particularly as a larger fraction of traffic within a local network is headed to destinations outside the network. They also usually span greater distances.

If you step back and forget the different origins of the Internet and the long-distance telephone/telecommunications networks, they resemble each other. Both carry signals long distances between nodes, organizations, or cities where users are concentrated. This has led each type of network to adapt concepts from the other, such as the layering of standards, with some for local transmission and others for interchange. However, specific standards differ, reflecting the important differences between the Internet and the telephone system.

Interchange Standards

Interchange standards such as asynchronous transfer mode (ATM) and the Internet Protocol (IP) are built around packet switching. Their function is to package information into packets that carry routing and other necessary information. Both were developed to make efficient use of network resources, but they differ because their designers did not share the same priorities or concerns and the two systems initially carried different types of traffic.

Asynchronous Transfer Mode (ATM)

ATM (asynchronous transfer mode) is a packet-switched format developed for telecommunications.

Asynchronous transfer mode (ATM) is a packet-switching format developed for the telecommunications industry to meet requirements for transmitting voice and video signals as well as data. In ATM, the packets are cells of 53 bytes—a 5-byte header, which identifies the data and its destination, and a 48-byte information field, which contains the user data. ATM functions as an interchange and data-packaging format, the third layer in Figure 19.1. Services that users see, such as voice, video, and data communications, are converted into ATM cells; then the ATM cells are packaged for efficient transmission through fiber-optic and other communication systems.

As a packet-switching system, ATM can intermingle high-speed video signals with low-speed voice signals, without users or network managers having to worry about the details of splitting transmission capacity into the proper fractions. The system assigns priorities to different services, depending on their sensitivity to delay. Thus high-bandwidth and delay-sensitive video signals have a higher priority than computer data. Voice, which is delay-sensitive but has a much lower data rate, has a different priority. ATM was designed to generate maximum throughput from limited transmission resources.

The packet-switching aspect of ATM should not be evident to users, who should receive signals at the same rate they would with a dedicated line or time slot. Its function is to help the service provider make the most efficient possible use of resources—that is, not spend as much on hardware as would be needed with dedicated lines. In short, ATM is a resource-allocation system that lets cheaper packet-switched circuits act like dedicated phone lines.

The ATM standard deliberately avoids mentioning speeds or the transmission medium, because its function is merely to package raw data. It can feed data to any kind of fiber-optic system, as well as coaxial cables, local area networks, or radio-transmission systems. Hypothetically, it could even work with pigeons, each carrying one cell, but it would require a huge flock to do the job—as well as a way to assure the pigeons arrived in the proper sequence.

Internet Protocol (IP)

The Internet also uses packet switching, but the Internet Protocol (IP) specifies different ways of breaking data into packets. Instead of fixed-length cells, it generates variable-length packets, with the header information indicating the frame length as well as the address.

The IP standard evolved over a number of years and was specifically designed for con-necting networks that transmit digital data. Because of that origin, the current IP does not assign a priority code to each packet. Instead, nodes attempt to transmit every packet on a best-effort basis. If they get overwhelmed, they may discard some of the packets. This happens more often than you might like to think, leading to long delays when the Net appears to go to sleep in the midst of downloading web pages.

IP transmission has spread rapidly with the growth of the Internet and works well for data transmission. It does work for voice and video, but they may suffer noticeable and annoy-ing transmission delays. A new version of the IP is being developed that may allow for priority codes, which could alleviate this need.

Although ATM and IP occupy the same level in Figure 19.1, the two standards do not exactly compete for the same niche in the telecommunications network. ATM is designed for resource optimization; IP is designed more for interfacing and transmitting signals across networks. In fact, IP signals may be converted into ATM format for transmission through some systems.

Fiber-Transmission Standards

The telecommunications and networking industries have developed a variety of standards for data transmission over fiber. These standards structure digital transmission, specifying signal transmission rates and how signals are structured to carry information such as their destinations.

Unlike interchange standards, these standards usually assume a particular transmission medium. Some are oriented toward long-distance transmission, others to networking or

Internet Protocol (IP) is a packet-switching system with variable-length frames, developed for the Internet.

connecting networks, and a few seek to cover both domains. I will describe a sampling of important standards, but you should remember that new ones are always being proposed, and some old ones are slowly fading from sight. Later chapters will give more details on their operation.

Digital Telephone Hierarchy

● The digital telephone hierarchy is a series of time-division-multiplexed rates.

Back in the days when AT&T was *the* telephone company for most of the United States, it devised a set of standards for the then-new idea of digital telephone transmission. This digital telephone hierarchy remains in use today, particularly at lower speeds. The International Telecommunications Union devised a similar—but not identical—standard that is used in much of the rest of the world. You'll learn more about these standards later in Chapter 21 on the global telecommunications network.

The starting point for the digital telephone hierarchy is electronics that convert a standard analog voice telephone signal into a digital signal at 56,000 bit/s. Other circuits interleave the bit streams from 24 digitized phone lines into a single sequence of 1.5 Mbit/s, called the T1 or DS1 rate. That, in turn, feeds into systems operating at successively higher T2 and T3 (or DS2 and DS3) rates. The top of that hierarchy, the T4 (sometimes DS4) rate, is 274 Mbit/s but is rarely used.

Single-mode fiber optics allow much higher speeds, but by the time they arrived in the early 1980s, the old Bell System was breaking up and no longer set standards for the North American telephone industry. Industry developed a series of higher-speed systems based on the same principles as the digital telephone hierarchy, some using higher rates standardized by ITU.

The digital telephone hierarchy is a sequence of time-division multiplexing steps, each one combining multiple signals at slower speeds and essentially interleaving them into fixed slots. As you learned earlier, these fixed slots guaranteed the capacity to carry voice telephone signals, at the cost of leaving some capacity unused. The data rates are at speeds that were convenient for telephone transmission when the systems were designed, but they don't necessarily meet the needs of other users, such as video transmission.

Another constraint of the digital hierarchy is that you have to step back down the ladder to extract a lower-speed signal. That is, you must break a high-speed signal into its component parts to extract one of the components. In addition, the format omits some control features that would aid in operation of a modern network.

SONET/SDH

● SONET/SDH is a packet-switched standard hierarchy of digital transmission rates.

The Synchronous Optical Network (SONET) is a packet-switching standard designed for telecommunications to use transmission capacity more efficiently than the old digital telephone hierarchy. SONET is the American standard; a similar international standard is called the Synchronous Digital Hierarchy, or SDH.

SONET/SDH organizes data into 810-byte "frames" that include data on signal routing and destination as well as the signal itself. The frames can be switched individually without breaking the signal up into its component parts.

The standards were developed primarily for fiber-optic transmission of mixed traffic, including telephone calls and other signals. Unlike ATM, SONET/SDH explicitly defines transmission speeds. The base rate (OC-1) is 51.84 Mbit/s, just a little higher than the widely used 45 Mbit/s T3 rate in the digital hierarchy. The next step is the 155.52-Mbit/s OC-3 rate, nominally produced by merging frames from three OC-1 signals. Beyond that are OC-12 at 622 Mbit/s, OC-48 at 2.5 Gbit/s, and OC-192 at 10 Gbit/s.

The SONET standard does more than specify data rates and frame sizes. It also configures transmission in ring topology such as that shown in Figure 18.10, rather than the traditional branching network. The ring connects all nodes on a SONET transmission system, which is designed to automatically sense a cable break and reroute traffic in the other direction. As long as there's only one break in the ring, the signals will continue to reach their destination.

Fibre Channel

Fibre Channel is a standard developed for transmission at speeds of 12.5, 25, 50, 100, 200, and 400 megabytes per second. It adds 2 bits to each 8-bit byte, so this corresponds to nominal data rates of 133, 266, 531, 1062, 2124, and 4125 Mbit/s. The European-style spelling of *fibre* is a deliberate choice, which the developers say symbolizes the use of metal cables in addition to single-mode and graded-index fibers. Fibre Channel transmits data in variable-length frames.

> ● Fibre Channel transmits variable-length frames at rates to 1062 Mbit/s, with 2- and 4-Gbit/s versions in development.

Fibre Channel operates on three layers, one that groups data in frames, a second that encodes and decodes the frames, and a third that provides physical transportation of signals over various media. You can think of these as the lower three levels in Figure 19.1. It can handle point-to-point transmission between a pair of devices (such as a high-speed disk array and a computer), transmission around a loop, or transmission through a switched network. Unlike SONET, it is intended primarily for short-distance transmission in a computer system, network, building, or campus situation. For example, it may be a successor to SCSI cabling for high-speed data transfer between computers and peripherals.

Ethernet and Gigabit Ethernet

Gigabit Ethernet is an extension of the old 10-Mbit/s Ethernet architecture for local area networks linking desktop computers with coaxial cables. Developers first introduced the 100-Mbit/s "Fast Ethernet" and more recently introduced the 1-Gbit/s Gigabit Ethernet. The actual data rate, including overhead bits, is 1.25 Gbit/s.

> ● Gigabit Ethernet is a 1-Gbit/s version of Ethernet, for networks and short internetwork links.

Like Fibre Channel, the Gigabit Ethernet standard covers multiple layers, but it can also interface with other standards such as IP. The transmission hardware is based on Fibre Channel equipment. Like Fibre Channel, signals can be transmitted over twisted-wire pairs, coaxial cables, multimode fiber, or single-mode fiber. As a networking technology, Gigabit Ethernet generally is intended for short-distance transmission on a local-area network or as a backbone system linking networks on a campus.

Fiber Distributed Data Interface (FDDI)

The Fiber Distributed Data Interface (FDDI) is a networking standard established for transmitting 100 Mbit/s. Up to 500 nodes can be included on a dual-ring FDDI network, with nodes separated by up to 2 km. Originally developed for graded-index multimode fibers, the standard has been expanded to cover single-mode fibers and copper wires. The wire version is sometimes called CDDI, for Copper Distributed Data Interface.

Initially intended to serve as a backbone connecting local-area networks operating at lower speeds, FDDI has been adapted for local-area networks as well. It and other computer networks are covered in Chapter 25.

Video Standards

Traditional video standards cover analog transmission. New standards cover digital and high-definition video.

Video-transmission standards are in a state of flux as the television industry tries to deal with digital television technology. The transition will take years and ultimately its success will depend on the public's willingness to pay for a whole new generation of television receivers and adapters.

Three different formats exist for analog television. North America and Japan use NTSC, with 525-line displays transmitted at the rate of 60 interlaced half-frames per second. Most of the rest of the world uses the PAL and SECAM standards, which transmit 625-line displays at the rate of 50 interlaced half-frames per second. The critical difference in frame rates comes from a difference in frequency of AC power lines—North America and Japan use 60 Hz, but most other countries use 50 Hz. Both these analog formats require a bandwidth of 6 MHz per channel.

Digital high-definition television (DTV or HDTV) standards are being adopted around the world. They offer much higher resolution, but by using digital data compression most systems are able to squeeze that higher resolution into the 6-MHz bandwidth of one analog channel. (The United States required this so it would not have to redivide the part of the radio spectrum allocated for television broadcasting.) Alternatively, one broadcast channel can carry two or more digital video signals at lower resolution.

Many details remain to be defined, notably how cable-television system will transmit digital video signals and which of many possible display formats will be used.

Optical Networking Standards

The advent of wavelength-division multiplexing and development of technology for optical switching and signal processing at different wavelengths is creating a need for optical networking standards.

Optical channel and multiplexing standards are in development.

The International Telecommunications Union is considering three levels, or layers, of optical networking standards that would extend the layers of telecommunication standards described earlier. The first proposed layer (just below the SONET/SDH layer) is the optical channel. This covers the end-to-end transport of a single optical channel, which is one wavelength in a WDM system. The concept assumes that the channel could be converted from one wavelength to another at one or more points along the line. The second layer is the optical multiplex section, which covers networking and processing of multiplexed optical signals—that is, the simultaneous processing of several optical channels at different wavelengths, which could be sent through the same fiber. The third layer is the optical transmission section, covering the actual transmission of WDM signals through fiber.

Most details have yet to be worked out. One controversy is whether transmission should be "optically transparent" or "optically opaque." The critical difference is whether the optical signals are switched and transmitted purely in the optical domain (transparently), or whether they must be converted into electronic form for some processing, making the transmission opaque. The choice depends on practical considerations such as how wavelengths can be converted.

Note that a few standards already have been developed for specific optical hardware. The most important is the ITU specification of a wavelength "grid" for wavelength-division multiplexing, starting with a frequency of 193.1 THz and separating signals by 100 GHz. However, some manufacturers have chosen to ignore this grid spacing, while others have adopted a 50-GHz optical channel spacing so they can pack more wavelengths into the 1550-nm band.

What Have You Learned?

1. Standards specify coding techniques so different systems can understand each other. The importance of standards increases with the scale of the system.

2. Modern standards are developed in layers, each of which serves a different function.

3. The major ways to combine digital signals for long-distance transmission are by time-division multiplexing and packet switching. TDM guarantees slots for service, but packet switching uses scarce resources more efficiently.

4. Headers carry information on how to route packets; they are followed by data.

5. Asynchronous Transfer Mode (ATM) is an interchange standard used to pack data efficiently in packets while providing service comparable to time-division multiplexing.

6. Internet Protocol is an internetworking standard developed to carry signals between networks connected by the Internet.

7. The digital telephone hierarchy is a series of time-division-multiplexed data rates developed as standards when the telephone network started carrying digital signals but was still dominated by monopoly carriers.

8. SONET/SDH specifies frame transmission at an ordered series of rates, starting at 52 Mbit/s, over optical fibers. It includes a ring topology to guarantee service in case of one cable break. It is mainly designed for long-distance service.

9. Fibre Channel carries data rates of 133 to 4125 Mbit/s over fibers or metal cables. Applications include point-to-point transmission, loops, switched transmission, and connections between networks.

10. Gigabit Ethernet is a derivative of the 10 Mbit/s Ethernet, but it operates at 1 Gbit/s using technology similar to Fibre Channel.

11. FDDI is the Fiber Distributed Data Interface, a network standard for transmission at 100 Mbit/s among up to 500 nodes.

12. Old analog television standards such as NTSC, PAL, and SECAM are being replaced by new standards for digital television.

13. Optical networking standards will cover three layers: optical channels, optical multiplexing, and optical transmission of WDM signals.

What's Next?

In Chapter 20, you will learn the basic elements of fiber-optic system design. Chapters 21 through 25 will cover major types of fiber systems.

Quiz for Chapter 19

1. Which of the following are not defined by telecommunications industry standards?

   a. Data transmission formats on optical fiber.

   b. Transmission speeds in digital telecommunications.

   c. Interchange formats for signals sent to other countries.

   d. Data transmission in local-area networks.

   e. Monthly telephone service charges.

2. What kind of a standard is Asynchronous Transfer Mode (ATM)?

    a. Data-interchange format.

    b. Fiber transmission.

    c. Analog television.

    d. Time-division multiplexing.

    e. Financial transfer for banking.

3. What data-transfer speed does ATM specify?

    a. T3, 45 Mbit/s.

    b. 100 Mbit/s.

    c. OS-3, 155 Mbit/s.

    d. 1 Gbit/s.

    e. No data rate is specified.

4. How does packet switching combine signals from different sources?

    a. Assigns each one a different wavelength.

    b. Packages them into a series of packets, with headers indicating destinations.

    c. Assigns each one a different time slot in a sequence of bits.

    d. Transmits them simultaneously at different frequencies.

    e. None of the above.

5. Packet switching has what advantage over time-division multiplexing?

    a. Packets always reach their destination on time.

    b. Packets use available transmission lines more efficiently, avoiding empty time slots.

    c. Packet switching assures line availability.

    d. Packets avoid signal interruptions.

    e. The two cannot be used for the same type of communications.

6. Which of the following are interchange formats? (More than one answer is possible.)

    a. ATM.

    b. FDDI.

    c. Fibre Channel.

    d. Gigabit Ethernet.

    e. Internet Protocol (IP).

    f. SONET.

7. Which of the following are fiber-transmission formats? (More than one answer is possible.)

    a. ATM.

    b. FDDI.

    c. Fibre Channel.

    d. Gigabit Ethernet.

    e. Internet Protocol (IP).

    f. SONET.

8. Which transmission format is primarily used for long-distance telecommunications?

    a. SONET.

    b. FDDI.

    c. Fibre Channel.

    d. Gigabit Ethernet.

    e. Ethernet.

9. How fast are data transmitted at the OC-192 rate?
   a. 51.84 Mbit/s.
   b. 100 Mbit/s.
   c. 155 Mbit/s.
   d. 1 Gbit/s.
   e. 10 Gbit/s.

10. Which of the following is an analog transmission standard?
    a. FDDI.
    b. Fibre Channel.
    c. NTSC.
    d. HDTV.
    e. SONET.

20

System Design

About This Chapter

Now that you have learned the general concepts of fiber-optic systems, it's time to see how communication systems are designed. This chapter covers general design concepts; Chapters 21 through 26 describe how fiber optics are used in various communication applications.

The top two technical considerations for communication systems are loss budget and transmission capacity, or bandwidth. You calculate loss budget to be sure enough signal reaches the receiver to give adequate performance. Likewise, you must calculate pulse dispersion, or bandwidth, to be sure the system can handle signals at the speeds you want to transmit. Some simple guidelines will give you rough assessments. In the real world, you also need to consider cost-effectiveness, which involves making trade-offs among various approaches, seeking the one that gives the best performance at the most reasonable cost.

This chapter won't prepare you for heavy-duty system design. However, it will prepare you to evaluate system designs and develop system concepts that should work. It concentrates on simple designs to give you a clear idea of how systems work.

Variables

Design of a fiber-optic system is a balancing act. You start with a set of performance requirements, such as sending 100 Mbit/s through a 5-km cable. You add some subsidiary goals, sometimes explicitly, sometimes implicitly. For example, you may demand cost as low as possible, less than another alternative, or no more than a given amount. Your system might need an error rate of no more than 10^{-15} and should operate without interruption for at least 5 years.

● **Design of fiber-optic systems requires balancing many cost and performance goals.**

You must look at each goal carefully to decide how much it is worth. Suppose, for instance, you decide that your system absolutely must operate 100% of the time. You're willing to pay premium prices for transmitters, receivers, and super-duper heavily armored absolutely gopher-proof cable. But how far should you go? If that is an absolute must because of national security and you have unlimited quantities of money, you might buy up the entire right of way, install the cable in ducts embedded in a meter of concrete, and post guards armed with tanks and bazookas to make sure no one comes near the cable with a backhoe. If its purpose is just to keep two corporate computers linked together, you might be satisfied with laying a redundant gopher-proof cable along a second route different enough from the first that no single accident would knock out both.

● **Many variables enter into system design.**

That somewhat facetious example indicates how many variables can enter into system design. In this chapter, I will concentrate on the major goals of achieving specified transmission distance and data rate at reasonable cost. Many design variables can enter into the equation, directly or indirectly. Among them are the following:

- Light source output power (into fiber)
- Coupling losses
- Spectral linewidth of the light source
- Response time of the light source and transmitter
- Signal coding
- Splice and connector loss
- Type of fiber (single- or multimode)
- Fiber attenuation and dispersion
- Fiber core diameter
- Fiber NA
- Operating wavelength
- Wavelength-division multiplexing
- Optical amplifiers
- Direct versus indirect modulation of transmitter
- Switching requirements
- Receiver sensitivity
- Bit error rate or signal-to-noise ratio
- Receiver bandwidth
- System configuration
- Number of splices, couplers, and connectors
- Type of couplers
- Costs

Many of these variables are interrelated. For example, fiber attenuation and dispersion depend on operating wavelength as well as the fiber type. Coupling losses depend on factors such as fiber NA and core diameter. Some interrelationships limit the choices available. For example, the need to achieve low fiber loss may require operation at 1300 or 1550 nm, and the need for optical amplification may dictate 1550 nm.

Some variables may not give you as many degrees of freedom as you might wish. For example, you may need to interconnect several computer terminals. You have enough flexibility to pick any of the possible layouts in Figure 20.1, but you still have to connect all the terminals, and that requires enough optical power to drive them all.

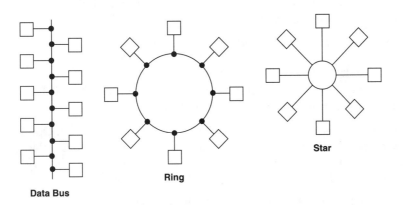

FIGURE 20.1

Three ways to interconnect computer terminals.

Data Bus

Ring

Star

In practice, the type of system dictates the features you consider. If your goal is to connect computer terminals on a single floor of an office building, coupling loss probably will be more important than fiber attenuation. If your goal is to span the Pacific, fiber attenuation and optical amplification will be your main concerns. Designers of transpacific systems must carefully consider how much wavelength-division multiplexing to use and what data rate to transmit on each optical channel, but the office network designer faces the more mundane-seeming choice between step-index plastic or graded-index glass fibers.

Usually you can reach the same performance goals in more than one way. A submarine cable can carry 10 Gbit/s either as one time-division-multiplexed channel or as four wavelength channels, each carrying 2.5 Gbit/s. The choice may ultimately depend on other factors, such as the cost, expected reliability, and potential for future upgrades. Room for future growth also can be critical for office networks, where demand for transmission capacity—like the need for hard disk space and computer memory—can expand at amazing speed.

Power Budgeting

> Power budgeting verifies that enough light reaches the receiver for proper system operation.

Power budgeting is much like making sure you have enough money to pay your bills. In this case, you need enough light to cover all optical transmission losses and deliver enough light to the receiver to achieve the desired signal-to-noise ratio or bit error rate. That design should leave some extra margin above the receiver's minimum requirements to allow for system aging, fluctuations, and repairs, such as splicing a broken cable. However, it should not deliver so much power that it overloads the receiver.

One note of warning: be sure you know what power is specified where. You can lose 3 dB if the transmitter manufacturer specifies output as peak power but the receiver manufacturer specifies average power.

In simplest form, the power budget is

> The difference between transmitter output and receiver input equals the sum of system losses and margin.

$$\text{Power}_{transmitter} - \text{total loss} + \text{amplification} = \text{margin} + \text{receiver sensitivity}$$

when arithmetic is done in decibels or related units such as dBm. The simplicity of these calculations is the main reason for using decibel units.

Remember that optical amplification can offset loss in the system budget. Optical amplifiers are expensive, but that high cost is justified in some cases. You wouldn't buy a $3000 optical amplifier so you could replace a $100 laser source with a $10 LED, but you would if you could avoid spending $10,000 on an electro-optic regenerator.

All losses in the system must be considered. These include

1. Loss in transferring light from source into fiber
2. Connector loss
3. Splice loss
4. Coupler loss
5. Fiber loss
6. Fiber-to-receiver coupling loss

Some of these losses have been covered in detail earlier, but others deserve more explanation.

Light Collection

MATCHING LEDS TO FIBERS

> Significant losses can occur in coupling light sources to fibers.

Typically, little light is lost in transferring from a fiber to a receiver, but large losses can occur in transferring light from the source into the fiber. The fundamental problem is matching the source emitting area to the fiber core. This is particularly true for LEDs with large emitting areas, as shown in Figure 20.2. If the emitting area is larger than the fiber core, some emitted light is lost in the cladding and dissipated from the fiber. In addition, some light rays are emitted at angles outside the fiber's acceptance angle. The smaller the fiber core and the numerical aperture, the more severe these losses. LEDs couple light efficiently into large-core step-index fibers, but losses are much larger for LEDs when coupled to 62.5/125 multimode graded-index fibers. LED output in the 1-mW range can be reduced to about 50 μW—a 13-dB loss—by losses in getting the light into the fiber. LEDs are almost never used with single-mode fibers.

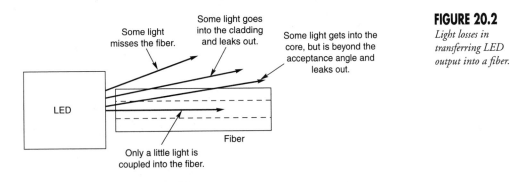

FIGURE 20.2

Light losses in transferring LED output into a fiber.

LASER SOURCES

Semiconductor lasers deliver more power into optical fibers. Their advantages are a smaller emitting area, smaller beam spread, and higher output power. The smaller beams fit better into fiber cores, particularly the tiny cores of single-mode fibers. Where a good LED might couple 50 μW into a 62.5/125-μm graded-index multimode fiber, a good edge-emitting semiconductor laser can transfer a milliwatt or more into a single-mode fiber.

If this makes lasers seem like better light sources, that's largely because they are. Semiconductor lasers can be modulated faster and deliver more power into a fiber than LEDs. However, cost counts in the real world, and LEDs are cheaper than edge-emitting lasers. They also last longer and generally do not require the cooling and stabilization needed by many edge-emitting laser transmitters.

VCSELs (vertical-cavity surface-emitting lasers) combine many of the advantages of LEDs and lasers. They are long-lived and inexpensive but generate higher power in a beam much smaller than that from an LED. VCSELs also can be modulated considerably faster than LEDs. This makes them attractive sources for systems operating at moderate distances and speeds.

Special high-power lasers, or laser sources followed by optical amplifiers, can deliver powers of around 100 mW into optical fibers. These strong light sources are used when signals must be distributed among many receivers, such as in cable television systems or

A good laser can transfer a milliwatt into a single-mode fiber.

other networks where couplers split signals among many nodes. Although these lasers or laser-amplifier combinations are considerably more expensive than individual ordinary semiconductor lasers, they are less costly than the multiple lasers that you would otherwise need to serve so many terminals.

FIBER CHOICE

Fibers with larger cores and/or numerical apertures collect more light.

The choice of fiber also affects the light-collection equation. The larger the core diameter and the numerical aperture, the more light a fiber can collect, assuming that the light source emits from a large enough area to fill the larger fiber core. You won't gain anything by switching from a 62.5/125-μm multimode graded-index fiber to a large-core step-index fiber if you have a laser source that emits from a 10-μm stripe.

You can estimate the difference in the efficiency of light collection by a pair of fibers—fiber 1 and fiber 2—using the equation

$$\Delta \text{Loss (dB)} = 20 \log_{10}\left(\frac{D_1}{D_2}\right) + 20 \log_{10}\left(\frac{NA_1}{NA_2}\right)$$

where the Ds are core diameters and the NAs are numerical apertures of the two fibers. You can use the formula as long as the emitting area is larger than the cores of both fibers and no optics are used to change the effective size of the emitting area or the effective NA of the source.

The difference can be significant with a large source. Consider, for example, the difference in how much light a step-index fiber with 100-μm core and 0.3 NA can collect compared to a graded-index fiber with 50-μm core and 0.2 NA. Substituting the numbers gives:

$$\Delta \text{Loss} = 20 \log\left(\frac{100}{50}\right) + 20 \log\left(\frac{0.3}{0.2}\right) = 9.6 \text{ dB}$$

That difference is nearly a factor of 10, well worth considering if you have run out of loss budget.

On the other hand, remember that larger core reduces transmission bandwidth as well as increasing light-collection efficiency. The sacrifices are largest in moving from single-mode to multimode graded-index fiber and from graded-index multimode to step-index multimode.

Loss in transferring light from an LED into a single-mode fiber is about 19 dB higher than into a 50/125 fiber.

SINGLE-MODE FIBERS

The preceding example was for multimode fibers. Carry it a step further to a single-mode fiber with a nominal core diameter of 10 μm and NA of 0.11, and you will immediately see a big problem. A single-mode fiber collects 19.2 dB less light from an LED than a 50/125-μm fiber.

If your first impulse is to say, "Forget it," you are in good company. However, there are ways to ease that coupling problem. Instead of just butting the fiber end against the LED or aiming LED output in the general direction of the fiber end, developers can focus the light onto the fiber end with tiny optics. Losses remain significant, but they are well below the exceedingly high levels predicted by this simple cookbook formula.

What about transferring diode laser output into fibers? The huge losses mentioned earlier go away because the light-emitting stripes of edge-emitting lasers are smaller than the cores of single-mode fibers. (VCSELs emit from larger areas, but their beams are smaller than the cores of standard graded-index fibers.) Laser light also does not spread out as fast as that from an LED. As shown in Figure 20.3, this makes light collection much simpler. In addition, lasers emit higher powers, so an edge-emitting laser can deliver a milliwatt or more into a single-mode fiber. Thus, with very rare exceptions, a laser is the only reasonable choice for use with single-mode fiber.

> Fibers collect laser output more efficiently because of the smaller emitting area and beam spread.

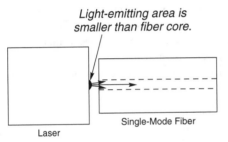

Light-emitting area is smaller than fiber core.

Single-Mode Fiber

Laser

FIGURE 20.3

Laser output couples easily into a single-mode fiber core.

Fiber Loss

Fiber loss nominally equals the attenuation (in decibels per kilometer) times the transmission distance:

$$\text{Total loss} = (\text{dB/km}) \times \text{length}$$

> Fiber loss equals attenuation times distance, sometimes plus transient losses.

However, this is only an approximation for multimode fibers. One problem is that measurements of fiber attenuation in dB/km do not consider transient losses that occur near the start of a multimode fiber. An LED with a large emitting area and high NA excites high-order modes that leak out as they travel along the fiber. Typically this transient loss is 1 to 1.5 dB, concentrated in the first few hundred meters of fiber following the transmitter. This loss becomes less significant after you go a kilometer or two, but graded-index multimode fibers are rarely used over such long distances. Thus, it's important to remember transient loss and allow for it in your system margin.

An additional problem that can occur with graded-index fiber is uneven and unpredictable coupling of modes between adjacent lengths of fiber. These concatenation effects make loss of long lengths of spliced graded-index fiber difficult to calculate; fortunately, such systems are extremely rare.

Single-mode fibers are much better behaved because they carry only one mode, avoiding differential mode attenuation.

Fiber-to-Receiver Coupling

> Losses are normally small in transferring light from fibers to receivers.

One of the rare places where the fiber-optic engineer wins is in coupling light from a fiber to a detector or receiver. The light-sensitive areas of most detectors are larger than most fiber cores, and their acceptance angles are larger than those of multimode fibers. Of course, if you're determined to screw things up, you can find a detector with a light-collecting area smaller than the core of large-core multimode fibers. But that isn't likely.

Receiver Sensitivity

> There are trade-offs among received power, speed, and bit error rate or signal-to-noise ratio.

In much of the discussion that follows, receiver sensitivity is taken as a given. That is, I assume that a receiver must have a minimum power input to work properly. Things aren't quite that simple because there are trade-offs between received power, speed, and bit error rate or signal-to-noise ratio. As data rate increases, a receiver needs more input power to operate with a specified bit error rate. If the data rate is held fixed but the input power is decreased, the error rate can increase steeply.

These trade-offs are not always useful. Error rate can increase steeply as input power decreases. At the margin of receiver sensitivity, a 1-dB drop in power can increase error rate by a factor of 1000 or more! You gain more by lowering data rate, particularly near the receiver's maximum speed. However, many system designs do not allow much flexibility in transmission speed. As I describe later in this chapter, some gains in sensitivity are possible by switching bit encoding schemes, but the simplest course may be using a more sensitive receiver or going back to reduce loss or increase power.

Remember, too, that more power is not always a good thing. Too much power can overload the detector, increasing bit-error rate.

Other Losses

> Total loss from connectors, couplers, and splices is their characteristic loss multiplied by the number in the system.

Splices, connectors, and couplers can contribute significant losses in a fiber-optic system. Fortunately, those losses are generally easy to measure and calculate. Connectors, couplers, and splices have characteristic losses that you can multiply by the number in a system to estimate total loss. However, there are two potential complications.

One is the variability of loss, particularly for connectors. A given connector may be specified as having maximum loss of 1.0 dB and typical loss of 0.5 dB. The maximum is the specified upper limit for that type of connector; no higher losses should show up in your system (unless the connector was installed improperly or is dirty). The typical value is an average, meaning that average connector loss should be 0.5 dB but that individual connectors may be higher or lower.

You can calculate total loss in two ways for a system with four connectors. The worst-case approach is to multiply the highest possible loss (1 dB) by the number of connectors to get 4 dB. On the other hand, if the average connector loss is 0.5 dB, the most likely total loss is four times that: 2.0 dB. The prudent approach for so few connectors is to take the worst-case value, but it's much more realistic to take the average loss for systems with many connectors or splices. Remember, because detector overload can cause problems, you can run into trouble by seriously overestimating loss as well as by underestimating it.

Transient losses following connectors can further complicate the picture for multimode fibers. Connectors near the transmitter may increase transient losses by effectively stripping away high-order modes, which otherwise would leak out further along the fiber. However, once light has traveled far enough to reach an equilibrium mode distribution (a kilometer or so), a connector can redistribute some light to higher-order modes, which tend to leak out of the fiber—a milder form of transient losses than experienced with light sources.

Margin

One quantity that always figures in the loss budget is system margin, a safety factor for system designers. This allows for uncertainties in calculating losses, for minor repairs, and for minor degradation of system components. Uncertainties are inevitable because component losses are specified within ranges and because components change as they age and are used. Margin also allows for repairs in case of cable damage, which typically add to cable loss.

System margin is a safety factor to allow for repairs and uncertainties.

Depending on the application, the performance requirements, the cost, and the ease of repair, the loss margin added by designers may be 3 to 10 dB.

Optical Amplifiers

Optical amplifiers can overcome losses by boosting signal strength, but practical concerns may offset this advantage. Optical amplifiers are expensive, are only available readily for the 1550-nm region, and as analog devices inevitably amplify background noise as well as signal. On the other hand, they can amplify gigabit signals and multiple wavelengths in their operating ranges. Thus they are mainly used in high-performance and WDM systems, where their high cost can be spread among many signals being amplified.

Optical amplifiers boost signal strength.

You can use optical amplifiers in several places:

- As post-amplifiers after transmitters, to generate high-power signals in fibers
- In the middle of long transmission systems, to boost signal strength for further transmission

● As preamplifiers before receivers, to raise signal strength to the proper level for the receiver

● Before 1-to-*n* couplers or WDM demultiplexers, which divide input signals among many outputs

Examples of Loss Budgeting

To see how loss budgeting works, I'll step through three simple examples. Example A, shown in Figure 20.4, is a short system transmitting 100 Mbit/s between two points in a building. Example B, shown in Figure 20.5, is a telephone system carrying 2.5 Gbit/s between two switching offices 300 km apart. Example C, shown in Figure 20.6, is an intra-building network linking 10 terminals with each other at a signal speed of 100 Mbit/s. The examples are arbitrary and are intended to show how design works rather than to illustrate actual systems. Note that in considering only the loss budget, you don't directly address whether or not the system can carry the data rate listed. We'll look at that issue later in this chapter.

EXAMPLE A

●
Connectors can contribute the dominant losses if several are in a short system.

In Figure 20.4, designers need to transmit signals through 200 m of fiber already installed in a building. That means that they must route the signal through patch panels with connectors. In the example, they have six connector pairs, three on each floor: one linking the terminal device to the cable network for that floor, and one pair on each end of a short cable in the patch panel. (Connectors also attach the fiber to transmitter and receiver, but their losses are included under LED power transfer and receiver sensitivity.) The 50/125 graded-index multimode fiber has attenuation of 2.5 dB/km at the 850–nm wavelength of the LED transmitter. The loss budget is as follows:

LED power into fiber	−16.0 dBm
Connector pairs (6 @ 0.7 dB)	−4.2 dB
Fiber loss (200 m @ 2.5 dB/km)	−0.5 dB
System margin	−10.0 dB
Required receiver sensitivity	−30.7 dBm

The calculation shows that the dominant loss is from the connectors. The fiber loss may underestimate transient loss, but the large system margin leaves plenty of room.

The calculated receiver sensitivity is a reasonable level, and system margin could be improved by picking a more sensitive receiver. This calculation started with a given loss, system margin, and input power, but you could start by specifying receiver sensitivity, system margin, and loss, to calculate the needed input power. Note that the LED transmitter provides a low input power, but that is adequate for this short system.

FIGURE 20.4
Example A.

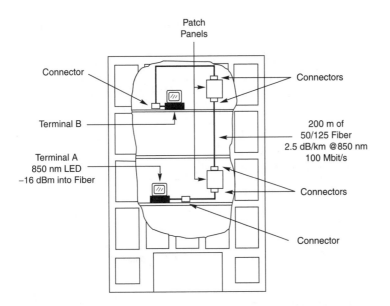

EXAMPLE B

Loss sources in the telephone system shown in Figure 20.5 are quite different. The system spans 300 km, with one splice every 10 km in single-mode fiber with loss of 0.25 dB/km at 1550 nm. It links two rural areas, carrying a single wavelength at 2.5 Gbit/s. The high speed and long distance demand a laser source and a more sensitive receiver. Signals go through two connector pairs in patch panels at each end. Although the fiber loss is very low at 1550 nm, the long distance makes fiber attenuation the dominant loss. The sample calculation shows the laser transmitter alone does not deliver enough power to span that distance:

Fiber attenuation dominates loss in a 300-km fiber system.

Laser power into single-mode fiber	0.0 dBm
Fiber loss (300 km × 0.25 dB/km)	−75.0 dB
Splice loss (29 × 0.1 dB)	−2.9 dB
Connector pairs (4 × 0.8 dB)	−3.2 dB
Power at receiver	−81.1 dBm
Receiver sensitivity	−32.0 dBm
System power deficit	−49.1 dB

The output power falls far short of system requirements. You need to insert optical amplifiers. Suppose you add a pair of optical amplifiers with 30-dB gain, one at the 100-km point and the second at 200 km. This requires four extra connector pairs (one on each end of each optical amplifier), which replace two splices. The loss budget then becomes:

Laser power into single-mode fiber	0.0 dBm
Fiber loss (300 km × 0.25 dB/km)	−75.0 dB
Optical amplifier gain	60.0 dB
Splice loss (27 × 0.1 dB)	−2.7 dB
Connector pairs (8 × 0.8 dB)	−6.4 dB
Power at receiver	−24.1 dBm
Receiver sensitivity	−32.0 dBm
System power margin	7.9 dB

FIGURE 20.5

Example B.

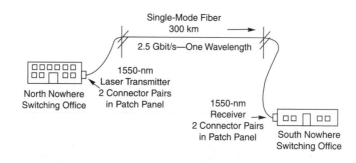

That looks much better. To verify that the loss budget works for the whole system, you should check the budget for each segment.

Segment 1:

Laser power into single-mode fiber	0.0 dBm
Fiber loss (100 km × 0.25 dB/km)	−25.0 dB
Splice loss (9 × 0.1 dB)	−0.9 dB
Connector pairs (3 × 0.8 dB)	−2.4 dB
Power at optical amplifier	−28.3 dBm
Gain of optical amplifier	30.0 dB
Output of segment 1	1.7 dBm

Segment 2:

Optical amplifier into single-mode fiber	1.7 dBm
Fiber loss (100 km × 0.25 dB/km)	−25.0 dB
Splice loss (9 × 0.1 dB)	−0.9 dB
Connector pairs (2 × 0.8 dB)	−1.6 dB
Power at optical amplifier 2	−25.8 dBm
Gain of optical amplifier	30.0 dB
Output of segment 2	4.2 dBm

Segment 3:

Laser power into single-mode fiber	4.2 dBm
Fiber loss (100 km × 0.25 dB/km)	−25.0 dB
Splice loss (9 × 0.1 dB)	−0.9 dB
Connector pairs (3 × 0.8 dB)	−2.4 dB
Power at receiver	−24.1 dBm
Receiver sensitivity	−32.0 dBm
System power margin	7.9 dB

For our purposes, 7.9 dB seems an adequate power margin. In practice, the system margin probably will be better, because I have assumed a relatively high connector loss of 0.8 dB.

Segment-by-segment calculations both check your result and make sure that placement of optical amplifiers doesn't get you into trouble. In practice, optical amplifiers saturate at high powers, so you may get only 25 dB of gain with 20 dBm input. In this example, suppose you put the second optical amplifier at the 170-km point because you happen to have a storage building at that point. Then the calculations for segments 2 and 3 are as follows.

Segment 2:

Optical amplifier into single-mode fiber	1.7 dBm
Fiber loss (70 km × 0.25 dB/km)	−17.5 dB
Splice loss (6 × 0.1 dB)	−0.6 dB
Connector pairs (2 × 0.8 dB)	−1.6 dB
Power at optical amplifier 2	−18.0 dBm
Reduced gain of optical amplifier	25.0 dB
Output of segment 2	7.0 dBm

Segment 3:

Laser power into single-mode fiber	7.0 dBm
Fiber loss (130 km × 0.25 dB/km)	−32.5 dB
Splice loss (12 × 0.1 dB)	−1.2 dB
Connector pairs (3 × 0.8 dB)	−2.4 dB
Power at receiver	−29.1 dBm
Receiver sensitivity	−32.0 dBm
System power margin	2.9 dB

Although the receiver power is above the required level, a system margin of 2.9 dB is inadequate for contingencies. This is a reminder that you can't simply add up the losses and gains of all components without considering the input conditions to components such as optical amplifiers.

EXAMPLE C

Coupling losses
are largest
in a network
distributing signals
to many terminals.

Complications also arise when you have to divide input signals among many outputs, as shown in Figure 20.6. In this case, you need to connect 10 terminals so the output of each one is divided among the receivers of all 10 terminals. You can do this with a 10×10 directional star coupler, which divides an input signal from any of the 10 incoming fibers (one from the transmitter end of each terminal) among the 10 output fibers going to the receiver end of each terminal. Assume the coupler divides the signals equally and has excess loss of 3 dB. Because the data rate is a modest 100 Mbit/s, let's calculate the loss budget with an LED source.

FIGURE 20.6

*Example C
10-terminal network.*

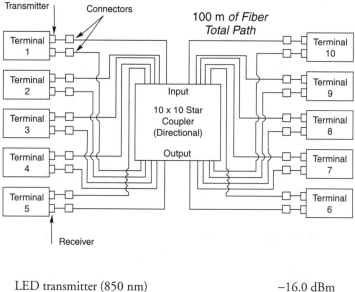

LED transmitter (850 nm)	−16.0 dBm
Fiber loss (100 m @ 2.5 dB/km)	−0.25 dB
Connector pair loss (2 @ 0.5 dB)	−1.0 dB
Coupler loss (includes its own connections)	−13.0 dB
Power at receiver	−30.25 dBm
Receiver sensitivity	−30.0 dBm
System power deficit	−0.25 dB

The calculations show that the coupler loss dominates the loss budget and that I'm in deep trouble. The system margin is negative, a power deficit. It's only −0.25 dB, but it's enough that the receiver may not work well under the best of circumstances. Performance will degrade even further if anything reduces receiver power.

A single component, the coupler, dominates the loss budget, but it is not easy to eliminate because it is needed to distribute the signal to all terminals. One way to overcome the power deficit is by replacing the LED with a more powerful laser source. In this case, the power budget becomes

Laser transmitter (850 nm)	0.0 dBm
Fiber loss (100 m @ 2.5 dB/km)	−0.25 dB
Connector pair loss (2 @ 0.5 dB)	−1.0 dB
Coupler loss (includes its own connections)	−13.0 dB
Power at receiver	−14.25 dBm
Receiver sensitivity	−30.0 dBm
System power margin	15.75 dB

This may be too much of a good thing, depending on the power level that overloads the receiver. If the receiver overloads at −15 dBm, you can add a 3-dB attenuator to bring the receiver power down to −17.25 dBm, well within the operating range of −15 to −30 dBm.

Transmission-Capacity Budget

The transmission capacity of a fiber-optic system is its analog bandwidth or the highest digital bit rate it can carry. Calculating a budget for transmission capacity is both simpler and more complex than calculating a loss budget. The simplicity comes from being able to ignore such components as couplers, connectors, and splices. The complexity comes from the various factors that limit transmission capacity in different ways.

If a system carries only one wavelength, its transmission capacity is limited by how fast the system responds to changes in input signals. The major time limitations are the rise and fall times of the transmitter and receiver and the dispersion of the fiber, which also depends on the light source. If the system carries multiple wavelengths, the ultimate limitations come from the number of wavelengths it can carry as well as from the speed of individual wavelength channels. I will concentrate on time limitations, which are better defined and important in more cases.

In my earlier description of system loss budgets, I did not need to define whether systems transmitted analog or digital signals. Both experience the same attenuation, although receiver sensitivities may differ. Transmission capacity is different, because if you are trying to calculate precise results, you need to know if the system carries analog or digital signals and even what digital coding is used. To simplify things here, I will concentrate on basic principles and assume digital NRZ coding as standard. The details may differ slightly for other systems, but the principles are the same.

Bandwidth or bit-rate budgets are more complex than loss budgets but depend only on source, fiber, and receiver characteristics.

To simplify calculations of system capacity, I will assume you can calculate everything you need to know from the time response to input signals, without directly considering frequency response. That is reasonable because there is a characteristic time, t, per bit at any transmission rate, R:

$$t = \frac{1}{R}$$

where R is the speed in bits per second. At 1000 Mbit/s, the bit time is 1 ns. Roughly the same relationship holds for analog signals, where there is a characteristic time that is the inverse of the frequency, ν:

$$t = \frac{1}{\nu}$$

Thus a 1-ns response time also corresponds to a 1-GHz analog bandwidth. These simplifications do not give exact results, but they are useful approximations.

Overall Time Response

For a signal to be received correctly, the overall time response must be less than the bit time. Time response in this case means the longer of rise or fall time of the signal emerging from the system. If the time response is too long, successive pulses start overlapping and the system starts performing poorly. (The same principle applies to analog transmission.) Thus, a system that transmits 1 Mbit/s must have a time response faster than 1 μs (one-millionth of a second).

The choice of time response simplifies calculations. The overall time response of a system is the square root of the sum of the squares of the response times of individual components:

$$\Delta t = \sqrt{\Sigma(\Delta t_i^2)}$$

where Δt is the overall time response and Δt_i is the time response for each component.

Connectors, splices, and couplers do not affect the time response significantly, and in practice optical amplifiers do not significantly limit response times in current commercial systems. The important response times are those of the transmitter, fiber, and receiver:

$$\Delta t = \sqrt{\Delta t^2_{transmitter} + \Delta t^2_{receiver} + \Delta t^2_{fiber}}$$

That is, the response time is the square root of the sum of the squares of the response times of the transmitter, receiver, and fiber.

Fiber Dispersion

Rise and fall times of transmitters and detectors are given on data sheets, ready to plug into the formula. Fiber response times must be calculated from the values of dispersion and transmitter spectral width. As you learned earlier, there are four types of dispersion:

The overall time response of a system is the square root of the sum of the squares of response times of transmitter, receiver, and fiber.

Fiber response time is determined by dispersion effects.

modal dispersion, material dispersion, waveguide dispersion, and polarization mode dispersion. The types that are important depend on the types of fibers. In multimode fibers, modal dispersion and material dispersion are important. In single-mode fibers, it is chromatic dispersion (the sum of material dispersion and waveguide dispersion), plus polarization mode dispersion if the others are low.

You calculate dispersion using a sum-of-squares formula similar to that for overall time response. However, dispersion is more complicated because other factors enter the equation. Modal dispersion is the characteristic value for a fiber (specified in ns/km) times the length of the fiber. Chromatic dispersion is the characteristic value for a fiber (specified in ns/km·nm) times the length of the fiber and spectral width of the light source. Polarization-mode dispersion is specified in units of ps/$\sqrt{km}$ and is harder to define.

Total dispersion is

$$\Delta t = \sqrt{\Delta t^2_{modal} + \Delta t^2_{chromatic} + \Delta t^2_{polarization}}$$

For multimode fiber, you can simplify this to

$$\Delta t = \sqrt{\Delta t^2_{modal} + \Delta t^2_{chromatic}}$$

For a single-mode fiber, you can simplify the equation to

$$\Delta t = \sqrt{\Delta t^2_{chromatic} + \Delta t^2_{polarization}}$$

In practice, you don't need to consider polarization-mode dispersion until data rates exceed 2.5 Gbit/s.

Each type of fiber has its own characteristic dispersion, D, which must be multiplied by the proper units of fiber length L and/or spectral width of the source $\Delta\lambda$. Substituting these numbers into the formula for multimode fiber gives:

$$\Delta t_{multimode} = \sqrt{(D_{modal} \times L)^2 + (D_{chromatic} \times L \times \Delta\lambda)^2}$$

For single-mode fiber, you can ignore modal dispersion. If you substitute the proper values into the formula, this leaves

$$\Delta t_{single\ mode} = \sqrt{(D_{chromatic} \times L \times \Delta\lambda)^2 + (D_{polarization} \times \sqrt{L})^2}$$

A couple of examples will show how dispersion calculations work.

MULTIMODE DISPERSION EXAMPLE

In Example A, considered earlier in this chapter, an 850-nm LED sends 100 Mbit/s through 200 m of 50/125-μm fiber. Modal bandwidth of a typical commercial 50/125-μm fiber is 400 MHz, which is equivalent to a modal dispersion of 2.5 ns/km. For a 200-m length, that corresponds to modal dispersion of 0.5 ns.

To that, you need to add the chromatic dispersion, calculated from the formula

$$\Delta t_{chromatic} = D_{chromatic} \times L \times \Delta\lambda$$

A typical value of chromatic dispersion is 100 ps/nm·km at 850 nm, which combined with a linewidth of 50 nm for a typical 850-nm LED, gives a chromatic dispersion of 1.0 ns for a 200-m length of fiber. This means that the chromatic dispersion is actually higher than modal dispersion because of the large LED spectral linewidth.

Adding modal and chromatic dispersion together according to the sum-of-squares formula indicates total dispersion is 1.1 ns. That leaves plenty of room for transmitting 100 Mbit/s, assuming the transmitter and receiver are fast enough.

If you wanted to transmit 1 Gbit/s, you could try using a laser source with a 1-nm linewidth. In that case, total dispersion is

$$\Delta t = \sqrt{(0.5 \text{ ns})^2_{\text{modal}} + (100 \text{ ps/nm·km} \times 0.2 \text{ km} \times 1 \text{ nm})^2} = \sqrt{0.25 + 0.0004} = 0.50 \text{ ns}$$

This is essentially equal to the modal dispersion of 0.5 ns and is adequate for gigabit transmission over 200 m.

SINGLE-MODE TRANSMISSION EXAMPLE

In Example B, we considered transmitting a 2.5-Gbit/s signal a total of 300 km through single-mode fiber at 1550 nm. For a typical dispersion-shifted fiber, chromatic dispersion is specified at below 3 ps/nm·km in this region. Let's consider two cases: a Fabry-Perot laser with linewidth of 1 nm and a distributed-feedback laser with linewidth of 0.001 nm. For a first approximation, ignore polarization-mode dispersion.

For the 1-nm laser, chromatic dispersion is

$$\Delta t_{\text{chromatic}} = 3 \text{ ps/nm·km} \times 300 \text{ km} \times 1 \text{ nm} = 900 \text{ ps}$$

This value is much too high for a 2.5-Gbit/s system, where the time per bit is 400 ps.

With the distributed-feedback laser, chromatic dispersion is

$$\Delta t_{\text{chromatic}} = 3 \text{ ps/nm·km} \times 300 \text{ km} \times 0.001 \text{ nm} = 0.9 \text{ ps}$$

That value leaves plenty of margin for operation at 1550 nm in dispersion-shifted fiber. In fact, you could get away with using step-index single-mode fiber with zero dispersion at 1310 nm, which has dispersion around 20 ps/nm·km at 1550 nm.

$$\Delta t_{\text{chromatic}} = 20 \text{ ps/nm·km} \times 300 \text{ km} \times 0.001 \text{ nm} = 6 \text{ ps}$$

This value still leaves plenty of room. However, we haven't considered polarization-mode dispersion. A typical value is no more than 0.5 ps/$\sqrt{\text{km}}$. Thus for 300 km of single-mode fiber, polarization dispersion is

$$\Delta t_{\text{polarization}} = 0.5 \text{ ps/}\sqrt{\text{km}} \times \sqrt{300 \text{ km}} = 8.7 \text{ ps}$$

This value is larger than the chromatic dispersion for a distributed-feedback laser, but combining the two gives total dispersion of 10.7 ps, no problem at a data rate of 2.5 Gbit/s.

Dispersion Compensation

As speeds increase and more wavelength channels are added, dispersion compensation becomes an important issue. As you learned earlier, one approach is to add extra lengths of compensating fiber, with dispersion that offsets that of the transmission fiber. An alternative is adding fiber gratings with grating spacing that varies along their length, so different wavelengths are delayed by different intervals when they travel along the fiber. The major application now envisioned for dispersion compensation is to increase the capacity of existing cables installed with step-index single-mode fibers, which have zero dispersion near 1310 nm and relatively high chromatic dispersion at 1550 nm.

Design rules are not yet established, but the basic goal is to produce net dispersion close to zero by delaying the wavelengths that travel the fastest in conventional fibers. Figure 20.7 shows the basic idea when using dispersion-compensating fiber. In this example, the dispersion of the compensating fiber is five times that of the step-index single-mode fiber being compensated. The net dispersion of a system segment that includes 5 km of step-index single-mode fiber and 1 km of dispersion-compensating fiber is zero at 1530 nm but not zero at shorter and longer wavelengths. (If the system were to be used for dense wavelength-division multiplexing, you would want the zero-dispersion wavelength to be longer than the transmission wavelengths, 1580 at 1600 nm.)

> ●
> Dispersion compensation is important for long systems at high speeds or with WDM.

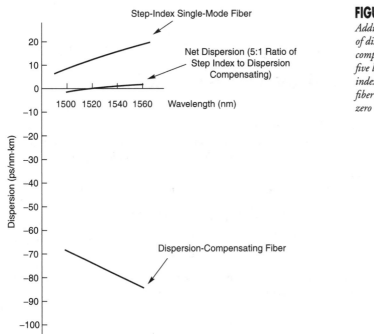

FIGURE 20.7

Adding one length of dispersion-compensating fiber to five lengths of step-index single-mode fiber produces near-zero net dispersion.

Note that the net dispersion is not equal to zero at all wavelengths, because you can't readily make dispersion-compensating fiber that exactly cancels out the dispersion of other fibers. A slight difference in slope leads to a difference in net dispersion at longer and shorter wavelengths. Although these numbers are not zero, they are small and are no problem over short distances. However, the matches cannot be made exact, so the differences accumulate over long distances, as shown in Figure 20.8. The steep slopes show the regions where dispersion-compensating fiber is used; the more gradual slopes show conventional step-index single-mode fiber. The further you go along the system, the larger the differential delay and dispersion among the three wavelengths.

FIGURE 20.8

Dispersion in system with short lengths of dispersion-compensating fiber. Note the dispersion at each wavelength gradually diverges with increasing distance, because compensation is not perfect at all wavelengths.

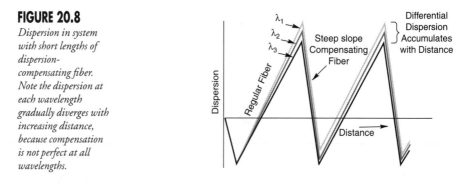

Fiber grating compensation works in a similar way, but the gratings needed to compensate for dispersion are much shorter than the special dispersion-compensating fiber.

Transmitter and Receiver Response Time

So far, I have largely neglected the response times of transmitters and receivers. You learned about them earlier in Chapters 10 and 11. Recall that external modulation is faster than direct modulation of semiconductor lasers and avoids wavelength chirp, which can be a significant limitation at high speeds. Suppose, for example, that direct modulation generates a modest-seeming wavelength chirp of 0.07 nm. If you're considering the 300-km telephone system of Example B, this means chromatic dispersion is

$$\Delta t_{\text{chromatic}} = 20 \text{ ps/nm·km} \times 300 \text{ km} \times 0.07 \text{ nm} = 420 \text{ ps}$$

That stretches pulses out slightly longer than the 400-ps pulse time of 2.5-Gbit/s signals and would effectively block transmission at 2.5 Gbit/s.

The response times of inexpensive sources and detectors can pose significant limits on some lower-speed systems. Suppose you pick an LED source with 7-ns response and an inex-

Wavelength chirp of directly modulated laser transmitters can limit transmission capacity at high speeds.

pensive silicon detector with 10-ns response. If you substitute the numbers into the sum-of-squares law, you get a total time response of 12 ns, too slow to handle 100-Mbit/s signals even before you worry about the fiber response, which we calculated earlier at 0.5 ns. To get adequate speed to handle 100-Mbit/s signals, you need source and detector response times of at most 5 ns, which gives total response time of

$$\Delta t = \sqrt{(5)^2 + (5)^2 + (0.5)^2} = 7 \text{ ns}$$

Wavelength-Division Multiplexing Design

The extent of wavelength-division multiplexing possible depends on the spectral range of any optical amplifiers used, the spectral width and dispersion of sources, the data rate per channel, and how precisely wavelength-selective couplers can select wavelengths during demultiplexing. Factors such as four-wave mixing, uniformity of amplifier gain, and non-linear effects also influence WDM design.

You learned earlier that the International Telecommunicaions Union established a WDM grid that starts at a frequency of 193.1 THz and increases in 100-GHz steps. As often happens, technology has moved faster than the standard-setting process, so some companies are already offering systems with wavelength channels spaced 50 GHz apart. Others are essentially ignoring the standard.

The most important factor to consider in WDM is how many wavelength channels are available. You can calculate this by dividing channel spacing into the spectral bandwidth of the whole communication system—in particular, the range of wavelengths amplified reasonably uniformly in the 1550-nm region. Assume that the usable range of wavelengths is λ_1 to λ_2 and the channel spacing is given in wavelength units as $\Delta\lambda$. Then the number of possible channels, N, is

$$N = 1 + \frac{\lambda_1 - \lambda_2}{\Delta\lambda}$$

Thus if the usable wavelength range is 1540 to 1560 nm and the channel spacing is 1.6 nm, you can fit 12.5 wavelength channel slots between them or allocate a total of 13 wavelength channels. You can use the same principle with frequency units:

$$N = 1 + \frac{\nu_1 - \nu_2}{\Delta\nu}$$

Remember, however, you have to convert between the two. If you're given channel spacing in frequency and the spectral width in wavelength, you should convert the end wavelengths to frequencies (using *exact* values for wavelength and the speed of light).

The number of WDM channels possible depends on channel spacing, amplfier spectral range, source spectral width, data rate per optical channel, fiber dispersion, and demultiplexer range.

If you're given a base wavelength (or frequency) and the number of channels, you can calculate the final step. For example, if you have a system that starts at 193.1 THz and has 12 channels separated by 100 GHz, the highest frequency is

$$\nu_{high} = \nu_1 + ((N-1) \times \Delta\nu) = 193.1 + (11 \times 0.1)\text{ THz} = 194.2\text{ THz}$$

(Remember that you have $N-1$ channel spacings between N channels.)

Upgrading Existing Cables

Installing new cables is expensive, so it is common to upgrade transmission capacity of existing systems containing single-mode fiber by adding new transmitters, receivers, and optical amplifiers. (You have few options with multimode fiber, but little of it was installed over distances of more than a kilometer or two.) You can enhance transmission capacity either by increasing the data rate on a single channel in a TDM system or by adding multiple wavelengths for WDM. The options depend on the type of single-mode fiber installed.

The bulk of the long-distance transmission system is step-index single-mode fiber, with zero dispersion at 1300 nm. Much of it still operates at 1300 nm, using electro-optic repeaters installed in the 1980s, but this equipment is being replaced to increase capacity. Step-index single-mode fiber can transmit 1550-nm signals at 2.5 Gbit/s with narrow-line laser transmitters, but at 10 Gbit/s dispersion becomes significant, and you need to add dispersion compensation if the transmission distance is over about 40 km. (The exact distance depends on the transmitter and fiber.) However, the same fiber can handle multiple WDM channels at 2.5 Gbit/s without dispersion compensation. This makes WDM the better choice for increasing capacity.

Some long-distance systems use dispersion-shifted fiber, with zero dispersion at 1550 nm. Single-wavelength transmission at 1550 nm does not require dispersion compensation in this fiber, even at TDM rates of 10 Gbit/s. However, four-wave mixing can make WDM difficult in dispersion-shifted fiber, making TDM the better choice.

Recently developed nonzero dispersion-shifted fiber avoids four-wave mixing problems by shifting the zero-dispersion wavelength beyond the region normally used in WDM systems, but because these fibers are new, you won't find them in existing systems being upgraded.

●
Cost is vital in real-world system design. It is up to the user to make cost-performance trade-offs for specific applications.

Cost/Performance Trade-offs

So far, I have only mentioned in passing one of the most important considerations in real-world system design—cost. Minimizing cost is an implicit goal in all system design; a few guidelines for doing so follow. However, no book can give hard-and-fast rules for the tough job of making trade-offs between cost and performance. Ultimately, it is your judgment as a system user or designer whether pushing bit error rate from 10^{-9} to 10^{-12} is worth an extra $1000. What I can do is give you some ideas to apply in working situations.

Choice of Fiber Type

The choice of fiber type will have a tremendous impact on the cost and performance of your system. The fundamental choice is between single- and multimode fiber, but on a more detailed level you need to consider the various types of each available. You've already learned about the types of fibers; let's look briefly at the deciding factors.

Choice of fiber type is crucial.

You need single-mode fiber if you're going more than a couple of kilometers. It is possible to go further if you're transmitting at low speeds, but you have to be sure you won't *ever* want to transmit a higher speed. The premium grade, preferred for new dense-WDM systems, is nonzero-dispersion-shifted fiber, with zero dispersion shifted to wavelengths longer than the standard erbium-doped fiber amplifier range—1580 nm or longer. Dispersion-shifted fiber with zero dispersion around 1550 nm is vulnerable to four-wave mixing in WDM systems. Step-index single-mode fiber requires dispersion compensation and/or expensive narrow-line lasers (typically externally modulated distributed feedback types), unless you're going to operate at 1300 nm.

You need multimode fiber if you are spanning only short distances. The shorter the distance, the more choices. Graded-index fibers typically are better for 100 m and up; 50/125-μm fibers have somewhat more bandwidth than 62.5/125-μm fibers, but the smaller cores may mean higher connector losses. Larger-core step-index fibers have limited range because of their high dispersion, but they collect light very well. Plastic fibers are easier to terminate than glass fibers, but their optical performance has been poorer. Consider plastic fibers when links are short and termination is likely to be important. Keep your eyes open for graded-index plastic fibers, which will improve bandwidth.

Other Guidelines

In earlier chapters, I examined some trade-offs that can affect cost and performance but skimmed over others. Examples include the relative costs of components—generally cheaper at shorter wavelengths—and the low marginal cost of adding extra fibers to multifiber cables. Many of these balances shift with the pricing of commercial equipment and go beyond the scope of this introduction to the field. Here are some other rough-and-ready (but not necessarily complete) guidelines.

I'll start with a few commonsense rules:

- Your time is valuable. If you spend an entire day trying to save $5 on hardware, the result will be a net loss.
- Installation, assembly, operation, and support are not free. For a surprising number of fiber-optic systems, installation and maintenance cost more than the hardware. You may save money in the long term by paying extra for hardware that is easier to install and service.

Don't forget to apply common sense in system design. Labor is never free.

- It can cost less to pay an expert to do it than to learn how yourself. Unless you need to practice installing connectors, it's much easier to buy connectorized cables or hire a fiber-optic contractor for your first fiber-optic system.
- You can save money by using standard mass-produced components rather than designing special-purpose components optimized for a particular application.

You should also learn some basic cost trade-offs that people often face in designing fiber-optic systems.

- The performance of low-loss fiber, high-sensitivity detectors, and powerful transmitters must be balanced against price advantages of lower-performance devices.
- Low-loss, high-bandwidth fibers generally accept less light than higher-loss, lower-bandwidth fibers. Over short distances, you can save money and overall attenuation by using a higher-loss, more costly cable that collects light more efficiently from lower-cost LEDs. (Because of the economics of production and material requirements, large-core multimode fibers are considerably more expensive than single-mode fibers.)
- The marginal costs of adding extra fibers to a cable are modest and much cheaper than installing a second parallel cable. However, if reliability is important, the extra cost of a second cable on a different route may be a worthwhile insurance premium.
- LEDs are much cheaper and require less environmental protection than lasers, but they produce much less power and are harder to couple to small-core fibers. Their broad range of wavelengths and their limited modulation speed limit system bandwidth.
- Fiber attenuation contributes less to losses of short systems than losses in transferring light into and between fibers.
- Topology of multiterminal networks can have a large impact on system requirements and cost because of their differences in component requirements. Coupler losses may severely restrict options in some designs.
- Light sources and detectors for 1300 and 1550 nm cost more than those for the 650- or 800–900-nm windows, although fiber and cable for the longer wavelength may be less expensive.
- 1550-nm light sources cost more than 1300-nm sources. To provide reasonable bandwidth, they must have extremely low bandwidth or be used with dispersion-shifted fiber.
- Fiber and cable become a larger fraction of total cost—and have more impact on performance—the longer the system.

- Balance the advantages of eliminating extra components with the higher costs of the components needed to eliminate them. For example, it's hard to justify two-way transmission through a single fiber over short distances unless wavelength-division-multiplexing couplers are cheap, large installation savings are possible, or system requirements permit only a single fiber.

- Optical amplifiers or high-power laser transmitters make sense in systems distributing signals to many terminals.

- Narrow-line distributed-feedback lasers are much more expensive than lasers with broader spectral linewidth.

- Generally, it makes sense to upgrade transmitters and receivers to work with step-index single-mode fiber already installed rather than to buy and install new cable.

- Compare costs of high-speed TDM on single channels or lower-speed TDM at multiple wavelengths.

- *Dark fibers*—extra fibers installed in the original cable that were never hooked up to light sources—are sometimes available in existing cables.

- Always think of future upgrade possibilities. To paraphrase one of Parkinson's laws, Communications requirements expand to fill the available bandwidth. If a small extra investment now can allow expansion to much greater capacity in the future, it's generally worthwhile unless cost constraints are severe or the route lifetime is limited. (You don't want to spend extra money on a building that will be torn down in 2 years.)

- Leave room to expand capacity by adding WDM.

- Installing extra dark fibers in a cable is usually worthwhile if feasible, because it allows more room for expansion.

- Leave margin for repair and expansion. It costs much less to design margin into the system than to add it afterwards.

- Remember to account for the costs of nonfiber hardware, such as splice enclosures and patch panels, and any extra losses they involve and to allow room for installing them.

- Remember that human actions—not defective equipment—cause most fiber-optic failures. Consider ring topologies that can survive a single break. Take the extra time and spend the extra money to make important systems less vulnerable to damage. This means labeling and documenting the system carefully, as well as not leaving cables where people can trip over them or contractors can damage them.

As you grow more familiar with fiber optics, you will develop some of your own guidelines based on your own experience.

What Have You Learned?

1. Design of fiber-optic systems requires balancing sometimes-conflicting performance goals as well as costs.

2. The system loss budget is calculated by subtracting all system losses from the transmitter output power plus the gain of any optical amplifiers. The resulting output power should equal the input power required by the receiver plus system margin.

3. Significant losses can occur in coupling light from sources into fibers. You need multimode fibers to collect light from LED sources and single-mode fibers to collect light from edge-emitting laser sources. Large-core fibers are more efficient for large-area LEDs.

4. Total fiber loss equals attenuation (dB/km) multiplied by transmission distance. Multimode fibers may suffer transient losses in the first 100 to 200 m.

5. Total loss from connectors, couplers, and splices is their characteristic loss multiplied by the number of each in the system. You calculate the most likely loss using average loss and the worst case using maximum specified loss.

6. System margin is a safety factor that allows for repairs and aging of components. Typical values are 5 to 10 dB.

7. Optical amplifiers boost signal strength, but because of their high cost they are best used in long, high-speed systems or systems that distribute signals from one source to many receivers.

8. Transmission capacity budgets calculate bandwidth or bit rate; they depend only on source, fiber, and receiver characteristics. You can estimate capacity by calculating response time.

9. Response time of a system is the square root of the sum of the squares of component response times. Calculations must include transmitter and receiver response times as well as fiber dispersion.

10. Modal dispersion and chromatic dispersion combine to limit capacity of multimode fibers. Because of these capacity limits, multimode fibers are rarely used over more than a couple of kilometers.

11. Chromatic dispersion and polarization-mode dispersion limit capacity of single-mode fibers, which usually transmit over a kilometer or more. Chromatic dispersion depends on source spectral width as well as fiber dispersion.

12. Dispersion compensation is important for high-speed, long-distance systems, especially with WDM, if they use standard step-index single-mode fibers, which have high dispersion at 1550 nm.

13. The number of WDM channels possible depends on channel spacing, amplifier spectral range, source spectral width, data rate per optical channel, fiber dispersion, and demultiplexer resolution.

14. Users must evaluate cost-performance trade-offs for system applications.

15. Installation can cost much more than hardware. With demand for transmission capacity rising, you must consider possible upgrade paths.

What's Next?

In Chapter 21, I will look at the fiber-optic backbone of the global telecommunications network, cables that span oceans and continents.

Quiz for Chapter 20

1. A large-area LED transfers 10 μW (10 dBμ) into an optical fiber with core diameter of 100 μm and numerical aperture of 0.30. What power should it couple into a fiber with 50 μm core and NA of 0.2?

   a. 10 dBμ.

   b. 9.5 dBμ.

   c. 3 dBμ.

   d. 1.0 dBμ.

   e. 0.4 dBμ.

2. A connector is specified as having loss of 0.6 dB ± 0.2 dB. What is the maximum connector loss in a system containing five such connector pairs?

   a. 0.6 dB.

   b. 3.0 dB.

   c. 4.0 dB.

   d. 5.0 dB.

   e. None of the above.

3. A 10-Mbit/s signal must be sent through a 100-m length of fiber with eight connector pairs to a receiver with sensitivity of −30 dBm. The fiber loss is 4 dB/km, and the average

connector loss is 1.0 dB. If system margin is 5 dB, what is the minimum power that the light source must couple into the fiber?

   a. −13.0 dBm.

   b. −13.4 dBm.

   c. −16.0 dBm.

   d. −16.6 dBm.

   e. −20.0 dBm.

4. A system is designed to transmit 565 Mbit/s through 50 km of cable with attenuation of 0.4 dB/km. The system contains two connector pairs with 1.5 dB loss, a laser source that couples 0 dBm into the fiber, and a receiver with sensitivity of −34 dBm. How many splices with average loss of 0.15 dB can the system contain if the system margin must be at least 8 dB?

   a. None.

   b. 10.

   c. 20.

   d. 30.

   e. 40.

   f. None of the above.

5. A 2.5-Gbit/s system must span a distance of 2000 km, with optical amplifiers every 80 km. If the fiber loss is 0.3 dB/km at 1550 nm and there is one 0.1 dB splice every 16 km, what must the amplifier gain be if the system is not to gain or lose signal strength across its entire length?

   a. 20 dB.

   b. 24.4 dB.

   c. 26.4 dB.

   d. 30 dB.

   e. 34.4 dB.

6. You need to transmit identical 1-Gbit/s signals to 200 homes using a 1310-nm laser source. The homes are 1 to 4 km from your transmitter and use receivers sensitive to 30 dBm. What transmitter power do you need to achieve a 5-dB system margin if your fiber has a 0.4-dB/km loss at 1310 nm, each signal path from transmitter to home includes 6 connectors with a 0.5-dB average loss, and you split the signal in a 1 × 200 tree coupler with no excess loss?

   a. 4.6 dBm.

   b. 9.6 dBm.

   c. 2.6 dBm.

   d. 0.0 dBm.

   e. −0.4 dBm.

7. What is the duration of a single-bit interval in a 1.7-Gbit/s signal?

   a. 1.7 ns.

   b. 1 ns.

   c. 0.588 ns.

   d. 0.294 ns.

   e. 0.170 ns.

8. What is the response time of a system with transmitter response of 2 ns, receiver response of 1 ns, and 100 m of multimode fiber with dispersion of 20 ns/km (including both modal and chromatic dispersion)?

   a. 2 ns.

   b. 2.236 ns.

   c. 2.646 ns.

   d. 2.828 ns.

   e. 3 ns.

9. What is the total dispersion of 10 km of graded-index fiber with modal dispersion of 2.5 ns/km and chromatic dispersion of 100 ps/nm·km when it is used with an 850-nm LED having a 50-nm spectral width?

   a. 5 ns.

   b. 25 ns.

   c. 50 ns.

   d. 55.9 ns.

   e. 75 ns.

10. What is the total dispersion of 10 km of single-mode fiber with chromatic dispersion of 17 ps/nm·km and polarization-mode dispersion of 0.5 ps/$\sqrt{\text{km}}$ at 1550 nm when used with a laser source with spectral width of 1 nm?

   a. 1.58 ps.

   b. 10 ps.

   c. 17 ps.

   d. 170 ps.

   e. 172 ps.

11. You need to provide dispersion compensation for a 100-km system using step-index single-mode fiber with chromatic dispersion of 17 ps/nm·km at 1550 nm. You can buy dispersion-compensating fiber with chromatic dispersion of −85 ps/nm·km and have places to install it every 12.5 km along your system. To completely compensate for dispersion at 1550 nm, how much dispersion-compensating fiber do you need to install at each point?

    a. 2 km.

    b. 2.5 km.

    c. 10 km.

    d. 12.5 km.

    e. 12.5 m.

12. Your system uses optical amplifiers with a usable bandwidth of 30 nm in the 1550-nm region. How many WDM channels can the system handle if they are spaced 0.8 nm apart?

    a. 30.

    b. 37.

    c. 37.5

    d. 38.

    e. 75.

Global Telecommunications Applications

About This Chapter

Now that you have learned about fiber-optic hardware, it's time to look at its major system applications. New technology and changes in regulations are breaking down traditional barriers, but fiber communications can still be loosely divided into several major realms: the global telecommunications network, national and regional networks, local telecommunications, video and cable television, and data networks of various scales. In this chapter, I will describe the global fiber-optic transmission systems that carry data, voice, video, and other signals around the world. They provide the backbone of the global telecommunications network, including ocean-spanning submarine cables and the global portions of the Internet. The following chapters will look at other aspects of this global system.

Types of Telecommunications
Defining Telecommunications

Before looking at how optical fibers are used in global telecommunications, I want to clarify what I'm talking about. The term *telecommunications* is deliberately broad. It dates back to the era when communication specialists were trying to lump telephones and telegraphs together under one heading. As the telegraph

●
Telecommunications
is a broad term,
encompassing
voice, data,
facsimile, video,
and other forms of
communication.

industry withered away, telephony became dominant, but the new word had caught on—and was useful because new types of communications were emerging. Telex became an accepted way to send messages around the globe. Facsimile systems began transmitting images of documents. Computer data communications grew rapidly. So did video transmission. They all fell under the broad heading of telecommunications.

Different types of telecommunications had different beginnings and have evolved differently, but they are now converging. The main reason is simple and compelling—it costs less to build a few common networks that can serve the same purpose than to build many separate ones with distinct functions.

●
Many
telecommunication
networks exist;
many (but not all)
interconnect.

The common purpose in modern telecommunications is to carry digitized signals around the world. At this writing, there are two somewhat distinct networks that serve this purpose: the telephone network and the Internet. I say *somewhat* distinct deliberately, because they both can carry much the same information. The difference is that the telephone network is optimized for telephone traffic, and the Internet is optimized for digital data. The two types of traffic have somewhat different requirements, as you learned in Chapter 18, but data can flow over telephone lines and telephone conversations can be routed over the Internet. Adjacent fibers in the same cable may carry Internet and telephone traffic. You also can find special-purpose long-haul systems that carry other kinds of traffic, particularly video signals.

The telecommunications industry is changing as well as the technology. Competition is already a reality in most of the American telecommunications industry outside of local phone and cable service. This means that there are many parallel national networks providing such services as Internet backbone transmission and long-distance telephone lines. This competition is possible because most networks are increasingly interconnected. This means that you can use a cable modem supplied by your cable-TV company to send a fax via the Internet to a friend across the street whose fax is connected to a phone line.

To understand the global telecommunications network, let's start by looking at various types of communications.

The Telephone Network

●
The telephone
network evolved
into the backbone
of the traditional
global telecommu-
nications system.

The telephone network spread around the globe in the twentieth century, supplanting electrical telegraphs to become the backbone of the international telecommunication system. Its original purpose was to carry conversations between any two phones connected to the network. To do this, it has a network of connections extending to individual homes and offices around the world. Signals from individual conversations—and from other services that share phone lines—are combined and routed to their destinations at telephone switching offices. Once mechanical switches connected electrical wires; now electronic switches route signals through optical fibers and other media.

Local and regional telephone systems interconnect with each other and with long-distance and international carriers to offer service around the block and around the planet. Telephone numbers provide the information needed for routing signals. In most of North America, you can direct calls within your area code by dialing seven digits. Long-distance calls within the United States, Canada, and parts of the Caribbean require dialing a long-distance code (1), a three-digit area code (XXX), and a seven-digit local number. To make overseas calls, you dial an international code (011), a 1- to 3-digit country code (e.g., 44 for Britain or 81 for Japan), usually a city code or other regional code (e.g., 171 for inner London or 3 for Tokyo), then a local number (usually 6 to 8 digits). Thanks to this system, you can call most of the phones in the world from your home or office, although you may regret it when you get the bill.

Each traditional twisted-wire-pair telephone line carries only a modest amount of information. A standard analog phone line carries sound frequencies of 300 to more than 3000 Hz, which the industry calls POTS, for Plain Old Telephone Service. (Phone lines can carry frequencies to 4000 Hz, but the upper frequencies are used for control signals.) That is enough for intelligible conversations, but it is far short of the 20- to 20,000-Hz range of the human ear. Pulse-code modulation converts the analog signal to digital format, with one voice channel equal to 56,000 bit/s in North America.

There are some important variations on POTS. Telephone wires also can carry digitized service called ISDN, for Integrated Services Digital Network. Upgraded phone lines can carry higher-speed digital signals called ADSL, for Asymmetric Digital Subscriber Loop. Radio signals from towers wired (or fibered) to the telephone network connect to mobile phones. Cellular phones use analog technology; a newer service called PCS uses digital technology. You will learn more about these services in Chapter 24.

Other Services over Phone Lines

Although the telephone network was designed to carry only voices, its wide reach makes it attractive to handle other types of signals that analog telephone lines can accommodate. The two most important examples are facsimile (fax) images and computer data transmitted via modems, shown schematically in Figure 21.1.

Fax machines digitally encode images and then transmit them as a series of sounds representing individual bits. Current-generation fax machines operate at 9600 bit/s, and computer-driven fax modems can operate at 14,400 bit/s. The use of phone lines allows faxes to reach anywhere within the telephone system, so faxes have their own dial-up phone lines or share phone lines with voice telephones. The telephone network converts the analog sounds from fax machines back into digital form at switches and then reconverts them to analog fax sounds for delivery to a subscriber.

Computer modems likewise encode digital data as analog sounds, which you hear as warbles, whines, and whistles. The signals must be clean and "robust," because the telephone network digitizes the sounds before routing them through the network and converts them back to analog form before delivering them to another analog modem, which has to reinterpret the data, as shown in Figure 21.1.

Computer modems and fax machines send signals over standard analog phone lines.

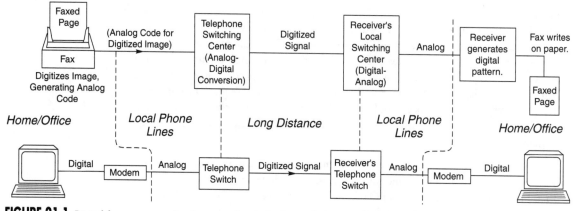

FIGURE 21.1 *Digital fax or computer data is converted to analog format for local telephone transmission and back to digital form for long distance.*

Both fax machines and modems have standardized codes for data transmission, so different models can talk with each other. (Fax-modems speak both languages.) Their signals can go over the Internet as well as through phone lines, but phone lines are often more convenient. At this writing, speeds are limited by the capacity of the analog phone lines to homes, although they are being improved, as you will learn in Chapter 24.

The Internet and Computer Networks

The Internet began as a network linking the computer networks at major research universities and laboratories but has since expanded to link many of the world's computers. It generally carries digital data more efficiently than phone lines. As with the telephone network, you can divide the Internet into a long-distance backbone system and regional and local transmission systems.

> The Internet carries digital data more efficiently than phone lines.

In practice, there is considerable overlap between computer networks and telecommunications networks. You can connect a personal computer to the following:

- A modem linked to the telephone network, which sends data to an Internet service provider over phone lines
- A cable modem connected to the cable-television network, which the cable company links elsewhere to the Internet
- A corporate or university network that links to the Internet
- Directly to the internet, usually via high-speed phone lines linking to a regional Internet node, *if* you have a powerful enough computer

The Internet interconnects with the phone system and with switches and routers that process Internet signals. How this all works could be the subject of another book. What is important is that Internet transmission is entirely digital, without having to convert to and from analog format, as in the present telephone system. This makes it inherently efficient for digital data.

Video Communications

Video signals are distributed by broadcasting through the air (or from satellites) or by transmission through cables. There are three types of video distribution—long-distance distribution from central sources to individual broadcasters and cable companies, direct broadcast from satellites to home receivers, and local distribution from cable companies and broadcast stations to individual homes. You will learn more about these in Chapter 23.

Traditionally, video distribution has been separate from the global telecommunications network, but this is changing. Much distribution of programs to broadcast stations or cable head-ends is via satellite, but some video signals are distributed over fiber. Cable companies link to the Internet to provide cable modem service and to the telecommunications network if they compete with the local telephone company to offer telephone service.

Television is starting to make a transition from analog to digital technology that will strongly impact video transmission. Unprocessed digital high-definition video signals require much more transmission capacity than lower-resolution analog signals—but digital signals can be compressed very efficiently, to occupy about the same bandwidth as analog video signals. What this will mean in practice for video transmission remains to be established.

Most video-signal distribution is one way, but video conferencing requires two-way transmission. Although video conferencing remains a limited application, streaming and two-way video signals can be routed through the Internet as well as through phone lines.

> Cable-television systems receive signals from distant sources for local distribution.

Other Communications

Some communication systems don't fit neatly into the categories described so far. For example, military organizations have their own high-speed networks designed to survive hostile attack. Utilities and railroads often have their own dedicated systems along their rights of way to meet special needs, such as monitoring their own operations. Often these networks interconnect with the global telephone network and/or the Internet. Many utilities and railroads lease telecommunications capacity along their rights of way to other companies, such as long-distance phone and Internet carriers.

Competing Carriers

Competition has made the global telecommunications network far more complex than it was in 1983, when AT&T was "the telephone company" to most Americans. Many systems exist, specializing in different areas but often overlapping in no easy-to-describe way. It's a bit like the choices you face when going out to buy a newspaper. In my neighborhood, I can buy a paper at a coin vending box, the drug store, the bakery, the convenience store, or the supermarket—but not all of them offer the same papers. The hard-and-fast rules are gone, and the choices can change tomorrow.

The Global Telecommunications Network

Diverse communication systems are interconnected to form a global network.

The pieces I have described so far are linked together, as shown in Figure 21.2, to form the global telecommunications network. Although many components were built separately, they have been interconnected, because connectivity is vital to communications.

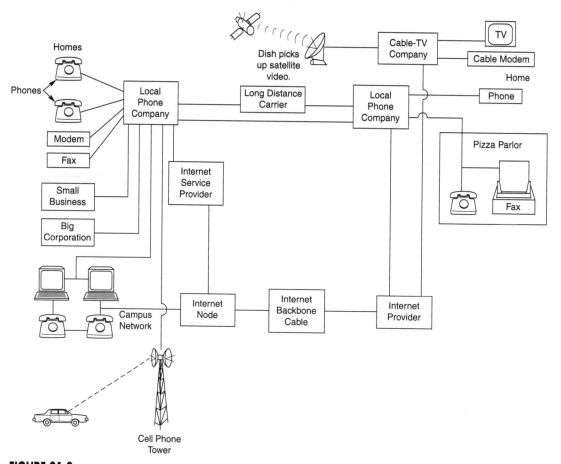

FIGURE 21.2 *Interconnection of telecommunication networks.*

The global telecommunications network operates on many levels and through many media. At the highest level, it connects national telecommunication networks. Submarine cables and satellite links cross oceans, linking continents with each other, at speeds of gigabits per second. Long-distance land cables connect adjacent countries. The nature of international links varies greatly, depending on geography, history, politics, economics, and a host of other factors. Closely allied countries, like the United States and Canada, are closely tied (to the extent that they share the same system of area codes). The countries of western Europe likewise are closely tied. On the other hand, only one submarine cable links the United States and Cuba, reflecting decades of political hostility. High-capacity land and submarine cables span heavily trafficked routes, such as between London and New York or London and Moscow. Networks branch out from major nodes to serve nations, states, or regions. A call from London to Rio de Janeiro may pass through a transatlantic cable to New York and then through another submarine cable crossing the Atlantic to South America. Alternatively, it might be routed from London to southern Europe and from there across the Atlantic to the Caribbean and south to Brazil. State-of-the-art submarine cables carry 5 Gbit/s on each fiber pair; systems now in the planning stages will carry up to 160 Gbit/s on each fiber pair and 640 Gbit/s in a single undersea cable.

Satellite links distribute video signals and provide telephone service to remote sites impractical to reach by cables. Calls to the Falkland Islands off the southern tip of South America or to Tuvali in the mid-Pacific will go via satellite. CNN reporters reporting live from remote battlefields send signals via satellites. Cable companies typically receive their video feeds by satellite. New satellite systems such as Iridium will provide mobile services available to individuals around the world.

National telecommunication networks differ in scale with the sizes of countries, but also usually operate at hundreds of megabits to tens of gigabits per second. The United States network rivals that of western Europe in size, for example. Submarine cables play only minor roles in national networks (except for countries made up of many islands). The backbones of the switched telecommunication networks that carry telephone and other traffic are land-based fiber-optic cables. Satellites broadcast signals to multiple points (particularly video feeds to cable television operators), and carry limited other signals, particularly data or traffic to remote sites. Land-based microwave radio and coaxial cable systems are becoming rare, made obsolete by high-speed fiber-optic systems.

> ●
> Fiber optics are the backbones of national telecommunication networks operating at speeds to tens of gigabits per second.

Regional networks are the next step down. In the United States, high-speed fiber-optic cables link major cities and then spread out to serve the surrounding area. Typically they branch out from points on the national backbone system, as you will see later.

Local telecommunication networks branch out from regional systems and in practice can be complex. As you saw earlier, there are actually multiple local networks that are to some extent linked together. I won't talk much about local broadcasting of television and radio signals or about cellular telephones, but later I will cover fiber-based services: telephone, digital data, and cable television. As you will see later, the technology behind these services is converging—thanks in part to fiber optics—and in coming years telephone and cable television networks will come to resemble and compete with each other.

> ●
> Local telecommunication networks branch out from regional systems.

Putting Networks Together

Putting the pieces together to make a single functional network requires combining many signals from diverse sources. There are two crucial concepts involved: multiplexing or combining many signals for transmission through a single carrier and conversion of signals into a common format. These can be addressed in various ways, but the basic concepts and reasoning are the same. It's cheaper and easier to combine signals traveling the same path than to send them separately. Likewise, all the signals traveling through the system have to be converted to the same format.

You can compare the telecommunication network with the circulation system of your body. Blood flows from tiny capillaries to larger veins, which in turn feed larger veins that can carry more blood. After the blood passes through your heart and lungs, it is divided up into smaller and smaller arteries and ultimately reaches the tiny capillaries. Individual phone lines are the capillaries of the old telephone network, upon which the modern telecommunication system is based. Low-speed lines feed into higher-speed systems, which go longer distances. There is a standardized hierarchy of transmission rates.

All the information handled by any transmission system has to be translated into the same format. As you will see later, the format is changing as the network evolves, but it has maintained a strong compatibility with older hardware. With a pair of wire cutters and a screwdriver, you can attach a massive 1950-vintage dial phone in basic black to the same standard analog telephone line as the latest 56-kbit/s fax-modem.

The Digital Telephone Hierarchy

The digital transmission hierarchy is itself evolving, with a new family of standards emerging. One old standard, still in wide use, is the North American digital telephone hierarchy of Figure 21.3, which was largely established in the days when AT&T was the only telephone company. The figure shows how low-speed signals (in units of voice channels) are multiplexed to higher speeds at each step of the hierarchy. In practice, all those slots in the higher-speed signals may not be filled. For example, rural areas may have too few telephone subscribers to use all the available slots. In addition, most phone companies now skip directly from the 1.5-Mbit/s DS1 rate to the 45-Mbit/s DS3 rate, not bothering with the intermediate DS2 rate. (For practical purposes, the DS and T signal hierarchies are identical.)

Figure 21.3 shows only the first few levels of the North American digital telephone hierarchy. Standards have evolved as transmission speeds have increased. In practice, there are three major families of standards, listed in Table 21.1: the North American Digital Hierarchy, the international telephone standard developed by the International Telecommunications Union to cover similar transmission rates, and the Sonet/SDH hierarchy, which is essentially uniform around the world.

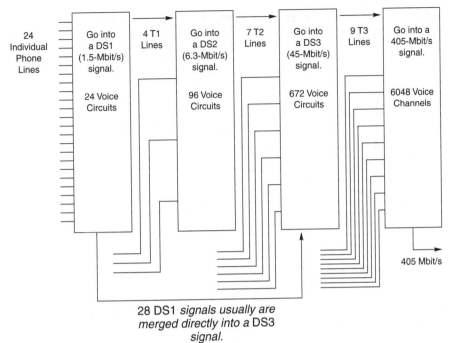

FIGURE 21.3

Multiplexing in the North American digital telephone transmission hierarchy.

28 DS1 *signals usually are merged directly into a* DS3 *signal.*

The North American and international digital hierarchy systems are based on time-division multiplexing of digital signals from multiple sources. Input signals are interleaved, with each allocated its own slot. As you learned earlier, SONET packages signals in frames or packets. SONET and the equivalent Synchronous Digital Hierarchy (SDH) speeds are higher than those of the other standards, and generally they are used for the fastest signals. The SONET/SDH standards go up to 10 Gbit/s on a single wavelength channel; in practice, higher speeds require wavelength-division multiplexing of separate signals at several wavelengths. Note that SONET covers only time-division multiplexed signals.

NORTH AMERICAN HIERARCHY

The North American Digital Hierarchy takes 56,000 bits/s as a single digitized voice channel and adds more bits for signal control. The most important rates in use are the 1.5-Mbit/s T1 rate and the 45-Mbit/s T3 rate. The 6.3-Mbit/s T2 rate is like second gear in a sports car, rarely used or quickly shifted through. For a variety of reasons, the 274-Mbit/s T4 rate is almost never used. In practice, the next step up is either 400 or 565 Mbit/s or switching to SONET rates. Note that rates of 400 Mbit/s and above are not formally part of the T-series hierarchy. They are de facto industry standards that have come into use since the early 1980s.

Table 21.1 Transmission rates in North America and Europe.

Rate Name	Data Rate	Nominal Voice Circuits
North American Digital Hierarchy		
Single circuit	56,000 bit/s	1
T1 or DS1	1.5 Mbit/s	24
T2 or DS2	6.3 Mbit/s	96
T3 or DS3	45 Mbit/s	672
T3C or DS3C	90 Mbit/s	1,344
T4 or DS4	274 Mbit/s	4,032
400 Mbit/s	405 or 417 Mbit/s*	6,048
565 Mbit/s	565 Mbit/s*	8,064 (56-kbit/s equiv.)
810 Mbit/s	810 Mbit/s*	12,098
1700 Mbit/s	1,700 Mbit/s*	24,192
2400 Mbit/s	2,400 Mbit/s*	36,290
European (CCITT standard)		
Single circuit	64,000 bit/s	1
Level 1	2.048 Mbit/s	30
Level 2	8.448 Mbit/s	120
Level 3	34.304 Mbit/s	480
Level 4	139.264 Mbit/s	1,920
Level 5	565.148 Mbit/s	7,680
SONET/Synchronous Digital Hierarchy		
STS-1/OC-1	51.84 Mbit/s	672 (28 DS1s or 1 DS3)
STS-3/OC-3(STM-1)	155.52 Mbit/s	2,016
STS-12/OC-12(STM-4)	622.08 Mbit/s	8,064
STS-48/OC-48(STM-16)	2,488.32 Mbit/s	32,256
STS-96/OC-96(STM-32)	4,976.64 Mbit/s	64,512
STS-192/OC-192(STM-64)	9,953.28 Mbit/s	129,024

*Actual line rate depends on design and overhead bits and is not standardized.

INTERNATIONAL STANDARDS

The International Consultative Commission of Telephone and Telegraph, an arm of the International Telecommunications Union, known as CCITT from the French version of its name, set its own family of standards built around digitization of single voice circuits at 64,000 bit/s (rather than 56,000 in North America). It also multiplexed different numbers of channels together, getting different data rates. These standards, listed in Table 21.1 along with other standard rates, are used in Europe. (Japan set its own standards.)

Different digital telephone hierarchies are used around the world.

SYNCHRONOUS DIGITAL HIERARCHY/SONET

Unhappy with old lower-speed standards, the telecommunications industry wrote a new generation of standards, which operate at higher speeds and can accommodate many kinds of signals besides telephone traffic. This is called SONET, the Synchronous Optical Network, in North America, and SDH, the Synchronous Digital Hierarchy, by CCITT. (I mentioned these earlier, in Chapters 18 and 19.) The two standards are functionally virtually identical, although they assigned different number levels to transmission rates. In Table 21.1 STM rates are for SDH; OC rates are for SONET. Both can be extended to higher transmission rates; I show up to 10 Gbit/s.

The SONET/ Synchronous Digital Hierarchy standards offer multigigabit data rates.

If you look carefully, you will note that the basic STS-1 SONET signal carries as many phone lines as a DS3 signal, but transmits more bits per second. The basic SONET rate was designed to have the same capacity as a DS3 carrier. The bit rates differ because more overhead information is added to the SONET signal to allow the system to monitor its transmission and direct signals properly.

FITTING INTO THE HIERARCHY

Although it was designed to transmit only telephone signals, the digital telephone hierarchy can handle other signals—as long as they're converted into a compatible format. That's what fax machines and modems do automatically—convert digital signals into analog tones compatible with the phone system. Digital signals can also be transmitted at higher speeds, including the 56-kbit/s equivalent of a voice channel and the 1.5- or 45-Mbit/s rates used for multiplexed phone signals.

Signals transmitted using the digital telephone hierarchy must meet standards of one level of the hierarchy.

The advantage of SONET/SDH over the old digital hierarchies is that the signals do not have to fit into rigid time-division-multiplexed slots. The frame-oriented SONET/SDH formats are inherently more flexible in accepting data rates that do not fit into the hierarchy levels or in processing bursty signals.

Packaging signals using asynchronous transfer mode (ATM) or Internet Protocol (IP) also can adapt signals at different speeds for transmission using either digital hierarchy or SONET standard rates. Recall that both ATM and IP are packet-switching technologies, which bundle data into packets for routing through the system.

WAVELENGTH CHANNELS

Wavelength-division multiplexing adds another layer by adding optical channels. You can think of each wavelength channel in a fiber as operating at its own data rate. In fact, optical channels can carry signals at different SONET (or other standard) speeds.

Wavelength-division multiplexing can push total capacity per fiber to hundreds of gigabits per second. You generally need more space between wavelength channels when operating at 10 Gbit/s than at 2.5 Gbit/s, but the total capacities are nonetheless impressive. Standards for optical channels have not been established, but Table 21.2 lists a sampling of possible rates, based on commercial systems announced or delivered as of spring 1998.

Table 21.2 Transmission rates with WDM.

Wavelength Channels	Data Rate per channel	Total Data Rate
4	2.5 Gbit/s	10 Gbit/s
8	2.5 Gbit/s	20 Gbit/s
8	10 Gbit/s	80 Gbit/s
16	2.5 Gbit/s	40 Gbit/s
32	2.5 Gbit/s	80 Gbit/s
40	10 Gbit/s	400 Gbit/s
80	2.5 Gbit/s	200 Gbit/s

If you consider multiple fibers in a single cable, you can get even higher transmission rates. However, that does not mean you should consider transmission at multiple wavelengths or through multiple fibers as equivalent to moving to a higher SONET speed. You should consider each wavelength channel as a separate bit stream with its own transmission rate. The goal is to be able to switch them separately, so you can talk of a single fiber in a WDM system as carrying eight "OC-48s", just as you would describe a cable with eight fiber pairs operating at that speed.

Submarine Cables

The largest-scale links in the global telecommunications network are submarine fiber-optic cables, which cross oceans and circle continents. They link whole continents, forming the critical backbone of the intercontinental telecommunications network. Since the age of the telegraph, they have been vital systems, linking and shrinking the world.

To keep discussions of the global network manageable, I will separate submarine cables from the national and regional telecommunications operating on land, described in Chapter 22. Later chapters will cover other aspects of the network: video communications in Chapter 23, local voice and digital telecommunications in Chapter 24, and computer networking in Chapter 25.

Submarine cables come in many types. Some cross the few kilometers of seawater separating an island from the mainland; one of the first to use fiber was an 8-km cable from Portsmouth, England to the Isle of Wight off the English coast. Many cross tens or hundreds of kilometers of sea; the Mediterranean and Caribbean seas are crisscrossed with submarine cables. Some span thousands of kilometers of ocean; the longest run across the bottom of the Pacific and from Europe to Japan.

Submarine cables must meet extremely tough requirements. Their transmission capacity should be as high as possible, because the cables are costly to make, lay, and operate. The cable, and any optical amplifiers or repeaters, must withstand harsh conditions on the bottom of the ocean for a design life of 25 years. Components must be extremely reliable, because it is very expensive to recover the cable from the sea floor and haul it to the surface for repairs. The cable should transmit digital signals cleanly to be compatible with modern equipment. These specifications veritably call out "fiber optics," and since the 1980s fibers have been standard for submarine cables.

A Short History of Submarine Cables

Designing submarine cables is a tremendous challenge, but they play a vital role in binding the world together. To understand their importance, you should understand a bit of their history, which began in the days when sailing the seas was still an adventure. Cable laying is now almost routine, but the technology is advancing so rapidly that several generations of fiber systems are operating on the ocean floor, with more planned, as shown in Figure 21.4.

TELEGRAPH CABLES

The need for electrical cables first arose with the electric telegraph in the early nineteenth century. It wasn't long before engineers laid waterproof cables underwater to carry telegraph signals. In 1850, the first submarine cable was laid in the open ocean between Britain and France, but it carried only a few messages before a fisherman caught it and hauled it to the surface. He thought it was a rare type of seaweed!

That experience taught submarine cable engineers an important lesson—waterproof isn't enough. The biggest dangers to cables in shallow waters still are fishing trawlers and anchors, so modern cables are buried a meter or so under the sea floor for protection in shallow water. The next telegraph cable laid between Britain and France in 1851 was armored with ten 7-mm wires of galvanized iron. That protected it from fishing trawlers well enough that it worked for many years.

> The first transatlantic cable carried telegraph signals more than a century ago.

FIGURE 21.4 *Submarine fiber-optic cables planned and in operation.* (Courtesy KMI Corp. Newport, RI)

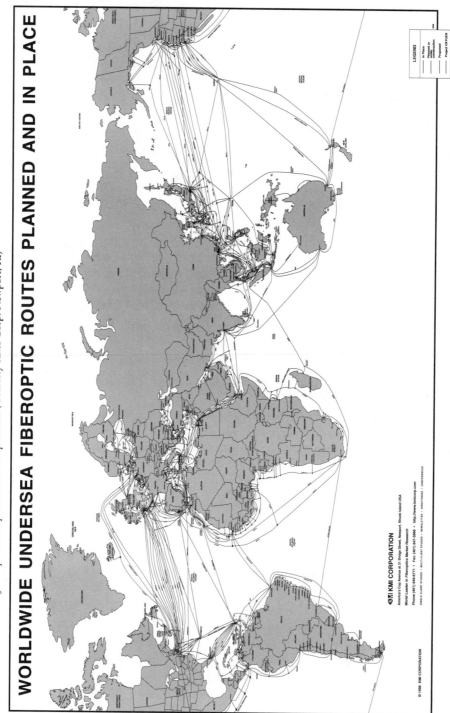

WORLDWIDE UNDERSEA FIBEROPTIC ROUTES PLANNED AND IN PLACE

The next bold step was to lay a cable across the entire Atlantic Ocean, which is far deeper and wider than the English Channel. Two efforts failed in 1857, but the following year a third worked for about 3 weeks. However, the principles of long-distance telegraphy were not well understood at the time, and an operator fried the cable by putting 2000 V across it. The Civil War and other problems slowed progress, and it was not until 1866 that the first transatlantic telegraph cable was working regularly.

TELEPHONE CABLES

The telephone came along soon afterward, but submarine telephone cables were much harder to build. One key problem was the need for a repeater to amplify telephone signals so the cable could carry them long distances. Mechanical relay amplifiers could handle the dots and dashes of the telegraph, but electronic amplifiers are necessary to handle voices. The required electronic technology wasn't available until well into the twentieth century. Instead, the first transatlantic phone calls were made by shortwave radio signals, or "wireless," which could travel long distances because they bounced off the atmosphere but were known for their crackle, static, and fade-out.

Britain laid the first submarine telephone cable with an underwater repeater in 1943 between Holyhead and Port Erin. The first such cable in North America—and the longest-operating—was laid between Key West, Florida, and Havana, Cuba, in 1950; it operated until 1989. The first transatlantic telephone cable, the TAT-1 (TransATlantic-1) cable between Britain and Canada, began operation in 1956.

Those early telephone cables were made of coaxial cable, which offers the highest bandwidth of any metal cable. However, coaxial cable has limitations. Its attenuation increases with the square root of transmission frequency, ν, and decreases as the inside diameter, D, of its outer conductor increases:

$$\text{Attenuation} = \frac{C \times \nu^{1/2}}{D}$$

where C is a constant depending on cable characteristics.

Increasing transmission frequency raises cable capacity but requires either a smaller repeater spacing (to compensate for higher losses) or a larger cable diameter (to reduce transmission losses). Either one is a problem. Repeaters are costly, can fail, and require electrical power. Thicker cables are hard to lay in the ocean.

The TAT-1 cable, which carried 36 telephone circuits, was 1.6 cm in diameter and had repeaters 70.5 km apart. The last transatlantic coaxial cable, TAT-7, which was put into service in 1983, is 5.3 cm in diameter and has a repeater each 9.5 km. Speech interpolation techniques could crowd 4200 analog phone circuits onto the cable, but even before TAT-7 was laid, engineers knew they had reached the practical limit of coax technology.

> Submarine telephone cables were not made until the mid-twentieth century because they needed submerged electronic repeaters.

> Transmission capacity and repeater spacing were limited in submarine coaxial cables.

SATELLITES VERSUS CABLES

Communications satellites arrived in the 1960s. The first transatlantic communications satellite, Intelsat I ("Early Bird"), was launched April 6, 1965. It could carry 240 phone calls, nearly twice as many as any extant transatlantic cable. By 1970, satellites offered more transatlantic voice circuits than cables, and cables were in trouble.

Coax had reached its limits, but submarine cable developers were not about to concede defeat to satellites. Satellite channels have some disadvantages. Radio waves take a quarter of a second to make the round-trip to and from geosynchronous orbit 37,000 km (22,000 mi) above the earth. That delay is barely perceptible, but it can be annoying, especially if a telephone call makes two bounces. Microwave transmission to and from satellites can be intercepted by electronic eavesdropping or spy satellites. Phone calls sent over analog satellite channels can suffer echoes that sound louder than the person at the other end.

Perhaps even more important was the fact that satellites and cables were owned and operated by different organizations through the 1970s and 1980s. Most submarine cables were owned by international consortia of telecommunications companies and government communication authorities, such as AT&T, British Telecom, and the French Ministry of Posts and Telecommunications. Most satellites were owned and operated by the International Telecommunications Satellite Organization (Intelsat) or by private companies. At the time, rigid regulations separated the two domains, so cable companies could not just shift their investment to satellites. They were not allowed into the satellite business. If they gave up on submarine cables, they would be forced out of the lucrative international communications business.

SUBMARINE FIBER CABLES

In the late 1970s, Bell Labs started looking seriously at fiber optics for submarine cable. By 1980, they had a design for TAT-8, the first transatlantic fiber-optic cable. They planned to transmit 278 Mbit/s at 1300 nm on each of two pairs of single-mode fibers, with a third pair kept in reserve. It was a daring design at the time, when single-mode fibers were not in practical use, but designers needed to stretch repeater spacing beyond 50 km because they wanted to reduce the number of repeaters, and at the time semiconductor lasers were not very reliable.

Their goal was to put the cable into service in 1988. Today, that sounds like a sluggish pace, but at the time it was a tight schedule to allay all the many concerns of understandably cautious cable operators. Fiber optics was an unproven technology in 1980, only recently installed for the first time in the terrestrial telephone network. Laser lifetimes were disturbingly short. And to make matters much worse, submarine cable designers proposed using a whole new generation of technology, with then-new single-mode fibers and 1300-nm lasers. Everything had to be tested again and again to verify it would work for 25 years on the ocean floor, with no more than two failures requiring recovery of the cable.

Over eight long years, development slipped only slightly behind the original schedule. The operators switched TAT-8 on at the end of 1988. Despite a couple of minor glitches the next year, the technology was a clear success. Anyone who made many transatlantic calls noticed the difference almost immediately. Submarine fiber-optic cables have grown explosively in the years that have followed, almost totally replacing satellites for international telephone service.

Types of Undersea Cables

Before I start looking at submarine cable designs, you should recognize that not all undersea cables are alike. They can be divided into three broad categories: short systems that are typically part of a national telecommunications network, moderate-distance systems connecting different countries but not crossing entire oceans, and transoceanic systems spanning thousands of miles (or thousands of kilometers). Each has somewhat different characteristics.

There are three type of submarine cables: short unrepeatered, moderate-distance repeatered, and long-distance repeatered transoceanic.

Short systems are typically 100 km or less and link islands with nearby continents or other islands. Examples include cables running between islands in the Japanese archipelago. Although some early fiber systems used repeaters, designers generally prefer to avoid repeaters or optical amplifiers. From the network standpoint, these cables are merely links in a national network that happen to run under water. Some countries have linked coastal cities with submarine cables because they are cheaper to install than land cables.

Moderate-distance cables run to more than 1000 km and include optical amplifiers or—in older cables—repeaters. Many cross the Caribbean, Mediterranean, and North Seas; others link islands in countries such as Indonesia and Malaysia. These are significant links in the global telecommunications network, with the amount of traffic depending on the areas served. Typically designers include extra capacity for future expansion.

Transoceanic cables run thousands of kilometers between or around continents and contain many optical amplifiers or—in older cables—repeaters. These are among the most critical links in the global telecommunications network. System requirements have consistently pushed fiber technology; innovations such as optical amplifiers have been developed in large part to meet their needs.

In the rest of this chapter, I will concentrate on intercontinental submarine cable systems. They must meet special requirements for capacity and reliability because they are critical links in the global telecommunications network. Their great lengths and their underwater location impose other design constraints that separate them from shorter submarine cables that are part of national or regional transmission networks. Those shorter submarine cables must meet requirements similar to those for other national and regional telecommunication systems.

Design of Intercontinental Submarine Cables

●
Long-haul
submarine fiber
cable design has
evolved very
rapidly.

The design of submarine fiber-optic cables has evolved very rapidly. Early work on TAT-8 helped launch the rapid spread of 1300-nm single-mode fiber-optic systems. The next major step was to 1550 nm, where fiber loss is lower, so repeaters could be spaced further apart. Then came optical amplifiers for systems transmitting a single channel at up to 5 Gbit/s. WDM followed, and as I write, the most ambitious plans are for dense-WDM with 16 10-Gbit/s channels per fiber in cables that include four fiber pairs. Some of the WDM systems in construction will be able to route individual wavelengths to particular destinations.

Table 21.3 summarizes the key design parameters of several major current and planned long-haul submarine cable systems. Looking only at the operational dates may somewhat overstate the rate of progress. The developers of TAT-8 were very cautious in testing every component of their system before installation, because the industry had to learn about the performance of submarine fiber cables. In fact, during the testing stages they encountered and overcame a major problem, excess attenuation caused when hydrogen accumulated in certain cables that contained fibers sensitive to hydrogen contamination.

Designers of later submarine cables have benefitted from experience accumulated over more years of operating undersea fiber cables. This greater knowledge allows shorter design cycles. At the same time, demand for more capacity is escalating rapidly, making installation of new cables an urgent matter.

At the time it was laid, TAT-8 represented a major advance, with raw data rate of 560 Mbit/s for the two operating fiber pairs (a third pair was kept as a spare) and electro-optic repeater spacing over 50 km, made possible by the use of single-mode fiber at 1300 nm. Its total capacity was 40,000 voice circuits, using speech-compression technology that originally was developed for analog cables. Submarine cables now carry increasingly large volumes of other signals, so the voice-channel equivalents have become less meaningful.

The next steps were to increase data rates through each fiber to 565 Mbit/s, and to use the longer 1550-nm wavelength where lower attenuation allows longer repeater spacing as long as narrow-line distributed-feedback lasers or dispersion-shifted fibers are used. The first regular uses of 1550-nm transmission were in shorter cables, where stretching repeater spacing well beyond 100 km could avoid the need for submerged electro-optic repeaters. This relieved the understandable concern about putting developmental hardware where it would have to be recovered if repairs were needed.

Rapid improvements in 1550-nm technology soon eased fears about using it in submerged repeaters. By 1992, submerged 1550-nm repeaters were carrying 565 Mbit/s across the Atlantic in the TAT-9 and -10 cables, using distributed-feedback lasers and standard step-index fiber with zero dispersion at 1300 nm. Repeater spacings were well over 100 km.

The next advance was the use of erbium-doped fiber amplifiers, avoiding the need for electro-optic regenerators under the ocean. Optical amplifiers offer two important advantages for submarine cable. They are much simpler than electro-optic regenerators, with a much

Table 21.3 Initial capacities of some major undersea fiber cables. Some systems with fiber amplifiers such as TAT 12/13 are upgradable by adding more wavelength channels.

System	TAT-8	TAT-10	TAT-12/13	SEA-ME-WE-3	Atlantic Crossing 1	Project Oxygen
Operational	Dec. 1988	1992	1996	1998	1998	2000–2002
Location	US–UK and France	US–Germany	US–UK–France–US loop	Germany to Singapore	US–UK–Netherlands–Germany loop	Global, 116 segments, 101 landing points
Initial Data Rate per Fiber Pair	278 Mbit/s	565 Mbit/s	5 Gbit/s	2.5 Gbit/s per optical channel	2.5 Gbit/s per optical channel	10 Gbit/s per optical channel
Working Pairs	2	2	2 each half of loop	2	4 each half of loop	4
Fiber	Single-mode	Single-mode	Dispersion-shifted to 1550 nm	Zero dispersion at 1580 nm	Zero dispersion at 1580 nm	To be determined
Repeater spacing	Over 50 km	Over 100 km	None	None	None	None
Wavelength	1300 nm	1550 nm	1550 nm	Up to 8 near 1550	4 near 1550 nm	16 near 1550 nm
Optical amplifiers	None	None	Yes	Yes	Yes	Yes
Total cable capacity	560 Mbit/s	1130 Mbit/s	10 Gbit/s	Up to 40 Gbit/s	40 Gbit/s	640 Gbit/s
Notes				Optical add-drop capability		158,000-km network, mostly undersea; optical add-drop

● **Erbium-doped fiber amplifiers elminated the need for undersea regenerators.**

lower component count, so they are more reliable. Eliminating the need for active electronic systems under the ocean is an attractive way both to reduce costs and to reduce the likelihood of failures. In addition, systems using optical amplifiers can be upgraded simply by replacing transmitters and receivers on the land ends, without touching the undersea portion of the system. This design quickly became standard. It uses dispersion-shifted fiber.

Wavelength-division multiplexing can multiply the capacity per fiber by transmitting multiple channels, although at lower data rates per individual channel. Although single-channel transmission in the 1550-nm window is at 5 Gbit/s, each WDM channel in early WDM systems will be at 2.5 Gbit/s. Nonetheless, overall speed is higher. These systems use nonzero-dispersion-shifted fiber, with the zero-dispersion wavelength shifted to 1580 nm, outside the range of wavelength channels.

Higher transmission speeds are in the works. The ambitious plans for the global network of Project Oxygen (see Table 21.3) call for transmitting 10 Gbit/s on each of 16 wavelength channels in each of four fiber pairs in a cable, for a total data rate of 640 Gbit/s. It probably will operate on nonzero-dispersion-shifted fiber, like other WDM systems, although definite plans have not been announced.

Submarine System Architectures

● **Submarine cables may be point-to-point links, loops, or trunk-and-branch systems.**

Traditional submarine cables merely connected two points, although some of them had branch points near the end to serve additional sites. For example, TAT-8 branches off the European coast, splitting into cables linking with Britain and France. Recent submarine cables, and others still in the planning stages, use other architectures.

One alternative is the ring system, shown in Figure 21.5. Like a SONET ring, a submarine cable ring can continue to function after a single cable failure. You might think submarine cables are safe at the bottom of the ocean, but they are anything but safe along the continental shelves. Fishing trawlers rake over most of the sea floor at depths less than about 200 m (660 ft) and can snag and break submarine cables that are not trenched into the ocean floor.

FIGURE 21.5

Undersea cable ring.

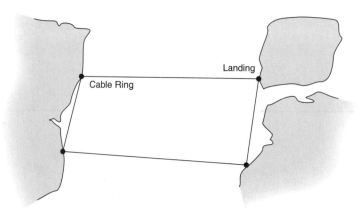

Another architecture is a trunk-and-branch system, shown in Figure 21.6. In this case, a trunk cable is laid around the coast of a continent and makes landings at locations around the continent. The connections to shore can be made by branch cables connected to the main trunk cable offshore, or the trunk cable can come to shore to serve a major traffic point, such as the Big Important Country in Figure 21.6.

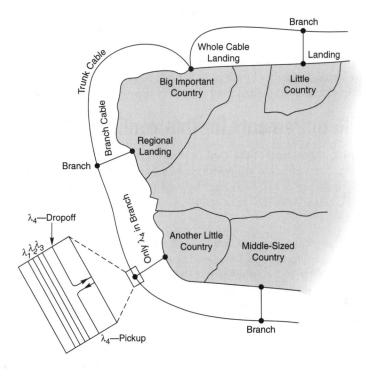

FIGURE 21.6

Undersea cable branch connections.

Modern WDM systems can add and drop single wavelength channels at individual drop points, as shown in the inset in Figure 21.6. In that example, the cable that loops offshore around the region carries four wavelengths, λ_1, λ_2, λ_3, and λ_4. The first three pass by Another Little Country at the lower left, but λ_4 is separated from the rest and routed to the landing. Signals from Another Little Country are collected and transmitted on λ_4, which is added to the cable as the signal travels toward the branch at Middle-Sized Country.

Note that branching points can be undersea or on land. Making the connections off the continent can offer political advantages if some countries worry that signals passing through unfriendly nations might be interrupted.

Traditionally, submarine cables have been laid individually to connect a few points or to make a number of connections along a single route. For example, SEA-ME-WE-3 runs from Germany to Singapore via Holland, Britain, France, Portugal, Morocco, Italy, Greece, Turkey, Cyprus, Egypt, Djibouti, Saudi Arabia, Oman, United Arab Emirates,

Pakistan, India, Sri Lanka, Burma, Malaysia, and Indonesia. The planned Project Oxygen is a departure in seeking to build a complete undersea telecommunications making connections to every continent but Antarctica.

Shorter Submarine Cables

At last count, there are more than 600 submarine fiber cables planned or in operation. Most are relatively short and essentially form part of the regional and national telecommunication networks described in Chapter 22. Figure 21.7 gives an example of submarine cables installed along the southwest coast of Italy that are part of the Italian telecommunication network. In such cases, it often is simpler and cheaper to lay a cable offshore between two coastal cities than to acquire right of way and run cable on land.

Design Requirements for Intercontinental Cables

Low-gain optical amplifiers are used on long submarine cables to reduce noise levels.

Intercontinental submarine cables pose serious design challenges because of their extreme length. As you learned earlier, noise can accumulate over long distances in a system using optical amplifiers. The higher the amplification at each stage, the higher the noise level. To avoid this extra noise, designers of submarine cables use more lower-power amplifiers.

Suppose, for example, you need to build a 6000-km fiber cable. You can build it using 30-dB amplifiers, one every 150 km, or using one 10-dB amplifier every 50 km. You would save money if you chose the 30-dB amplifiers, but it would come at the cost of a noise level about 30 times higher. That is not an acceptable trade-off, so submarine cable designers prefer to install more fiber amplifiers, with each one having lower gain. This is particularly important with WDM systems.

Note that noise accumulation increases sharply with distance, because optical amplifiers are analog devices that amplify noise along with the signal they receive. Once you get the noise in, you can't get it out with optical amplifiers. This is not a problem you see on land, because it usually takes more than a thousand kilometers for it to accumulate to significant levels, and few land cables run that far without an interruption to serve a major population center. Thus optical amplifiers generally are spaced further apart on land lines than on submarine cables.

Another important practical limitation is that WDM submarine cables *require* gain equalization across the spectrum of optical amplifiers. The longer the chain of amplifiers, the more important equalization becomes. Suppose each amplifier has 0.3 dB more gain at 1550 than at 1560 nm. This wouldn't amount to much if the signals had to pass through only five amplifiers. However, a 6000-km transatlantic cable might contain 120 amplifiers, each 50 km apart. In that cable, the 1550-nm signal would experience 36 dB more gain than the 1560-nm signal and would essentially overwhelm the longer wavelength in optical amplifiers, leaving it too weak to be detected reliably.

FIGURE 21.7
Submarine fiber cables link coastal cities in Italy. Land lines also are shown. (Courtesy of Corning Inc.)

What Have You Learned?

1. The global telecommunications network carries voice, data, video, and other signals. It is largely an outgrowth of the global telephone network, but it also includes the Internet. It is heavily interconnected and includes fiber links, satellite channels, and other cable transmission systems.

2. The telephone network evolved into the backbone of the traditional global telecommunications system. It connects local, regional, and long-distance telephone networks so you can dial phones around the world.

3. POTS is plain old telephone service, usually over analog phone lines. New digital services are an alternative to POTS.

4. Computer modems and fax machines convert digital signals into analog form for transmission over analog phone lines.

5. The Internet was developed to interconnect large computer networks. It carries bursty digital data more efficiently than digital telephone lines. It also interconnects with the telephone system.

6. Cable-television systems receive signals from distant sources for local distribution. Some signals come via fiber, but many are delivered by satellite broadcasting systems.

7. Television is starting to convert from analog to digital technology.

8. Optical fibers are the backbone of the global telecommunications network, both for telephone and Internet traffic.

9. Telephone systems transmit at a hierarchy of digital data rates, with bits from several slow signals interleaved to generate successively higher-speed signals. The digital hierarchies of North America and Europe transmit at different data rates.

10. SONET in North America and SDH elsewhere are standards for transmission over fiber at speeds of 52 Mbit/s and up. There are only very minor differences between the SONET and SDH standards.

11. Wavelength-division multiplexing multiplies total transmission capacity by adding optical channels.

12. Submarine fiber-optic cables are backbones of the global telecommunications network. The largest interconnect continents; smaller systems link countries with offshore islands or cross smaller seas, such as the Mediterranean.

13. The first submarine cables carried telegraph signals, starting in the 1860s. Telephone cables are much harder to build because they require electronic repeaters. The first transatlantic telephone cable was put into service in 1956, using coaxial cables.

14. Fiber-optic submarine cables replaced coaxial cables because fibers have higher capacity and allowed longer repeater spacing. Submarine fiber cables replaced satellites for telephone calls because they avoided annoying satellite-bounce delays.

15. Optical amplifiers replaced electro-optic repeaters in submarine fiber cables in the 1990s. Amplifiers are simpler to install undersea and allow upgrading transmission to higher speeds. Wavelength-division multiplexing allows much higher transmission capacity per fiber.

16. WDM submarine fiber systems can add or drop wavelengths at various points.

17. Submarine cable designs include point-to-point, loop, and trunk-and-branch designs.

18. Amplifier gain is lower in submarine cables to prevent noise from accumulating. Amplifier gain must be equalized across wavelengths to process WDM signals properly.

What's Next?

In Chapter 22, you will learn about the national and regional telecommunications networks, which interconnect with the global network.

Quiz for Chapter 21

1. What types of signals travel on the global telecommunications network?
   a. Voice telephone.
   b. Digital data.
   c. Facsimile.
   d. Video.
   e. All the above.

2. How are signals carried on the global telecommunications network?
   a. They are digitized and multiplexed to generate high-speed signals that can be routed long distances.
   b. Analog and digital signals are carried on separate networks.
   c. Local networks feed signals to regional networks, which route them to national backbone systems and international lines.
   d. a and c.
   e. a, b and c.

3. How does the Internet relate to the global telecommunications network that evolved from the telephone system?
   a. The two interconnect, and both carry digital data along separate paths.
   b. The telephone network carries only analog signals; the Internet transmits only digital data.
   c. The two are identical.
   d. The Internet is replacing the global telecommunications network.
   e. Only the Internet can carry packet-switched signals.

4. A single voice channel in the North American Digital Hierarchy corresponds to a speed of
   a. 4000 Hz.
   b. 4000 bit/s.
   c. 14,400 bit/s.
   d. 56,000 bit/s
   e. 1.5 Mbit/s.

5. How many T1 signals go into a SONET OC-3 signal?

    a. 84.

    b. 96.

    c. 672.

    d. 2016.

    e. 155 million.

6. Which of the following signals can feed a SONET OC-3 system?

    a. ATM format.

    b. Packet-switched Internet Protocol.

    c. T3 from the Digital Telephone Hierarchy.

    d. Multiple T1 circuits.

    e. All the above.

7. How does SONET differ from the Digital Telephone Hierarchy?

    a. The only difference is that SONET is at higher speeds.

    b. SONET uses packet switching; the telephone hierarchy allocates slots for multiplexed signals at slower speeds.

    c. SONET is pure time-division multiplexing; the telephone hierarchy uses packet switching.

    d. The digital telephone hierarchy can handle digitized analog signals, but SONET cannot.

    e. There are no differences; they are identical.

8. What is the total data rate in a cable containing four fiber pairs, two carrying four wavelength channels each at OC-48, one carrying a single wavelength channel at OC-192, and one unused?

    a. 10 Gbit/s.

    b. 22.5 Gbit/s.

    c. 30 Gbit/s.

    d. 32.5 Gbit/s.

    e. 40 Gbit/s.

9. Which type of transmission has not been used in a transatlantic fiber cable already laid or planned?

    a. Single-mode transmission at 850 nm.

    b. Single-mode transmission at 1300 nm.

    c. Wavelength-division multiplexing at 1550 nm.

    d. Electro-optic repeaters at 1550 nm.

    e. Nonzero-dispersion-shifted fiber.

10. For a submarine fiber-optic cable to operate properly, all WDM channels must have power within 12 dB of each other at the receiver end of the cable. If the cable is 6200 km long and identical optical amplifiers are separated by 50 km, how uniform must the gain be at each optical amplifier?

    a. 0.1 dB.

    b. 0.125 dB.

    c. 0.13 dB.

    d. 0.2 dB.

    e. 1.2 dB.

National and Regional Telecommunication Networks

About This Chapter

Now that you have learned about the global telecommunication network, it is time to look at national and regional networks that connect to it. These networks are a complex array of interconnected systems, which route signals among widely separated users. They integrate on a larger scale with the global systems described in Chapter 21 and on a smaller scale with the local subscriber systems described in Chapter 24. They carry mainly digitized voice and data signals, but they also transmit some video.

Network Structure

You can think of national and regional telecommunications networks as the part of a network that links many local switching centers or interconnection points. Figure 22.1 shows the basic idea for a telephone network. It is composed of a number of building blocks: cables that carry signals and switching or regional offices that receive, process, and direct signals. They operate at various levels, from switching offices that serve individual communities to regional centers that serve large areas. Although the network originated from the telephone system, it can carry other types of traffic as well. (The Internet is a separate network that delivers signals in a different way but functions similarly in many other ways. This chapter concentrates on the switched public telecommunications network, which evolved from the old telephone system.)

●
National and regional networks link many local switching centers or connection points.

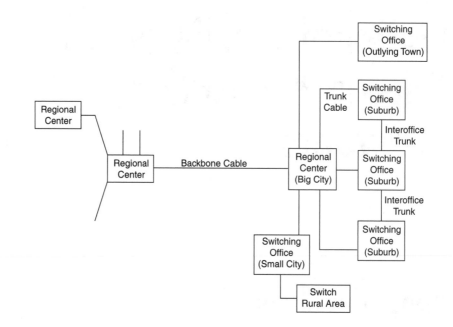

FIGURE 22.1

A regional telecommunications network.

The basic concept of the telecommunications system shown in Figure 22.1 is relatively simple. Local switching offices collect and process signals and then switch them to other switching offices in the area (local calls) and to regional centers that process long-distance traffic. Trunk cables carry traffic to and from switching centers.

Regional centers collect and process signals from local switching centers much as the switching centers collect and process signals from individual telephone users. They direct long-distance signals to other regional centers and local calls to the local switching offices they serve. Backbone cables carry signals between regional centers.

Naturally, life and the telecommunication network are not quite that simple. The switching centers serving small rural towns may be linked to switching offices in a nearby small city, not to a regional switching center in a distant large city. The splitting of area codes and the addition of competitive telephone carriers has muddied the picture, obscuring the original definitions of local and long-distance telephone service.

●
Telecommunication networks collect signals locally, package them together, and direct them to their destinations.

However, the organizing principles of the network remain the same. Signals are collected locally, concentrated and packaged into convenient form, and directed to their destinations. The more people served, the higher the capacity of the switch and the higher the capacity of the cable. Backbone cables have more capacity than trunk cables; regional switching centers have more capacity than switching offices. Fiber optics provide most of the transmission capacity.

This structure was developed for telephone transmission, but it also is used for Internet transmission and for other types of telecommunications covering large areas. In fact, you often find parallel networks providing services using different telecommunications protocols. For example, a single backbone cable may include one fiber pair carrying Internet traffic in IP format, another fiber pair carrying SONET-framed data for corporate clients who lease capacity from the carrier, and a couple of fiber pairs carrying nominally "telephone" traffic from the public switched network.

Competitive carriers offer a second level of parallelism. AT&T, MCI, and Sprint all have separate backbone networks that span the nation. Some regional long-distance carriers have their own networks that span large areas. These backbone cables are not completely parallel in the sense that they don't run exactly the same routes, but they do provide the same service. (For example, one carrier might lease right-of-way along a major highway, and another might lease right-of-way along a railroad.)

Network Design Principles

Because this is a book about fiber optics, I cannot go into detail about network design. However, you should be aware of a few basic design principles that underlie the structure of the telecommunications network.

- Transmission is digital. Input analog signals are digitized, generally at or before the switching office, and remain digital as they travel through the network. They are converted back into analog format at the other end.

- Digitized signals are concentrated into bit streams at higher and higher rates for longer distances and higher-capacity systems. You can think of this network as a collection of digital "pipes," with smaller pipes feeding larger ones. Natural analogies are the array of small streams feeding into large rivers or the concentration of blood into larger and larger blood vessels.

- Transmission systems are essentially hierarchical, with the smaller ones feeding into bigger ones serving larger areas. You could think of it as analogous to town governments that belong to counties, counties that belong to states, states that belong to countries, and countries that share the same continent. The analogies and levels are not exact; just as New York City includes several times more people than the whole state of North Dakota, so New York City requires many times more telecommunications capacity.

- Signals must be directed to diverse destinations. Depending on your system architecture, you can do this with a switch, which establishes a path

> Signals are digitized and combined for transmission and then reconverted at the other end.

for signals to follow, or a router, which directs data packets to their destinations. In general, telecommunications systems that grew from the telephone system use switches, and the Internet uses routers.

- Switching and routing are done at various points in the network to send signals to their destinations.

- System designers assume a certain loading—that is, a level of traffic to expect. The telephone network does not have enough capacity to handle the calls if everyone picks up the phone at once and tries to call his or her mother (something that can happen nationally on Mother's Day or locally when an earthquake hits California without knocking out the phone lines).

- Different networks are optimized for different types of service. Telephone conversations differ fundamentally from the best-effort packet switching of the Internet. A conventional telephone network makes a connection between a pair of phones, reserving a voice channel for the users whether or not they say anything. In contrast, the Internet routes packets of data to their destinations, without *guaranteeing* that they will ever get there.

Keeping these design principles in mind, let's look at the different levels and functions in national and regional telecommunication networks. I'll start with long-distance backbone systems and then focus on successively smaller systems. Once you've seen the various levels, I'll put the pieces together with a couple of examples.

Long-Haul Fiber Systems on Land

Long-distance telecommunication systems on land, like submarine cables, carry high-speed signals and serve as backbones of the global telecommunications network. You can divide these land backbone systems into international and national networks, although the major differences are in who operates them rather than in how they work. For example, an international cable connecting France and Germany serves the same function as a cable linking New York State and the Midwest in the United States.

Long-haul land telecommunication systems differ from current submarine systems in that they are *networks* rather than point-to-point links. You can see the difference in Figure 22.2, which shows Sprint's long-haul fiber systems providing telephone service in the United States. The long-distance system links many population centers, marked by junctions and bends in the lines.

Submarine versus Long-Haul Land Cables

Note that the long-haul land networks do not have the long uninterrupted cable runs of submarine cables. A cable that crosses the Atlantic has no logical stopping point between Europe and North America. However, a fiber cable crossing North America from New York might stop in Pittsburgh, Cleveland, Chicago, Omaha, Denver, and Salt Lake City to distribute signals in those regions before continuing to San Francisco.

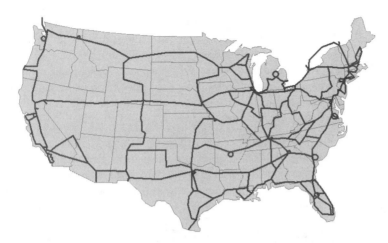

FIGURE 22.2
*Sprint's long-distance
fiber system.*
(Courtesy of Sprint).

These shorter cable runs have important practical implications. One is that the signals do not have to go thousands of kilometers between transmitter and receiver, only several hundred kilometers. This relaxes many requirements on optical amplifiers, because noise, pulse dispersion, and differences in gain as a function of wavelength do not accumulate over such distances. Instead of limiting optical gain to around 10 dB per amplifier, land-based cables can use the full 30 dB possible, without severe noise penalties. Instead of one amplifier every 50 km, you might have one amplifier every 100 or 150 km.

● Long-distance land cables do not go as far as transoceanic cables, so their design is different.

A second critical difference is that land systems are much easier to access than submarine cables. Most long-haul land cables are buried (often in ducts) along railroad rights of way, highways, or utility lines. The urban terminations usually are buried under the streets. A service crew can reach and repair a damaged cable much easier on land than at the bottom of the ocean. On the other hand, submarine cables laid in the ocean depths or buried on the continental shelves are safely out of the way of careless contractors, who might accidentally break land cables.

Transmission Speeds

Backbone long-haul systems on land operate at high speeds. The first American systems transmitted 400 Mbit/s over standard step-index single-mode fiber at 1300 nm, with typical repeater spacings 40 km. During the 1980s, maximum data rates increased first to 565 Mbit/s, then to 800 Mbit/s, and later to 1.7 Gbit/s. By the early 1990s, the highest speeds were 2.5 Gbit/s. Today, the highest time-division multiplexing speeds for a single wavelength channel are 10 Gbit/s, and the highest total speeds today are 80 Gbit/s, achieved by wavelength division multiplexing signals at 2.5 or 10 Gbit/s. Higher speeds are likely by the time you read this. Transmission speeds of the fastest terrestrial long-distance systems generally have been somewhat higher than those of the fastest submarine cables, because the technology is moving fast and submarine cables have longer lead times.

● Long-distance land systems operate at high speeds.

In the 1980s, telecommunications companies built their national networks using step-index single-mode fiber with zero dispersion at 1310 nm, and this fiber remains in use today. In addition, many companies installed cables containing spare fibers, called *dark fibers,* which they did not initially connect to light sources. This took advantage of the economics of multifiber cables and left room for future expansion. New transmitters and receivers can upgrade transmission through step-index single-mode fibers by WDM much more cheaply than you could add capacity by laying new cable.

Comparatively few networks use fiber with zero dispersion shifted to 1550 nm, which is difficult to upgrade to WDM because of four-wave mixing effects. However, zero-dispersion-shifted fiber can be upgraded to TDM at 10 Gbit/s. New systems designed for WDM use nonzero-dispersion-shifted fiber, which has its zero-dispersion point close to 1600 nm, so it avoids four-wave mixing effects.

Long-Haul Network Connections

The long-haul land network has two types of connections. It receives signals from regional networks and ultimately delivers them to other regional networks. It also connects with submarine cables for intercontinental transmission. In the United States, regulators have divided telephone transmission between companies that provide local service (*local exchange carriers*) and long-distance companies. This means that a call from Boston to Miami will go through the lines of three carriers: the local Boston carrier, a long-distance carrier, and the local Miami carrier.

High transmission speeds make it possible to send an incredible volume of signals through a single fiber. Unfortunately, it also means that a single cable break can disrupt tens of thousands of phone conversations. To prevent such disruption, long-distance carriers have organized their land networks in SONET rings, so signals can be switched around failure points. For example, if someone breaks the main Sprint cable across Missouri in Figure 22.2, calls can be routed through Iowa to the north or Arkansas to the south.

Types of Long-Haul Networks

There are three basic types of long-haul networks.

- The public switched telecommunications network, which has grown from the long-distance telephone network to provide service on a call-by-call basis. It switches signals, making temporary paths between pairs of terminals.

- The Internet, which transfers data packets among computer networks and among Internet services. It provides service to all people with accounts on Internet service providers. It routes data packets, reading header information and using that to direct them through the network.

- Private leased lines, service which long-distance carriers provide by subdividing transmission capacity and leasing it to other companies, such as airlines and banks.

These systems may run on separate fiber pairs through the same cable, but they function separately. They may go down together in case of an unprotected cable break, but if other equipment fails, one system may crash while the others continue operating.

To further complicate the picture, in the United States and some other countries companies that compete in offering long-distance service build separate networks, which may offer all three types of long-distance transmission. AT&T and MCI have their own long-distance networks, which cover the whole United States, but follow different routes than Sprint's. Other companies have long-distance networks that span only certain parts of the country. And many long-distance "carriers" are actually resellers, which lease capacity from companies that own networks and transmit signals over those leased lines.

Regional Telecommunication Networks

Regional telecommunications networks link the local switching centers that serve individual communities with each other and with long-distance networks. They function as intermediaries between purely local and long-distance systems. (In reality, the distinctions are a bit vague, but the concept is nonetheless important.) I will concentrate on switched telecommunications networks rather than on the Internet; the details differ but the principles are similar.

Parts of the Regional Network

Figure 22.3 shows the elements of a regional telecommunications network. The solid lines connecting boxes are parts of the regional system; the boxes are switching centers for each area. (We'll get to them shortly.) The regional network runs among switching centers in the area. The dashed lines are not part of the regional network. They include parts of the long-distance system (that is, links to the national networks of long-distance carriers) and lines connecting individual homes and businesses to switching centers in each community.

Regional networks link local switching offices with each other and with long-distance providers.

In general, the company that provides local telephone service operates the regional network as well as the lines to your home and business. This regional network connects to long-distance lines. If two or more companies offer local telephone service, they may have parallel networks in your area. That may mean they have their own separate sets of cables running among switching centers or that they lease space on cables from other companies. Unless you are a large customer, competing local carriers rarely will string their own cables to your home or office.

Back in the 1980s, when AT&T broke up and the United States deregulated long-distance telephone service, the difference between regional and long-distance carriers was defined according to area codes. Any calls between those area codes had to be handled by long-distance carriers, while calls within the area codes were regional, billed by your local phone company—even if you were billed separately for each call as a toll call. However, the definitions of what's regional and what's long distance have not changed as area codes split, so calls to some nearby area codes may be handled by your regional carrier, but calls to other area codes go through your long-distance carrier.

FIGURE 22.3

A regional telecommunications network.

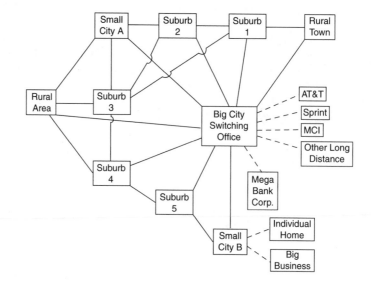

Switching Offices

Switching offices make connections to and from individual telephone subscribers.

A switching office or central office is the interface between the regional network and the *local loop*—cables running to individual homes and businesses. Nominally, all telephone circuits run from subscriber phones to the central office, but in practice they often run to remote concentrator nodes, where the signals from many homes are multiplexed together for transmission to the central office. (You'll learn about the subscriber loop in Chapter 24.)

The local switching center contains special-purpose computers that switch your call based on the numbers you dial, as shown in Figure 22.4 for a region with seven-digit local dialing. First, it checks to see if the first digit is 1, meaning the call is long distance. If not, it reads the first three digits and sets electronic switches to send the signal to the appropriate local exchange. In the figure, the call goes from the 679 exchange to 555. This means it passes through the regional phone network from the 679 exchange switch to the 555 exchange switch. Then the 555 switch sends it to the proper phone line.

The same principles apply if you have 10-digit dialing—that is, if you have to dial the area code for local as well as long-distance numbers. In that case, the outgoing call switch decides if the call is local or long distance by comparing the area code with internal tables.

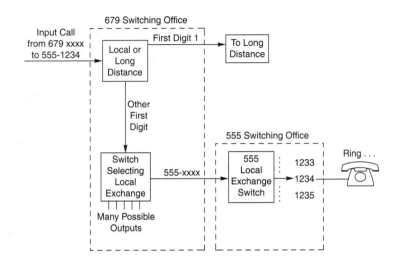

FIGURE 22.4

Directing calls in a switching office.

The arrangement of switching centers depends on the locality. In rural areas, you may find them in small buildings or even trailers, serving only a single telephone exchange. Small cities and suburbs typically have a single switching office serving multiple exchanges. Large cities may have several switching offices, each serving multiple exchanges.

Regional Transmission

The phone lines running between switching offices are called *interoffice trunks.* They run at 45 Mbit/s and up—mostly higher—through fiber-optic cables that may be buried directly in the ground, run through underground ducts, or—in some areas—strung on overhead poles. In urban and suburban areas, switching offices typically are no more than several kilometers apart, but in rural areas they can be much more widely separated. Except in sparsely populated areas or where cables run long distances to regional centers, they do not require optical amplifiers or repeaters.

Interoffice trunks connect telephone switching offices.

Trunk cables were the first application for fiber-optic communications, with the first few installations in the late 1970s. The oldest of these systems use graded-index fiber to transmit at 850 nm; a few use graded-index fiber at 1300 nm. By the late 1980s, the industry had switched completely to single-mode fiber at 1300 nm. Now some systems operate at 1550 nm, particularly those carrying high-speed signals.

Table 22.1 shows typical performance of various generations of trunk cables. The first and second generations are now obsolete, and you're unlikely to find them. Third- and later-generation systems are still being installed and used. Fifth-generation systems offer the highest capacity, but their use in regional systems remains limited. Optical amplifiers or repeaters are rarely needed in urban or suburban areas but may be used in rural areas where long cables are needed to link widely spaced population centers.

Table 22.1 Typical performance of fiber-optic trunk systems.

	First Generation	Second Generation	Third Generation	Fourth Generation	Fifth Generation
Wavelength	850 nm	1300 nm	1300 nm	1550 nm	1550 nm, multiple
Fiber	Graded-index, multimode	Graded-index, multimode	Step-index, single-mode	Single-mode	Nonzero dispersion-shifted, or step-index, single-mode
Typical data rates	45 Mbit/s	90 Mbit/s	400–2500 Mbit/s	2.5 or 10 Gbit/s	2.5 Gbit/s per wavelength
Fiber loss	3–4 dB/km	1 dB/km	0.35 dB/km	0.25 dB/km	0.25 dB/km
Repeater/amp spacing, where needed	Repeaters, 8 km	Repeaters, 20 km	Repeaters, 40–150 km	Amplifiers, 50–150 km	Amplifiers, 50–150 km

Fiber optics are standard for interoffice trunks.

Fibers have become the standard transmission medium for regional telecommunications because they offer several important advantages over other media. Higher transmission speeds and longer transmission distances are at the top of the list today. Small size of fiber cables is a closely related advantage. As shown in Figure 22.5, ducts made to handle one thick metal cable can carry four smaller-diameter fiber cables, each with much more capacity than a metal cable. This can save phone companies the large costs of digging up urban streets to install new ducts. Fiber cables also are much less vulnerable to water damage than metal cables and are immune to power surges and electromagnetic interference.

The choice among cable types depends on the environment. Rural cables normally are strung on overhead utilities or buried directly by trenching into the ground. (Buried cables must be armored in regions where gophers live.) In urban areas, the cables may also be installed in buried utility ducts. Nonmetallic cables are used in lightning-prone areas; although the fibers don't carry current surges, any metal elements in the cable can carry surges that damage terminal equipment.

Electric utilities have built regional fiber-optic networks both to control and monitor their own networks and to capitalize on their rights of way by offering telecommunication services. They often install fibers in special ground wires for high-voltage power lines, such as one shown in Figure 22.6. The outer metal part of the cable serves as a ground wire. The fibers at the core of the cable are unaffected by high electric fields associated with power transmission. Adding the fibers to the core of the metal cable increases cost only a modest amount but adds the important capacity to transmit signals optically.

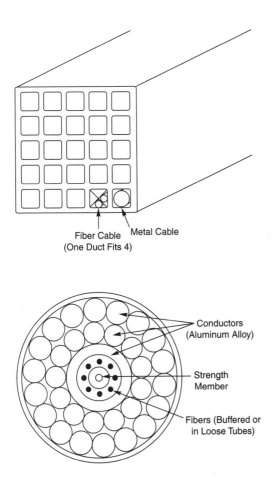

Fiber Cable
(One Duct Fits 4)
Metal Cable

FIGURE 22.5

Hollow plastic ducts can house more fiber cables than metal cables.

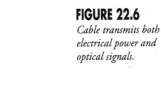

Conductors
(Aluminum Alloy)

Strength
Member

Fibers (Buffered or
in Loose Tubes)

FIGURE 22.6

Cable transmits both electrical power and optical signals.

Regional Switching Centers

Regional switching centers are the places where local telephone companies deliver signals to long-distance carriers. Typically these are in or near major population centers. The long-distance carriers pick up outgoing signals and drop off incoming signals for that region. Trunk lines feed into regional switching centers from local switching offices, either directly or through intermediate switching centers.

In addition to switching signals, regional centers concentrate signals, combining them where necessary to generate higher-speed signals for long-distance transmission.

Types of Regional Carriers

There are multiple networks for regional transmission as well as for long-distance transmission. However, most of us don't see them because they offer their services primarily to large businesses that generate large volumes of traffic. These often are called *bypass* systems because they bypass the regional telephone network. You can think of them as alternatives to your regional telephone company, although they generally are not interested in doing business with individuals.

A few companies have begun to compete with local phone companies for individual customers. They are essentially alternatives to the telephone company that has traditionally operated as a local monopoly in your area. Some have their own networks, but often they merely lease transmission capacity from the older phone companies under terms set by state and local regulators.

Network Operation

The telecommunications network continues to function as a single entity, although deregulation and competition have split it into a sometimes bewildering array of companies with various responsibilities. Let's put the pieces together for a brief review of the bigger picture.

The Telephone Network

Figure 22.7 shows a simplified view of how telephone calls are switched for local and long-distance calls. Don't worry too much about the details of the subscriber loop, which is between your home and the switching office; you'll learn more about that in Chapter 24.

Local calls are inherently simple, because all the switching is done locally. If you call the local pizza parlor, the call goes from your home through a concentrator to the local switching office. There an electronic switch decodes the number you dialed and connects your line to the line going to the pizza parlor. If you wanted to call your dentist in the next town, your local switch would connect your line to the next town's switching center, which in turn would connect your line to your dentist's phone, at the bottom of the figure.

Suppose your neighbor wanted to call the Super Corporation on the other side of the country. Her call would go through the same concentrator as yours to the switching office. There, a switch would identify the call as long distance, identify her carrier (AT&T in the example), and switch her call to the AT&T long-distance lines. Her call may go through a regional switching center, but that isn't shown in the diagram. AT&T lines would carry the call to a local switching office that serves Super Corporation, which would connect her line to the company's. If she dialed an incorrect digit, the switch might instead connect her to someone's home.

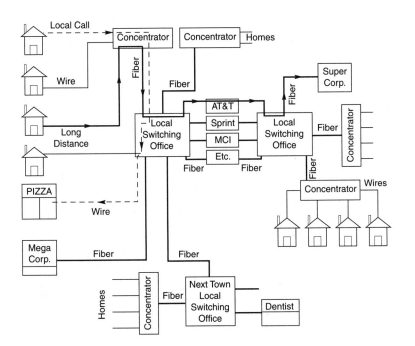

FIGURE 22.7

Switching telephone calls.

If your neighbor was sending a fax to the Super Corporation, her call would follow exactly the same path through the telephone network, but it would end up at a fax machine.

Internet Connections

The Internet makes connections in similar ways through multiple layers of networks. Figure 22.8 shows how it works.

Suppose you're sitting at home in Fort Worth and want to send e-mail to a friend working at the University of Texas in Arlington. Your modem dials your local Internet service provider and sends the message over local phone lines. The Internet provider sends the message over leased lines to an Internet node in Dallas, which routes it to the university's campus network, which routes it to your friend's computer on a local-area network. (Note that the signals are routed according to their address header rather than switched by connecting lines.)

Now suppose that your friend is trying to send e-mail to a geologist on a field trip to Tasmania. Her local-area network relays the message to the university network, which routes it to the Internet node in Dallas. The Internet router then sends the signal to Los Angeles over Internet lines, where another router packages it with signals going through a submarine cable to Australia. In Sydney, an Internet node reads the message header and routes the message to an Internet service in Tasmania, where the geologist set up an account. The geologist can reach the Internet service either using a cellular telephone modem from field camp or by borrowing a computer at a friend's home and calling over ordinary phone lines.

FIGURE 22.8

Routing e-mail over the Internet.

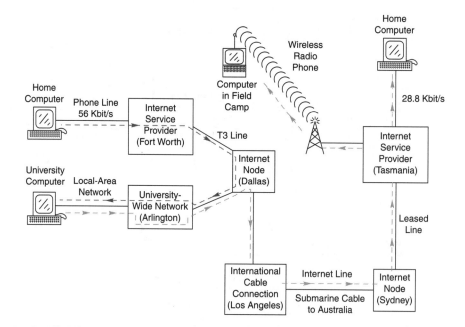

What Have You Learned?

1. National and regional telecommunications networks link many local (telephone) switching centers or (Internet) connection points.

2. Telecommunication networks collect signals locally, package them together, and direct them to their destinations. The Internet and the telephone system do this in different ways.

3. Parallel networks offer different services over the same area, sometimes using different fibers in the same cable.

4. Regional and national networks transmit digital signals. They are arranged in hierarchies that transmit signals at increasing speed the longer the distance.

5. Interoffice trunks connect telephone switching offices, which in turn connect to individual telephone subscribers.

6. Long-distance telecommunication systems on land are networks connecting many points; most submarine cables are point-to-point transmission links.

7. Terrestrial systems span up to several hundred kilometers, so their design requirements differ from those of submarine cables, which can be much longer.

8. The fastest long-distance terrestrial systems generally are faster than any operating submarine cable, because lead times are shorter for land systems and the technology is advancing rapidly.

9. Long-haul networks include the public switched telecommunications network (originally just telephones), the Internet, and private leased lines (data, voice, and/or other signals).

10. Regional telecommunication networks link local switching centers with each other and the long-distance network.

11. A switching office is the interface between the regional telecommunications network and the local loop of the telephone system. Interoffice trunks link switching offices with each other and with regional switching centers, where signals transfer to long-distance lines.

12. National and regional telephone systems differ in architecture from the Internet.

What's Next?

In Chapter 23, you will learn about video transmission and cable-television systems.

Quiz for Chapter 22

1. The long-distance telecommunications network includes
   a. the Internet.
   b. the public switched network that carries telephone traffic.
   c. lines leased to large corporations to carry their own signals.
   d. b and c.
   e. a, b, and c.

2. Telecommunication switches do which of the following?
   a. Create temporary paths between pairs of terminal devices.
   b. Route data packets to their destinations based on information in their headers.
   c. Turn telephone systems off and on.
   d. Turn light transmission in an optical fiber off and on.
   e. Use electro-mechanical relays to complete electrical circuits.

3. Routers do which of the following?
   a. Create temporary paths between pairs of terminal devices.
   b. Route data packets to their destinations based on information in their headers.
   c. Turn telephone systems off and on.
   d. Turn light transmission in an optical fiber off and on.

e. Use electro-mechanical relays to complete electrical circuits.

4. What are the longest distances that terrestrial long-distance cables normally span?

a. 150 km.

b. Several hundred km.

c. Coast-to-coast across North America.

d. 10,000 km.

e. The circumference of the earth.

5. Local switching offices connect with which of the following? (More than one answer is possible.)

a. Regional telecommunication systems.

b. Telephone lines to individual homes and businesses.

c. Intercontinental submarine cables.

d. Other nearby local switching offices.

6. 1300-nm single-mode fiber-optic systems

a. were never installed in national or regional telecommunication systems.

b. are still used for long-distance transmission but are being replaced for regional transmission.

c. are being upgraded for WDM transmission near

1550 nm on backbone systems.

d. are incompatible with Internet routers.

e. are replacing 1550 nm systems used for interoffice trunks.

7. Which of the following is a major difference between Internet transmission and long-distance telecommunications?

a. Internet data are transmitted only at 1550 nm; telephone signals are transmitted only at 1300 nm.

b. Internet signals are transmitted digitally; the telephone network is analog.

c. Routers direct Internet data packets; switches make telephone connections.

d. Switches direct Internet data packets; routers make telephone connections.

e. There are no significant differences.

8. Advantages of fiber optics for national and regional telecommunication systems include

a. fiber cables that are smaller than copper, so more can fit in existing ducts.

b. higher transmission capacity.

c. digital transmission.

d. less vulnerable to lightning strikes.

e. all the above.

9. Telephone calls are directed to other phones within your local community by

  a. regional switching centers.

  b. long-distance carriers.

  c. Internet routers.

  d. local switching offices.

  e. all the above.

10. You try to call a friend whose area code has just changed to 456 and get a recording saying that the number 456-xxxx in your area code is not a working number. What went wrong?

  a. Hackers got into an Internet router.

  b. Your long-distance service was shut off because you forgot to pay your long-distance bill.

  c. Your local switching office was not reprogrammed for the new area code.

  d. You cannot dial an area code if those three digits are assigned as a telephone exchange in your area code.

  e. Your long-distance carrier did not program its switch for the new area code.

Video Transmission

About This Chapter

Video transmission technology is in a state of flux. Traditionally, video signals have been in analog format and have been transmitted separately from voice and digital data. Now the industry is attempting to switch to digital video systems, known variously as advanced television (ATV), digital television (DTV) and high-definition television (HDTV). In this chapter, I will cover the basics of video transmission, concentrating on fiber-optic applications, particularly in cable television. As you will see later in this chapter and in Chapter 24, the old distinctions between cable television and the local telephone network are fading.

Video Basics

Video transmission is more complex than sending voice or data signals. Old-fashioned analog voice telephones simply convert the continuous variations in sound intensity of your voice into continuous variations in an electrical signal. Digital systems translate this time-varying signal into a series of 1s and 0s that correspond to the binary data. Video signals must encode continually changing pictures and sound, and that gets complicated.

Video images are based on the principle of raster scanning. Look closely at a television screen, and you find that the pictures consist of many parallel lines, with the intensity varying along the line. The signals are transmitted point by point along the line, with one line following the next. In a simple black-and-white set with an old-fashioned picture tube, an electron beam scans one line after the next, its intensity varying with the brightness of each point recorded

●
Video signals encode continually changing pictures and sound.

by the television camera. Color picture tubes write the three primary colors, red, green, and blue, with three separate electron beams, but otherwise the principle is the same.

Video signals carry the information needed to draw these lines. You can think of them as recording the intensity of the original scene point by point, so the same image is reconstructed on the picture tube. The signal encodes brightness and color of each point and the accompanying sound. The way the signal carries that information depends on the encoding format. Traditional formats were analog, but new digital standards have been developed that will require new transmission equipment. As you will soon learn, the wide variety of possible formats can create many complications.

Video-Transmission Requirements

●
Video requires much more transmission capacity than sound or equivalent digital data.

Video requires much more transmission capacity than telephone sound or equivalent digital data. It's often said that one picture equals a thousand words, but Table 23.1 shows that the picture requires considerably more transmission capacity than 1,000 words of written text. Sophisticated digital compression can reduce data rates by factors of 10 to 60 for video transmission, but they depend on transmitting a series of pictures, so single images cannot be compressed as much. Note that the spoken word is much less efficient when converted into digitized sound.

Table 23.1 Comparison of approximate video, voice, and text transmission requirements.

Transmission	Analog Equivalent	Digital Equivalent (No Compression)	Digital Equivalent (Compressed)
Standard U.S. analog television (NTSC)	6.3 MHz	100 Mbit/s	2–10 Mbit/s
HDTV (U.S. format)	About 100 MHz	1.2 Gbit/s	20 Mbit/s
Voice telephone	4 kHz	56 kbit/s	About 10 kbit/s
One standard TV video frame		3.3 Mbits	
One HDTV video frame (1/60 s)		About 20 Mbits	
1000 spoken words (5 min on phone)		20 Mbits	
1000-word text file		60 kbits	

You can appreciate what these differences mean if you use a 28.8-kbit/s modem to access the World Wide Web with your personal computer. A page of pure text loads quickly. A page with a fair-sized static image may take a minute. And you know you've hit the World Wide Wait when you find a page with a video clip that takes many minutes to download, even though the image is small and the sequence lasts less than a minute. You don't find speech much on the Web, because digitized audio files also are large.

Transmission Standards

Video signals are transmitted in standardized formats so transmitters can talk to receivers. These formats have evolved for historical reasons and are often not ideal. One difference in analog video formats is the number of frames per second, originally chosen to be half the different frequencies used for alternating current (60 Hz in North America and 50 Hz in Europe). The North American standard for broadcast color television was chosen to be compatible with older black-and-white receivers, because broadcasters did not want to lose that audience.

New standards are emerging for digital television. The original goal was higher screen resolution, or high-definition television (HDTV), but the standards were broadened to cover *advanced television* (ATV), for sets with smaller screens. The technology comes in part from high-resolution computer monitors. Importantly, the digital standard signals are *not* compatible with existing analog television sets, which will require adapters when television broadcasters shift completely to digital television.

Other video standards also are in use, such as those for computer monitors, but I will concentrate mostly on television standards.

Standard Broadcast Analog Video

The present analog standard for broadcast television programs in North America is the NTSC format, from the National Television System Committee. The analog signals carry information representing the lines that compose the screen images. Pictures are displayed as 525-line frames (although a few lines do not actually show up on the screen). Nominally, NTSC shows 30 frames a second, but to keep the image from flickering to the eye, NTSC uses an interlaced scanning technique. First it scans odd lines on the display, then the even lines, then the odd lines again, as shown in Figure 23.1. Technically, this interlaced scan displays 60 half-images (called fields) a second, with only 267 lines of resolution each, but this fools the eye, giving the appearance of high resolution while avoiding the flicker of slower scanning speeds.

Nominally, the NTSC video bandwidth is 4.2 MHz, with the sound carrier at a higher frequency. However, for broadcast the video signal is used to modulate a radio-frequency signal, a process that increases overall bandwidth to 6 MHz, which is the amount of radio-frequency spectrum allocated to each broadcast television channel in the United States. Figure 23.2 shows the structure of this signal, which extends from 1.25 MHz below the

Video is transmitted in standardized formats.

NTSC video displays 30 analog 525-line frames a second.

carrier frequency to 4.75 MHz above the carrier. The NTSC format is used in North America, Japan, Korea, the Philippines, and much of South America.

FIGURE 23.1

Interlaced and progressive scanning.

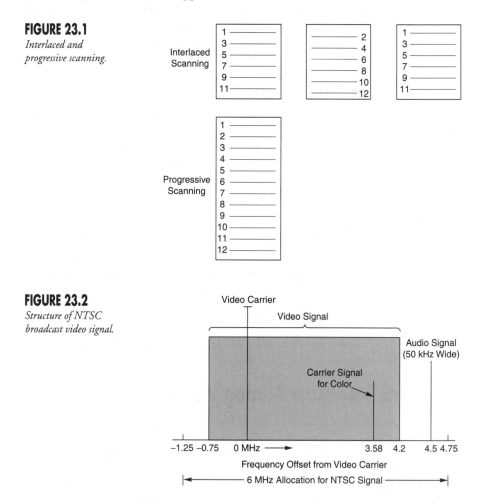

FIGURE 23.2

Structure of NTSC broadcast video signal.

Two other broadcast television standards are in wide use: PAL and SECAM. Both are interlaced scanning systems that show 25 frames (50 fields) per second, each frame with 625 lines. These have nominal video bandwidth of 5 to 6 MHz and broadcast channel bandwidth of about 8 MHz. PAL and SECAM systems are used in Europe, mainland Asia, Africa, and parts of South America.

> PAL and SECAM are interlaced scanning systems showing 25 frames of 625 lines each per second.

These standards were set for television broadcasting from ground-based transmitters. National and international standards set aside specific frequencies for television broadcasting, with each channel allocated the required bandwidth (6 MHz for NTSC channels). These standards have come into wide use for other types of video because NTSC, PAL, and SECAM equipment is readily available.

Remember that broadcast video standards were established decades ago, when color television came on the market. (The NTSC standard was a modified version of the original North American standard for black-and-white television, which goes back to 1948.) This means that these standards were developed to deal with the limitations of the vacuum-tube technology available in the electronic stone age.

Standard video formats are decades old.

Computer Displays and Video Formats

It might seem logical to use standard television displays for computers, but the two technologies are not readily compatible. Television sets are adequate displays for computer-based video games, and sufficed for some early personal computers. However, text displayed on a screen does not show up well with interlaced scanning, because the interlacing effectively mixes information from successive frames for part of the time. The best displays for computers use progressive scanning, in which all lines are scanned one at a time, then the entire screen is rescanned, shown in Figure 23.1.

Computer displays require progressive scanning to show text clearly, not NTSC format.

Progressive scanning demands more bandwidth and faster electronics than interlaced scanning, because it transmits 60 (or sometimes more) complete frames a second to avoid flicker, compared to the 60 fields (or half-frames) for NTSC video. The benefit is higher resolution than interlaced scanning.

Multimedia or interactive video displays are hybrids, based on a combination of computer and television technologies. At this writing, they don't have their own special display standards; those that play on computers use computer formats, those played on television sets use television formats. The American HDTV standard allows both progressive and interlaced scanning.

Digitized Video and Compression

Like voice signals, video can be digitized. The raw data rate is considerably higher than the corresponding analog bandwidth, as shown in Table 23.1. However, raw image data contains much redundant information, and suitable software can compress it to occupy less space.

Advanced television systems will use compressed digital video.

Some compression is possible with all files, by software that recognizes long strings of identical bits or bytes and replaces them with shorter codes containing the same information (e.g., a code indicating that the next 20 digits are 1s). However, only limited compression is possible for a single image or data file. Video signals that contain a series of images can be compressed much more efficiently by using other techniques that transmit the changes between images rather than an entire new image. Most images do not change completely between frames, so it takes much less information to convey the changes than to send a whole new image.

Impressive progress has been made in video compression, and the American HDTV standard assumes that transmitted signals will be compressed from the raw 1.2 Gbit/s to about 19 Mbit/s, which can fit into the 6-MHz bandwidth allocated for broadcast video. Compression inevitably degrades the signal slightly, with the damage depending on the extent of compression and the type of signal. Compression works best for images that change little between frames, such as videoconferences or news broadcasts showing talking heads. Rapid motion and changing scenes, such as in broadcasts of sports, are the hardest.

Studios expect to use various levels of compression at different stages of production, as shown in Table 23.2. Video producers try to maintain the highest possible quality during production but accept lower quality for transmission. In addition, they must avoid compression techniques that depend on a sequence of frames, because editing could change the sequence.

Table 23.2 Compression levels proposed for HDTV in a video studio.

Task	Compression Ratio
Video production	4:1
Archival storage	25:1
Transmission	60:1

High-Definition Television (HDTV)

HDTV will greatly increase resolution for large-screen sets.

Since the 1980s, the electronics industry has been pressing for a new generation of television technology. Their goal is to offer larger, wider images of much better quality and—not incidentally—to make more money by selling a new and more expensive generation of large-screen television sets. After initially proposing an analog standard, the industry switched to a digital standard, which the Federal Communications Commission accepted in the United States. Canada, South Korea, and some other countries are adopting the American standard. European countries have developed their own standard, based on similar ideas. (Japan developed an analog HDTV system called MUSE, which found limited use in video production but seems likely to be replaced by digital systems.)

Officially, the standard is known as the Digital Television (DTV) standard of the Advanced Television Systems Committee. It includes 18 distinct digital video formats, with different numbers of scan lines and screens per second. Six are classed as high definition, and the other 12 are standard definition television (SDTV), which offers somewhat better image quality than NTSC analog television. The HDTV formats are intended for large-screen sets; the SDTV formats are for smaller screens. Table 23.3 lists these formats.

Table 23.3 Advanced television digital formats.

Picture Size (Lines High by Pixels Long)	Frames per Second	Aspect Ratio
1080 × 1920 (HDTV)	60 interlaced 30 progressive 24 progressive	16:9 (wide-screen)
720 × 1280 (HDTV)	60 progressive 30 progressive 24 progressive	16:9 (wide-screen)
480 × 704 (SDTV)	60 interlaced 60 progressive 30 progressive 24 progressive	16:9 (wide-screen) 4:3 (conventional)
480 × 640 (SDTV)	60 interlaced 60 progressive 30 progressive 24 progressive	4:3 (conventional)

This long list of formats represents the type of compromise committees arrive at. Stations will not transmit different signals simultaneously in each of these formats. Instead, they will transmit a single compressed digital signal, which digital electronics in new sets can interpret to produce displays in any of these formats.

The compromise gives something for almost everyone in the industry. The television industry retains some interlaced scanning, at twice the screen rate of present televisions (60 interlaced screens per second rather than 30). The computer industry gets progressive scanning at lower speeds and also at some higher speeds. The standard supports the big wide-screen sets the electronics industry would love to sell, as well as smaller conventional-width screens on less costly sets.

The government agreed to give every television broadcaster a new broadcast channel for digital television transmission—on the condition that they return their present analog channel to the Federal Communications Commission starting in 2006. When analog transmission stops, existing analog sets will become useless without digital converters.

Although the standard has been adopted officially, it remains to be seen how television broadcasters will implement it. Many broadcasters are more interested in using their

Digital television supports several screen formats with various levels of resolution.

digital channels to transmit multiple standard-definition digital video signals; about five will fit on one existing 6-MHz channel.

Transmission Media

So far I haven't said much about how video signals are distributed. Although our main interest is fiber optics, you should understand other important transmission media: ground-level broadcast at radio frequencies, satellite broadcast at microwave frequencies, and coaxial cables.

Terrestrial Broadcast

Television began as a broadcast medium, with radio-frequency signals transmitted from tall antennas. NTSC, PAL, and SECAM standards were all based on the assumption that signals were broadcast from terrestrial towers to receivers, which could be tens of miles away, depending on frequency, power, antenna height, and local obstacles. Stations are allocated specific frequency channels for their broadcasts in a given area; those frequencies may also be used by other stations outside their broadcast range.

The American HDTV standard is also designed for terrestrial broadcast in a 6-MHz frequency channel. HDTV channels are in the same block of frequencies used by NTSC stations, but their broadcast areas do not overlap. HDTV signals are not supposed to interfere with NTSC signals.

Direct Broadcast Satellites

A direct broadcast satellite is essentially a television transmitter located in geosynchronous orbit, so it stays in place above the same point on the equator as the earth rotates. From the ground, it looks like a stationary satellite, so it can broadcast signals over a large area on the ground. The signals are transmitted at microwave frequencies (above 1 GHz) to dish-shaped antennas on the ground aimed at the satellite. As satellites have moved to transmitting at higher microwave frequencies, satellite dishes have become smaller. Satellite signals generally are encrypted, so you need special decoding electronics to view them.

Direct broadcast satellites essentially compete with cable television systems by offering a broad choice of national channels. Unlike cable systems, they don't carry local channels and do not offer two-way services such as cable modems. However, satellites can inexpensively serve large areas because no expensive cable plant is needed. This makes satellite broadcast particularly attractive in rural areas where cable is impractically expensive. Satellite services are now available in urban areas as well, where they offer premium channels. Some direct-broadcast satellites transmit digital signals, but they have not begun transmitting in HDTV format—and HDTV receivers are not yet on the market.

● Television began with radio broadcasts from local stations on the ground.

● Satellites can broadcast signals over large areas from space using microwaves.

Cable Television

Cable television began as community antenna television (CATV, an acronym still used by the industry) to serve areas not normally reached by broadcast television signals. The idea was to build one big antenna to pick up remote broadcasts and then distribute the signals via coaxial cables to local homes. Eventually the concept spread to urban and suburban areas where broadcast quality was better, but the choices were limited. Economics and interference limit the number of broadcast channels in a metropolitan area, but cable systems can pick up many more channels (from satellites and distant stations) and distribute them to homes along with signals from local stations. Cable systems can also offer extra-cost "premium" services to customers who rent special decoders. (The signals are scrambled and sent to all subscribers, but only those who pay the premium for the decoders can unscramble them.) Existing cable television systems serve essentially the same function as broadcast television—they distribute the same signals to everyone.

Present cable systems carry analog video signals in NTSC format. Each channel is assigned a frequency slot and signals are multiplexed together for transmission over the cable. Typical cable systems carry dozens of 6-MHz channels, but some new ones can carry up to 100. The signals are carried through fiber and coaxial cables at a broad range of radio frequencies to about 750 MHz. Set-top cable boxes demultiplex the signals, picking out the one selected by the viewer.

Cable systems have evolved considerably in the past several years. Many now have some capability to transmit signals from as well as to homes; some offer digital data transmission, as I will explain later in this chapter. However, it remains to be seen how cable systems will handle HDTV signals.

Fiber optics has come to play an important role in cable television, and that role is likely to expand as systems continue to evolve. To help you understand the importance of fiber, I will first look at traditional cable systems, then describe new cable technology.

> Cable TV systems carry dozens of analog video signals on fiber and coaxial cable.

The Present Cable Network

Cable-television networks traditionally have been designed to do different things than local telephone systems. Cable systems were built to distribute the same high-bandwidth signals to all subscribers. In that, they serve the same function as broadcasters. Although they don't advertise the fact, they actually distribute even their premium channels to all cable subscribers—but they scramble the premium channels electronically. Only subscribers who pay for the premium channels get set-top boxes with the electronics needed to decode the signals. This is a different function than telephone networks, which switch low-bandwidth signals to individual subscribers. Unless you're one of the last people with a party phone line, your telephone signals go only to your home, not to your neighbors.

Traditional Cable Architecture

Figure 23.3 shows the traditional architecture for cable television systems. Signals from satellites and television stations are collected at a control center or head-end, which functions as the heart of the system. The head-end may connect with other cable networks in the area, reflecting the growing integration of cable companies. The head-end combines video signals from various sources and sends them to regional hubs, which distribute them to distribution nodes and then to homes. The number of levels depends on the size of the community served.

FIGURE 23.3

A traditional cable television system.

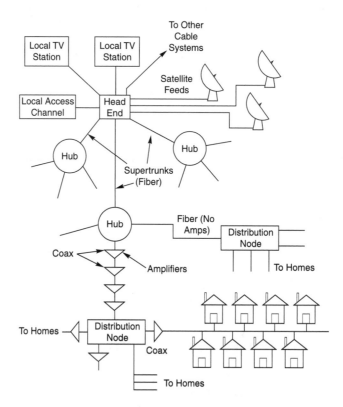

Fiber-optic links are used as supertrunks between head ends and distribution hubs.

The links between cable head-ends and hubs are called supertrunks. They must carry 30 to 100 video channels from a cable system head-end to remote points many kilometers away, from which signals are distributed to subscribers. A key requirement is that signal-to-noise ratio at the output be at least 53 dB to ensure that signal quality is adequate when it reaches subscribers. Early cable systems used coaxial cables or terrestrial microwave towers to send signals across such distances. However, those systems were comparatively noisy, a problem for cable television systems trying to market better transmission quality than broadcast stations. Coaxial cable systems also required many amplifiers or repeaters—one about every 0.5 to 0.6 km (0.3 to 0.4 mi)—and failure of any one of those repeaters could knock out the whole system. Optical fibers offered ways around those problems, and by the late 1980s, fibers had become standard for supertrunks. Typically the signals are divided among multiple fibers in a single cable sheath.

A critical technical development came at about the same time. Practical distributed-feedback lasers reached the market, and their prices began dropping. This was vital because cable television requires analog transmission, which is inherently sensitive to laser noise. The more controlled emission from distributed-feedback lasers reduced noise and made system response more linear, greatly improving analog video transmission quality, without a huge price premium.

> Distributed-feedback lasers give analog fiber systems a linear response.

High-quality analog fiber systems soon began spreading further into the cable distribution network shown in Figure 23.3, replacing coaxial cables between hubs and distribution nodes. For cable companies, the big improvement was eliminating long chains of amplifiers between the hub and the distribution node, which caused noise and made the system prone to failure. Newer cable systems now have fibers running out to each node, serving between 500 and 2000 households.

Cable Evolution

Older analog cable systems carry signals at frequencies between 400 and 550 MHz. As cable companies expand their capacity, they are adding digital channels at higher frequencies, up to about 750 MHz, to take advantage of new capacity added by the expansion of fiber links.

Older cable systems do not carry signals at the low end of the spectrum, at frequencies below about 50 MHz. Those frequencies can carry return signals, originated in the subscriber's home, to offer additional services.

> Digital signals are being added to existing cable systems at higher frequencies.

Hybrid Fiber/Coax (HFC)

The spread of fiber in the cable-TV network has led to an architecture called hybrid fiber/coax (HFC), built around both fiber and coaxial cable. As in older cable networks, fiber carries signals from the head-end toward the subscriber. However, in hybrid fiber/coax, fiber runs all the way to an optical node, relatively near to subscribers, where an optical-to-electronic interface transfers the signals to coaxial cables running to homes, as shown in Figure 23.4.

Look closely and you can see some significant differences between this and the older cable system of Figure 23.3. There are no regional hubs in hybrid fiber/coax, and the only coaxial amplifiers are on long cable runs between the optical node and the most distant subscribers. Fiber runs all the way to the optical nodes, each of which serves about 500 subscribers via coax. Note also that the hybrid fiber/coax design provides a return path for signals from homes. This is critical, because one purpose of hybrid fiber/coax is to transmit data and telephone signals as well as video.

FIGURE 23.4

Hybrid fiber/coax network.

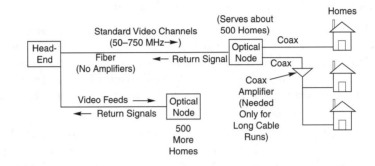

Hybrid fiber/coax systems divide their transmission bandwidth into four segments, shown in Figure 23.5. Frequencies of 5 to 42 MHz are allocated for "upstream" signals from the subscriber, including video, data and telephone traffic. These frequencies are below those normally used for television broadcast or video on cable. Standard analog NTSC video is transmitted at 50 to 550 MHz, the same frequencies used for that service on traditional cable-TV networks. Frequencies from 550 to 750 MHz are used for "downstream" digital signals to subscribers, including voice, video, and data. The space above 750 MHz is reserved for future two-way services, as yet undefined. System bandwidth should extend beyond 1 GHz.

FIGURE 23.5

Frequency allocation in hybrid fiber/coax.

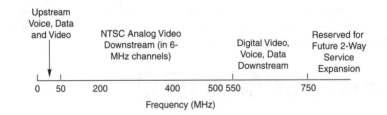

You can think of hybrid fiber/coax as a system that delivers signals to a neighborhood over fiber and then distributes them within the neighborhood over coaxial cable. This design is intended to take advantage of the best features of both fiber and coaxial cable. Fiber offers high-quality, low-loss, wideband transmission to the neighborhood. That doesn't cost too much, because many homes share the cost of the fiber link. It retains existing coaxial cables from the optical node to homes, avoiding the high cost of installing new fiber cable and optical equipment in every home. It also offers a logical path for system growth by running fiber cables from neighborhood nodes to smaller nodes that would serve clusters of less than 500 homes, taking fiber to each block rather than just to the neighborhood.

New Services on Hybrid Fiber/Coax

One service made possible by hybrid fiber/coax is data transmission through cable modems. A radio-frequency carrier transmits data over a 6-MHz channel set aside for digital data, with total capacity typically 10 to 30 Mbit/s. This channel circulates data among terminals—cable modems in individual homes—and delivers it only to the one terminal that has requested it. In this way, it functions like a local area network (LAN) in an office, a technology you will learn about in Chapter 25.

Like office LANs, cable modems can carry data all the time, without tying up a phone line. They also operate at much higher speeds, as long as other terminals don't tie up the network. Cable companies promote them for high-speed Internet access, and often cable modems work quite well for this purpose. However, as with office LANs, installation can be complex, and speeds can be limited by the interface with the terminal. In addition, Internet access speeds often are limited by traffic jams at other points in the Internet, not merely by your modem speed. (You can see this if your telephone modem has indicators that light up during data transfer. If they're on or flickering rapidly, your modem is working as fast as it can. If they're off, the modem is waiting for some other part of the network to deliver data.)

Another possible extension of hybrid fiber/coax is voice telephone service, putting the cable company into direct competition with the local phone company. However, few cable companies have taken this step yet.

Cable companies have talked about other possible services, but most have been demonstrated only in small test systems rather than offered widely. One is near video on demand, which would transmit a premium movie simultaneously on several channels with staggered starting times. For example, the show might start at 8:00 P.M. on one channel, 8:15 on a second, 8:30 on a third, and 8:45 on a fourth. With enough digital channels, cable companies could provide video on demand, allowing individual users to request specific programs from an online video library at times they select.

Upgraded versions of the local telephone network also could offer many of these services, as you will learn in Chapter 24.

Architecture of Hybrid Fiber/Coax

Hybrid fiber/coax systems use single-mode fiber and lasers at either 1310 or 1550 nm. They retain the essential design of the cable-TV network, which distributes signals to all subscribers rather than switching them to individual lines like the telephone network. This is true even for services nominally delivered only to one subscriber; as in a local-area network, the signal physically passes through the whole network, but only the person who requested it receives that signal. Others don't know it's there.

One attraction of this architecture is that a single powerful laser source can produce optical signals for distribution to multiple nodes, significantly reducing transmitter

Hybrid fiber/coax supports telephone and Internet services.

A single powerful laser transmitter can serve multiple HFC optical nodes.

costs. In this case, the laser output is split among the fibers delivered to separate nodes, each of which receives the same signal. As long as there are extra channels available at the high-frequency end, separate channels can be dedicated to each node for signals transmitted to individual users, such as data and telephone service. For example, if a single laser served 10 nodes and had optional channels 1–20 in the 550–750-MHz band, channels 1 and 2 would be directed to node 1, channels 3 and 4 to node 2, and so on. Each node would receive signals for all nodes but would ignore those intended for other nodes.

If data traffic increased, requiring more capacity, the system could add more channels if they were available, so each optical node would receive 4 data channels. Or the operator could install a second transmitter and modulate it with a separate set of signals on high-frequency channels 1–20. Likewise, optical nodes could be split, dividing them into subnodes, each serving a smaller number of homes, with the optical signals divided among the smaller nodes, which in turn would distribute signals to individual homes.

The optical nodes also include transmitters to relay signals from subscribers back to the head end—vital for Internet and telephone service. Nominally these return signals are sent in the low-frequency band at 5 to 42 MHz, an approach originally devised for two-way transmission on coaxial cable. However, as long as the optical signals are transmitted on separate fibers—or at separate wavelengths on the same fiber—there is no reason signals can't be transmitted at higher frequencies. Suppose, for example, that traffic had grown to a point where an optical node needed more capacity. It could be split into four subnodes serving homes with coaxial cables, as shown in Figure 23.6. The coax would return signals at 5 to 42 MHz from each group of homes, but those from one group would be kept at the base band, those from a second group would be shifted up 50 MHz, those from a third shifted up 100 MHz, and those from a fourth shifted up 150 MHz, generating a composite signal to modulate the transmitter in the optical node at 0 to 200 MHz. The receiver could shift the frequencies back to their original level or convert the signals into other forms for processing.

Impact of New Television Formats

New digital television standards inevitably will affect cable television, although the rules and transmission format have yet to be determined.

The most direct approach is to replace analog channels with digital transmission over the same 6-MHz bands and to install a new generation of digital set-top boxes to process the signals in homes. As a practical matter, new set-top boxes will need both analog and digital feeds to televisions, because new digital sets will not instantly replace old analog sets. There inevitably will be a mixture of sets in use, with digital sets initially few and far between—but owned by the most attractive customers, those eager to pay substantial sums for new entertainment technology. On the other hand, cable companies cannot afford to snub their existing customers with analog sets.

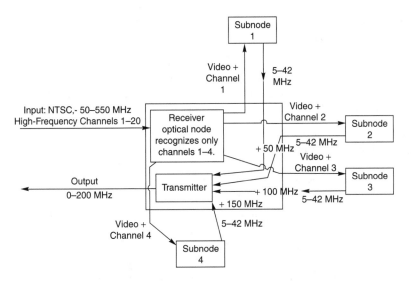

FIGURE 23.6
Optical node with four subnodes.

Other Video Applications

Cable television is the largest-volume video application for fiber optics, but there are many other cases where fiber is used for video transmission. Table 23.4 lists a sampling of important applications, with brief descriptions. Most involve point-to-point transmission.

Small, light, and durable fiber cables are valuable for portable systems.

Table 23.4 Other video-transmission applications for fiber optics.

Application	Requirements	Special notes
Electronic news gathering, special-event coverage	Light, durable cable to link mobile camera to fixed equipment	Camcorder an alternative
Security video	Vary; low cost important	Often low resolution
Studio and production transmission	High-quality link inside studio	
Feeds to and from remote equipment (e.g., antennas)	High transmission quality	

Transmission requirements vary widely for these systems. Although many require high transmission quality, security video systems must be low in cost. Although metal cables can do many of these jobs, fibers offer benefits of lighter weight, smaller size, higher signal quality, longer transmission distances, immunity to electromagnetic interference, better durability, and avoidance of ground loops and potential differences.

Small, light, and flexible, fiber cables offer important benefits where portability is important, such as in remote news gathering and when covering special events. Many systems use rugged cables and connectors developed to meet rigid military specifications for durability. Any time cables are strung anywhere, they are vulnerable to damage.

Fiber transmission also offers more subtle advantages, notably avoiding the need to adjust transmission equipment to account for differences in cable length. Television studio amplifiers are designed to drive coaxial cables with nominal impedance of 75 Ω. However, actual impedance of coaxial cables is a function of length. As cable length increases, so does its capacitance, degrading high-frequency response if the cable is longer than 15–30 m (50–100 ft). Boosting the high-frequency signal, a process called equalization, can compensate for this degradation, but proper equalization requires knowing the cable's length and attenuation characteristics. Compensation also becomes harder with cable lengths over 300 m (1000 ft) and is impractical for cables longer than about 900 m (3000 ft). There is no analogous effect in optical fibers, so operators need not worry about cable length.

What Have You Learned?

1. Video signals encode continually changing pictures and sound. They are transmitted in standard formats and require considerably more capacity than voice or digital data.

2. Analog NTSC video displays 30 analog 525-line frames a second with interlaced scanning. Each NTSC channel requires 6 MHz of broadcast spectrum. PAL and SECAM are interlaced scanning systems that each second show 25 analog frames of 625 lines each. These formats are decades old.

3. Computer displays need progressive scanning to show text clearly, not the interlaced scanning of NTSC, PAL, or SECAM. Progressive scanning demands more bandwidth and faster electronics.

4. Digitized video signals can be compressed by up to a factor of 60 without seriously degrading quality.

5. Digital television standards cover both high-definition (HDTV) and standard-definition (SDTV) video in 18 distinct formats. The HDTV formats have 720 or 1080 lines and a wide-screen format.

6. Digital television broadcasting is being phased in to replace analog broadcasts in the United States.

7. Video signals can be broadcast from a ground station to serve a local area. Microwave transmission from direct broadcast satellites can serve a much larger area; customers need satellite dishes and converters.

8. Modern cable television systems now carry dozens of analog NTSC video channels over fiber-optic and coaxial cables; the fiber runs from the head end to distribution points or optical nodes. Coaxial cables run from those points to homes. Customers need set-top converters to access premium channels.

9. Hybrid fiber/coax systems transmit NTSC video to subscribers at 50 to 550 MHz. Digital services are transmitted to optical nodes at 550 to 750 MHz, and signals from subscribers return at 5 to 42 MHz. Each optical node serves about 500 homes.

10. Hybrid fiber/coax can deliver services including Internet connections, telephony, and special subscription video services. Internet connections via cable modem work like local-area networks.

11. Hybrid fiber/coax can be upgraded by splitting optical nodes to serve fewer subscribers.

12. Video transmission generally is over single-mode fiber at 1300 or 1550 nm.

13. Small, lightweight fiber cables are valuable for portable news gathering and sports event coverage.

What's Next?

In Chapter 24, you will learn about the role of fiber optics in telephone service to homes and how that role is changing with new technology and competition from cable companies.

Quiz for Chapter 23

1. What is analog bandwidth of one standard NTSC television channel?

   a. 56 kHz.

   b. 1 MHz.

   c. 6.3 MHz.

   d. 25 MHz.

2. How many lines per frame do standard analog European television stations show, and how many full frames are shown per second?

   a. 525 lines, 25 frames per second.

   b. 625 lines, 25 frames per second.

   c. 625 lines, 30 frames per second.

   d. 1125 lines, 25 frames per second.

3. The HDTV standard in the U.S. transmits about 20 Mbit/s after digital compression. How much compression is used, and what would the data rate be without it?

   a. 3-to-1 compression, 90 MHz.

   b. 10-to-1 compression, 200 Mbit/s.

c. 60-to-1 compression, 1200 Mbit/s.

d. None of the above.

4. What key development made the quality of analog fiber-optic transmission adequate for cable television trunks?

a. Highly linear distributed-feedback lasers.

b. Inexpensive single-mode fiber.

c. Dispersion-shifted fiber.

d. Digital video compression.

e. Optical amplifiers for 1550 nm systems.

5. What is the most important advantage of fiber optics over coax for distributing cable television signals from head-ends to optical nodes.

a. Fiber optics are hard to tap, so they reduce signal piracy.

b. Fiber repeater spacing is much longer, avoiding noise and reliability problems with coax amplifiers.

c. Fiber can be extended all the way to subscribers.

d. Fiber cables are less likely to break.

6. How are video signals distributed to subscribers on present cable television systems?

a. All subscribers receive the same signals, which require set-top decoders to show premium services.

b. Signals from set-top controls are used to switch designed signals to the home.

c. Equipment at the head end switches selected services to each subscriber.

d. One pair of optical fibers runs directly from head end to home.

7. What signal format is used by present cable television systems?

a. Each system has a proprietary format.

b. Analog NTSC signals, with 6 MHz bandwidth, assigned to radio frequencies between 50 and 550 MHz.

c. Digitized compressed video at 20 Mbit/s.

d. Analog PAL format in North America.

8. What frequencies are used for signals from the subscriber to the head end in hybrid fiber/coax?

a. 50–550 MHz.

b. 0–1 GHz.

c. 550–750 MHz.

d. 5–42 MHz.

e. None of the above.

9. How do cable modems work on hybrid fiber/coax networks?

a. They switch signals directly from the head end to individual subscribers.

b. They transmit signals in one direction only.

c. They function like a local-area network, addressing high-speed signals to one of many subscriber terminals served by the same network.

d. They digitize video images for videoconferencing but cannot be used for other purposes.

e. They are incompatible with hybrid fiber/coax.

10. How will cable television handle HDTV transmission?

a. Tear up its entire system to build a new all-digital network.

b. Encode digital signals for transmission at frequencies now used for NTSC video and convert them with new set-top boxes.

c. Transmit signals in present analog format and digitize them with new set-top boxes.

d. Ignore it because the standard does not specify cable transmission.

Local Telephone Networks

About This Chapter

The part of the telephone network most visible to all of us is the subscriber loop, the portion from your home or office phone to the local switching office described in Chapter 22. Like the cable-television system you learned about in Chapter 23, the local telephone network is evolving. In this chapter, you will learn where fibers already are used for local telephone service, where wires are used, and the advanced services made possible as fibers spread closer to homes and businesses. I'll close the chapter by looking a bit into the future, to new services envisioned by phone companies and suggestions for bringing fibers all the way to your home.

The Subscriber Loop

In telephone-industry jargon, the *subscriber loop* is the circuit that forms a loop from the switching office through your local phone lines and your phone back to the switching center. It began as a loop of wire, back in the days when switching was done by people plugging wires into switchboards. Since then it has evolved considerably as both technology and services have changed.

Structure of the Subscriber Loop

Figure 24.1 shows services radiating outward from a local telephone switching office. Large organizations, such as big companies or universities, have cables that connect directly to the switching center; generally these are fiber cables operating at the 45-Mbit/s T3 rate or above. If the switching office serves cellular phones, another fiber cable connects it to a local cellular antenna.

Individual phone lines run over copper wire pairs—two wires per phone circuit. Few individual phone lines run directly to the switching office. Generally they run to boxes called concentrators, placed on telephone poles, in manholes, or in small service boxes on the ground. Inside the concentrator, up to 24 individual phone lines feed into a multiplexer, which digitizes them and interleaves them to produce a 1.5-Mbit/s T1 signal. As the figure shows, these individual phone lines may include lines carrying fax and data signals as well as voices.

> The subscriber loop radiates outward from a telephone switching center.

FIGURE 24.1

The telephone subscriber loop.

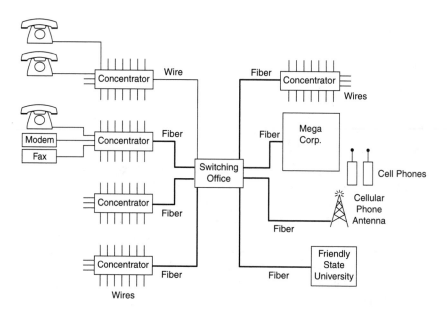

You can think of a concentrator as serving about a block of an ordinary suburban neighborhood, while a switching office serves an entire suburban town of 25,000 to 50,000 people, as well as local business and industry. Phone lines run from concentrators serve small businesses as well as homes, but larger businesses (or phone-intensive businesses such as an Internet service provider) usually have dedicated lines from the phone company.

Figure 24.1 doesn't show all services available today, such as ISDN, the Integrated Services Digital Network, a digital 144-kbit/s service that runs over copper-wire phone lines. Nor does it show other emerging digital services that also run over copper-wire pairs. These services are not widespread, and I'll describe them and their operating requirements later.

Copper and Fiber in the Subscriber Loop

As Figure 24.1 shows, the subscriber loop includes both fiber and copper wires. Fiber carries most signals at the T1 rate and above, although wires are used for some T1 transmission. The fiber cables may come into your neighborhood and often reach within a few blocks of your home. They may be installed in underground ducts, buried, or strung from overhead poles. At the concentrator, the signals are demultiplexed and transferred to copper cables, which run along overhead poles, run through underground ducts, or are buried underground.

In practice, the connection from your home phone to the switching office may go through two levels of concentration, as shown in Figure 24.2. The wires from your home phone go to a serving terminal, probably within a block of your door. Wires from several serving terminals go to a serving area interface in a concentrator somewhere in the neighborhood. The concentrator multiplexes the signals and transmits them to the switching office, usually over fibers. You can think of the different levels as your home, your block, your neighborhood, and your town.

Both optical fibers and copper wires are in the subscriber loop. Fibers usually carry signals between the switching office and neighborhood concentrators; wires carry signals between concentrators and phones.

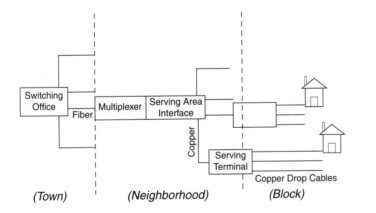

FIGURE 24.2

Path of phone signals between home and central office.

Although the figure shows the wires as separate, they typically are combined in a single cable that runs along your street. The wires are called twisted-wire pairs, or *twisted pairs,* because within the cable they are wound around each other in a helix to give them the proper transmission characteristics. "Drops" from the cable go to your home, either from overhead wires or underground if your neighborhood has buried utilities. Although phone jacks have places for four wires, only two are used for most connections today (the red and the green wires, if you poke around inside).

Copper-wire phone connections date back to Alexander Graham Bell, although their design has changed over the past century—as you can verify if you look around in the basement of a century-old house. Wires are inexpensive, easy to install, and reasonably durable. Once they are in place, phone companies do not want to spend extra money to replace them.

Copper phone
wires were
designed to
transmit 300- to
4000-Hz analog
signals.

However, copper-wire phone lines have some serious limitations. At the top of the list is limited bandwidth. Telephone lines were designed to transmit analog signals at 300 to 4000 Hz, not high-speed digital signals. It turns out copper cables can do much better over short distances, particularly if carefully adjusted. With proper conditioning, twisted-wire pairs can transmit 1.5 Mbit/s a kilometer or two. That's usually enough to reach a concentrator in urban or suburban areas. As we will see later in this chapter, this allows phone companies to offer new digital services that transmit data much faster than ordinary phone lines.

Other limitations affect signal quality. As electrical conductors, wires can pick up electromagnetic interference, such as the local AM radio station or the whirring of noisy motors. Moisture can work its way inside cables, corroding wires and causing sporadic noise that can affect transmission. Such noise can affect modem or fax transmission more than human conversations. Although your mind can filter out the background static, modems and faxes can't tell the static from the signal.

Trends in the Subscriber Loop

Deregulation and competition are changing the telephone subscriber loop, along with the rest of the telecommunications industry. For the first time, your local telephone company is faced with the prospect of competition from a local cable company or from other carriers. Most new carriers simply lease lines from the local phone company, which is forced to sell space by new rules designed to encourage competition. However, some new carriers are beginning to install new cables to connect directly to homes. They may be affiliated with other local utilities, such as electric companies, or they may be independent companies.

Traditionally, telephone and cable-television companies were blocked from competing with each other in most of the United States. However, new rules have changed that, and now both new and existing carriers would like to offer both telephone and cable-television services. As you learned in Chapter 23, cable companies can use new technology such as hybrid fiber/coax systems to provide telephone services. Likewise, telephone companies are trying to adapt their networks to offer cable television service. So far, there is little real competition, but both groups of companies keep saying they want to compete.

Internet access and
high-speed digital
communications
are growing in
importance.

Another important trend is the growing importance of the Internet and high-speed, two-way digital communications. Cable companies have capitalized on the high bandwidth of their networks to offer high-speed access via cable modems. Telephone companies are expanding their subscriber-loop bandwidth by bringing fiber closer to homes and by conditioning twisted-wire phone lines to carry signals at speeds higher than the fastest available with conventional modems, nominally 56 kbit/s.

Thanks to digital video compression, the improved phone lines have enough capacity to carry two-way videotelephone conversations, a service that was supposed to be the future of communications over half a century ago, as shown in Figure 24.3. However, no one but telephone engineers and science-fiction writers have ever seemed very interested in video telephones, and their modern business incarnation, video conferencing, has found only limited use. Even with cheap video cameras available for around $100 and software readily available for Internet video calls, few people bother.

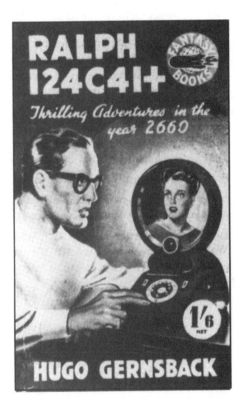

FIGURE 24.3

Videophones were part of the background Hugo Gernsback, publisher of the first science-fiction magazines in the 1920s, used for his first science-fiction novel. However, the cover artist's vision still included a dial. (Courtesy of Fantasy Books)

Present and Emerging Subscriber Loop Services

Through the subscriber loop, the telephone system offers a different capability than a cable-television network. The telephone system uses its communication lines and switches to make temporary connections between pairs of terminals attached to the network. The subscriber loop is not as big an information pipeline as the cable network, but it is one that is more precisely directed. It also has generally higher reliability standards than cable systems.

The telephone system was built to offer voice communications, but it has proved versatile enough to provide other services. Some of them can fit within the same format as voice telephone calls; others work differently. To understand the present state of the subscriber loop and its future evolution, let's take a look at these services.

Plain Old Telephone Service (POTS)

Most home telephone service is still voice telephony, or POTS.

The telephone industry was built around analog voice telephone lines, now called *POTS*, for plain old telephone service, which require an analog bandwidth of 4 kHz to give what telephone companies consider to be intelligible speech. Intelligible is not high fidelity. Telephone lines transmit audio frequencies from 300 Hz to a little more than 3000 Hz; a good stereo can reproduce sound beyond the limits of human hearing, 20 to 20,000 Hz. The 4-kHz bandwidth also includes control signals and the sounds of rotary and push-button (Touch-Tone) dialing. (By the way, tone dialing is analog, based on unique pairs of audio-frequency tones transmitted when each button is pushed. Old-fashioned rotary dials send phone numbers as a series of 1 to 10 clicks—an approach that is more digital than tone signals.)

Engineers have found that POTS lines can carry other things besides telephone conversations. They can relay digital signals, if you convert the digital signals to analog tones at frequencies transmitted by phone lines. This is what fax machines and computer telephone modems do. They fool the telephone system into thinking that their sounds are conversations.

Facsimile and Data Modems

Fax and data modem signals travel as analog signals on POTS lines.

Fax machines conforming to the group 3 (G3) standard of the International Telecommunication Union became common during the late 1980s, and the group 3 format has remained the universal fax standard. Most computer telephone modems (called fax-modems) can generate the same signals. They operate at a series of speeds including 14,400, 9600, 7200, 4800 and 2400 bit/s, initially attempting to establish communications at the highest rate, and then dropping down to lower speeds if the receiver cannot accept the signal or if the line quality is too poor.

Manufacturers of computer data modems have steadily pushed the maximum speed possible over phone lines to higher and higher levels. In 1985, the best you could do was 1200 bit/s; today, the highest standard is 56,000 bit/s, and virtually all modems on the market operate at 28,000 bit/s or more. Data modems slow to fax speeds when operated in fax mode. Their speed also can be limited by line noise and other phone-line problems.

If you're sending data over a phone line, the copper wires from your home to the concentrator or switching center are, very literally, a bottleneck. The present limit is 56,000 bit/s, carefully encoded onto a 4-kHz analog bandwidth, and reaching that speed is an impressive engineering achievement. As long as the data travel over the ordinary phone system, that signal is likely to be converted to digital format (at 56,000 bit/s) and then converted back to analog form before it reaches the receiving modem.

Integrated Services Digital Network (ISDN)

The telephone industry realized the potential for digital services many years ago and devised a standard called the Integrated Services Digital Network, or ISDN. It has been essentially sitting on the shelf ever since, offered only half-heartedly by most phone companies until recently.

The idea behind ISDN is to digitize voice and data signals right at the subscriber's home or office and combine them into a single bit stream that the telephone system could switch just as it switches digitized analog phone signals today. The standard calls for transmitting 144 kbit/s, including two 64-kbit/s channels (equivalent to digitized voice channels) and one 16-kbit/s data channel. The twisted wires that carry present analog phone signals should be able to carry ISDN if they don't stretch more than 3.4 mi, or 5.5 km, from the central office, although some may require conditioning.

One big attraction of ISDN is that it digitizes signals right at the start, so the entire telecommunications network can switch them efficiently. Another is that it gives customers a digital pipeline able to carry any digital signal at that rate. However, it was delayed for many years by the need for special equipment both in the telephone switching office and at the customer premises. Telephone companies finally have installed the required equipment in many switching offices, but they have made little effort to market it and generally charge a steep premium. Customers also are discouraged, because they must buy special phones and other equipment to take advantage of ISDN; because ISDN is not widely used, that equipment is made in small quantities and is quite expensive. Even more discouraging, ISDN does not offer a dramatic improvement over a conventional phone line with a 56-kbit/s modem and falls far short of cable modem performance.

ISDN is used in some other countries, but it generally has failed to catch on in North America. Barring unforseen circumstances, telephone customers are likely to move directly to higher-speed services now in development.

> ● ISDN offers 2 64-kbit/s digitized voice channels and a 16-kbit/s data channel over twisted-wire pairs.

Digital Subscriber Line (DSL)

A new generation of digital technology for copper wires to the subscriber loop is the digital subscriber line (DSL). It transmits digital signals to and from subscribers over one or two pairs of twisted-wire pairs. At this stage, there are many variations on the idea, and many of them involve transmitting data at unequal rates to and from subscribers. Those with unequal speeds are called *asymmetric digital subscriber lines,* or ASDL. The asymmetric approach assumes that subscribers will receive more information than they send for most services. A prime example is the Internet, where virtually all users download and receive more information than they send.

Unlike ISDN, there is no single DSL standard. Table 24.1 compares several approaches in development with each other and with the existing technologies of ISDN and T1 carrier over copper wires. Note the multiple existing and proposed standards. In practice,

> ● DSL is a new generation of digital technology, much faster than ISDN.

phone companies may not offer the maximum capacity or may charge different prices for different speeds. Many of the formats simultaneously transmit an analog voice telephone signal in addition to the digital signal.

Table 24.1 Digital subscriber line variations.

Technology	Standards	Maximum Data Rate	Maximum Distance
ISDN (integrated services digital network)	ANSI/ITU	144 kbit/s both ways	18,000 ft (5.5 km)
ADSL (asymmetric digital subscriber line)	ANSI (proposed)	6 Mbit/s downstream; 640 kbit/s upstream	12,000–18,000 ft (3.6–5.5 km)
HDSL (high bit rate digital subscriber line)	ANSI	768 kbit/s (one pair); 1.5 Mbit/s (two pairs) both ways	12,000 ft (3.6 km)
RADSL (rate adaptive digital subscriber line)	None	Adaptive, up to 9 Mbit/s downstream, 1 Mbit/s upstream	12,000 ft (3.6 km)
T1	Digital telephone hierarchy	1.5 Mbit/s	3000 ft (900 m)
VDSL (very high bit rate digital subscriber line)	ANSI (proposed)	52 Mbit/s downstream, 2.3 Mbit/s upstream	300–1000 ft (90–300 m)

The higher the speed, the shorter the distance digital signals can travel on copper.

Look carefully, and you can see a fundamental trade-off between speed and distance possible on copper. The higher the signal speed, the shorter the distance it can travel before requiring regeneration. The newer DSL technologies do better than the older ones, but they still suffer the same limitation.

You can think of this distance limitation as the maximum length of wire between the end of the optical fiber at the distribution node and the end of the drop wire at the home. For ADSL, this means the optical node should be somewhere in your neighborhood. (Remember, the wires run along streets, not in the shortest possible straight lines.) The limits for VDSL are very stringent indeed. If your house is set back on a large suburban lot, it may mean that the optical node should be no more than one or two houses down the street—if not right opposite your home.

Remember also that this assumes existing wires are in good condition. This is not a safe assumption anywhere, especially in older communities. Moisture may have seeped into the cable, the insulation may have degraded, or squirrels doing gymnastics on overhead cables may have loosened connections or cracked wires inside. Telephone companies will be learning the extent of these problems as they start to install these new digital services.

Switched Digital Video and High-Speed Internet Access

The two major applications envisioned for digital subscriber line are high-speed access to the Internet and switched digital video services, which deliver digitized video signals requested by the subscriber.

Switched digital video was the first idea proposed, as a way for telephone companies to compete with cable television. The idea was that subscribers could request transmission of a specific video signal, which the phone company would digitize and deliver over high-capacity lines without tying up the voice telephone. One possibility is video-on-demand service, transmission of a program stored in an on-line library, which would compete directly with video rentals. However, switched digital video has important limitations, notably the limited number of video channels possible with most DSL schemes. VDSL can overcome this problem but will require fiber service to come quite close to homes.

An earlier variation on switched digital video was called *video dial tone.* The idea was that a phone company could provide access to video services offered by other companies, the video equivalent of a dial tone. However, regulatory issues and other problems damped interest in that idea.

The main purpose now expected for most DSL systems—at least in the near term—is high-speed access to the Internet. A dedicated DSL line operating at 300 kbit/or more could be a viable competitor to cable modems for high-speed access. Although cable modems offer a higher overall speed, like other local area network architectures, that capacity is shared among all users and is not necessarily available to everyone.

Two-Way Video and Videoconferencing

Digital subscriber lines that provide service at the same speed in both directions could be used for two-way video transmission or videoconferencing, if anyone were interested in that service. So far there are few signs that many home or small-office telephone subscribers want video telephones. The only significant use of two-way video is in business teleconferences.

High-speed Internet access is the most likely use for DSL.

Broadband-ISDN (B-ISDN)

The ultimate vision for the telephone network a few years ago was broadband-ISDN, or B-ISDN, which would bring a 155-Mbit/s OC-3 SONET signal to homes that could include voice, video, and data signals transmitted via ATM. The B-ISDN standard was developed along with SONET and ATM, but it has never gained wide acceptance. It is designed to work with broadband fiber-optic links that reach all the way to homes.

New Subscriber Loop Architectures

Telephone companies hope that the existing subscriber network can provide many of the digital subscriber line services I have described. It costs money to install new equipment that offers higher capacity, and they don't want to spend that money unless they have to. However, as the demand for transmission capacity increases, phone companies will have to upgrade their plants.

●
Phone networks can upgrade incrementally or by complete rebuilds.

Two types of upgrading are possible: incremental upgrading and complete rebuilds. In an incremental upgrade, a phone company (or the network operator) replaces obsolete parts that limit transmission capacity. Suppose, for example, the underground ducts to your neighborhood are clogged with old wire cables that limit total service to 1500 phone lines. About 20% of the circuits are unusable because of noise, damaged insulation, or broken wires. If all 600 homes in the neighborhood decide they want separate second phone lines, they will use every available circuit.

The easiest way to upgrade is to replace the old metal cables with higher-capacity fiber cables serving new concentrators. A single fiber cable with 8 pairs, each carrying a T3 signal, can deliver up to 5376 (8×672) voice circuits. That might seem like plenty—but not if the phone company wants to offer DSL service at 6 Mbit/s. For that, the phone company might prefer to install the same eight-fiber cable but send 2.5-Gbit/s OC-48 SONET signals through the fibers instead. A single OC-48 could carry 336 DSL signals, enough to serve half the neighborhood, so the phone company could start with one live fiber pair and seven dark fiber pairs, ready if and when it needs the extra capacity. As demand increased, the phone company could string fiber from the neighborhood optical node to concentrators on each block, close enough that wires could carry the high-speed signals to homes.

It costs much more to replace the entire cable plant at once, pulling out all the old copper cable and replacing it with fiber all the way to the home. However, because labor costs account for a large share of installation costs, phone companies building networks to serve new developments may install fiber close to homes.

We've already seen how far fiber has spread in the present telephone network. Let's look at the next couple of steps needed to expand transmission capacity.

Fiber to the Curb (FTTC)

You can think of the modern telephone system as providing fiber to the neighborhood. That is, fiber-optic cables deliver signals to a distribution node somewhere within a few blocks of your home. Fiber generally comes closer to offices in a business district, because businesses use a lot of phone capacity; some businesses may have dedicated fiber lines. On the other hand, if you live in a sparsely populated or older neighborhood, the fiber may be further away. You saw that system architecture in Figure 24.1.

The next step is bringing fiber past your home and distributing signals from a local node on your block. Figure 24.4 shows one version of such a system, which the industry calls *fiber to the curb.* Each neighborhood has its own add-drop multiplexer along a fiber ring; the ring design protects service against cable breaks. Fibers branch out from the multiplexer to every block, where optical interface units serve several homes. The fiber literally runs down every street, with the optical network unit in a box somewhere along the street. Wires need run only a few hundred feet to homes. The same system also serves cellphones and corporate networks.

Fiber to the curb brings fibers within a few hundred feet of homes.

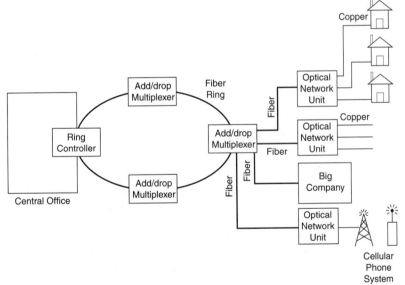

FIGURE 24.4
Fiber-to-the-curb system, with fiber ring.

Nippon Telegraph and Telephone is installing fiber-optic cables throughout its network, with the target of completing a fiber to the curb system throughout all of Japan by 2010. This does not mean fiber will connect to every home, but it means that fiber will *pass by* every home. The Japanese network is designed so that it is complete, NTT can install fiber links to individual homes whenever customers are ready.

Fiber to the curb also can be combined with copper wires in various ways to provide high transmission capacity. As you learned earlier, VDSL can deliver up to 52 Mbit/s over short copper cables running from a nearby fiber concentrator to the home. Figure 24.5 shows a different design for fiber to the curb, where an optical network unit distributes switched voice, high-speed data, and videophone services to homes over twisted-wire pairs and unswitched cable television over coaxial cable.

FIGURE 24.5

Fiber to the curb, with unswitched video fed over coax and telephone and digital data delivered over twisted-pair DSL.

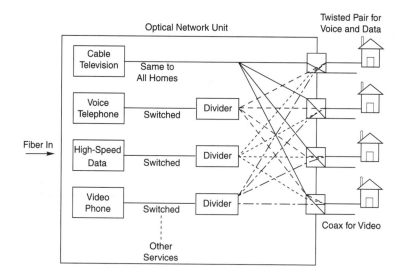

Fiber to the Home (FTTH)

Fiber to the home promises high bandwidth, but only at high cost.

The ultimate step for fiber optics is all the way to the home. Telecommunication visionaries have been considering ways to bring fiber to the home (FTTH) since 1972, when John Fulenwider first suggested the idea for a wired-city project being studied by General Telephone and Electronics. The first experimental system, called Hi-OVIS, began operation in Higashi-Ikoma, Japan, in 1978. Canada, France, and a few U.S. telephone companies also have tested fiber to the home since then. In most cases, the technology worked, but the economics didn't. No one could find a combination of services that could generate enough revenue to pay the high cost of installing fibers to every home.

That problem remains with us today. Optical hardware is expensive. So is the labor needed to install it. In most present systems, you can't just install fiber to one home; you need to rebuild subscriber lines to the entire block or neighborhood to support the high-speed service. That adds to the cost. Maintenance is another concern. In the trunk and the long-haul network, fiber generally costs less to maintain than copper wires. However, phone companies worry that fiber links to homes could prove much more troublesome to maintain, especially if do-it-yourself homeowners get there first.

Costs scare telecommunications companies, because they do not see how they can recover them. The hottest new service possibility is high-speed Internet access, but various types of digital subscriber lines can deliver that service much less expensively than fiber to the home. Another possibility is video-on-demand service, which retrieves video programs from large on-line libraries, giving you the same choice you would have renting a video tape, but without the trip. However, on-line video libraries turn out to be very expensive, and market studies predict the revenue would be limited.

Another mundane but important issue in fiber-to-the-home systems is supplying power to telephones. Most current telephones are powered by electricity that flows through phone wires (many multiline office phone systems are exceptions and run from local electric lines). There are no major technical problems in powering home telephones from electric lines in the house, but that would make phone lines go down when power failed. This is a concern for phone companies and customers who expect the phones to stay in service during power failures (giving them a lifeline service—if only to call the power company and report the failure).

Passive Optical Networks

Development engineers continue investigating technologies to reduce the costs of bringing fiber closer to homes, either for fiber to the curb or fiber to the home. The current favorite is the passive optical network (PON).

The goal of the passive optical network is to reduce the number of costly "active" components, particularly laser transmitters. Figure 24.6 shows two possible approaches.

Figure 24.6(a) shows the use of a single expensive laser transmitter to deliver high-speed signals to many homes, dividing the signals among them with a splitter or $1 \times n$ coupler. You could use a high-power laser or follow a lower-power amplifier with an optical amplifier. All subscribers would receive the same signals, but you could send signals to individual subscribers by allocating them particular time slots in a time-division-modulated component of the signal. The receiver in each home would detect and process only signals in that particular time slot.

Return signals would be sent from the home using inexpensive, lower-speed laser transmitters. In the example, each home transmitter would be allocated its own time slot for transmission, which the receiver at the optical network unit would automatically process so the system knew which home sent the signal. The result would be a time-division-multiplexed return signal, with each home allocated one time slot in the signal.

Figure 24.6(b) shows a similar system, in which a single expensive laser transmitter again sends signals to many homes. However, in this case a part of the high-speed signal is split off and passed through a modulator in each home, which superimposes a slow return signal on the high-speed input signal. Receivers at the optical network would filter out the high-speed signal to detect only the low-speed signal. This removes laser sources from the

Passive optical networks reduce the number of costly active components.

FIGURE 24.6

Passive optical networks for fiber to the home.

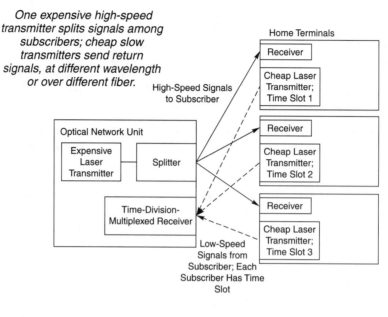

One expensive high-speed transmitter splits signals among subscribers; cheap slow transmitters send return signals, at different wavelength or over different fiber.

Home Terminals

High-Speed Signals to Subscriber

Optical Network Unit

Expensive Laser Transmitter

Splitter

Time-Division-Multiplexed Receiver

Receiver

Cheap Laser Transmitter; Time Slot 1

Receiver

Cheap Laser Transmitter; Time Slot 2

Receiver

Cheap Laser Transmitter; Time Slot 3

Low-Speed Signals from Subscriber; Each Subscriber Has Time Slot

a.

One expensive high-speed transmitter splits signals among home subscribers; that signal is split and modulated at slow speed by home terminals. Receiver at the optical network filters to detect only signals from homes.

Home Terminals

High-Speed Signals to Subscriber

Optical Network Unit

Expensive Laser Transmitter

Splitter

Receiver (Detects Only Modulation from Home, Filters Out High-Speed Signal); Could Be One per Home

Splitter   Receiver

Modulator

Splitter   Receiver

Modulator

Splitter   Receiver

Modulator

Low-Speed Signals, Derived by Modulating Split Part of High-Speed Signal

b.

home completely, leaving a modulator as the only active component. This is a more passive network than the first example, but in practice modulators may cost more than inexpensive laser transmitters.

Future Trends

Future trends in the subscriber loop are both easy and difficult to predict. The easy prediction is that bandwidth delivered to individual subscribers will increase. The market exists, and the technology is being developed. The hard part is to predict how that bandwidth will be delivered. Cable television networks soon will be able to deliver voice and data services that look much like those supplied by the telephone network. Conversely, telephone-based systems may soon offer cablelike services. New companies promise hybrids of both cable and telephone service plus Internet access.

Fiber will come closer to homes, but how close remains to be seen. If you live in a typical community, fiber lines from the telephone switching office and the cable head-end come closer to your home now than they did a decade ago. When—and if—fibers will come to your curb or arrive at your house remains unclear. The choice of fiber technology also is uncertain. The decisions depend on factors that remain uncertain: demand for new services that require new hardware, competition in the turbulent telecommunications industry, and success in translating new laboratory ideas into practical new hardware. What is clear is that the fiber-optics industry realizes the subscriber loop could be a tremendous market, and developers are working on ways to reach that market.

What Have You Learned?

1. The subscriber loop radiates outward from a local telephone switching center to serve homes and businesses. It includes both twisted pairs of copper wires and optical fibers. The wires carry signals from individual phones to concentrators, where the analog signals are digitized, multiplexed, and transmitted via optical fibers to the switching office.

2. Copper wire pairs were designed to transmit analog voice signals at 300 to 4000 Hz.

3. Deregulation and competition are changing the telephone subscriber loop along with the rest of the telecommunications industry.

4. Internet access and high-speed digital data transmission are of growing importance.

5. Most home telephone service is still POTS, analog voice telephony. Digital signals from fax machines and computer modems are converted to analog form and travel on POTS lines.

6. ISDN offers two 64-kbit/s digitized voice channels and one 16-kbit/s data channel over a twisted-wire pair.

7. Digital Subscriber Line (DSL) is much faster than ISDN. Asymmetric DSL (ADSL) transmits signals at higher speed to subscribers than from them, with speeds to 6 Mbit/s downstream. VDSL (very high bit rate DSL) transmits downstream at rates to 52 Mbit/s, but only over distances of several hundred feet.

8. Broadband-ISDN (B-ISDN) is a standard developed for fiber links to the home at speeds to 155 Mbit/s; it has yet to come into practical use.

9. The subscriber loop can be upgraded incrementally or rebuilt completely to increase capacity. Phone companies prefer incremental upgrades to save money.

10. Fiber to the curb brings fiber distribution nodes within a few hundred feet of homes.

11. Fiber to the home promises high bandwidth, but the high cost has deterred telephone companies from offering it.

12. Passive optical networks are in development to reduce the need for expensive active components.

13. The future subscriber loop will increase its transmission capacity, but the details remain uncertain.

What's Next?

In Chapter 25, we'll look at a different family of fiber-optic networks that distribute signals, local-area networks that distribute data among computers.

Quiz for Chapter 24

1. What area is served by a typical switching office?
    a. A major city of over 1 million people.
    b. An entire area code.
    c. 25,000 to 50,000 phone lines.
    d. 500 phone lines.
    e. One large corporation.

2. What is the bandwidth and format of the signal from a standard voice telephone?
    a. 300–4000 Hz, analog.
    b. 20–20,000 Hz, analog.

    c. 56,000 bit/s, digital.
    d. 64,000 bit/s, digital.
    e. 6 MHz, analog.

3. What is the Integrated Services Digital Network?
    a. A meaningless marketing buzzword.
    b. The existing telephone network is an integrated digital network.
    c. A future all-fiber network.
    d. Digital services over existing twisted-pair phone lines at 144 kbit/s.

4. What is the main service offered over home telephone lines?

   a. High-speed digital data.

   b. POTS, Plain Old Telephone Service.

   c. Video telephone.

   d. Cable television.

   e. Teleshopping.

5. What format do facsimile machines transmit over phone lines?

   a. Facsimile does not work over analog phone lines.

   b. Digital signals at the 144-kbit/s ISDN rate.

   c. Analog signals carrying digital data at 2400 to 14,400 bit/s.

   d. Analog signals carrying digital data at 56 kbit/s.

   e. Any of the above, depending on how you set the machine.

6. Which of the following best describes Asymmetric Digital Subscriber Line?

   a. Transmission over fiber of higher speeds in one direction than the other.

   b. Transmission over twisted pairs of higher speeds downstream to subscribers than upstream.

   c. Transmission over twisted pairs of higher speeds upstream to the switching center than downstream to the subscriber.

   d. A defective subscriber line unable to transmit evenly shaped pulses.

   e. An old and obsolete standard.

7. If you want to provide VDSL (very high bit rate digital subscriber line) service, how close does the customer have to be to the end of the fiber portion of the subscriber line?

   a. Within 10 mi (16 km).

   b. Within 12,000 ft (3.6 km).

   c. Within at most 3000 ft (900 m).

   d. Within at most 1000 ft (300 m).

   e. Fiber must terminate at the home.

8. How close to the end of the fiber portion of the subscriber loop must a customer be to receive HDSL (high bit rate digital subscriber line)?

   a. Within 10 mi (16 km).

   b. Within 12,000 ft (3.6 km).

   c. Within at most 3000 ft (900 m).

   d. Within at most 1000 ft (300 m).

   e. Fiber must terminate at the home.

9. What area is served by each fiber drop in a fiber to the curb system?

   a. A small town.

   b. 500 phone lines.

   c. One business.

d. One home.

e. About a block.

10. If an HDTV signal can be compressed to 19 Mbit/s, how many HDTV channels can you transmit on a single VDSL line operating at peak speed?

    a. None.

    b. 1.

    c. 2.

    d. 3.

    e. 500.

11. What do you need in order to provide B-ISDN service?

    a. Tons of money.

    b. Fiber to the home.

c. 155-Mbit/s input signals.

d. None of the above.

e. a, b, and c.

12. What is the goal of developing passive optical networks?

    a. Greater reliability, because active components fail.

    b. Passive technology is perfect for couch potatoes.

    c. Higher transmission speeds.

    d. Avoiding the cost of expensive active components.

    e. Meeting safety requirements and fire codes.

Computers and Local-Area Networks

About This Chapter

Fiber-optic data communication has been considered promising since the late 1970s, but only in recent years have fiber optics become important in local area networks and other computer communications. The major reason has been that few computer applications needed the speeds and long transmission distances fibers offer. Fiber optics have spread as local area networks have moved to higher speeds and spread over larger areas. Some fiber-based networks are already in commercial use; others are in development for the higher transmission speeds that come with more powerful computers. To understand the use of fiber optics for data communications, I will first review computer communication basics and relevant fiber capabilities. Then I will look at how fibers meet system requirements.

Basic Concepts

Computers think and communicate in binary bits—1s and 0s. Identical computers—and circuit boards within the same computer—decode binary information in the same way. Different computers must convert information to a common format before they can interchange it. This is the job of data communications software and hardware.

Computers require a common digital format to interchange information.

Computer data rates are normally measured in baud, which means signal-level transitions per second. In coding schemes where there is one transition per bit, such as nonreturn to zero, baud equals bit rate. This is the usual case with most modems and other data communications equipment. However, in schemes such as Manchester coding, where there are two transitions per bit, the baud rate is twice the bit rate. Most computer data transfer speeds are slow by the standards of fiber-optic telecommunications. The fastest personal computer data interchange over phone lines is 56,000 baud, but high-speed transfers to and from hard disks are measured in megabaud. Electrical wires can handle those data rates as long as distances are modest or there are no special problems such as electromagnetic interference.

Point-to-Point Transmission

Much data transmission simply moves information between pairs of devices (e.g., from a computer to a printer or external hard disk), as shown in Figure 25.1. Even if data goes from the external disk to the printer, it must pass through the computer, as shown in Figure 25.1.

FIGURE 25.1

Point-to-point connections between a personal computer and individual external devices.

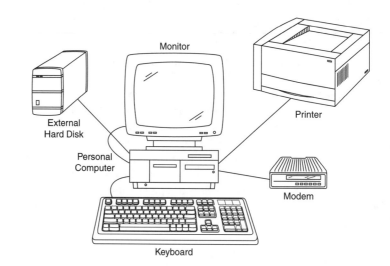

Point-to-point transmission is the simplest of tasks for fiber optics because it requires only a transmitter, a receiver, and some fiber. However, in most cases, wires are even simpler because they can carry the electrical output from one device directly to the other without a special transmitter or receiver. Some devices have infrared parts. Optical fibers enter the picture when data rates become too high, distances too long, or the environment too noisy, or when other factors make it hard for wires to work. Such cases are becoming more common.

Local-Area Networks

Networks link many terminals, nodes, or devices. Many personal computers are linked to local-area networks (LANs), which serve many nodes or devices in the area, as shown in Figure 25.2. (You might think that the array of devices attached to a single personal computer forms a network, but in practice local-area networks connect multiple computers and other terminal devices.) Typically, a local-area network serves a work group, department, or small business, whereas a wide-area network links many local area networks to serve an entire large company. Local-area networks typically have interfaces with other communication services; the example in Figure 25.2 has links to a wide-area network and (through a fax-modem) to the telephone network.

A local-area network interconnects many nodes.

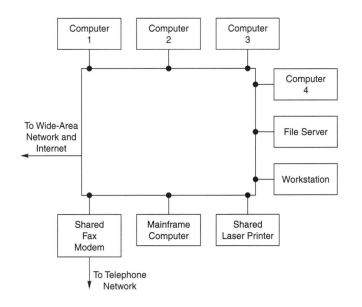

FIGURE 25.2

A LAN interconnects many nodes that can send messages to any other node.

Details vary widely among local-area networks, but the key idea is that all nodes can interchange data with each other. A single medium—wires, optical fibers, or radio waves—carries signals to all nodes on the system. Data packets carry header information to route them to particular nodes. Many terminals can use the network at the same time. For example, the users of computers 1 and 2 could each retrieve data from the file server at the same time, computer 3 could print a report on the laser printer, and computer 4 could access the corporate wide area network to communicate with another department.

Local-area networks can take a variety of forms. Three basic approaches to LANs are shown in Figure 25.3. In the star topology, all signals pass through a central node, which

●
Common LAN
types are the
ring, the star,
and the bus.

may be active or passive. (An active star, which switches signals to particular nodes, functions like a telephone switch.) In a ring network, the transmission medium passes through all nodes, and signals can be passed in one or both directions (sometimes over two parallel paths for redundancy). In the data-bus topology, a common transmission medium connects all the nodes but is not closed to form a loop (i.e., the signal does not pass through all nodes in a series). Variations on these approaches make classification more complex than it might sound, but I will ignore those here.

FIGURE 25.3

*Star, bus, and ring
LAN architectures.*

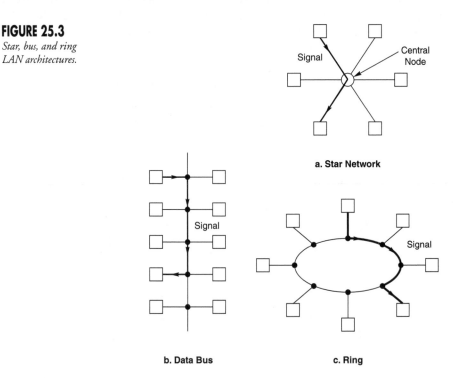

a. Star Network

b. Data Bus

c. Ring

The major media used for LANs are twisted wire pairs (shielded or unshielded), coaxial cables, and optical fibers. (Wireless LANs transmit via radio waves or infrared, but their use remains limited.) The difficulty of tapping into optical fibers at nodes makes some designs awkward or uneconomical. To overcome this problem, fiber LANs may be made with fiber-optic cable connecting nodes, at which signals are converted back into electrical format; those electrical signals can be sent to the terminal equipment and used to drive a transmitter sending optical signals to the next node. This approach avoids excess losses, but the use of extra transmitters and receivers drives up costs. One result is that completely fiber networks are usually used only at high speeds, although fibers are often used as segments of slower networks.

Wide-Area Networks

The next step up from the local-area network is the wide-area network, or WAN (sometimes called a metropolitan-area network, or MAN). A wide-area network links local-area networks, and often other terminals, over a large area. For example, a wide-area network in a large company may connect departmental LANs and have a direct link to a corporate mainframe computer. This arrangement clusters groups that work together and need to communicate more intensely in local-area networks, while still allowing communication among different groups. It avoids performance degradation that comes from adding too many terminals to a local area network.

You can think of a wide-area network as a network linking networks instead of linking terminals. To do that job, it has higher transmission speeds than local-area networks.

Wide-area networks are not inherently limited to data communications. In fact, the term is often used for networks that carry voice and data signals over a large area—for example, to all company plants in a large metropolitan area. This covers metropolitan networks operated by some telecommunications carriers that are really alternative telephone companies—another indication of how telephone networks are evolving into other forms.

I covered the networks oriented toward local telephone communications in Chapter 24. Here I will concentrate on corporate or campus networks that nominally carry mainly data communications. Remember, however, that the technological boundaries are hazy.

● Wide-area networks link local area networks.

● WANs are not inherently limited to data communications.

Optical Interconnection

All data transfer is not between separate boxes. Data must be moved between circuit boards in computers, between chips on circuit boards, and even within chips. In some cases, such as supercomputers, data must be transferred at very high speeds, and wires and other circuit components must be very tightly packed. Fibers can help both by allowing faster data transmission and by avoiding interference between adjacent wires. Gigabit data rates may require fiber optics over all but very short distances.

Optical links may also carry information directly to and from integrated-circuit chips. Electronic connections grow harder as the scale of integration increases, because the number of circuit elements on the chip surface can increase much faster than the room to make electrical connections along the edges of the chip. Optical interconnection offers a way around this problem.

One possibility is to multiplex several digital signals together, forming a single high-speed signal that could be transmitted through one fiber rather than several wires. Other alternatives involve optical devices that emit and receive light from the chip surface, with or without fibers. Vertical-cavity semiconductor lasers (VCSELs) are attractive because they emit light from their surfaces. External optics or fibers could collect this

● Optical signals can make interconnections within computers and even between chips.

light and focus it onto a detector on another chip, which would convert the signal into electrical form.

Some current high-performance computers already use high-speed fiber-optic connections between circuit boards. More such links are likely as computer speeds increase.

Why Use Fiber Optics?

Copper wires are adequate for the vast bulk of computer data transmission over point-to-point links and local-area networks. As you saw earlier, copper wires can transmit high-speed signals a short distance and slower signals considerably further. Optical fibers make more sense in wide-area networks and are used in many more of them. However, wires remain the usual choice for data transmission.

The main advantage wires offer is lower cost. Wires can directly carry the electrical signals generated by computers and peripheral devices over short to moderate distances. Optical transmitters and receivers are needed to convert those signals to and from optical form for transmission through an optical fiber. You don't want to pay that premium where you don't have to. The inherent limitations of signal splitting in fiber-optic couplers can also drive up costs, especially for networks that connect many devices.

A more subtle advantage of wires is their compatibility with existing computer and data-transmission equipment. The back of your personal computer has wire connections but no fiber-optic sockets. Likewise, many high-speed computer ports are designed for parallel transmission through multiwire cables, not for serial transmission of bits through a fiber-optic cable. You can always add adapters, but they cost extra and can be hard to find.

Conventional wiring also is easy to install, particularly because technicians are used to working with copper cables. Terminating fibers is generally more difficult than installing copper cables, although plastic fibers are not as difficult as glass. (On the other hand, plastic fibers have their own limitations, as you learned earlier.)

Despite these limitations, fiber optics are spreading for data transmission. Data rates continue increasing, with new networks operating at higher speeds and Internet connections demanding ever-higher transmission capacity. Meanwhile, fiber costs are coming down, and the technology is being included in more standards. Let's look at the cases where fibers offer performance advantages that offset their higher costs.

High-Speed and/or Long-Distance Transmission

The most common reason to use fiber optics is to transmit signals at higher speeds than copper can handle over the required distance. Each new generation of computer hardware and software seems to require faster transmission than the old. Internet access and graphics-intensive applications also drive an increasing demand for bandwidth. Local-area networks are requiring higher transmission capacity; so are wide-area networks that link local-area networks.

As you learned in Chapter 24, the higher the data rate, the shorter the distance copper wires can carry a signal. The reason is that attenuation increases with frequency, as shown in Figure 25.4. The figure plots typical loss per 100 m (*not* per kilometer, as is usual for fiber) as a function of signal frequency for four types of unshielded twisted-pair wires designed for data transmission. Categories 3 and 5 are unshielded twisted pairs meeting standards established by the TIA and EIA; the shielded twisted pair is a cable from the same manufacturer in which the wire pairs are shielded by a metal foil layer. As you learned earlier, optical fibers do not suffer the same limit.

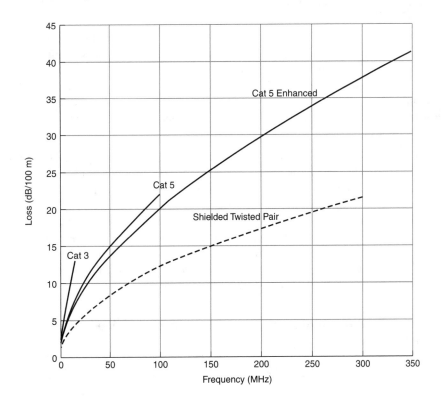

FIGURE 25.4

Typical loss of twisted-pair wiring designed for high-frequency use.

Category 5 cable was designed specifically for short-distance, high-speed data transmission, and it can indeed carry signals up to 1 Gbit/s over short distances. One qualification is that installation must confine to rigid rules, which limit such factors as how much wire can be exposed at the end of the cable when stripping insulation. These factors are not important at low frequencies but become significant at high frequencies and, in practice, can affect transmission at high speeds. In short, Category 5 can work, but you have to do it just right.

Fibers get around these distance limits, whether for individual remote terminals requiring high-speed transmission or for backbone links between local-area networks at different locations. You don't have to install an entire fiber-optic network; as with residential telephone systems, you can install fiber only for the longer, higher-speed parts of the network. For example, in a large office building high-capacity fiber cables may run to each floor and than branch out on each floor to serve several local nodes—like fiber lines to telephone concentrators. Copper wires can branch out from local nodes to distribute signals the short distance to desktops. Alternatively, easy-to-install plastic fibers with limited-bandwidth can be used for the desktop connections.

Upgrade Capability

Fiber-optic cables make future upgrades easier.

Even if the high capacity of fiber is not absolutely necessary now, you may want it in the future. You aren't going to rip out a functioning copper system to make room for fiber that will be needed at some indefinite date in the future. However, if you are installing cable in new facilities, you should consider the prospects for future expansion. Labor accounts for a large part of the cost of cable installation, and it takes much less labor to install cable in a new building than to string new cable through existing walls, where access is limited.

Suppose, for example, you were moving into a new building that you expected to occupy for 25 years. You know that you can get away with copper cables now, but if you plot current trends of network use, you can see that within 5 to 10 years, you are likely to need higher capacity. Assume that the fiber hardware costs 50% more than copper cabling and that fiber installation costs an added 20%. You know that fiber costs are coming down, but you also know that installation in a finished building is going to be twice as expensive as installation in a new plant. Table 25.1 shows that copper is much cheaper today, but you'll pay a lot more altogether if you have to go back and retrofit fiber cables later. (My figures are purely illustrative, not from actual installations.)

Table 25.1 Hypothetical costs of installing copper and fiber in new building.

Costs	New Copper	New Fiber	Retrofit Fiber Later
Hardware	$5000	$7500	$5000
Labor	$12,000	$14,400	$28,800
Total costs	$17,000	$21,900	$33,800

Immunity to Electromagnetic Interference

Fibers are immune to electromagnetic interference, unlike wires.

One advantage of optical transmission is its immunity to electromagnetic interference (EMI), a common source of noise. EMI arises from the basic properties of electromagnetism. Changing currents generate magnetic fields, and magnetic field lines can generate (or induce) an electrical current when they cut across a conductor. This can generate noise, as shown in Figure 25.5, when two wires come close together. The strong current in the upper wire induces a current in the lower wire, which added to the input signal becomes noise. If the noise power is high enough, it can overwhelm the input signal. A noise spike, caused by a sudden surge of current, can add a spurious data bit to a digital signal.

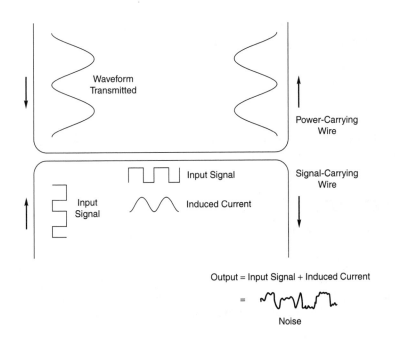

FIGURE 25.5

Induction of noise currents in a wire carrying an electrical signal.

You don't need two wires next to each other to get EMI. All you need is passage of magnetic flux through a conductor. That's how a radio or television antenna picks up broadcast signals. Stray magnetic fields can induce a current in any wire exposed to them. Often those currents are simple noise (e.g., the crackle on AM radio when a nearby light is switched on). Sometimes the result is crosstalk (e.g., a radio program in the background on your telephone line).

Shielding, as in coaxial cables, can reduce electromagnetic interference by weakening the magnetic field that reaches the inner conductor, but even coax isn't immune to EMI. Optical fibers are immune because they transmit signals as light rather than current. Thus, they can carry signals through places where EMI would otherwise block data transmission—from power substations to hospitals with radio paging systems.

(I should note, however, that fiber-optic transmitters and receivers include electronic circuits that can pick up EMI, so fiber systems are not perfectly immune to EMI. Careful design is required to shield transmitters and receivers exposed to EMI.)

Data Security

Fibers do not emit electromagnetic fields that can be tapped by eavesdroppers.

Magnetic fields and current induction work two ways. They don't just generate noise in a signal-carrying conductor; they also let information leak out. Changes in signal current cause fluctuations in the induced magnetic field outside a conductor, which carry the same information as the current passing through the conductor. That's good news for potential spies because they can eavesdrop on these magnetic fields without cutting the cable. Shielding the wire, as in coaxial cable, can alleviate the problem, but bends and imperfections can let some signals leak out.

There are no radiated magnetic fields around an optical fiber—the electromagnetic fields are confined within the fiber. That makes it impossible to tap the signal being transmitted through a fiber without bending the fiber (to induce bend losses) or cutting into the fiber.

That would increase fiber loss sharply, in a way easy for users of the communication channel to detect, making fibers a much more secure transmission medium. This has led to fiber-optic links in some secure government data networks.

Nonconductive Cables

Nonconductive fiber-optic cables are immune to ground loops and resistant to lightning surges.

Subtle variations in electrical potential between buildings can cause problems in transmitting electrical signals. Electronic designers assume that ground is a uniform potential. That is reasonable if ground is a single metal chassis, and it's not too bad if ground is a good conductor that extends through a small building (e.g., copper plumbing or a ground wire in electrical wiring). However, the nominal ground potential can differ by several volts if cables run between different buildings or sometimes even different parts of the same building.

That doesn't sound like much—and in the days of vacuum tube electronics, it wasn't worth worrying about. However, signal levels in semiconductor circuits are just a few volts, creating a problem called a ground loop, which isn't mentioned in many engineering textbooks. When the difference in ground potential at two ends of a wire is comparable to the signal level, stray currents start to cause noise. If the differences grow large enough, they can damage components. Electric utilities have the biggest problems because their switching stations and power plants may have large potential differences. Fiber optics can avoid these problems, as long as the nonconductive glass fiber is enclosed in a nonconductive cable with no metal elements. Many sellers of computer data links recommend that fibers be used for interbuilding connections to avoid noise and ground-loop problems.

Nonconductive cables can also alleviate a serious concern with outdoor cables—lightning strikes, which can cause power and voltage surges large enough to fry electronics on either end.

Eliminating Spark Hazards

In some cases, transmitting signals electrically can be downright dangerous. Even modest electric potentials can generate small sparks, especially at switches. Those sparks ordinarily pose no hazard, but they can be extremely dangerous in an oil refinery or chemical plant where the air contains potentially explosive vapors. One tiny spark could make one very large and deadly boom. Again, nonconductive fiber-optic cables can avoid this hazard.

Sparks from electrical wires can be dangerous in explosive atmospheres.

Ease of Installation

Increasing transmission capacity of wire cables generally makes them thicker and more rigid. Shielding against EMI or eavesdropping has similar effects. Such thick cables can be difficult to install in existing buildings where they must go through walls and cable ducts. Fiber cables are easier to install because they're smaller and more flexible. This helps reduce installation costs, especially in cases where only fiber cables are small and flexible enough to fit through existing ductwork in buildings or underground.

Fiber cables can be much easier to install than metal cables.

The small size, light weight, and flexibility of fiber-optic cables also make them easier to use in temporary or portable installations.

Point-to-Point Fiber Links

I mentioned earlier that fibers are used both for point-to-point data links and in computer networks. The two applications differ in important ways, and I'll talk about them separately.

Point-to-point fiber data links work on the same principles as point-to-point telecommunications, but they operate over shorter distances. Some operate at standard rates in the digital telephone hierarchy, usually 1.5 and 45 Mbit/s, but most operate at rates used in data communications. Their design is less standardized than networks, but most are made to interface with standard computer equipment, and some standards do exist, such as SCSI and Fibre Channel. Fiber data links do not compete with copper links for general applications because of their higher cost, but they are used in cases where fiber performance offers important benefits, such as those described earlier.

An array of point-to-point links can function as a network if the nodes attached to them can route the signals. This forms what is called a switching fabric. For example, the central node of a star local-area network could route signals between pairs of other nodes. You could even think of a personal computer as having similar capabilities, such as sending data from a disk to a printer.

Technology

Point-to-point data communications rarely push the limits of fiber-optic technology in distance or data rate, and cost is usually a major design constraint. This leads to widespread

Point-to-point fiber data links rarely push technical limits.

use of multimode fibers at 850 or 1300 nm and sometimes to the use of all-plastic fiber. LED sources are used as long as they meet performance requirements.

The Fibre Channel standard, described in Chapter 19, was developed partly for fast two-directional (or full-duplex) data interchange among computer system components. Despite the name, it allows use of both twisted-pair and coaxial cables over short distances. It also provides for fiber transmission at 780 to 850 and 1300 to 1550 nm.

Many other commercial point-to-point fiber links are designed to behave much like conventional electrical data links. The transmitters and receivers on such systems accept input and deliver output in standard electrical signal formats and often come with integral electronic connectors. The goal is to be functionally transparent, so users don't see any difference between the fiber data link and a standard electronic data link. The user sees a data link with bulky connectors that feed into fiber-optic cables; the bulky connectors include an electrical connector, an electrical-to-optical converter, and an optical connector. This packaging serves to "hide" the fiber—or at least prevent the user from worrying about new and unfamiliar technology. Some of these data links are called fiber-optic "modems," because they function somewhat like electronic modems in converting signals into a different form for transmission, but they cannot be used instead of electronic modems.

In practice, some fiber-optic data links are semicustomized products assembled from standard components. The transmitter and receiver are standard components, adaptable for use with various connector types. Specifications indicate allowable transmission loss through different fibers. Often there is a minimum acceptable loss (to prevent receiver overload), as well as a maximum loss. Typical loss budgets are 10 to 15 dB for LED sources. Suppliers cut the cable to length, mount the desired components, and plug the proper pieces together to produce a system.

Security requirements may dictate the use of fiber for sensitive links at military or security agencies or in financial institutions.

Many point-to-point fiber applications are quite routine, arising from the fiber-optic advantages I described earlier. For example, the only readily accessible path between equipment on two floors may run along machinery that generates strong electromagnetic noise, or ground loops may leave two nearby buildings at slightly different electrical potentials. Space constraints, interference problems, and high data rates lead to the use of fiber links inside high-performance computers and electronic telephone switching systems.

Some applications can be quite unusual. One example is in electromagnetic testing, where equipment is operated in a screen room shielded from electromagnetic fields, and the shielding prevents electronic transmission. Another was in the underground testing of nuclear weapons, where high-speed cables were hung down deep, narrow shafts to collect data from instruments during the milliseconds between bomb detonation and the time the blast destroyed the instruments.

Fiber-Optic Data Networks

Networks are making increasing use of fiber optics as their data rates and transmission distances expand. Small local-area networks are unlikely to use fibers, but high-speed wide-area networks are more likely to use fibers to link smaller LANs or devices requiring high-speed connections. Many network architectures have been developed and tested, but only a few have gained wide acceptance. These common networks have standardized designs and interfaces, so they can connect various devices in a uniform way. This gives users vital flexibility in connecting different equipment as well as helping them predict behavior of hardware and software.

The first generation of local-area networks used standards such as standard Ethernet and the IBM Token Ring network, transmitting about 10 Mbit/s. That seemed adequate a decade ago, and many such networks are still operating. However, transmission rates have pushed steadily upward for local-area networks and are even higher for wide-area networks interconnecting LANs. A 100-Mbit/s Fast Ethernet followed the original 10-Mbit/s Ethernet, with Gigabit Ethernet emerging in 1998. Fibers are important elements of the faster Ethernets, as well as of networked versions of Fibre Channel and of the 100-Mbit/s Fiber Distributed Data Interface (FDDI) standard. Let's look at the most important of these network standards.

> Fibers play various roles in different standardized networks.

10-Mbit/s Ethernet

The first LAN to gain much acceptance was the original Ethernet standard codified as IEEE (Institute of Electrical and Electronics Engineers) standard 802.3. It distributes digital data packets of variable length at 10 Mbit/s to transceivers dispersed along a coaxial cable bus, as shown in Figure 25.6. Separate cables up to 50 m long, containing four twisted-wire pairs, run from the transceivers to individual devices (e.g., personal computers, file servers, or printers). The network can serve up to 1024 terminals.

> The 10-Mbit/s Ethernet LAN was designed for coax, but fiber can be added.

An Ethernet network has no overall controller; control functions are handled by individual transceivers. If a terminal is ready to send a signal, its transceiver checks if another signal is going along the coaxial cable. Transmission is delayed if another signal is present. If not, the terminal begins transmitting and continues until it finishes or detects a collision—the transmission of data at the same time by a second terminal. Such collisions happen because it takes time—several nanoseconds a meter—for signals to travel along the coax. If the delay is 6 ns/m, a collision would occur if two terminals 300 m apart on the coax started sending within 1.8 µs of each other. The terminal stops transmitting if it detects a collision and waits a random interval before trying again.

An address header specifies the destination for every data signal. All the transceivers on the network see every data signal, but they ignore the signals not directed to them. The only signals the transceiver relays to the terminal attached to it are those with the terminal's address.

FIGURE 25.6

Basic elements of Ethernet.

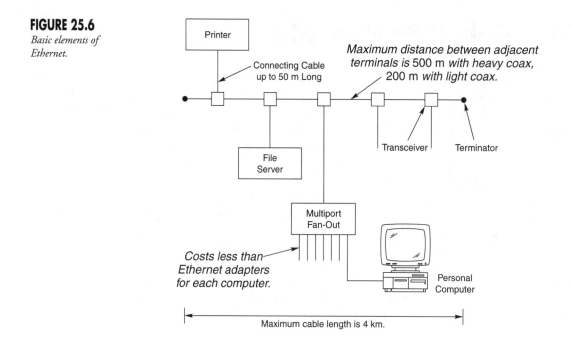

There are some important variations on the basic 10-Mbit/s Ethernet design. The original standard heavy coaxial cable allows transceivers to be up to 500 m apart, but it is expensive. Substituting a lighter grade of coax limits transceiver spacing to 200 m, but this "thin" Ethernet is adequate for most purposes. Another alternative is using twisted-wire pairs, which can carry signals up to about 100 m. In addition to the data bus configuration shown in Figure 25.6, Ethernet often is arranged in a star configuration, with cables radiating outward from a hub, which relays signals to other terminals.

Optical fibers can stretch transmission distances beyond the limit imposed by the loss of coaxial cable to distances limited by other factors, such as the time signals take to travel through the network. Often, a point-to-point fiber link may connect two coaxial segments of an Ethernet or a remote terminal with a central Ethernet. This allows a single Ethernet to link terminals in different buildings, which is difficult with the 500-m limit of coax.

The maximum transmission distance depends on whether the network is operating in half-duplex mode, so terminals either transmit or receive at any one time, or in full-duplex mode, where they simultaneously send and receive data. In half-duplex mode, the maximum distance is 2 km for either multimode or single-mode fiber. In full-duplex mode, multimode fiber allows cable runs to 2.5 km, and single-mode allows spacing to 15 km. (For reference, light takes roughly 75 μs to travel a 15-km fiber, meaning the terminal on the end of a 15-km fiber lags 75 μs behind the rest of the network.)

Fast Ethernet (100 Mbit/s)

As the name implies, Fast Ethernet is a faster version of Ethernet, using interface cards that operate at 100 Mbit/s but retain the same frame format and transmission protocols as the original 10-Mbit/s Ethernet. The Fast Ethernet standard was approved in 1995. It uses the same network configurations and cabling as 10-Mbit/s Ethernet; the major change is replacing 10-Mbit/s Ethernet cards with Fast Ethernet cards. However, the faster speed limits coax runs to 100 m.

The Fast Ethernet specification limits half-duplex transmission to 412 m over either single- or multimode fiber, a travel time of 2 µs. Full-duplex transmission stretches the maximum distance to 2 km for multimode fiber and 10 km for single-mode. The differences arise because of differences in the nature of half- and full-duplex transmission.

- Fast Ethernet operates at 100 Mbit/s.

Gigabit Ethernet (1 Gbit/s)

The latest step to higher speeds is Gigabit Ethernet, and you probably won't be surprised that it operates at 1 Gbit/s. At this writing, the final standard has yet to be approved, but the developers have set ambitious goals. The new standard will use the same protocols and frame format as slower Ethernets but with only full-duplex transmission. However, because of the high speed, the node spacing for Gigabit Ethernet is shorter. A special *twinax* cable—a coaxlike cable with a twisted pair at the center instead of a single metal wire—is used for jumper cables running up to 25 m. Four twisted-wire pairs in a Category 5 cable will combine to span up to 100 m. Note that this does not mean one pair in Category 5 cable—the 1-Gbit/s signal is split among four pairs.

- Gigabit Ethernet operates at 1 Gbit/s; it needs fiber to transmit beyond 100 m.

Fiber is expected to be the backbone for Gigabit Ethernet, with copper used only for short connections. The draft standard specifies different maximum distances for four types of fiber cable:

Short-wavelength (780–850 nm) in 62.5/125-µm fibers:	260 m
Short-wavelength (780–850 nm) in 50/125-µm fiber:	525 m
Long-wavelength (1300–1500 nm) in 62.5- or 50-µm fiber:	550 m
Single-mode, long-wavelength:	3 km

Modal dispersion dominates the limit on multimode fibers; it is larger in the larger-core 62.5/125-µm fiber.

The Gigabit Ethernet standard is built around components developed for 1-Gbit/s transmission using the Fibre Channel standard, but it is not itself covered by Fibre Channel.

- Gigabit Ethernet uses Fibre Channel components.

Advocates of Gigabit Ethernet see it as the best choice for backbone networks and a logical choice for transmitting Internet Protocol signals between networks. In their more enthusiastic moments, they envision it replacing almost everything else, but you'll hear that from people promoting other standards as well.

Fibre Channel

Fibre Channel is another ambitious standard, which covers a wide range of signal transmission. You learned about some of its uses in Chapter 19. In addition to covering the point-to-point transmission I emphasized earlier, Fibre Channel also covers switched networks and transmission around loops and other network topologies. Hubs connect nodes to form loops; switches are interconnected to make a fabric that functions somewhat like the phone system in routing signals between devices. However, Fibre Channel processes signals as frames, rather than allocating dedicated channels.

●
Fibre Channel uses 10-bit coding for each byte; top speeds are 4.25 Gbit/s.

To review quickly, Fibre Channel uses a 10-bit coding for each 8-bit byte. The bits can enter the system in parallel, but Fibre Channel transmits them in series. Data rates can be specified either as megabits per second (Mbit/s, sometimes abbreviated Mb/s) or megabytes (Mbytes, sometimes abbreviated MB), which can be confusing. Overhead bits increase the bit rate by 6.25%. Table 25.2 lists the speeds in both formats.

Table 25.2 Fibre channel speeds.

Assigned Number	Megabytes/Second	Megabits per Second (with Overhead)
12.5	12.5	133
25	25	266
50	50	531
100	100	1062
200	200	2125
400	400	4250

Like Gigabit Ethernet, Fibre Channel allows transmission over copper as well as fiber. Twisted pair, coax, and twinax are the major alternatives for speeds of 1 Gbit/s and below; at the higher rates only fiber is specified. Transmission can be in the short- or long-wavelength bands.

Like Ethernet, the Fibre Channel protocol specifies limits on the numbers of terminals in a loop and the arrangement of hubs and switches. The details are beyond the scope of this book, but you should remember Fibre Channel as a high-speed digital transmission standard useful in networks as well as point-to-point transmission.

●
The 100-Mbit/s FDDI standard LAN is based on fiber optics.

Fiber Distributed Data Interface (FDDI)

The Fiber Distributed Data Interface (FDDI) network standard operates at 100 Mbit/s. The FDDI standard calls for the ring topology shown in Figure 25.7, with two rings that can transmit signals in opposite directions to a series of nodes. It also specifies concentrator-type terminals that allow stars and/or branching trees to be added to the main FDDI backbone ring. Normally one ring carries signals while the other is kept in reserve in case of component or cable failure.

FDDI transmission is controlled by a scheme of "token passing" used in slower-speed token ring networks, covered by the IEEE 802.5 standard. Terminals do not contend for space to send signals, as does Ethernet, but instead pass around the loop an authorization code called a *token*. When a node with a message to send receives the token, it holds the token and sends the message, which includes a code identifying its destination. All other nodes ignore the message, which is canceled when it completes its path around the ring. Then the terminal that sent the message begins passing the token around the ring again. You can think of this as a somewhat more orderly scheme than Ethernet transmission, although it has its own limitations.

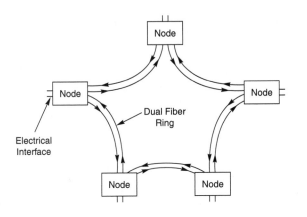

FIGURE 25.7

FDDI's dual fiber ring.

FDDI uses a 4 of 5 transmission code, which adds one extra bit for every four data bits. This means the actual data rate is 125 Mbaud for 100 Mbit/s of user data. This coding scheme balances transmission between on and off bits to enhance operating efficiency.

The standard was developed around fiber-optic transmission, but copper wires can be used to carry 100-Mbit/s signals short distances, and wired versions of FDDI have been developed. (They are sometimes called CDDI, with the C from copper substituted for the F from fiber.)

● Copper wires can carry FDDI signals short distances.

FDDI is nominally a local-area network, but in practice it often serves as a backbone network, linking LANs that operate at slower speeds. In that case the nodes are gateways to other networks. Devices called concentrators area attached to FDDI nodes to combine signals from many terminals, or to collect signals from a LAN for transmission to the FDDI network. Higher data rates and the growth of video- and graphics-intensive applications may lead to more use of FDDI as a local-area network.

NODES

●
FDDI nodes
include transmitter,
receiver, bypass
switch, and a
terminal interface.

Each FDDI node includes a transmitter, receiver, and possibly an optional optical bypass switch, as well as an electronic interface to the terminal, as shown in Figure 25.8, for one fiber in the ring. In normal operation, the receiver/transmitter pair acts as a repeater that monitors the signal it receives. The receiver detects and amplifies the signal and passes it along to be decoded. If the message is not addressed to that terminal, the signal is regenerated and passed along to the next terminal, but not processed by the terminal. If the signal is addressed to that terminal, it is passed on to the terminal (via the electronic connections on top) as well as regenerated and transmitted to the next terminal. This approach allows transmission of signals through up to 2 km of fiber between nodes. The maximum length of the entire ring, constrained by default settings of recovery timers, is 200 km, passing through a thousand nodes.

FIGURE 25.8

*A node in an FDDI
network.*

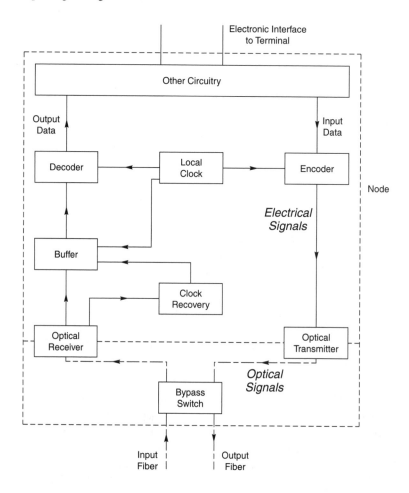

The dual counterrotating ring topology of FDDI allows the network to continue operating in the event of a failure, such as a cut cable or a failed node. When the failure is detected, the FDDI network bypasses the problem area, doing a "wraparound" that converts the network into a single ring until the problem is fixed. An optional optical bypass switch can be used as an extra network survival tool for nodes that may be turned off (such as individual computer terminals). More typically, terminals that may be turned off are connected to the network via an FDDI concentrator, avoiding the need to bypass turned-off nodes.

FIBERS

The FDDI standard specifies some details of the transmission equipment:

- Multimode graded-index fiber with 62.5-μm core and 125-μm cladding is recommended, but 50/125 and 100/140 fiber can also be used. Modal bandwidth should be at least 500 MHz-km at 1300 nm. Attenuation between nodes must not exceed 11 dB (or 7 dB for the low-cost FDDI standard).
- 1300-nm transmission, to take advantage of low fiber loss and dispersion and allow use of inexpensive LED sources.
- *Pin* photodiode detectors because of their lower cost and better reliability than 1300-nm APDs. Minimum power needed at the detector for a bit error rate of 1 in 2.5×10^{10} bits must be no higher than −27 dBm.
- The FDDI standard also provides for the use of single-mode fiber with four combinations of laser transmitters and receivers, depending on transmission distance.

FDDI uses multimode fiber and 1300 nm LEDs.

Other Fiber Networks

Other fiber-optic networks are in development. Most are proprietary or in the research stage, but a few may emerge as standards. Many concepts are still evolving, such as basing data networks on the asynchronous transfer mode (ATM). If history is any guide, most of these ideas will fall by the wayside, but a few may emerge eventually as important new systems.

What Have You Learned?

1. Computers may exchange data over point-to-point links between pairs of devices or over local-area networks (LANs), which link many nodes or devices. Wide-area networks link many LANs and may connect directly with other devices. Networks allow pairs of devices attached to the network to communicate directly with each other.

2. Local-area networks come in star, ring, and bus configurations.

3. Most data communications is over wires because wire systems are cheaper than fiber equipment.

4. Fibers are used in applications where wires will not meet speed and/or distance requirements. Fibers may also be installed when new networks are built to provide capacity for future upgrades. Continuing increases in data-transmission requirements are leading to wider use of fiber data links and networks.

5. Fibers are immune to electromagnetic interference, so they are used where EMI would degrade transmission on wires. Fibers also do not radiate electromagnetic fields, so they are used where data security is critical. The small size and flexibility of fiber cables can simplify installations.

6. Fiber links are recommended between buildings because they are not affected by small variations in the ground voltage level at separate locations, which can cause problems over electric wiring.

7. The nonconductive nature of fibers avoids spark hazards and damage to electronic equipment from power surges.

8. The original Ethernet was a 10-Mbit/s local area network. Fast Ethernet operates at 100 Mbit/s; the new Gigabit Ethernet transmits at 1 Gbit/s. Fibers are sometimes used for long cable runs on standard and Fast Ethernet. Gigabit Ethernet uses copper only for short distances; fiber is standard for longer distances.

9. Gigabit Ethernet uses components developed for Fibre Channel.

10. Fibre Channel includes point-to-point, loop, and switched transmission. Transmission speeds are 133 Mbit/s to 4.25 Gbit/s. Fiber is required for transmission above 1 Gbit/s, but short copper cables can be used at 1 Gbit/s and below.

11. The transmission loss of all copper cables increases with operating frequency. Category 5 twisted-pair cable is a high-capacity copper cable designed for data transmission.

12. The FDDI LAN is based on fiber-optic transmission of 100 Mbit/s over a ring network. FDDI is often used as a wide-area network to connect smaller LANs. FDDI nodes convert optical signals to electronic form to drive terminal equipment and optical transmitters.

What's Next?

In Chapter 26, I will look at some interesting fiber-optic communications outside the normal world of telecommunications and data transmission—military and vehicle systems.

Quiz for Chapter 25

1. Point-to-point data transmission involves

   a. transmission of signal from a central computer to remote nodes.

   b. interchange of data between pairs of devices.

   c. communication between any two devices connected by a common transmission network.

   d. the connection of two devices through a switched network like the telephone system.

2. Which of the following is a local-area network (LAN)?

   a. A system that interconnects many nodes by making all signals pass through a central node.

   b. A ring network with a transmission medium that passes through all nodes.

   c. A common transmission medium or data bus to which all nodes are connected but which does not form a complete ring.

   d. All the above.

   e. None of the above.

3. What makes optical fibers immune to EMI?

   a. They transmit signals as light rather than electric current.

   b. They are too small for magnetic fields to induce currents in them.

   c. Magnetic fields cannot penetrate the glass of the fiber.

   d. They are readily shielded by outer conductors in cable.

4. The most important drawback of optical fibers for point-to-point data transmission is

   a. that they require switches.

   b. the higher costs of fiber equipment.

   c. that fiber cannot provide electrical grounding.

   d. that they do not operate properly at low data rates.

   e. that it is difficult to upgrade.

5. Why would you install a fiber-optic network in a new building rather than a less expensive wire system if both could meet current requirements?

   a. To avoid ground loops.

   b. Fiber is simpler to install in a new building.

   c. To provide future upgrade capability at a cost much lower than retrofitting later.

   d. To get a big kickback from the fiber supplier.

   e. Fiber costs are always lower.

6. Why are fiber-optic cables recommended for connections between buildings?

   a. To avoid ground loops.

   b. Fiber is simpler to install between new buildings.

c. To provide future upgrade capability.

d. To avoid eavesdropping by industrial spies.

e. Fiber costs are always lower.

7. When would optical fibers be used in a standard (10-Mbit/s) Ethernet?

a. Never, the standard requires coaxial cable.

b. To extend transmission distance to reach remote terminals.

c. Routinely, all Ethernet standards require fiber for distances beyond 10 m.

d. When the network includes a hub.

e. When the stockroom is out of coaxial cable.

8. When would optical fibers be used in a Gigabit Ethernet?

a. Never, the standard requires coaxial cable.

b. Always, the standard requires fiber-optic cable at all points.

c. In most cases beyond short distances.

d. Only if the Gigabit Ethernet network had to be connected to an FDDI network.

e. Only when making connections to the Internet.

9. Gigabit Ethernet components are adapted from those developed for which other standard?

a. FDDI.

b. 10-Mbit/s Ethernet.

c. ATM.

d. SONET

e. Fibre Channel.

10. Fibre Channel can be used for which type of transmission?

a. Point-to-point.

b. Ring or loop.

c. Switched.

d. None of the above.

e. All the above.

11. How can you transmit Gigabit Ethernet through Category 5 cable?

a. Under all conditions; it is required by the standard.

b. By adding fiber pairs to the Category 5 cable.

c. By electrically insulating the Category 5 cable.

d. By dividing the signal among four twisted pairs in the Category 5 cable, over 100 m.

e. Only through a miracle.

12. One data rate is specified as a standard in Fibre Channel, FDDI, and the various Ethernet standards. It is

a. 10 Mbit/s.

b. 100 Mbit/s.

c. 250 Mbit/s.

d. 500 Mbit/s.

e. 1 Gbit/s.

Vehicle and Military Fiber Communications

About This Chapter

In the past few chapters, I have examined a wide range of fiber-optic applications in voice, data, and video communications. Some important fiber-optic communication applications do not fall neatly into these categories. One broad area is vehicle communications, including cables to moving vehicles (from remotely controlled submersibles to guided missiles), and cables installed in various types of vehicles (planes, ships, cars, and spacecraft). A second—often overlapping—category is military communications. I'll talk first about vehicle communications, including many military systems. Then I'll cover other military communications that are either portable or fixed in place permanently. This chapter will show you why fibers are used and how these special technologies differ from those in more conventional communication systems.

Remotely Controlled Robotic Vehicles

When we think of remotely controlled vehicles, most of us think first of radio-controlled toys that zip across the floor until the batteries run down. Radio controls are cheap and simple, but limited. You can command your radio-controlled car to go faster, slower, forward, backward, or turn right or left—but not much more.

●
Fiber-optic cables carry signals to control robotic vehicles.

Control of advanced robotic vehicles is a far more demanding job. The operator needs video transmission from a camera in the robot to see the local environment. Other environmental sensing information may also be needed, such as temperature and pressure readings. Signals must flow in the opposite direction so the operator can control the vehicle. Fiber-optic cables carry signals in both directions for a variety of remotely controlled vehicles, often using wavelength-division multiplexing so two signals can travel in opposite directions through a single fiber at different wavelengths. Although care must be taken to protect them, fiber-optic cables can work in places where radio signals cannot, including underwater and in electromagnetically noisy environments. Small single-fiber cables can also be made quite rugged and better able to survive being run over than heavier metal cables. Other fiber advantages include their ability to carry high-bandwidth signals over greater distances and their light weight.

Remotely controlled robots are not widely used today, but they are attractive for a variety of applications. Their prime advantage is that they can go into places unsafe for humans. Robots can probe the radioactive parts of nuclear reactors, to make measurements or repairs, or to dissemble old reactors at the ends of their operating lifetimes. Robots can descend deep into the ocean or explore the surface of the moon or Mars. Robots can be scouts for armies, and they can even deliver weapons to their target (we call them guided missiles). Let's look at how some of this technology works.

Fiber-Optic Guided Missiles

●
A fiber can send images from a television camera in a missile back to a soldier guiding the missile to its target.

Guided missiles are, in a sense, simple robots with rather deadly missions—to deliver bombs to their targets. The Pentagon has developed a system that uses a ruggedized optical fiber to carry control signals to and from a short-range missile on the battlefield, letting a soldier guide it to its target from a safe hiding place. Called FOG-M, for fiber-optic guided missile, the program gives a good idea of how remote control through optical fibers works.

The idea of FOG-M, shown in Figure 26.1, is to send images from a video camera in the missile to a soldier on the ground, who guides the missile to its target. The missile is launched toward the target with a single ruggedized bare optical fiber trailing from it to the launcher. Looking at the video image, the soldier operates controls that direct the missile to its target. The soldier can follow the missile right to impact.

Military agencies like FOG-M because the soldier operating it keeps safe under cover. This is an advantage over laser-guided bombs, where the laser operator must be in line with the target to project a laser spot onto it. Missiles can be guided by wire, but the wires can't carry video images, which allow more accurate guidance. Only an optical fiber has the combination of small size, light weight, strength, low attenuation, and bandwidth needed to transmit video signals over the 10 or 20 km needed for missile guidance.

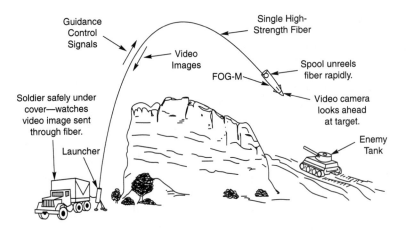

FIGURE 26.1

A soldier guiding a FOG-M missile to its target.

The basic hardware for FOG-M is shown in Figure 26.2. The missile contains a video camera, a fiber-optic video transmitter, a low-bandwidth receiver, and a special reel of fiber. One end of the fiber is mounted on the launcher, so it remains behind when the missile is fired. As the missile speeds toward its target, the fiber rapidly unwinds from the reel, forming a long arc over the battlefield. The reel is a critical component, because the fiber will tangle or break if not unwound at the right rate. The camera transmits a video image to a soldier at the launcher, who sends control signals back through the fiber to guide the missile to keep the target in the proper place in his field of view.

Fiber unwinds from a special reel on the missile.

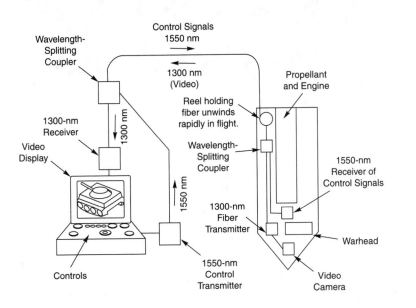

FIGURE 26.2

FOG-M components.

FOG-M uses wavelength-division multiplexing to send signals in opposite directions. In this drawing, video signals from the missile are sent at 1300 nm through fibers with low dispersion at that wavelength. Low-bandwidth control signals are sent at 1550 nm in the opposite direction.

Robotic Vehicles on Land

Fiber cables can control robotic land vehicles for scouting or weapon delivery.

The same principles can be applied to robotic vehicles for use on land. Much of the work is military. The Marine Corps has tested unmanned ground vehicles, linked to a controller through a fiber-optic cable, like the one shown in Figure 26.3. In addition to video, the controller receives signals from sensors on the vehicle. Those inputs let the controller drive the vehicle, and even fire machine guns mounted on it. Fiber cables are immune to electromagnetic interference and electromagnetic pulse effects that could block radio or wire communications, vital considerations on the battlefield.

FIGURE 26.3

Remotely operated vehicle is controlled by fiber cable. (Courtesy of AT&T)

Ruggedization of the cable is critical for military systems because the vehicle is virtually certain to run over it. In the Marine Corps experiments, a ruggedized 2.5-mm cable carried signals to and from a modified "HMM-WV," or "hummer"—the high-mobility multipurpose wheeled vehicle that is replacing the venerable military jeep. The Army is working on a robotic tank, called ROBAT for Robotic Obstacle Breaching Assault Tank, which may require an even more rugged cable 4 mm in diameter.

The high bandwidth of fiber cables makes it possible to consider using virtual reality techniques to remotely operate robotic ground vehicles. Sensors on the vehicle would scan the area, serving as the operator's "eyes," while other sensors would listen for sounds and "feel" the terrain. The sights, sounds, and feel would be conveyed to the operator—far from the vehicle—using screens, speakers, and perhaps a moving chair. The goal would be to make the operator feel as if he or she were driving the vehicles, but without being exposed to the dangers faced by the vehicle.

Remote-controlled robots could also serve many nonmilitary purposes in environments hostile or dangerous to humans. Robots could inspect the "hot" interiors of nuclear power plants or perform needed repairs inside the reactor. The robots could be left inside the reactor permanently if they became contaminated. Specialized robots could be used to dismantle old reactors, without exposing people to the highly radioactive materials inside. Likewise, remotely controlled robots could clean up hazardous wastes. A fiber-optic cable was used to control a multilegged robot built to climb into a hazardous Antarctic volcano and collect data. As with military vehicles, the immunity of fiber-optic cables to EMI and EMP effects is a big plus.

> Remotely controlled robots could clean up hazardous wastes and dismantle old nuclear reactors.

Submersible Robots

Radio links can substitute for cables in many land applications, but most radio waves don't penetrate far into water. Cables or acoustic signaling are required to maintain contact with submerged vessels. Although crewed submersibles can operate without a continuous link to the surface, only cables can provide the transmission capacity needed to remotely operate a sophisticated submerged vessel. Fiber cables are preferred because of their high bandwidth and durability.

> Hybrid fiber-electrical cables carry signals and power to remotely operated submersibles.

Hybrid fiber and electrical cables carry the signals and power needed to steer and accelerate submerged vessels, as well as bring video signals and telemetry to the surface, where shipboard operators can monitor them.

Fiber cables also allow operators aboard a submersible to control robotic vehicles that can be sent into small spaces or dangerous areas. The most famous example came when Robert Ballard's team from the Woods Hole Oceanographic Institution discovered the sunken wreck of the *Titanic* in 1985. The scientists discovered the wreck with *Alvin,* a submersible that carried three people. However, they did not dare to explore the inside of the deteriorating wreck. Instead, they used a 250-lb robot, tethered to *Alvin* with a fiber-optic cable that carried control signals. It was this fiber-controlled robot that photographed details of the dark interior of the wreck. Ballard remains enthusiastic about the use of fiber-controlled robot submarines.

Fibers in Aircraft

It was not too long ago that most aircraft were controlled by hydraulic systems. When the pilot moved a lever, it would cause hydraulic fluid to move a control surface (e.g., a wing flap), much as hydraulic brakes work in an automobile. Newer planes have fly-by-wire electronic controls that send electronic signals to motors that move control surfaces. Modern aircraft—particularly military planes—also use many electronic systems

> Fibers can serve as the control networks for aircraft.

and sensors, adding to signal transmission requirements. These include radars, navigation and guidance systems, and—in military planes—weapons systems with automatic targeting capabilities and electronic countermeasure equipment.

Like many other users faced with increasing communication requirements, the aerospace industry and the military began investigating fiber optics. In fact, the Pentagon began looking seriously at airborne fiber-optic transmission in the 1970s. An added motivation was development of composite nonmetallic materials for aircraft skins. Such materials are stronger per pound than metals, but unlike a metal fuselage they cannot shield the inside of the plane from electromagnetic interference and potential enemy countermeasures. Using fiber could overcome such problems, as well as reduce cable weight.

● *New military planes use some fiber links, but fibers are not yet standardized for aircraft.*

It takes years for new technology to work its way into military hardware, and complete military specifications have yet to be completed for aircraft fiber optics. Some optical fiber was used in the B-1 bomber, which was originally designed in the 1970s when fiber was new and largely untested. Other planes also use some short lengths of fiber. A 6-m (20-ft) length of fiber cable carries sensor data in the Marine Corps' AV-8B harrier attack aircraft. Future aircraft might benefit from more extensive use of fiber. Calculations indicate that the B-1's weight could have been reduced by as much as a ton if fiber had replaced all its wire cables. Such weight reductions could mean greater range, lower fuel requirements, or higher load capacity.

Few design details have been released on Stealth aircraft, but they probably make much more extensive use of fibers. Stealth technology depends on reducing radar visibility, and that, in turn, requires minimizing the use of metal. The lack of a metal fuselage leaves advanced electronic systems vulnerable to electromagnetic interference and enemy countermeasures, pushing a shift to fiber. Fiber transmission would also help prevent EMI radiation by aircraft wiring which an enemy might spot.

The short distances involved in systems installed on single aircraft make multimode fibers the logical choice for on-board fiber systems. Standard military specifications call for radiation-hardened fiber, a heritage of the cold war. Most military specifications call for radiation hardening of all electronic and communication equipment.

Light weight and immunity to electromagnetic interference are also crucial for spacecraft, making fiber-optic systems attractive, and some are used in the international space station.

Shipboard Fiber Systems

● *Big ships have massive communication requirements.*

The communication requirements of a big ship rival those of an office building. Ships have their own telephone networks to keep officers and crew in contact. They have a variety of sensing and weapon systems, as well as radars, sonar systems, and radio links with military communication systems. Modern ships have computer rooms, both to control weapon systems on board and to analyze their situation. Computers have become so important that the Navy uses local area networks that are essentially militarized versions of FDDI. Figure 26.4 shows how optical fibers can link some of these systems together.

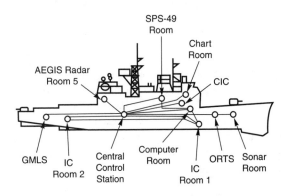

FIGURE 26.4

Cabling in a large ship. (Courtesy of AT&T)

For example, the *U.S.S. Washington,* launched in July 1992 from Newport News Shipyard, makes extensive use of fibers. Fibers provide the backbone of the ship's telephone system. Fiber links reach all the way to the desks of officers. Fibers collect signals from cameras on the exterior of the ship and carry information to and from many other systems.

Weight is not as critical on ships as it is on aircraft, but scrapping metal cable systems can save space. Fibers are also immune to electromagnetic interference, which can be a problem when mechanical and electronic systems are crammed together on a ship. EMI immunity is also important to avoid potential enemy countermeasures designed to knock out electronic systems.

As in aircraft, the usual choice of fiber is radiation-hardened 62.5/125 fiber, although the Navy is looking at single-mode fiber. The Navy systems use special water-blocking cables, designed to prevent water from flowing through empty parts of the cable itself.

Military Systems

The Pentagon has developed a host of fiber-optic systems with cryptic code numbers and acronyms and has deployed some of them. Some systems are fixed strategic-communication networks that operate much like civilian telecommunication lines. Others are large programs that use a small amount of fiber. Some are classified. It is impossible to describe the whole range of military systems, but I will give a few examples of how and why fibers are used.

Radar Remoting

Fibers carry signals from remote radars to control centers.

Radar is invaluable in spotting and tracking enemy aircraft, but it also has an important drawback. Microwave emissions from radar dishes are a target for enemy radiation-seeking missiles. Military planners figure they are bound to lose a few radar dishes in a battle, so they want to put the dishes far from ground control centers. That lets the control center—and the soldiers operating it—survive if a radiation-seeking missile takes out a radar dish.

That was difficult when only metal cables were available. Military radar generates an analog intermediate-frequency output at 70 MHz. That frequency is high enough to carry the signal but too high to go far through metal cable. The only way to locate the radar dish a comfortable distance from the control center was to install repeaters, which created other problems. However, single-mode fiber optics can easily transmit the 70-MHz radar signals a few kilometers without repeaters, so fiber cables have become standard—and radar dishes have been safely moved to remote locations.

Battlefield Communication Systems

The military is now turning to wireless communications on the battlefield, because cables take time to deploy and once they are deployed, can get in the way. Mobility is vital on the battlefield, and military engineers have developed wireless systems that can withstand enemy jamming. The new generation of wireless technology will replace an earlier generation of portable fiber-optic systems that military engineers developed to overcome serious problems with metal cables.

The Army Communications and Electronics Command developed the portable fiber system for temporary field headquarters. Field command centers require extensive communication capabilities, and the equipment to provide those capabilities must be rugged and easy to deploy. Cables may be laid in the dirt, or strung from trees or buildings. Soldiers may step on them, and vehicles may drive over them. The Army had been using cables containing 26 copper wire pairs or coax, but these were bulky, cumbersome to install, and very vulnerable to damage during use or installation. To avoid these problems, engineers working for the Army and military contractors developed rugged fiber cables able to survive being run over by heavy vehicles. One sample survived being run over by 30,000 cars at the entrance to a contractor's parking lot.

Shifting to fiber greatly simplified logistics. It takes a few trucks to carry enough 26-pair cable for a regional command center, and a couple of hefty soldiers to carry a reel full of the thick cable. A single truck can carry all the fiber cable needed, and a single soldier or a helicopter can easily lay the thin two-fiber cable. By fiber-optic standards, the system is simple, using 850-nm LED sources, silicon *pin* receivers, and radiation-hardened 50/125 μm fibers. Yet it was entirely adequate for military needs until wireless systems promised a way to dispense with cables altogether.

Automotive Fiber Optics

Once upon a time, automotive engineering took a nap reminiscent of Rip Van Winkle's, and automotive innovation was confined mostly to sculpting tail fins. The industry finally woke in the early 1970s, kicked awake, perhaps a bit brutally, by government and public concern over pollution, safety, and fuel economy. After some angry and sometimes befuddled protests, automotive engineers found that electronics could solve many of their problems and enhance their products in many ways.

They also discovered that automobiles are not friendly environments for electronics. Semiconductor electronics are quite vulnerable to electromagnetic interference because they need only a few volts to switch states, and EMI can make strange things happen on the road. Radio signals bouncing from the metal deck of a Chicago bridge confused the control systems of early electronic brakes being tested on buses, even though the transmitter was half a mile away. Delicate electronics were vulnerable to extremes of heat and cold; cars must survive in conditions ranging from a sun-scorched Miami parking lot in mid-summer to a frozen Anchorage snowdrift in mid-winter.

The proliferation of automotive electronics, like those cited in Table 26.1, have complicated matters. Many of these systems use microprocessors, even for such simple-seeming tasks as control of intermittent windshield wipers. The more electronic systems involved, the more complex the wiring harnesses needed to deliver power and control signals. Because many electronic systems are optional, automakers must stock many different harnesses in their plants and make sure the proper one is installed in each car. Servicing them can be even more of a problem, as you quickly learn if you try to find and fix a defective electrical connection somewhere in an automobile.

Automobiles use many electronic systems but have been very slow to adapt optical fibers.

Table 26.1 Some electrical and electronic systems available in cars.

Speedometer	Odometer	Light-on warning
Battery guard	Interior lights	Illuminated entry
Dimming control	Exterior lights	Fuel monitor
Transmission control	Clock/calendar	Alarm
Climate diagnostic panel	Airbag	Air conditioner
Rear-window defogger	Cruise control	Cellular phone
Automatic latch release	Cigarette lighter	Windshield wipers
Instrument panel	Coolant fan control	Horn
Electronic fuel injection	Windshield washer	Hazard flashers
Seat-belt warning buzzer	Radio/tape player/CD player	Power windows
Power door locks	Navigation aids	Radar detector
Automatic seat belts		

Frustrated automotive engineers turned to fiber optics as one possible solution. Fibers can't carry electrical power, but they can carry control signals. Engineers realized that those control signals could be used to switch electrical power off and on to accessories such as power windows. That would let them send a signal from the dashboard to roll down the window, without passing current to drive the motor through the dashboard switch—one of the things that makes wiring harnesses very complex. The control signals don't require much bandwidth, so they could be multiplexed together on a single fiber network with modest bandwidth of 1 Mbit/s. Engineers have demonstrated such systems, and they work—but you won't find them in 1998 cars.

● *Fiber optics can carry control signals, but not power.*

Fiber-Optic Limitations

What happened to automotive fiber optics is a mixture of technical and organizational problems. The giants of the U.S. auto industry have long been slow to change established technology—especially technology critical for safety. You can drive your car safely without a working radio or power door lock, but not if the steering, fuel injection, or windshield wipers don't work. They want to make sure that new technology can stand up to the rigors of automotive use. They don't want to take big risks, or spend extra money.

● *Automakers want to use plastic fibers, but their temperature range is limited.*

They also try to make sure that cars are easy to assemble and can be fixed by trained mechanics. They are not about to equip every auto shop in the country with fusion splicers for single-mode fibers. They want instead to use large-core all-plastic fibers that could be cut with a razor blade and spliced together (if necessary) with an inexpensive mount. Plastic fibers can handle the data rate over the required distance, but automotive engineers worry if they can withstand the extreme high temperatures in engine compartments.

Future Prospects

Will automakers ever overcome the formidable technical barriers—and their own conservatism? Probably. Fiber optics reportedly have been used in a few high-end cars in Japan, but they evidently have not been successful enough to spread or to be heralded as an important new feature in car advertisements. Some progress has been made on plastic fibers, although the biggest automotive challenge is the toughest to surmount—making plastic fibers that can withstand the hostile conditions inside an engine compartment over the lifetime of a modern automobile.

Every few years, I hear rumors that someone has at last surmounted the technical problems and that a carmaker is ready to install fibers. The word I've heard is to watch for the 2000-model Mercedes. It's certainly possible, but I'm not holding my breath.

What Have You Learned?

1. Optical fibers can carry signals to control robotic vehicles on land, in air, or in the water. Fibers' advantages are their small size, light weight, immunity to EMI, and high bandwidth. Ruggedization of cables is critical for vehicle applications.

2. A fiber can transmit images from a television camera in a missile back to a soldier guiding the missile to its target. Fiber unwinds from a special reel on the missile.

3. Remotely controlled robots could serve as scouts or deliver weapons in the battlefield. In civilian applications, remotely controlled robots could clean up hazardous wastes and dismantle old nuclear reactors.

4. Fibers can be used for signal transmission in aircraft because of EMI immunity, small size, and light weight. Fibers are also attractive for transmission in large satellites.

5. Fiber-optic communication networks are used on military ships, which have large communication needs.

6. Because fibers can transmit signals farther without repeaters than other cables, they can be used to put radar dishes far from military battlefield control centers, reducing risks to soldiers.

7. Fiber-optic cables replaced bulky 26-pair wire cables for portable battlefield communication networks, but are now being replaced by wireless communications.

8. The automobile industry has tested plastic fibers for carrying control signals and other information between the many electronic systems in automobiles. However, engineers worry if plastic fibers can withstand the extreme environments in cars.

What's Next?

In Chapters 27 and 28, I will look at the many uses of fiber optics outside of communications.

Quiz for Chapter 26

1. What kinds of remotely operated vehicles cannot be controlled by operators through fiber optics?

    a. Guided missiles.

    b. Submersibles.

    c. Battlefield scouting systems.

    d. Guns mounted on vehicles.

    e. Satellites.

2. What signals are transmitted from fiber-guided missiles to the operator?

    a. Video images of the target.

    b. Control commands.

    c. Data on temperature and pressure.

    d. Data on fiber attenuation.

3. How are signals transmitted to and from a fiber-guided missile?

    a. Separately through two fibers in a single cable.

    b. Bidirectionally through one fiber by time-division multiplexing.

    c. Bidirectionally through one fiber by wavelength-division multiplexing.

    d. Signals are transmitted only one way.

    e. From the missile through the fiber; to the missile via radio.

4. Which of the following attributes of fiber optics are important for remote control of land vehicles?

    a. Secure data transmission.

    b. Lightweight, durable cable.

    c. EMI immunity.

    d. b and c.

    e. a, b, and c.

5. Which of the following reasons do not influence the use of fibers for signal transmission in aircraft?

    a. Optical fibers are immune to EMI.

    b. Optical fibers are lighter than wires.

    c. Aircraft lack adequate power supplies for wire-based communications.

    d. Military aircraft must be hardened against enemy electronic countermeasures.

    e. Fiber optics can help reduce aircraft visibility to radar.

6. Why are fiber-optic cables used to connect radar dishes to battlefield control centers?

    a. Because they carry radar signals far enough that the dishes can be placed a few kilometers from the control centers.

    b. Because they are immune to electromagnetic eavesdropping.

    c. Because they are inexpensive.

    d. Because the control centers already use fiber optics.

    e. Because a top military official's brother-in-law sells fiber-optic cable.

7. What did fiber-optic cables replace in portable battlefield communication systems?

    a. Obsolete plastic fibers that have become brittle with age.

    b. 26-pair cable and coax.

    c. Telephone cables.

    d. Microwave transmission.

    e. Nothing—without fibers such systems were not practical.

8. What type of fiber systems were used in portable battlefield networks?

  a. Plastic fibers transmitting in the red.

  b. Multimode fibers transmitting 850 nm.

  c. Multimode fibers transmitting 1300 nm.

  d. Single-mode fibers transmitting 1300 nm.

  e. Single-mode dispersion-shifted fibers transmitting 1550 nm.

9. What is the major disadvantage of fiber-optic cables for portable battlefield communications?

  a. They cannot be repaired in the field.

  b. They are not durable enough.

  c. They are vulnerable to EMI and jamming.

  d. They are cables and they can get in the way.

  e. They lack enough bandwidth.

10. What problem has limited the use of fiber optics in automotive control systems?

  a. Optical fibers cannot conduct electric power.

  b. The high cost of single-mode connectors.

  c. Temperature limitations of plastic fibers.

  d. Pollution regulations.

  e. Automotive engineers don't like anything electronic.

Fiber-Optic Sensors

About This Chapter

So far, I have concentrated on how optical fibers are used for communications. However, fiber optics also have other important uses. This chapter will show how fibers are used as sensors. Fiber sensors work in a variety of ways, sometimes just using fibers to deliver light, other times monitoring changes induced in light transmission caused by external effects. Fiber sensors can measure pressure or temperature, serve as gyroscopes to measure direction and rotation, sense acoustic waves at the bottom of the sea, and do many other tasks.

Fiber-Sensing Concepts

The label *fiber sensors* covers a broad range of devices that work in many different ways. The simplest use optical fibers merely as a probe, to detect changes in light outside the fiber. The fiber may collect light from a given point, to see if an object (such as a part on an assembly line) is present or not. The fiber also may collect light from another type of optical sensor that responds to its environment in a way that changes the light reaching the fiber. For example, a prism in a tank of liquid may start reflecting light back into a fiber probe if the liquid level drops below the prism's reflective surface, exposing it to air so total internal reflection occurs.

Other fiber sensors detect changes in light passing through a fiber that is affected by changes in the outside world, such as the temperature or pressure. That may seem strange if you're used to communications fibers, which generally do not respond significantly to outside effects. However, you can design special fibers or special structures within fibers to respond more strongly to outside effects. You also can use optical effects such as interference to detect small effects that accumulate over long lengths of fiber. In these ways, fiber sensors can detect changes in quantities such as temperature, pressure, and rotation.

● **Fibers can serve as probes or as sensors themselves.**

There is an amazing multitude of fiber sensors, most used only for a few special purposes. This book can't cover them all. Instead, I will concentrate on simple examples and important types of sensors. I will first survey simple fiber sensors, where the fiber merely probes the environment. Then I will describe sensing mechanisms and some important types of fiber sensors and their applications.

Fiber-Optic Probes

Fiber-optic probes collect light from remote points, often sampling light that was delivered there by fibers. They come in two broad families that perform different sensing functions. The simpler ones look to see if light is present or absent at the point they observe. Others collect light from remote optical sensors, bringing it back to a place where it can be analyzed.

Simple Probes

● **Fiber probes can detect objects when they block or reflect light.**

Figure 27.1 shows a simple fiber-optic probe checking for parts on an assembly line. One optical fiber delivers light from an external source, and a second fiber collects light emerging from the first, as long as nothing gets between the two. When a part passes between them on the assembly line, it blocks the light. Thus light off indicates that a part is on the assembly line, and light on indicates that no part is passing by.

FIGURE 27.1

Fiber-optic probe checks for parts on an assembly line.

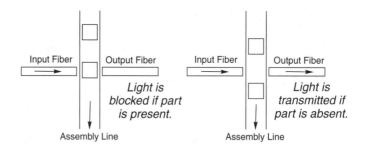

This concept can be used in many ways and is not new. One early example was reading holes in the punched cards used to input data to early mainframe computers, although in this case a detector directly sensed the transmitted light without a light-collecting fiber. The card passed an array of fibers at a fixed speed, and detectors monitored light transmission as a function of time. When a hole passed the end of the fiber, light reached the detector. When there was no hole, the card blocked the light. The technique was simple and effective, but punched cards are now museum pieces.

More refined variations are possible, such as measuring the size of parts to make sure they meet tolerances. An array of fibers can be mounted beside the production line, so passing parts block the light to some of them. The parts pass inspection if all the fibers above the maximum height receive light and all those below the minimum height do not. Parts that are too small or too tall are rejected when light reaches fibers that are supposed to be dark or does not reach fibers that are supposed to be illuminated.

Optical Remote Sensing

Fiber probes can also collect light from other types of optical sensors. In this case, the fibers function like wires attached to an electronic sensor. The optical sensor (which is not a fiber) responds in some way to the environment, changing the light that reaches the fiber probe. The fiber carries that light to a detector, which senses the change.

Fibers can collect light from other optical sensors.

One example is the liquid-level sensor shown in Figure 27.2, which senses when the gasoline in tank trucks reaches a certain level. Many tank trucks are filled from the bottom so vapor left in the tank can be collected to control pollution, and the liquid level must be sensed to prevent overfilling. One fiber delivers light to a prism mounted at the proper level. If there is no liquid in the tank, the light from the fiber experiences total internal reflection at the base of the prism and is directed back into the collecting fiber. If the bottom of the prism is covered with gasoline, total internal reflection cannot occur at the angle that light strikes the prism's bottom face, and no more light is reflected back into the fiber. When the light signal stops, the control system shuts off the gas pump.

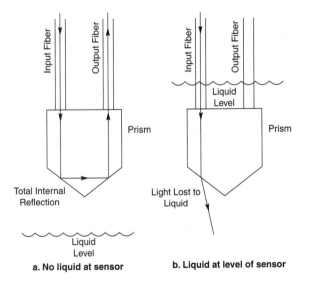

FIGURE 27.2

A liquid-level sensor.

Another example senses temperature changes by observing the response of a phosphor in a glass blob at the end of a fiber. Ultraviolet light transmitted by the fiber stimulates fluorescence from the phosphor at several wavelengths. The ratio of fluorescence at the different wavelengths changes with temperature. The fiber collects the fluorescent light and delivers it to an optical analyzer that compares intensities at different wavelengths and thus measures the temperature.

Fiber-Sensing Mechanisms

Some effects can
change how fibers
transmit light.

Outside influences can directly affect light transmission in fibers in a variety of ways, depending on the type of fiber and how the fiber is mounted. For communications, you design fibers and cables to be isolated from the environment. For sensing, you design fibers to respond as strongly as possible. For example, you may dope fibers with materials that change their refractive index as temperature or pressure change. Or you may mount fibers between grooved plates, so increasing pressure on the plates causes microbending.

Countless fiber sensors have been demonstrated in laboratories around the world. A variety are used for practical measurements, although none are in true mass production. It's impossible to cover all the diverse types of fiber sensors here, but I will give you an overview of the basic principles of intrinsic fiber sensing, which depends on properties of the fiber.

The Idea of Sensing

Sensors convert
something hard to
measure into units
easier to observe.

The basic idea of sensing is to convert a physical effect you want to observe into a form you can measure. Let's start with a familiar sensor, a thermometer filled with mercury or some other liquid. As temperature changes, the liquid expands. Most liquid in the thermometer sits in the hollow bulb at the bottom; the hollow tube calibrated with temperatures has a much smaller volume. (It looks big because the glass or plastic cylinder magnifies the apparent width of the tube.) The engineers who design thermometers know how much the liquid expands per degree, so they can calculate how much liquid they need to expand to fill the extra tube.

Suppose, for example, mercury expands 0.01% per degree Celsius. Then, if you start with a volume of 1 cm^3 of mercury, it grows 0.0001 cm^3 larger for each degree it is warmed. To make a mercury thermometer, you can attach a bulb containing 1 cm^3 of mercury to a thin tube marked with lines that indicate 0.0001-cm^3 units of volume inside the tube. If the tube's cross-sectional area is 0.001 cm^2, each 0.1 cm—or 1 mm—represents a 1° temperature change. It isn't quite that simple, because a careful designer must consider thermal expansion of the tube itself, but that's the basic idea. The thermometer converts a hard-to-measure unit, temperature, into one that is easier to measure, length of a column of mercury.

Fiber sensors work in the same way, but they measure properties like temperature by observing the light transmitted through the sensor. They make the property they are trying to measure modulate the light in some way.

Measurement Methods

Most fiber sensors work by modulating the light passing through them in one of three ways:

- Directly altering the intensity
- Affecting the polarization of the light
- Shifting the phase of the transmitted light

To actually measure that modulation, you have to convert those changes to variations in intensity. Let's look a bit closer to see how that works.

DIRECT INTENSITY MODULATION

Sensors that directly change light intensity are conceptually simple. The simplest of all is a crack sensor based on a fiber embedded in a material. As long as the material is intact, the fiber transmits light without impediment. A crack breaks the fiber, reducing light intensity or cutting the light off altogether, depending on how large the crack is. You can think of it as a simple on-off sensor. If the light is on, you can drive a heavy truck across the bridge, but if the light stops coming through the fiber, you need to check the structure.

> Some fiber sensors directly modulate transmitted light intensity.

A more subtle type of intensity sensor depends on microbending. Figure 27.3 shows a simple pressure sensor based on a fiber passing between a pair of grooved plates. If there's no pressure on the plates, the fiber remains straight, and light passes through it. Pressure on the plates causes microbending—the more pressure, the more microbending—and microbending makes light leak from the fiber core. The more pressure, the less light out.

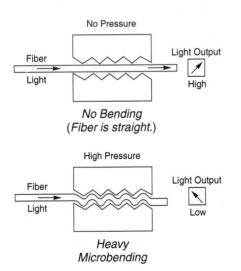

FIGURE 27.3

Increasing pressure on the plates causes microbending, reducing light transmission.

POLARIZATION SENSING

Some fiber sensors affect light polarization.

Other sensors affect the polarization of light in the fiber. There are a number of possible variations. One example is sensing of magnetic fields, using a process called Faraday rotation, which rotates the plane of polarized light by an angle proportional to the strength of the magnetic field. If you send vertically polarized light through a sensitive fiber, you can measure the magnetic field by measuring the angle the polarization is rotated.

In practice, you don't directly measure the angle of polarization, however. You actually measure the changes in the intensity of light transmitted by another polarizer. If the second polarizer is also vertical, the decrease in transmitted light intensity measures the degree of rotation. This converts a change in polarization to a change in intensity, which is easier to measure.

Other fiber sensors produce effects that affect light of different polarizations differently. For example, pressure may change the refractive index for vertically polarized light differently than that for horizontally polarized light. This leads to a phase change in the intensities of the light in different polarizations, which requires another kind of measurement, as I describe next.

PHASE OR INTERFEROMETRIC SENSING

Interferometric sensors can detect very small changes.

Sensors also can modulate the phase of light to cause interference effects that modulate light intensity. To understand how this works, let's continue with the example of the pressure sensor that changes the phase of polarized light. By changing the refractive indexes of different polarizations by different amounts, the sensor effectively delays one polarization relative to the other. To measure this, you can separate the two polarizations at the output end, rotate one by 90°, equalize the path lengths, and then mix them together, as shown in Figure 27.4. If the two polarizations are in phase—that is, there is no delay between the two of them—the output is high. If one is 180° behind the other, the output is low.

Interferometric sensors are very sensitive to small changes, but they have a few specific limitations. One is that the light has to be coherent enough that interference occurs. Thus you need either laser sources or very carefully equalized path lengths. In addition, there is an inherent ambiguity because a 360° delay produces the same effect as no delay or a 720° delay. You have to keep track of how many cycles of shifting occur or just measure a small shift.

Note also that to convert the phase shift to a change in intensity for this sensor, you need to compare two signals. In the case of the polarization sensor, these signals are two polarizations of light affected differently by pressure-induced changes in refractive index.

Another approach is to compare the phases of light passing through two fibers, one isolated from the environment and the other exposed to it. If the effective length of the fiber exposed to the environment changes, the phase changes, which can be measured by mixing light from the two fibers in an interferometric detector.

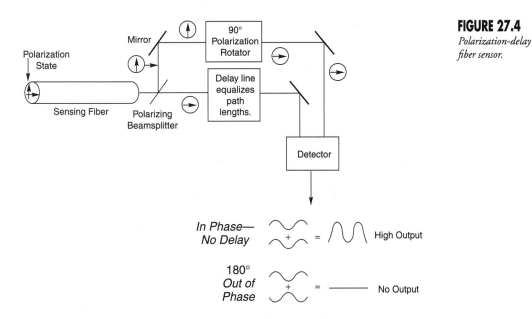

FIGURE 27.4
*Polarization-delay
fiber sensor.*

A third approach is to make a sensor that is itself an interferometer, which changes its resonance wavelengths as pressure, temperature, or other conditions change. I'll describe an example of that type of sensor later.

Constant versus Changing Measurements

One of the many subtleties of sensing is the difference between measuring long-term values and changing quantities. From a physical viewpoint, sound waves are really short-term variations in atmospheric pressure. However, you can't use the same instruments to measure the two. A microphone picks up sound waves but not atmospheric pressure. On the other hand, a barometer measures pressure but not sound waves.

The same is true for fiber sensors. Acoustic sensors work on different principles than pressure sensors. An interferometric fiber sensor on the seabed could pick up undersea sounds, but you'd need a different sensor to measure the pressure there.

Some Fiber Sensor Examples

Now that you've learned the basic principles of fiber sensing, let's look at a few examples. I will first cover a few general examples, then look at some promising specific cases.

Microbending Sensors

One attraction of microbending sensors is their simplicity. Microbending directly affects loss of a fiber; the more microbending, the higher the loss and the less light transmitted.

Therefore, microbending sensors require only a simple measurement of light intensity, not a sophisticated interferometric setup to measure phase.

Pressure is the most straightforward quantity to measure with a microbending sensor, as shown in Figure 24.3. You can adapt microbending sensors to measure both static pressure and acoustic waves by designing and calibrating them differently. For total pressure—such as detecting whether a seat is occupied—you could use a fairly small sensor that would not respond to a 10-lb briefcase but would respond to a small 80-lb person. On the other hand, you would use a longer length of more sensitive fiber to detect acoustic waves, monitoring output continuously to detect their variation in time.

Length and Refractive Index Changes

● Changing length or refractive index causes a phase shift.

A large family of sensors depend on changes in the effective length of the sensor, which depends on both the refractive index and the physical length. Recall that the time, t, it takes light to travel through a length, L, of material with refractive index n is

$$t = \frac{nL}{c}$$

where c is the speed of light in a vacuum. You can think of nL as the "effective length" of the material. A change in temperature can affect both refractive index and physical length, giving

$$t = \frac{(n + \Delta n)(L + \Delta L)}{c} \approx \frac{nL + n\Delta L + L\Delta n}{c}$$

as long as the changes are small. The result is a change in transit time,

$$\Delta t = \frac{n\Delta L + L\Delta n}{c}$$

which is equivalent to a phase shift in the light emerging from the sensor.

Interferometric detection can sense this phase change. Note that the principles of operation are the same whether the sensor is detecting a temperature change that affects only physical length of the fiber, a pressure change that affects only its refractive index, or something that affects both. (In practice, temperature change may affect refractive index as well as physical length.)

Changes in Light Guiding

Refractive index change also can be measured if it affects light guiding in the fiber. Suppose, for example, the refractive indexes of core and cladding vary with temperature in different ways. At 0°C, the core index is 1.50 and the cladding index is 1.49. As temperature increases, the core index decreases by 0.0005 per degree, but the cladding index decreases by 0.0004 per degree. At 100°C, the two refractive indexes would both equal 1.45. At that point, the fiber would stop confining light to the core, so output light intensity would drop to near zero.

In practice, light intensity might decrease as the core and cladding indexes approached each other, because at smaller index differences total internal reflection would trap an increasingly narrow range of light rays in a large-core fiber. However, the principle has been demonstrated in a sensor that can measure temperature within a few degrees.

Fiber Fabry-Perot Interferometer Sensors

The fiber Fabry-Perot interferometer is a sensor that detects a phase shift within a resonant cavity rather than by comparing the phase shifts of light taking two different paths. The sensing element is a section of fiber that has reflective layers on each end, as shown in Figure 27.5. Light passes through a partly reflecting layer and is reflected by a totally reflecting mirror some distance behind it. The layers can be made by splicing fiber segments together at those points.

A fiber Fabry-Perot interferometer detects a phase shift in a resonant cavity in the fiber.

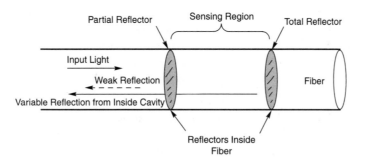

FIGURE 27.5

Fiber Fabry-Perot interferometer sensor.

These two mirrors form a Fabry-Perot interferometer, which has a series of resonances at characteristic wavelengths defined by the cavity length and refractive index. Recall from earlier that the round-trip distance must equal an integral number of wavelengths in the material, with refractive index included to account for the difference between the vacuum wavelength, λ, and the wavelength in the material, λ/n.

$$N\lambda = 2Ln$$

If the wavelength stays fixed and the cavity is long compared to the wavelength, the intensity of the reflected light changes with variations in length or refractive index. In temperature sensors, the change in refractive index is about 20 times larger than the change in length, so it dominates the phase shift. The same approach can be used to sense pressure and strain.

Fiber Grating Sensors

The fiber gratings you learned about in Chapter 7 also can be used in sensors. As in a fiber Fabry-Perot interferometer, changes in the refractive index change reflective properties such as the wavelength of peak reflectivity.

Fiber-Optic Gyroscopes

The fiber-optic gyroscope is probably the most successful fiber sensor so far. It relies on optical processes to sense rotation around the axis of a ring of fiber. Rotation sensing is vital for aircraft and missiles, which have traditionally used gimbaled mechanical gyroscopes as references. Fiber gyroscopes (and laser gyroscopes that serve a similar purpose but operate on different principles) offer a number of advantages, including no moving parts, greater reliability, and no need for a warm-up period to start the gyro.

Figure 27.6 shows the workings of a fiber gyro. Light from a single source is split into two beams directed into opposite ends of a loop of single-mode fiber. In actual sensors, the fiber is wound many times around a cylinder, but the drawing shows only one turn. Light takes a finite time to travel around a fiber loop with radius r, and in that time the loop can rotate an angle θ, which in practice is very small. This rotation moves the starting point a distance Δ. Light going in the direction of the rotation must travel a distance $2\pi r + \Delta$ to get back to its starting point, but light traveling in the opposite direction travels only $2\pi r - \Delta$. That slight difference in distance will mean a difference in a phase when the two beams are superimposed. This difference, called the Sagnac effect, can be detected by interferometry if the beams travel through a suitable single-mode fiber.

Fiber gyros are not as accurate as laser gyros, which are used on recent civilian and military aircraft. However, fiber gyros are good and inexpensive, making them suitable for applications such as guiding missiles (which you don't want to load with lots of expensive equipment) and short-range aircraft. Without any moving parts, they pose fewer operational problems than mechanical gyros. Fiber gyros can also be used with global positioning satellite (GPS) receivers in navigation systems for automobiles.

Smart Skins and Structures

Fiber sensors can be embedded in composites and other materials such as concrete to create "smart structures" or "smart skins." The goal is to create a structural element (including the skins of aircraft) equipped to monitor internal conditions. The initial emphasis is on verifying that components meet initial structural requirements, but the fiber sensors could be used throughout the life of the component. Figure 27.7 shows how fibers can be embedded between layers of a composite material; in this case, they are encased in an epoxy layer.

The initial use of the fiber sensors is to monitor fabrication and curing of the composite. The fiber sensors can monitor temperature to be sure curing conditions meet requirements. They can also monitor strain, to verify that the component is not stressed excessively. Detection of cracked fibers indicates serious stress problems. Later, the fiber sensors can provide data on stresses and strains that occur after the composite component is mounted in final position. Eventually this information may be used by operating engineers, but currently its main use is in studying properties of structures and aircraft.

FIGURE 27.6
Workings of a fiber-optic gyroscope.

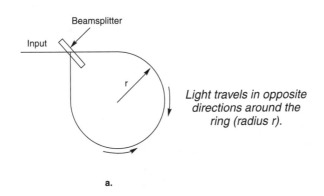

Input
Beamsplitter
r

Light travels in opposite
directions around the
ring (radius r).

a.

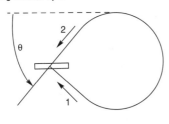

Ring Rotates by θ

θ

2

1

Because the speed of
light is constant, light
traveling clockwise (1),
which goes a shorter
distance, gets back to
the starting point before
light going counter-
clockwise (2).

b.

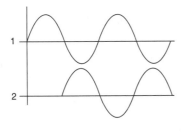

1

2

This shifts the phase of
wave 1 *ahead* of wave
2, in this case by 180°

c.

Once a smart-skin or smart-structure system is in operation, engineers could use the fiber sensors for periodic checks of performance and structural integrity. For example, fibers embedded in aircraft wings could be plugged into monitoring equipment in the service bay, to make sure they suffered no invisible internal cracks that could cause catastrophic failure. Dams and bridges likewise could be monitored with fibers.

FIGURE 27.7

Sensing fibers in a smart skin are embedded in an epoxy matrix between layers of a composite material.

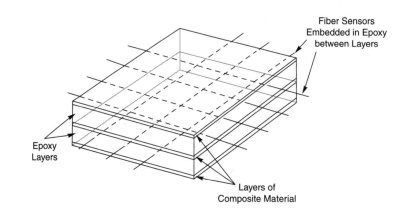

Some military planners think the ultimate step would be to plug the fiber sensors into a real-time control system designed to optimize performance. The performance limits of aircraft materials and structures are not known precisely, so engineers err on the side of safety and avoid pushing too far. Real-time fiber monitors could tell computers how well components were withstanding stresses in operation. Ultimately, perhaps, the computers could use the sensor data to apply corrections in real-time that would push the performance envelope further, without endangering pilots or aircraft.

What Have You Learned?

1. Fibers can serve as probes that collect light for sensing. Fibers can also function as sensors themselves.

2. Fiber probes can detect objects that block or reflect light. This lets them measure shapes, count parts, and do other simple tasks.

3. Fiber optics can collect light from remote optical sensors so it can be measured.

4. Sensors convert something hard to measure into units easier to observe.

5. Intrinsic fiber sensors detect changes in the way fibers transmit light. Unlike communication fibers, these fibers are designed to respond to changes in the environment.

6. Fiber sensors work by modulating light they transmit, either directly, changing intensity, by affecting polarization properties, or by shifting the phase of the light.

7. Interferometric sensors measure phase changes; they can detect very small shifts.

8. Placing a fiber in a place where pressure can cause microbending allows the fiber to sense pressure; the more pressure, the more light lost from the fiber.

9. Temperature and pressure can change the refractive index of glass in a fiber, causing phase shifts and other effects.

10. A fiber Fabry-Perot interferometer detects a phase shift within a resonant cavity in a fiber.

11. Loops of fiber can measure rotation by sensing differences in the time light takes to travel in opposite directions around the loop. Such fiber gyroscopes can be used in guidance systems.

12. Fiber sensors can be embedded in composite materials to make smart structures and smart skins.

What's Next?

In Chapter 28, I will look at other noncommunication applications of fiber optics in a wide variety of fields.

Quiz for Chapter 27

1. How do fiber-optic probes work?

    a. They detect the presence or absence of light at a point.

    b. They detect the pressure of objects placed on top of them.

    c. Changes in temperature make them expand or contract.

    d. None of the above.

2. Which of the following is an example of a fiber collecting light from a remote optical sensor?

    a. Fiber-optic gyroscope.

    b. Liquid-level sensor based on total internal reflection from a prism.

    c. Acoustic sensor based on microbending.

    d. Fiber grating used as a pressure sensor.

    e. Smart skins.

3. How can microbending effects be sensed?

    a. By observing tension along the length of the fiber.

    b. By monitoring changes in light transmitted by the fiber.

    c. By looking for changes in data rate of a signal transmitted through the fiber.

    d. By measuring light emitted by the fiber.

4. Which of the following can change the refractive index of a fiber?

    a. Temperature changes.

    b. Pressure changes.

    c. Sound waves.

    d. All the above.

    e. None of the above.

5. Which sort of change in a fiber sensor can be measured by interferometry?

    a. Changes in the wavelength of light.

b. Changes in intensity of light.

c. Changes in refractive index caused by pressure.

d. Changes in optical absorption.

6. An example of an interferometric sensor is

   a. a punched card reader.

   b. a microbending sensor of acoustic waves.

   c. a fiber-optic gyroscope.

   d. a sensor that measures the height of parts on a production line.

7. How do fiber grating sensors work?

   a. Microbending causes increased attenuation.

   b. They alter wavelengths transmitted and reflected.

   c. They change polarization.

   d. They modulate light with a digital code.

8. A 1° increase in temperature reduces the refractive index of the glass in a sensing fiber by 0.000005 at a wavelength of 1 μm. Assuming the length of the fiber does not change significantly, how much does a 10° temperature shift the phase of 1-μm light passing through a 10-mm sensor?

   a. 1.8°

   b. 90°

   c. 180°

d. 360°

e. 1800°

9. How do fiber-optic gyroscopes detect rotation?

   a. By measuring changes in the wavelength of light in the fiber.

   b. By interferometrically measuring differences in the paths of light going in opposite directions around a fiber loop.

   c. By detecting changes in polarization of light caused by inertial changes in the moving fiber loop.

   d. By measuring intensity changes caused by microbending.

   e. By detecting changes in the refractive index induced by acceleration.

10. What can fiber sensors measure when embedded in a smart structure?

   a. Curing conditions of a composite material.

   b. Internal strain in a composite material.

   c. Structural integrity of a completed component.

   d. Stresses on a component during use.

   e. All the above.

Imaging and Illuminating Fiber Optics

About This Chapter

Communications and sensing were latecomers in the world of fiber optics; the early developers of optical fibers had other things in mind. You have seen some of these other uses of fibers in passing, but now it's time to take a closer look at applications including light piping, imaging, inspection, and medical treatment. Many require fibers quite different from those used for communications, or bundled together in a particular way. If you are going to work regularly with fiber optics, you should know about such applications, although many are limited to specialized fields. The major applications—classical fiber-optic light piping and imaging, and medicine—differ in important ways, so I will look at each separately. First, however, I will look at light guiding in bundled fibers.

Basics of Fiber Bundles

As you read in Chapter 1, optical fibers were invented for imaging and were soon applied to illumination as well. Imaging requires a bundle of fibers, one to carry each point on the image. For imaging the bundle must be coherent, which in this case means that the ends of the fibers must be arranged in the same way on both ends of the bundle. Project an image onto one end of a coherent bundle, and the same image appears on the other end.

If you want to visualize how a coherent bundle works, you can start with a handful of drinking straws all the same length. With a little care, you can hold the straws so they are aligned parallel to each other. Look through the straws at a printed page, and you'll see the words through the array of little pipes. The smaller the straws, the smaller the bit of the page you see through each one. Individual fibers are like individual straws, but they are much thinner and far more flexible. Fibers guide light by total internal reflection, but straws only transmit light straight along their axes.

The original goal of the first generation of fiber-optic developers was to make long, thin, flexible bundles that could transmit images. Soon, two basic variations appeared: rigid and flexible bundles and coherent and incoherent bundles.

Assembling loose fibers into a coherent bundle can be tricky and tedious. It is much simpler to fuse many glass rods together, as you will see later. That process leads to a family of rigid bundles, with many fibers aligned parallel to each other in a solid block of glass. You wouldn't want one used as an endoscope to look down your throat, but they are very useful for many other applications.

A second variation is not bothering to align the fibers on opposite ends of the bundle. You don't need to align the fibers if all you want to do is deliver light to the other end, rather than an image.

For some illumination applications it doesn't matter how the fibers are aligned, but for others you want even illumination, so you want the distribution of fibers to be truly randomized. In general, most incoherent bundles are flexible.

Imaging and illuminating fibers almost always are multimode step-index types with a thick core covered by a thin cladding. Individual fibers may be drawn quite thin, but the cores account for a large fraction of the fiber diameter, and the claddings are thin.

Making Fiber Bundles

●
Long, thin flexible bundles are made by winding a fiber around a spool and cutting through a glued region.

Figure 28.1 shows one way to make coherent fiber bundles. You loop a single long, thin fiber many times around a spool, glue the fibers together in one spot and remove them from the spool. Then you cut through the glued region. This gives you a flexible bundle, with fibers loose in the middle and fixed on both ends. Because the two ends were originally adjacent to each other, the fibers are all in the same positions.

This approach is simple in concept and dates back to the mid-1950s, when it was used to make the first flexible fiber bundles. However, it is a demanding process and is difficult for very thin fibers, because they may break.

●
Fused imaging bundles are drawn jointly into solid rods.

An alternative approach is to draw many fibers simultaneously to finer and finer diameters in a series of stages. The first step is drawing a step-index fiber with a diameter about 2.5 mm. These fibers are easy to handle, and a group of them—typically 37 to 169—are grouped together, heated until they melt, and stretched out into a rigid "multifiber" about 2 mm in diameter, as shown in Figure 28.2. Then a number of multifibers (typically 61 to 271) are packed together, heated, and drawn again to produce a rigid fiber bundle, containing many thousands of fibers. Each fiber is about 3 to 20 μm in diameter.

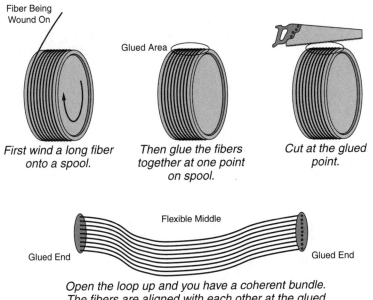

FIGURE 28.1

Flexible bundle made by winding fiber around a spool.

Fiber Being Wound On

Glued Area

First wind a long fiber onto a spool.

Then glue the fibers together at one point on spool.

Cut at the glued point.

Flexible Middle

Glued End

Glued End

Open the loop up and you have a coherent bundle. The fibers are aligned with each other at the glued point where it was cut and are loose in the middle.

The numbers of fibers packed together are chosen to make geometric patterns that pack well together. The difference between core and cladding refractive indexes is larger than for communication fibers, so even smaller-core fibers transmit multiple modes at visible wavelengths. You don't want to operate near the single-mode cutoff in imaging bundles, because mode patterns appear that distribute light unevenly across the fiber ends.

The same basic process can be used to make both rigid and flexible bundles, with a few important differences. Look carefully at Figure 28.2, and you will note that the large core is surrounded by two rings of cladding. One is the conventional low-index cladding that confines light to the core in all fibers. The composition of the other depends on the type of bundle being made.

For rigid bundles, that outer layer is a dark absorptive glass that keeps light from leaking between the cores in the bundle. Remember that a certain amount of light always leaks into the fiber cladding. Usually this stays in the inner part of the cladding, but for imaging bundles the cladding is quite thin. If the claddings were all fused together—as they would be without the dark glass—the light could freely disperse through the whole bundle within the fused cladding glass. Then it could leak back into the cores and degrade the image.

FIGURE 28.2

Stages in making a fiber bundle. (Courtesy of Schott Fiber Optics Inc.)

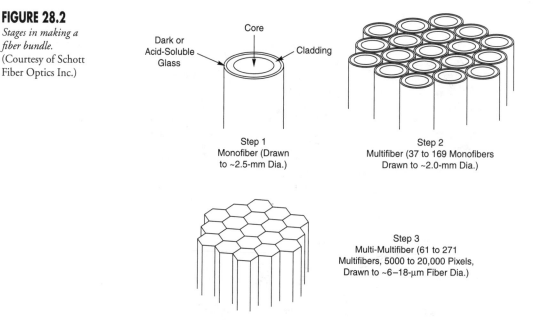

For flexible bundles, that outer layer is a glass that is soluble in acid. Manufacturers cover the ends of the rigid rod and then dip it in an acid that dissolves away that leachable layer in the middle of the rod, leaving a flexible bundle of many thin fibers, which are arranged so their ends are aligned for imaging.

Individual fibers in a flexible coherent bundle can be small, but not quite as small as in a fused bundle. Some performance limits of flexible bundles are comparable to those of rigid bundles. When flexible bundles are used, an added concern is breakage of individual fibers, which does not occur in fused bundles. Each fiber break prevents light transmission from one spot on the input face. The loss of a single fiber is not critical, but as more fibers break, the transmitted light level drops and resolution can decline as well. Eventually breakage reaches a point where the image-transmitting bundle is no longer usable. Because of the breakage problem, plastic fibers are often used in flexible bundles.

Randomly aligned bundles serve as "light pipes."

Randomly aligned bundles are made by collecting many fibers into a bundle, much like collecting strands of spaghetti. This would be very difficult if the fibers were as thin as those in imaging bundles, but such fine fibers are not needed because the resolution does not matter; random bundles serve purely as "light pipes." Typically, random bundles are made of fibers with diameters in the 100-μm range, which are flexible enough to bend freely with minimum fiber breakage.

Imaging and Resolution

So far, I've glossed over the crucial issue of resolution in an imaging fiber bundle. Figure 28.3 shows how an image is carried from one end of the bundle to the other. Each fiber core carries its own segment of the image to the other end, maintaining their alignment.

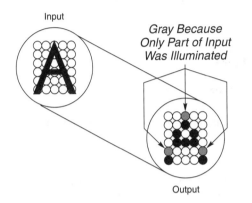

FIGURE 28.3

Image transmission through a fiber bundle.

To visualize what happens, imagine that each fiber core captures a chunk of the image and delivers it to the other end of the bundle. This process averages out any details that fall within a single core. For example, if the input to a single core is half black and half white, the output will be gray. Thus, the fiber cores must be small to see much detail. For a static fiber bundle, the resolution is about half a line pair per fiber core, meaning two fiber core widths are needed to measure a line pair. Numerically, that means 10 μm fiber cores could resolve 50 line pairs per millimeter (1 line pair per 20 μm). Imaging bundles have fiber cores as small as 3 μm. Resolution is significantly higher—about 0.8 line pair per fiber core diameter—if the fiber bundle is moving with respect to the object.

Before you wonder too much about the quality of fiber-bundle images, you should realize that if fiber cores were a common size of 10 μm, the letter A in Figure 28.3 would be only 60 μm high, less than 1/16 mm tall. That's many times smaller than the finest of fine prints used in legal documents. You have to look very hard, and may need a strong magnifying lens, to see the individual fiber spots on a good imaging bundle.

> Bundle resolution depends on the core sizes of the fibers it contains.

Cladding Effects

The cores conduct light in fiber bundles, but they are surrounded by cladding layers. Bundles are made with thin cladding layers, but some light must fall onto the cladding rather than the core. The fate of that light depends on the bundle design. Rigid bundles have a dark outer cladding layer that absorbs light so that little can pass between fiber cores. Light that leaks out of the cores of individual fibers in flexible bundles cannot easily enter other fibers. However, neither type can completely prevent any light from leaking between fibers.

> Light that falls into fiber claddings in bundles is lost, but typically 90% falls onto fiber cores.

Most light entering the cladding is lost, which can limit transmission efficiency. This makes the fraction of the surface made up by fiber cores an important factor in a bundle's light-collection efficiency. That is, the collection efficiency depends (in part) on the packing fraction, defined as

$$\text{Packing fraction} = \frac{\text{total core area}}{\text{total surface area}}$$

A typical value is around 90%.

Transmission Characteristics

> Typical attenuation of bundled fiber is around 1 dB/m.

The fibers used in bundles do not have as low attenuation as communication fibers, because bundles carry light no more than a matter of meters. Typical attenuation of bundled fiber is around 1 dB/m, over a thousand times higher than that of communication fibers at 1300 nm.

Likewise, operating wavelengths differ. Visible light is needed for imaging and illumination, and even for other applications the short distances make it unnecessary to operate at wavelengths where fibers are most transparent. Glass fiber bundles are typically usable at wavelengths of 400–2200 nm, and special types made from glass with good ultraviolet transmission are usable at somewhat shorter wavelengths. Plastic fibers are usable at visible wavelengths, 400–700 nm. Some special-purpose bundles are made of other materials, but they are not widely used.

> Bundled fibers are step-index multimode types with large NA.

Bundled fibers generally have higher numerical apertures than communication fibers, because light-collection efficiency is critical and pulse dispersion is irrelevant. In general, the difference between core and cladding index is larger for imaging and illumination fibers than for communication fibers. This gives bundled fibers typical NAs of 0.35 to 1.1 and means that transmission is multimode. The same holds true for large-core single fibers used in illumination; larger NAs are better because they boost light-collection efficiency.

Optics of Bundled Fibers

> Some simplifying assumptions valid for single communication fibers are not valid for bundles.

The basic principles of fiber optics are the same if fibers are separate or bundled. However, some implicit assumptions always hide behind any discussion of basics. In describing communication fibers earlier, I made some assumptions that don't always work for bundles or other noncommunication fibers. It's time to go back and face some complications that I earlier simplified away.

Light Rays in Optical Fibers

Looking at individual light rays, as in Figure 28.4, gives a slightly different view consistent with what you learned earlier. If a light ray enters the fiber at an angle θ within the fiber's acceptance angle, it will emerge at roughly the same angle to the fiber axis, although not necessarily in the same direction. "Roughly" is the operative word, because the ray will emerge in a ring of angles centered on θ because of imperfections in the fiber, effects of fiber length, and other factors.

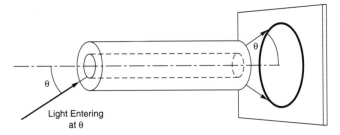

FIGURE 28.4
Light rays emerge from a fiber in a diverging ring.

This does not conflict with what you learned earlier, because then you looked at light guiding only collectively, for a large number of rays. If you had broken down the cone of light entering the fiber into individual rays, you would have seen the same effect. At that point, there was no need to do so.

One other thing should be pointed out: step-index fibers with constant-diameter cores do not focus light. (As you will see later, graded-index fibers can focus light passing along their length.) All light emerges from a step-index fiber at roughly the same angle that it entered, not at a changed angle, as would happen if it did focus light. As long as the fiber's sides and ends are straight and perpendicular to each other, a step-index fiber or a fiber bundle can no more focus light than a pane of flat window glass can. This has one important practical consequence that you'll discover the first time you look through an imaging bundle. You have to put the distant end up very close to what you want to see, or the image will become blurred. You see the image on the close end, because light travels straight through each fiber, but the bundle does not rearrange light rays that got into the wrong fibers, because the far end was not close enough to the object.

If the fiber's output end is cut at an angle not perpendicular to its axis, light entering at an angle θ still emerges in a cone, but the center of the cone is at an angle to the fiber axis. If the slant angle (from the perpendicular) is a small value φ, the angle β by which the rays are offset is approximately

$$\beta = \phi(n - 1)$$

where *n* is the refractive index of the fiber core.

Tapered Fibers

I assumed earlier that fiber cores are straight and uniform, but they could also be tapered (although not over long distances). Figure 28.5 shows what happens to a light ray entering such a fiber at an angle θ_1. If the ray meets criteria for total internal reflection, it is confined in the core. However, it meets the core-cladding boundary at different angles on each bounce so each total internal reflection is at different angles from the axis. The result is that it emerges from the fiber at a different angle, θ_2. If input core diameter is d_1 and output core diameter is d_2, the relationship between input and output angles is

$$d_1 \sin \theta_1 = d_2 \sin \theta_2$$

The same relationship holds for the fiber's outer diameter as long as core and outer diameter change by the same factor, d_2/d_1.

FIGURE 28.5

Light passing from the narrow to the broad end of a tapered fiber.

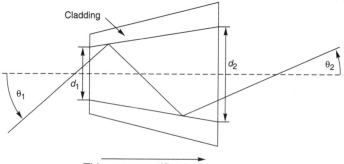

This way magnifies image.

As a numerical example, suppose the input angle is 30° and the taper expands diameter by a factor of 2. The output angle would be about 14.5° (the inverse sine of 0.25). Thus, light exiting the broad end of a taper would emerge at a smaller angle to the axis than at which it entered (and, conversely, light entering the broad end would leave the narrow end at a broader angle). This effect lets fiber tapers magnify or demagnify objects. Images are magnified if light goes from the narrow end to the broad end, and are shrunk if light goes from the broad end to the narrow end.

In practice, single fibers are not used as tapers. Instead, fiber tapers are rigid bundles of fibers, each expanding or shrinking by the same factor. You can also use this viewpoint to see why a taper magnifies. All the light from each core on the small end is spread out over the larger core area on the larger end—making the image larger (although not increasing resolution measured as the number of lines across the image). Essentially, the taper makes each spot larger. The effect is somewhat like a lens, but not exactly the same.

Focusing with Graded-Index Fibers

Graded-index fibers can focus light in certain cases.

Unlike step-index fibers, graded-index fibers can focus light in certain cases. This does not make graded-index fibers useful for image transmission or other fiber-bundle applications, but as described later in this chapter, segments of graded-index fibers can function as components in some optical systems.

In Chapter 4, you saw that light follows a sinusoidal path through graded-index fiber. When you looked at how a cone of light was transmitted through a long fiber, you saw output as a cone of the same angle. Now look instead at the path of an individual ray through a short segment of graded-index fiber, shown in Figure 28.6, and compare that with the path of a light ray in step-index fiber.

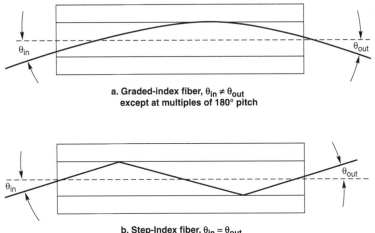

FIGURE 28.6
Rays in graded-index and step-index fibers.

There is an important but subtle difference. Total internal reflection from a step-index boundary keeps light rays at the same angle to the fiber axis all along the fiber. However, graded-index fibers refract light rays, so the angle of the ray to the axis is constantly changing as the ray follows a sinusoidal path. If you cut the fiber after the light ray has gone through 180° or 360° of the sinusoid, the light emerges at the same angle that it entered. However, if the distance the light ray travels is not an integral multiple of 180° of the sinusoid, it emerges at a different angle. This property allows segments of graded-index fiber to focus light.

In design of graded-index fiber lenses (usually sold under the trade name Selfoc), the key parameter is the fraction of a full sinusoidal cycle that light goes through before emerging. That fraction is called the pitch. A 0.23-pitch lens, for instance, has gone through 0.23 of a cycle, or $0.23 \times 360° = 82.8°$. The value of the pitch depends on factors including refractive-index gradient, index of the fiber, core diameter, and wavelength of light.

Although the lenses are segments of fiber, they are short by fiber-optic standards, just a few millimeters long. Thus, they can be considered as rod lenses as well as fiber lenses. These tiny lenses are used in a variety of optical systems.

● Pitch is a critical parameter of graded-index lenses.

Light Piping

The simplest application of optical fibers of any type is light piping. The term describes the process—piping light from one place to another. The light can be carried by one or many fibers without regard to how the fibers are arranged, as long as they collect light and deliver it to the same places. Thus, alignment of individual fibers need not be the same at the two ends of a fiber bundle. It doesn't matter if a fiber is at the center of the input end and at the outer edge of the output end. In fact, you don't always need a bundle for light piping; sometimes a single fiber does the job better.

ILLUMINATION

A fiber bundle can illuminate small or hard-to-reach areas.

Most light piping is for illumination, the delivery of light to some desired location. Why bother with optical fibers to do a lightbulb's job? A flexible bundle of optical fibers can efficiently concentrate light in a small area or deliver light around corners to places it could not otherwise reach (e.g., inside machinery). A bundle can illuminate places where lightbulbs cannot be used (e.g., areas where explosive vapors are being used). And fiber bundles can be divided to deliver light from one bulb to many places.

Such illumination fibers are also used in indicators. And illumination fibers—in the form of fiber-optic lamps and displays—gave many of us our first real view of fiber technology.

OPTICAL POWER DELIVERY

Single large-core fibers can carry optical power for medicine and materials-working.

Some light-piping fibers can carry enough optical power to do more than illuminate. They carry laser beams used for medical treatment or industrial materials-working.

Conventional laser systems use lenses or mirrors to focus their beams on the desired point. However, these beam-delivery systems are bulky and can be cumbersome for fine tasks, such as delicate surgery. Fiber systems for beam delivery are much easier to manipulate. Some are designed for surgeons to use with their hands. Others are built for robotic control in factories.

Power delivery requires single fibers with large cores or bundled fibers. Single fibers are best for many applications if the input fiber can be concentrated into a single core. Power transmission capacities are surprisingly high for single large-core fibers with losses measured in decibels per kilometer, which can easily carry tens of watts over a few meters.

Signs

Fiber arrays can create illuminated signs.

If all the fibers in an illumination bundle wind up in the same place, they illuminate a single spot. If they are routed to different places, they can form a patterned image, such as the fiber-optic display shown in Figure 28.7. All the fibers are brought together in one place to collect light from a bulb, then they are splayed out to create the desired pattern. Diffusing lenses at the ends of the fiber can spread light out to make large spots.

FIGURE 28.7
A fiber-optic sign.

Fused and Imaging Fibers

Like incoherent bundles for illumination, coherent fiber bundles are not the standard means of image transmission or projection. Conventional lenses and optical systems generally are much less costly, and typically project better images. However, lenses and conventional optics cannot be used everywhere. Imaging fiber bundles can probe inaccessible areas, from the interior of the human body to the interiors of machines. Fiber bundles fit into places where lenses can't and offer other capabilities, such as directing light from a display in a particular direction. I'll take a look at a sampling of these applications.

Faceplates

Image transmission does not have to be over a long distance. One of the most common uses of fiber-optic image transmission uses thin slices of coherent bundles in which individual fibers are only a fraction of an inch long. This is the fiber-optic faceplate, cut like a slice of salami from a longer fused coherent bundle.

The purpose of a faceplate is to concentrate light along the direction of the fibers. You can mount a faceplate on the curved screen of a display tube to make a flat display, as

Fiber-optic
faceplates
concentrate light.

shown in Figure 28.8. You also can butt the output side of the faceplate against the input side of an imaging detector if you want to make sure virtually all the light reaches the detector.

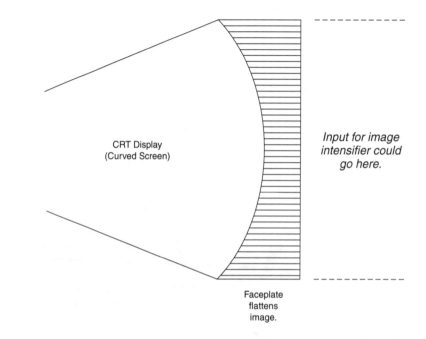

CRT Display
(Curved Screen)

Input for image
intensifier could
go here.

Faceplate
flattens
image.

The big advantage of the faceplate is that it transfers light very efficiently between two surfaces that otherwise can't be butted face to face. Suppose, for example, you're trying to detect some very weak light from a scene illuminated only by starlight. A single-stage image-intensifier camera makes the image brighter, but not bright enough to see clearly. You want to add a second stage, but the output of the first stage is on a curved screen. Put a fiber faceplate between that output and the input of the second-stage tube, and you lose very little light. An imaging lens would lose much more light. The first fiber-optic faceplates were developed for such military imaging tubes, and they remain in use for newer equipment.

Faceplates also can help flatten the curved image generated by some display screens, correct for distortion, and make the display appear brighter by concentrating light toward the viewer.

Image Manipulation, Splitting, and Combining

Coherent fiber
bundles can
manipulate
images.

Coherent fiber bundles can do more than just transmit images; they can also manipulate them. Twisting a coherent bundle by 180° inverts the image. You can do the same with lenses, but a fiber-optic image inverter does not require as long a working distance, which is of critical importance in some military systems. (Some image inverters are less than 1 in. long.)

Another type of image manipulation possible with fused fiber optics is the image combiner/splitter shown in Figure 28.9. This is made by laying down a series of fiber-optic ribbons, alternating them as if shuffling a deck of cards. One ribbon goes from the single input to output 1, the next from the input to output 2, the next to output 1, and so on. Put a single image into the input, and you get two identical (but fainter) output images. Put separate images into the two outputs, and you get one combined image.

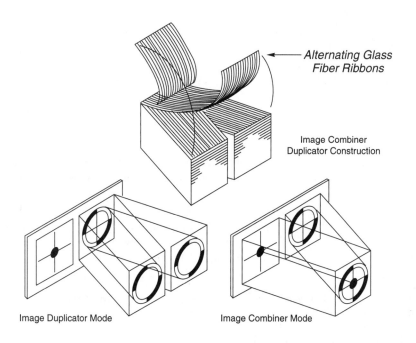

Alternating Glass Fiber Ribbons

Image Combiner Duplicator Construction

Image Duplicator Mode   Image Combiner Mode

FIGURE 28.9

A fiber-optic image combiner and duplicator. (Courtesy of Galileo Electro-Optics Corp.)

Similar ideas could be used in other image manipulators or in devices to perform operations on optical signals. However, before you rush out for a patent application on your own bright idea, you must face the ugly reality of cost. Manufacture of the fiber-optic image combiner in Figure 28.9 requires time and exacting precision, making it too expensive for most uses. Image inverters are used in some systems, but only where less costly lens systems won't do the job.

Tapers

Earlier you saw how tapered fiber cores could bend light rays. The same principle could be used for imaging with tapered bundles. Controlling the degree of tapering across the area of the taper can vary the degree of magnification. For example, the center of the image can be magnified more than the outer part, or vice versa. However, the practical problems are similar to those with other fiber-optic image manipulators—lenses cost much less and have higher resolution, so they are used for most applications.

Medical Endoscopes

The most important use of imaging fiber bundles is in medicine, to let physicians look inside the body without surgery. These special-purpose coherent fiber bundles, up to a couple of meters long, are called endoscopes. Endoscopes may be rigid or flexible, but flexible types are preferred for many purposes, because they are easier to insert and manipulate through body orifices.

Suppose a physician wants to examine a patient's bronchial tubes. He passes an endoscope down the patient's throat toward the lungs. Some fibers in the bundle transmit light from a lamp to illuminate the airway. Others return light so the physician can see conditions inside. Similar instruments are used to examine the stomach and colon.

Miniature CCD (charge-coupled-device) imaging cameras have replaced many fiber-optic endoscopes for viewing inside the body, but fiber optics still deliver the light picked up by the CCD.

Optical fibers also can deliver laser light to perform surgery inside the body. Thin fibers can be inserted through small incisions to perform keyhole surgery, speeding patient recovery. For example, a fiber can deliver laser pulses to remove lesions inside the knee joint. The surgeon looks through an endoscope to align the fiber, fires the pulse, and looks back to check each step. (Surgeons do not look while the laser pulse is firing to protect their eyes.) For some types of surgery, the fibers delivering the laser light may be part of the endoscope that the surgeon uses to examine the patient.

Optical fibers can direct laser energy to many parts of the body in minimally invasive surgery. One example is threading a fiber through the urethra to shatter kidney stones with laser pulses.

Industrial Inspection Instruments

Fiber-optic imaging scopes also are used in industry to inspect dangerous or otherwise inaccessible areas. Suppose, for example, you wanted to inspect the inside of a tank that had only one small opening on the top. You could insert a fiberscope to get a close-up view of the area in question.

Graded-Index Fiber Lenses

The graded-index fiber segments described earlier in this chapter have uses quite different from imaging fiber bundles and faceplates. Their applications are as lenses.

Some uses are in fiber optics. A graded-index fiber microlens can focus output from an LED or diode laser so it could be coupled efficiently into a fiber. However, most transmitters have light sources butted up against the collecting fiber, without intermediate components. In addition, many fiber pigtails could serve the same function without the need of any other discrete component.

Most applications of graded-index fiber microlenses are in optical systems such as photo-copiers. One example is the use of a linear array of fiber-optic microlenses to focus light reflected from a small area of a page being copied onto individual sensors in a linear array that detects reflected light.

What Have You Learned?

1. Rigid or flexible bundles of optical fibers can transmit images if the fibers that make them up are properly aligned at the ends (coherent). Rigid bundles are made of fibers fused together; flexible bundles contain separate fibers bonded at the ends. Resolution is limited by the size of the fiber cores, typically around 10 μm.

2. Bundles of fibers in which the ends are not aligned with one another serve as "light pipes" to illuminate hard-to-reach places. The bundle can be broken up on one end to form an image or display (e.g., a WALK sign).

3. Light that falls into fiber claddings in bundles is lost, but typically 90% falls onto fiber cores.

4. Imaging and other short-distance fibers generally have much higher attenuation than communication fibers. Bundled fibers are step-index multimode types with large NA.

5. Step-index multimode fibers do not focus light, but segments of graded-index fiber do focus light and can serve as lenses. Tapered fibers magnify or demagnify objects seen through them; they are used in bundles.

6. Thin fiber-optic faceplates are used to concentrate light from certain displays in a particular direction. They are used with certain high-performance imaging tubes, but not for ordinary cathode-ray tubes.

7. Coherent fiber bundles can invert, split, and combine images.

8. Endoscopy is the use of coherent fiber bundles to view inside the body without surgery.

9. Large-core fibers can deliver laser power for medicine or materials-working.

Quiz for Chapter 28

1. Which of the following statements is false?

    a. Coherent fiber bundles can transmit images.

    b. Coherent fiber bundles can focus light.

    c. Graded-index fiber segments can focus light.

    d. Imaging fiber bundles contain step-index multimode fibers.

2. A graded-index fiber lens has a pitch of 0.45. How much of a sinusoidal oscillation cycle do light rays experience in passing through it?

   a. 27°.

   b. 45°.

   c. 81°.

   d. 162°.

   e. 180°.

3. What does it mean to say that a fiber bundle has a packing fraction of 90%?

   a. 90% of the fibers are intact.

   b. 90% of the input surface is made up of optical fibers.

   c. 90% of the input surface is made up of fiber core.

   d. 90% of the input surface is made up of fiber cladding.

   e. It transmits 90% of the incident light through its entire length.

4. You want to resolve an image with 8 line pairs per millimeter. In theory, what is the largest fiber core size that you could use in a stationary coherent bundle?

   a. 8 μm.

   b. 50 μm.

   c. 62.5 μm.

   d. 100 μm.

   e. 125 μm.

5. Endoscopes used in medicine to view inside the body

   a. usually are flexible fiber-bundles.

   b. sometimes transmit laser beams to treat disease.

   c. examine stomach, lungs, or colon.

   d. all the above.

   e. none of the above.

6. Fiber-optic faceplates are

   a. specialized sensors that detect temperature variations across a surface.

   b. thin rigid fiber bundles used to transfer light efficiently in image intensifiers.

   c. assemblies of graded-index fiber lenses that focus light in photocopiers.

   d. used on most television sets.

7. Average attenuation of bundled fibers is

   a. 0.5 dB/km.

   b. 1–5 dB/km.

   c. 10–100 dB/km.

   d. around 1 dB/m.

8. What types of fibers are used in imaging bundles?

   a. Step-index multimode.

   b. Graded-index multimode.

   c. Step-index single-mode.

   d. All the above.

9. The practical use of fiber-optic bundles to manipulate images is limited by what?

   a. Poor resolution.

   b. High attenuation.

   c. Fragility.

   d. High cost.

10. Which of the following is the most important advantage of random fiber bundles for illumination?

   a. Flexibility.

   b. Low cost.

   c. Disposability.

   d. Durability.

Laser Safety

With the exercise of reasonable common sense, fiber-optic systems are inherently reasonably safe. From a practical standpoint, the main hazard is sticking yourself with sharp fiber fragments—and like any fine, stiff fiber fragments, they can do serious damage in the wrong place, such as your eye. However, you may be more likely to hear about the special rules that cover the safe use of lasers and optical amplifiers. Their most visible impact is in warning labels printed on many light-source data sheets and packages to meet rules imposed by the Center for Devices and Radiological Health, which is part of the Food and Drug Administration.

Why are there so many warnings when even a couple hundred milliwatts from the most powerful optical amplifiers will not burn holes through anything? Because the eye focuses laser light at wavelengths shorter than about 1400 nm onto a tiny spot on the retina, the light-sensitive area at the back of the eye. Focusing even a 1-mW laser beam onto such a small spot produces a light intensity comparable to the intensity produced if you look directly at the sun. Just as with the sun, a momentary glance into a milliwatt-level laser beam will not blind you, but staring into it for a long period could leave a blind spot.

Nature is fairly kind in some ways. The 1550-nm band of erbium-doped fiber amplifiers does not penetrate to the retina, offsetting the higher powers from optical amplifiers. In addition, light from semiconductor lasers, optical amplifiers, and optical fibers spreads out rapidly (at least by laser standards), so a fiber a few feet away is no real threat if the power is in the milliwatt range or the wavelength is longer than 1400 nm. (Laboratory lasers are quite another matter. Many of them can fire powerful pulses or generate high-power beams, so you must wear safety goggles when using them.)

However, there are a couple of potential exceptions. The 980-nm pump lasers used with many erbium-doped fiber amplifiers can deliver much higher powers, at a wavelength that is a serious eye hazard. You're fine as long as they stay inside the amplifier package, but be careful if you open the case. A few systems that distribute identical signals to many points, particularly for cable television, may include 1300-nm lasers with powers well above a milliwatt. You should not be afraid of light from fiber-optic systems, but neither should you be careless.

Glossary

Absorption   Loss of light energy that is absorbed and converted to heat. Not equal to loss or attenuation, which include other effects.

Acceptance Angle   The angle over which the core of an optical fiber accepts incoming light; usually measured from the fiber axis. Related to numerical aperture (NA).

ADSL   Asymmetric digital subscriber line, digital transmission at high rate to subscribers and at a lower rate from subscribers, over twisted-wire pairs.

All-Dielectric Cable   Cable made entirely of dielectric (insulating) materials without any metal conductors, armor, or strength members.

Analog   A signal that varies continuously (e.g., sound waves). Analog signals have frequency and bandwidth measured in hertz.

Ångstrom (Å)   A unit of length, 0.1 nm or 10^{-10} m, often used to measure wavelength but not part of the SI system of units. Often written Angstrom because the special symbol is not available.

Armor   A protective layer, usually metal, wrapped around a cable.

ATM (Asynchronous Transfer Mode)   A digital transmission switching format, with cells containing 5 bytes of header information followed by 48 data bytes.

Attenuation   Reduction of signal magnitude, or loss, normally measured in decibels. Fiber attenuation is normally measured per unit length in decibels per kilometer.

Attenuator   An optical element that reduces the intensity of light passing through it (i.e., attenuates it).

Avalanche Photodiode (APD) A semiconductor photodetector with integral detection and amplification stages. Electrons generated at a *p/n* junction are accelerated in a region where they free an avalanche of other electrons. APDs can detect faint signals but require higher voltages than other semiconductor electronics.

Average Power The average level of power in a signal that varies with time.

Axis The center of an optical fiber.

Backbone System A transmission network that carries high-speed telecommunications between regions (e.g., a nationwide long-distance telephone system). Sometimes used to describe the part of a local area network that carries signals between branching points.

Backscattering Scattering of light in the direction opposite to that in which it was originally traveling.

Bandwidth The highest frequency that can be transmitted in analog operation. Also (especially for digital systems), the information-carrying capacity of a system.

Baud Strictly speaking, the number of signal-level transitions per second in digital data. For some common coding schemes, this equals bits per second, but this is not true for more complex coding, where it is often misused. Telecommunication specialists prefer bits per second, which is less ambiguous.

Beamsplitter A device that divides incident light into two separate beams.

Bel A relative measurement, denoting a factor of ten change. Rarely used in practice; most measurements are in decibels (0.1 bel).

BER See *bit error rate*.

Bidirectional Operating in both directions. Bidirectional couplers split or combine, light the same way when it passes through them in either direction. Bidirectional transmission sends signals in both directions, sometimes through the same fiber.

Birefringent Having a refractive index that differs for light of different polarizations.

B-ISDN See *Broadband-Integrated Services Digital Network*.

Bistable Optics Optical devices with two stable transmission states.

Bit Error Rate (BER) The fraction of bits transmitted incorrectly.

Broadband In general, covering a wide range of frequencies. The broadband label is sometimes used for a network that carries many different services or for video transmission.

Broadband-Integrated Services Digital Network (B-ISDN) A standard for digital telecommunications integrating voice, video, data, and other services.

Broadcast Transmission Sending the same signal to many different places, like a television broadcasting station. Broadcast transmission can be over optical fibers if the same signal is delivered to many subscribers.

Bundle (of fibers)   A rigid or flexible group of fibers assembled in a unit. Coherent fiber bundles have fibers arranged in the same way on each end and can transmit images.

Byte   Eight bits of digital data. (Sometimes parity and check bits are included, so one "byte" may include 10 bits, but only 8 of them are data.)

Category 5   A type of twisted-pair copper cable that meets standards for transmitting high-speed signals.

CATV   An acronym for cable television, derived from Community Antenna TeleVision.

CCITT   International Consultative Commission on Telephone and Telegraph, an arm of the International Telecommunications Union, which sets standards.

Cells   Blocks of data transmitted in Asynchronous Transfer Mode.

Central Office   A telephone company facility for switching signals among local telephone circuits; connects to subscriber telephones. Also called a switching office.

Chromatic Dispersion   Pulse spreading arising from differences in the speed that light of different wavelengths travels through materials. Measured in picoseconds (of dispersion) per kilometer (of fiber length) per nanometer (of source bandwidth), it is the sum of waveguide and material dispersion.

Cladding   The layer of glass or other transparent material surrounding the light-carrying core of an optical fiber. It has a lower refractive index than the core and thus confines light in the core. Coatings may be applied over the cladding.

Coax   Coaxial cable, cable with a central metallic conductor surrounded by a metallic sheath that runs the length of the cable.

Coherent Bundle (of fibers)   Fibers packaged together in a bundle so they retain a fixed arrangement at the two ends and can transmit an image.

Coherent Communications   In fiber optics, a communication system where the output of a local laser oscillator is mixed with the received signal, and the difference frequency is detected and amplified.

Compression   Reducing the number of bits needed to encode a digital signal, typically by eliminating long strings of identical bits or bits that do not change in successive sampling intervals (e.g., video frames).

Connector   A device mounted on the end of a fiber-optic cable, light source, receiver, or housing that mates to a similar device to couple light into and out of optical fibers. A connector joins two fiber ends or one fiber end and a light source or detector.

Copper   Industry slang for metal wire, either twisted-pair or coaxial cable.

Core   The central part of an optical fiber that carries light.

Coupler   A device that connects three or more fiber ends, dividing one input between two or more outputs or combining two or more inputs into one output.

Coupling   Transfer of light into or out of an optical fiber. (Note that coupling does not require a coupler.)

Critical Angle   The angle at which light in a high-refractive-index material undergoes total internal reflection.

Cut-Back Measurements   Measurement of optical loss made by cutting a fiber to compare loss of a short segment with loss of a longer one.

Cutoff Wavelength   The longest wavelength at which a single-mode fiber can transmit two modes, or (equivalently) the shortest wavelength at which a single-mode fiber carries only one mode.

Cycles per Second   The frequency of a wave, or number of oscillations it makes per second. One cycle per second equals one hertz.

Dark Current   The noise current generated by a photodiode in the dark.

Dark Fiber   Optical fiber installed without transmitter and receiver, usually to provide expansion capacity. Sometimes carriers lease dark fibers to other companies that add equipment to transmit signals through them.

Data Link   A fiber-optic transmitter, cable, and receiver that transmit digital data between two points.

dBm   Decibels below 1 mW.

dBµ   Decibels below 1 µW.

Decibel (dB)   A logarithmic comparison of power levels, defined as ten times the base-ten logarithm of the ratio of the two power levels. One-tenth of a bel.

Demultiplexer   A device that separates a multiplexed signal into its original components; the inverse of a multiplexer.

Dense Wavelength Division Multiplexing (D-WDM)   Transmitting multiple closely spaced wavelengths through the same fiber. In practice, this often means wavelengths 200 GHz or less apart.

Detector   A device that generates an electrical signal when illuminated by light. The most common in fiber optics are photodiodes.

Dielectric   Nonconductive.

Digital   Encoded as a signal in discrete levels, typically binary 1s and 0s.

Digital Subscriber Line (DSL)   A service that transmits digital signals to homes at speeds of hundreds of kilobits to tens of megabits per second over twisted-pair wires. There are several variations.

Diode   An electronic device that lets current flow in only one direction. Semiconductor diodes used in fiber optics contain a junction between regions of different doping. They include light emitters (LEDs and laser diodes) and detectors (photodiodes).

Diode Laser   A semiconductor diode in which the injection of current carriers produces laser light by amplifying photons produced when holes and electrons recombine at the junction between *p*- and *n*-doped regions.

Directional Coupler   A coupler in which light is transmitted differently when it goes in different directions.

Dispersion   The spreading out of light pulses as they travel in an optical fiber, proportional to length.

Dispersion Compensation   The use of fiber segments with different dispersions to reduce total dispersion.

Dispersion-Shifted Fiber   Optical fiber with nominal zero-dispersion wavelength shifted to 1550 nm from the 1310 nm in step-index single-mode fiber. This is distinct from nonzero-dispersion-shifted fiber.

DSL   See *digital subscriber line.*

DS*x*   A transmission rate in the North American digital telephone hierarchy. Also called T carrier.

DTV   Digital television.

Duplex   In cables, one that contains two fibers. For connectors, one that connects two pairs of fibers. For data transmission, full-duplex transmitters and receivers simultaneously send and receive signals in both directions, but half-duplex cannot do both at the same time.

D-WDM   See *dense wavelength-division multiplexing.*

Edge-Emitting Diode   An LED that emits light from its edge, producing more directional output than LEDs that emit from their top surface.

Edge-Emitting Laser   A semiconductor laser that emits light in the plane of its junction from the edge of the chip.

Electromagnetic Interference (EMI)   Noise generated when stray electromagnetic fields induce currents in electrical conductors.

Electromagnetic Radiation   Waves made up of oscillating electrical and magnetic fields perpendicular to one another and traveling at the speed of light. Can also be viewed as photons or quanta of energy. Electromagnetic radiation includes radio waves, microwaves, infrared, visible light, ultraviolet radiation, X rays, and gamma rays.

EMI   See *electromagnetic interference.*

Endoscope   A fiber-optic bundle used for imaging and viewing inside the human body.

Erbium-Doped Fiber Amplifier   Optical fiber doped with the rare earth element erbium, which can amplify light in the 1550-nm region when pumped by an external light source.

Ethernet   A local-area network standard. The original Ethernet operates at 10 Mbit/s, Fast Ethernet operates at 100 Mbit/s, and Gigabit Ethernet operates at 1 Gbit/s.

Evanescent Wave   Light guided in the inner part of an optical fiber's cladding rather than in the core.

Excess Loss   Loss of a passive coupler above that inherent in dividing light among the output ports.

External Modulation   Modulation of a light source by an external device.

Extrinsic Loss   Splice losses arising from the splicing process itself.

Eye Pattern   A pattern displayed when an oscilloscope is driven by a receiver output and triggered by the signal source that drove the transmitter. The more open the eye, the better the signal quality.

Faceplate   A rigid array of short fibers fused together to direct light, used in image-intensifier tubes.

FDDI   See *Fiber Distributed Data Interface*.

Ferrule   A tube within a connector with a central hole that contains and aligns a fiber.

Fiber Amplifier   An optical fiber doped to amplify light from an external source. The most important type is the erbium-doped fiber amplifier.

Fiber Distributed Data Interface (FDDI)   A standard for a 100-Mbit/s fiber-optic local-area network.

Fiber Grating   An optical fiber in which the refractive index of the core varies periodically along its length, scattering light in a way similar to a diffraction grating, and transmitting or reflecting certain wavelengths selectively.

Fiber-Optic Gyroscope   A coil of optical fiber that can detect rotation about its axis.

Fiber To The Curb (FTTC)   Fiber-optic service to a node that is connected by wires to several nearby homes, typically on a block.

Fiber to the Home (FTTH)   A network in which optical fibers bring signals all the way to homes.

Fibre Channel   A standard for transmitting signals at 100 Mbit/s to 4.25 Gbit/s over fiber or (at slower speeds) copper.

FITL   Fiber in the loop.

Fluoride Glasses   Materials that have the amorphous structure of glass but are made of fluoride compounds (e.g., zirconium fluoride) rather than oxide compounds (e.g., silica).

FOG-M   Fiber-optic guided missile.

Frames   Blocks of data transmitted in the SONET format; also individual images shown in sequence on video screens.

Frequency-Division Multiplexing   Combining analog signals by assigning each a different carrier frequency and merging them in a single signal with a broad range of frequencies.

Full Duplex   In data transmission, transmitters and receivers that simultaneously send and receive signals in both directions.

Fused Fibers   A bundle of fibers melted together so they maintain a fixed alignment with respect to each other in a rigid rod.

Fusion Splice   A splice made by melting the tips of two fibers together so they form a solid junction.

GaAlAs   Gallium aluminum arsenide.

GaAs   Gallium arsenide.

Gallium Aluminum Arsenide (GaAlAs)   A semiconductor compound used in LEDs, diode lasers, and certain detectors.

Gallium Arsenide (GaAs)   A semiconductor compound used in LEDs, diode lasers, detectors, and electronic components.

Gbit/s   Gigabits (billion bits) per second.

Graded-Index Fiber   A fiber in which the refractive index changes gradually with distance from the fiber axis, rather than abruptly at the core-cladding interface.

Graded-Index Fiber Lens   A short segment of graded-index fiber that focuses light passing along it.

Half-Duplex   In data transmission, a system in which transmitters and receivers cannot simultaneously send and receive signals.

Hard-Clad Silica Fiber   A fiber with a hard plastic cladding surrounding a step-index silica core. (Other plastic-clad silica fibers have a soft plastic cladding.)

HDTV   High-definition (or high-resolution) television; digital television with higher resolution than present systems.

Head-End   The central facility where signals are combined and distributed in a cable television system.

Hertz   Frequency in cycles per second.

Hierarchy   A set of transmission speeds arranged to multiplex successively higher numbers of circuits.

Hybrid Fiber/Coax   A system developed for cable-television distribution, with fiber bringing signals to distribution nodes from which coaxial cables take them to homes.

Index of Refraction   The ratio of the speed of light in a vacuum to the speed of light in a material, usually abbreviated n.

Index-Matching Gel   A gel or fluid with refractive index close to glass that reduces refractive-index discontinuities that can cause reflective losses.

Indium Gallium Arsenide (InGaAs)   A semiconductor material used in lasers, LEDs, and detectors.

Indium Gallium Arsenide Phosphide (InGaAsP)   A semiconductor material used in lasers, LEDs, and detectors.

Infrared   Wavelengths longer than 700 nm and shorter than about 1 mm. We cannot see infrared radiation but can feel it as heat. Transmission of glass optical fibers is best in the infrared at wavelengths of 1100–1600 nm.

Infrared Fiber   Colloquially, optical fibers with best transmission at wavelengths of 2 μm or longer, made of materials other than silica glass.

InGaAs   Indium gallium arsenide.

InGaAsP   Indium gallium arsenide phosphide. Properties depend on composition, which is sometimes written $In_{1-x}Ga_xAs_{1-y}P_y$.

Injection Laser   Another name for a semiconductor or diode laser.

Integrated Optics   Optical devices that perform two or more functions and are integrated on a single substrate; analogous to integrated electronic circuits.

Integrated Services Digital Network (ISDN)   A digital standard calling for 144-kbit/s transmission, corresponding to two 64 kbit/s digital voice channels and one 16-kbit/s data channel.

Internet Protocol (IP)   Standard format for transmitting data on the Internet; it uses packet switching.

Intensity   Power per unit solid angle.

Interferometric Sensors   Fiber-optic sensors that rely on interferometric detection.

Intrinsic Losses   Splice losses arising from differences in the fibers being spliced.

Irradiance   Power per unit area.

ISDN   See *Integrated Services Digital Network*.

Junction Laser   A semiconductor diode laser.

Kevlar   A strong synthetic material used in cable strength members; the name is a trademark of the Dupont Company.

LAN   See *local-area network.*

Large-Core Fiber   Usually, a fiber with a core of 200 μm or more.

Laser   From *light amplification by stimulated emission of radiation,* one of the wide range of devices that generates light by that principle. Laser light is directional, covers a narrow range of wavelengths, and is more coherent than ordinary light. Semiconductor diode lasers are the usual light sources in fiber-optic systems.

LED   See *light-emitting diode.*

Light   Strictly speaking, electromagnetic radiation visible to the human eye at 400 to 700 nm. Commonly, the term is applied to electromagnetic radiation with properties similar to visible light, including the invisible near-infrared radiation in most fiber-optic communication systems.

Light Piping   Use of optical fibers to illuminate.

Light-Emitting Diode (LED)   A semiconductor diode that emits incoherent light at the junction between *p-* and *n-*doped materials.

Lightguide   An optical fiber or fiber bundle.

Lightwave   An an adjective, a synonym for optical, often (but not always) meaning fiber-optic.

Linewidth   The range of wavelengths in an optical signal, sometimes called spectral width.

Local-Area Network (LAN)   A network that transmits data among many nodes in a small area (e.g., a building or campus).

Local Loop   The part of the telephone network extending from the central (switching) office to the subscriber.

Longitudinal Modes   Oscillation modes of a laser along the length of its cavity. Each longitudinal mode contains only a very narrow range of wavelengths, so a laser emitting a single longitudinal mode has a very narrow bandwidth. Distinct from transverse modes.

Loose Tube   A protective tube loosely surrounding a cabled fiber, often filled with gel.

Loss   Attenuation of optical signal, normally measured in decibels.

Loss Budget   An accounting of overall attenuation in a system.

Margin   Allowance for attenuation in addition to that explicitly accounted for in system design.

Mass Splicing   Simultaneous splicing of many fibers in a cable.

Material Dispersion   Pulse dispersion caused by variation of a material's refractive index with wavelength.

Mbit/s   Megabits (million bits) per second.

Mechanical Splice   A splice in which fibers are joined mechanically (e.g., glued or crimped in place) but not fused together.

Microbending   Tiny bends in a fiber that allow light to leak out and increase loss.

Micrometer   One-millionth of a meter, abbreviated μm.

Micron   Short for the preferred form, micrometer.

Modal Dispersion   Dispersion arising from differences in the times that different modes take to travel through multimode fiber.

Mode   An electromagnetic field distribution that satisfies theoretical requirements for propagation in a waveguide or oscillation in a cavity (e.g., a laser). Light has modes in a fiber or laser.

Mode-Field Diameter   The diameter of the one mode of light propagating in a single-mode fiber, typically slightly larger than core diameter.

Mode Stripper   A device that removes high-order modes in a multimode fiber to give standard measurement conditions.

Multimode   Transmits or emits multiple modes of light.

Multiplexer   A device that combines two or more signals into a single output.

***n* Region**   A semiconductor doped to have an excess of electrons as current carriers.

NA   See *numerical aperture.*

Nanometer   A unit of length, 10^{-9} m. It is part of the SI system and has largely replaced the non-SI Ångstrom (0.1 nm) in technical literature.

Nanosecond   One-billionth of a second, 10^{-9} second.

National Electrical Code   A wiring code that specifies safety standards for copper and fiber-optic cable.

Near Infrared   The part of the infrared near the visible spectrum, typically 700 to 1500 or 2000 nm; it is not rigidly defined.

Network   A system of cables or other connections that links many terminals, all of which can communicate with each other through the system.

No Return to Zero (NRZ)   A digital code in which the signal level is low for a 0 bit and high for a 1 bit and does not return to 0 between successive 1 bits.

Noise Equivalent Power (NEP)   The optical input power to a detector needed to generate an electrical signal equal to the inherent electrical noise.

Nonzero-Dispersion-Shifted Fiber   Single-mode optical fiber with the zero-dispersion wavelength shifted to beyond 1580 nm, so it is not zero in the 1550-nm range of erbium fiber amplifiers.

Normal (angle)   Perpendicular to a surface.

NRZ   See *no return to zero.*

NTSC   The analog video broadcast standard used in North America, set by the National Television System Committee.

Numerical Aperture (NA)   The sine of half the angle over which a fiber can accept light. Strictly speaking, this is multiplied by the refractive index of the medium containing the light, but for air the index is almost equal to 1.

OC-*x*   Optical Carrier, a carrier rate specified in the SONET standard.

Optical Amplifier   A device that amplifies an input optical signal without converting it into electrical form. The best developed are optical fibers doped with the rare earth erbium.

Optical Loss Test Set   An optical power meter and light source calibrated for use together.

Optical Node   The point where signals are transferred from optical fibers to other transmission media, typically twisted pair wires or coaxial cable.

Optical Time-Domain Reflectometer (OTDR)   An instrument that measures transmission characteristics by sending a short pulse of light down a fiber and observing backscattered light.

Optical Waveguide   Technically, any structure that can guide light. Sometimes used as a synonym for optical fiber, it can also apply to planar light waveguides.

***p* Region**   Part of a semiconductor doped with electron acceptors in which holes (vacancies in the valence electron level) are the dominant current carriers.

Packet Switching   Organizing signals by dividing them into data packets, each containing a header that specifies its destination and a packet of data intended for that destination. Separate data packets then are directed to their destinations.

Packing Fraction   The fraction of the surface area of a fiber-optic bundle that is fiber core.

PCS Fiber   See *plastic-clad silica fiber.*

Peak Power   Highest instantaneous power level in a pulse.

Phase   The position of a wave in its oscillation cycle.

Photodetector   A light detector.

Photodiode   A diode that can produce an electrical signal proportional to light falling upon it.

Photonic   A term coined for devices that work using photons or light, analogous to "electronic" for devices working with electrons.

Photons   Quanta of electromagnetic radiation. Light can be viewed as either a wave or a series of photons.

Picosecond   One trillionth (10^{-12}) second.

***pin* Photodiode**   A semiconductor detector with an intrinsic (i) region separating the p- and n-doped regions. It has fast linear response and is used in fiber-optic receivers.

Planar Waveguide   A waveguide fabricated in a flat material such as a thin film.

Plastic-Clad Silica (PCS) Fiber   A step-index multimode fiber in which a silica core is surrounded by a lower-index plastic cladding.

Plenum Cable   Cable made of fire-retardant material that meets electrical code requirements (UL 910) for low smoke generation and installation in air spaces.

Point-to-Point Transmission   Carrying a signal between two points, without branching to other points.

Polarization   Alignment of the electric and magnetic fields that make up an electromagnetic wave; normally refers to the electric field. If all light waves have the same alignment, the light is polarized.

Polarization-Maintaining Fiber   Fiber that maintains the polarization of light that enters it.

Polarization Mode Dispersion   Dispersion arising from differences in the speed of the two polarization modes of light in a fiber (vertical and horizontal).

POTS   Plain Old Telephone Service, analog voice telephone lines.

Preform   A cylindrical rod of specially prepared and purified glass from which an optical fiber is drawn.

Pulse Dispersion   The spreading out of pulses as they travel along an optical fiber.

Pump Laser   The semiconductor laser that provides the light that excites atoms in a fiber amplifier, putting them in the right state to amplify light.

Quantum Efficiency   The fraction of photons that strike a detector which produce electron-hole pairs in the output current.

Quaternary   A semiconductor compound made of four elements (e.g., InGaAsP).

Radiation-Hardened   Insensitive to the effects of nuclear radiation, usually for military applications.

Radiometer   An instrument, distinct from a photometer, to measure power (watts) of electromagnetic radiation.

Rays   Straight lines that represent the path taken by light.

Receiver   A device that detects an optical signal and converts it into an electrical form usable by other devices.

Recombination   Combination of an electron and a hole in a semiconductor that releases energy, sometimes leading to light emission.

Refraction   The bending of light as it passes between materials of different refractive index.

Refractive Index   Ratio of the speed of light in a vacuum to the speed of light in a material; abbreviated n.

Refractive-Index Gradient   The change in refractive index with distance from the axis of an optical fiber.

Regenerator   A receiver-transmitter pair that detects a weak signal, cleans it up, then sends the regenerated signal through another length of fiber.

Repeater   A receiver-transmitter pair that detects, and amplifies a weak signal for retransmission through another length of optical fiber.

Responsivity   The ratio of detector output to input, usually measured in units of amperes per watt (or microamperes per microwatt).

Return to Zero (RZ)   A digital coding scheme where signal level is low for a 0 bit and high for a 1 bit during the first half of a bit interval and then in either case returns to zero for the second half of the bit interval.

Ribbon Cables   Cables in which many fibers are embedded in a plastic material in parallel, forming a flat ribbon-like structure.

Ring Architecture   A network scheme in which a transmission line forms a complete ring. If the ring is broken, signals can still be sent among the terminals.

Rise Time   The time it takes output to rise from low levels to peak value. Typically measured as the time to rise from 10% to 90% of maximum output.

Router   A device that directs data packets to their destinations using information in their headers to pick the best path. Sometimes in WDM, a device that routes wavelengths to separate destinations.

RZ   See *return to zero*.

Scattering   Loss of light that is scattered off atoms in different directions, so it escapes from the fiber core. A major component of fiber attenuation.

SDH   See *Synchronous Digital Hierarchy*.

Selfoc Lens   A trade name used by the Nippon Sheet Glass Company for a graded-index fiber lens; a segment of graded-index fiber made to serve as a lens.

Semiconductor Laser   A laser in which injection of current into a semiconductor diode produces light by recombination of holes and electrons at the junction between p- and n-doped regions.

Sheath   An outer protective layer of a fiber-optic cable.

SI Units   The standard international system of metric units.

Signal-to-Noise Ratio   The ratio of signal to noise, measured in decibels; an indication of signal quality in analog systems.

Silica Glass   Glass made mostly of silicon dioxide, SiO_2, used in conventional optical fibers.

Simplex   Single element (e.g., a simplex connector is a single-fiber connector).

Single-Frequency Laser   A laser that emits a range of wavelengths small enough to be considered a single frequency.

Single Mode   Containing only one mode. When dealing with lasers, beware of ambiguities because of the difference between transverse and longitudinal modes. A laser operating in a single transverse mode typically does not operate in a single longitudinal mode.

Single-Polarization Fibers   Optical fibers capable of carrying light in only one polarization.

Smart Structures (or Smart Skins)   Materials containing sensors (fiber-optic or other types) to measure their properties during fabrication and use.

Soliton   An optical pulse that naturally retains its original shape as it travels along an optical fiber.

SONET (Synchronous Optical Network)   A standard for fiber-optic transmission.

Splice   A permanent junction between two fiber ends.

Splitting Ratio   The ratio of power emerging from output ports of a coupler.

Standard Single-Mode Fiber   Step-index single-mode fiber with zero dispersion at 1310 nm, the first type used in fiber-optic communications, still widely used.

Star Coupler   A coupler with more than three or four ports.

Step-Index Multimode Fiber   A step-index fiber with a core large enough to carry light in multiple modes.

Step-Index Single-Mode Fiber   A step-index fiber with a small core capable of carrying light in only one mode; this type has zero dispersion at 1310 nm.

Submarine Cable   A cable designed to be laid underwater.

Subscriber Loop   The part of the telephone network from a central office to individual subscribers.

Surface-Emitting Diode   An LED that emits light from its flat surface rather than its side. Simple and inexpensive, with emission spread over a wide angle.

Surface-Emitting Laser   A semiconductor laser that emits light from the wafer surface.

Switch   A device that directs light or electricity along different physical paths, such as fibers or wires.

Switched Network   A network that routes signals to their destinations by switching circuits, such as the telephone system.

Synchronous Digital Hierarchy (SDH)   The international version of SONET, the Synchronous Optical Network standard. The biggest difference is in the names of the transmission rates.

Synchronous Optical Network   See *SONET.*

Tbit/s   Terabits (trillion, or 10^{12} bits) per second.

T Carrier   A system operating at one of the standard levels in the North American digital hierarchy.

T Coupler   A coupler with three ports.

TDM   See *time-division multiplexing.*

Ternary   A semiconductor compound made of three elements (e.g., GaAlAs).

III-V (3-5) Semiconductor   A semiconductor compound made of one or more elements from the IIIA column of the periodic table (A1, Ga, and In) and one or more elements from the VA column (N, P, As, or Sb). Used in LEDs, diode lasers, and detectors.

Threshold Current   The minimum current needed to sustain laser action in a diode laser.

Tight Buffer   A material tightly surrounding a fiber in a cable, holding it rigidly in place.

Time-Division Multiplexing (TDM)   Digital multiplexing by taking one pulse at a time from separate signals and combining them in a single bit stream.

Total Internal Reflection   Total reflection of light back into a material when it strikes the interface with a material having a lower refractive index at an angle below a critical value.

Transceiver   A combination of transmitter and receiver providing both output and input interfaces with a device.

Transverse Modes   Modes across the width of a waveguide (e.g., a fiber or laser). Distinct from longitudinal modes, which are along the length of a laser.

Tree   A network architecture in which transmission routes branch out from a central point.

Trunk Line   A transmission line running between telephone switching offices.

Twisted Pair   Pair of copper wires twisted around each other. The standard way to connect individual voice telephones, widely used for other low-speed communications.

Ultraviolet   Electromagnetic waves invisible to the human eye, with wavelengths about 10-400 nm.

VCSEL   Vertical Cavity Surface Emitting Laser, a semiconductor laser in which light oscillates vertically (perpendicular to the junction plane) and light emerges from the surface of the wafer rather than from the edge of the chip.

Videoconferencing   Conducting conferences via a video telecommunications system.

Video on Demand   A service that delivers individuals specific video programs that they request from an on-line library.

Videophone   A telephone-like service with a picture as well as sound.

Visible Light   Electromagnetic radiation visible to the human eye at wavelengths of 400–700 nm.

Voice Circuit   A circuit capable of carrying one telephone conversation or its equivalent; the standard subunit in which telecommunication capacity is counted. The U.S. analog equivalent is 4 kHz. The digital equivalent is 56 kbit/s in North America and 64 kbit/s in Europe.

Waveguide   A structure that guides electromagnetic waves along its length. An optical fiber is an optical waveguide.

Waveguide Couplers   A coupler in which light is transferred between planar waveguides.

Waveguide Dispersion   The part of chromatic dispersion arising from the different speeds light travels in the core and cladding of a single-mode fiber (i.e., from the fiber's waveguide structure).

Wavelength   The distance an electromagnetic wave travels in the time it takes to oscillate through a complete cycle. Wavelengths of light are measured in nanometers (10^{-9} m) or micrometers (10^{-6} m).

Wavelength-Division Multiplexing (WDM)   Multiplexing of signals by transmitting them at different wavelengths through the same fiber.

Window   A wavelength region where fibers have low attenuation, used for transmitting signals.

Y Coupler   A variation on the T coupler in which input light is split between two channels (typically planar waveguide) that branch out like a Y from the input.

Zero-Dispersion Wavelength   Wavelength at which net chromatic dispersion of an optical fiber is nominally zero. Arises where waveguide dispersion cancels out material dispersion.

Index